THE STRUGGLE FOR DEVELOPMENT AND DEMOCRACY
VOLUME 2

Studies in Critical Social Sciences Book Series

Haymarket Books is proud to be working with Brill Academic Publishers (www.brill.nl) to republish the *Studies in Critical Social Sciences* book series in paperback editions. This peer-reviewed book series offers insights into our current reality by exploring the content and consequences of power relationships under capitalism, and by considering the spaces of opposition and resistance to these changes that have been defining our new age. Our full catalog of *SCSS* volumes can be viewed at https://www.haymarketbooks .org/series_collections/4-studies-in-critical-social-sciences.

THE STRUGGLE FOR DEVELOPMENT AND DEMOCRACY

VOLUME 2

A General Theory

ALESSANDRO OLSARETTI

Haymarket Books
Chicago, IL

First published in 2023 by Brill Academic Publishers, The Netherlands
© 2023 Koninklijke Brill NV, Leiden, The Netherlands

Published in paperback in 2024 by
Haymarket Books
P.O. Box 180165
Chicago, IL 60618
773-583-7884
www.haymarketbooks.org

ISBN: 979-8-88890-241-7

Distributed to the trade in the US through Consortium Book Sales and
Distribution (www.cbsd.com) and internationally through Ingram Publisher
Services International (www.ingramcontent.com).

This book was published with the generous support of Lannan Foundation,
Wallace Action Fund, and the Marguerite Casey Foundation.

Special discounts are available for bulk purchases by organizations and
institutions. Please call 773-583-7884 or email info@haymarketbooks.org for more
information.

Cover design by Jamie Kerry and Ragina Johnson.

Printed in the United States.

Library of Congress Cataloging-in-Publication data is available.

Contents

Acknowledgments

I repeat here the same acknowledgments as in Volume 1, with a few modifications and additions. This book is part of a project that took shape during the course of a long and difficult intellectual journey that lasted thirty years. It is simply impossible for me to recall all those who influenced my work in one way or another during these thirty years, whether through teaching, stimulating conversations, friendly advice, or support of one type or another. Moreover, this book, including these acknowledgments, were written in the time of COVID, under time constraints made worse by financial constraints, with no time to sit down and carefully try to remember the names of all those I should acknowledge. Therefore, I limit myself here to acknowledging only those who just cannot be left out. Flora Dura, my mother, just cannot be left out. As a mother, she was my Prime Mover, as it were, the beginning of all things, because a child is borne by his mother and first socialized by his mother. Moreover, while I was growing up, and later as I tried to build my own nest, she had an uncanny and unfailing ability to be there at important times, especially all difficult times, in my intellectual journey. It was only later in life that I understood the level of commitment, single-mindedness, and intelligence, that it takes to be such a presence in the life of a son. Renato and Renzo Olsaretti, my two paternal uncles, also just cannot be left out. Renato was my actual godfather, who died as I was a child, while Renzo was my number one fan, and the real godfather to me, who helped me financially while I was finishing my PhD and later as I searched for a new career, despite the fact that he often jokingly described himself as a Pantalone, after the character in Italian popular theater known for his stinginess, similar in some ways to Moliere's character Harpagon.

I had to go my own way to pursue my principles and ideals, and this required cutting some bridges and devoting myself to research rather than pieties. With these acknowledgments I want to spell out my appreciation of what my mother and my two paternal uncles have done, an appreciation that I only came to in the last few years, especially as I wrote this book, down to this day, as I completed this second volume. In particular, I have learned my mother's lessons in tough love, and put them to good use, although I am sure it is not the use that she expected, since my education ended up being so different than hers. It is true that I have wondered, tongue in cheek of course, about the meaning of the Latin phrase *nomen est omen*, which suggests that one's name presages one's future, since dura in Latin and in Italian means 'hard'. But it is also true that I gained through her an appreciation of Latin and the subtleties of grammar, which she instilled in me as a child by teaching me clever oracle pronouncements like the sibylline phrase *ibis redibis, nunquam per bella peribis*, which means 'you will go and return, never die in war,' and which completely changes meaning if only one shifts the comma to *ibis redibis nunquam, per bella peribis*, which then means 'you will go to never return, and die in war'. Most importantly, later in life she proved to be an incredibly good 'nonna' or grandmother, and she even went out of her way to be listening and understanding, to the point of showing interest in my research in social history, social theory, and even sociology, which is so far from her classical education. For years, both her and Renzo lent a sympathetic hear to, and seemed bemused by, my efforts to formulate a theory, and my efforts to make sense of contemporary Italian history, periodically rocked by government scandals such as Tangentopoli or the SISMI scandal, bigger than any CIA, DIA, or NSA scandals, and yet which never led to a reform of the Italian state.

I had to go my own way to pursue my principles and ideals, simply because there are turning points in life after which, without any drama or doubt on my part, it is better to be independent than not to be independent. One such turning point for me was my research trip to Italy in 2010, other turning points came while I was writing up my dissertation and searching for a new career. In 2010 Maurilio Buffone, a school friend of mine who had been in touch with me, died after a long fight with cancer. As a youth I had been struck by the irony in another sibylline phrase I had been taught, 'he whom the gods love dies young,' but this marked for me the beginning of maturity. We all act recklessly when we are young, to a greater or lesser extent, because we feel invulnerable, or because we think we have such a long time ahead of us. Maturity brings the realization that it is important to make the most of the time we have especially if the 'gods' are against us. In my 2010 trip to Italy my mother and Renzo showed me hospitality, also through my mother's childhood friends Claudia and Salvatore Esposito and their children Luciana, Valeria, and Luca Esposito, all bright professionals, and through Silvia Olsaretti and Egidio Podda, all of whom bemusedly put up with my efforts to formulate a theory, which must have seemed so distant from their concerns, or even foreign. There is one other person not tied to me by institutional ties who just cannot be left out, Fabio Frosini, an Italian philosopher I met by chance, who is a leading expert on Gramsci, and who was very generous with his time while I was a graduate student and influenced everything I have written on Gramsci, except this book. This book is outside his area of expertise, as I have ventured to extend Gramsci's theory introducing concepts from contemporary sociology, and in the index I refer to Gramscian concepts, rather than to Gramsci, in order to avoid entering into a debate as to whether the interpretation that I provide is really supported by Gramsci's text.

I believe it is, but I argue this elsewhere. Fabio and Dolores Frosini also showed me hospitality in Bilbao.

Other persons who just cannot be left out are the scholars who taught me at McGill University. Most importantly, these scholars are John Anthony Hall, Axel van den Berg, Steven Rytina, and also Matthew Lange, Suzanne Staggenborg, Rodney Nelson, Alberto Cambrosio, and to some extent Lucia Benacquisto, who supervised my dissertation or the readings and research that contributed to my dissertation. These scholars are also Uner Turgay, and Wael Hallaq, who were once at the Institute of Islamic Studies, and Elizabeth Elbourne, and Daviken Studnicki-Gizbert in the department of history, and also other historians at McGill University who showed an interest in my work, most importantly James Delbourgo and Nicholas Dew, Malek Abisaab and Rula Abisaab Jordi. The history tutors who taught me at St Anne's College, Oxford University, namely, Gill Lewis, Jean Dunbabin, and Peter Ghosh, also just cannot be left out. They supervised my readings for a degree in modern history that I never completed, and yet which greatly influenced my later research. Ghosh also supervised my first research on Gramsci.

As for references to others' work, this book was written in the time of COVID and under many constraints, one of which was that I did not have access to libraries and books. Another one is that I am still working under strict time constraints, made even worse by mounting financial constraints. I have cited sources for all the important concepts conveyed to me in conversation that I could remember, by Hall and by other scholars at McGill University of course, since I know their work well. However, during the past thirty years I have read very widely, and it is possible that I derived some concepts from a book that I have long forgotten. If anyone has a genuine case to have arrived at a key concept that I discuss in this book before me, I will gladly acknowledge them, if they contact me and point me to the work that they published. In any case, the originality of this book lies not so much in a ground-breaking new concept, which is what makes an academic star or an eminent scholar, who can seize upon a new concept and fly with it, as it were. This book is first and foremost a work of analysis, critique, and synthesis, based on long and painstaking work on the existing literature, and on informal observation of culture in all different walks of life. This is humble work that does not make one an academic star, but can provide a very important synthesis. There are some original concepts and diagrams that I came up with, by combining sociology and engineering as part of a social engineering for democracy, but these are part of another book. I believe these concepts and diagrams constitute a significantly new approach to development and democracy, that I begin to define in this book, but I make the main argument regarding these concepts and diagrams elsewhere. In this volume, the second volume, the formulation of development and democracy as part of a unified theory of power, and the concepts of embedded autonomy between arenas that are based on distinct types of behavior, *Homo Oeconomicus*, *Homo Culturalis*, and *Homo Politicus*, are concepts that I arrived at independently, through my reading of Gramsci, and my readings in history, Islamic studies, and sociology.

As it turned out, I was able to make this synthesis also because I was willing to learn from all different walks of life, and from popular culture as much as from high culture, in a difficult process that I describe in my novel *The Caravaggio Code*, and that I begin to explain in a forthcoming series of essays titled *Towards a Humanist Social Science*. Another friend of mine, Colin Goldin, classically trained but with an interest in film, introduced me many years ago to work by the Taviani brothers, especially *The Night of the Shooting Stars*, which uses imagery from Italian popular culture and from Italian history that I related to. The Italian title of the film refers to the night of Saint Lawrence, and the film uses a frame story whereby a mother narrates to her child memories from the Second World War, which constitute the main story. The narration of memories from one generation to another is an important part of popular culture, and the imagery of the night of Saint Lawrence is an integral part of Italian popular culture. Every child in Italy knows that if you are patient and look at the sky long enough and hard enough on that night you might see a *shooting star*, or even more than one. They might not make your wishes come true, but seeing those shooting stars might be a wish in itself. Such imagery and such timeless human wishes were also a source for Dante's *Divine Comedy*, which although considered today a canonical text, once challenged high culture because it was written in Italian, or the Tuscan dialect that is the source of Italian, rather than Latin. I had an opportunity to re-read passages from the Divine Comedy recently, including passages from the *Inferno,* after Setrag and Claudia Manoukian thoughtfully gave me a copy of it as a present at my graduation party. Dante follows the conventional Catholic wisdom of the Middle Ages, which I presume was sanctioned by Vatican doctrine, and frames his description of Odysseus as a condemnation of a fraudulent advisor who led his men away from ordained truth. But the form of the text and its poetic imagery tell a different story. In Dante's memorable phrase, 'O frati [...] considerate la vostra semenza: fatti non foste a viver come bruti, ma per seguir virtute e canoscenza'. This is hard to translate, because of inherent difficulties in cross-cultural communications that I sketch in *The Caravaggio Code*, but the phrase essentially constitutes a sympathetic depiction of Odysseus' thirst for knowledge.

The true Odysseus in Dante's *Inferno* is not a fraudulent advisor, but a mortal who defied both the gods of Olympus and the conventional Catholic wisdom of the Middle Ages, and yet managed to speak words that break through the frame imposed upon him by the times.

Figures and Tables

Figures

Tables

Introduction

This book has two main goals. The first is to provide theoretical alternatives to neoliberalism, while the second is to explain the social origins of neoliberalism and the populism. Populism does not need theoretical alternatives, since it is based on plainly bad theory or no theory at all. It requires instead that we combat the anti-intellectualism that fuels populism, also by providing better and more intelligible theories. Understanding *the social origins of neoliberalism and populism* is important, together with providing theoretical alternatives to neoliberalism, because theories succeed, not *just* because of their inherent merits as theories, but also because certain social conditions favor their diffusion and acceptance. This entails that some theories that have few merits, and even make recurrent errors, are likely to be widely accepted because of favorable social conditions. Neoliberalism is one such theory. As emphasized by critics of neoliberalism, including economist Joseph Stiglitz in his *Globalization and its Discontents* and later work, neoliberalism made dubious claims regarding development that predictably led to instability, and ultimately led to the 2008 economic crisis. The claims made by neoliberalism look all the more dubious when we consider the similarities between neoliberalism and the earlier free-trade liberalism that eventually led to the 1929 economic crisis. These similarities suggest that there are deep flaws in our cultural institutions, because these institutions have been unable to move beyond some very serious errors made by past theories, to the point that it seems appropriate to claim that these errors are due to the lack of social conditions for objectivity in social science. In order to move beyond these errors, it is necessary to formulate significantly new theories, also by carefully scrutinizing how development works, down to the basic assumptions regarding what motivates human beings, whether profit, truth, or service to the community. It is also necessary to apply these theories reflexively to what motivates intellectuals, including economists and social scientists more in general.[1]

The theoretical alternatives to neoliberal economic theories consist chiefly in a theory of development and democracy that is alternative both to neoliberal economic theories, which call for market deregulation as the only way to

---

1   I address many of the arguments that I introduce here in: Alessandro Olsaretti, *The Struggle for Development and Democracy, Volume 1: New Approaches* (Leiden and Boston: Brill, 2022). I go into greater detail in the arguments regarding methodology, social science, and theory, in a forthcoming series of essays titled: *Towards a Humanist Social Science*, Essays on Philosophy, Sociology, and the History of Culture and Politics (forthcoming).

produce growth, and also to Keynesian theories, which call for injecting money in an economy without much regard for the institutions and social networks involved. There are historical links between Keynesian and neoliberal theories. They are two theories, or groups of theories, one of which led to or reinforced the other, with Keynesian theories calling for unrestricted state spending, and then neoliberal theories reacting by calling for all state spending to be cut off. These links extend to policies, as one bad policy reinforced the other, and both reinforced uneven development. In countries in which there are powerful and entrenched patronage networks, typically political patronage networks, the money injected in the economy following Keynesian theories fueled these networks and the influence and private wealth of powerful politicians, resulting in little beneficial investment in the economy, and thus in very little development. In many developing countries, including Italy in the 1960s and southern Italy to this day, the disregard for patronage networks led to a ballooning debt that the economy was unable to repay. This forced many countries to ask for bailouts from institutions like the International Monetary Fund that imposed draconian conditions following neoliberal economic theories, cutting off all money to institutions, and thus further hampering development in these countries. In Italy this resulted in strengthening uneven development within the country, since political patronage networks have historically affected southern Italy especially badly, and they arguably became even stronger, leading to the enduring underdevelopment of this part of the country compared to northern Italy, and in particular compared to north-western Italy. There is a similar link between Marxist and neoliberal theories to the link between Keynesian and neoliberal theories, whereby Marxist theories overemphasized the state as the only way to produce an equitable development, and in the case of developing countries as the only driver of development, leading to disastrous development policies in many cases, and eventually to a complete rejection of the state that was supported by neoliberal theories arguing that unrestricted markets are the only driver of development, reducing the role of the state to a guarantor of markets.

Besides historical links, there are also theoretical commonalities between neoliberal, and Keynesian and Marxist theories, as they are *all one-sided theories that are part of false dichotomies*, or artificial oppositions between two stark alternatives, making it seem as if one has to choose between *either* markets, *or* the state, with no intermediate positions, nor third ways like those emphasizing civil society as an important driver of development. In addition, they all oversimplify and misrepresent the very real need for regulation of markets that, as emphasized by Stiglitz, is necessary to avoid instability and catastrophes like the 2008 economic crisis. In contrast to neoliberal, and also to Keynesian and

Marxist theories, I propose a general theory of development and democracy based on the sociology multidisciplinary approach to social questions, and on my reading of work by Antonio Gramsci, the anti-fascist political theorist, including his insights into the social origins of uneven development across regions within Italy, particularly southern Italy compared to northern Italy, a question known in Italian political discourses as the Southern Question. One of these insights was that southern Italy was deeply affected by social disaggregation, which includes the loss of community and other social ties amongst individuals pushed to the margins of society, who often fell into poverty and violence traps. Another insight was that a better and more accountable state and civil society were needed to obviate these problems of development and democracy. Unlike neoliberalism, Keynesianism and Marxism, I propose that it is crucially important not to waste public money, but the answer to this important need is not to cut down all public spending, nor to reduce the role of the state to a mere guarantor of markets. The answer is instead to *build better states and find better ways for the state to interact with both civil society and markets*, guaranteeing both stability and equitable growth, that is, a stable development not subject to fluctuations, and also a more equitable development that benefits all of the population, not just the elites and their patronage networks. Therefore, in response to equally one-sided neoliberal, and Keynesian and Marxist theories, and to the problem of patronage networks, I propose that development needs markets, and also a well-built and smoothly functioning civil society and state. In addition, there should be suitable coordination between markets, civil society, and the state, as well as democracy in all three. This coordination requires certain types of networks, and an interaction that I describe below using the sociological concept of embedded autonomy.

1   The Approach to Theory and the Goals of the Book

This book is a work of theory. Theory is very important to social science, and in this project I argue that good theory, properly formulated and conveyed through good rhetoric, gives to social science some very important contributions. These contributions include: clear summaries of, and preliminary answers to, big questions such as the origins of development and democracy; broad pictures regarding how the whole of a country works that are necessary to formulate successful policies; and clearly phrased hypotheses supported by preliminary evidence that are necessary for carrying out empirical tests. Volume 1 defines theory and good rhetoric in greater detail, proposes a methodology to formulate general theory, and introduces some key theses of the general theory of development and democracy that I propose. Volume 2, this volume, sets out the entire theory. This theory is a *general* theory, because it provides the broadest or most high-level pictures, and it is based upon fairly general assumptions. It thus has wide application to countries in the West. However general, this is still empirically informed theory, not pure theory with few or no applications, and I defend general theory in Chapter 1 below, explaining why it is indispensable to understand phenomena such as globalization that affect many countries at any one time. The social science that this general theory contributes to is *based on the sociology multidisciplinary approach*, as both the general theory and this approach focus on producing broad pictures of society that include markets, civil society, and the state, not just markets, nor just the state. This volume argues, more in general, that culture and politics are very important to development, as much as the economy, and that they complement reliance on the economy alone which, without culture and politics, leads to failures in development. It also argues that *institutions and organizations are very important* to understand how each of these domains of human activity work, and that in order to understand culture and politics, and the positive contributions that they can give to the economy, we have to understand civil society and its institutions and organizations, including cultural institutions like universities, and cultural associations and other non-profit organizations (NPOs), and also the state and its institutions and organizations, including political institutions like ministries, and political associations and other non-governmental organization (NGOs), and of course political parties.

The models of the sociology multidisciplinary approach that I build upon are works by Gramsci and by sociologist Max Weber, the latter strictly as a scientific model, since Weber was otherwise politically close to imperialist and totalitarian ideologies. There are several aspects of Weber's work that complement scientifically Gramsci's work. A key aspect of Gramsci's *Prison Notebooks* that I build upon is an effort to formulate a multidisciplinary social science, an effort that is complemented by Weber's work in comparative historical sociology and his theory of development that sought to understand the emergence of capitalism in the West in a comparative context with other civilizations, and included a multidisciplinary approach to development, aimed at understanding how the whole of a country works, not just markets. In addition, both Gramsci and Weber, in different ways, emphasized that a certain type of culture and state were key factors for the emergence and functioning of capitalism, in particular a culture that contributed to legitimating and enabling the functioning of modern states, and that together with the state sanctioned certain behaviors that were very important for the emergence of capitalism, including self-discipline and honesty in the pursuit of profits, as well as the acquisitive individualism associated with market behavior. Weber also emphasized the modern bureaucratic state as an important contribution to capitalism, because both are based upon frequently repeated standard transactions, and calculations of profits or utility become possible only where such transactions predominate. As emphasized by sociologist Thomas Ertman and a number of historians, Weber's concept of the bureaucratic state is important also in contrast to the patrimonial states that had preceded it. In patrimonial states office-holders treated their offices as their property, in a manner that led to the emergence of huge patronage networks in some states that remained mired in patrimonial practices.

The models of general theory that I build upon in this volume are works by philosopher and political theorist Gerald Allan Cohen, and by sociologist Immanuel Wallerstein. These might seem very different models, but like Gramsci's and Weber's approaches to a multidisciplinary social science, they are arguably complementary. Works by Cohen and Wallerstein respectively represent two approaches to theory-building that I describe in Volume 1: the axiomatic-deductive approach, and theoretical groundwork. Their works are arguably also some of the most important contemporary works in political and social theory that have proposed general theories of development, and I advance their approach to formulating theory, while differing from them in very important ways that will become clear in the course of this volume. Elsewhere in this project, I propose an anthropological-sociological view of philosophy, language, and science, including social science, that can be applied to works by these two theorists.[2] Borrowing concepts from cultural anthropology to describe theory, I see Cohen's *Karl Marx's Theory of History* as representative of an approach to theory that relies on what anthropologists call *thin descriptions*. It is very rigorous and internally coherent, and it makes very clear statements that are useful to formulate hypotheses to submit to empirical tests. However, it also makes for very hard reading, as it shares the style of legal documents, and it is little informed by empirical research, relying instead, largely or even exclusively, upon deriving statements from axioms. If some of these axioms are incorrect, and I believe that at least some axioms in Cohen's work are incorrect, the entire theoretical edifice is deeply flawed, and even faulty. Cohen's argument is that the development of productive forces drives human history, and that states that promote this development will eventually prevail. Evidence from development in the past decades suggests that this is not the case.

---

2   *Towards a Humanist Social Science.*

Incorrect, and also misapplied axioms, are a flaw that Cohen's work shares with much of game theory, and also to some extent with mainstream economics, including neoliberal theories. The general theory that I propose in this book relies instead upon a broader view of human beings than just profit-seeking, and more in general utility-maximizing, individuals. It emphasizes instead that we are all to a greater or lesser extent capable of acting in the pursuit of profit, or truth, or service to the community. The general theory also emphasizes that in modern societies there emerge three fairly distinct arenas, the economic, cultural, and political-military arenas, which respectively overlap in capitalist societies with markets, civil society, and the state. In these arenas different organizational forms come to prevail, together with different principles of individual behavior. In the economic arena, the utility-maximizing principles of individual behavior come to prevail. They are described by the concept of *Homo Oeconomicus*, a concept that is arguably still central to economic theory, although rarely spelled out. In the cultural and the political-military arenas, in which behavior is more collaborative than the individualistic behavior that prevails in markets, and public goods are more important, the pursuit of truth, and service to the community and in modern times the nation, come to prevail. Various names have been proposed for these types of behavior, but for uniformity of nomenclature with the expression *Homo Oeconomicus* I refer to them as *Homo Culturalis* and *Homo Politicus*. The general theory that I propose argues that the different organizational forms and different principles of behavior maximize development in each arena, and ultimately also overall development.

In contrast with Cohen's work, I see Wallerstein's *The Modern World System* as representative of an approach to theory that relies on what anthropologists call *thick descriptions*, as it is based upon theoretical groundwork that uses a vast amount of empirical literature on specific times and places, and makes generalizations from this literature that are more generally applicable than the local theories put forward in this literature. It is thus a theory that is more empirically informed than Cohen's theory. It led to a theoretical paradigm called World Systems Theory that has played a major role in the sociological study of development, bringing to the fore such key concepts as underdevelopment and uneven development. Two arguments in World Systems Theory are especially important to the general theory that I propose in this volume. One is the suggestion that there is a world economy, world culture, and a state system, which roughly correspond, on the world stage, to the economic, cultural, and political-military arenas within countries. However, building partly upon arguments by sociologist Christopher Chase-Dunn, and partly upon arguments by Gramsci, I suggest that the world stage is dominated chiefly by logics (or mechanisms) in the world economy and the state system, with world culture lagging sorely behind them in influence, and with the state system and raw political-military power driving the expansion of the world economy, not the other way around. Another important argument by World Systems Theory that I build upon is that the world economy, world culture, and the state system are part of a world system that is divided into a core, semi-periphery, and periphery, in what is essentially a hierarchy of power. In the world economy, and at the lowest level in the hierarchy of power, the periphery is chiefly a provider of agricultural goods, raw materials, and more recently of cheap labour for industries that relocated from the core. This is enriching what I suggest is an emergent imperialist world-elite that has close ties to national elites in countries around the world.

2   The General Theory in Comparison to Other Theories

This volume is divided into four parts, each consisting of two chapters. These parts contain respectively: first, a detailed summary of all the theory, with all the theses presented together, spelling out the hypotheses that they support; second, a critical review of the key approaches and concepts in sociology and geography that I use; third, a general theory about the sources of development and democracy within countries; and fourth, an extension of the general theory to international development and international relations that focuses on the sources of imperialism and uneven development. Part 1 is the summary at the beginning of this volume that presents definitions of key concepts, and most importantly a summary of all hypotheses and theses put forward by the general theory. It is followed by three other parts that discuss the theory in detail. The entire Part 2, and the first chapter in each of Part 3 and 4 (Chapter 5 is the first chapter in Part 3, and Chapter 7 is the first chapter in Part 4), are general theory on the Wallerstein model, or theory that relies upon thick descriptions. They include what I define in Volume 1 as theoretical groundwork, which serves as the basis for Theses I to XV of the general theory. These are set out in the second chapter in each of Part 3 and 4 (Chapter 6 is the second chapter in Part 3, and Chapter 8 is the second chapter in Part 4), both of which are general theory on the Cohen model, or theory that relies upon thin descriptions, implementing an axiomatic-deductive approach to theory. All the theses rely upon an axiomatic-deductive procedure to propose mechanisms that explain phenomena and social processes introduced by the theoretical groundwork. This organization of the book is meant to highlight the complementary nature of the two approaches to theory that I implement, the theoretical groundwork that is necessary to identify important phenomena and processes that require an explanation, and the axiomatic-deductive approach that is necessary to suggest the mechanisms that constitute the explanation of the important phenomena and processes.

The following chapter by chapter overview of the arguments in this volume locates the arguments of this volume vis-a-vis some of the most important contemporary theories in sociology, geography, political science, and economics that address the same questions concerning development and democracy that I address in this book. It is useful to begin by introducing these theories. The general theory that I propose can aptly be described as a continuation and extension, using contemporary social science, of Gramsci's theory of hegemony, which was arguably part of *a broader theory of power that Gramsci had begun to outline*. This theory of power included both hegemony and domination, it implied that there are different types of hegemony, and pointed out that domination often degenerates into violence, in what Gramsci described as the social equivalent of a war of maneuver that I refer to below as a *social war of maneuver*, a war that includes revolutions and violent social movements. Gramsci's theory also took into consideration the different ability of social groups to engage in collective action, and problems of cooptation and defection of the leadership of social groups that I describe in Volume 1 as meso collective action problems.

I complement this broader theory of power with *a number of important concepts from contemporary sociology and geography* that I revise throughout this volume in the process of integrating them within the theory of hegemony. Both the degeneration into violence, and meso collective action problems, were especially stark in certain geographical locations that I suggest can be aptly described as locations in the semi-periphery and periphery of the world system. Below I focus in particular upon the contributions that macro historical sociology, and macro historical geography, as well as World Systems Theory, can give towards theories of development and democracy. The *macro historical sociology* that I build upon includes chiefly work by Charles Tilly on states, democracy and social movements, and in particular the arguments that European states were shaped by war, and democracy emerged out of a long process of democratization that involved contention, and sometimes open conflict, between states and social movements. The *World Systems Theory* that I build upon is the one proposed by Wallerstein, and revisions of it proposed by sociologist Giovanni Arrighi, who began the task of including Gramsci's theory of hegemony within World Systems Theory, and within the study of international relations more in general. The *macro historical geography* includes work by geographer Jared Diamond on the origins and sources of European imperialism, a work that drew attention to the geographical factors that explain why some European countries were able to build large colonial empires, taking over much of the world. Diamond especially drew attention to the favorable ecosystems and consequent high population densities, and location alongside trade routes and exchange of innovations, that many parts of Europe benefited from, leading to the emergence of states and advanced military technology, and also of deadly diseases, all of which enabled imperialists from Europe to conquer many countries outside Europe, especially in the Americas and Africa.

All of these approaches and concepts are very relevant to the sociology of development, and especially to *contributions in the sociology of development that are part of a trend to bring the state back into sociological research,* a trend that includes studies of the negative and also positive effects that states can have on development. I especially focus upon contributions by sociologists Matthew Lange and Peter Evans. Recent work in the sociology of development has drawn attention to the negative legacy for the development of countries outside Europe of conquest by European states. This often left a legacy of post-colonial states that are either failed states or weak states mired in problems of violence and underdevelopment. Lange has especially drawn attention to the legacy associated with the rule of imperialists from Europe upon the countries they conquered, and to the violence that is rife in failed states and weak states. This volume begins to generalize Lange's findings and to theorize the effects of violence on development and democracy in all geographical locations, including locations in the semi-periphery and periphery in or near Europe, in which the social war of maneuver led to the emergence of poverty and violence traps, and of violent social movements. Violence in its turn led to underdevelopment and dictatorship in these countries. I suggest that a number of different social phenomena, from crime like banditry and the mafia, to violent social movements like fascism, nazism, populism, and islamofascism, are all related to the degeneration of social conflict into violence in certain locations of the world system, a degeneration that has disastrous consequences for development and democracy. These effects explain the origins of those states that Evans described as predatorial states, which continued, and still continue, this legacy of violence initiated by imperialists from Europe.

Part 2 and Chapters 3 and 4 provide important concepts concerning the state, the systems that it participates in, and networks across institutions and organizations, as part of a critical appraisal of key approaches and concepts from contemporary theories in sociology, geography, and World Systems Theory, as well as the sociology of development, that I have just introduced. Part 2 provides the broadest framework and concepts for the arguments of this book. *Chapter 3* introduces all the key concepts from macro historical sociology, macro historical geography, and from World Systems Theory, that I use in this volume, suggesting that they are all part of what might be called *a return of general theory in social science*. These are the broadest approaches and concepts, with the widest applicability, either because they are most general, or because they concern globalization. In particular, the chapter discusses the concepts of world system and state system. This chapter also defends general theory understood as a type of theory that, in conjunction with macro historical sociology and geography, covers large time spans and vast geographical distances, both of which are indispensable to understand globalization. *Chapter 4* provides an appraisal of sociological theories of development and democracy, within the framework defined in Chapter 3. It suggests that Lange's theory and Evans' theory are part of a *trend towards a rediscovery of the role of the state in development*. Their main contribution is the argument that not all states are bad for development, some actively promote it, and that the state in general is indispensable to provide defense and also to avoid the degeneration of social conflict into violence. To this I add the consideration that, in addition to state type, the different systems that a state participates in also affect development. These different systems can be external to the state, as in the ecosystems studied by Diamond, and the state systems studied by Wallerstein, or they can be internal to the state, and constitute a state-society system and a state-markets system, respectively systems that include institutions and organization active between the state and civil society, and between the state and markets. This chapter also introduces the concepts of political-military development, which is promoted by states, and of cultural development, which is promoted by civil society. I suggest that political-military development and cultural development are important in their own right, and also because they contribute to economic development. Different states can lead to altogether different levels of political-military development and cultural development, and ultimately of economic development. They also have different degrees of ability to coordinate amongst these types of development.

The arguments in Part 2 of this volume lead to two main revisions of important arguments regarding the social origins of democracy in civil society and its impact on development, in particular political scientist Robert Putnam's work on democracy and civic traditions in Italy. I suggest *two revisions to Putnam's theory regarding development and democracy in Italy,* a theory that sought to explain uneven development across regions of Italy. Putnam argued that the greater number of civil society organizations in northern Italy led to greater democracy, and ultimately to greater development, compared to southern Italy. I also bring out the importance of arguments in this part of the book to revise a similar theory to Putnam's that was formulated by sociologist

Harvey Molotch and his collaborators for the specific case of urban planning and the built environment in two counties in the United States, whereby the county with the greater civil society also had better urban planning and a better built environment, which attracted investment and a greater participation from the citizenry, and thus ultimately contributed to greater development. The arguments in this part of the volume also begin a revision of institutional theories of economics and politics, like Elinor Ostrom's later work on these topics. This first revision emphasizes the *importance of institutions in relation to the whole of a country*, not just the economy, focusing in particular upon cultural as well as political institutions, and upon networks between institutions and organizations within markets, civil society, and the state This includes the view that the state interacts with social groups, and while it is closer to elites, particularly aristocratic-military elites, it is the subject of contention with the masses, which try to get the state to recognize and address their grievances and implement a more broadly based and just development. Evans started theorizing the manner in which the sociological concept of embedded autonomy applies to the interaction between states and markets, to produce what Evans called developmental states, that is, states that actively advance development. Embedded autonomy entails a relationship whereby states and markets remain autonomous of each other, but through appropriate social networks that provide embeddedness, are capable of sharing information and coordinating activities. The second revision entails *an international dimension to development and democracy*. These networks and embedded autonomy are impossible in those geographical locations and social conditions in which there is heightened conflict and violence is rife, where violent social movements and a social war of maneuver prevail. This suggests that we have to add an international dimension to the study of networks, because as Gramsci suggested, civil society and democracy are strong in the core, and weak in those locations that World Systems Theory calls the semi-periphery and periphery of the world system.

Part 3 and Chapters 5 and 6 argue that *the Durkheimian division of labour in society is a major source of development, which is stable only where democracy and embedded autonomy prevail. Chapter 5* sets out the theoretical groundwork for the general theory. It suggests that *the division of labour in society in modern times entails the emergence of three distinct arenas, the economic, cultural, and political-military arenas*, encompassing respectively much of the economy, culture, and politics and the military. In modern *capitalist* societies these arenas roughly correspond to markets, civil society, and the state, all of which are indispensable to development. This is because the cultural and political-military arenas advance their own distinctive types of development, and also provide both capital and regulation to the economic arena that are indispensable to it, for example in the form of values and laws. Embedded autonomy is important to development, because it enables the sharing of information and coordination of activities that ensure this provision of capital and regulation. Embedded autonomy complements democracy understood as a balance of power in society, and a division of powers in society, whereby economic, cultural, and political-military power remain autonomous of each other yet in constant dialogue. *Chapter 6* contains the theses that constitute the main theory of development and democracy put forward in this volume, proposing what amounts to a unified approach to development and democracy as part of a theory of power. It argues that *development and democracy are closely related, as they both involve power*, since development is the growth of power, while democracy is the distribution of power in society. These theses also suggest the mechanisms whereby the division of labour in society leads to development, arguing that organizational forms and principles of behavior distinctive to each arena maximize development in each arena, that is, the development that is distinctive to each arena, and that each arena is best at producing, and through embedded autonomy there arise efficiencies and synergies that maximize overall development in a country.

The arguments in Part 3 of this volume lead to three main revisions of important arguments regarding what constitutes development, and what are the sources of development, including in particular revisions of the capability approach to development proposed by philosopher Martha Nussbaum and economist Amartya Sen. The first revision consists in *approaching development as the growth of power, not just capabilities*, specifically locating capabilities within a theory of power. This extension follows logically from the capability approach. Evans began studying collective capabilities, as well as the individual capabilities that Sen focuses on, and I propose that military capabilities are an important instance of collective capabilities, and are part of political-military development, which includes also other important components such as the capability to formulate and express one's views and grievances, as well as the organization necessary to pursue them through deliberate and sustained collective action with others who share one's views and grievances. This extension also follows from a conflict view of society, which entails that capabilities, whether in politics and the military, culture, or the economy, are always relative, and should be measured in comparison to the capabilities of other individuals, social groups, or states, or relative to the needs of a harsh environment, and are thus part of power in society and over nature. Therefore, development is not *just* the expansion of capabilities, but the growth in power, including economic, cultural, and political-military power. The second revision of the capability approach that I propose begins to study the sources of collective capabilities that arise chiefly from organizational, as well as technological, innovation. This leads me to a revision of *the Smithian division of labour in a factory as part of a broader division of labour in society.* The latter includes a division of labour in industrial districts, between factories and cultural institutions such as high schools and universities, and a division of labour within a country, between the economic, cultural, and political-military arenas, and their respective organizations and institutions. The third revision concerns the *Smithian concept of the self-regulating market,* suggesting that all rapidly expanding markets, and the large markets associated with modern capitalist societies, are not self-regulating, but require regulation from both culture and politics, without which markets are imperfect and dominated by coercion rather than competition, and even fail to arise, for example in geographical locations rife with violence, whether from criminality or violent social movements.

Part 4 and Chapters 7 and 8 argue that *the division of labour in the world system is associated with imperialism and uneven development, and leads to major distortions in development and democracy within countries,* including countries in the semi-periphery and periphery, and also countries in the core, at least in the long run. This complements another revision of Smithian economic theory, which argues that out of competition between countries on international markets, an ideal division of labor between countries emerges. This is not the case. *Chapter 7* sets out the theoretical groundwork for a theory about the origins of imperialism and uneven development. These arose from conflict in the core, which led to a marked expansion that negatively affected countries in the semi-periphery and periphery through a combination of social disaggregation initiated by the expansion of the world economy and capitalism, and conquest or being brought under the sphere of influence of states in the core. Focusing on uneven political-military development across countries, and on the projection of power by states in the core, the chapter suggests that the social disaggregation that accompanied incorporation in the world economy, together with a skewed balance of power in society associated with the projection of power by states in the core, led to poverty and violence traps, violent social movements, and underdevelopment and dictatorship in countries outside the core, with enduring negative influences for development and democracy. *Chapter 8* contains the theses that constitute the main theory regarding the origins of imperialism and uneven development. It suggests the mechanisms whereby, out of a combination of social conflict and interstate conflict in the core, there emerged a marked tendency towards imperial expansion in colonial ventures alongside sea lanes. This led to the survival of mixed organizational forms that combined market competition with violence, a combination clearly visible in European trading companies, and later in neocolonial corporations, that were active in long-distance trade. The main argument is that the division of labour in the world system is far from ideal, as it is based upon various forms of exploitation based on violence, and is associated with rents, or easy profits, that should not be confused with development, and in fact undermine it.

The arguments in Part 4 of this volume lead to a major revision of World Systems Theory that is relevant to questions of international development, and to a revision of theories of development that emphasizes the concept of *social rents*, that I suggest arise from a skewed distribution of power in society. This argument continues the unified approach to development and democracy as part of a theory of power by applying it to international relations, and their effect on countries and the distribution of power within countries. This revision of World Systems Theory argues that the origin of the division of the world system into a core, semi-periphery, and periphery, was due uneven political-military development across countries, and to geopolitical and geocultural features of the core of the state system, which led to the creation and survival for a long time of social rents. This argument also revises a theory of development associated with neoliberalism that was put forward by political scientist Robert Bates regarding development in Africa, which was undermined by states protecting local markets and thus keeping local prices for agricultural products artificially high. Bates suggested that states thus created rents, that is, easy profits without investment and any improvement in the economy, which can aptly be called state rents. Building upon a number of insights introduced by Gramsci, I propose the more general concept of social rents, or rents that I define as rents arising in all geographical locations in which the balance of power in society is so skewed that one social group is entirely dominated by another, and it has no bargaining power, which enables elites to extract profits without promoting development, often by keeping the cost of labour artificially low. The states policies identified by Bates, and the failed states and weak states identified by Lange, create state rents that are part of these social rents, as they arise from them, and further contribute to them. This affects development for the entire country, as part of the effects of a geographical location in which the elites dominate the masses, because elites can extract profits without increasing development, that is, without focusing upon introducing efficiencies and synergies through better organization and more advanced technology, or more investment in economic capital and cultural capital, like a better trained and more skilled workforce. These elites and their states were closely associated with European aristocratic-military elites which, when challenged at home, just moved further away in their search for social rents, which they created or accentuated through the mix of trade and conquest that they employed, and through their alliances with local elites.

PART 1

Summary of the Hypotheses and Theses of the Theory

∴

Introduction to Notebook 12, Remarks and miscellaneous notes for a group of essays on the history of intellectuals
In England the development [of intellectuals and politicians who led industrialization] is very different than in France. The new social groups that were born on the terrain of modern industrialization have a surprising economic-corporative development, but proceed tentatively in the intellectual and political field[s]. The group of organic intellectuals, born on the same terrain of industrial development as the economic group, [the bourgeoisie directly involved in industrialization], is vast, but in the highest levels [of power] we can find the old landholding class, preserved in the position of near monopoly [that it traditionally enjoyed]. [...] The English phenomenon [of survival of the landholding class] is present also in Germany, [where it is] complicated by other historical and traditional elements. Germany, like Italy, was the seat of a universalist institution and ideology (the Holy Roman Empire) and it gave a certain number of intellectuals to the medieval cosmopolis [...] Industrial development took place under a semi-feudal wrap that lasted until November 1918, and the Junkers maintained a politico-intellectual supremacy [even] greater than the comparable English social group [of landholders].

ANTONIO GRAMSCI, *Prison Notebooks*, Notebook 12, Note 1, p.1526. My emphasis.[1]

∴

---

1 Antonio Gramsci, *Quaderni del Carcere*, ed. Valentino Gerratana, 4 vols. (Torino: Einaudi, 2007), 1526. This and other passages where I cite Gramsci are my translations from the Italian original. They reflect my interpretation of Gramsci's work.

CHAPTER 1

Hypotheses on Neoliberalism and Elites and Collective Action

This volume proposes a general theory of development and democracy that is alternative to neoliberal economic theories. This general theory argues that we need to provide *comprehensive development*, that is, development across all domains of human activity, namely, the economy, culture, politics, and the military, and not just in the economy. It also argues that *development needs democracy*, and that uneven development can lead to loss of both development and democracy in the long run. At the same time as making these arguments, the general theory tries to explain the success of neoliberalism, and the populist backlash that followed it, in an effort to understand the place of neoliberalism and the populist backlash in the contemporary history of the West and its effect upon uneven development in the West. Neoliberalism is rooted in phenomena, and more specifically processes, that affect our culture and politics. In the project that this book is part of, I argue that an important reason for the wide diffusion and acceptance of neoliberalism is that neoliberalism was aided by cultural phenomena such as increasing specialization within universities and the increasing remoteness of academics from the rest of culture, and ultimately from the rest of society.[1] I also argue that another important reason for the wide diffusion and acceptance of neoliberalism is that it was aided by such political phenomena as imperialism, which led to, or at least contributed to, uneven development. The overall argument regarding neoliberalism and development is that, together with other phenomena (neoliberalism, populism, imperialism, and uneven development) they are the product of, or have been largely exploited and amplified by, Western elites and other elites that are active on both the national and international stages. A key part of these elites is an emergent imperialist world-elite that coordinates amongst disparate national elites. What made these elites successful, and their ideologies including neoliberalism widely accepted, was the ability of these elites to drive globalization to their advantage, and to continue increasing their collective

---

[1] I argue this point in: Olsaretti, *The Struggle for Development and Democracy, Vol. 1.* I also address it in the essays *Towards a Humanist Social Science.*

action advantage, that is, their greater ability to engage in collective action compared to the masses, and thus to dominate politics.

1   Definitions of the Main Concepts of the General Theory

This volume seeks to explain four concepts, namely, neoliberalism, populism, imperialism, and uneven development, addressing also other key phenomena in the modern history of the West, like fascism and nazism, that have affected countries throughout the world. Since these four concepts are widely used in the vast literature that studies development, and in somewhat different manners, I want to begin by providing definitions of these four concepts that clarify what I am referring to when I use these concepts. *Neoliberalism and populism* are closely related in the theory that I propose, since it emphasizes that populism is at least in part a backlash against neoliberalism.[2] I use the term *neoliberalism* to refer to an economic theory that argues unregulated markets are the only way to provide the greatest economic growth, and seeks to diminish state intervention to the absolute minimum that is necessary to guarantee the functioning of markets.[3] I include in the concept of neoliberalism also the claim that markets can be applied to other domains of human behavior, that is, to culture and politics, a claim that builds upon neoliberal theories that unregulated markets are more efficient than other forms of organization. Neoliberalism was initially closely associated with the department of economics at the University of Chicago, where Milton Friedman taught, but has since been accepted in many other universities and departments.[4] I use the term *populism* to refer to a political ideology distinguished by three features: proposing simple solutions to complex problems through unscrupulous

---

2   The idea of a populist backlash is discussed by Rawi Abdelal, in: Rawi Abdelal, "Dignity, Inequality, and the Populist Backlash: Lessons from America and Europe for a Sustainable Globalization," *Global Policy* 11, no. 4 (2020).

3   The concept of neoliberalism is treated in similarly broad terms by David Harvey in: David Harvey, *A Brief History of Neoliberalism* (Oxford and New York: Oxford University Press, 2007).

4   The importance of Milton Friedman and the department of economics at the University of Chicago is discussed by: Edward Nik-Khah, "Chicago Neoliberalism and the Genesis of the Milton Friedman Institute (2006–2009)," in *Building Chicago Economics: New Perspectives on the History of America's Most Powerful Economics Program*, ed. Robert Van Horn, Philip Mirowski, and Thomas A. Stapleford (Cambridge and New York: Cambridge University Press New York, 2011). All contributions in this edited volume are interesting. See also: Edward Nik-Khah and Robert Van Horn, "The Ascendancy of Chicago Neoliberalism," in *The Handbook of Neoliberalism*, ed. Simon Springer, Kean Birch, and Julie MacLeavy (London and New York: Routledge, 2016).

politicians; xenophobic nationalism that presents migrants and developing countries as the main threat to development; and bad rhetoric, including inflammatory rhetoric used by unscrupulous politicians who propose quick and drastic solutions that include blaming scapegoats, typically migrants and developing countries. When I refer to populist *backlash*, I do so in order to draw attention to the fact that most populism occurred as a reaction to other ideologies or policies, especially neoliberalism in the course of the 1990s, and was amplified by the 9/11 attacks and other terrorist attacks, which created a perception of Arab countries as a threat.[5]

As I use the term, *imperialism* refers to the combination of an ideology and practices whereby empires are built. The ideology justifies the conquest and exploitation of other countries, through military or other means, and it is associated with imperialist practices, that is, ways to conquer and exploit other countries that are routinized. The imperialist practices include divide-and-conquer and divide-and-rule tactics. Both ideologies and practices are part of the way in which imperialist elites operate in building empires.[6] Imperialism is not a new phenomenon, as it has been present in much of modern European history. This raises some important questions. Why has democracy been combined with imperialism in much of the modern history of the West? Why was Great Britain the country that advanced the most both democracy and imperialism? What does this mean for the prospects of development and democracy in the West? Sociology at its inception sought to understand the social features that affected development and democracy in the history of the West.[7]

---

5   A discussion of populism that reviews its various aspects is provided by: Jan-Werner Muller, *What Is Populism?* (Philadelphia: University of Pennsylvania Press, 2016).

6   The following two studies are complementary. They are respectively a study focused upon the ideology associated with empire and the practices associated with state formation or state-building, and a study based on the institutional approach that focuses on state formation itself: David Armitage, *The Ideological Origins of the British Empire*, Ideas in Context (Cambridge and New York: Cambridge University Press, 2000); Michael J. Braddick, *State Formation in Early Modern England, C.1550–1700* (Cambridge and New York: Cambridge University Press, 2000). I consider building an empire to be a particular practice that affects state formation. In the process of state formation whereby states developed into full-blown semi-autonomous or autonomous organizations above society, different social groups tried to build different types of states. I addressed state formation in parts of the Ottoman empire in: Alessandro Olsaretti, "Political Dynamics in the Rise of Fakhr al-Din, 1590–1633: Crusade, Trade, and State Formation Along the Levantine Coast," *The International History Review* 30, no. 4 (2008). My approach in this article was informed by the view that in the sixteenth century there was a process of state formation in the core of the Ottoman empire, in competition with other processes of state formation alongside the Levantine coast.

7   The involvement of sociology in studies of empire, and in some cases in imperialism itself, is the subject of the many interesting contributions in: George Steinmetz, ed. *Sociology*

The association between the West and imperialism was formulated as a socio-logical question known as the Rise of the West, a question that also asked what were the causes and consequences of European colonial expansion. I argue that it is still very important to understand the reasons for the association between democracy and imperialism, and also more specifically to answer this question.

Lastly, I use the expression *uneven development* to refer to a number of dif-ferent social phenomena, not just uneven development across countries, on the international stage, which is what is usually meant by uneven develop-ment. The latter definition, still common amongst development planners, was made famous by Soviet theorists.[8] Some authors today study uneven development across individuals, whereby measures of development such as a high average income and high life expectancy, nevertheless present a large spread when measured across individuals within a country. Sen is amongst these authors, and so are sociologists who focus on measuring life expectancy within the United States.[9] By contrast, I emphasize both *uneven development across countries*, whereby some countries are more developed than others, and also *uneven development within countries*, within which I address three types of uneven development that are little studied and are undertheorized in much of the literature on uneven development. The first type is uneven development across arenas, whereby high economic development might not be accompa-nied by political development and cultural development, in the form of large numbers of NGOs and NPOs. The second type is an uneven development across social groups, whereby the middle class, or upper middle class, benefits from development and increases its income and life expectancy, whereas the working class does not. This is an alarming phenomenon in different countries in the West.[10] The third type is an uneven development across geographical

---

and Empire: The Imperial Entanglements of a Discipline (Durham and London: Duke University Press, 2013). For an critical overview of Marxist contributions to the study of imperialism, see: Anthony Brewer, *Marxist Theories of Imperialism: A Critical Survey* (London and New York: Routledge, 1990). Interestingly, Barrington Moore Jr was an expert on Soviet politics.

8   A more general approach to uneven development was introduced in: Neil Smith, *Uneven Development: Nature, Capital, and the Production of Space* (Athens: University of Georgia Press, 2008).

9   Sen has criticized the wide spread in life expectancy within the United States in: Amartya Sen, *Development as Freedom* (Oxford and New York: Oxford University Press, 2001).

10   The problem of uneven development in the United States was addressed by: Theda Skocpol, *The Missing Middle: Working Families and the Future of American Social Policy* (New York: W.W. Norton, 2000). On similar processes affecting the middle class in Italy, particularly the lower middle class, see: Arnaldo Bagnasco and Doug Thompson, "The

areas, which can be different parts of a city, different counties or regions, or even different macro regions, in a given country. The Southern Question introduced in the first volume is a question regarding the origins of the relative underdevelopment of the whole of southern Italy compared to northern Italy. A similar question has been raised for the American South.[11] I argue that it is very important to understand the sources of uneven development across regions, and especially to explain why this type of uneven development is so hard to overcome.

I relate all of the above concepts to democracy. *Democracy* involves the distribution of power in society. Democracy in the political-military domain of human activity, which is what we typically refer to when we refer to democracy, is *a distribution of power favorable to the masses that depends upon the ability to engage in collective action*, since this is the main type of activity in this domain. I develop at some length in this book a theory first put forward by Sydney Tarrow and Charles Tilly, which suggests that modern democracies arose thanks to the ability of the masses to engage in collective action and demand and achieve political freedoms and political democracy from powerful states as part of a process of democratization.[12] These freedoms were further expanded also thanks to the ability of the masses to engage in collective action, and this expansion arguably contributed to the trends in the expansion of citizenship in modern states, since citizenship evolved out of struggles between civil society and states, particularly struggles between, on the one hand, social groups that were part of the masses and the social movements they gave rise

---

Question of the Middle Class," *Italian Politics* 20 (2004). Bagnasco and Thompson are more optimistic that these processes have not yet greatly affected the entire middle class in Italy, just the lower middle class.

11   I address the Southern Question in sections 1.4, 1.5, and 2.7 of: Olsaretti, *The Struggle for Development and Democracy, Vol. 1*. For a recent review of the state of this question in Italian scholarship, see: Guido Pescosolido, *La Questione Meridionale in Breve: Centocinquant'Anni di Storia* (Rome: Donzelli Editore, 2017). For a comparison between the United States and Italy, see: Don Harrison Doyle, *Nations Divided: America, Italy, and the Southern Question* (Athens, Georgia, and London: University of Georgia Press, 2002).

12   The theory is set out in several books and edited volumes: Charles Tilly, *Social Movements, 1768–2004* (Boulder: Paradigm Publishers, 2004); Charles Tilly, Sydney Tarrow, and Doug McAdam, *Contention and Democracy in Europe, 1650–2000*, Cambridge Studies in Contentious Politics (Cambridge and New York: Cambridge University Press, 2004); Charles Tilly and Sidney G. Tarrow, *Contentious Politics*, (Oxford and New York: Oxford University Press, 2015). This theory contributed a number of important concepts for social movements research: Jacquelien van Stekelenburg, Conny Roggeband, and Bert Klandermans, *The Future of Social Movement Research: Dynamics, Mechanisms, and Processes*, Social Movements, Protest and Contention (Minneapolis: University of Minnesota Press, 2013).

to and, on the other hand, the elites that were engaged in building modern states. I differ from Tarrow and Tilly in many important ways that I describe below, but the insight that democracy is related to collective action and social movements, an insight that was already present in Gramsci's work and was theorized and researched at length by Tarrow and Tilly, is very valuable and it is important to elaborate upon it. I also build upon the insight proposed by Tilly that *the elites' participation in state formation shared similarities with organized crime*.[13] This was in part because the same social conditions that favored elites favored also organized crime, and in part because some elites made use of crime in order to keep some of their power outside the state and under their exclusive control. This was a deviation from Weber's concept of state formation, whereby states claimed the monopoly of legitimate violence over a territory, a monopoly that was closely related to the emergence of citizenship, and the associated rights and duties.

2   Gramsci's Theory of Hegemony and Uneven Development

My approach to uneven development builds upon Gramsci's essay titled *The Southern Question*. This essay sets out a number of points that Gramsci took up and further elaborated upon in the *Prison Notebooks*, within the context of a broader theory of hegemony and power. It is useful to begin this discussion with a clarification regarding nomenclature. I use the expression the Southern Question to refer to the social science question, addressed by several authors in Italy in the past, while the title *The Southern Question* refers to Gramsci's essay that he wrote shortly before being imprisoned.[14] As explained in Volume 1, the Southern Question is a question regarding the origins of the relative underdevelopment of the whole of a macro region of Italy, southern Italy, compared to another macro region, northern Italy, although there are other important differences, for example between north-western and north-eastern

---

13   Charles Tilly, "War Making and State Making as Organized Crime," in *Bringing the State Back In*, ed. Peter Evans, Dietrich Rueschemeyer, and Theda Skocpol (New York: Cambridge University Press, 1985).

14   Antonio Gramsci, *La Questione Meridionale* (Roma: Editori Riuniti, 1974). There are numerous editions of The Southern Question. It was translated into English as: Antonio Gramsci and Pasquale Verdicchio, *The Southern Question*, trans. Pasquale Verdicchio, Picas (Toronto, Buffalo, Chicago, Lacaster: Guernica Editions, 2005). Amongst the intellectuals who worked on this question, there was also historian Gaetano Salvemini: Salvatore Lucchese, *Federalismo, Socialismo e Questione Meridionale in Gaetano Salvemini*, Meridiana (Manduria, Taranto: Piero Lacaita, 2004).

Italy, and between the models of development known as the First, Second, and Third Italy. The First Italy typically refers to the industrialized north-west, the Second Italy to the underdeveloped south, and the Third Italy to parts of the center and the north-east in which a model of development based upon Small and Medium Enterprises, or SMES, and industrial districts prevailed.[15] Michelangelo Vasta and his collaborators have emphasized the importance of new forms of organization to the Italian economy that emerged from the decline of both mass production as emphasized by Michael Piore and Charles Sabel, and of the Second Italy.[16] There have also been important changes in the relationship between the banking sector in Italy and Italian companies. Raising capital outside family sources has been a major challenge for Italian companies, many of which are SMES.[17]

The Southern Question is of especial interest beyond Italy because there is *uneven development across regions in other countries in the West.* The uneven development between southern Italy and the rest of Italy that is central to the Southern Question is perhaps one of the most marked and enduring instances of this type of uneven development.[18] However, there is a similar

---

15   See sections 1.4, 1.5, and 1.6 in: Olsaretti, *The Struggle for Development and Democracy, Vol. 1.*

16   Alberto Rinaldi and Michelangelo Vasta, "The Italian Corporate Network after the 'Golden Age' (1972–1983): From Centrality to Marginalization of State-Owned Enterprises," *Enterprise & Society* 13, no. 2 (2012). On new forms of organization, see the many contributions in: Renao Giannetti and Michelanelo Vasta, eds., *Evolution of Italian Enterprises in the 20th Century* (Physica-Verlag, 2009); Andrea Colli and Michelangelo Vasta, *Forms of Enterprise in 20th Century Italy: Boundaries, Structures and Strategies* (Cheltenham, UK and Northampton, Massachusetts: Edward Elgar, 2010). Both Vasta and Giannettti worked also on technological innovation: Renato Giannetti, ed. *Nel Mito di Prometeo. L'innovazione Tecnologica Dalla Rivoluzione Industriale ad Oggi. Temi, Inventori e Protagonisti dall'Ottocento al Duemila* (Firenze: Ponte alle Grazie, 1996). The decline of Fordist methods of mass production in relation to SMES was studied by: Michael Piore and Charles Sabel, *The Second Industrial Divide: Possibilities for Prosperity* (New York: Basic Books, 1986).

17   Michelangelo Vasta et al., "Reassessing the Bank–Industry Relationship in Italy, 1913–1936: a Counterfactual Analysis," *Cliometrica* 11, no. 2 (2017); Michelangelo Vasta and Alberto Baccini, "Banks and Industry in Italy, 1911–36: New Evidence Using the Interlocking Directorates Technique," *Financial History Review* 4, no. 2 (1997). On the difficulties in small business finance, see: Luigi Guiso, "Small Business Finance in Italy," *EIB papers* 8, no. 2 (2003). For a comparison between Italy and Great Britain/UK in SMES, see: Thorsten Beck and Asli Demirguc-Kunt, "Small and Medium-Size Enterprises: Access to Finance as a Growth Constraint," *Journal of Banking & finance* 30, no. 11 (2006).

18   On the enduring differences in income between north and south, see: Emanuele Felice, "Regional Income Inequality in Italy in the Long Run (1871–2010): Patterns and Determininants," in *The Economic Development of Europe's Regions: A Quantitative History since 1900*, ed. Joan Ramon Rosés and Nolf Wolf (London and New York: Routledge, 2018).

divide in Spain between the capital Madrid, the center-north including Bilbao, and Catalonia including Barcelona, all of which have high economic development, and the south-west of Spain, whose economic development is comparable to southern Italy.[19] Even amongst countries with advanced capitalism and high *average* economic development, there is significant uneven development across regions. In Great Britain, the country/regions Northern Ireland, Scotland, and Wales, all historically had lower economic development than England. In the United States, the American South has been historically less developed economically than the north-east and the west of the country.[20]

What is especially interesting about Gramsci's views on the Southern Question is that he introduced *a number of insights and began to approach the question of uneven development within a country in a general way*, as part of a theory of hegemony and power. Historian Peter Gran has begun applying Gramsci's insights to a comparative historical sociology of uneven development, comparing the enduring uneven development across regions in Italy to similar phenomena in Egypt and India.[21] In this volume I focus upon three insights by Gramsci that he began to elaborate upon in *The Southern Question*, all of which concern *the difficulties of the masses in southern Italy in lifting themselves out of poverty*, whether by forming class alliances, or by pursuing deliberate and sustained collective action on their own. The first insight regards *divisions across social groups*. Gramsci observed that most of the working class was concentrated in northern Italy, and most of the peasantry in southern Italy.[22] This insight can be reformulated using the modern concept of social formation, a concept that has been adapted to World Systems Theory. It suggests that a purely industrial country, or even a purely industrial region of

19   Alfonso Diez-Minguela, Julio Martinez-Galarraga, and Daniel A. Tirado-Fabregat, *Regional Inequality in Spain: 1860–2015*, Palgrave Studies in Economic History (London and New York: Palgrave MacMillan, 2018).

20   Philip McCann, *The UK Regional-National Economic Problem: Geography, Globalisation and Governance*, Regions and Cities (London and New York: Routledge, 2016). Frank Greary and Tom Stark, "150 Years of Regional GDP: United Kingdom and Ireland," in *The Economic Development of Europe's Regions: A Quantitative History since 1900*, ed. Joan Ramon Rosés and Nolf Wolf (London and New York: Routledge, 2018); Alexander Klein, "Regional Inequality in the United States: Long-Term Patterns, 1880–2010," ibid.For a discussion of the contested nature of these divides, see: Sara González, "The North/South Divide in Italy and England: Discursive Construction of Regional Inequality," *European Urban and Regional Studies* 18, no. 1 (2011).

21   Peter Gran, *Beyond Eurocentrism: A New View of Modern World History* (Syracuse: Syracuse University Press, 1996). This book, while containing interesting insights, is not very successful at theory building.

22   Gramsci, *La Questione Meridionale*.

a country, is rarely encountered in practice. What one encounters are various combinations of industrial areas and agrarian areas.[23] In the early twentieth century, southern Italy was predominantly agrarian, and the most numerous class was the peasantry, which worked either on large estates, or in small farms with sharecropping. At that time, northern Italy was agrarian too, at least compared to France and Great Britain, but had important industrial centers that would continue growing, later attracting migration from southern Italy.[24] These industrial centers included Turin, the regional capital of Piedmont, and Milan, the regional capital of Lombardy. The social division just introduced was compounded by geographical distance, linguistic differences, and cultural stereotypes, all of which made it very hard to form alliances between the working class and the peasantry.

The second insight by Gramsci regards *the inability of the masses in southern Italy to participate in any hegemony*. This point can be divided into two parts. One part emphasizes that *the masses in southern Italy were unable to articulate and pursue their grievances, and also to formulate their own hegemony* that would be alternative to the hegemony of the elites and the vision for Italy that these elites formulated and implemented. Gramsci suggested that this inability was due to the lack of intellectuals. High intellectuals from southern Italy like Benedetto Croce and Giustino Fortunato were detached from the masses in southern Italy, and closer in their vision for the country and in political alliances to industrialists from northern Italy like Senator Agnelli, the owner of one of Italy's most important car manufacturers at the time.[25] The other part emphasizes that *some of the masses in southern Italy had undergone social disaggregation*, and had been reduced to poverty, some pushed into poverty and violence traps, so that they lost all community, all or most social ties, and all

---

23   Chase-Dunn extended Luis Althusser's concept of social formation to the world system in: Christopher Chase-Dunn, *Global Formation: Structures of the World-Economy* (Oxford: Basil Blackwell, 1991).

24   For an overview of the history of the north-south divide in Italy, see: Gianni Toniolo, "An Overview of Italy's Economic Growth," in *The Oxford Handbook of the Italian Economy since Unification*, ed. Gianni Toniolo (Oxford and New York: Oxford University Press 2013); Giovanni Iuzzolino, Guido Pellegrini, and Gianfranco Viesti, "Regional Convergence," ibid. For the role that access to markets played in this divide, see: Brian A'Hearn and Anthony J. Venables, "Regional Disparities: Internal Geographies and External Trade," ibid. Important north-west/south inequalities were found also by: Giovanni Federico, Alessandro Nuvolari, and Michelangelo Vasta, "The Origins of the Italian Regional Divide: Evidence from Real Wages, 1861–1913," *The Journal of Economic History* 79, no. 1 (2019).

25   This point is central to: Gramsci, *La Questione Meridionale*. Croce and Fortunato were Senators and possibly cooperated in the Italian Senate with Agnelli.

ability to engage in collective action. They were therefore completely dominated by elites whose vision for development in Italy largely excluded the
masses in southern Italy. The massive migration from southern Italy to Latin
America and North America in the past was due to this condition of the peasantry in southern Italy as a dominated social group whose region of origin
offered few or no possibilities for employment.[26]

The third insight by Gramsci regards *the importance of education to lift the
masses in southern Italy out of poverty*, as part of efforts to formulate their own
hegemony. Education is important both to the masses themselves, as it enables
them to participate consciously in social movements, and also to the masses'
ability to organize by creating a group of organic intellectuals drawn from the
masses and working for the masses. Gramsci's own activism, as well as his theoretical work on education, addressed all these questions.[27] Theorist of education Aziz Choudry, has been elaborating upon parts of this insight by Gramsci,
and is focusing on the importance of intellectual work to social movements,
and of organizations such as Non-Governmental Organizations, or NGOs, that
participate in these social movements. The latter also raise concerns regarding the professionalization of activism, and the move away from civil society
volunteering.[28] Other theorists of education, Rachel Zellars and Rosalind

---

26   For an overview that includes the benefits of migration for the Italian economy through
      remittances, see: Matteo Gomellini and Cormac Ó Gráda, "Migrations," in *The Oxford
      Handbook of the Italian Economy since Unification*, ed. Gianni Toniolo (Oxford and
      New York: Oxford University Press 2013). Piore's earlier work emphasized the economic
      problems that migration is associated with: Michael Piore, *Birds of Passage: Migrant Labor
      and Industrial Societies* (Cambridge and New York: Cambridge University Press, 1979).

27   Mayo has focused on Gramsci's approach to education: Peter Mayo, *Gramsci, Freire and
      Adult Education: Possibilities for Transformative Action* (London and New York: Zed Books,
      1999); *Hegemony and Education under Neoliberalism: Insights from Gramsci* (London and
      New York: Routledge, 2015). See also the many contributions in: Carmel Borg, Joseph
      A. Buttigieg, and Peter Mayo, eds., *Gramsci and Education*, Culture and Politics Series
      (Lanham, Boulder, New York, and Oxford: Rowman & Littlefield, 2002); Nicola Pizzolato
      and John D. Holst, eds., *Antonio Gramsci: A Pedagogy to Change the World*, Critical Studies
      of Education (Cham, Switzerland: Springer, 2017). I address the importance of organic
      and traditional intellectuals to Gramsci in: Alessandro Olsaretti, "Beyond Class: The Many
      Facets of Gramsci's Theory of Intellectuals," *Journal of Classical Sociology* 14, no. 4 (2014).

28   Aziz Choudry, *Learning Activism: The Intellectual Life of Contemporary Social Movements*
      (Toronto, Buffalo, London: University of Toronto Press, 2015). On the successes and
      organizational problems facing activists involved in knowledge production, see the
      many contributions in: Dip Kapoor and Aziz Choudry, eds., *Learning from the Ground
      Up: Global Perspectives on Social Movements and Knowledge Production* (London
      and New York: Palgrave Macmillan, 2010); Aziz Choudry and Dip Kapoor, eds.,
      Ngoization: Complicity, Contradictions and Prospects (London and New York: Zed Books,

Hampton, have focused more specifically on problems facing activists in black communities trying to promote education within these communities. They have focused in particular on the combination of organizational problems, and bias and exclusion due to racial prejudices, that black activists are faced with.[29] Sociologist Rabab AbdulHadi has similarly focused on Palestinian activists and campus politics, in particular on Palestinian women, as well as on the negative framing of their activities in the literature and press, which can affect any activists.[30] I begin to address in this book the importance of education and in particular of such cultural institutions as schools for industrial districts and universities for regions, which participate in both development and democracy.

In this volume I begin to elaborate upon these points made by Gramsci within the context of a general theory of development and democracy that is part of a theory of power. I also begin to integrate in this theory of power questions of international relations, and in particular questions regarding

---

2013). The latter edited volume discusses the problems with the professionalization of organizations involved in social movements.

29   Rachel Zellars, "'Too Tedious to Mention:' Pondering the Border, Black Atlantic, and Public Schooling in Colonial Canada," *Left History: An Interdisciplinary Journal of Historical Inquiry and Debate* 23, no. 1 (2019); Rachel B. Zellars, "'As If We Were All Struggling Together:' Black Intellectual Traditions and Legacies of Gendered Violence," *Women's Studies International Forum* 77 (2019). Hampton has focused both on public schools and higher education: rosalind hampton, "Nous Who? Racialized Social Relations and Quebec Student Movement Politics," in *The University and Social Justice: Struggles across the Globe*, ed. Aziz Choudry and Salim Vally (Toronto: Between the Lines publisher, 2020); rosalind hampton and Désirée Rochat, "To Commit and to Lead: Black Women Organizing across Communities in Montreal," in *African Canadian Leadership: Continuity, Transition, and Transformation*, ed. Tamari Kitossa, Erica S. Lawson, and Philip S.S. Howard (Toronto, Buffalo, London: University of Toronto Press, 2019). She also focused specifically on McGill University: rosalind hampton, *Black Racialization and Resistance at an Elite University* (Toronto, Buffalo, London: University of Toronto Press, 2020). Hampton prints her name all in small letters, like black activist bell hooks.

30   AbdulHadi's work focused initially upon social movements and exile: Rabab Abdulhadi, "The Palestinian Women's Autonomous Movement: Emergence, Dynamics, and Challenges," *Gender & Society* 12, no. 6 (1998). "Where Is Home? Fragmented Lives, Border Crossings, and the Politics of Exile," *Radical History Review* 86, no. 1 (2003). She later focused also on the corporate university, and on framing in literature: Rabab Ibrahim AbdulHadi and Saliem Shehadeh, "Resisting the US Corporate University: Palestine, Zionism, and Campus Politics," in *The University and Social Justice: Struggles across the Globe*, ed. Aziz Choudry and Salim Vally (Toronto: Between the Lines publisher, 2020). Rabab Ibrahim Abdulhadi, "Framing Resistance Call and Response: Reading Assata Shakur's Black Revolutionary Radicalism in Palestine," *Women's Studies Quarterly* 46, no. 3 & 4 (2018).

hegemony amongst states, in addition to hegemony amongst social groups, along the lines of the theory proposed by the neogramscians at York University in Toronto, chiefly Stephen Gills, and by Arrighi's work in this field.[31] In this volume I especially emphasize that *hegemony and domination are related to uneven development.* The poverty of the masses in southern Italy, and their inability to articulate and redress their grievances, had serious consequences, both for the masses in southern Italy, and also for the country as a whole. This was part of two general mechanisms that are still at work, in Italy, and arguably also elsewhere. As far as development is concerned, social disaggregation and the inability to participate in any alternative hegemony means that elites do not have to innovate and rely on advanced technology in order to be competitive, nor do they have to be efficient to be competitive, they simply pay the workforce less, relying upon what are for all intents and purposes social rents. After wages and standards of living slowly rose in Italy, and a minimum wage was imposed, these elites simply moved their factories elsewhere, in search of cheaper labour, rather than trying to improve the Italian state and Italian universities, both of which are arguably responsible for the lack of organizational and technological innovation in Italy. Had there been organizational and technological innovation, it would have enabled Italian industry to pursue other strategies of development than reducing labor costs by relocation of industry. As far as democracy is concerned, social disaggregation leads both to large numbers of volunteers who participate in violent social movements like fascism, and also to widespread criminality and organized crime like the mafia. These are military volunteers, whose social origins and conditions overlap with those of groups in shifting military employment, and with terrorists.

---

31   Stephen Gill, *American Hegemony and the Trilateral Commission* (Cambridge and New York: Cambridge University Press, 1991). Gill also edited a book advocating the integration of Gramscian concepts in international relations studies: *Gramsci, Historical Materialism and International Relations*, Cambridge Studies in International Relations (Cambridge and New York: Cambridge University Press, 1993). This book became the founding manifesto for a school of thought in international relations based on Gramsci's theory that is sometimes referred to as 'neogramscians.' Another view on this school is: Andreas Bieler and Adam David Morton, "A Critical Theory Route to Hegemony, World Order and Historical Change: Neo-Gramscian Perspectives in International Relations," *Capital & Class* 28, no. 1 (2004). Gill's most recent statement of his theory of international relations is: Stephen Gill, *Power and Resistance in the New World Order*, 2nd ed. (Palgrave Macmillan, 2008). This book was first published in 2002. For critical reviews of the neogramscians and their approach to questions in international relations, see: Peter Ives and Nicola Short, "On Gramsci and the International: a Textual Analysis," *Review of International Studies* 39, no. 3 (2013); Mark McNally, "The Neo-Gramscians in the Study of International Relations: an Appraisal," *Materialismo Storico* 2, no. 1 (2017).

The focus of this book is on military volunteers. Moreover, these problems of development and democracy reinforce themselves, in a downward spiral that has been very hard to counteract.

3   Hypotheses on Neoliberalism and the Hegemony of Elites

This book began with a large amount of theoretical groundwork, including the above points that I derived from my reading of Gramsci's essay *The Southern Question*, and of the *Prison Notebooks*. This led me to formulate a number of hypotheses regarding the role of elites in neoliberalism, populism, imperialism, and uneven development. In this summary I lay out all the hypotheses that I set out in Volume 1, in the final form that I arrived at after many iterations. These hypotheses suggest that neoliberalism is driven by elites that enjoy a collective action advantage compared to the masses, that is, a greater ability than the masses to engage in collective action. This collective action advantage could be found in Italian elites compared to the masses in Italy, and arguably also in the elites compared to the masses in many other countries in the West, with variations that apply to the case. The hypotheses and theses regarding elites that I put forward all contribute to the study of elites and their role in development initiated by sociologist Richard Lachmann.[32] I lay out in Volume 1 the methodology that I followed in formulating the hypotheses and theses of the general theory, here I just want to emphasize that in formulating the theory I followed many iterations, moving back and forth from case studies to general theory, and from theoretical groundwork to axiomatic-deductive work. I also want to emphasize that I present below both hypotheses and theses in bullet form, and with two or more levels, namely, main hypothesis and sub-hypotheses, and main thesis and sub-theses, because I want to spell out clearly the hypotheses to submit to empirical tests, and the theses to be validated or rejected, as the case may be, by further empirical tests. I believe that a very important task of theory is to formulate precise hypotheses and theses, in order to aid empirical tests. Another important task is to provide a broad picture of the manner in which an entire country works, for example in order to enable formulating cultural policies that aid economic policies. In this volume

---

32   Richard Lachmann, *Capitalists in Spite of Themselves: Elite Conflict and Economic Transitions in Early Modern Europe* (Oxford and New York: Oxford University Press, 2000); "Elite Self-Interest and Economic Decline in Early Modern Europe," *American Sociological Review* (2003); "Hegemons, Empires, and Their Elites," *Sociologia, Problemas e Práticas*, no. 75 (2014).

I also attempt to provide a broad picture that suggests what drove globalization and how it might negatively affect entire countries and in particular their development and democracy.

I began writing this book with four generic hypotheses in mind that I refined with time. These four hypotheses all concern the elites that might be involved in neoliberalism, and also in globalization and the relocation of industry, since neoliberalism played a key part in the relocation of industry, as part of a globalization driven by elites in the West to their own exclusive advantage. *Hypothesis 1* concerns national elites, like the Italian elite that drove the process of national unification, and the earlier industrialization and subsequent relocation of industry.

1. *There are national elites in many or even in all countries that are part of the West, and they are responsible for formulating neoliberal theories and implementing neoliberal policies.* The national elites are distinguished by the following features.

    a.   The national elites are divided into economic, cultural and political-military elites, each of which derives power from a different source, respectively: the economy, culture, politics and the military.

    b.   These elites however have ties to each other, or are building ties to each other, that enable them to cooperate more or less closely.

    c.   Parts of these elites are consolidating into establishments, which can be described as social groups that are closed and not affected by democratic pressures, compared to social groups that are open and recruit from below.

    d.   There are already in countries that are part of the West economic, cultural, and political-military establishments.

Hypothesis 2 suggests that there is likely an elite active on the international stage that helps drive globalization to the advantage of elites, because the relocation of industry required coordination across countries, in order to open up foreign markets to investment from industrialists in the West, and at the same time open up markets for consumer goods in countries in the West after these investments were made. This also required substantial investment in transportation infrastructure. The relocation of industry might have started as a piecemeal process, but then took on a wide and systemic dimension, as it involved many or even most countries in the West, with elites tapping into the cheap labour in many developing countries, so that a world-elite emerged out of this process. Parts of this world-elite might be consolidating into an emergent imperialist world-elite.

2.   *There is an emergent world-elite that coordinates between national elites to make neoliberalism possible.* The emergent world-elite is distinguished by the following features.

   a.   The emergent world-elite derives its power from globalization processes that transcend countries, in such a manner that its power is not based in just one country, but in many countries around the world.

   b.   It has ties to the national elites or establishments of different countries and cooperates with them.

   c.   Parts of it are imperialist elites and are consolidating into an emergent imperialist world-elite or have consolidated into an imperialist world-elite.

Hypothesis 3 suggests that the power of the emergent imperialist world-elite is at least partly based upon culture, and that this world-elite exercises hegemonic leadership over the national elites. This world-elite and the national elites are together responsible for neoliberalism and the subsequent policies that led to the relocation of industry.

3.   *The emergent imperialist world-elite exercises a form of hegemonic leadership over the establishments of different countries that includes sharing the same culture and worldview.* The power of this emergent imperialist world-elite is distinguished by the following features.

   a.   The emergent imperialist world-elite and the national establishments of different countries are scattered over vast territories, but they share the same views regarding economic growth, and development more in general, that enable cooperation amongst them.

   b.   They also share the same imperialist worldview that gives them a sense of superiority and entitlement compared to the masses and that predisposes them to pursue development in ways that exclusively benefit them, or even that benefit them at the expense of the masses.

   c.   The emergent imperialist world-elite cooperates with national establishments to gain acceptance for policies that benefit them most of all, rather than imposing them by coercion.

   d.   It is these elites, the imperialist world-elite and the establishments, who are responsible for neoliberalism, market deregulation policies and the relocation of industry.

Hypothesis 4 suggests that organizational means, including in particular cultural institutions like academies, institutes, and universities, are key to hegemonic leadership.

4. *Elites that exercise hegemonic leadership do so thanks to organizational means.* The following are features of these organizational means that contribute to hegemonic leadership.
    a.   Cultural institutions are important to formulate a shared world-view and culture and to educate members of the hegemonic social group and allied social groups in this worldview and culture.
    b.   Humanistic studies that provide a broad picture of society and history are important to this worldview and culture.
    c.   Education of new generations that provides long-term continuity in policies and a build-up of knowledge from one generation to the next is also important.

4   Refined Hypotheses on the Italian and British Case Studies

Case studies help corroborate the above hypotheses, constituting a *prima facie* case that the hypotheses might be true, and that therefore they are worth researching in greater detail. In particular, case studies also help both to refine each hypothesis, and also to suggest where to carry out empirical tests, by suggesting places where the hypothesis can be tested initially, to establish a *secunda facie* case, which consists in the claim that preliminary tests of the hypothesis in one or a few locations confirmed the hypothesis, thus suggesting that the hypothesis might be true, and therefore that it is worth researching it in more locations, and ultimately in many other locations or even in all locations, if sufficient data is available or can be gathered. Below I present hypotheses 1 to 4 that I have refined using two case studies of elites, the Italian elite involved in the Risorgimento, the process of national unification of Italy and the founding of the modern Italian state, and the British elite involved in creating the British empire. These refined hypotheses are based on my reading of Gramsci's work, and on theoretical groundwork using recent historical studies of Italy and Great Britain. I suggest that the Italian elite is an instance of an earlier national elite that consolidated into an establishment, while the British elite is an instance of an earlier imperialist world-elite. I also suggest that the Italian elite is an instance of minimal hegemony, as this elite relied largely upon domination of the masses in Italy for its power, whereas the British elite is an instance of integral or broader hegemony, over the masses in Great Britain, and over national elites throughout the world.

The hypotheses on the Italian elite are all formalizations of Gramsci's hypotheses, and refinements of Hypothesis 1 in the light of theoretical ground-work. I propose three refined hypotheses that I refer to as 1′, 1″, 1‴, as each hypothesis is a further refinement of Hypothesis 1, adding more details regarding the sources of power that enabled the Italian elite to drive the process of national unification to its advantage, resulting in the foundations of a unified Italian state as a Kingdom of Italy, rather than an Italian Republic. These elites also influenced the early industrialization of Italy, that they similarly drove to their advantage, industrializing northern Italy, and using southern Italy largely as a captive market and provider of labour.[33] They thus relied on what Bates calls state rents. However, they were able to do so because they dominated the masses in Italy through their marked collective action advantage, that is, their far greater ability to engage in collective action compared to the masses in Italy, since the latter were deeply divided by geographical distance, different languages and cultures, as well as the inability to formulate their own hegemony that Gramsci highlighted in *The Southern Question*. The state rents were thus ultimately due to social rents associated with collective action and a very skewed distribution of power, that the elites exploited and amplified through their policies, enabling their complete domination over the masses in Italy, and especially in southern Italy.

Hypothesis 1ʹ focuses on the *Piedmontese* elite that drove the process of national unification in Italy and the creation of the modern Italian state. Piedmont is one of the current 20 regions of Italy, and was a key part of the Duchy of Savoy and the Kingdom of Sardinia, under the House of Savoy, which took a leadership role in the process of creation of the modern Italian state and became the ruling house of the Kingdom of Italy that it created.

1ʹ.   *The Piedmontese elite that drove the process of national unification in Italy became an early instance of a national elite, emerging from a process that brought together several elites.* This early national elite was distinguished by the following features.

    a.   The national elite included economic, cultural, and political-military elites, respectively landowners, secular intellectuals and an aristocratic-military elite.

    b.   These elites cooperated thanks to count Cavour's leadership, a leadership that was enabled in part by the ties between Cavour and other individuals in key positions within the elites.

    c.   During the course of the nineteenth century, and until the early twentieth century, these elites consolidated into establishments.

---

33   I make these arguments in Chapter 6 of: Olsaretti, *The Struggle for Development and Democracy*, Vol. 1.

The next hypothesis, *Hypothesis 1″*, is a further refinement of *Hypothesis 1′*, reformulating Gramsci's insights, and specifying for each sub-hypothesis, a to c, the basic mechanisms that explain the minimal hegemony of the Piedmontese elite, based on its collective action advantage compared to the masses in Italy. For example, sub-hypothesis *1′.a* states that the Piedmontese national elite emerged out of a process that unified economic, cultural, and political-military elites, and the further refined sub-hypothesis *1″.a* points out that despite these initial internal divisions, this elite was more unified than the masses because more socially homogeneous, since power is relative to the capabilities of other social groups. *Hypothesis 1″* also adds two further sub-hypotheses, namely, sub-hypotheses d and e. These two additional sub-hypotheses explicitly make the point that power is relative, and also draw a conclusion regarding the different mechanisms that unified the elites compared to the masses, all of which were based on a combination of greater social homogeneity, more coherent ideology, and better political-military organization, as stated respectively in sub-hypotheses a to c.

1″. *The Piedmontese elite that drove the process of national unification in Italy was able to do so thanks to the fact that they enjoyed a collective action advantage.* This collective action advantage was derived from the following features of this elite social group, actually several elites initially, that were progressively unified.

  a. The elites were more socially homogenous than the masses.

  b. The elites shared a more coherent ideology than the ideology of the masses.

  c. The elites had better political-military organization than the masses, and this was at least partly thanks to the better leadership provided by Cavour compared to Garibaldi and Mazzini.

  d. All of this made the elites into a relatively cohesive bloc of social groups, compared to the disparate social groups that were part of the masses.

  e. The elite bloc can be described as a hegemonic bloc because its power was partly based upon a coherent ideology and also because it was able to pursue economic development based on this ideology, even though only a limited development.

Hypothesis 1‴ is a further refinement of *Hypothesis 1″*, spelling out the exact mechanisms that might have been involved in each of the sub-hypotheses 1″.a to 1″.c.

1‴. *The Piedmontese elite that drove the process of national unification in Italy was able to do so thanks to the fact that they enjoyed a collective action advantage.* This collective action advantage was derived from the following features of the organization of this elite social group, actually several elites initially that were progressively unified, compared to the divided masses.

a. *The elites were more socially homogenous than the masses.* This hypothesis can be refined as:

    i.   The three elites within Piedmont, the aristocratic-military elite, the cultural elite, and the economic elite, were more homogeneous than the masses within Piedmont.

    ii. The Piedmontese elite had ties, through personal networks, to elites in other parts of Italy, and this made the resulting elites more unified by alliances than the masses within Italy as a whole.

b. *The elites shared a more coherent ideology than the ideology of the masses.* This hypothesis can be refined as:

    i.   The Piedmontese elites and other elites in Italy shared a common language, which could have been either literary Italian, a language that before unification was spoken by 1 to 2 % of the population, or French, the language of diplomacy at that time.

    ii. There was a common ideology justifying elite power in terms of the right of kings, which was being replaced by a common ideology justifying elite power in terms of natural law and improving the realm.

c. *The elites had better political-military organization than the masses, and part of this was thanks to the better leadership provided by Cavour compared to Garibaldi and Mazzini.* This hypothesis can be refined as:

    i.   There were actual diplomatic ties and informal military alliances, for example with other states in the Italian peninsula that held plebiscites to unite with the newly formed Italy.

    ii. There were sources of intelligence in states that were conquered, like the Kingdom of Naples. These sources could be the survivors of the Pisacane expedition, which was similar to Garibaldi's expedition, but took place a few years earlier and failed. Or it could be intelligence through networks that reached from other parts of Italy into the Kingdom of Naples.

The case study based on the British elite can be used to refine the remaining three hypotheses, all concerning the emergent imperialist world-elite, since the British elite was associated with empire-building. There are some aspects of British history, and of the power of the elite that led the British state, that can be used to refine *Hypothesis 1*, but in a different direction, since the national elite of Great Britain was a peculiar case compared to other national elites. It exercised its power internally mostly through hegemony, rather than domination, arguably because it did not enjoy internally as great a collective action advantage compared to the masses as the Italian elite did. As pointed out in Volume 1, the Piedmontese elite is an instance of minimal hegemony, an hegemony that extends only to members of the elite, and is used to keep together the narrow hegemonic bloc that led the process of Italian unification and later of Italian industrialization. By contrast, the British ruling elite is an instance of integral hegemony, which extended to most of British society, at least most of British society that was engaged in politics. However, parts of this British elite became engaged in a process of empire-building that eventually resulted in the creation of the largest empire in European history.

The parts of the British elite that built the British empire are an instance of an early imperialist world-elite, and are most useful theoretically as a case study of an imperialist elite. This elite arguably still relied on hegemony, vis-à-vis other parts of the elite in Great Britain, and also vis-à-vis other elites throughout the world that became its clients. These other elites were in the colonies that it conquered and ruled in part with the help of local elites, or in parts of Europe that were brought under the sphere of influence of the British imperialist world-elite, or more appropriately its hegemonic leadership. This influence included institutional design, as Great Britain pioneered modern constitutional monarchies and also modern nationalism, both of which were taken as models by other countries in Europe during the nineteenth century, and even by military leaders like Garibaldi. In its turn, the British imperialist world-elite bolstered some of these leaders, as Garibaldi was lionized in the British press of the time. *Hypothesis 2´* is a refinement of *Hypothesis 2*.

Hypothesis 2´. The British aristocratic-military elite that built the British empire became an early world-elite. This early world-elite was distinguished by the following features.

a. It derived its power from an early process of globalization that it encouraged by building trade networks around the world that involved many different countries.

b. It ruled to a greater or lesser extent through local elites that cooperated with it.

c. In this process of expansion, this world-elite became an *imperialist* world-elite distinguished by a worldview with racial overtones, such as Rudyard Kipling's 'white man's burden,' which justified conquest in the name of bringing civilization to other parts of the world, somehow seen as lacking civilization.

Hypothesis 3´ is a refinement of *Hypothesis 3* that suggests what were the means whereby the British imperialist world-elite exercised hegemonic leadership over other elites, including elites in other countries involved in empire-building in Europe, like Portugal, and later France, which changed from a contender for the role of hegemon in the state system to a close ally of Great Britain.

3´.   *The British imperialist world-elite exercised a hegemonic leadership over other elites also through cultural leadership and its ability to justify its rule through ideologies.* The power of this early imperialist world-elite was distinguished by the following features.

    a.   The British imperialist world-elite and the other Western imperialist elites that became its clients shared similar views regarding economic growth, and development more in general.

    b.   The British imperialist world-elite and other Western elites, and some of the elites of the countries they conquered, shared a sense of superiority and entitlement compared to the masses of these countries that predisposed them to extract wealth from the masses rather than create wealth and share it with the masses.

    c.   The British imperialist world-elite cooperated with parts of the cultural elite in Great Britain to gain acceptance for policies that benefited them most of all, rather than imposing them by coercion, because it faced strong opposition within Great Britain.

    d.   It is these elites, including the imperialist world-elite, and parts of the cultural elite in Great Britain, who developed the academic discipline of economics and free-trade liberalism.

    e.   These ideologies, combined with political-military means, helped the British aristocratic-military elite exercise hegemony within Great Britain and gain acceptance of policies that favored it. They justified an early opening of markets, which flooded Great Britain with cheap agricultural products at the time of the repeal of the Corn Laws, and with cheap textiles produced abroad, like calico prints imported by the East India Company, an opening of markets that became the object of prolonged political and economic struggles in Great Britain.

Hypothesis 4´ is a refinement of *Hypothesis 4* that details the organizational means used by the British imperialist world-elite to build the British empire.

4´.   *The British aristocratic-military elite that built the British empire was able to exercise hegemonic leadership thanks to organizational means.*

a.   Cultural institutions like elite universities played an important
     role in the formation of the British imperialist world-elite, bring-
     ing together disparate members of the upper classes into one elite
     through a shared culture, including a shared worldview.

b.   Amongst humanistic studies, historical studies and language stud-
     ies have played an especially important part in the education of
     the British aristocratic-military elite and in its success.

c.   The British aristocratic-military elite might have left to later elites
     the learning and knowledge of how to build an empire, and even
     specific techniques of power, that they perfected over centuries.
     This knowledge might have been handed down to later elites in
     Great Britain and elites from around the world who were educated
     in Great Britain. It might also have been handed down to elites in
     institutions based on the model of British elite institutions.

CHAPTER 2

The Theses and Additional Hypotheses of the General Theory

At the same time as formulating and refining the above hypotheses, in this book I propose a number of theses that explain hegemony and domination, both within and across countries, with a focus upon development and democracy. I introduce the theses here with short explanations, simply in order to provide a summary of the entire general theory at a glance, and in order to relate the theses to the above hypotheses. While the hypotheses consist of short statements to be subjected to empirical tests, the theses are more elaborate statements that constitute the theory. In order to help distinguish hypotheses from theses, the hypotheses are numbered using Arabic numerals, whereas the theses are numbered using Roman numerals. The theses corroborate the hypotheses by answering the general question: what are the conditions under which social and interstate conflict can spiral out of control and lead elites to imperial expansion and to create uneven development in a search for social rents? What are the consequences of this imperial expansion and uneven development across countries for countries in the West? Volume 1 introduced Theses IX to XII, which served to corroborate Hypotheses 2 to 4, and laid the groundwork for Hypotheses 2′ to 4′. More in general, the theses corroborate the hypotheses by spelling out the mechanisms whereby certain social conditions lead to imperialism and uneven development. Since these social conditions are still found in the West, it is plausible that new processes of imperial expansion are continuing previous processes, but with the changes that are applicable to a later historical period, including a more advanced globalization, and more advanced technology that enables Intelligence and Communications, or IC, and Command and Control, or C2, with a speed and on a scale unthinkable before. In addition, the theoretical groundwork for the theses, and the theses themselves, corroborate some of the hypotheses introduced above. The theses suggest that a combination of social conflict and interstate conflict can lead to imperial expansion and uneven development, even in countries in the core, as they did in the past.

1   Theses about the Sources of Development and Democracy

Theses I to VII are all the theses that are introduced and discussed in detail in Chapter 6 below. They constitute the unified approach to development and democracy as part of a theory of power. They suggest that the division of labour in society is a major source of development, but it requires embedded autonomy to function smoothly. They all concern the definitions and sources of development and democracy for a country that is able to develop largely free of outside interference. This is a hypothetical case, and an ideal case. Nevertheless, it is a useful way to begin to state the general theory, if only as a counter-factual of what countries could achieve in terms of development and democracy had there not been imperialism and uneven development. Moreover, there are some cases of countries in Europe that roughly approximate this ideal case. Countries in the core of the world system, especially Great Britain, France, and Spain, and to some extent the Netherlands and Portugal, influenced each other through interstate conflict that initially took the form of numerous wars, and also through a process of learning and imitation of each other's military technologies, and of military and economic organizational innovations like the trading companies. However, none of these countries were able to conquer each other, and eventually by 1648 or 1714 at the latest, they reached a balance of power within Europe that was to continue undisturbed until 1914, with the only major exception of the Napoleonic Wars. During this period these countries participated in a massive expansion outside Europe, in colonial ventures over sea lanes, and in a type of imperialism that they perfected, colonialism. This was the only expansion that succeeded, and it eventually altered the balance of power within Europe too.

Theses I and II respectively propose definitions of power, development, and democracy, that underpin the entire theory. Both development and democracy are defined in terms of power. The theses emphasize that development is the growth of per-capita capabilities, thus differentiating development from demographic growth and from territorial expansion that simply adds more population or more territories with relatively little population. The latter is the basis of what Mann calls extensive power, and it is associated with imperialism. It is also the basis for *some* social rents. Demographic growth involves more competition lower down social hierarchies of power, including more market competition, which enables the elites who control the economy to live off social rents simply by paying less for labour. Conquest of more territories either adds population, and leads to these social rents, or adds mostly territories with less population. The latter still leads to social rents, because a very powerful elite can easily dominate even a large population, if the latter is scattered over a large territory, and through domination can live off social rents. *Thesis 1* defines power.

I. *There are different types, measures, and forms of power that are especially important to countries and populations within them.* They are all based upon capabilities, which constitute the bases of power when they are compared to the capabilities of others, or to the capabilities required in a harsh environment, or to the capabilities required at a certain historical conjuncture.

    a.   There are *three main types of power,* each based on specific capabilities produced in a different arena, with each arena being specialized in producing a different type of capabilities and ultimately of power:

        i.   The economic arena, specialized in economic capabilities.

        ii.   The cultural arena, specialized in cultural capabilities.

        iii.   The political-military arena, specialized in political and military capabilities.

    b.   It is useful to distinguish between *two measures of capabilities, namely, total and per-capita capabilities.* These are two ways of measuring the capabilities available to a country that can lead to very different types of growth:

        i.   *Total capabilities* are the sum of all capabilities available to a country, regardless of their source. In practice, because of the specificity of capabilities, it makes sense to measure separately the total economic, cultural, and political-military capabilities.

        ii.   *Per-capita capabilities are the capabilities per individual* in a country, which can vary more or less greatly around a country average. For the same reason as with total capabilities, it makes sense to measure separately the per-capita economic, cultural, and politica-military capabilities.

    c.   There are *two forms of power that define a country*, depending upon the distribution of capabilities within the country across individuals or social groups, and thus depending upon the distribution of power within the country, since the capabilities are compared across individuals or social groups. There are two forms of power.

        i.   There is an *extensive form of power*, with power concentrated in the hands of the elites, which derive their power from large numbers of individuals with low per-capita capabilities, for example low per-capita income. These elites can still raise total capabilities by expanding territory or population.

    ii.   There is an *intensive form of power*, with less concentration of power in the hands of elites, which derive their power from a small number of individuals with high per-capita capabilities, for example high per-capita income. It tends to be associated with elites that could not greatly expand territory or population.

Thesis 11 presents the definition of development and democracy in terms of power. It includes different types of development corresponding to each arena, and also different types of democracy. Social development includes development in social capital. This type of development includes networks that facilitate sharing of information and coordination of activities, and as such it affects all other types of development. *Overall development* is a composite measure of development that takes into consideration development in all arenas, and it can be quantified via suitable indexes.

11.   *Development and democracy are both related to per-capita capabilities within a country*, and ultimately to power within that country.

    a.   There are *five main types of development,* each consisting in the growth of per-capita capabilities in one of the three arenas specialized in a specific type of capabilities, plus a fourth one consisting in the growth of per-capita basic capabilities that are based on social capital, and lastly an aggregate measure of the overall development of a country:

        i.   *Economic development* is the growth of economic per-capita capabilities;

        ii.   *Cultural development* is the growth of cultural per-capita capabilities;

        iii.   *Political-military development* is the growth of political and military per-capita capabilities.

        iv.   *Social development* is the growth in basic per-capita capabilities that are needed by individual to function in society and engage in social interaction, and it includes social capital.

        v.   *Overall development* is the growth in all of the above per-capita capabilities that a country can achieve given its population and resources, whereby there is not just great economic development and little or no cultural development or political-military development, but considerable or even maximum development in each and every type of development.

    b.   *It is useful to distinguish between different distributions of per-capita capabilities* according to the set of individuals across whom we measure the distribution. There are the following useful distributions:

   i.   *A distribution of capabilities across individuals within the whole country,* whereby the distribution is measured across all individuals in a country. In practice, it makes sense to measure this distribution across all individuals in each of the different arenas in the whole country.

   ii.   *Distributions of capabilities across individuals within a region, or social group,* whereby the distribution is measured across all individuals in a region, or across all individuals in a social group, that are part of a country.

   iii.   *A distribution of capabilities across regions or social groups, not individuals,* within the whole country, whereby for example the average capabilities in one region are compared to the average capabilities in other regions, and whereby one measures the distributions of all the averages across regions.

c.   *Democracy consists in a distribution of per-capita capabilities favorable to the masses.* Depending on how we measure the distribution, it is useful to distinguish between the following different types of democracy.

   i.   There are *different types of democracy associated with each arena,* each of which is based upon the distribution of per-capita capabilities measured for one arena within the whole country:

      1.   *Economic democracy* is based upon the distribution of economic capabilities.

      2.   *Cultural democracy* is based upon the distribution of cultural capabilities.

      3.   *Political and military democracy* is based upon the distribution of political and military capabilities.

   ii.   *The intensive form of power is most often associated with democracy,* although there can be some democracy also in countries characterized by the extensive form of power. However, the likelihood of an intensive form of power and ultimately of democracy varies with the arena. Even in the case of a country in which intensive power predominates:

      1.   *The economic arena tends to be based upon intensive power.*

2. *The cultural arena tends to be based upon a mix* of intensive power and extensive power, varying greatly with the geography and history of the country.

3. *The political-military arena tends to be based upon extensive power,* since the military, and all legitimate violence more in general, is a natural monopoly, and those who ran this monopoly can most readily concentrate power in their own hands, even where the intensive form of power predominates in the rest of society.

Theses III and IV both concern the sources of development. Thesis III proposes that the division of labour in society is a source of development, suggesting that the division of labour in society can be divided into the division of labour in an organization, in a district, and in a country, increasing in geographical scale. Different mechanisms are at work in producing greater capabilities, all related to organization, and the manner in which organization leverages technology, which is another important driver of development. I do not address technology for reasons of space, and also because this is a book of social science, concerned with social processes, rather than technological processes, studying the latter only as they interact with society.

III. *The division of labour in society leads to a growth in capabilities through differentiation or specialization.* We can distinguish between three different types of division of labour, which co-exist and complement each other in the division of labour in society, as they lead to growth in capabilities through different mechanisms.

   a. *There is a division of labour in an organization.* This type of division of labor leads to growth in capabilities through differentiation or specialization. It is necessary to distinguish between differentiation within a production process, and human specialization, since in some cases differentiation and specific equipment require less skills and thus less human specialization.

      i. *At the level of the production process and equipment,* differentiation in processes enables the maximum development of capabilities for that activity, by minimizing waste of time in switching between different activities and by using very specific machinery.

      ii. *At the level of the workforce, and its knowledge, know-how, and skills*, specialized workers and often entire specialized departments maximize capabilities through the specific knowledge, know-how, and skills that are needed for greater output in certain production processes.

b. *There is a division of labour in a district.* In a district there are several, and sometimes numerous, organizations that compete and cooperate with each other at the same time, with differentiation combined with specialization leading to growth in capabilities in the following manners, each corresponding to a somewhat different mechanism.

   i. *Differentiation and specialization in economic and cultural capabilities,* between on the one hand factories and offices, and on the other hand universities and schools associated with training.

   ii. *Differentiation and specialization affecting the demand-side,* associated with product innovation, carving out market niches, or supplying variable demand, for a variety of different products, associated with economies of scope.

   iii. *Differentiation and specialization affecting the supply side,* as part of more or less long supply chains that provide different inputs needed for a given product, which contributes to economies of scale.

c. *There is a division of labour in a country.* Within a country with a large territory and population, there are two divisions of labour that lead to growth in capabilities through different mechanisms.

   i. *There is a division of labour associated with products* that is an extension to the entire country of the division of labour in a district, in which there emerges a single nation-wide market for a certain product, or group of similar products, that is produced in one or more districts.

   ii. *There is a division of labour in arenas* that involves different activities, in which the three different arenas, namely, the economic, cultural, and political-military arenas, each become heavily specialized in a different domain of human activity. The growth in arena-specific capabilities emerges from a combination of principles of behavior and organizational forms.

      1. *Arena-specific principles of behavior emerge that guide individual and organizational behavior in each arena,* and become widespread within that arena, as the type of behavior that is most successful within that arena comes to predominate, and is sanctioned by law and values.

2. *Arena-specific organizational types emerge and become predominant in each arena*, as each type is best at developing the capabilities distinctive to that arena, and becomes sanctioned by law. In the West the organizational types that prevailed are:
    a. Private companies in the economic arena.
    b. Non-governmental organizations, or NGOs, and non-profit organizations, or NPOs, in the cultural arena, which overlaps with civil society.
    c. Nation-states, political parties, and social movement organizations, or SMOs, in the political-military arena.

Thesis IV defines embedded autonomy as a certain type of interaction between arenas, and also suggests the mechanisms that are necessary to ensure embedded autonomy, including certain types of social networks, and certain types of social areas in which more fleeting interactions occur that are associated with networks characterized by weak ties and even transient networks, some of which can nevertheless be very important for sharing information. Embedded autonomy, and the networks and social areas that enable it, contribute to a smoothly functioning division of labour in society, to regulation, and ultimately to stable and lasting development. These are facilitated if development is *comprehensive development*, that is, if each arena develops to a large extent, enough to maximize efficiencies and synergies with other arenas.

IV. *Embedded autonomy between arenas in a country contributes to development.* Embedded autonomy consists of a type of interaction between arenas whereby there is smooth functioning of the division of labour between arenas, and also the greatest possible contribution to development from each arena.
    a. *The definition of embedded autonomy* is that it is a type of interaction that involves both autonomy and embeddedness between arenas and contributes to the smooth functioning of the division of labour between arenas.
        i.   *Through autonomy* each arena can adopt the principles of behavior and organizational forms that maximize the growth in capabilities that are distinctive to that arena.
        ii. *Through embeddedness* there can be sharing of information and coordination of activities with the other arenas that maximize the contributions needed by other arenas from that arena.

b. *Embedded autonomy leads to the greatest growth in per-capita capabilities* through the following mechanisms involving the division of labour.

    i. *There is the most efficient use of resources by arenas,* since each arena is capable of optimizing the production of its distinctive type of capabilities through autonomy, and to receive the most capabilities that it needs from the other arenas through embeddedness.

    ii. *There are synergies in development if comprehensive development is pursued,* because different arenas can share common pools of resources that these arenas contribute to and draw from, ensuring the greatest advances in such shared resources as human resources and technological base.

c. *Embeddedness ensures the sharing of information and coordination of activities that is necessary to capitalize on efficiencies and synergies, and also to ensure regulation.* Within the mechanisms involved, it is useful to differentiate between the structures and the processes that these structures enable.

    i. *The structures that enable embeddedness facilitate interaction amongst institutions and organizations* like NGOs, NPOs, and SMOs, and also private companies and corporations, which exchange information and coordinate activities through all of the following structures and means.

        1. *Networks amongst institutions and organizations,* which can be permanent or transient, and strong or weak, with degrees in between these parameters, for example from most permanent to most transient.

        2. *Shared social areas and forums,* in which institutions and organizations more freely interact, typically through public goods and transient networks, and in which there is transparency and accountability of all the networks, whether permanent or transient.

        3. *A shared language and mutually intelligible professional dialects or jargons* are an integral means of interactions used in the networks and in the shared areas and forums, without which the networks and shared areas and forums cannot properly function.

    ii. *Embeddedness enables important processes,* which include the following processes involving the contributions needed by other arenas.

1. *The formulation of new policies or adjustments to policies,* which guarantee that new capabilities are produced, and that the right type of capabilities needed by the other arenas are produced, in the right amount, and when and where they are needed.

2. *The formulation of new laws and values or adjustments to laws and values* that punish criminal behaviors, or put pressure on behaviors deemed unacceptable, and ensure productive social conflict free of violence, as well as rules of civility in debates and ultimately in all interactions.

3. *The implementation of existing procedures within a given policy and legal framework* for addressing problems or needs that arise in the ordinary provision of capabilities from one arena to another, like the routine assignment of more policemen to an area, or of more funds to some NGOs, if the need arises.

Theses V and VI define democracy and the manner in which democracy interacts with development. Thesis V provides what I call a full definition of democracy that emphasizes a distribution of power both within arenas and across arenas. This serves to set the stage for the argument that there must be some democracy in each arena, and also across arenas, in order to prevent loss of democracy.

V. *The full definition of democracy includes structures amongst institutions and organizations, as well as a certain distribution of power both within each arena and across arenas,* all of which act as the social conflict equivalent of checks and balances, ensuring advances in democracy and preventing losses in democracy.

a. *Democracy emerges in the course of a long democratization process involving both cultural and organizational components,* chiefly a political culture and a large civil society with many SMOs, all of which interact to advance democracy, and help maintain democracy.

    i. *A political culture emerges that regulates interactions between protesters and the state,* and ensures that protesters seek voice, and also that they seek voice through productive social conflict, from which all violence was removed, and that the state too avoids resorting to violence.

    ii. *A large civil society emerges in which many SMOs participate in democratization,* and in which there are specific structures amongst NGOs, SMOs, and the state that ensure communication and coordination across all these organizations and the state in order to prevent the escalation of conflict into violence.

b. *Democracy includes a distribution of power within each and every arena that is favorable to the masses*, a distribution of the power that is specific to that arena. This distribution of power ensures that democracy within each arena does not come to an end for reasons *internal* to that arena. This distribution depends upon specific capabilities.

    i. *Political-military democracy* is a distribution of power in the political-military arena that is favorable to the masses, and it depends upon the capability to engage in collective action.

    ii. *Cultural democracy* is a distribution of power in the cultural arena that is favorable to the masses, and it depends upon the capability to engage in collective action within the cultural arena, for example by student groups within colleges, or by associations of colleges, and upon the capability to formulate and spread philosophies and scientific theories.

    iii. *Economic democracy* is a distribution of power in the economic arena that is favorable to the masses, and it depends upon the capability to engage in collective action in the economy arena, for example by cooperatives, unions, or industrialists' associations, and upon the distribution of wealth and the capability to engage in entrepreneurship, which requires access to economic capital.

c. *Democracy includes an even distribution of power across arenas that ensures the autonomy of arenas*, since an even distribution of power guarantees both the autonomy of each arena, and democracy within each arena, in order to make sure that autonomy and democracy do not come to an end for reasons *external* to that arena. The distribution of power across arenas has the following features.

    i. *Each arena is able to resist takeover by other arenas*, for example by agents in other arenas.

    ii. *Each arena is able to exercise some influence over the other arenas*, and thus to contribute to restoring democracy if democracy is lost in another arena.

Thesis VI suggests that the interaction between development and democracy is mediated by embedded autonomy. Democracy guarantees embedded autonomy, and through it guarantees also a smoothly functioning division of labour in society, thus also contributing to development. This argument is in addition to other arguments, for example the argument that democracy provides the criticism necessary for better theories and better policies. Arguably the latter is the product of embedded autonomy and is an instance of one important contribution that embedded autonomy gives to development, since criticism requires a cultural arena that is autonomous of the political-military arena, yet closely interacts with it through embeddedness.

VI.   *There is an interaction between development and democracy, with embedded autonomy as an intermediate factor,* which includes several processes that belong to each arena conceived of as a system, or to systems that cross arenas, like society-markets and state-society systems.

    a.   *The interaction between development and embedded autonomy occurs in each arena and also in a society-markets system,* a system in which civil society organizations interact with private companies and other economic organizations; this interaction can be conceptualized as consisting of two processes.

        i.   *Development contributes to embedded autonomy,* by creating the wealth that enables financing a large and thriving civil society, including the organizational means that contribute to democracy, namely, NPOs, NGOs, and SMOs, all of which benefit either from donations or from volunteering by individuals who have disposable wealth or time.

        ii.   *Embedded autonomy contributes to development,* as institutions emerge, and develop ties to each other and to civil society organizations that enable them to share information and coordinate activities, and thus to provide the club goods and public goods that are needed, and also the regulation that is needed, to ensure development.

    b.   *The interaction between democracy and embedded autonomy occurs in each arena and also as part of a state-society system,* a system in which state institutions interact with civil society organizations; this interaction can be conceptualized as consisting of two processes.

        i.   *Democracy contributes to embedded autonomy,* because a certain distribution of power helps maintain the autonomy of arenas that is part of embedded autonomy, and also guarantees such important rights as the right to free speech, and to freedom of enterprise, which contribute to a thriving civil society.

      ii.   *Embedded autonomy contributes to democracy,* because it ensures that each arena retains its independence but still contributes to preventing loss of democracy within that arena, or in other arenas.

  c. *Several systems come to interact within a country, including state-society and society-markets systems, giving rise to more complex interactions,* which can be part either of virtuous or vicious circles between different systems, that is, interactions that mutually reinforce or undermine each other. The virtuous or vicious circles can be conceptualized as involving feed and feedback mechanisms that participate in, or undermine, comprehensive development.

      i.   *There can be a virtuous circle between democracy and development,* whereby democracy guarantees embedded autonomy and contributes to development, which in its turn contributes to embedded autonomy and democracy. Two mechanisms are involved in this virtuous circle between development and democracy, a feed mechanism and a feedback mechanism, which mutually reinforce each other.

      ii.   *There can be a vicious circle between democracy and development,* whereby loss of democracy leads to loss of embedded autonomy, which leads to loss of development, and a further loss of embedded autonomy and democracy. These two mechanisms reinforce each other, but with signs reversed, as the feed and feedback mechanisms mutually undermine each other, and loss in one increases loss in the other.

Thesis VII suggests that a positive interaction between development and democracy through embedded autonomy can be reversed through a combination of uneven development and imperfect embedded autonomy due to conflict. This sets the stage for the arguments in the last part of this volume, which suggest that imperialism, by creating uneven development, and by contributing to neoliberalism, which undermines institutions and thus undermines embedded autonomy or prevents the emergence of embedded autonomy, ultimately undermines both development and democracy.

  VII. *There can be reversals of the democratization process whereby loss of democracy, or loss of embedded autonomy, or loss of development, lead to further losses in the other factors,* undermining both development and democracy in the long run. There are numerous combinations of these three factors that can lead to loss of development democracy understood as per the full definition of democracy. Reversal of a virtuous circle can occur at one or more of the following points.

a. *Reversal can occur at development,* with changes in the feedback mechanism, so that loss of development leads to loss of embedded autonomy, and ultimately of democracy. This can be initiated by the following different types of uneven development within a country.

    i.   *Uneven development across arenas,* which can lead to loss of comprehensive development, which in its turn can lead to loss of embedded autonomy, because an arena can be more easily taken over by the other arenas.

    ii. *Uneven development across social groups,* which creates social rents that enable companies that are not competitive to survive by leveraging a large reservoir of cheap labour, and thus leads to less economic development, and also to heavy reliance upon labour, which subtracts labour resources from other arenas, and thus leads to less comprehensive development.

    iii. *Uneven development across regions,* which creates social rents similar to uneven development across social groups, and also specific social rents that use other large reservoirs of cheap factors such as cheap land and cheap existing real estate, that are widely available in the underdeveloped regions.

b. *Reversal can occur at embedded autonomy,* which stops reinforcing democracy. This is loss of embedded autonomy that is caused by other factors than uneven development, like purely institutional considerations, or considerations regarding the manner in which institutions interact with organizations. This can be initiated by the following failures in institutions and their interactions with society.

    i.   *Lack of networks amongst institutions and organizations,* which can be due to purely institutional factors such as specialization, whereby for example cultural institutions become very remote from the rest of culture and from other arenas.

    ii. *Lack of shared social areas and forums,* in which institutions and organizations can freely interact, which can be due to the same factors that lead to lack of networks amongst institutions and organizations, and also to more specific factors affecting the provision of public spaces, like the emergence of suburban sprawl that comes to dominate real estate, in which there are only private spaces linked to economic activities, and no truly public spaces in which economic, cultural, and political activities interact.

    iii.   *Lack of a shared language and mutually intelligible professional dialects or jargons*, which can be due to specialization within institutions, and also to turf wars, which compound the lack of networks, and of shared areas and forums, between institutions and organizations.

c.   *Reversal can occur at democracy*, that is at the distribution of political-military power, and it can affect the types of conflict, including how widespread is violence, which affects all other processes. This can be initiated by the following failures in the regulation of conflict, all of which undermine productive conflict, or can lead to conflict spiraling out of control, to the point that one social group or one organization can impose semi-permanent social rents.

    i.   *Wars amongst social groups,* whereby there is sustained large scale conflict, with or without violence, and with or without direct participation of the state, which can take sides, or attempt to moderate or even solve the conflict. There can be different types of war amongst social groups, all of which undermine democracy.

        1.   *Social wars*, or wars amongst *entire* social groups, which can include class conflict, or inter-ethnic conflict.

        2.   *Economic wars*, in which one side deliberately tries to prevent gains by the other side, for example by employers using *caporalato*, fascists, or mafias, in order to break strikes and intimidate workers, or by workers creating groups to break machinery and intimidate employers.

        3.   *Culture wars*, in which different groups of intellectuals take extreme positions, and forsake the goal of contributing to public goods like a shared stock of knowledge, and also forsake rules of civility, aiming first and foremost at putting down adversaries.

        4.   *Political wars,* or partisan wars, in which different groups of activists or politicians behave like intellectuals in culture wars, and sometimes cooperate with these intellectuals.

ii. *Diffuse violence, or diffuse thieving, associated with social disaggregation*, which lead to particular types of wars amongst social groups, in which there is no regulation and complete failure to play by acceptable rules of the game that are necessary for conflict to be productive.

1. *Social banditry*, or social wars in which both sides involved in the conflict act outside the law, and small organized groups resort to banditry at the borderline between social conflict and thieving.

2. *Illegal employment*, or economic wars in which employers completely dominate the other side, who have no contracts, and no resort to the law in case of grievances, and are completely subjected to *caporalato*, fascists, or mafias.

2 Theses about Imperialism and Uneven Development

Theses VIII to XV are all the theses that are introduced and discussed in detail in Chapter 8 below. These theses constitute a general theory of international relations relevant to understand international development and in particular imperialism and uneven development. The latter introduce significant deviations from the ideal case of development and democracy in a country that develops free of outside interference. The main argument is that there is a division of labour in the world system that is far from ideal, and is based upon the predominance of political-military power in international affairs, and of widespread violence, which was removed from interactions internal to countries, but allowed to continue in interactions external to countries. The division of labour in the world system introduces deviations from the division of labour in society, and could impose reversals of development and democracy, via imperialism and uneven development, even in countries in the core in which development and democracy are advanced and supposedly strong. There is a combination of social conflict and interstate conflict that prevails in international relations, and leads to imperialism and uneven development by encouraging violence and destructive conflict more in general. The first three theses, Theses VIII to X, concern the combination of social and interstate conflict in countries in the core, which leads to uneven political-military development across countries, whereby some countries became considerably more powerful than other countries, and ultimately leads to imperialism.

Thesis VIII defines the social conditions for democracy, reformulating a central insight of elite theorists in a manner compatible with Gramscian theory and contemporary political sociology. It suggests that a balance of power in society that is favorable to the masses is an important condition for democracy, and this balance of power depends upon the ability to engage in collective action, whereby elites tend to have a collective action advantage, and greater power, because they are better able to engage in collective action than the masses.

VIII.   *The balance of power between social groups in society affects the likely outcomes of social conflict.* In particular, the outcomes of social conflict depend upon the following factors influencing the balance of power between social groups.

　　a.   *The balance of power between social groups in society affects democracy.* A group that is powerful, if it is faced by an even more powerful group, will not achieve democracy.

　　　　i.   *Political-military power is immediately decisive in social conflict,* since quickly raising this power can settle open social conflict or routinized social conflict such as elections;

　　　　ii.   *Political-military power still requires contributions from other sources of power,* without which it cannot achieve decisive victories in the long run.

　　　　　　1.   *Cultural power provides the cultural means to engage in collective action,* including the theories needed to guide deliberate and sustained collective action, and a sense of identity needed to sustain collective action.

　　　　　　2.   *Economic power provides the economic means to engage in collective action,* such as the means needed to take time off from work, the means to finance strikes, and the donations to pay for campaigns and organizations.

　　b.   *The balance of power between social groups in society depends upon the ability to engage in collective action* of different social groups, and it is the difference in this ability from one social group to another, or collective action advantage, that affects democracy.

　　　　i.   *The ability to engage in collective action in large countries* in which many different social groups participate in political life depends upon the relative unity of different blocs of social groups. The following factors affect the ability of each social bloc to engage in collective action.

1. The number, type, and relative position of social groups within the social bloc.
2. The existence within the social bloc of organizations of one type or another enables coordination of the different social groups.
3. Features of each social group within the social bloc such as the group's cohesiveness, which is related to the presence of community and of dense networks, and also to the presence of organizations such as NPOS, NGOS, and SMOS.

ii. *The collective action advantage depends upon both of the following factors* regarding two blocs involved in social conflict.

1. The comparison in the abilities to engage in collective action of the two different blocs.
2. The ability of one bloc to compound the collective action problems of the other bloc, whether micro or meso collective action problems, also by cooptation and defection.

c. *The collective action advantage of the elites can be very different between one type of society and another,* in particular between agrarian-artisanal society and capitalist society.

i. *In agrarian-artisanal society the elites enjoy a marked collective action advantage* over the masses that is very hard to undo, except in cities.

ii. *In capitalist society the elites see their collective action advantage reduced* and a long period of social conflict starts in which there can be both victories and reversals for democracy.

The next two theses explain that in transitions from agrarian-artisanal society to capitalist society the collective action advantage of elites is reduced, and this leads to heightened conflict, and a window of opportunity for elites to expand their power. *Thesis IX* specifies the sources of elites' collective action advantage in agrarian-artisanal society.

IX. *The elites in agrarian-artisanal society enjoy a marked collective action advantage over the masses* because of the following organization and social structures that act on a meso scale.

a. *Social organization,* including social stratification considerations such as the number and relative position in the hierarchy of power of social groups. This is affected by culture and social boundaries, both of which affect the number and relative position of different social groups in the hierarchy of power.

    i.   Social boundaries amongst the elites are fewer, are porous, and are less affected by geographical distance, enabling the elites to engage in collective action even across large distances.

    ii.   Social boundaries amongst the masses are more numerous, are stronger, and are more affected by geographical distance, making it harder for the masses to engage in collective action because they are divided into many communities.

b.   *Political-military organization*, which includes networks of individuals and networks of organizations like SMOs and political parties, can reinforce the effects of social organization by providing, or failing to provide, IC and C2 capabilities.

    i.   Social networks across the elites can be of the same form as the above stratification, and are such as to endow them with C2 capabilities that enable them to coordinate their forces across large distances and also with IC capabilities that enable them to identify which community amongst the masses poses the greatest threat.

    ii.   Social networks across the masses, from one community to another, are non-existent or weak or do not stretch very far.

c.   *International alliances*, which can range from alliances of equals, all the way to conquest, and provide support to one elite or another. All have the effect of altering the balance of power in society, through external support, and sometimes through the transfer of organizational innovations and technology.

    i.   *Alliances of equals*, in which different elites participate who help each other, sharing in the benefits and costs of the alliance.

    ii.   *Hegemony*, in which one elite leads politically and culturally, and other elites follow the leadership and implement the policies of the leading elite without compulsion.

    iii.   *Incorporation in a sphere of influence*, in which there is some compulsion, or the threat of compulsion, which can have negative effects compared to hegemony, depending upon the timing and the manner of incorporation.

    iv.   *Conquest*, whereby the elite of the conquered country is left partially in command, but is under the compulsion to implement all the orders of the conquering elite.

Thesis X, which was introduced in Volume 1 in a shorter form, explains why the balance of power does not shift decisively in favor of the masses with the transition to capitalism, because elites have greater political-military organization than the masses, which struggle to build this organization.

X.   *The elites in capitalist society see their collective action advantage reduced because of changes in social boundaries* that make mass political mobilization possible and favor collective action by the masses on a large scale.

   a.   There is however a *tradeoff between social organization and political-military organization*. A favorable social organization to the masses, a social organization with fewer boundaries, requires also greater political-military organization and the accompanying 1C and C2 capabilities, both of which arise from networks that take time and resources to build.

      i.   *A favorable social organization to the masses is especially undermined by social disaggregation*, which entails at the level of individuals lack of social capital, and at the level of social groups lack of community, both of which remove safety nets and also make collective action harder, through lack of knowledge and trust.

      ii.   *Rapid urbanization initially destroys the favorable social conditions for collective action that existed in cities*, as it destroys neighborhoods with strong communities, and leads to anonymous interaction.

   b.   This tradeoff creates a *window of opportunity for the elites*. At least initially, the masses lack the required political-military organization to make use of the favorable changes in social boundaries, and this offsets their advantage in numbers. The elites can take advantage of this opportunity to expand their extensive power before the masses could build sufficient political-military organization and intensive power to challenge elite rule.

      i.   During this window of opportunity the elites can especially implement the following *political-military tactics outside control of the state*, control of which is changing in favor of the masses:

         1.   *Create irregular forces controlled by the elites* that can range from thugs and hit squads, to more or less large armed retinues, to private armies and private police forces, all using volunteers or cheap military labour more in general.

2. *Divide-and-conquer and divide-and-rule tactics* that involve setting one social group against another, to prevent the emergence of social blocs amongst the masses that could challenge elite power.

ii. Elites can also implement the following *criminal tactics that make use of criminals or encourage criminality*, that are also outside control of the state.

1. *Banditry* that either undermines a region by preventing investment, or directly targets some inhabitants of that region.

2. *Pogroms and other riots* against specific individuals or specific social groups, as part of crowd behavior that is manipulated by elites.

The next two theses, Theses XI and XII, were both introduced in Volume 1, and both explain the tendency towards expansion of some states, due to conflict. *Thesis XI* explains the tendency towards expansion due to social conflict within states.

XI. *In modern Europe there was competition between two forms of power, the intensive power distinctive of democracies and the extensive power distinctive of empires. There was no decisive victory between these forms of power, but a dynamic balance of power that kept changing.*

a. *This balance of power was internal to states* and consisted in a dynamic balance of power between social groups within the state, whereby if some groups increased their power, so did the other groups.

b. *The balance of power between social groups overlapped with the balance between intensive and extensive forms of power.* It was distinguished by the following features.

i. Democracies achieved a breakthrough in developing intensive power by advancing economic development in city-states, where population was concentrated, and proved a match for feudal lords.

ii. Feudal lords, and later imperialist elites, reacted by further extending their power, typically in areas that were poorer and less densely populated and were thus easier to conquer, but they developed this extensive power to the point that they could fight back against democracies and conquer some of them.

iii. This social conflict led to a first tendency towards state expansion. This is because there was no fixed balance of power between the intensive and extensive forms of power, but a tendency whereby each form tried to outgrow the other, leading to both economic development and imperial expansion.

Thesis XII explains the tendency towards expansion due to interstate conflict in the core of the state system, which was initially the whole of western Europe, and would later consolidate to include just north-western Europe, as Spain and Portugal were set on an altogether different path to development.

XII.   *In modern Europe there emerged a number of powerful states of a new kind for Europe, namely, proto nation-states.* These were *England, France, Spain, with the Netherlands and Portugal as intermediate cases* between city-states and proto nation-states. There was no decisive victory nor permanent peace amongst these states, or between these states and other states, but a dynamic balance of power that kept changing.

   a.   *This balance of power was external to states* and consisted in a dynamic balance of power between states, whereby if one state increased its power, so did the other states.

   b.   *The balance of power between these states kept changing slowly* through a mix of external and internal factors. It was distinguished by the following features.

      i.   There was, post 1648, a relatively stable balance of power between states, whereby major wars within Europe were rare compared to the previous two centuries.

      ii.   The proto nation-states concentrated in expanding outwards, in areas outside Europe, by a mix of trade and conquest, expanding extensive power.

      iii. The net effect was that European proto nation-states engaged in a sustained outward expansion, and then occasional very destructive wars in Europe when expansion altered the balance of power between states.

      iv.   Some of these proto nation-states also developed the internal economy to a great extent, and this led to more of the competition highlighted in thesis IX and thus even more expansion, especially within one state, England, which went through a historically unprecedented expansion.

Thesis XIII suggests the mechanism whereby uneven political-military development across countries led to imperialism, arguing that imperial expansion was subject to rules of projection of power that included the balance of power in the state core and other features of the state core. The projection of power led to the division of the world system into a core, semi-periphery, and periphery.

XIII.   *Uneven political-military development across states leads to imperialism,* because of the dynamic balance of power between states in north-western Europe, initially throughout western Europe. Imperialism has the effect of producing or accentuating uneven social and economic development within countries that are conquered, thus strengthening uneven political-military development.

    a.   *The balance of power that was distinctive to the core of the modern state system,* had the following features that affected its dynamics.

        i.   *State type,* which includes differences in size, and varies with both time and geographical distance. The following classification is important to understand states in early modern Europe.

            1.   *North-western European proto nation-states,* which proved more successful than the other state types, and were initially all concentrated in western Europe.

            2.   *City-states,* like the city-states in Italy, Germany, and Switzerland, which were concentrated in the first geopolitical band, and initially acted as buffer states.

            3.   *Territorial empires,* like the Habsburg, Ottoman, and Romanov empires, which were concentrated in the second geopolitical band, and initially threatened proto nation-states.

        ii.   *Geopolitics,* which includes more than just logistics, and in particular the following important factors.

            1.   Geographical position relative to each other as a bloc of territories that shared land borders or were within close proximity of each other by sea.

            2.   Physical conformation as a state system dominated by three large states of approximately equal size and power, namely England, France, and Spain, and two smaller states, namely, the Netherlands and Portugal.

            3.   A mix of extensive power with intensive power, whereby these states were fairly large territorially, and also included pockets of capitalism, which would continue expanding.

        iii.   *Geoculture,* which includes the uses of culture made by states, whatever the origins of the culture. In particular, proto nation-states had begun using culture to ensure loyalty, and at most also voice, but not exit.

1.   The use of religion for political purposes to ensure loyalty to the ruling houses, whose rule was claimed to be sanctioned by God.

2.   The beginnings of nationalism as a non-religious identity that ensured attachment to a specific state, initially overlapping with a specific religious identity, such as Anglicanism in England.

b.   *The projection of power by north-western European states was subject to rules due to the balance of power, and also to the geography and history of individual states and of the state system* that they were part of, which led to expansion alongside sea lanes, first into the Americas, then into Asia, and lastly into Africa, because of the following factors.

i.   Geographical position alongside the Atlantic coast of Europe, such that they could not easily tap into Levantine ports and the trade across Asia, in which there was much competition by more established players, including Genoa and Venice, but they could easily expand into the Atlantic.

ii. Cost-benefit tradeoffs associated with the fact that expansion across sea lanes, while increasingly possible, was still expensive, and the Americas offered the greatest opportunities to get rich from conquest, Asia the greatest opportunities but also the greatest costs, and Africa fewer opportunities as well as fewer costs.

c.   *The effects of the projection of power were disastrous upon the countries that were conquered or colonized,* because of the following factors, all of which contributed to either uneven social development, or uneven economic development across countries, or both these types of uneven development.

i.   *Colonies,* which can be more or less extensive, whereby a number of colonists move permanently to the country that has been taken over, and form part of the elite and sometimes also of the subaltern social groups that are necessary for the exercise of power by the elite, who are much more militarily powerful, and live off of social rents rather than developing the countries they colonized.

    ii.   *A mix of trade and conquest,* whereby trade pays for and thus facilitates conquest, and later pays for keeping the country under foreign control, and also facilitates domination and living off of social rents, because the introduction of capitalism creates social disaggregation.

    iii.   *Techniques of power,* including widespread use of divide-and-conquer and divide-and-rule tactics, which heightened conflict in already volatile situations associated with social disaggregation.

The last two theses, Theses xiv and xv, suggest the mechanisms whereby uneven development across countries caused by imperialism can lead to uneven development in the core, and also to imperfect embedded autonomy, and loss of democracy. *Thesis XIV* suggests that the division of labour in the world system, in conjunction with neoliberalism, which is strengthened by this division of labour, leads to migration, relocation of industry, and populism, all of which lead to uneven development within countries in the core.

xiv.   *The division of labour in the world system brings about uneven development in countries in the core through the following mechanisms,* all of which involve social rents.

    a.   *Elites can tap into, and compound through political means, two different types of social rents outside the core,* which enable elites to extract profits and even be competitive, not by introducing organizational and technological innovations, but by paying less for certain factors.

        i.   *Social rents associated with low population density and cheap land in the periphery,* which typically lead to export of agricultural goods from the periphery to the core that benefit from cheap land.

        ii.   *Social rents associated with high population density and cheap labour in the periphery,* which typically lead to export of industrial goods from the periphery to the core that benefit from cheap labour, such as goods in labor-intensive industries.

    b.   *Social rents outside the core lead to uneven development* in the core through the following mechanisms:

        i.   *Migration,* which lowers the costs of labour in the core, and in the case of illegal immigration creates social disaggregation lower down the hierarchy of power in society, and also a vast pool of cheap labour with no rights that is exploited through such practices as *caporalato.*

    ii.   *Relocation of industry* from countries in the core to coun-
tries in the periphery, which affects especially the working class and the lower middle class of countries in the
core.

   c.   *Neoliberalism and populism compound these effects by providing
ideological legitimation* to policies that enable these effects, or
that make them worse.

     i.   *Neoliberalism* provides ideological legitimation to reliance
upon international markets, and to cuts in state funding
rather than making it efficient, thus enabling social rents
and imperfect markets in which some social groups have
no bargaining power.

    ii.   *Populism* enables social rents to continue by blaming
scapegoats, and by encouraging divisions amongst social
groups that belong to the masses, especially between the
middle class and the working class, and the existing population and migrants.

Thesis XV suggests the mechanism whereby dictatorship and violent social
movements in the semi-periphery and periphery, due to uneven social and
economic development, lead to imperfect embedded autonomy and loss of
democracy in the core through interstate conflict.

xv.   *The division of labour in the world system brings about imperfect embedded autonomy and loss of democracy in countries in the core through the
following mechanisms,* all of which involve macro conflict.

   a.   *There is a political side to uneven social development in the world
system, which leads to a social war of maneuver* in semi-peripheral
and peripheral locations of the world system. This social war of
maneuver has different effects depending upon uneven economic
development.

     i.   *In the case of Italy and Germany in the 1920s-40s,* it gave rise
to violent social movements, and when the violent social
movements seized power, they could pose a symmetric
threat to countries in the core because of fairly advanced
economic development.

    ii.   *In the case of countries in the Middle East and North Africa
in the 1980s-2000s,* it gave rise to dictatorships and violent social movements, which lead to asymmetric threats
because of low economic development, and often inability to seize the state, so that the threat remained
asymmetric.

b. *Macro conflict leads to imperfect embedded autonomy* through international pressures on institutions, some of which are reinforced by neoliberalism and populism.

  i. *High military expenditures can lead to pressures to make savings on expenditures by institutions,* which can harm institutions and reduce their ability to interact with organizations.

  ii. *Security threats can reduce investment,* both because investors are directly concerned by the security threats, and because they are concerned by the effects of the security threats on markets, including international markets for strategic resources like oil, and markets that the investment would produce for.

c. *Macro conflict leads to loss of democracy* through pressure on social conflict within countries in the core, which can escalate into war, in conjunction with migration, neoliberalism, and populism, whereby violent social movements stoke up social conflict inside countries in the core, and turn it into war.

  i. *Economic wars* lower down hierarchies of power are stoked up by increasing numbers of immigrants.

  ii. *Culture wars* between different ideological camps, or between the state and churches, are stoked up by populism, aided indirectly by large numbers of immigrants, as well as by foreign dictatorships, and by violent social movements which contribute to creating a perception of imminent threats by immigrants, instead of by elites or by more complex problems.

  iii. *Political wars* between politicians, *some* of whom tap into culture wars, participate in populism, and cooperate with intellectuals engaged in culture wars, and are indirectly aided by dictatorships and violent social movements.

3   Additional Hypotheses on Other Countries as Case Studies

A number of additional hypotheses can be formulated based upon the theoretical groundwork for the above theses and the theses themselves. I present here additional hypotheses focusing on state type and cultural power, and in particular upon the power of the Catholic Church since early modern times, down to our *own* times. These additional hypotheses concern Germany and the Habsburg empire, straddling Austria-Hungary, and Spain and Portugal. Whereas in Volume 1 the main comparison was between Italy and Great Britain, as instances respectively of minimal and integral (or wide-ranging) hegemony, Germany and the Habsburg empire are part of another set of comparisons, as Germany provides an interesting case to compare to Italy, and the Habsburg empire an interesting case to compare to the British empire. Germany was part, together with Italy, of a geopolitical area just outside western Europe that shared with western Europe a long political border. Both Italy and Germany in early modern times were divided into numerous small states, mostly city-states and derived state types like leagues of city states. This was in contrast to the larger territorial states in western Europe, all of which were proto nation-states. Both Italy and Germany were only unified in the nineteenth century, and were initially both in the semi-periphery of the world system, suffering from imperfect democracies, and falling prey to totalitarian dictatorships, buttressed by the ideologies of fascism and nazism respectively. There are similarities between the cases of Italy and Germany, summarized in the following hypothesis, suggesting that Germany's elite is an instance of a national elite similar to Italy's.

1g'. *The Prussian elite that drove the process of national unification in Germany became an early instance of a national elite, which emerged out of a process that brought together several elites.* This early national elite was distinguished by the following features.

a.   The Prussian elite included economic, cultural, and political-military elites, respectively landowners, secular intellectuals and an aristocratic-military elite.

b.   These elites cooperated thanks to prince von Bismarck's leadership, which was enabled in part by the ties between Bismarck and other individuals in key positions within the elite.

c.   During the course of the nineteenth century, and until the early twentieth century, these elites consolidated into establishments.

However, Germany arguably was based on a different dominant hegemony than Italy, in which cultural and economic elites played a greater role, an hypotheses summarized in a further refinement of the above hypothesis.

1g''. *The Prussian elite that drove the process of national unification in Germany was able to do so thanks to the fact that* they *enjoyed a collective action advantage*, which was not however as great as the advantage of the Piedmontese elite over the masses in Italy. The collective action advantage of the Prussian elite was derived from the following features of this elite social group, actually several elites initially, that were harder to unify compared to Italian elites.

a.   The landowners and aristocratic-military elites known as Junkers were as socially homogenous, but secular intellectuals and the emerging bourgeoisie were more powerful and less easily coopted into the hegemonic bloc.

b.   The Prussian elites shared a cohesive ideology, but the masses in Germany were better able to develop their own ideology and a large social democratic party.

c.   The Prussian elites still had better political-military organization than the masses.

d.   All of this made the Prussian elites into a relatively cohesive bloc of social groups, that was however faced by a more unified social bloc comprising the masses.

e.   The elite bloc can be described as a hegemonic bloc, but it was faced with a stronger alternative hegemony, with its distinctive ideology and political organization.

f.   The alternative hegemony was challenged by nazism, which built a counter-hegemony outside both of the Catholic Church and of social democracy, and through irredentism launched into a series of conflicts that eventually led to the Second World War.

The Habsburg empire, which at the height of its power combined Austria and Hungary, and also for a time Spain and Portugal through marriage alliances, was in its time the largest empire in European history. It had vast colonies throughout the Americas, and in the Pacific Ocean and the Philippines. It thus provides an interesting case to compare to the British empire.

2h'. The Habsburg aristocratic-military elite that built the Habsburg empire became an early world-elite.

This early world-elite was distinguished by the following features.

a.   It derived its power from a process of conquest, reliant more upon extraction of tribute than trade, and thus with fewer shared economic interests amongst the elites involved.

b.   It ruled to a greater or lesser extent through colonial elites originally from Europe that cooperated with it.

c.   In the process of expansion that it drew, this world-elite became an *imperialist* world-elite distinguished by a worldview with religious overtones formulated by the Catholic Church.

Further additional hypotheses *3h'* and *4h'* can be formulated around the case study of the Habsburg aristocratic-military elite, and the Spanish colonial empire, and the Austro-Hungarian territorial empire in Europe, focusing on the details whereby this elite exercised domination, an especially brutal domination, and on the details whereby its hegemony was built around the Catholic

Church, which was, and arguably still is, extremely centralized. Its ties to other imperialist elites would be an important point to research.

4   Additional Hypotheses on Neoliberalism and Populism

The main reason why ties amongst diverse imperialist and national elites are important to research is that, in the wake of the Napoleonic Wars, there emerged with the Concert of Europe a cooperation and coordination amongst different elites in maintaining the social status quo in Europe, and to some extent the political status quo, which greatly strengthened reactionary forces. The Concert of Europe saw western European colonial empires cooperate with territorial empires, chiefly the Habsburg empire, but also the Romanov empire of Russia, in a vast hegemonic bloc uniting elites at the very top of hierarchies of power in Europe. It is not unthinkable that a similar bloc could emerge again, and it is sensible to ask what the consequences could be for development and democracy if such a bloc was to emerge. The following hypothesis, *Hypothesis 5*, suggests that the emergent imperialist world-elite might have such organizational means that would enable this elite to reverse development and democracy even in countries in the core, by setting off a vicious circle like the one described in Theses VII and XV. These organizational means consist of networks between this elite and national elites in the semi-periphery and periphery. The sub-hypotheses suggest that these network might be ties, that is, more or less strong networks, rather than transient networks, which could lead to uneven development, imperfect embedded autonomy, and loss of democracy in the core.

5.   *The organizational means of the emergent imperialist world-elite could include networks that enable coordination of activities,* which could be used to reverse development and democracy in the core. The following are possible instances of these organizational means that could enable this world-elite to bring development and democracy to an end.

   a.   *The world-elite has ties to economic elites in fast-developing countries,* especially in the BRICS countries, the Asian Tigers (or Four Asian Dragons), and the Tiger Cubs, that have enabled it to undermine the economy and society in the core.

   b.   *The world-elite has ties to political-military elites in countries that are dictatorships for all intents and purposes,* including Russia and China, that could pose a severe military threat, especially if there was coordination amongst their military operations, for example through pan-Asian alliances.

c. *The world-elite has ties to political-military elites that are dictator-ships in countries that are still largely underdeveloped in Africa, Latin America, and the Middle East,* and could pose a threat through criminal organizations and violent social movements that have destabilizing and polarizing effects.

d. *The world-elite has ties to international institutions* like the World Bank, and the International Monetary Fund, which can impose austerity measures and undermine economies trying to develop, and the United Nations, which can fail to prevent regional wars.

The BRICS countries include Brazil, Russia, India, China, and South Africa, two of which, India and China, have been major providers of labour respectively for IT companies and call centers that relocated, besides industry that relo-cated. Other countries in Asia that have been sources of cheap labour are the Asian Tigers (or Four Asian Dragons), namely, Honk Kong, Singapore, South Korea, Taiwan, and the Tiger Cubs, which include Indonesia, Malaysia, the Philippines, Thailand, and Vietnam. All are part of the Pacific Rim area that includes most of the fast-developing countries in the world. The next hypothe-sis, *Hypothesis 6,* suggests what might be the sources of the networks tying the emergent imperialist world-elite to economic and political-military elites in these fast-developing countries.

6. *The main sources of these organizational means would likely be ties to past elites,* since such networks take a very long time to build and to consol-idate into more or less strong ties. The emergent imperialist world-elite could have inherited the following ties from past elites.

a. *Ties to past aristocratic-military elites of western European countries, and the successor states of the Habsburg, Ottoman, and Romanov empires,* all of which only officially ceased to exist over the past 50 to 100 years, and had vast organizational means, some of which could have survived over the years.

b. *Ties amongst the existing ruling houses of Europe, all of which have vast organizational means at their disposal through their respective states,* chiefly the British, Danish, Dutch, Norwegian, Spanish, and Swedish royal houses, and the peerages and knightly orders with ties to these royal houses, and former ruling houses with ties to these royal houses, like the House of Braga of Portugal, the House of Bourbon of France, and the House of Savoy of Italy.

c. *Ties amongst aristocrats in the Catholic Church and their networks,* including such groups as the Black Nobility, and the many cru-sading and knightly orders of the Catholic Church that are still in existence.

d.   *Small European principalities that have historically acted as meeting places and resorts for past elites*, including Andorra, Liechtenstein, Luxemburg, Monaco, and small republics that can play a similar role like Cyprus, Malta, and San Marino.

e.   *International lobbying organizations and their venues for meetings*, like the World Economic Forum and the Davos resort in Switzerland.

The aristocratic-military elites of the past were united both by vast networks across royal houses, and by centuries of intermarriage, visits, and the occasional wars that brought about changes in the hierarchies amongst these families, but rarely led to the demise of any family, at least rarely since the emergence of the Concert of Europe. For example, the ruling house of Great Britain originated and has strong historic ties to Germany, as well as ties to aristocratic families as far as Russia, and the royal family of Italy originated in France and has strong historic ties to France. These elites of the past also cultivated patronage networks to elites lower down hierarchies of power, and thus had vast networks of clients, effectively patronage networks.

PART 2

Key Approaches and Concepts from Sociology and Geography

∵

The Age of the Risorgimento
There is a period of foreign domination in Italy, [that] for a certain time [consisted of] direct domination, and later [consisted
of] hegemonic domination [via incorporation into the sphere of
influence] (or mixed direct domination and hegemonic domination). The fall of the [Italian] peninsula under foreign domination
in the 1500s already provoked a reaction [within the peninsula]
[...] and the will to fight to regain [independence] in a historically
more advanced [state] form [...] In the 1700s the European balance
of power, [based on] the Austria [Habsburg empire]-France [axis]
enters a new phase as far as Italy [is concerned]: there is a mutual
weakening of these two great powers, and there arises a third great
power [in continental Europe], Prussia. *Therefore, the origins of the
Risorgimento movement, that is, the process of formation of the
[social] conditions and international relations that would enable
Italy to come together as a nation and the internal national forces to
develop, are not to be sought in this or that event that took place on a
given date, but in the historical process whereby the European system
[of states] is transformed.*

ANTONIO GRAMSCI, *Prison Notebooks*, Notebook 19, Note 2, pp.1962–1963.
My emphasis.[1]

∴

1   Gramsci, *Quaderni del Carcere*, 1962–1963.

Macro Historical Sociology and Geography and World Systems Theory

This chapter provides a *framework that emphasizes globalization as a very important overarching process* within which processes affecting development and democracy take place. The overarching process constitutes the context within which key factors affecting development and democracy play out. This chapter specifically introduces a number of key concepts from World Systems Theory, historical sociology, and historical geography that I argue are necessary to understand development and democracy, and shows how these key concepts are relevant to a high-level summary of the explanations proposed in this volume. I also introduce a number of additional concepts that complement World Systems Theory, and emphasize how geopolitics and a combination of interstate conflict and social conflict are especially useful to understand development and democracy, and also to *nuance and expand upon Putnam's insight regarding democracy and development in Italy.* In a landmark book on this topic, Putnam argued that the geographically uneven development of civil society in Italy explains the north-south division within Italy, a division marked by uneven economic development within one country, that has proven extremely hard to eradicate. This uneven economic development is central to the debate over the Southern Question. Putnam showed that northern Italy has a larger number of NGOs for given numbers of the population, compared to southern Italy. Putnam inferred that *the extent of civil society is correlated with the extent of democracy*, whereby the greater number of organizations of civil society, such as NGOs, correlates with greater democracy. Putnam further inferred that *the greater extent of civil society led to greater development*, as democracy can affect development through a number of mechanisms, for example through greater and better criticisms of policies, which improves policies, which in their turn lead to greater development.[1]

---

1 Robert D. Putnam, Robert Leonardi, and Raffaella Y. Nanetti, *Making Democracy Work: Civic Traditions in Modern Italy* (Princeton and Oxford: Princeton University Press, 1994). Harvey Molotch addresses similar points in: John R. Logan and Harvey L. Molotch, *Urban Fortunes: The Political Economy of Place. With a New Preface*, 20th Anniversary ed. (Berkeley, Los Angeles, and London: University of California Press, 2007).

It is useful for the arguments of this chapter to clarify my view of World Systems Theory, and the parts of it that I focus upon. I focus mostly upon the contributions to World Systems Theory given by Wallerstein and Arrighi. Wallerstein is one of the founders of World Systems Theory, and Arrighi is a sociologist who began integrating Gramscian concepts in this theory. Wallerstein argued that World Systems Theory was not really a theory, and preferred to call it an approach to sociology, including the sociology of development, which was the central focus of Wallerstein's early work.[2] Both Wallerstein and Arrighi began their careers by studying problems of development in developing countries, and both focused upon Africa in particular, and included in their theories from the very beginning the study of colonialism and its negative effects upon development, which include underdevelopment, a concept that emphasizes colonialism amounts to reducing the development that a country would otherwise be capable of.[3] I view World Systems Theory more specifically as a school of thought that includes a number of key concepts that are part of a set of related theories, all sharing both key concepts and a certain approach, and all having various ties to postcolonial theory, if the latter is understood not only

---

2   Wallerstein set out his interpretation of World Systems Theory in: Immanuel Maurice Wallerstein, *The Modern World-System: Capitalist Agriculture and the Origins of the European World-Economy in the Sixteeth Century*, Studies in Social Discontinuity (New York: Academic Press, 1976); "A World-System Perspective on the Social Sciences," *The British Journal of Sociology* 27, no. 3 (1976). It emerged out of his work on development, and he set out his views on the concept of development in: "The Development of the Concept of Development," *Sociological Theory* (1984). Wallerstein argued that he did not want World Systems Theory to become a theory: "The Itinerary of World-Systems Analysis; or, How to Resist Becoming a Theory," in *Uncertain Worlds*, ed. Immanuel Maurice Wallerstein, Carlos Aguirre Rojas, and Charles C. Lemert (London and New York: Routledge, 2015). World Systems Theory is arguably a paradigm that includes loosely related theories, including Wallerstein's work. Wallerstein's full work has been recently re-published as: *The Modern World-System, Vol. I: Capitalist Agriculture and the Origins of the European World-Economy in the Sixteenth Century* (Berkeley and Los Angeles: University of California Press, 2011); *The Modern World-System, Vol. II: Mercantilism and the Consolidation of the European World-Economy, 1600–1750*; *The Modern World-System, Vol. III: The Second Era of Great Expansion of the Capitalist World-Economy, 1730s–1840s, with a New Prologue*; *The Modern World-System, Vol. IV: Centrist Liberalism Triumphant, 1789–1914*.

3   Wallerstein's early work on Africa includes: *Africa, the Politics of Independence* (New York: Vintage Books, 1961); *The Road to Independence: Ghana and the Ivory Coast* (Paris and the Hague: Mouton, 1964); *Africa: The Politics of Unity* (New York: Random House, 1967). His more recent work on Africa includes: *The World-System and Africa* (New York: Diasporic Africa Press, 2016). Arrighi's early work on Africa includes: Giovanni Arrighi, *The Political Economy of Rhodesia*, vol. 16 (Mouton The Hague, 1967); "Peripheralization of Southern Africa, I: Changes in Production Processes," *Review (Fernand Braudel Center)* 3, no. 2 (1979). Arrighi taught in Zimbabwe and Tanzania for a number of years.

as a literary theory about literature and other cultural products from postcolonial locations, but also more in general as a theory about the culture, economy and politics of these locations.[4] An important part of the approach of World Systems Theory was emphasized by Christopher Chase-Dunn, who introduced the question as to whether the world system includes one logic (I refer to it below as a mechanism), namely an economic logic central to the economy, or two logics, including a political logic central to states.[5] I argue in this book that there are three logics, each of which is central respectively to the economy, politics, and culture. The rest of this chapter focuses upon key concepts in World Systems Theory, and adds a number of other concepts, including the concepts of state core and frontier and their effects on social conflict, and Gramsci's concepts of war of maneuver and war of position. All these concepts are especially important to understand processes that undermine civil society, and ultimately undermine development and democracy, also by giving rise to violent social movements and other violent phenomena like social banditry and diffuse criminality.

1 General Theory and Macro Historical Sociology and Foundations

World Systems Theory is part of a group of theories in sociology that can aptly be characterized as macro historical sociology. World Systems They also makes use of macro geography. The reason why I make use of macro historical sociology and geography is that they are especially useful to general theory, and I want to begin here by *defending general theory* and explaining why macro historical sociology and geography are useful to it. This should be clear already from *the preliminary definition of theory* that I introduced in Volume 1 of this book, where I introduced also a preliminary definition of humanist social science. This definition can be extended to a humanist general theory, and

---

4 An historical overview of postcolonial literary theory is provided in: Robert J. C. Young, *Postcolonialism: An Historical Introduction* (Chichester, West Sussex and Malden, Massachusetts: Wiley-Blackwell, 2016). This book was first published in 2001. For the place of World Systems Theory compared to postcolonial theory, see: Julian Go, *Postcolonial Thought and Social Theory* (Oxford and New York: Oxford University Press, 2016).

5 Christopher Chase-Dunn, "Interstate System and Capitalist World-Economy: One Logic or Two?," *International Studies Quarterly* 25, no. 1 (1981). There is a paradigm known as political Marxism that gives pride of place to politics: Alex Callinicos, "The Limits of "Political Marxism"," *New Left Review* 184, no. 1 (1990); Samuel Knafo and Benno Teschke, "Political Marxism and the Rules of Reproduction of Capitalism: A Historicist Critique," *Historical Materialism* 29, no. 3 (2020).

emphasizes that a humanist general theory includes all domains of human activity, namely, the economy, culture, politics and the military, and also different dimensions of human activity, namely, time and space. Thus I propose a general theory that seeks to explain how the whole of a country works. Such a general theory is both feasible and useful, and in particular it is the type of theory that is most useful to all citizens in democracies, yet there is a misconception regarding general theory that discredits it and makes it seem as if general theory is of little or no practical use. It is important therefore to clarify that general theory is both feasible and useful. It is especially important to differentiate general theory from grand theory. In doing so, I also want to differentiate the approach adopted here from the approach of mainstream economics, particularly neoclassical economics, which underpins neoliberal theories.

I want to begin here by defining grand theory and explaining why it important to *differentiate between general theory and grand theory, and suggest that there should be a return to general theory*, not to grand theory. I want to emphasize, in particular, that the general theory that I propose is useful, and even indispensable, to understand development. This work proposes a general theory of development and democracy that is applicable to explain social change and the prospects for development and democracy in countries that are part of the West during the modern era, covering the period 1500–2000 approximately. It might be further extended and be made useful to other parts of the world. Historian Quentin Skinner, a critic of this approach, has called it 'grand theory.'[6] Sociologist Robert K. Merton's critique of Talcott Parson's theory similarly involved framing it as grand theory.[7] This is implicitly dismissive because it suggests that those who formulate such a theory do not have their feet on the ground and their theories are not useful. The most famous use of the expression 'general theory' is possibly by Albert Einstein, who is often portrayed as the quintessential scientist without his feet on the ground.[8] These criticisms of general theory as grand theory actually entail two different criticisms, namely, that general theory is not feasible, and that it is not useful. I answer both of these criticisms below, and I argue that the general theory proposed in this

---

6   Quentin Skinner, *The Return of Grand Theory in the Human Sciences*, Canto (Cambridge and New York: Cambridge University Press, 1990).

7   On Merton's dismissal of grand theory, see: M. Waters, *Modern Sociological Theory* (London, Thousand Oaks, New Delhi: SAGE Publications, 1994). The conclusion of Waters' book lays out clearly Merton's position.

8   On Einstein's biography, see: Walter Isaacson, *Einstein: His Life and Universe* (New York, London, Toronto, Sydney, New Delhi: Simon & Schuster, 2017). Einstein's most famous theory is known as the 'general theory of relativity.' Interestingly, Einstein also made contributions to quantum theory that have direct and important practical applications.

book is a completely different kind of general theory that is both feasible and useful.

This book, in both volumes, seeks to contribute instead to *a return of general theory in social science* seen as including both theory and empirical research. Here I begin by rejecting the criticism that general theory is grand theory and thus not feasible, *defining in greater detail general theory* and at the same time clarifying why, despite being general, it is still feasible. The theory that I propose is general because of the method that I used to formulate this theory and also because, in using this method, I have used a more general framework than mainstream social science and neoliberal economic theory, and also more general assumptions. Let us consider first the framework that I use. This framework is feasible, and not part of grand theory. It is a broader and thus *more general framework that includes macro and meso, as well as micro scales of social interaction.* Here I want to emphasize that social interaction occurs on all different scales, namely, the micro, meso, and macro scales, and that this entails that there are micro-foundations, meso-foundations, and macro-foundations of human behavior that must be used to explain social processes. There are in sociology two main approaches to formulating theory that are usually considered separately, as if they were two irreconcilable approaches, but in this project I argue that they are complementary and have to be used together. The *micro-foundational approach* to theory building in sociology is an approach that is analogous to game theory and is called micro-foundational because it claims that all social processes have foundations in individual behavior and can be explained starting from individual behavior, using such assumptions regarding individual behavior as *Homo Oeconomicus*.[9] Cohen's theory of history can be described as based upon a micro-foundational approach to the theory of history, at least from the way in which Cohen presents his theory. The macro historical sociology advocated by Tilly in his studies of social movements and states can instead be described as a *macro-foundational approach* because it focuses on processes that are considered to be largely independent of individual behavior and dominate the macro scale of social interaction.[10]

---

9   This is a definition given by Daniel Little in: Daniel Little, *Microfoundations, Method, and Causation: On the Philosophy of the Social Sciences* (Transaction Publishers, 1998).

10   Tilly's work on states spans the whole of Europe and covers a millennium of history: Charles Tilly, *Coercion, Capital and European States: AD 990–1992*, Studies in Social Discontinuity (Oxford: Blackwell, 1993). So does his edited volume on cities involved in these macro processes: Charles Tilly and Willem Pieter Blockmans, *Cities and the Rise of States in Europe, AD 1000 to 1800* (Boulder, Colorado: Westview Press, 1994). Tilly's work on social movements and democratization similarly spans the whole of Europe and covers half a millennium of history: Tilly, *Social Movements*; Tilly, Tarrow, and McAdam,

Other notable examples of macro sociology than Tilly's work are the study of world civilizations in Weber's theory, and the study of state systems and the world-economy in Wallerstein's theory. Sociologist Karen Barkey has begun theorizing also intermediate scales of social interaction, in what might be called a *meso-foundational approach* that is implicit in Gramsci's notes on political parties, workers' movements, and their relations to social groups.[11]

In this volume I focus upon *the macro scale of social interaction and upon macro processes*. By macro processes I mean social processes that span very large areas and that last decades or even centuries. An important macro-phenomenon addressed is globalization, which affects the whole world and also spans decades or even centuries. This approach is still feasible, because in order to consider globalization, a vast phenomenon, I narrow the focus of the theory and I seek to explain only those aspects of globalization, like trade flows, and interstate conflict, that are common to and affect all countries in the West. This entails that the general theory that I propose is not a grand theory, because I do not try to explain the whole of globalization, but only parts of it. I also want to emphasize that using a broad framework that encompasses macro processes does not mean that the general theory that I propose is limited to these processes. To the contrary, I consider *all scales of social processes, namely, micro, meso, and macro scales*. In this volume I focus on the interaction between processes on the macro scale and processes on the other scales. This interactions affects *economic processes*. In considering the division of labour on society, I focus on a micro scale that involves individuals and companies interacting in a local market that is part of the local economy, and also on the meso scale involving interaction in nation-wide markets that are part of the national economy, as well as on the macro-scale that involves interaction in global markets that are part of the globalized world-economy, which is arguably distorted by interstate conflict and violence. The interaction amongst processes on all three scales also affects *political processes*. I especially focus below on the interactions between macro processes such as interstate conflict, which is affected by such features of macro social interaction as the number, type, and relative hierarchy of states, with such meso processes as social conflict

---

       Contention and Democracy in Europe. Tilly also theorized and defended the methodol-
       ogy of macro historical sociology in: Charles Tilly, *Big Structures, Large Processes, Huge
       Comparisons* (New York: Russell Sage Foundation, 1984).

11   Karen Barkey drew my attention to the importance of the meso scale in a seminar
       that I took as an external student at Columbia University. I discuss her work in Section
       4.3 below. I address Gramsci's approach in Chapter 6 of: Olsaretti, *The Struggle for
       Development and Democracy, Vol. 1*.

amongst social groups within a state and between social movements and the state, and such micro processes as processes involving individuals that participate in diffuse violence and social disaggregation. The latter is affected by interstate conflict, and in its turns affects it by providing large numbers of volunteers who man irregular forces used in social conflict and interstate conflict alike. These political processes also affect economic processes involved in the division of labour in society, and of course also affect the proper functioning of markets, which is distorted by diffuse violence, and by the organized crime that arises in some cases in which there is social disaggregation and elites who are ready to make use and even encourage social disaggregation. Similarly, the creation of elites and establishments in many countries in the West, regardless of whether we believe they are a cohesive group or a loosely coordinated bloc of social groups, involves interactions on a meso scale, and interacts with the emergence of a world-elite on a macro scale, which affects establishments by providing them with the coordination and the ability to defeat the masses in social conflict.

Let us consider now *the general assumptions that I use for the axiomatic-deductive method.* The general theory proposed here started with extensive theoretical groundwork expressly aimed at revising assumptions. I then used a specific method for building general theory, the axiomatic-deductive method. The axiomatic-deductive method is widely used in social science, particularly in economics, including neoliberal economic theory, and it is therefore a tried-and-tested method, that has been used before to formulate theories that have influenced policies. What sets this theory apart is not so much the method, but the assumptions, as well as the framework that complements these assumptions. I differ from most of economic theory because I use more general assumptions that describe behavior in the economy, and also in culture and politics, and their interactions with the economy.[12] The approach of neoliberal economic theory, and also of game theory, narrows down individual behavior, which has many aspects or sides, by selecting only one type of behavior. It assumes that individuals are motivated chiefly or even only by material gains as part of acquisitive individualism, in other words by profit, a behavior that is

---

12   This approach has been pioneered by AnnaLee Saxenian: AnnaLee Saxenian, *Regional Advantage: Culture and Competition in Silicon Valley and Route 128, with a New Preface by the Author* (Cambridge, Massachusetts and London: Harvard University Press, 1996); *The New Argonauts: Regional Advantage in a Global Economy* (Cambridge, Massachusetts and London: Harvard University Press, 2007). Interestingly, in her later work, Saxenian has begun studying flows of knowledge and skilled workforce in the global economy, a very important topic.

described by the concept of *Homo Oeconomicus*. This is a feature of economic behavior in markets, which does not include commitment to truth for example. The latter is instead an important feature of individual behavior in culture. The assumptions of economics are also too narrow for politics. Cohen, who initially formulated a theory of history based chiefly on assumptions associated with game theory, in his later work conceded that this approach is not sufficient, because individuals are motivated by identity, and in particular by national identity, rather than just material gains.[13] Therefore the assumptions described by the concept of *Homo Oeconomicus* are not universally valid, and to broaden my assumptions I introduce more assumptions that I describe below as *Homo Culturalis*, and *Homo Politicus*. The resulting approach is still feasible, because at the same time I narrow the focus of the theory, and I seek to explain only development and democracy, and to explain even these two phenomena only in the broadest terms. Therefore, this is not a grand theory, but a feasible theory that does not pretend to explain the whole of history. It simply seeks to explain the interactions between, on the hand culture and politics, and on the other hand economics, in favoring or delaying development.

With its broad framework and general assumptions, *the general theory that I propose is still very useful.* General theory that considers macro processes is especially *useful for policies set by states.* I want to pre-empt, in particular, the criticism that we cannot do anything about macro-phenomena or phenomena that last a long time, and that therefore there is no need for a general theory that addresses these phenomena. To the contrary, such a theory is very useful for policy. Globalization provides an especially clear example. It is probably true that by this time it is impossible to stop globalization. Two important points follow from this consideration, both of which relate to the usefulness of general theory. The first is that it is *necessary to take into account globalization in formulating theories and policies.* For example, if globalization has already reached a point at which it spans the entire world and makes use of billions of low-paid workers, to focus only or even chiefly, in countries that are part of the West, on how to make a local market more competitive by lowering labour costs, is doomed to failure. This local market will be swamped by competition from abroad in any case, and to compete by lowering wages and reducing job security will only hasten this failure. Furthermore, to save money by cutting on education would only compound this failure. The second point is that, although it is impossible to stop globalization, *it might be possible to steer*

13   Gerald Allan Cohen, *Karl Marx's Theory of History: A Defence*, Princeton Paperbacks (Princeton and Oxford: Princeton University Press, 2001). This books was first published in 1978.

globalization in different directions that are more favorable to the masses. The general theory of development and democracy that I propose in this book suggests ways in which development can be made less uneven, and globalization less unjust, so that it can be made to work for democracy. This raise a number of questions related to politics and collective action, because it is through politics and collective action that we can steer globalization and other processes in different directions.

General theory that considers macro processes is also especially *useful for activists and social movements* active in communities and at the local level. A naïve objection to general theory and the study of globalization might suggest that in a globalized economy all that matters is the world economy and the macro scale. This is not true. There are arguably very tangible processes that have been described by the term *glocalization*, because they involve both global and local scales, not just global processes that are part of globalization.[14] These processes are important scientifically, and I seek to generalize the insight that different scales of social processes are important by suggesting that it is necessary to formulate a theory that considers micro, meso, and macro scales. Simplifying the argument somewhat, the main agents are individuals at the micro level, social groups and social movement organizations at the meso level, and states at the macro level. The processes at these scales interact with each other, for example because micro interactions involving individuals are affected by social movements and states. Conversely, meso interactions involving social movements are affected by the beliefs and values of individuals. These processes are also important normatively, because community exists chiefly at a local level and we should not lose community. I argue in this project that community and the local level are especially important because they can be used to build stronger and thus better democracies, that can serve as the bases for a more comprehensive or all-round development that advances all human faculties and capabilities.[15] They can also be used to formulate a more equitable development that benefits the masses as well as the elites. This is an instance of how general theory can contribute to policy.

---

14   The concept of glocalization is described in: Victor Roudometof, *Glocalization: A Critical Introduction*, Routledge Studies in Global and Transnational Politics (London and New York: Routledge, 2016). It is addressed also in work by sociologist Saskia Sassen, who emphasizes the importance of processes at the local and the national level, as well as the world level, in her approach to globalization: Saskia Sassen, *Sociology of Globalization*, Contemporary Societies (w.w. Norton, 2007); *Deciphering the Global: Its Scales, Spaces and Subjects* (New York and London: Routledge, 2013).

15   I make this argument in the forthcoming series of essays: Olsaretti, *Towards a Humanist Social Science*.

2   World Systems Theory and the Maximum Systems in the World

World Systems Theory, and the concept of system that it proposes, is very important to the arguments of this book because this is the one school of thought within sociology in which the ancient Greek concept of hegemony, understood as the influence of one state over other states, has been further elaborated. This ancient concept is important to nuance and expand upon Gramsci's concept of hegemony understood as the influence of one social group over other groups, in order to produce *a contemporary theory of hegemony*.[16] Arrighi began introducing in World Systems Theory a number of concepts from Gramsci's theory of hegemony, including its focus on social conflict amongst social groups within a state, in order to complement the modern study of hegemony in interstate conflict that is the main focus of World Systems Theory. However, Arrighi never got much further than a few preliminary remarks. I want to pursue this line of research much further, instead, since part of my goal is to develop a contemporary theory of hegemony that is a comprehensive theory taking into consideration how hegemony works amongst states, on the macro scale, which is a central concern of World Systems Theory, and also how hegemony works amongst social groups, on the meso scale, which is a central concern of Gramsci's theory. The contributions of World Systems Theory to a contemporary theory of hegemony consist in the way in which it has integrated *concepts from historical sociology and historical geography* within the study of hegemony. World Systems Theory is the main school of thought that has been promoting a historical social science and the sub-field of historical sociology, of which it is part. World Systems Theory also introduced a spatial dimension to sociological research that is very close to historical geography, as will become clear below in discussions of such concepts as core, semi-periphery, and periphery of the world system, all of which I suggest are essentially geopolitical and geoeconomic concepts.

World Systems Theory builds upon *key concepts in historical sociology*, and in particular macro historical sociology, as it is one of several schools of historical sociology that build upon *the concept of system*. This concept is proposed amongst others by two leading historical sociologists today, Mann and Wallerstein, and it is especially relevant to, and can be incorporated into, a contemporary theory of hegemony. The most useful interpretation of the

---

16   Benedetto Fontana has begun the task of studying Gramsci's work on hegemony in relation to the ancient Greek concept of hegemony: Benedetto Fontana, "Logos and Kratos: Gramsci and the Ancients on Hegemony," *Journal of the History of Ideas* 61, no. 2 (2000).

concept of system arguably emphasizes *system as a complementary concept to the concept of organization*. An organization is distinguished by a formal hierarchical structure, command chains, and very precise and extensive rules of behavior that cover most behaviors and relations within the organization. A system is constituted of a number of different organizations, amongst which there is neither a formal hierarchy, nor command chains, and relatively few rules of behavior, compared to an organization. Some loose hierarchies can develop, in which one organization issues commands and sets broad rules that are followed by some of the other organizations. If these hierarchies are based upon cultural influence, then this organization can be said to be hegemonic. The concept of system in conjunction with hegemony is especially relevant to understand the social problems and political phenomena that this book addresses, including globalization. World Systems Theory claims that, with globalization, systems have emerged that span the entire world, all of which are part of an overarching modern world system.

It is useful to distinguish between *three different maximum systems* that *coexist and interact with each other within a single overarching modern world system*. By maximum systems I refer to systems that act on the greatest geographical scale, and thus require the maximum geographical framework in order to be studied accurately.[17] There are systems that act on a global and near-global scale. Arguably, there is a single world system today that includes a world economy, a world culture, and a state system. These three systems are each defined by a different type of organization that participates in the system, whether it is economic, political-military, or cultural organizations. Wallerstein suggested that *a world-economy* dominated by large economic organizations has been developing since the 1500s. This world-economy emerged through a progressive expansion of trade flows that initially spanned long distances and included mostly luxury items like spices and silk, until our own day, when we can speak of a globalization that spans the entire world and affects many or even most economic items.[18] Wallerstein also pointed out that states played a major role

---

17   Galileo Galiei, the scientist, used the concept of 'massimi sistemi' to refer to the systems of maximum extent or maximum scale that he was studying. In social science today, the world system is the maximum system.

18   Wallerstein called it the world economy, at a time when the word globalization had not yet come into widespread use. He wrote a book focusing just upon it: Immanuel Maurice Wallerstein, M. Aymard, and J. Revel, *The Capitalist World-Economy*, Studies in Modern Capitalism (Cambridge and New York: Cambridge University Press, 1979). For Wallerstein's views on globalization as an old phenomenon, see: William I. Robinson, "Globalization and the Sociology of Immanuel Wallerstein: A Critical Appraisal," *International Sociology* 26, no. 6 (2011).

in the expansion of the world economy, and that they constituted a system of their own, *a state system* that from its beginnings in the 1500s has become the modern state system.[19] The modern state system consists of powerful political-military organizations and it is arguably very important. States contributed to the expansion of the world economy, and to exploitation within it, in a number of ways that ranged from securing trade routes, to opening up markets, and also to outright conquest.

I want to emphasize that there is also *a world culture* that is emerging alongside the world economy, and that, similarly to the world economy, is affected by the state system.[20] This world culture includes world literature, a concept introduced by Marx that has been recently gaining renewed attention, and is beginning to be integrated into World Systems Theory.[21] World literature includes economically driven phenomena like global markets for books, and the export of literature from the West to other parts of the world. It also includes politically driven phenomena like postcolonial literature, which emerges in countries that freed themselves from colonialism, and by some accounts it includes also purely cultural phenomena like the emergence of a 'world republic of letters.'[22] Arguably, however, world culture was dominated for a long time by religious organizations. These were the Christian Churches active in proselytizing in lands conquered by European powers, or penetrated by European merchants. Sometimes the Catholic Church achieved great influence over the new countries that were created, Quebec and Mexico most

---

19   Wallerstein's views on the modern state system are set out in: Immanuel Maurice Wallerstein, *The Politics of the World-Economy: The States, the Movements and the Civilizations* (Cambridge and New York: Cambridge University Press, 1984); "The Inter-State Structure of the Modern World-System," *International theory: positivism and beyond* (1996).

20   For an overview of the concept of world culture, see: Frank J. Lechner and John Boli, *World Culture: Origins and Consequences* (Oxford: Blackwell, 2008). Wallerstein focused mostly on the study of the world economy, and to some extent of the state system.

21   On Marx and world literature, see: S. S. Prawer, *Karl Marx and World Literature* (London and New York: Verso, 2014). For an overview of the concept of world literature see: David Damrosch, *What Is World Literature?* (Princeton and Oxford: Princeton University Press, 2003). The many contributions in a more recent volume edited by Damrosch highlight the different approaches to world literature in the history of this concept: *World Literature in Theory* (Chichester, West Sussex and Malden, Massachusetts: Wiley-Blackwell, 2014).

22   Markets and global flows of books are studied by: Franco Moretti, *Atlas of the European Novel: 1800–1900* (London and New York: Verso, 1999); *Distant Reading* (London and New York: Verso, 2013). The concept of a world republic of letters, building upon the Enlightenment precedent to this concept, was proposed by: Pascale Casanova, *The World Republic of Letters*, trans. M.B. DeBevoise (Cambridge, Massachusetts and London: Harvard University Press, 2004).

obviously, but also El Salvador and Santo Domingo.[23] Universities participate in this world culture, and the emergence of new disciplines like oriental studies and other area studies, and of disciplines like anthropology and sociology, was part of this emergent world culture, and was deeply affected by differences in power within it.[24]

World Systems Theory also builds upon *key concepts in historical geography*. Wallerstein argued that in the modern world system there are three geographically distinct areas: the core, the semi-periphery, and the periphery. These are three key concepts for World Systems Theory, although Arrighi has criticized a tendency within this school of thought to use the classification into core, semi-periphery, and periphery to explain all social processes.[25] I agree with this criticism but for completely different reasons. Wallerstein's classification of the world actually combines a number of different concepts that I think are best kept separate. I think it is necessary to distinguish between three different hierarchies of power, namely, the economic, cultural, and political-military hierarchies, and to emphasize that they are only loosely related. I elaborate upon this point at some length in Chapters 5 and 6 below. Wallerstein's theory is still very useful because of three very important insights that it conveys: the

---

23   I address some of these points in: Olsaretti, *Towards a Humanist Social Science*. On Catholic missions in the New World, see: Catherine Ballériaux, *Missionary Strategies in the New World, 1610–1690: An Intellectual History* (London and New York: Routledge, 2016); John Frederick Schwaller, *The History of the Catholic Church in Latin America: From Conquest to Revolution and Beyond* (New York and London: New York University Press, 2011). Michael Pasquier, *Fathers on the Frontier: French Missionaries and the Roman Catholic Priesthood in the United States, 1789–1870* (Oxford and New York: Oxford University Press, 2010).

24   Institutions have played an important role in world culture: John Boli and George M. Thomas, "World Culture in the World Polity: A Century of International Non-Governmental Organization," *American Sociological Review* 62, no. 2 (1997). The importance of universities to capitalists active on a world stage is addressed in: Leslie Sklair, *The Transnational Capitalist Class* (Oxford: Blackwell, 2000). On the participation of universities in globalization, see the many contributions in: Janice K. Currie and Janice Newson, eds., *Universities and Globalization: Critical Perspectives* (Thousand Oaks, London, and New Delhi: SAGE, 1998); Sheryl Bond and Jean-Pierre Lemasson, eds., *A New World of Knowledge: Canadian Universities and Globalization* (Otttawa, Cairo, Dakar, Johannesburg, Montevideo, Nairobi, New Delhi, Singapore: International Development Research Centre, 1999).

25   Giovanni Arrighi, "Capitalism and the Modern World-System: Rethinking the Nondebates of the 1970's," *Review (Fernand Braudel Center)* 21, no. 1 (1998). A criticism of World Systems Theory has suggested that it should take into consideration geopolitics: Aristide R. Zolberg, "Origins of the Modern World System: a Missing Link," *World Politics* 33, no. 2 (1981). In his later work, Wallerstein did begin to consider geoculture and geopolitics: Immanuel Maurice Wallerstein, *Geopolitics and Geoculture: Essays on the Changing World-System* (Cambridge and New York: Cambridge University Press, 1991).

first is that there emerged in modern times a European state system that has a tendency to expand both economically and militarily, and thus to engage in imperialism, potentially spanning the entire world through a combination of conquest and trade, and leading to the creation of the modern world system; the second insight is that this modern world system is constituted of a state system and a world economy that includes trade flows between states; the third insight is that, in describing imperialism and trade flows, it is necessary to distinguish between core, semi-periphery and periphery of the world system, in what is essentially a geographical distribution of power, roughly corresponding to a hierarchy of power, whereby power is greatest in the core, and least in the periphery. The concepts of core, semi-periphery, and periphery, are also useful because they are very important to understand both the context and the reference frame, and through them contribute to the explanations that I put forward in this book.

3   Causal Chains and Reference Frames within the Main Arguments

It is useful, in order to formulate a theory with many concepts, to introduce some important distinctions. This book seeks to provide explanations of development and democracy, which *entail using more basic factors that act as causal factors to explain development and democracy*. Basic factors include *social processes and entities in the world*. Social processes include globalization, whereas entities include states and social groups. The causal factors are part of a causal chain, which plays out within a given context. When thinking in terms of a high-level summary of the explanations that one provides, it is useful to divide the causal factors into two categories, whereby *causal factors are either part of the explanandum or the explanans*, a distinction emphasized at McGill University by Axel van den Berg. The explanandum are the concepts that one seeks to explain, whereas the explanans are the concepts that are used to explain. They occupy different places in a causal chain. The explanans is at the beginning of the causal chain, whereas the explanandum is at the end of the causal chain, which leads from the explanans to the explanandum. Figure 1 shows the case of a simple cause and effect in which there is just an explanans and an explanandum with no intermediate factors.

For the arguments of this book, it is necessary to introduce *other categories of causal factors: ambivalent concepts and intermediate concepts*. These other categories are necessary to a theory that addresses complex social processes like development and democracy, and thus uses many causal factors that are part of a long causal chain. *Ambivalent concepts could be legitimately classified*

Explanans or cause: *Explanandum or effect:*
collective action   ----------------------➤   neoliberalism
advantage

FIGURE 1   The relationship between explanans and explanandum I: simple cause and effect
             with no intermediate causal factors

as either explanans or explanandum. The ambivalent status of some concepts
at the beginning of the research is fairly obvious, because before one starts
studying a topic in depth, one could legitimately classify certain concepts as
either explanans or explanandum, simply because one does not know as yet
their place in the causal chain. Democracy is a good example that applies
to this study. One could see democracy as part of the explanans, that is, as a
factor that explains neoliberalism, for example neoliberals might argue that
democracy leads to neoliberalism. Alternatively, one could see democracy as
the explanandum, suggesting that failures of democracy, reinforced by lack of
the social conditions for objectivity in social science departments, lead to both
neoliberalism and populism, each being a type of non-valid or plainly bad theories, of economics and politics respectively.

   *Intermediate concepts can be classified as being both an explanans and an
explanandum.* In a complex scientific model, there are more or less long causal
chains, in which an intermediate concept is at one and the same time both
an explanans and an explanandum, depending on the segment of the causal
chain that one considers. Figure 2 shows a causal chain with two segments,
with democracy as an intermediate factor. Democracy is capitalized in the diagram in order to highlight the fact that it is an intermediate factor.

   Democracy is an explanandum in segment 1, the first part of the causal
chain, which leads through social conflict from the basic factors of hegemony,

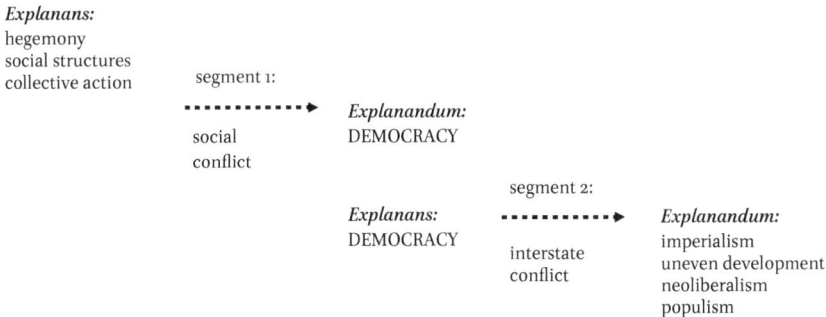

Explanans:
hegemony
social structures
collective action   segment 1:

                      ············➤   *Explanandum:*
                        social   DEMOCRACY
                        conflict

                                              segment 2:
                            Explanans: ···········➤   *Explanandum:*
                            DEMOCRACY   imperialism
                                        interstate   uneven development
                                        conflict   neoliberalism
                                                               populism

FIGURE 2   The relationship between explanans and explanandum II: causal chain with two
             segments and one intermediate causal factor

collective action and social structures, to democracy. It is instead an explanans in segment 2, the second part of the causal chain, which leads through inter-state conflict from democracy, or more specifically the struggle for democracy, to imperialism, uneven development, neoliberalism, and populism. Democracy is also capitalized because it is a complex concept that includes many other concepts, for example in this theory I define democracy as a distribution of power both within arenas and across arenas, two separate concepts, both of which are integral to the definition of democracy. Figure 2 also provides a high-level summary of the argument of this book that I introduce in Volume 1 and elaborate at greater length in this volume, namely, that hegemony, social structures and collective action lead to more or less democracy, which leads to imperialism, uneven development, neoliberalism, and populism. At this point in the argument the relationships amongst these last four concepts remain unspecified. In Chapter 8 I argue that they reinforce each other through different causal chains. The exact mechanism by which failures of democracy lead to these four factors is also at this stage unspecified.

Other concepts yet like *the context and the reference frame do not neatly belong to a causal chain, but still take part in explanations*. These two concepts are especially important to the arguments of this book. *A context can be a broad social process* that encompasses other social processes. It participates in causal chains, chiefly by changing one or more causal factors that are part of causal chains. The main context that is important to this book is the context of globalization, which interacts with and changes several causal factors. Globalization arguably leads to greater uneven development within countries in the West that are affected by it, and through it, or indirectly through migration and populism, it affects democracy. Globalization changes the way in which causal factors play out, for example because it increases social conflict, since market competition under some circumstances destroys the livelihood of entire social groups, which then engage in greater conflict with other social groups. *The concept of reference frame, whether geographic or semantic, describes features of the context* and is thus associated with the context. The geographic and semantic reference frames are both very important to the arguments of this book, as they enable me to revisit the concept of the West.

In this book I use *a geographic reference frame*, that is, a frame whereby we measure distances that are important to describe key features of the context. In mathematics, the expression reference frame denotes two or more axes by reference to which measurements are made. In this book, I make use of a distinct geographic reference frame that is based upon the concepts of core, semi-periphery and periphery, that I nuance and expand upon below by adding geopolitical concepts. Similarly to mathematical reference frames, the geographic reference frame that I use in this book has a zero point, corresponding to the center of the core, and it has axes with dimensions. In particular the reference frame uses a large scale necessary to describe the dimensions of globalization. I want to *emphasize the differences of this approach from Eurocentrism*. Measuring geographical distance from the core is not an instance of seeing one's culture as the center of the world. It is due instead to the fact that *the theory tries to understand how power works, and this includes how power is projected*, and as a rule of thumb, the further one moves from the place from which power is projected, namely the core, the riskier and the costlier it is to project power. It is thus useful to place the zero point of the geographic reference frame in the core, and measure distance from the core. The definition of the core that I use overlaps with the West in modern times, but this too is not an instance of Eurocentrism since *I approach the West as a political construct reinforced by cultural features*, whereby the concept of the West is based on the concept of state system, which emphasizes that states in the system are in competition with each other, a competition that is often adversarial competition and thus constitutes interstate conflict. Cultural definitions of the West follow from this political definition. This conflict can turn violent and thus includes war, but there is also cultural contact, which leads to the emergence of some common culture amidst all the differences, so that the West is reinforced by cultural features. This political construct can change. As the state system changes, the core expands, and might even move outside Europe, to be centered in North America, and might even move outside the West altogether.

Since the West is a key concept in this book, it is important to *define the concept of West precisely and in some detail*. I especially want to explain the choice to approach it as a political construct, because I want to make clear that my focus on the West is *not* a fallback upon Eurocentric, or orientalist and more in general racist, views that essentialize the West and see it as an entity instead of a system, and as the depositary of democracy, science, and capitalism. I use the word West to refer instead to a more or less clearly defined *political and military alliance shaping the state system within the modern world system*. Over the years this alliance has acquired specific cultural connotations. Throughout this book, when I refer to the West, I mean Western Europe and Anglophone and Francophone North America. It overlaps with the early signatories of NATO and, more recently, with the West European Union, or WEU, whose importance as a military alliance and intelligence sharing alliance I fear is underestimated and is likely to be overlooked now that it has officially ceased to exist.[26] The

---

26   Joint collective efforts by the European Union today bring to mind first of all CERN, the
      massive particle physics laboratory in Geneva, or the Fusion Project, first headquartered

mantle of the WEU is carried on today by European battlegroups, military forces of about 1,500 men that are available for quick deployment and for rotation to trouble spots around the world. In December 2017 a new union was set up, similar to NATO, and parallel to the earlier WEU, and to all the armed forces and agencies of European countries, referred to in English as Permanent Structured Cooperation, or PESCO. It seeks to bring together the military projects, and to harmonize the strategies, of 25 out of the 27 countries that are part of the European Union, and could one day form the basis for a new WEU. PESCO is also parallel to NATO, which has been expanding to include much of Europe, and could one day perhaps form its own agency, also parallel to those of NATO countries, if only because of the growing importance of intelligence in the modern military.[27]

In this book I also use a *semantic reference frame, which is useful to describe cultural processes that are part of globalization*, a frame that changes the meaning of concepts, and thus deeply affects theory, because one has to revisit and sometimes redefine concepts. In particular, the semantic reference frame that I use changes the definition of the four concepts of imperialism, uneven development, neoliberalism, and populism, or puts them in a different light. In addition, globalization, especially early globalization, is intertwined with imperialism, and this changes the perception and meaning of science itself.[28] Imperialists from Europe used science in two ways. The first was largely a *practical-scientific use of science*, for example an understanding of how markets work, based on scientific theories, enabled these imperialists to introduce or expand markets in a way that benefited them over and above all others. I refer to it below simply as a scientific use of science or of scientific concepts. The second way was also practical, but largely ideological, and implicated in the exercise of political-military power, and can thus be aptly described as *a practical-ideological use of science*. I refer to it below simply as an ideological use of science or of scientific concepts. An example of this way is that imperialists from Europe claimed that science made them superior to non-European

---

in Barcelona, now located mostly in southern France, where this project aims to build a working fusion reactor. However, for many years the European Union had a military and intelligence arm, the Western European Union, arguably an important organization of the European Union, despite its ostensibly small size.

27   An overview of PESCO, CSP in French, is provided in: Delphine Deschaux-Dutard, "L'Europe et Sa Défense: La Coopération Structurée Permanent, Est-Elle une Panacée?," *Défense & Sécurité Internationale*, no. 149 (2020).

28   I addressed this point at some length in Chapter 2 of Volume 1, and in a series of essays: Olsaretti, *The Struggle for Development and Democracy, Vol. 1; Towards a Humanist Social Science*.

cultures, and justified their imperialism by claiming to be bringing a 'superior' civilization that includes science to other countries. Imperialists from France claimed this was part of their *mission civilizatrice*, or civilizing mission, towards other parts of the world that were somehow seen as missing civilization.[29]

4   The Semantic Reference Frame and the Rise of the West

It is useful to begin by addressing the semantic reference frame, because *a different semantic reference frame helps us revisit the concept of science and its association with civilization.* It is thus also helpful to address problems raised by Eurocentrism. This is important because the practical-ideological uses of science can lead to a knee-jerk reaction against science, ultimately rejecting all uses that sciences can be put to, and thus rejecting the scientific, as well as the ideological uses of sciences. It is also important to emphasize that the practical-ideological uses of science can be made to work for democracy. This is especially clear when we consider globalization. Let us *define globalization first and address how it relates to scientific explanation.* Some aspects of globalization are obviously important to this book because neoliberalism is tied to globalization. Neoliberalism encouraged trade flows and furthered globalization, leading to a massive relocation of industry on a truly global scale, which fueled the discontent associated with the populist backlash in many countries in the West. Here I want to introduce some aspects of globalization that are important but not in an obviously way. A key point made by Wallerstein is that globalization is not a new phenomenon. It was preceded by, and perhaps we could say it continued, an earlier globalization that started a very long time ago, in the 1500s, in conjunction with colonialism, a type of imperialism.[30]

---

29   Overviews from different viewpoints of the *mission civilizatrice* of imperialists from France are provided by: Nick Harrison, *Our Civilizing Mission: The Lessons of Colonial Education*, Contemporary French and Francophone Cultures Series (Liverpool: Liverpool University Press, 2019). Alice L. Conklin, *A Mission to Civilize: The Republican Idea of Empire in France and West Africa, 1895–1930* (Stanford, California: Stanford University Press, 1997). On the connection between paternalism and colonialism in the case of Lebanon, see: Elizabeth Thompson, *Colonial Citizens: Republican Rights, Paternal Privilege, and Gender in French Syria and Lebanon* (New York: Columbia University Press, 2000).

30   On globalization and World Systems Theory, see: Thomas D. Hall, *Comparing Globalizations: Historical and World-Systems Approaches*, World-Systems Evolution and Global Futures (Cham, Switzerland: Springer, 2017). Some authors have suggested that the world system predates the 1500s: Albert James Bergesen, "Pre Vs. Post 1500ers," *Comparative Civilizations Review* 30, no. 30 (1994). On this point, see also the many contributions in: Andre Gunder Frank and Barry K. Gills, eds., *The World System: Five Hundred*

This begins to suggest a *relationship between, on the one hand imperialism, and on the other hand uneven development, neoliberalism, and populism,* namely, the other three concepts that are part of the explanandum. All three are related to globalization and the *imperialism that was associated with the earlier globalization,* an imperialism that might have been continued to this day in new forms of imperialism. To understand this earlier globalization, we need to reconsider the question of the rise of West, since both imperialism and this early globalization were driven by Western powers.[31] As proposed here, this question can be reinterpreted in such a way that we *approach civilization in an altogether different manner.* This is an instance of how the context of globalization and the associated semantic reference frame change the perception of science and its practical-ideological uses, in particular of the concept of civilization used by science. Focusing on the earlier globalization enables reconceptualizing civilization by going back in time, before the practical-ideological uses made of this concept by imperialists from Europe distorted it. This has scientific value, because it introduces an altogether new concept of civilization. It also has an ideological value, because this new concept of civilization, and its relationship to globalization, can help us define new political approaches to civilization that can inform an emancipatory and subaltern politics. For example, it can ultimately help us approach the association between European civilization, science, and modernity, in ways that are less culturally specific and more inclusive.

The question of the Rise of the West was a central question to sociology at its inception. Sociologists, including Max Weber, debated what could explain the remarkable fact that in the modern era parts of Europe had introduced economic innovations like capitalism and conquered much of the world.[32] This is

---

Years or Five Thousand? (London and New York: Routledge, 1996). One of the key argument in these debates is whether the many changes that occurred in the 1500s, including the expansion of capitalism, the emergence of proto nation-states with their military forces, and the Reformation, alongside the voyages of exploration and the new trade routes opened, amount to the emergence of an altogether new world system. I believe they do, especially compared to the world system that had begun to emergence in the Middle Ages with the expansion of overland trade through Asia, as described by: Janet L. Abu-Lughod, *Before European Hegemony: The World System A.D. 1250–1350* (Oxford, New York, Toronto: Oxford University Press, 1991). The economic and political importance of the north-western European proto nation-states was certainly a new phenomenon in European history that shaped Europe for centuries after the 1500s and had a major impact on other parts of the world.

31   For a review of this question, see: Jonathan Daly, *Historians Debate the Rise of the West* (London and New York: Routledge, 2014).

32   Wolfgang Schluchter and Guenther Roth, *The Rise of Western Rationalism: Max Weber's Developmental History,* trans. Guenther Roth (Berkeley, Los Angeles, and London: University

more remarkable if we consider that Great Britain alone was able to conquer all of India, which was much larger and much more populous than Great Britain, and that eventually Great Britain and other European powers were able to subject much of the world, including China, another large and populous country, to some form of colonial tutelage. This is even more remarkable if we consider that Europe in the Middle Ages was relatively backwards compared to China, for example. How could a relatively backward periphery of Eurasia, less populous and less powerful than many other Eurasian countries, come to conquer much of the world, including most other Eurasian countries? Diamond has written an insightful study of the way in which some countries in the West were able to conquer other parts of the world. This study focuses on the conquest of less densely populated continents like Africa and the Americas.[33] It incorporates in a broader picture that includes many recent advances in geography, some of the concerns and insights by economic historian Carlo M. Cipolla. Diamond's study however ignores the fact that some countries in the West were able to conquer also densely populated countries throughout Eurasia.[34] In particular, the British empire, in addition to large parts of North America, and much of Africa, included the whole of South Asia, from which it derived much wealth.

The question of the Rise of the West lost its original importance to sociology with the decline of European colonial empires and it has been marginalized following the publication of Edward Said's *Orientalism*.[35] Said argued that the work of nineteenth century scholars who focused on understanding Asian countries was in many ways subservient to imperialists from Europe and was biased in always comparing Asian countries to the West and always finding them wanting, implicitly assuming a Eurocentric point of view whereby Europe was the only standard of progress. Today *the study of the Rise of the West survives in only a few departments of sociology,* for example at McGill University, where

---

of California Press, 1985). Daniel Chirot, "The Rise of the West," *American Sociological Review* 50, no. 2 (1985).

33   Jared Diamond, *Guns, Germs, and Steel: The Fates of Human Societies* (New York and London: W. W. Norton, 1999). I address Diamond's argument in some detail in Chapter 2.

34   Carlo M. Cipolla, *Guns, Sails and Empires: Technological Innovations and the Early Phases of European Expansion, 1400–1700* (New York: Pantheon Books, 1965). Cipolla also began studying questions of epidemiology in a historical context: *Miasmas and Disease: Public Health and the Environment in the Pre-Industrial Age*, trans. Elizabeth Potter (New Haven and London: Yale University Press, 1992). He also focused on European colonial empires in Asia, and on such questions as the decline of the once powerful Ottoman empire: *The Economic Decline of Empires*, Economic History (London and New York: Routledge, 2013).

35   Edward W. Said, *Orientalism* (Vintage Books, 1994). Said's book was first published in 1978. It has become a classic.

John Anthony Hall, who has built his fame with a work on the rise of the West, continued addressing questions related to it, and where younger scholars like Matthew Lange to this day study the impact of the British empire on other parts of the world.[36] Scholars working on more fashionable questions might argue that McGill University is a bastion of old ways of thinking, and dismiss Hall and Lange as old-fashioned scholars who are nostalgic of the heydays of the British empire. However, there has been in recent years a *renewal of interest in the Rise of the West* amongst both sociologists and historians working on world history, which has nuanced this question by focusing on a number of different factors, not just culture, and also by questioning whether the West diverged in any fundamental way from East Asia.[37]

I am afraid that *the wholesale dismissal of the Rise of the West debate as Eurocentric is associated with a knee-jerk reaction* which, while capturing a basic truth, leads to errors that must be avoided.[38] There are two such errors that are closely related and are associated with both orientalism and reverse-orientalism: essentialism, and dismissing important concepts. *Essentialism* is based on narrow and undifferentiated views of the occidental 'other' similar to those denounced by Said. An example of essentialism that we must avoid is that, by seeing the entire West as an undifferentiated other, we could miss *important differences within the West, and even just within Europe*. This leads to the *dismissal of important concepts*. This is the second error, which can aptly be described as throwing out the baby with the bathwater, something that one

36   John Anthony Hall, *Powers and Liberties: The Causes and Consequences of the Rise of the West* (Berkeley and Los Angeles: University of California Press, 1986). I address Lange's work in the next chapter.

37   McNeill's classic has more recently been reprinted: William H. McNeill, *The Rise of the West: A History of the Human Community* (Chicago and London: University of Chicago Press, 2009). Important instances of this renewal of interest are: Jack A Goldstone, "The Rise of the West—or Not? A Revision to Socio-Economic History," *Sociological Theory* 18, no. 2 (2000); "Efflorescences and Economic Growth in World History: Rethinking the 'Rise of the West' and the Industrial Revolution," *Journal of world history* (2002). There has also been an interesting exchange between Bryant and Goldstone: Joseph M Bryant, "The West and the Rest Revisited: Debating Capitalist Origins, European Colonialism, and the Advent of Modernity," *Canadian Journal of Sociology/Cahiers canadiens de sociologie* 31, no. 4 (2006); Jack A Goldstone, "Capitalist Origins, the Advent of Modernity, and Coherent Explanation: a Response to Joseph M. Bryant," ibid. 33, no. 1 (2008); Joseph M Bryant, "A New Sociology for a New History? Further Critical Thoughts on the Eurasian Similarity and Great Divergence Theses," ibid.

38   Hall himself weighed in on the argument and described himself as a Eurocentric, suggesting that Eurocentrics were being prevented from speaking by a rising anti-Eurocentric consensus: John Anthony Hall, "Confessions of a Eurocentric," *International Sociology* 16, no. 3 (2001). I find the argument that Eurocentrics are being muted unconvincing.

should never do. In the eagerness to reject apologies of European imperialism, we should not reject also important concepts that happen to be historically associated with European imperialism. In particular, we could miss out on the important point that *some European countries and states were bypassed and to some extent the victims of the rise of the West.* This is true both of Italian city-states, and later of southern Italy, and of large territorial empires in Europe, like the Ottoman empire, which included the Balkans and the Middle East, leading to enduring forms of underdevelopment that are still visible in successor states of the Ottoman empire like Greece, Lebanon, and Syria.[39] Below I refer to the Rise of the West, all in capital letters, as the sociological question, and the rise of the West, or more specifically the rise of north-western Europe, as the actual social process.

Essentialism also misses the point that, *even within countries that participated in the rise of north-western Europe, there were important differences* that I argue, here and elsewhere, were important to the rise of imperialism. The following arguments suggest views that avoid essentialism and that better reflect the realities of power. There were within the West poorer areas that have been described as *internal peripheries*, which ended up being exploited as reservoirs of manpower, and serving as proving grounds for the imperialism that was launched abroad at a later stage.[40] The concept of internal peripheries can be applied equally well to describe the fate of Northern Ireland, Wales and Scotland within Great Britain. Imperialists from England first conquered these internal peripheries, then moved on to take over much of the world.

---

39   There are numerous works that study the decline of the Ottoman empire and ask whether this decline was inevitable. A socio-economic approach to this question is provided by: Halil Inalcık and Donald Quataert, eds., *An Economic and Social History of the Ottoman Empire. Volume Two: 1600–1914* (Cambridge and New York: Cambridge University Press, 1994); Sevket Pamuk, *A Monetary History of the Ottoman Empire*, Cambridge Studies in Islamic Civilization (Cambridge and New York: Cambridge University Press, 2000). An institutional approach is provided by: Ayse Y. Evrensel and Tiffany Minx, "An Institutional Approach to the Decline of the Ottoman Empire," *Cogent Economics & Finance* 5, no. 1 (2017).

40   In sociology the concept of internal periphery, in relationship to colonialism, was first studied by: Michael Hechter, *Internal Colonialism: The Celtic Fringe in British National Development*, Sociology, History, Political Science (New York: Columbia University, 1972). Nolte has addressed the concept of internal periphery also with specific reference to southern Europe: Hans-Heinrich Nolte, "Internal Peripheries: From Andalucia to Tatarstan," *Review (Fernand Braudel Center)* 18, No. 2 (1995); "Why Is Europe's South Poor? A Chain of Internal Peripheries Along the Old Muslim-Christian Borders," *Review (Fernand Braudel Center)* 26, No. 1 (2003).

They also first devised modern colonialism in these internal peripheries.[41] Similarly, imperialists from northern Italy trying to parrot their more powerful counterparts from England, first conquered southern Italy, then started foreign conquests and imperial expansion abroad. Racist and condescending attitudes were part of these hierarchical power relationships. The argument introduced by some scholars, that In Italy there was 'orientalism in one country,' aptly describes the condescending ideologies, sometimes veering into open racism, that were part of the imperialism towards southern Italy of elites from northern Italy, who encouraged or even formulated the racist ideologies, and engaged in imperialism, with the cooperation of at least some elites from southern Italy.[42]

Another example of essentialism that we must avoid is that, by focusing on very visible cultural differences, and by conceiving of civilization as defined exclusively by culture, or defined exclusively as religion, we could miss out on the point that *there were different types of civilizations. Material culture is especially important to a different concept of civilization.*[43] Historian Fernand Braudel, by focusing on material culture, such as the type of agriculture practiced, the types of textiles manufactured, and on patterns of trade that involved exchange of material artefacts, made a convincing case that *before the 1500s there existed a single Mediterranean civilization that included disparate cultures and religions* that interacted as part of an earlier world system centered on the Mediterranean, which traded with other world systems in East Asia and South

---

41   Hechter points out that there were internal peripheries in European states analogous to the peripheries in the world economy: Hechter, *Internal Colonialism*. This book was republished in 1999 and 2017.

42   Jane Schneider, ed. *Italy's 'Southern Question': Orientalism in One Country* (London and New York: Routledge, 2020). In a study of travelogues to the Levant, I argued that the exoticism and curiosity towards Middle Eastern cultures continued and repeated stereotypes and cultural tropes that British elites had towards parts of the working classes of their countries: Alessandro Olsaretti, "Urban Culture, Curiosity and the Aesthetics of Distance: The Representation of Picturesque Carnivals in Early Victorian Travelogues to the Levant," *Social History* 32, no. 3 (2007).

43   Braudel proposed the concept of 'material civilization,' a concept that is central to his volumes on the material culture of capitalism: Fernand Braudel, *Civilization and Capitalism, 15th-18th Century, Volume 1: The Structure of Everyday Life*, trans. Sian Reynolds (New York: Harper & Row, 1981); *Civilization and Capitalism 15th-18th Century, Volume 2: The Wheels of Commerce*, trans. Sian Reynolds (New York: Harper & Row, 1982). For a discussion of this concept, and a comparison between Braudel's and Elias' work, see: Tim Dant, "Material Civilization: Things and Society," *The British Journal of Sociology* 57, no. 2 (2006). On the material culture of First Nations, or Native American peoples, see: Judy Thompson, Judy Hall, and Leslie Heyman Tepper, eds., *Fascinating Challenges: Studying Material Culture with Dorothy Burnham* (Ottawa: University of Ottawa Press, 2001).

Asia, and in Africa.[44] This argument and concept of civilization contributed to Wallerstein's concept of the modern world system. It leads to a different view of the rise of north-western Europe than views emphasizing cultural traits or religion alone. After the 1500s the entire Mediterranean system, including much of Italy and all the lands that were part of the Ottoman empire, that is, Greece, the Balkans, the Middle East and North Africa, was displaced by a newly-created Atlantic world system, as patterns of trade changed and the earlier system centered on the Mediterranean was replaced by what was to become the modern world system, a single world system that today spans the entire world and was and arguably still is dominated by states in north-western Europe.[45]

The other error associated with the knee-jerk reaction encouraged by eagerness to reject apologies of European imperialism is that it could lead to the *dismissal* of *important concepts associated with the Rise of the West.* One such concept is *the rise of north-western Europe*, an actual process that needs explanation. It is an undisputed fact that some European states built massive colonial empires that spanned most of the globe within a relatively short historical time span, and lasted through most of the modern era, over the period 1500–1950 approximately. It is also undisputed that this had profound consequences for development and democracy throughout the world, in the rest of the world, and I suggest also in Europe. It is important to reject the idea that any European, including north-western European, countries were inherently superior to countries in other parts of the world or in Europe. This is both false and has been used as an apology for European imperialism. But we should still try to understand what exactly made European colonial empires possible, both in order to understand what happened in a recent part of our past, and

---

44 This argument is central to Braudel's work on the Mediterranean: Fernand Braudel, *The Mediterranean and the Mediterranean World in the Age of Philip II, Vol. 1*, trans. Sian Reynolds (New York: Harper & Row, 1972); *The Mediterranean and the Mediterranean World in the Age of Philip II, Vol. 2*, trans. Sian Reynolds (New York: Harper & Row, 1973).

45 Braudel's later work, on capitalism, included the view that there was a shift in patterns of trade from the Mediterranean to the Atlantic: *Civilization and Capitalism, Vol. 1*; *Civilization and Capitalism, Vol. 2*; *Civilization and Capitalism, 15th-18th Century Volume 3: The Perspective of the World*, trans. Sian Reynolds, 1st ed. (New York: Harper & Row, 1984). For a review of the literature on the Atlantic world system, by topic, from migration and class, to civility, authority, and empire, see: David Armitage and Michael J. Braddick, eds., *The British Atlantic World, 1500–1800*, Problems in Focus Series (London and New York: Palgrave Macmillan, 2002). The concept of 'Atlantic world' is useful also for studies of science: James Delbourgo and Nicholas Dew, eds., *Science and Empire in the Atlantic World*, New Directions in American History (New York and London: Routledge, 2008).

also in order to prevent this and other similar forms of imperialism from ever arising again.

Two key concepts are associated with the rise of north-western Europe. The first key concept that we might miss because of the knee-jerk reaction is that the notion of *social organization* is important to understand social processes like the rise of north-western Europe. Social organization is a key concept for sociological explanation. This concept is indispensable to understand differences between Europe and other Eurasian countries, and within Europe itself. It is intuitive that a large nation-state or proto nation-state that includes many cities is organized in a manner different than a city-state centered around a single city. The relationship between, on the one hand, these two different types of social organization and, on the other hand, capitalism, is less intuitive. For example, Weber drew attention to the fact that the rise of capitalism was made possible by the presence in Europe of many relatively independent city-states. This proved important for the rise of both democracy and capitalism, but the relationship and the sequence of events might be more complex than allowed by Weber. For example, Italian city-states, despite pioneering both democracy and capitalism within Europe, went into a long period of decline starting in the early 1500s. Gramsci drew attention to this phenomenon and sought to understand its causes, emphasizing the way in which culture interacted with social organization and social structures in Italian city-states, enabling an aristocratic reaction against Italian city-states that in many cases put an end to democracy, to the flourishing of culture in the Renaissance, and slowed down development, turning once thriving democracies into duchies and marquisates.[46]

The second important concept associated with the *rise of north-western Europe* is that a *macro scale of analysis* is necessary to understand phenomena affecting development and democracy. This is the scale of analysis that is necessary to understand the shift in patterns of trade from the Mediterranean world system to the Atlantic world system. This scale was central also to Weber's inquiry comparing civilizations and state types across Eurasia. This macro scale of analysis complements the meso scale introduced in Volume 1 of this book in order to explain collective action problems in the Risorgimento, which can be extended to explain the decline of Italian city-states. I want to introduce here the idea that in order to understand development and democracy we have to combine the micro questions that are central to most studies of development,

---

46   An overview of Gramsci's notes on the Renaissance and Reformation (he studied the two together as instances of cultural movements, or social movements within culture), is provided in: Fabio Frosini, "Riforma e Rinascimento," in *Le Parole di Gramsci: Per un Lessico dei Quaderni del Carcere* ed. Fabio Frosini and Guido Liguori (Roma: Carocci, 2004).

with macro questions that used to be central to sociology, and also with meso questions, representing an intermediate scale of analysis.[47] Examples of these different scales, from the smallest to the largest, are: the functioning of one market in one area, which involves a micro scale of analysis; the functioning of a region of a country or the entire country, up to a wide geographical area like Europe, the Mediterranean, or East Asia, all of which involve a meso scale; entire continents like the Americas, Africa, Eurasia and, increasingly important, the world scale, on which phenomena like globalization act, all of which involve a macro scale. I want to emphasize that macro questions involving a macro scale of analysis, far from being irrelevant, have a direct bearing upon meso and micro questions, and that all three of these scales of analysis are indispensable to understand development and democracy.

5   The Geographic Reference Frame and Interstate and Social Conflict

A different geographic reference frame can help us understand hegemony and social movements. The concepts from World Systems Theory introduced above, including in particular the concepts of state system and modern world system, are especially useful concepts to explain violent social movements, including fascism, nazism, and populism.[48] Below I expand upon these concepts and introduce additional concepts, all of which are useful to reconceptualize islamofascism and the relationships between all these four social phenomena. This answer builds upon the framework provided by Wallerstein and Arrighi. Although I differ in very important ways from Wallerstein and Arrighi, there are parts of their theories that are very useful to understand development

---

47   Hechter, amongst others, has tried to combine macro sociology with the micro-foundational approach typical of rational choice theory, which shares important similarities with game theory: Debra Friedman and Michael Hechter, "The Contribution of Rational Choice Theory to Macrosociological Research," *Sociological Theory* 6, no. 2 (1988).

48   There is a growing literature on violent social movements that focuses on contemporary cases. See the many contributions in: Seraphim Seferiades and Hank Johnston, eds., *Violent Protest, Contentious Politics, and the Neoliberal State* (London and New York: Routledge, 2016); Julie M. Mazzei, ed. *Non-State Violent Actors and Social Movement Organizations: Influence, Adaptation, and Change*, Research in Social Movements, Conflicts, and Change (Bingley, United Kingdom: Emerald Publishing Limited, 2017). For a comparison of violence by social movements in Italy and Germany, see: Donatella Della Porta, *Social Movements, Political Violence, and the State: A Comparative Analysis of Italy and Germany*, Cambridge Studies in Comparative Politics (Cambridge and New York: Cambridge University Press, 1995).

and democracy, and I want to sketch here those useful parts of World Systems Theory that I build upon. In addition to the concept of system, there are several *features of the state system and of conflict within the state system* that were highlighted by Wallerstein and Arrighi and that I build upon. They are all important to understand the interaction between interstate conflict and social conflict, which in its turn is important to understand the tendency towards expansion of countries in north-western Europe and the rise in imperialism, and the great impact it had upon development and democracy, both outside Europe and within it.

The following *characterization of the state system and interstate conflict* proposed by World Systems Theory is especially useful to understand European imperialism. I focus in this book on the concept of tendency towards expansion, which is not the same as imperialism, but leads to it and underpins it. It is a simpler concept to study and a promising place to start in order to understand imperialism. There have been numerous state systems in history. They are all characterized by interstate conflict, often escalating to war. Thus *systems are characterized by a tendency to be taken over by a successful state* that conquers all other states in the system and incorporates them into a single empire, describable as a world empire. *The modern world system is somewhat unique in this respect. No single empire has emerged* spanning the whole of Europe or the whole of the West thus far. Instead, *states in the modern world system have achieved relatively long truces* during which their efforts at imperial expansion were directed, not towards other states in the core of the state system, but towards states and stateless countries in the periphery of the system, in pretty much the rest of the world.[49] These long truces are one of the reasons why some European states have been able to build massive colonial empires, exporting at gunpoint various types of capitalism and various types of exploitation to many parts of the world. The truces were made possible by the fact that *there emerged an hegemonic state or hegemon* within Europe. In the case of hegemonic states, being hegemonic still includes a form of cultural power, as in Gramsci's theory of hegemony, to the extent that the hegemonic state proposes a model of development and an ideology that tend to have great influence. Another distinctive feature of a hegemonic state is that it exercises

---

49   Wallerstein introduced the difference between empire and world system at the beginning of his work on world systems: Wallerstein, *The Modern World-System, Vol. 1.* The contrast between empire and world system has also been applied to empires outside Europe: Michael E. Smith, "The Aztec Empire and the Mesoamerican World System," in *Empires: Perspectives from Archaeology and History,* ed. Susan E. Alcock, et al. (Cambridge and New York: Cambridge University Press, 2001).

power over the state system, and influences other states, without however taking them over and incorporating them into an empire. Different states have been hegemonic at different times.[50] Eventually, sufficiently powerful challengers to the hegemonic state emerge and interstate conflict in the core flares up. Sometimes this interstate conflict leads to the replacement of the hegemonic state by another hegemonic state.

The above characterization of the state system and interstate conflict by World Systems Theory can be nuanced and made even more useful to understand development and democracy if we *combine the concept of interstate conflict with the concept of social conflict*, that is, conflict between social groups, and relate hegemony between states to hegemony between social groups. This contributes to the argument that the tendency towards expansion was driven by both social conflict within the states that expanded, and by interstate conflict that affected these states. Below I suggest that the two are related also through their effects on social movements. Here I want to emphasize the relevance of this approach to understand social movements. Some scholars have begun exploring the connections between conflict in the world system and social movements by proposing the concept of *antisystemic movements, defined as social movements that oppose the way in which power within the world system works and its injustices*, a working that is affected by a combination of features of the state system, and of social organization within each state.[51] These movements engage in social conflict with the hegemonic social group, or in asymmetric conflict with the hegemonic state, or in a mix of both of these types of conflict. Following a common use in military theory, I use the expression asymmetric conflict to refer to conflict between actors that are of different types, typically a violent social movement and the hegemonic state. This is asymmetric conflict because of the difference between the types of actors, a non-state actor and a state actor respectively (an actor is an agent with a defined organizational or institutional role), and also because of the differences in means and rules of conduct, whereby violent social movements tend

---

50   Giovanni Arrighi, *The Long Twentieth Century: Money, Power, and the Origins of Our Times* (London and New York: Verso, 1994). Despite its title, this book focuses on the different hegemons in the modern world system since the 1500s. For Arrighi, these were the Netherlands, Great Britain, and the United States. Arrighi focuses partly upon status in trade flows, and partly upon economic and political influence in advancing capitalism on a global scale.

51   Giovanni Arrighi, Terence K. Hopkins, and Immanuel Maurice Wallerstein, *Antisystemic Movements* (London and New York: Verso, 2012). I introduce below the concept of state-society systems to describe this combination.

to be economically backwards and also to operate outside the law and resort to terrorism.[52]

The following *broad characterization of phases of conflict in the modern state system*, and in particular of interstate conflict within it, is also especially useful to understand European imperialism. It proposes the following changes in the main participants in interstate conflict within the state system, focusing on the hegemons in the last two phases. *Great Britain was the hegemonic state during the eighteenth and the nineteenth century, the last phase.* During this time, it presided over a period of relative peace in Europe following the Napoleonic Wars, after which France became an ally rather than a challenger, many European states cooperated in what became known as the *Concert of Europe* under the watchful eye of Habsburg foreign minister Klemens von Metternich, and there occurred an historically unprecedented expansion of European colonial empires. *The United States began to emerge as the hegemon in the current phase.* The twentieth century saw the progressive emergence of the United States as the hegemonic state, replacing Great Britain in the wake of the First and the Second World War.[53] This is where I begin to diverge in very important ways from Wallerstein and Arrighi, and also from Mann, as I reinterpret World Systems Theory using concepts derived from Gramsci.

World Systems Theory predicts that states in the core engage in imperialism towards the periphery, against the countries and states that are easiest to conquer. One of my major differences from Wallerstein's and Arrighi's theories regarding empire is that *I believe an empire could emerge in the core of the modern state system*, that is, an empire could emerge that spans the whole of Western Europe, and even North America, and ultimately the entire West. Michael Hardt and Antonio Negri have suggested as much in their book *Empire*, which was published in 2000 and showed remarkable prescience in foreseeing

---

52   Different approaches to asymmetric conflict are provided in: Ivan Arreguín-Toft, *How the Weak Win Wars: A Theory of Asymmetric Conflict* (Cambridge and New York: Cambridge University Press, 2005); Larisa Deriglazova, *Great Powers, Small Wars: Asymmetric Conflict since 1945* (Woodrow Wilson Center Press, Washington D.C.: Johns Hopkins University Press, Baltimore, 2020). On terrorism and asymmetric conflict, see: Ekaterina Stepanova, *Terrorism in Asymmetrical Conflict: Ideological and Structural Aspects*, Stockholm International Peace Research Institute (Oxford and New York: Oxford University Press, 2008).

53   Arrighi, *The Long Twentieth Century*. Arrighi describes what he sees as a crisis in United States hegemony in: "Hegemony Unravelling," *New Left Review* 32 (2005); "Hegemony Unravelling–II," *New Left Review* 33, no. May–June (2005). Wallerstein similarly sees the United States as heading for an inevitable decline: Immanuel Maurice Wallerstein, *The Decline of American Power* (New York and London: New Press, 2012).

the upsurge in imperialism that followed the 9/11 attacks.[54] I find their theory otherwise fundamentally flawed. One of their flaws has to do with the *concept of multitude*, which they suggest might be agents engaged in antisystemic movements. I see the multitude as a tool in the hands of imperialist elites instead, because it is closer to an underproletariat, or *lumpenproletariat*, that is, a working class that has lost all group cohesion.[55] Working classes and other classes that lost their group cohesion, including parts of the petite bourgeoisie, and were reduced to a multitude of many isolated individuals, very likely contributed to the rise of fascism and nazism, and today of populism. This is because an underproletariat is poorer, less organized, and completely lacking its own means including ideas, compared to a working class, petite bourgeoisie, or a middle class, and is thus incapable of deliberate and sustained collective action. For this reason, it cannot challenge the system and it cannot be the basis for antisystemic movements. Moreover, it can be manipulated by elites and it can take part in dramatic and polarizing movements for brief periods of time, including violent social movements like fascism, nazism and populism, also by providing volunteers to these movements.

By contrast with the concept of multitude, I emphasize *the concept of class, in conjunction with the concept of masses*, and conflict between elites and masses. By *masses* I mean all the social groups that are not part of the elites. It is a concept that I borrow from American political traditions, but I do not see it as alternative to class.[56] The masses include the *main laboring classes*,

---

54   Michael Hardt and Antonio Negri, *Empire* (Cambridge, Massachusetts and London: Harvard University Press, 2000). Negri was the ideologue of the Red Brigades terrorist organization in Italy, similar to the Red Army Faction in Germany.

55   *Multitude: War and Democracy in the Age of Empire* (London: Penguin, 2005). For different takes on the concept of multitude, see: Nicholas Brown and Imre Szeman, "What Is the Multitude? Questions for Michael Hardt and Antonio Negri," *Cultural Studies* 19, no. 3 (2005); Nicholas Tampio, "Assemblages and the Multitude: Deleuze, Hardt, Negri, and the Postmodern Left," *European Journal of Political Theory* 8, no. 3 (2009); Finn Bowring, "From the Mass Worker to the Multitude: A Theoretical Contextualisation of Hardt and Negri's *Empire*," *Capital & Class* 28, no. 2 (2004). Hardt and Negri answered some of the earlier criticisms to the concept of multitude in: Michael Hardt and Antonio Negri, "Adventures of the Multitude: Response of the Authors," *Rethinking Marxism* 13, no. 3–4 (2001). See also the other contributions in this special issue of *Rethinking Marxism*.

56   The concept of 'masses' is an integral part of American political thought, which has focused far less than European political thought upon the concept of class. A rare exception to this lack of focus on class is work by two members of G. A. Cohen's September Group. Economist John Roemer proposed a general theory of class: John E. Roemer, *A General Theory of Exploitation and Class* (Cambridge, Massachusetts and London: Harvard University Press, 1982); *Value, Exploitation, and Class*, Fundamentals of Pure and Applied Economics (Harwood Academic Publishers, 1986). The latter has been

namely, the working class, the middle class, and the petite bourgeoisie. They also include *non-class laboring social groups,* that is, social groups that do not count as classes because they have no cohesiveness and no organizations of their own, such as the lumpenproletariat or under-proletariat made up of workers in shifting employment, and migrants in similar situations. These groups are the product of social disaggregation. Following a tradition of theorizing that Gramsci contributed to, I emphasize that *the laboring classes include also the peasantry and organized groups of agricultural laborers.*[57] The concept of mass thus defined is associated with the insight that the most important conflict in Western countries in modern history is between elites and masses, not between the working class and the bourgeoisie, as suggested by Marx, nor between one laboring class and another, as suggested by fascism and populism.[58] The elites try to prevent this conflict from arising through divide-and-conquer and divide-and-rule tactics, including by fostering conflict between one laboring class and another, for example between the petite bourgeoisie and the working class, a conflict that was important at the time of fascism.[59] Populism similarly

re-published in 2001. More recently, sociologist Erik Olin Wright has argued that social science should focus more on the study of class: Erik Olin Wright, *Approaches to Class Analysis* (Cambridge and New York: Cambridge University Press, 2005); *Understanding Class* (London and New York: Verso, 2015). Some works have started combining the study of class with the study of the masses: Mike Hill and Warren Montag, *Masses, Classes and the Public Sphere* (London and New York: Verso, 2000). Here I employ a simple but useful way to combine the concepts of masses and classes.

57   Gramsci's politics was driven by the need to create an alliance between the working class of northern Italy and the peasantry in the south of the country. A theoretical framework for this is set out in: Gramsci, *La Questione Meridionale.* For a discussion of the importance that Gramsci attached to the peasantry, see: Alastair Davidson, "Gramsci, the Peasantry and Popular Culture," *The Journal of Peasant Studies* 11, no. 4 (1984).

58   Marx and Engels proposed that the conflict between bourgeoisie and proletariat (the working class) was central to modern history already in *The Communist Manifesto,* which was published in 1848, and went through various editions, including a recent one by Greek politician Yanis Varoufakis: Karl Marx, Friedrich Engels, and Yanis Varoufakis, *The Communist Manifesto. Introduction by Yanis Varoufakis,* Vintage Classics (New York: Vintage Books, 2019).

59   The association between fascism and the petite bourgeoisie has been argued from the 1930s to our day by various authors: Patrick L. Gallagher, "Andreu Nin on Fascism in Italy: Translator's Introduction," *Historical Materialism* 30, no. 2 (2022). Manlio Graziano, *The Failure of Italian Nationhood: The Geopolitics of a Troubled Identity* (London and New York: Palgrave Macmillan, 2010). This association has been rightly challenged: Linda Weiss, "Demythologising the Petite Bourgeoisie: The Italian Case," *West European Politics* 9, no. 3 (1986); Geoffrey Crossick and Heinz-Gerhard Haupt, *The Petite Bourgeoisie in Europe 1780–1914: Enterprise, Family and Independence* (London and New York: Routledge, 2013). This book was first published in 1997. A critical appraisal of this association, which was central to the interpretation of fascism put forward by the Third International

tries to obscure this conflict because, if this conflict comes to the fore, and is widely seen as the main conflict, it has the potential to undermine elite power. This is an insight that has to be proven, of course, first of all by providing a full explanation based upon more basic concepts. This can then be compared to other explanations, to check how well it explains such phenomena as fascism and populism, and can then be tested empirically.

Another flaw of Hardt and Negri's theory, which they share with Wallerstein, Arrighi, and Mann, is in the *sources and definition of the post-9/11 imperialism*. This is another one of my major differences from Wallerstein's and Arrighi's theories. The wars waged by G. W. Bush have been denounced by geographer David Harvey as a new American imperialism, which would have replaced a British imperialism that seemed to have waned from the world stage. Arrighi subscribes to this view, and suggests this new American imperialism is the unraveling of American hegemony.[60] I differ from all five authors, Wallerstein, Arrighi, Mann, Hardt, and Negri, in my interpretation both of the novelty of this imperialism and of the current status of the United States in the state system. As far as *the novelty of the post-9/11 imperialism* is concerned, I believe that this imperialism is not something altogether new. If the military adventures pursued by G. W. Bush constitute a new form of imperialism, it is a form that is directly descended from, and in a sense the contemporary implementation of, the form of imperialism first developed by the British aristocratic-military elite. Whatever differences there might be between these imperialisms are minor, even just cosmetic, and they hide basic continuities. I differ from all the five authors above also in my interpretation of *the current status of the United States in the state system*. Although the United States is the hegemon, or hegemonic state, I believe that it has not yet freed itself completely from the colonial tutelage of the British aristocratic-military elite, their allies, and their

---

(the Comintern), is provided by: Nicos Poulantzas, *Fascism and Dictatorship: The Third International and the Problem of Fascism* (London and New York: Verso, 2019). Here I am drawing attention to the fact that this interpretation itself participated, whether unwittingly or by design, in elite divide-and-rule tactics.

60 The concept of a new imperialism is put forward in David Harvey, *The New Imperialism* (Oxford and New York: Oxford University Press, 2003). Arrighi's articles that portray G. W. Bush's imperialism as a new American imperialism leading to the unraveling of American hegemony are: "Hegemony Unravelling."; "Hegemony Unravelling–11." See also: Giovanni Arrighi, "Hegemony and Antisystemic Movements," in *The Modern World-System in the Long Duree*, ed. Immanuel Maurice Wallerstein (2004). Amsden has also argued that the imperialism we are living through is an American imperialism: Alice H. Amsden, *Escape from Empire: The Developing World's Journey through Heaven and Hell* (MIT Press, 2009).

descendants or heirs in the world system, the imperialist world-elite that is emerging and consolidating its power, if it has not done so already.

6   Geopolitics and the Social War of Position and Maneuver

Geopolitics and a number of additional concepts that contribute to the geographic reference frame can further help us understand hegemony and social movements. Geopolitics and the additional concepts are very useful to nuance the concept of the West introduced above. As I explained above, I use the word West to refer to a political alliance, or more accurately a series of political alliances, today including chiefly NATO and the European Union. These alliances roughly coincide with the core of the state system. However, and this is the important point that I especially want to emphasize, the core and the corresponding set of alliances has changed over time, and during the past two hundred years the core has continued expanding. During this long time span the series of alliances has been *reinforced by a more or less clearly defined cultural identity* that emerged over the years as part of political projects, associated with a view of the West as the cradle of democracy and capitalism, which are seen unreflectingly as good. Throughout this project I emphasize instead that capitalism and democracy are complex phenomena, and that *there are different types of capitalism and democracy, and varieties and models of capitalism and democracy,* and that not all are good.[61] Monopoly capitalism, to take a clear example, is a type of capitalism widely recognized not to be good for development. Worse still, it is related to imperialism. Oligopoly capitalism is often accepted, but is subject to strict regulation in order to prevent the formation of cartels and price fixing.[62] The varieties of capitalism arguably include the Anglo-Saxon

---

61   The argument that that there are varieties of capitalism focuses on the different institutions that underpin capitalism in different countries. This argument is central to the many contributions in: Peter A. Hall and David W. Soskice, eds., *Varieties of Capitalism: The Institutional Foundations of Comparative Advantage* (Oxford and New York: Oxford University Press, 2001). See also: Bruno Amable, *The Diversity of Modern Capitalism* (Oxford and New York: Oxford University Press, 2003).

62   On the regulation of monopoly and oligopoly capitalism in public enterprises, see: Ingo Vogelsang, *Public Enterprise in Monopolistic and Oligopolistic Industries*, Fundamentals of Pure and Applied Economics (Chur, London, Paris, New York, and Melbourne: Harwood academic publishers, 1990). Monopoly capitalism has been a focus of many classics of Marxism, including: Vladimir Ilych Lenin, *Imperialism, the Highest Stage of Capitalism: A Popular Outline*, Unabridged with Original Tables and Footnotes ed. (Auckland, United Kingdom: Aziloth Books, 2018). Paul A. Baran, *Monopoly Capital* (New York: Monthly Review Press, 1966). Lenin's book was first published in 1917. More recent discussions

model of development, based on large capitalist enterprises with minimal regulation, and arguably also the Third Italy model of development, based on family-owned small and medium-sized capitalist enterprises, or SMEs.[63] Gosta Esping-Andersen has made a similar argument for the varieties of welfare capitalism, or capitalism coupled with a Keynesian welfare state, which produced rather different outcomes in different countries.[64]

One problem with Putnam's argument regarding the impact of democracy on development, and with the similar argument proposed by Molotch, and their respective collaborators, is that they focus on a count of NGOs per number of population, largely *ignoring social structures.* I suggest in Volume 1 that Putnam's theory can be further improved by a structural-foundational approach to social interaction that emphasizes structures in civil society, for example structures amongst NGOs, and between NGOs and institutions, all of which can greatly help both democracy and development.[65] Here I want to add that conflict can undermine civil society, democracy, and through it also development. Conflict that turns into diffuse violence also directly undermines all activities in society, including economic activities, and hampers the expansion and growth of markets, which require both stability and transparency. I want to suggest here an addition to this argument, based upon geopolitics and *Gramsci's concepts of social war of position and social war of maneuver.*[66]

---

include: Harry Braverman and John Bellamy Foster, *Labor and Monopoly Capital: The Degradation of Work in the Twentieth Century. New Introduction by John Bellamy Foster* (New York: Monthly Review Press, 1998). John Bellamy Foster, *The Theory of Monopoly Capitalism: An Elaboration of Marxian Political Economy* (New York: Monthly Review Press, 2014).

63   On the Anglo-Saxon model and alternatives to it, see: John B. Kidd and Frank-Jurgen Richter, eds., *Development Models, Globalization and Economies: A Search for the Holy Grail?* (London and New York: Palgrave Macmillan, 2005). Trigilia and Burroni treat the Italian model as including the Third Italy: Carlo Trigilia and Luigi Burroni, "Italy: Rise, Decline and Restructuring of a Regionalized Capitalism," *Economy and Society* 38, no. 4 (2009). As of the year 2000 the Italian model had not converged on the Anglo-Saxon model: Vincent Della Sala, "A New 'Confindustria' for a New Model of Italian Capitalism?," *Italian Politics* 16 (2000). I discus the three models of development known as the First, Second, and Third Italy in Chapter 1 of: Olsaretti, *The Struggle for Development and Democracy, Vol. 1.*

64   Gosta Esping-Andersen, *The Three Worlds of Welfare Capitalism* (Princeton and Oxford: Princeton University Press, 1990).

65   Putnam, Leonardi, and Nanetti, *Making Democracy Work.* I make the arguments regarding the structural-foundational approach to social interaction, including social interaction within civil society, in Chapter 1 of: Olsaretti, *The Struggle for Development and Democracy, Vol. 1.*

66   Gramsci, *Quaderni del Carcere,* 1616. See also the entries for 'guerra di movimento' and 'guerra di posizione' in: Guido Liguori and Pasquale Voza, eds., *Dizionario*

These two concepts describe the types of violent conflict that prevail in differ-ent parts of the state system and that have completely different effects upon democracy, and ultimately upon development. This is part of a *broader argu-ment that democracy is affected by the intensity of social conflict and the type of social war*, both of which can favor or harm democracy, and that the type of social war largely depends upon geopolitics.

Geopolitics emphasizes that there is a combination of geography and politics that affects conflict. It is very useful to understand interstate conflict. In par-ticular, I want to introduce here *three closely related concepts that are part of geopolitics*, as I use geopolitics in this book.[67] These concepts serve to qualify and nuance the concepts of core, semi-periphery, and periphery proposed by World Systems Theory. The first is a simpler and more useful concept of core, based only upon the hierarchy of political-military power: *the core of the state system*, that I refer to as the state core, not the core of the world system, that also includes a world economy and a world culture, whose cores have their own boundaries that do not necessarily coincide with the boundaries of the state core, and when they coincide they only do so approximately and never neatly. The second is a concept closely related to the concept of state core: *the frontier of the core of the state system*, that is, the political boundary between the core and nearby countries. The frontier is a boundary across which there is much military interstate conflict, and in particular competition that involves armies more than navies, because countries on either side of the frontier share a land border. The third concept is the concept of *semi-periphery of the state system*, a concept that is related both to the concept of frontier, and to the concepts of hemisphere and north-south divide. The last two concepts where involved in debates regarding north-south uneven development across coun-tries, and also in debates over uneven development within countries, one of which was especially important in Italy in the form of the Southern Question, the debate over north-south uneven development within Italy.[68]

Gramsciano: 1926–1937 (Roma: Carocci, 2009). Gramsci dealt mostly with social conflict, and thus what he referred to as 'war of maneuver' was a *social* war of maneuver. Since this project seeks to study both social conflict and interstate conflict, it is necessary to use dif-ferent expressions for the two types of conflict, each of which might or might not escalate into war. Thus I add the adjective 'social' when dealing with social conflict that spills into a 'social war of maneuver' or a 'social war of position.'

67   The importance of geopolitics to World Systems Theory is outlined in: Wallerstein, *Geopolitics and Geoculture*.

68   Arrighi addresses the north-south divide in international development in: Giovanni Arrighi, Beverly J. Silver, and Benjamin D. Brewer, "Industrial Convergence, Globalization, and the Persistence of the North-South Divide," *Studies in Comparative International Development* 38, no. 1 (2003). On the differences affecting workers in these locations,

It is useful to define each of these three concepts in greater detail and sketch their inter-relationships. They are all geopolitical concepts specifically aimed at understanding political dynamics related to interstate conflict, including conflict and war.[69] *The state core* is best defined by political-military power and proximity, as the group of states in close proximity with each other that includes the most militarily powerful states. Below, I also add as a defining characteristic of the core a certain state type, namely, proto nation-states that later became nation-states, a type of state that first emerged in the state core. State type arguably affected, and still affects, how much political-military power a state can produce and use in interstate conflict. The state core is defined also by geographical proximity relative to the hegemon, or hegemonic state, the most militarily powerful state within the state system. In the state core we find the hegemon, and also its geographically closest allies and competitors. This geopolitical definition of the state core suggests that there are political dynamics whereby these three different parameters, namely, political-military power, state type, and proximity, are all inter-related, because once these three parameters have certain values, namely, high political-military power, produced by proto nation-states, in close proximity with each other, they lead to conflict that strengthens some of these parameters, since the states form a system with competition and exchange of information and cultural influences within the system.

The other two concepts that I propose are geopolitical concepts aimed at understanding these political dynamics, and they too focus on the state core, as opposed to the core of the world system, since the latter includes also considerations regarding the world economy and world culture. *The frontier of the state core* changes with interstate conflict. The state core consolidates, as competitors are taken over or become allies, and expands, by incorporating states that were initially outside the core, including competitors that emerged outside the core. As the core expands, the frontier shifts in location. The *semi-periphery of the state system* is related to both of the above concepts. On the other side of the frontier, just outside the state core, we find states that are of altogether different types than nation-states, and are drawn into conflict in the core. These states can be either in the semi-periphery or periphery in terms of

---

see: Beverly J. Silver and Giovanni Arrighi, "Workers North and South," *Socialist Register* 37 (2001). This was seen as a divide that affected Italy, and also the state system. In World Systems Theory it is explained by the concept of internal peripheries, and the claim that hierarchies of power are nested.

69   I address questions related to political dynamics in the early modern Mediterranean in: Olsaretti, "Political Dynamics in the Rise of Fakhr al-Din."

power, and occasionally one of them increases its power to the point that it becomes a contender for the status of hegemon. The overall political dynamics that involves all three of the concepts can be summarized in the following manner. States in the core where all proto nation-states and later nation-states, and being in close geographic proximity, they were in intense conflict, often escalating into war. States outside the core were also initially involved in this conflict, up to 1648 and the truce that followed the end of the Thirty Years War. From that time until the Napoleonic Wars in the early 1800s there was no other *major* war that changed the balance of power within Europe, and the main territorial boundaries within it.

Political dynamics involving the core, that the above three concepts help us conceptualize and explain, can be illustrated with the following *interpretation of political dynamics in near-contemporary and contemporary European history*. Throughout the 1800s and up until the 1920s the hegemon was Great Britain. Two other states should be considered as part of the state core by the 1920s, France and the Netherlands, on account of geographical distance and political-military status: they were both near to Great Britain, and although former rivals, they were by then both close allies of Great Britain's. They also were powerful militarily, in the case of the Netherlands relative to the size of the state. The United States began being incorporated into the core, as with the First and Second World War it started participating in conflict involving the hegemon, Great Britain. On the other side of the frontier, outside the core, there were three states, namely, Germany, Italy and Spain, that were building up power and were potential competitors of the states in the core, their political status as competitor or ally of the state core depending upon who was in power. I propose that these states were part of the semi-periphery, together with Russia, Japan, and later South Korea. The semi-periphery at that time overlapped roughly with the northern hemisphere, or more accurately with the northern part of the northern hemisphere.[70] By the 1980s the state core had changed. Politically, the core had expanded. The United States had joined the core by the First World War, expanding its power both economically and

---

70   Terlouw has proposed that we study the semi-periphery as a way to describe change, rather than as a well-defined geographical area: Kees Terlouw, "Semi-Peripheral Developments: From World-Systems to Regions," *Capitalism Nature Socialism* 14, no. 4 (2003). I take a slightly different approach emphasizing change that affects states and sometimes entire countries in certain areas. On changes in the semi-periphery, see the contributions in: Owen Worth and Phoebe Moore, eds., *Globalization and the 'New' Semi-Peripheries*, International Political Economy Series (London and New York: Palgrave Macmillan, 2009).

militarily, and becoming an ally of Great Britain's. New states were added to the core starting with the end of the Second World War, Italy, Germany, Spain, Japan, and South Korea. In Europe, the frontier had now shifted eastward and southward, towards Russia and the Middle East. Culturally, the United States had begun converging with Great Britain on a model of Anglo-Saxon capitalism in economics, and of Thatcherism-Reaganism in politics, a conversion that led to neoliberalism.

The ways in which geopolitics affects interstate conflict are complex. I argue in this project that civil engineering is very important for geopolitics, because it affects logistics and communications, through means of transportation and means of communication, that always use a physical infrastructure, even in the case of modern means of communications like the internet and telecommunications, which use cables. I expand upon the concept of infrastructure proposed by Ertman, who referred to the networks between institutions and organizations as infrastructure. I emphasize that there is both a physical infrastructure and a social infrastructure.[71] However, the frontier is not a neat circle drawn from the hegemon, with greater radius corresponding to greater means of transportation and communication.[72] The core expands with both outcomes of previous conflict and with the availability of transportation, as well as with technological innovations that introduce greater means of transportation and communication, or new means of transportation and communication that place new geographical areas within easy reach. It is common in the literature on the rise of the Atlantic world system to emphasize the importance of a revolution in naval technology and the introduction of ocean-going vessels.[73] Here I just want to emphasize a simpler concept: there is *heightened conflict at the frontier, including war*, which entails that wars are either more

---

71   Thomas Ertman, *Birth of the Leviathan: Building States and Regimes in Medieval and Early Modern Europe* (Cambridge and New York: Cambridge University Press, 1997).

72   The concept of 'political radius' was introduced in historical studies by Laila Fawaz regarding social conflict in and around Beirut: Leila Tarazi Fawaz, "The City and the Mountain: Beirut's Political Radius in the Nineteenth Century as Revealed in the Crisis of 1860," *International Journal of Middle East Studies* 16, no. 4 (1984). This is a very useful concept, but we should not conceive of it as if it were a blast radius that reaches everywhere around a certain distance from it. The concept that I am proposing also takes into account available means of transportation and communication. It is intuitive that a nearby town not connected by a good road is harder to reach than a town further away connected by a good road.

73   The importance of technology and in particular of ocean-going vessels in the rise of the Atlantic world system is placed in a broader context in: Michael John Seymour, *The Transformation of the North Atlantic World, 1492–1763: An Introduction*, Studies in Military History and International Affairs (Wesport, Connecticut, and London: Praeger, 2004).

frequent or more intense, because the contenders are within easier reach of transportation and communication lines, and larger armies can be mobilized for longer periods of time.

At the frontier of the state core there are also *different types of war*, which consist of different combinations of interstate conflict and social conflict. Here I focus on social conflict that is affected by interstate conflict. This can be usefully conceptualized through the *two Gramscian concepts of social war of position, and social war of maneuver*, which complement the concepts of state core and frontier. Both types of war involve violent social conflict, including class war, and sometimes civil war, and also class war combined with civil war.[74] Gramsci suggested that *within the core a social war of position prevails*. This is because within the core there was also a greater development of civil society that Gramsci compared to the trenches in a war of position. Civil society makes a quick seizure of political power difficult and necessitates instead slow and progressive inroads into the other side, sapping its strength, in a manner analogous to the slow movement of the frontline in a military war of position. Gramsci also suggested that *outside the core a social war of maneuver prevails*, and that it is possible to seize power speedily through a revolution or a military coup, a speedy seizure of power, in a manner analogous to successful operations in a military war of maneuver that conquer the enemy's headquarters or capital.[75] This is because outside the core there was little or no autonomous civil society. Gramsci was drawing attention to the fact that the sheer number of institutions of civil society make social war, and social conflict more in general, very different in different parts of the world.

The different types of social war affect development and democracy in different ways, with the social war of maneuver being potentially disastrous for both development and democracy. Outside the core, and especially on the other

---

74   For a review of Gramsci's military metaphors, see: Daniel Egan, *The Dialectic of Position and Maneuver: Understanding Gramsci's Military Metaphor* (Leiden and Boston: Brill, 2016). Pavone has suggested that the Italian Resistance during the Second World War was a mix of military conflict, with civil war, and class war: Claudio Pavone and Stanislao Pugliese, *A Civil War: A History of the Italian Resistance*, trans. Peter Levy and David Broder (London and New York: Verso, 2013).

75   The geographical locations in which a social war of maneuver prevail do not correspond to those in which a military war of maneuver prevail. The *blitzkrieg*, the military doctrine implemented by German generals during the Second World War, was a war of maneuver doctrine that was implemented both against France and against Russia, that is, against both core and periphery, or dense and sparse civil society. On the *blitzkrieg*, see: Robert Michael Citino, *Blitzkrieg to Desert Storm: The Evolution of Operational Warfare* (Kansas: University Press of Kansas, 2004); *The Path to Blitzkrieg: Doctrine and Training in the German Army, 1920–39* (Mechanicsburg, Pennsylvania: Stackpole Books, 2007).

side of the frontier, where a war of maneuver prevails, there are often fewer institutions of civil society, and they are rapidly undermined by revolutions and military coups, which can be especially harsh and divisive, inflicting casualties and also creating divisions within society, and in the case of prolonged violence, creating conditions that undermine social interactions and market interactions alike. By contrast, a war of position is less of a threat to development and democracy, because rapid violent revolutions and military coups are harder, and institutions can change and become more inclusive without major upheavals. The latter are harmful for both development and democracy, since they can completely undermine the way an economy works, and lead to even more brutal dictatorships than the ones that some movements fight against, so that upheavals can have an enduring negative impact.[76] However, a war of position might still be associated with culture wars that can be very divisive, even if they do not immediately lead to revolutions and seizures of power.

Democracy is also affected by *social organization problems and transition problems, both of which can make the social war of maneuver considerably worse.* Here I just want to mention that *social organization problems* include social disaggregation, which leads both to diffuse criminality, and also to the availability of large numbers of volunteers who can be recruited to create large irregular forces that can be used in both social conflict and interstate conflict. Both criminality and the availability of large numbers of volunteers are affected by the number and wealth of organizations of civil society, since the lack of sufficient civil society to provide a safety net, and help pursue other options than criminality and shifting military employment contributes to diffuse criminality and large numbers of volunteers joining irregular forces, which can undermine democracy in conditions of heightened conflict. This is in marked contrast with wealthier countries, like the United States, in which volunteering like the one described by Tocqueville was enabled by wealth, not induced by poverty, and led to the flourishing of civil society instead of irregular forces, contributing to both democracy and development.[77] These social organization problems can

---

76   This is a different view than the view proposed by Sen in: Sen, *Development as Freedom*. Sen, in comparing China to India, suggested that social revolutions make rapid development possible. Sen attributes the rapid development of China to a social revolutions that swept away all obstacles to economic growth.

77   For an overview of volunteering in the United States in a comparative perspective, see: Helmut K. Anheier and Lester M. Salamon, "Volunteering in Cross-National Perspective: Initial Comparisons," *Law and Contemporary Problems* 62 (1999). The relation of volunteering to country wealth is argued in: K. Praveen Parboteeah, John B. Cullen, and Lrong Lim, "Formal Volunteering: A Cross-National Test," *Journal of World Business* 39, no. 4 (2004). This project seeks to contribute to a more general approach to volunteering.

be compounded by *transition problems*, because countries that do not have a strong civil society face the problem that, when they try to build one, while at the same time trying to introduce capitalism, which can finance the expansion of civil society, but initially impoverishes large numbers of the population, this leads to social organization problems. These *transition problems can be worse if the country is at the frontier*, because this position is associated with greater interstate conflict, which can interact with social conflict, so that a social war of maneuver follows, with violence and instability lingering on for prolonged periods of time, whether the violence comes from above, in the form of state repression by dictators who seized power, or from below, in the form of violent social movements, and of social banditry and diffuse criminality by large numbers of individuals.[78] In order to understand both of these problems, namely, social organization and transition problems, we have to introduce concepts that pertain to the manner in which social conflict changes as globalization advances and international trade reaches new countries.

In social science literature in English-speaking countries, volunteering refers mostly to volunteering for civil society organizations. In Gramsci's work, and in the literature on Italian history at the time when Gramsci was writing, volunteering referred mostly to volunteering for military organizations like Giuseppe Garibaldi's military forces. Both types of volunteering are unpaid labour. In the vast literature on volunteering, military volunteering is a marginal topic. For example, it is only touched upon by the contributors in: David Horton Smith, Robert A. Stebbins, and Jurgen Grotz, eds., *The Palgrave Handbook of Volunteering, Civic Participation, and Nonprofit Associations* (London and New York: Palgrave Macmillan, 2017).

78   I address these questions in greater detail in Chapter 6 of: Olsaretti, *The Struggle for Development and Democracy, Vol. 1*. I expand upon these concepts in Chapters 5 and 6 below.

CHAPTER 4

The Sociology of Development and Political and Cultural Sociology

This chapter introduces a number of key concepts from the sociology of development that are necessary in order to explain development, and that help formulate a significantly new theory of development. These key concepts build upon and complement the key concepts introduced in the previous chapter, although those who proposed these key concepts did not explicitly relate them to World Systems Theory or Gramsci's theory of hegemony. I emphasize instead that the key concepts in this chapter all complement the concept of modern world system, and the concept of state system more in particular, and that they are especially useful to understand the effects of globalization on the development of countries in areas of the world outside the state core. Many of these key concepts are part of an academic trend initiated in the 1980s that aimed to 'bring the state back in' social theory, after the neglect of the state that followed the diffusion within sociology of Marx's theory or approach (there was a dismissal of the state even amongst those who did not embrace Marx's theory wholesale, but simply shared his approach), both of which emphasized the economy above all else, and denounced the state as a tool of exploitation, ignoring its necessary role in human affairs.[1] By contrast, the key concepts introduced in this chapter serve to explain the following insights that emphasize the importance of the state: firstly, the state can contribute to the economy and its contribution differs depending upon state type; secondly, the systems that a state is part of also affect the economy. Below I introduce typologies both of states and of systems. One typology of states that is especially important to understand European history is a typology contrasting city-states with nation-states and empires. Each of these state types had very different effects upon development. Important systems that states participate in include state systems, as pointed out by Wallerstein, and ecosystems, as pointed out

---

1   Peter B. Evans, Dietrich Rueschemeyer, and Theda Skocpol, *Bringing the State Back In*, Papers from a Conference Held at Mount Kisco, New York, in February 1982 (Cambridge and New York: Cambridge University Press, 1985). Around the same time as this rediscovery of the role of the state was being advocated, van den Berg provided a critique of the neglect of the state in Marxism: Axel Van den Berg, *The Immanent Utopia: From Marxism on the State to the State of Marxism* (Princeton and Oxford: Princeton University Press, 1988).

by Diamond. I also begin to define how states participate in a state-society system, and a state-markets system, both of which are important for development. In countries in which civil society has developed institutions that are autonomous of the state, there are also society-market systems that are equally important for development.

In this chapter I focus upon the concepts of political-military development and cultural development, because they are under-theorized, and on the manner in which institutions, whether state institutions or civil society institutions, interact with each other to encourage development. State-society systems are systems that involve different institutions and organizations, namely the state and civil society organizations. This approach complements Putnam's theory by pointing to the importance of the state and its interaction with civil society organizations such as NPOs, in producing development. Putnam suggested there were ancient origins of the differences in development between northern and southern Italy.[2] In this project I suggest that these differences, some of which can be traced back to the Middle Ages and Renaissance, were arguably part of a different route to state formation taken by these different parts of Italy, republics in northern Italy, a kingdom in southern Italy. These differences were affected by the state, as well as by civil society, as part of what have been called 'lineages of despotism and development.'[3] The concept of state-society system that I introduce in this book contributes to this reformulation of Putnam's argument. It also contributes to reformulating key arguments in institutional economics, for example in work by Ostrom, particularly her study of states as providers of public goods, and her study of systems.[4] The approach that I take emphasizes that institutions are part of state-society systems in

---

2 Putnam, Leonardi, and Nanetti, *Making Democracy Work*. Putnam's argument on these ancient origins is criticized and nuanced in: Filippo Sabetti, *The Search for Good Government: Understanding the Paradox of Italian Democracy* (Montreal, Kingston, London, Ithaca: McGill-Queen's University Press, 2000).

3 The concept of 'lineages of despotism and development' has been proposed by Lange in: Matthew Lange, *Lineages of Despotism and Development: British Colonialism and State Power* (Chicago: University of Chicago Press, 2009). The concept of lineages in relation to states, and what today we call state formation, was proposed by: Perry Anderson, *Lineages of the Absolutist State* (London: Verso, 2013). I address the concept of state formation, and suggest that it is applicable also to the eastern Mediterranean, in particular the Levant, in: Olsaretti, "Political Dynamics in the Rise of Fakhr al-Din."

4 Ostrom's approach to these subjects is outlined in: Elinor Ostrom, "A General Framework for Analyzing Sustainability of Social-Ecological Systems," *Science* 325 (2009); "Beyond Markets and States: Polycentric Governance of Complex Economic Systems," *American Economic Review* 100, no. 3 (2010); Michael D. McGinnis and Elinor Ostrom, "Social-Ecological System Framework: Initial Changes and Continuing Challenges," *Ecology and Society* 19, no. 2 (2014).

which state institutions and civil society institutions such as NPOs interact with each other, in order to produce public goods. The emphasis upon state-society systems also complements Sen's work, and in particular an approach to study development together with democracy, because they affect one another, also through education, a crucially important public good that contributes to both development and democracy.[5] In this book I propose an approach to the interaction between states and civil society, and between development and democracy, that builds upon World Systems Theory, while using some key insights by Sen. The concepts of political-military and cultural development emphasize that these are forms of development valuable in their own right, for example because literacy and numeracy enrich a person's life and contribute to their capabilities, not just for their economic value. Below, I also begin to suggest that they greatly contribute to economic development.

In proposing this argument, I draw from disparate sub-fields within sociology. The sociology multidisciplinary approach has greatly suffered in the century since Weber's and Gramsci's times. The problem with sociology today is that it is affected by fragmentation of the discipline. Therefore, to outline a broad picture, it is necessary to draw from many different contributions that help understanding development, which remained thus far a collection of disparate contributions, each focusing upon a specific social mechanism or even just one specific causal factor in explaining development. Below I begin to combine these contributions into more complete pictures, paving the way for the synthesis and the single broad picture proposed in the next chapters. Thus, in this volume I propose a theory that I call the Diamond-Wallerstein theory, showing how shortcomings in Diamond's theory can be remedied by combining it with Wallerstein's theory. Similarly, I propose what I refer to as a Cohen-Tilly theory of conflict between states in a state system, and what I refer to as a Gellner-Smith-Conversi theory of the origins of nationalism. The discussion of these theories that I undertake below shows both the shortcomings of the theories proposed by each one of these scholars, and the usefulness of combining these theories in such a manner that a number of key concepts complement each other in explaining important social processes. I also show the importance of both political sociology and cultural sociology for a greater understanding of nationalism, and of its impact upon development. Nationalism is a product of the interaction between the state and culture, and nationalism is very important to state conflict.

---

5 Sen addresses education in: Sen, *Development as Freedom.*

1   The Sociology of Development and the Role of the State

Within sociology, the economy is studied as part of *two sub-fields: economic sociology; and the sociology of development*. There is a bias in this division, because economic sociology focuses upon developed countries, whereas the sociology of development focuses mostly upon developing countries, as if the concept of development only applied to countries with low per-capita income. I want to suggest, instead, that there should be a single field, the sociology of development, that studies the impact upon development as a whole of the main factors affecting the economy, culture, politics and the military of a country, no matter where the country is located, or what its per-capita income is. The sociology of development would thus combine contributions from economic sociology, political sociology, and cultural sociology. The sociology of development as it is conceived today is the smaller sub-field compared to economic sociology, but it has arguably provided a number of very important contributions to our understanding of development. They all amount to *a more nuanced understanding of the role of states in development*. These contributions are all related to the role of the state in a country, focusing in particular upon the interaction between state, society and markets, although not always describing it in these terms, and continuing the effort to 'bring the state back in.'[6] Two important theories in the sociology of development have started reconceptualizing the role of states in development by drawing attention to the fact that different states are distinguished by different types of rule and thus have very different effects upon development, some favoring, others hampering development. I use the expression type of rule to refer to features of rule such as absolutism and despotism, both of which relate to the manner in which elites or states rule.

　　These theories begin to provide an answer to neoliberal theories of development. Political scientist Robert Bates wrote an important book for neoliberalism and for the application of neoliberal tenets to developing countries throughout the world, titled *Markets and States in Tropical Africa*.[7] Bates' book

---

6　For examples of this approach that continue the effort to 'bring the state back in,' see the many contributions in: Matthew Lange and Dietrich Rueschemeyer, eds., *States and Development: Historical Antecedents of Stagnation and Advance*, Political Evolution and Institutional Change (London and New York: Palgrave Macmillan, 2005).

7　Robert Hinrichs Bates, *Markets and States in Tropical Africa: The Political Basis of Agricultural Policies*, California Series on Social Choice and Political Economy (Berkeley and Los Angeles: University of California Press, 1981). This book has been republished in an expanded version in 2014.

put forward the argument that the agricultural policies of states in tropical Africa were dictated by political considerations over and above economic considerations. States created *rents*, effectively easy profits, for industrialists who processed agricultural goods, because markets were so protected from foreign goods that these industrialists could make an easy profit at the expense of the farmers who provided the raw materials and at the expense of the population, who had no choice but to buy local goods that were expensive or inferior compared to goods on international markets. States thus distorted markets and impoverished farmers and the population of countries in tropical Africa, instead of helping them. The overarching argument of Bates' book, as with many other neoliberal books, is that if markets had been left to their own devices, they would have produced greater wealth. Bates' book arguably contributed to formulating and spreading views that supported the austerity measures imposed by the IMF upon many countries and criticized by Stiglitz.[8] Bates and neoliberals see states reductively, as introducing only distortions in markets, and contributing little or nothing else.

Sociologist Peter Evans has provided the first theory in the sociology of development that started reconceptualizing the role of states in development, by drawing attention to the positive as well as the negative effects of states, and to the type of rule that is associated with these different states. The type of rule emphasized by Evans focuses on *whether the state gives back to society, or simply extracts resources* giving nothing in return.[9] Evans created a typology of states that included, at one end of the spectrum, developmental states like South Korea that greatly contribute to development, and at the other end of the spectrum predatory states like Zaire that underdevelop countries also by extracting large amounts of resources and providing little or nothing in return.[10] This approach has blossomed into a paradigm, the developmental state paradigm, emphasizing the importance of states, and in particular of state policies, contrasting developmental to predatory states. There have been many contributions to this paradigm, some critical, but most reiterating the

---

8   Joseph E. Stiglitz, *Globalization and Its Discontents* (New York: W.W. Norton, 2003). I address Stiglitz' work in relation to its times in Section 5.7 of: Olsaretti, *The Struggle for Development and Democracy, Vol. 1.*

9   Peter B. Evans, *Embedded Autonomy: States and Industrial Transformation* (Princeton and Oxford: Princeton University Press, 1995).

10   Ibid. The typology is specifically discussed in: Peter B. Evans, "Predatory, Developmental, and Other Apparatuses: A Comparative Political Economy Perspective on the Third World State," *Sociological Forum* 4, no. 4 (1989). South Korean industrialization is an especially interesting case that has also been studied by: Alice H. Amsden, *Asia's Next Giant: South Korea and Late Industrialization* (Oxford and New York: Oxford University Press, 1992).

importance of states in negotiating transformations, such as initiating indus-trialization.[11] Evans considered Brazil and India as intermediate cases of states that contributed to industrialization to some extent, or at least in some sectors, specifically the Information and Communications Technology, or ICT, sector that progressed in Brazil as well as India, the latter enjoying more recently a spectacular success in ICT thanks in part to a large educated middle class created by good cultural institutions providing public education and favora-ble policies.[12] Brazil and India are also part of the emerging BRICS countries. These are all large or fairly large developing countries that have made signifi-cant gains in development, in part by following the pioneering example set by Brazil that Evans described.[13] Predatory states are often the legacy of European colonialism, which prevented or greatly distorted political-military and cul-tural development. It is necessary to complement Evan's study of predatory states with postcolonial theory and other studies of the legacy of colonialism that I address below. Imperialists from Belgium in Zaire, and imperialists from Italy in Libya, Ethiopia and Somalia, especially though not exclusively fascists, imposed a form of colonialism that was especially brutal, even by the stand-ards of brutal European colonial empires, in Italy's case building strong but oppressive states, after Italy was drawn into belated imperialist enterprises fol-lowing unification.[14]

---

11   An introduction to this paradigm is provided by: Stephan Haggard, *Developmental States*, Elements in the Politics of Development (Cambridge and New York: Cambridge University Press, 2018). Three edited volumes have brought together many recent con-tributions to this paradigm: Michelle Williams, ed. *The End of the Developmental State?* (London and New York: Routledge, 2014); Yin-wah Chu, ed. *The Asian Developmental State: Reexaminations and New Departures* (London and New York: Palgrave Macmillan, 2016); Meredih Woo-Cumings, ed. *The Developmental State*, Cornell Studies in Political Economy (Ithaca and New York: Cornell University Press, 2019).

12   Evans, *Embedded Autonomy*. Evans addresses Brazil also in his earlier work, specifically in relation to ICT: *Dependent Development: The Alliance of Multinational, State, and Local Capital in Brazil* (Princeton and Oxford: Princeton University Press, 1979). This book was republished in 2018. On Brazil as an instance of a social developmental states that integrates a social agenda in development, see: Celia Lessa Kerstenetzky, "The Brazilian Social Developmental State: A Progressive Agenda in a (Still) Conservative Political Society," in *The End of the Developmental State?*, ed. Michelle Williams (London and New York: Routledge, 2014).

13   The model was export-led industrialization, and greater local participation in govern-ance, together with transfer of technologies. On the significance of the BRICS coun-tries in the world economy, see: Deepak Nayyar, "BRICS, Developing Countries and Global Governance," *Third World Quarterly* 37, no. 4 (2016). William I. Robinson, "The Transnational State and the BRICS: a Global Capitalism Perspective," ibid. 36, no. 1 (2015).

14   Recent scholarship has confirmed that Belgian colonialism had an especially neg-ative effect on the development of Zaire through a state that was a failure both in

Lange has provided the second theory in the sociology of development that started reconceptualizing the role of states in development, by similarly drawing attention to the fact that states can have a range of different effects upon development. These effects depend upon the type of rule that is associated with these different states, leading to despotic or predatorial states, where the difference emphasizes *the predictability or erratic behavior of the state*, which makes despotic states even worse than absolutist states, in which there is a similar concentration of power, but the exercise of power is predictable. Lange's theory is useful in order to understand the effects of divide-and-conquer and divide-and-rule tactics that enabled a few imperialists from Europe, at the very top of the hierarchies of power in the colonies, to rule over vast countries, and large populations, extracting resources from them.[15] Lange' study of the impact of the British empire on states throughout the world distinguished between *two different types of rule* practiced by imperialists from Great Britain, that had different impacts upon local elites, leading to despotic or developmental states. These different types of rule were: *direct rule*, which involved taking over and running the state directly and incorporating these elites in a modern bureaucratic state, and was thus associated with more or less well-run and rule-bound bureaucratic states; and *indirect rule*, which involved ruling the state indirectly by placing local rulers faithful to imperialists from Great Britain at the head of states, a form of rule that was especially associated with divide-and-conquer tactics and patrimonial states often rife with conflict, and was also unpredictable and erratic. Lange has shown that where imperialists from Great Britain practiced direct rule, they built states that subsequently favored development, whereas where they practiced indirect rule, they built states that had negative,

---

comparison to Indonesia and to other countries in Africa: Leigh Gardner, "Fiscal Policy in the Belgian Congo in Comparative Perspecctive," in *Colonial Exploitation and Economic Development: The Belgian Congo and the Netherlands Indies Compared*, ed. Ewout Frankema and Frank Buelens (London and New York: Routledge, 2013). Andreas Exenberger and Simon Hartmann, "Extractive Insitutions in the Congo: Checks and Balances in the *Longue Durée*," ibid. On the similar impacts of French and Italian colonialism in Tunisia and Libya respectively, see: Lisa Anderson, *The State and Social Transformation in Tunisia and Libya, 1830–1980* (Princeton and Oxford: Princeton University Press, 1986). This book has been republished in 2014.

15 This is both through detailed case studies and statistical analysis. Colonialism varied considerably, but divide-and-conquer and divide-and-rule tactics did affect development in at least some cases: Matthew Lange and Andrew Dawson, "Dividing and Ruling the World? A Statistical Test of the Effects of Colonialism on Postcolonial Civil Violence," *Social Forces* 88, no. 2 (2009).

even disastrous, effects on development.[16] Indirect rule was especially harmful
in preventing the rise of modern bureaucratic states emphasized by Ertman
and a number of historians, who build upon Weber's work on this topic. It
aided instead patrimonial states in which the rulers threated public offices as
their own property.[17]

For all its strengths, there are some *glaring omissions from Lange's theory*
of the effects of states on development. *One such omission regards the vast
discretion that individual imperialists had* and the effects that this discretion
had on populations in European colonies. For example, despite his remarkable insights into the politics of imperialists from Great Britain, Lange does not
explain the involvement of *individual imperialists* like Charles George Gordon
in brutal repressions during wars, like putting down the Taiping rebellion,
which had a huge human cost for the people of China, and through this cost
would have affected development.[18] Lange does not explain either the discretion that private individuals like Gordon and sir Cecil Rhodes, and *private companies* more in general, exercised in at least some colonial enterprises. These
interventions perhaps disappear in a statistical analysis, but are nevertheless
ethically unacceptable, and can be politically, culturally, and economically disastrous for the populations that these imperialists and their private companies
sought to bring under their control. These private individuals and companies
practiced what amounted to *personal rule* in some areas, a form of absolutist
rule with disastrous effects upon development, that ruined these areas, just
like indirect rule did.[19]

---

16   The difference between direct and indirect rule was that direct rule involved building a
      whole state bureaucracy staffed with administrators committed to a bureaucratic instead
      of a patrimonial state, whereas indirect rule relied upon local rulers. For Lange's defini-
      tion, see: Lange, *Lineages of Despotism and Development.*

17   Ertman, *Birth of the Leviathan*; John Brewer and Eckhart Hellmuth, eds., *Rethinking
      Leviathan: The Eighteenth-Century State in Britain and Germany*, German Historical
      Institute London (Oxford and New York: Oxford University Press, 1999).

18   For a modern account of the Taiping Rebellion, see: T. Meyer-Fong, *What Remains: Coming
      to Terms with Civil War in 19th Century China* (Stanford, California: Stanford University
      Press, 2013). The death toll is estimated by some sources to have been between 20 and
      30 million lives. I do not think it is important to engage in an exact count, as if one was a
      pedantic bank manager accounting for money. The death toll was in the millions, and had
      it been even just a thousand, it would disprove rosy pictures of European colonialism.

19   Lange has a benign vision of imperialists from Europe, at least from Great Britain, very
      similar to that of Charles George Gordon, who promoted himself and his imperialist
      enterprises by providing his own benign account. For a popular account by a former
      soldier, portraying Gordon as a hero, and imperialist wars as if they were an adven-
      ture, see: Michael Asher, *Khartoum: The Ultimate Imperial Adventure* (London: Penguin,
      2005). For a popular account by a BBC journalist who instead portrays Gordon as a more

Lange's theory also omits *some important points regarding the rule of imperialists from Great Britain in India*. India too was conquered and administered for a long time by a private company, the East India Company, until it was placed directly under the British crown, and Queen Victoria was declared empress of India, alongside her title as British monarch. The impact on India might have been less favorable than Lange suggests, and it points to the *importance of counterfactuals* in social science: development in India might look favorable compared to that of failed states in Africa, but it would look unfavorable if compared to the development that India could have achieved if it had not been colonized. This is a counterfactual, a concept emphasized at McGill University by Steven Rytina, although he did not apply it to the effects of empires. Counterfactuals are important to conceptualize causation and also development.[20] It seems likely that, if counterfactuals were used, the effects of divide-and-conquer and divide-and-rule tactics in India by imperialists from Great Britain would appear as harmful and disruptive of development as the similar tactics associated with indirect rule in Africa. Ethnic divisions were often used by imperialists from Europe in divide-and-conquer and divide-and-rule tactics in their colonies, and this was facilitated by socio-economic changes that accompanied the expansion of trade. Thus incorporation in European colonial empires often stoked up social conflict, and specifically ethno-religious conflict, both by creating economic grievances, and by manipulating ethno-religious divisions, as part of divide-and-conquer and divide-and-rule tactics.

Both Evans' and Lange's theories can be reformulated as suggesting that *the positive as well as negative effects of states on development depend upon the provision of public goods* that the state provides or fails to provide. Evans' typology of rule contrasted developmental states like South Korea, which played a positive role in economic development by providing important public goods, especially education and research that helped provide a skilled workforce and technology, contrasting these states with predatory states like Zaire, which extracted

---

controversial figure, see: F. Nicoll, *Gladstone, Gordon and the Sudan Wars: The Battle over Imperial Invention in the Victorian Age* (Pen & Sword Books, 2013). The BBC, also via the BBC World Service, has played an important role in British culture.

20   Philosophers have been debating since 1973 the importance of counterfactuals to causation, some arguing that the very concept of causation implies counterfactuals. The many arguments by philosophers debating this point have been collected in: John Collins, Ned Hall, and L. A. Paul, eds., *Causation and Counterfactuals* (Cambridge, Massachusetts and London: MIT Press, 2004). For an instance of the use of counterfactuals in development studies, see: Bridget O'Laughlin, "Making People 'Surplus Population' in Southern Africa," in *Reclaiming Development Studies: Essays for Ashwani Saith*, ed. Murat Arsel, Anirban Dasgupta, and Servaas Storm (London: Anthem Press, 2021).

resources providing nothing in return.[21] This argument can be extended to include the internal peace and stability emphasized by Lange, which can be conceptualized as a public good, although I will argue below that it is more than *just* a public good. Lange used statistics to show empirically that there is a correlation between these two sets of phenomena: direct rule correlates with development; indirect rule correlates with underdevelopment. He then used a mix of empirical case studies and deductive procedures to show that the mechanism responsible for this correlation has to do with the provision of a crucially important public good, namely, internal stability and peace, thanks to a functioning state and laws that guarantee peace, without which violence thoroughly undermines development.[22] In my interpretation, the important point introduced by Lange compared to the economics literature, although he does not explicitly describe it in these terms, is to emphasize the concept of society in the discussion of development. Some states had a negative effect upon development because they destroyed civil society, and society more in general, while others had a positive effect because they encouraged peaceful societies, which made possible, and even positively advanced, development.

---

21   Fred Block and Peter Evans, "The State and the Economy," in *The Handbook of Economic Sociology*, ed. Neil J. Smelser and Richard Swedberg (Princeton and Oxford: Princeton University Press, 2010). Evans highlights the importance of Sen's work on public debates, and diversification of sources of information, as a public good that contributes to development: Peter B. Evans, "The Challenges of the Institutional Turn: New Interdisciplinary Opportunities in Development Theory," in *The Economic Sociology of Capitalism*, ed. Victor Nee and Richard Swedberg (Princeton and New Jersey: Princeton University Press, 2005). Arguably, many of the policies that distinguish developmental states build upon such public goods.

22   Recently, Lange has begun studying in detail the disastrous effects on development of violence that is due to continuous lack of stability and to education that emphasizes ethnic differences: Matthew Lange, *Educations in Ethnic Violence: Identity, Educational Bubbles, and Resource Mobilization* (Cambridge and New York: Cambridge University Press, 2011); *Killing Others: A Natural History of Ethnic Violence* (Ithaca, New York: Cornell University Press, 2017); Matthew Lange and Andrew Dawson, "Education and Ethnic Violence: a Cross-National Time-Series Analysis," *Nationalism and Ethnic Politics* 16, no. 2 (2010). Abernethy provided an earlier negative assessment of the effects that education had on violence in Southern Nigeria: David B. Abernethy, *Education and Politics in a Developing Society: The Southern Nigerian Experience* (Harvard University, 1965); *The Political Dilemma of Popular Education: An African Case*, Stanford Studies in Comparative Politics (Stanford, California: Stanford University Press, 1969). I do not believe these are conclusive arguments against the importance of education for development. These are arguments about bad education that is politically manipulated, as in Lange's study, or about the lack of coordination between cultural policies that focus on education and economic policies that focus on employment, as in Abernethy's studies.

2 Embedded Autonomy and Types of State Systems

It is useful to expand upon both Evans' theory and Lange's theory, by complementing these theories with additional theories and arguments. Here I bring into a broader picture the above theories about the contribution to development that states give as providers of public goods, focusing in particular upon *the manner in which states provide public goods*, not just whether they provide public goods or not. States, in addition to providing public goods, have to provide the public goods that are needed the most, at the time and place they are needed, and in the amounts that are needed. This requires significant coordination and sharing of information between the state and private companies, and also between the state and other organizations like NGOs, together with internal peace and stability, within the context of peaceful interaction between the state and other organizations, which avoids the disruptions that violence brings to economic activity and ultimately to all activities in a country.[23] The sociological concept of *embedded autonomy helps us conceptualize the manner in which developmental states provide public goods*. Embedded autonomy emphasizes that the state is embedded in markets, while both remain autonomous. It is also a major improvement upon Bates' theory and other neoliberal theories, which tend to approach state involvement in markets as a discrete variable, whereby either there is, or there isn't any, state involvement. By contrast, the entire approach adopted by Evans and Lange, and the concept of embedded autonomy, emphasize that the *extent*, as well as the manner, of state involvement in markets varies, and that both the extent and manner of state involvement are very important to the provision of public goods.

Evans' theory suggested also *the mechanism that ensures embedded autonomy, namely, networks between the state and companies or other organizations,*

---

23 The importance of information sharing between the state and the economy is the subject of research on Open Data. A recent volume by the IDRC brought together contributions on just about every facet and application of Open Data to development: Tim Davies et al., eds., *The State of Open Data: Histories and Horizons* (Cape Town and Ottawa: African Minds and the International Development Research Center, 2019). Information sharing is especially important to finance, including finance for SMEs, which have difficulties in financing themselves also because there is little information about them: Patrizio Messina, *Finance for SMEs: European Regulation and Capital Markets Union: Focus on Securitization and Alternative Finance Tools*, European Monographs (Alphen aan den Rijn, the Netherlands: Wolters Kluwer, 2019). Since they can contribute to information sharing, modern ICT technological advances have a major impact on markets: Swati Bhatt, *How Digital Communication Technology Shapes Markets: Redefining Competition, Building Cooperation* (London and New York: Palgrave Macmillan, 2016).

which give a crucially important contribution to the manner in which a state provide public goods. Evans has first drawn attention to the importance of *networks* between state and markets in his study of Brazilian industrialization. Some of these networks involved what were essentially organic intellectuals directly involved in markets, computer scientists and engineers trained in the United States and known as 'barbudos,' besides networks that stretched from the state to corporations.[24] More recently, he has placed the study of these networks within a broader sociological context. Sociologist Mark Granovetter proposed the concept of embedded autonomy to conceptualize that all activity in society, including economic activity, takes place as part of social relations, which can often be modeled as part of social networks.[25] Evans applied the concept of embeddedness to understand the positive effects of states on development, whereby embeddedness between states and markets is ensured by specific types of networks between state and markets that enable effective communications that are necessary for sharing of information and coordination of activities, while the state and society remain autonomous.[26] It is through these networks that the state knows what public goods are needed, where and when they are needed, and in what quantities they are needed. It is also through these networks that the state coordinates activities with organizations like NGOs to provide public goods, and with companies to change the type and quantity of public goods in response to changing needs. Lastly, it is through these networks that common strategies for growth are formulated. These networks are arguably *in addition to public communications by states* in the form of bulletins, press conferences, state-run news, etc. etc., all of which

---

24   Evans, *Dependent Development*.

25   Mark Granovetter, "Economic Action and Social Structure: The Problem of Embeddedness," *American Journal of Sociology* 91, no. 3 (1985). This concept built upon work by Karl Polanyi and has generated a large sociological literature, some of which arguably abused the concept: Greta Krippner et al., "Polanyi Symposium: a Conversation on Embeddedness," *Socio-economic Review* 2, no. 1 (2004). For a review of this sociological literature, see: Greta R. Krippner, "The Elusive Market: Embeddedness and the Paradigm of Economic Sociology," *Theory and Society* 30, no. 6 (2001); Greta R. Krippner and Anthony S. Alvarez, "Embeddedness and the Intellectual Projects of Economic Sociology," *Annual Review of Sociology* 33 (2007). On the geographical aspect of embeddedness, see: Martin Hess, "'Spatial' Relationships? Towards a Reconceptualization of Embeddedness," *Progress in Human Geography* 28, no. 2 (2004).

26   This is one of the arguments of: Evans, *Embedded Autonomy*. Samford has drawn attention also to the importance of the private sector, and thus of markets, in the information sharing between states and companies: Steven Samford, "Networks, Brokerage, and State-Led Technology Diffusion in Small Industry," *American Journal of Sociology* 122, no. 5 (2017).

are important. Networks are important because they enable rapid sharing of information, which moves both ways, from companies to the state, as well as from the state to companies, and enable coordination of activities, for example setting up educational institutions that companies hire from. The most important point about this sharing of information is that it works in both directions, also from companies to the state, and this makes these networks very different than patronage networks, for example, in which the state hands down money in return for votes from individuals, or hands down state rents in return for monetary contributions from companies, imposing its own political logic on markets.

It is useful *to expand the concept of embedded autonomy to the interaction of state and society, as well as states and markets*, and furthermore to conceptualize this interaction as a system. Society, particularly civil society, plays a major role both in communications and the sharing of information, for example by newspapers, and also in the provision of public goods like education. It is also very important for the provision of welfare and various services to the poorer parts of a population, as emphasized by the growing literature on public-private welfare mixes and NGOs more in general.[27] Sociologists, including Carlo Trigilia, have highlighted the importance of the *interaction of state, society, and markets as a key factor for development*. Both the appreciation of the autonomous power of the state, and its interaction with society as well as markets, can contribute to a more nuanced and useful approach to development.[28] Wallerstein unwittingly contributed to neoliberalism and to one-sided views of development by making the argument that the distinction between state, society, and markets was an artificial distinction, due to disciplinary turf wars, and rejecting the importance of considering markets alongside civil society

---

27 Carrie A Meyer, "The Political Economy of NGOs and Information Sharing," *World Development* 25, no. 7 (1997); Arne Hintz, *Civil Society Media and Global Governance: Intervening into the World Summit on the Information Society* (Münster: Lit Verlag, 2009). The importance of information to welfare is discussed in: Joe Soss, *Unwanted Claims: The Politics of Participation in the U.S. Welfare System* (Ann Arbor: University of Michigan Press, 2002).

28 Carlo Trigilia, *Economic Sociology: State, Market, and Society in Modern Capitalism* (Oxford: Blackwell, 2008). I emphasize here the importance of the state, markets, and *civil* society, also because of the centrality of the concept of civil society to Gramsci's work, and more recently to Putnam's work. This entails that policy-makers in developing countries have to be free to implement the right mix of markets and states, and I would add civil society, that is necessary for their country at a specific conjuncture. See also: Amsden, *Escape from Empire*.

and the state.[29] He dismissed arguments that use markets, civil society, and the state in order to explain development as the 'dominant liberal ideology of earlier times, which had argued that the state, the market, and civil society, were the three separated pillars upon which modern social structures were built,' likely because Wallerstein, in a manner analogous to Cohen, saw the economy as all important, and emphasized only one logic in the world system, the world economy.[30] By contrast, this book argues that the three separate arenas are necessary for both development and democracy, and that they have nothing to do with false dichotomies between liberal and conservative ideological alternatives. It also argues that we need to complement the study of the three arenas with the study of institutions, the latter approached in their relations to the whole of a country, through networks that are effectively social structures, and relations that vary across a territory. I also expand upon and reformulate arguments by Trigilia, and propose that state institutions participate in different extents of autonomy at different times, and that this affects development.[31] In the next part of this volume I further expand upon these points, highlighting that there are very important cultural institutions, especially universities, and also think tanks, that are more or less independent of the state, and have their own way to interact with markets.

The interaction between state and society is important for development. This interaction involves *looking at state institutions differently*, as they relate to

---

29   Wallerstein refers to the division between these three arenas as a 'trinity of arenas of social action—the economy or market; the polity, or state; the society, or culture,' however Wallerstein emphasizes the importance of the world system and of the macro scale of analysis over and above these three arenas: Immanuel Maurice Wallerstein, "World-Systems Analysis: The Second Phase," *Review (Fernand Braudel Center)* 13, no. 2 (1990): 292–93. Wallerstein later argued that the trinity 'State/Market/Civil Society' had become the basis of artificial disciplinary differences between, respectively, political science, economics and sociology: "What Are We Bounding, and Whom, When We Bound Social Research," *Social Research* 62, no. 4 (1995): 848–851.

30   "What Are We Bounding, and Whom, When We Bound Social Research," 851. Wallerstein is not openly in favor of neoliberalism, but like many other high intellectuals who started a school of thought, he focus exclusively on his key concepts. For Wallerstein, the world system, based on a world economy, is all that matters to development. In some other formulations, he seems to be more conciliatory towards the existence of separate economic, cultural, and political-military arenas, but still focuses exclusively on the world scale.

31   Carlo Trigilia, *Sviluppo Senza Autonomia. Effetti Perversi delle Politiche nel Mezzogiorno* (Bologna: Il Mulino, 1992). In this book Trigilia suggests an argument similar to Putnam's, but also emphasizes civic culture and the combined effects of civic culture and NGOs on local institutions, concluding that development in southern Italy was not autonomous from the state. This argument can be reformulated in terms of the lack of autonomy of both markets and civil society in southern Italy from the state.

society. It has become a subject of research in its own right, and it is central to work by political scientists, including Joel Midgal, who pioneered this study.[32] The success of developmental states in promoting development can best be studied using a combination of institutional analysis, together with studies of social structures or networks of individuals, specifically networks of individuals that link institutions to companies that the institutions interact with. This can be generalized to suggest that developmental states are distinguished by two sets of interactions, between state and markets, and between state and society, that *require both the right institutions for development and the right networks between these institutions and markets, and society.* It is important to add to this picture that state institutions are not monolithic.[33] In particular, providing an adequate account of the different relations between state institutions and society within a country requires that we introduce in the picture two important differences within state institutions that lead to variations in state-society relations. One difference involves *different institutions defined by function,* for example different ministries, that are concerned with different functions of a state, like a ministry of defense and a ministry of development, which can relate to society in very different ways. The other difference involves *different institutions defined by geography,* like different regional administrations within a state, which can be considerably different from one region to another, and can have considerably different relations to society in their region, compared to other such relations in other regions.

These interactions can be aptly described as part of systems, whether state-markets, state-society, or society-markets systems, the latter being especially important in countries in which society has developed its own independent institutions. This is for several reasons, all related to the fact that the networks between state institutions and companies, or other organizations in society like NPOs and universities, all participate in what is effectively a system

32   Joel S. Migdal, *Strong Societies and Weak States: State-Society Relations and State Capabilities in the Third World* (Princeton and Oxford: Princeton University Press, 1988).

33   This point is made by Michael Mann in: Michael Mann, *The Sources of Social Power, Vol. 1: A History of Power from the Beginning to AD 1760* (Cambridge and New York: Cambridge University Press, 2012). This is a very important point that I address in the book on the humanist theory of society. I also address throughout this project Mann's theory of power, as set out in Mann's volume above and in: *The Sources of Social Power, Vol. 2: The Rise of Classes and Nation-States, 1760–1914,* The Sources of Social Power (Cambridge and New York: Cambridge University Press, 2012); *The Sources of Social Power, Vol. 3: Global Empires and Revolution, 1890–1945* (Cambridge and New York: Cambridge University Press, 2012); *The Sources of Social Power, Vol. 4: Globalizations, 1945–2011* (Cambridge and New York: Cambridge University Press, 2012).

involving several organizations without formal command chains governing their interactions, as opposed to the command chains that govern all interactions in a single centralized organization. One of the reasons why it appropriate to speak of state-markets, state-society, and society-markets systems, is that *institutions within a state sometimes resemble a system*, since the state is not always a monolithic organization, but at times resembles to a greater or lesser extent a system without formal command chains for all activities. In cases in which society has developed autonomous institutions from the state this is obvious. For example, in Canada, Great Britain, and the United States, universities are more or less autonomous from the state, although they receive substantial funds from the state and are subject to some rules set by the state, compared to other countries, especially Italy.[34] In these cases it is clearly appropriate to speak of a state-society system involving, on the one hand the state and its political institutions, and on the other hand a large number of cultural institutions, chiefly universities, but also colleges and institutes, all of which interact with the state without being part of a formal hierarchy. Some of these cultural institutions also interact with markets, and in these cases it is appropriate to speak of a society-markets system. In the United States, where universities have traditionally been, and are still, more independent from the state than in other countries, there are also strong state universities, all part of a state-society system that is especially important for development.[35]

---

34   The question of university autonomy is an important and complex question. Autonomy
      refers to four pillars: organizational autonomy, financial autonomy, human resources
      autonomy, and academic or research autonomy, but these have to be understood as a
      whole, in relation also to the ties between universities and organizations such as companies: Romeo V. Turcan, John E. Reilly, and Larissa Bugaian, "The Challenge of University
      Autonomy," in *(Re)Discovering University Autonomy: The Global Market Paradox of
      Stakeholder and Educational Values in Higher Education*, ed. Romeo V. Turcan, John
      E. Reilly, and Larissa Bugaian (London and New York: Palgrave Macmillan, 2016). The
      recent loss of autonomy of universities in Italy, if they ever had any, sparked a conference
      whose many contributions were published in: Margrit Seckelmann et al., eds., *Academic
      Freedom under Pressure?: A Comparative Perspective* (Cham, Switzerland: Springer, 2021).

35   The United States has the most independent universities, although undergraduate education is still funded by the state, which does not *necessarily* erode university autonomy: OECD, Education Policy Analysis, (Paris: OECD Publishing, 2003). Contrary to
      what one might expect, there are important state universities, like the State University
      of New York, the University of California, and the University of Michigan, that are
      (nearly) as successful as completely independent universities. Some, like the University
      of California, have been especially important for development, as the University of
      California at Berkeley has participated in Silicon Valley. On the University of California,
      see: Patricia A. Pelfrey and Margaret Cheney, *A Brief History of the University of California*
      (Berkeley: University of California Press, 2004). There have been social movements to
      expand state universities and promote development in the American South: Michael

State-markets, state-society, and society-markets systems are most obviously at work in federal states, because the provinces or states that exist within such federal states as Canada and the United States, rather than being part of a monolithic, that is, single tightly centralized state organization, have some autonomy and thus resemble a system. There are many forms that these systems can take.[36] This can be especially important to bring the state closer to society and markets. The whole concept of multi-level governance promoted by the European Union is a way to recognize the need for different institutions over a territory that complement different policy approaches, and are not organized as part of a centralized state with a rigid hierarchy.[37] Another reasons why it is appropriate to speak of state-markets, state-society, or society-markets systems, is that *the networks and associated rules of conduct between state and society can be different* depending upon the state institutions involved. For example, there can be different networks that cross from one state institution to the rest of the state and to society, compared to the same networks from another state institution to the rest of the state and to society. Moreover, even within the same state institution there can be different networks that have different ties to the rest of the institution, to other institutions in the state, and to society. Yet another reason is that *the institutions themselves can be different.* Even in centralized states, state institutions are not always tightly centralized and can be considerably different from one region to another.

Some concrete examples can help clarify these points regarding state institutions that are not monolithic and resemble a system. *Spain is a state*

Dennis, *Lessons in Progress: State Universities and Progressivism in the New South, 1880–1920* (Urbana and Chicago: University of Illinois Press, 2001).

36   For a review of the concept of federal system, see: Ronald L. Watts, "Federalism, Federal Political Systems, and Federations," *Annual Review of Political Science* 1, no. 1 (1998). I classify the systems that the state participates in as state-markets and state-society systems. The question of the autonomy of individual states from the federal state is in addition to the question of the autonomy of the state from social groups. The idea that the state in the United States is autonomous from private interests has been challenged by authors who argue that corporations and wealthy individuals still exert considerable influence on the state: G. William Domhoff, *State Autonomy or Class Dominance?: Case Studies on Policy Making in America*, Social Institutions and Social Change (Hawthorne, New York: Aldine de Gruyter, 1996).

37   Serafin Pazos-Vidal, *Subsidiarity and EU Multilevel Governance: Actors, Networks and Agendas* (London and New York: Routledge, 2019). Multilevel governance can be extended to institutions within individual states, as well as institutions of the European Union: Nathalie Behnke, Jörg Broschek, and Jared Sonnicksen, "Introduction: The Relevance of Studying Multilevel Governance," in *Configurations, Dynamics and Mechanisms of Multilevel Governance*, ed. Nathalie Behnke, Jörg Broschek, and Jared Sonnicksen (London and New York: Palgrave Macmillan, 2019).

characterized by asymmetric federalism, whereby some regions like Catalonia elect their own parliament and have a government and legislature similar to states in a federal state, whereas other regions like Andalusia or Extremadura are directly under the central Spanish government and are subject to all its laws.[38] Interestingly, *even a centralized state like Italy has institutions that are not monolithic* and share some features of a system. Amongst the twenty regions of Italy there are five regions, namely the border regions Friuli-Venezia Giulia, Trentino-Alto Adige/Südtirol, Val D'Aosta, and the island regions Sardinia and Sicily, all of which were granted special status and the ability to issue some of their own laws, or to introduce substantial modifications to laws, especially concerning education, thus effectively introducing a measure of asymmetric federalism in Italy.[39] The different relations between state and society in these regions stem from a combination of political and cultural reasons. In the case of Friuli-Venezia Giulia, Trentino-Alto Adige, and Val d'Aosta, they are due to *linguistic differences* and in particular to the presence of fairly large non-Italian-speaking populations, in border areas that were cultural intermediaries between Italy and nearby states like Austria and Yugoslavia, the latter now replaced by Slovenia and Croatia, and between Italy and France. In the case of the islands Sardinia and Sicily, it is due to *cultural differences*, as each island historically had its own strong cultural identity, even though the local dialect is not considered a separate language, and is not taught in schools. These five regions have played a more important role than one might assume in contemporary Italian history, if only because today the idea of a federal state, proposed both by populists like the Northern League, and by ostensibly left-leaning politicians like Matteo Renzi, has been aided by the precedent set by the special status regions.[40]

Besides being part of state-markets, state-society, and society-markets systems, *the interactions between state, society, and markets, all participate also in*

---

38   On federalism in Spain, see: Luis Moreno, *The Federalization of Spain* (London and New York: Routledge, 2013). Spanish federalism in a comparative perspective is the focus of the many contributions in: Alberto Lopez-Basagueren and Leire Escajedo San Epifanio, eds., *The Ways of Federalism in Western Countries and the Horizons of Territorial Autonomy in Spain*, Cham, Switzerland (Springer: 2013).

39   Denita Cepiku, "A Network Approach to Asymmetric Federalism: The Italian Case Study," in *Making Multi-Level Public Management Work: Stories of Success and Failure from Europe and North America.*, ed. Denita Cepiku, Dabvid K. Jesuit, and Ian Roberge (Boca Raton, Florida: CRC Press, 2013).

40   Recent moves towards federalism in Italy are addressed by the contributors to: Stelio Mangiameli, ed. *Italian Regionalism: Between Unitary Traditions and Federal Processes: Investigating Italy's Form of State* (Cham, Swiztzerland: Springer, 2014).

ecosystems and state systems, both of which affect these interactions. Lange's theory suggests that there has to be internal peace and stability for development to occur. This is also because peace and stability are the necessary conditions for embedded autonomy, as well as for purely economic interactions. It is useful to expand upon Lange's theory by emphasizing that social conflict inside states is affected by interstate conflict. To understand this point it is necessary to take into account both ecosystems and state systems. Diamond has pioneered the application of ecosystem analysis to human societies. This is part also of a growing field of historical studies that focuses on the interactions between human societies and the environment in the course of history.[41] Diamond has applied *ecosystem analysis* to macro-studies of development, which explain the broadest trends in human development, spanning millennia and the entire globe. He has also introduced, within this very broad geographical picture, concerns about sustainable development, showing how the environment can bring to and end certain types of development, leading to societal collapse.[42] Diamond's theory explicitly sought to understand the success of imperialists from Europe in conquering other parts of the world. The concept of *state system* is necessary to understand the interaction between social conflict and interstate conflict, especially as it affected Africa and India. World Systems Theory included at the beginning an attempt to understand the underdevelopment of many countries in Africa by considering the political causes of underdevelopment within an international framework that emphasizes interstate conflict.[43] As interstate conflict can heighten social conflict, and compound social organization problems and transition organization problems, it can lead to diffuse violence and criminality, and also to dictators who create predatory states. To understand these effects it is necessary to combine the study of both ecosystems and state systems in one theory.

---

41 Notable instances of this growing field include: J. R. McNeill, *Something New under the Sun: An Environmental History of the Twentieth-Century World* (New York and London: W. W. Norton, 2001). See also the contributions in: Alf Hornborg, J. R. McNeill, and Joan Martinez-Alier, eds., *Rethinking Environmental History: World-System History and Global Environmental Change* (Lanham, New York, Toronto, Plymouth: AltaMira Press, 2007). Both Braudel's and Marx's work contributed to environmental history: Jason W. Moore, "Capitalism as World-Ecology: Braudel and Marx on Environmental History," *Organization & Environment* 16, no. 4 (2003).

42 Diamond, *Guns, Germs, and Steel*; *Collapse: How Societies Choose to Fail or Succeed: Revised Edition* (London: Penguin, 2011).

43 Wallerstein, *Africa, the Politics of Independence*; *The Road to Independence*; *Africa: The Politics of Unity*.

Diamond has made a convincing argument that *the rise of north-western Europe was a consequence of advantageous environmental factors that can be found in Eurasia,* not of the alleged superiority of European societies. Most Eurasian societies, or more precisely countries, in comparison to countries in Africa and in the Americas, benefited from the fact that in several parts of Eurasia, in particular in the Middle East, South Asia and East Asia, the environment provided the bases for an early introduction of agriculture, thanks to plant and animal species that were particularly easy to domesticate.[44] These animal and plant species also favored intensive agriculture with higher yields of calories per unit area under cultivation, whether from cereal or rice cultivation, compared to other types of cultivation. This led to higher population densities than anywhere else in the world. Diamond argues that high population densities then led to important innovations, including military innovations like steel weapons, political innovations like states, and the rise of diseases that Eurasian populations eventually developed some immunity against, but that populations in other parts of the world were very vulnerable to. Additionally, *geographical factors in Eurasia favored the development of trade routes* that greatly enhanced both trade and communications, in comparison to Africa and the Americas, leading to the relatively rapid spread of innovations and diseases to areas that were initially peripheral within Eurasia, like Europe, but benefited both from their own innovations and from innovations they received from China and India, for example. Diamond argues that when European countries encountered other countries in Africa and the Americas, they easily conquered them because they had weapons and states that enabled a speedy conquest of other societies, and in the case of the Americas, because they introduced diseases that decimated the local population following first contact.[45]

While Diamond has made important contributions to our understanding of development, there are *shortcomings in Diamond's argument that call for taking into consideration important points made by Wallerstein* regarding the state system and the world economy. I refer to the reformulation of Diamond's theory that takes into account Wallerstein's theory and the concepts of state system and world economy as *the Diamond-Wallerstein theory.* Wallerstein has suggested that already in the course of the sixteenth century there was an

---

44   This is the main argument of: Diamond, *Guns, Germs, and Steel.* I prefer to refer to countries rather than societies, since countries include society and sometimes also a state that governs the country, but here I present Diamond's argument in its form as an argument about societies.

45   Ibid.

emerging world economy based on long distance trade that was driven by a system of states in competition with each other. [46] These states were England, France, Spain, as well as the Netherlands and Portugal, and they incorporated other parts of the world in a world economy whose trade flows they controlled through their navies and merchant marines, but they did so on terms advantageous to themselves, often leading to the underdevelopment of other parts of the world with disastrous long-term consequences. The *concepts of underdevelopment and incorporation in the world economy are necessary to complement Diamond's argument* in order to explain the enduring underdevelopment of countries in West Africa, for example. It has been convincingly argued that parts of West Africa had rice cultivation.[47] This should have enabled countries in West Africa to develop high population densities and to develop in a manner similar to Eurasian countries. But they did not, and this raises the question of the negative impact that incorporation in a world economy dominated by north-western European states could have.

The Diamond-Wallerstein theory incorporates concepts from World Systems Theory that enable us to provide an answer to this question. *Incorporation in the world economy could lead to especially harsh forms of exploitation and lasting underdevelopment.* One explanation as to why countries in West Africa did not develop like many Eurasian countries is that they were incorporated into the world economy before they could develop significantly high population densities. Additionally, the manner in which they were incorporated into the world economy was especially damaging, for entire societies, as well as for the individuals affected by it. West Africa became the source of slaves in the slave trade that linked Europe to Africa and to the Americas.[48] This was especially damaging for development because it drastically reduced the population, furthermore removing the younger persons, in the prime of life, who could

---

46   Wallerstein, *The Modern World-System, Vol. 1:.*

47   Judith Ann Carney, *Black Rice: The African Origins of Rice Cultivation in the Americas* (Cambridge, Massachusetts and London: Harvard University Press, 2001). This book was republished in 2009. It points to the ingenuity of West African peoples and it adds to our understanding of contributions from Africa to American culture.

48   For an overview of West Africa's history with a focus on the slave trade, see: John Thornton, ed. *Africa and Africans in the Making of the Atlantic World, 1400–1800* (Cambridge and New York: Cambridge University Press, 1998). For a more general overview, see: Toby Green, *A Fistful of Shells: West Africa from the Rise of the Slave Trade to the Age of Revolution* (London: Penguin, 2019). The negative impacts of the slave trade on development were profound: Warren Whatley, "The Transatlantic Slave Trade and the Evolution of Political Authority in West Africa," *Africa's Development in Historical Perspective* (2014). Nonso Obikili, "The Impact of the Slave Trade on Literacy in West Africa: Evidence from the Colonial Era," *Journal of African Economies* 25, no. 1 (2016).

have started families and contributed to their societies' growth through both labour and demographic growth. Moreover, the slave trade had similar effects to indirect rule, since it made use of several African rulers who were the heads of states that waged wars on their neighbors and captured subjects of other states to sell them to European slave merchants. Some of these African rulers developed states specialized in the slave trade.[49] This set off a vicious circle for development involving demographic growth, increasing even more the negative impact of the slave trade, because wars to capture subjects for this trade led to more deaths and destruction that further depressed the population and economic growth of West Africa. It was possible for imperialists from Europe to exploit and underdevelop West Africa in this manner because West Africa had not achieved political-military development sufficient to protect itself from external aggression, and the states that existed in West Africa were part of a regional state system lacking institutions to regulate conflict.[50] Therefore, conflict could be stoked up by external aggression using divide-and-conquer tactics, which led some states to cooperate in the European slave trade, thus increasing conflict, and further dividing countries in West Africa and making them powerless against external aggression.

The Diamond-Wallerstein theory can be further extended *by introducing considerations regarding state type* that are implicit in Wallerstein's work, in such a way as to expand upon the explanation just proposed for West Africa and place it within a broader geographical framework. There were *dynamics of the state systems that were conquered which explain weaknesses* and are necessary to formulate in greater detail the concept of political-military development, without which cultural development and economic development can be undermined. These dynamics are also important to understand conquest, which did not rely exclusively upon military superiority.[51] These features

---

49   The arguments that the slave trade had a major impact on development by depressing demographics are reviewed in: Paul E. Lovejoy, "The Impact of the Atlantic Slave Trade on Africa: A Review of the Literature," *The Journal of African History* 30, no. 3 (1989). On the participation of *some* African states and rulers in the slave trade, see: Winston McGowan, "African Resistance to the Atlantic Slave Trade in West Africa," *Slavery and Abolition* 11, no. 1 (1990); Robin Law and Kristin Mann, "West Africa in the Atlantic Community: The Case of the Slave Coast," *The William and Mary Quarterly* 56, no. 2 (1999).

50   On the history of states in West Africa before colonialism, see: Basil Davidson, *West Africa before the Colonial Era: A History to 1850* (London and New York: Routledge, 2014). Braudel addresses the participation of West Africa in the Mediterranean world economy in: Braudel, *Civilization and Capitalism, Vol. 3.*

51   Thompson has argued that sheer military superiority is not enough to explain European conquests, most of which involved also local allies and exploited local weaknesses: William R. Thompson, "The Military Superiority Thesis and the Ascendancy of Western Eurasia in

apply to the case of Italian city-states, which suffered from a similar, albeit less severe, weakness and subsequent underdevelopment as states in West Africa. Italian city-states were divided, lacked sufficient institutions to regulate conflict amongst themselves, and ultimately lacked sufficient political-military development to defend themselves.[52] It is necessary to *add the concept of state type* also in order to answer another question. Diamond explains what advantages Eurasian countries had over other countries but does not explain differences amongst Eurasian countries. State type, as well as dynamics of the state system, both of which appear in Wallerstein's theory, are necessary to account for these differences. State type is a likely candidate to explain the fate of Italy and China in the modern world system. In the case of Italy, the Italian peninsula was divided into numerous small city-states that proved unable to cooperate for sufficient time to resist conquest by larger north-western European proto nation-states. In the case of China, internal conflict was limited by the emergence of a single state, but this was an empire that in the long run hampered development from within, which calls for another type of explanation regarding the manner in which state type affects development.[53]

State type is necessary to understand the *differences amongst Eurasian countries*, including what advantages north-western Europe had over Italy. By the early modern period Italy had high population densities, advanced technologies, and sophisticated states for the time. However, the whole of southern Italy and parts of northern Italy were conquered by other European states and entered a long period of decline. All the most important Italian city-states, namely, Florence, Genoa, and Venice, were displaced from the world economy and their trade was taken over by states in north-western Europe within

---

the World System," *Journal of World History* (1999). The approach that I take complements Diamond's argument that colonialists from Europe drew an important advantage from having states: Diamond, *Guns, Germs, and Steel*. This is because well-functioning states are a crucially important organization to enable collective action, and to prevent divide-and-conquer tactics by outsiders.

52   There were the beginnings of diplomacy, in order to prevent and regulate conflict: Garrett Mattingly, *Renaissance Diplomacy* (New York: Dover Publications, 1988). However, these were not enough to avoid conquest from outside powers. On the Italian Wars and the escalation in conflict set off by the French invasion led by Charles VIII, see: Michael Edward Mallett and Christine Shaw, *The Italian Wars, 1494–1559: War, State and Society in Early Modern Europe* (London and New York: Routledge, 2012). Some Italian states cooperated with Charles VIII and this spelled the doom of the entire system of states in the Italian peninsula.

53   World Systems Theory emphasizes the stifling effects of centralized empires on economic growth. Historical research has confirmed this in the case of China: William Guanglin Liu, *The Chinese Market Economy, 1000–1500* (State University of New York Press, 2015).

a short time span, or had to find niches in the new world trade.[54] They too were sidestepped by the Rise of the West which, as pointed out in the previous chapter, was really only the rise of north-western Europe. Eventually, these city-states too were reduced to vassal status of north-western European states.[55] Similarly, by the beginning of the early modern period, around 1500, China had high population densities, advanced technologies and a state that was especially sophisticated for its time. Yet China was not involved in any expansion comparable to the rise of north-western Europe. China also had the means to sail to the Americas and conquer a colonial empire like the British or French empires, but it never did.[56] Eventually, China itself was subjected to a semi-colonial tutelage by several European states. The fact that China was unified into a tightly centralized empire arguably explains its failure to develop as much as it could have, had it not been such an empire. Historical sociologists compare the many innovations introduced in China when it was divided into

---

54 This is a common viewpoint in both the history and the sociology literature. The decline of Italian city-states coincided with two historical phenomena. One was related to the decline of the entire Mediterranean system, replaced in international trade by the emerging Atlantic system. The other was specific to the Italian peninsula and saw the decline of all democracies that had flourished in the Middle Ages and early Renaissance in Italian cities, as part of a phenomenon sometimes referred to as re-feudalization. For an overview of the history of Italian city-states and their decline as they turned into lordships, see: Philip Jones, *The Italian City-State: From Commune to Signoria* (Oxford: Clarendon Press, 1997).

55 Both the Kingdom of Naples and the Duchy of Milan were conquered. Most of northern Italy, namely, Piedmont/Savoy, Mantua, Parma, Ferrara, Urbino, and their respective states, came to be ruled by Marquises or Dukes who were under the influence, sometimes as vassals, of the ruling houses of the kingdom of France or of the Habsburg empire. Cochrane charts this change in the course of the sixteenth century: Eric Cochrane, *Italy 1530–1630*, Longman History of Italy (London and New York: Routledge, 2014). Sella argues that Italian states had not gone into decline, and that there were still important cultural achievements: Domenico Sella, *Italy in the Seventeenth Century*, Longman History of Italy (London and New York: Routledge, 2014). However, politically and economically these states were all side-stepped by other European states. Both Cochrane and Sella speak of system, and Sella suggests that the Italian system had survived the Italian Wars, but the states in these systems had largely lost autonomy to their more powerful European neighbors.

56 Some authors have reversed interpretations of the rise of the West and pointed out that in many ways China was more economically advanced than Europe at the beginning of the modern era. For variants of this argument, see: John M. Hobson, *The Eastern Origins of Western Civilisation* (Cambridge and New York: Cambridge University Press, 2004). Andre Gunter Frank, *Reorient: Global Economy in the Asian Age* (Berkeley and Los Angeles: University of California Press, 1998). R. B. Wong, *China Transformed: Historical Change and the Limits of European Experience*, Cornell Paperbacks (Ithaca, New York: Cornell University Press, 1997).

states in competition with each other, to the stagnation after it was unified into an empire.[57]

3 Political Sociology and Interstate Conflict in State Systems

Political sociology has introduced a number of *important concepts that are useful to understand the dynamics of state systems*, and in particular the form and destructiveness of interstate conflict. The study of politics within sociology is the preserve of a recognized sub-field often referred to as political sociology. The study of social movements, which constitute an important part of politics in democratic countries, is closely related to political sociology and is sometimes conducted by political sociologists, although the sociology of social movements is sometimes considered as its own separate sub-field.[58] Political sociology is a small sub-field within sociology, in which there have been nevertheless a number of important contributions, for example to our understanding of democracy and how it relates to development. As in the sociology of development, these contributions too have remained thus far a collection of disparate contributions from a number of different scholars who are seen, I believe erroneously, as proposing mutually opposed theories. These theories are instead complementary. Here I want to suggest why some specific contributions are important that share a *common focus on understanding the dynamics of state systems, and how they affect both development and democracy*. Interstate conflict is an important part of this dynamics. The dynamics of state systems that it is important to address in order to understand the impact of state systems on development can usefully be summarized as consisting of two arguments. The first argument is that interstate conflict in a state system can lead to the selection of a particular state type, which becomes the predominant state type in that system. The second argument is that the state type that

---

57   This is one of the arguments of: Dingxin Zhao, *The Confucian-Legalist State: A New Theory of Chinese History*, Oxford Studies in Early Empires (Oxford and New York: Oxford University Press, 2015). Key Western historical sociologists, including Goldstone, Hall, Mann, have engaged with this work in the editorial forum introduced by: Richard Lachmann, "Chinese Powers: A Critical Appreciation of Dingxin Zhao's *the Confucian-Legalist State*," *Chinese Sociological Review* 51, no. 1 (2019).

58   Notable instances of this work are: Tilly, *Social Movements*. Sidney Tarrow, *Power in Movement: Social Movements and Contentious Politics* (Cambridge and New York: Cambridge University Press, 1998). An overview of both the social theory and empirical sociological literature on social movements is provided by: Suzanne Staggenborg, *Social Movements*, 2nd ed. (Oxford and New York: Oxford University Press, 2016).

emerges from interstate conflict is the state type best suited to development, that is, a developmental state in Evans' definition, or the state best suited to democracy, or best suited to both development and democracy. The overarching argument is that interstate conflict can lead to the selection of developmental states or democracies. A central question raised by this argument regards the form that interstate conflict has to take in order to lead to the selection of developmental states or democracies.

There have been several contributions that can help answering this question. Cohen's *Karl Marx's Theory of History* was an important book for the theory of history that has often been characterized as a form of economic-technological determinism.[59] It was actually more nuanced than that. Its main argument was not that the economy and technology, a key factor in economic development, directly lead to a certain type of state. Cohen allowed for states to be different and suggested that eventually *the state that develops the economy and technology the most would prevail and be adopted throughout the world.*[60] The overarching argument proposed by Cohen can be reformulated and summarized as an argument that in the long run the type of state described as developmental states will prevail and will become the predominant state type. Similar arguments that are similarly optimistic have been put forward regarding democracy. Not all states promote democracy, but the states that do will eventually prevail and be adopted throughout the world. This could be because democracy is best for development, or because democracy is most desired by citizens.[61] Cohen suggested a functional explanation to explain why the state type that best promotes development will prevail and become the prevalent state type. However, Cohen did not explain how exactly the functional explanation would select states. Functional explanations, including Cohen's, are like black boxes. Inside these black boxes there is a *selection mechanism* whereby,

---

59   Cohen, *Karl Marx's Theory of History*.
60   Ibid. The introduction to this newer edition presents new concepts compared to the 1978 edition, highlighting the importance of identity. Cohen's book sparked debates in Marxism and in the theory of history. Cohen himself introduced in these debates the importance of freedom in history, as part of development, although he does not use the word development: Gerald Allan Cohen, *History, Labour, and Freedom: Themes from Marx* (Oxford: Clarendon Press, 1988). This part of Cohen's work presages Sen's work, especially: Sen, *Development as Freedom*.
61   On the importance of democracy for development from an analytic perspective, see: Adam Przeworski et al., *Democracy and Development: Political Institutions and Well-Being in the World, 1950–1990*, Cambridge Studies in the Theory of Democracy (Cambridge and New York: Cambridge University Press, 2000). Przeworski had ties to Cohen's September Group.

out of many different states of several different state types, the states of one state type come to prevail. We need a clearer explanation of what might be the selection mechanism that selects out of the different states that compete in a state system the ones that promote development or democracy the most.

Important theories in political sociology have suggested concepts that can contribute to formulating this selection mechanism. Sociologist Barrington Moore Jr is amongst the sociologists who contributed to the birth of political sociology, and is the representative of what could be called a *Harvard school of political sociology* that is closely associated with the study of states, war and democracy. Moore is also associated with modern historical sociology, his work preceding and paving the way for Wallerstein's work. Some of the main exponents of this school are Theda Skocpol and Charles Tilly.[62] Hall, who participated in the rebirth of historical sociology, and to some extent van den Berg, who participated in the rediscovery of the state in sociology, are indirectly associated with this school of political sociology.[63] This school pioneered the rediscovery of the role of states in history, at the same time as the rediscovery within the sociology of development, but with an exclusive emphasis upon war and its impact on states. Moore's famous argument in *The Social Origins of Dictatorship and Democracy* contained the seeds of this rediscovery of the role of states in history. This rediscovery was foreshadowed by Gramsci, but these authors do not cite him. For Moore, countries like England and France developed capitalism first, and this led to bourgeois revolutions and democracy. Other states like Italy, Germany, Japan and Russia, desiring greater wealth and power to match those of England and France, carried out revolutions from above that led to what can be characterized as a state capitalism that resulted

---

62 Barrington Jr Moore, *Social Origins of Dictatorship and Democracy: Lord and Peasant in the Making of the Modern World* (Boston: Beacon Press, 2015). This work, first published in 1966, was republished in 1969, 1993 and then in 2015. Barrington Moore Jr was Theda Skocpol's supervisor. I learned from sociologist Donald von Eschen that Moore had worked on a Russia chapter for his book on dictatorship and democracy. A landmark volume for the Harvard School of political sociology was: Evans, Rueschemeyer, and Skocpol, *Bringing the State Back In*. An edited volume gathered work from all Barrington Moore's students and associates as a festschrift of sorts that was published in 1998, and re-published more recently: Theda Skocpol, *Democracy, Revolution, and History*, The Wilder House Series in Politics, History and Culture (Ithaca, New York: Cornell University Press, 2018).

63 John Anthony Hall dedicated his essay on nationalism to Barrington Moore Jr: John Anthony Hall, "Nationalisms: Classified and Explained," *Daedalus* 122, no. 3 (1993). Hall can be said to have built upon Barrington Moore Jr's work, recognizing him as an intellectual mentor, although Hall has had higher scholarly output.

in dictatorship rather than democracy.[64] Interstate conflict is important to Moore's theory, at least implicitly, because other states introduce capitalism from above in response to interstate conflict.

Later theories by the Harvard school of political sociology emphasized *war as a key element of interstate conflict*. Skocpol argued that modern revolutions that had a major impact upon important states, the French, Russian and Chinese revolutions, were caused, not by economic grievances alone, but at least in part by war, which exacerbated economic grievances through taxation and also weakened the state.[65] Tilly has generalized this argument in what has been called a 'bellicist' theory of the state, a theory that emphasizes war as a major activity defining and shaping the state. In Tilly's famous formulation 'war made the state and the state made war.'[66] Tilly essentially argued that the European states that emerged out of the Middle Ages had been shaped by war and were effectively war machines. In later centuries, the populations of these states began demanding a voice in the running of the state in return for the taxes they paid and also for their participation through conscription in the wars waged by these states. Tilly argued that there was a long process of contention between states and their populations, sometimes escalating into violence, other times taking more benign and ritualized forms that turned some states into democracies. Tilly characterized this process as a democratization process. Sydney Tarrow's and Tilly's argument that modern social movements engaged in contention with states played a key role in the emergence of democracy in modern states in the West fits within this broader bellicist argument.[67] Social movements fought for democracy because of the pressure that states waging wars applied on their population, in the form of taxation and conscription.

The bellicist theory of the state proposes a mechanism that explains the emergence of developmental states. Cohen's argument could be reformulated using complementary arguments from the bellicist theory of the state. I call this reformulation, for conciseness, the *Cohen-Tilly theory*. The main argument of this theory is that *war selects the states that are best for economic development and that encourage democratization*, out of the many states competing in a state system in which war is the main form of interstate conflict. This would

---

64   Moore, *Social Origins of Dictatorship and Democracy*.

65   Theda Skocpol, *States and Social Revolutions: A Comparative Analysis of France, Russia, and China*, Canto Classics (Cambridge and New York: Cambridge University Press, 2015).

66   Tilly, *Coercion, Capital and European States*.

67   Tilly, Tarrow, and McAdam, *Contention and Democracy in Europe*; Tilly and Tarrow, *Contentious Politics*.

be because the states that promote economic development become wealthier and thus also more militarily powerful. As implied by Moore, other states will be forced to promote economic development too or they will be defeated and in some cases taken over by the states that have already started promoting economic development. In other words, war provides the main selection mechanism. A similar mechanism would select states that promote democracy. More war would lead to more demands from the population for a voice in running the state, and this would lead to more democracy, at least under some circumstances. More democracy would further strengthen these states by creating consensus within the state. Other details of this selection mechanism have to be specified.

Tilly added to this argument the point that interstate conflict through war and the selection of a state type are related also to state size and pointed to the *tendency in European history towards the creation of larger states*. Arrighi made a similar argument for the hegemonic state in the modern state system.[68] Tilly's argument can be summarized as stating that *around the year 1,000 there were in Europe many different states, of many different types*, ranging from principalities to republics, from the smallest to relatively sizeable ones, many containing polities within themselves with varying degrees of autonomy, for example because many monarchies contained vassal fiefdoms within significant autonomy. These states included proto-nation-states that Tilly describes as national states to emphasize that they were different than nation-states, but eventually led to nation-states. Tilly was writing in the early 1990s, and argued that *nearing the year 2,000 Europe* was *divided into just a few nation-states, all relatively large, and all relatively centralized*, at least compared to their predecessors, with only a few remaining small states. Tilly emphasized that, out of the many competing different types of states, there emerged a new state type, the nation-state, that favored both economic development and democratization, and thus became the prevalent state type.[69] This state type would have been widely adopted because it was more successful than empires or city-states.

There are still limitations to the Cohen-Tilly theory, even in this form refined using the bellicist theory of the state. One limitation is that it *underestimates the continued importance of some small states* and the role they play in interstate

---

68 Arrighi pointed out that in the series of hegemonic states Netherlands, England, the United States, each was larger than its predecessor: Arrighi, *The Long Twentieth Century*. This is not a statistical series, but arguably still shows that, as the world economy and the state system increased in size, the hegemonic state had to be larger and more powerful in order to exercise hegemony.

69 Tilly, *Coercion, Capital and European States*.

conflict. Although there are only a few surviving principalities and small states, that are negligible in terms of both geographical area and population, small states like Luxemburg, and arguably also Liechtenstein and Andorra, nevertheless have acquired great importance, as tax havens, and also as playgrounds for elites, acting as sites that facilitate the emergence of international and ultimately world-elites. In these small states geographical proximity encourages close interaction, communication, and the emergence of ties amongst disparate elites, and ultimately of an elite culture and identity.[70] States like Ireland, larger but still relatively small, have become especially rich by acting as tax havens. Switzerland has acted sometimes as a tax haven, and it has a particular status vis-à-vis the European Union, not being part of it, but hosting very important European scientific centers like CERN. If other countries like Austria followed suit after Ireland in acting as tax havens, this could create problems for the European Community.[71] Other small European countries like Cyprus and Malta pose another problem yet, as they are small but have a vote in the European Community. Other small countries yet, like the San Marino Republic in Italy, have become the proving ground for experiments in education. *The Cohen-Tilly theory also cannot account for a very important feature of interstate conflict in the state system.* Arguably, in interstate conflict war has tended to predominate for a very long time, and thus destructive interstate conflict predominated over productive interstate conflict, and still does to our day. However, war is not the only selection mechanism at work in interstate conflict. *War is destructive and some states at least try to minimize it.* This is both because war is bad for economic development, and because it is bad for the population that pays the toll in human life and suffering that war takes. There are important examples of states that seek cooperation and peace rather than war, such as the expansion of diplomacy to limit conflict amongst Italian city-states, the creation of dynastic states by European aristocratic-military elites

---

70   It would be interesting to compare the role of these states in Europe to the role of territories in Great Britain, like the Isle of Man and Guernsey, that have enjoyed a special legal status. In Great Britain's case the crown is ultimately above these territories.

71   Small states in Europe present an especially serious challenge for the European Union, which could be characterized by the expression 'the tail wags the dog.' On these states, see: P. Christiaan Klieger, *The Microstates of Europe: Designer Nations in a Post-Modern World* (Lanham, Boulder, New York, Toronto, and Plymouth UK: Lexington Books, 2012). For a critique of the effects of tax havens, see: Gabriel Zucman and Thomas Piketty, *The Hidden Wealth of Nations: The Scourge of Tax Havens*, trans. Teresa Lavender Fagan (Chicago and London: University of Chicago Press, 2016). Margaret Thatcher's retrenchment policies arguably encouraged the strategy of some European states to attract investment by lowering taxes, thus acting effectively as tax havens.

through marriage alliances, and lastly, the creation of supra-national institutions like the European Union.

Italian Renaissance city-states are an early example of diplomacy aimed at limiting interstate conflict through war. Already during the Renaissance, Italian city-states were not just war machines but also provided public services like water to the urban population and recruited engineers and artists to build aqueducts, public buildings and to embellish cities. They had also begun to find a balance of power amongst themselves and pioneered permanent embassies, for example, to reduce the use of war in interstate conflict within the Italian peninsula.[72] The states in the Italian peninsula arguably formed a mini system, a small state system, fairly self-contained by the presence of the Alps, a very tall mountain range, acting as a natural barrier between Italy and the rest of Europe. For a number of reasons, this small state system was not as stable as it should have been. It was eventually incorporated into the emerging modern world system dominated by larger and more powerful north-western European proto nation-states. Why a proto nation-state did not emerge in the Italian peninsula, and Italian city-states did not manage to find permanent forms of cooperation, as the European Union has done in Europe in recent times, is an important question. They were arguably faced with macro collective action problems that were very difficult, or even impossible, to overcome. The number and type of states in the Italian peninsula was arguably such as to prevent the peaceful emergence of a proto nation-state, and also of permanent forms of cooperation, simply because there were too many states, that furthermore were very different, including city-state republics, kingdoms, and a theocratic state, the Vatican state centered in Rome.

European aristocratic-military elites, which sometimes acted as non-state agents, other times through their influence on the states that they ruled, constitute a special case in this effort to limit war. It has been suggested that European aristocracies at the head of dynastic states similarly found ways to cooperate with each other, and expanded state power by marriage alliances, as much as by war.[73] Moreover, at the end of major wars that engulfed Europe in

---

72   The idea that Renaissance Italian states pioneered diplomacy in Europe was first proposed by: Mattingly, *Renaissance Diplomacy*. This book was first published in 1955 and went through numerous reprints. Cipolla drew attention to the Florentine health board, set up in the late 1500s: Cipolla, *Miasmas and Disease*.

73   Lange suggested to me that this was a new and important topic in historical sociology, part of a critique of the bellicist school that several historical sociologists were working on. This critique involved making statistics regarding the expansion of European states due to marriage alliances, as opposed to expansion due to war. Philip Gorski has also drawn attention to another phenomenon, whereby state power expanded thanks to

the modern era, such as the Thirty Years War in the seventeenth century and the Napoleonic Wars at the turn between the eighteenth and the nineteenth centuries, there were settlements that sought to prevent the recurrence of war that were fairly successful for relatively long periods of time. The nineteenth century was characterized by what has been called the *Concert of Europe*, a name that describes the fact that interstate conflict through war declined, and cooperation prevailed over interstate conflict, thanks to a rapprochement between ruling aristocratic houses.[74] However, these ruling houses also presided over the senseless slaughter that occurred during the First World War and signally failed to prevent the rise of fascism and nazism and the even greater slaughter during the Second World War. It was partly for this reason that the European Union was established, in order to ensure cooperation and peace amongst European states, after the equilibrium found with the *Concert of Europe* failed and led to these two massively destructive world wars, which set economic development back by decades and caused huge loss of life and untold suffering.[75]

Nation-states in the European Union are a clear example of states trying to limit destructive interstate conflict and encourage competition instead of war. Political competition for greater influence in regional alliances like the West European Union, or in international institutions like the United Nations, is arguably an example of political competition that does not use war.[76] Some interstate conflict takes the form of economic competition and influence through economic power, and Germany within the European Union today is an example of this approach. In this context, it is important to remember that the small tax havens are a challenge both politically and economically because

---

culture: Philip S. Gorski, *The Disciplinary Revolution: Calvinism and the Rise of the State in Early Modern Europe* (Chicago: University of Chicago Press, 2003). This argument lends further weight to the idea that hegemony is very important to states.

74   John Lowe, *The Concert of Europe: International Relations 1814–70* (London: Hodder & Stoughton, 2000).

75   Martin Dedman, *The Origins and Development of the European Union 1945–1995: A History of European Integration* (London and New York: Routledge, 1996). Peace in Europe and social development were arguably the goals of the Ventotene Manifesto: Matthew D'Auria, "The Ventotene Manifesto: The Crisis of the Nation State and the Political Identity of Europe," in *European Identity and the Second World War*, ed. Menno Spiering and Michael Wintle (London and New York: Palgrave Macmillan).

76   The manner of enforcing interstate competition in Europe is debated by: Roland Vaubel, "Enforcing Competition among Governments: Theory and Application to the European Union," *Constitutional Political Economy* 10, no. 4 (1999). My point here is simply that the goal has to be interstate competition without war.

they undermine this competition.[77] Small island states or promontories like Gibraltar, Malta and Cyprus can also be crucially important from a strategic point of view. Gibraltar, at the entrance of the Mediterranean, is a dependency of the British crown and has always played a key role in controlling access to the Mediterranean and in facilitating supply lines. Malta, in the middle of the Mediterranean, was once very important strategically as a base for the Royal Navy. Cyprus, in the eastern Mediterranean, was also strategically important, and still today hosts a permanent base of the Royal Air Force, in Akrotiri.[78] Interestingly, now that Malta is part of the European Union, it has expanded cultural activities, and there is a Maltese institution, Link Campus University, based in Rome, despite being officially a Maltese institution.

The Cohen-Tilly theory can be *expanded to explain why nation-states are good for economic development and why they were established in cases like Italy and Germany.* Part of the answer is that nation-states were larger than city-states and regional states, and in many cases there was for nation-states a favorable *cost-benefit tradeoff* between the cost of maintaining a geographically large state, and the benefit of such a state, as emphasized by Alberto Alesina and Enrico Spolaore.[79] The benefit of larger states is that they encouraged industrial capitalism. Both Italy and Germany were created in the second half of the nineteenth century by unifying a number of smaller states, and then creating large internal markets and promoting industrialization.[80] This

---

77 Simon Bulmer and William E. Paterson, *Germany and the European Union: Europe's Reluctant Hegemon?* (London: Red Globe Prss, 2018).

78 On the importance of bases, see: Robert E. Harkavy, *Bases Abroad: The Global Foreign Military Presence,* SIPRI: Stockholm International Peace Research Institute (Oxford and New York: Oxford University Press, 1989). Navies needed bases to resupply, and more recently to refuel, and since they could easily defend small and medium-sized islands, the latter were ideal as bases.

79 Alberto Alesina, "The Size of Countries: Does It Matter?," *Journal of the European Economic Association* 1, no. 2–3 (2003). A discussion of these arguments for countries of all sizes is presented in: Alberto Alesina and Enrico Spolaore, *The Size of Nations* (Cambridge, Massachusetts, and Lndon, England: MIT Press, 2005).

80 The state, both through policies and customs union, and ultimately through removal of barriers, played a key role in German industrialization: Richard H. Tilly and Michael Kopsidis, *From Old Regime to Industrial State: A History of German Industrialization from the Eighteenth Century to World War I*, Markets and Governments in Economic History (Chicago and London: University of Chicago Press, 2020). In Italy an imperfect post-unification state did not help as much, and in some sectors even delayed industrialization: Gianni Toniolo, *An Economic History of Liberal Italy: 1850–1918*, Routledge Revivals (London and New York: Routledge, 2014). For a review of the debates on the role of nation-states in industrialization, see: Lars Magnusson, *Nation, State and the Industrial Revolution: The Visible Hand*, Routledge Explorations in Economic History (London and New York: Routledge, 2009).

is an instance of the positive contribution that political-military development gives to economic development. A very important driver of economic development in the modern era has been industrial capitalism. This involves the mass production of goods using advanced technology and large factories that benefit from economies of scale, whereby the greater the scale of production, the greater the economy. Industrial capitalism needs large and stable markets to absorb all of the goods it produces in a steady manner, without fluctuations. Small states, each with its currency, laws, and boundaries, are unable to promote industrial capitalism. This is because they lack sufficiently large internal markets to absorb a large number of mass-produced goods, and their access to external markets can be subject to fluctuations, particularly in a state system in which there is interstate conflict dominated by war. This is associated with embargos, which might have been a cause of the difficulties experienced by smaller states in early modern Europe, in the course of the 1500s and 1600s.[81]

By contrast, the fate of European territorial empires is a conundrum that simply cannot be answered using the Cohen-Tilly theory. At around the same time as Italy and Germany were created, *large European territorial empires tried to introduce industrial capitalism, but they all failed.* Territorial empires consisted of a large block of adjacent territories. They relied more upon land transportation than colonial empires. The European territorial empires were: the Habsburg Empire, consisting of Austria-Hungary and subject countries further east (in early modern times it included also Spain); the Ottoman Empire, consisting of Turkey and subject countries in the Balkans, the Middle East and North Africa; and the Romanov Empire, consisting of Russia and subject countries in Eastern Europe and throughout northern Eurasia.[82] These territorial empires present a problem for the Cohen-Tilly theory, because the introduction of industrial capitalism was accompanied by the splintering of these empires into many smaller states, a tendency that is exactly the opposite to the tendency towards larger states highlighted by Tilly, and towards capitalist states introduced by Cohen. Furthermore, large territorial empires were in

---

81   Ottoman treaties included trading agreements that were used as foreign policy tools. See Chapter 10 in: Gabor Agoston, *The Last Muslim Conquest: The Ottoman Empire and Its Wars in Europe* (Princeton and Oxford: Princeton University Press, 2021). Embargoes emerged as a policy tool in the Middle Ages, also in Ottoman-Western conflict: Stefan Stantchev, "The Medieval Origins of Embargo as a Policy Tool," *History of Political Thought* 33, no. 3 (2012).

82   The current comparative historical sociology of these empires was started by the edited volume: Karen Barkey and Mark von Hagen, eds., *After Empire: Multiethnic Societies and Nation-Building. The Soviet Union and the Russian, Ottoman, and Habsburg Empires* (London and New York: Routledge, 1997).

theory better suited to promote industrial capitalism than proto nation-states, because they had larger internal markets. In particular, they had large internal markets in one or more areas to begin with, as large as the internal markets that were created in Italy and Germany, and moreover their internal markets had the potential to become even larger, if the territorial empires thoroughly unified their territories. In a sense, this is what the European Union has been doing. The territorial empires in theory should have been able to do so too, even earlier, and should have been capable of promoting even more effectively industrial capitalism than the proto nation-states. Arguably, they were unable to do so because of the interaction between social conflict and interstate conflict during the transition to capitalism.

4   Cultural Sociology and Nation-States and Development

From the above discussion it should have become clear that state type is important, both to understand the dynamics of state systems, and also the effects of each state type on development. *The interaction between state and society, and also between state and markets,* including the provision of public goods, depends in part upon the state type. In brief, nation-states are better than empires at promoting cultural development, and through this, at promoting political-military and economic development. Cultural sociology can help us understand both why nation-states are better than empires at promoting development and why European territorial empires failed to advance industrial capitalism and broke up. Like political sociology, cultural sociology is another small sub-field within sociology in which there have been however a number of important contributions. Some of these contributions exclusively concern culture and cultural phenomena. I focus here instead on the interaction between culture and politics, and *how* both affect development. Some contributions, like those made to the study of nationalism, are *at the intersection between cultural sociology and political sociology.* I classify them as cultural sociology here because culture is central to them both as an important aspect of society and as something that explains other phenomena that are part of society. These theories are important to explain why nation-states are better than empires at promoting economic development, namely, because *nationalism, through cultural development, promotes capitalism,* and thus promotes economic development. They are also important to understand why European territorial empires broke up, which was due at least in part to the fact that their internal dynamics were susceptible to pressure from outside, since empires were less cohesive because they lacked nationalism. Furthermore, the internal dynamics of territorial empires started interacting with the dynamics of the world system. Territorial empires tried to introduce capitalism after states in the core had already done so and were seeking markets abroad. Territorial empires were thus incorporated into a world economy dominated by core states at around the same time they were trying to introduce capitalism, and later were drawn into the First World War, and were broken up as a result.

The contemporary sociological study of nationalism has come from what can arguably be described as *a London School of Economics, or LSE, school of the study of nationalism*. This school has drawn attention to the social bases of nationalism, with different members of the school drawing attention to different bases. Ernest Gellner, one of the three Gs of anthropology, namely, Gellner, Geertz, and Gilsenan, has led the emergence of the contemporary sociological study of nationalism.[83] This was through a landmark book that argued there are socio-economic bases of nationalism, which emerges in modern times due to the cultural requirements of modern industrial capitalism. Gellner suggested that nationalism arises only in countries with industrial capitalism, as a consequence of the occupational mobility required of individuals in industrial capitalism, which requires in its turn that citizens share a single culture enabling mobility. Gellner called this culture a 'universal high culture' because it is shared by all and it shares such traits of high culture as literacy.[84] Anthony

---

83   I address Gellner's work below. Geertz is one of the initiators of the cultural turn, and a promoter of interpretive anthropology: Clifford Geertz, *The Interpretation of Cultures* (New York: Basic Books, 1973); *Local Knowledge: Further Essays in Interpretive Anthropology* (New York: Basic Books, 1983). The latter is comparable to *verstehen* sociology, which involves understanding the motivations of individuals, including their culture. *Verstehen* sociology was advocated by Max Weber: William T Tucker, "Max Weber's Verstehen," *The Sociological Quarterly* 6, no. 2 (1965). It has recently made a comeback: Ronald Hitzler and Reiner Keller, "On Sociological and Common-Sense Verstehen," *Current Sociology* 37, no. 1 (1989); Catherine J. Turco and Ezra W. Zuckerman, "Verstehen for Sociology: Comment on Watts," *American Journal of Sociology* 122, no. 4 (2017). Some have argued that *verstehen* sociology can assist with the incorporation of local knowledge in sociology and in development policies: Akinpelu Olanrewaju Olutayo, "'Verstehen,' Everyday Sociology and Development: Incorporating African Indigenous Knowledge," *Critical Sociology* 40, no. 2 (2014). Michael Gilsenan has provided a landmark cultural study of narratives of violence in parts of Lebanon: Michael Gilsenan, *Lords of the Lebanese Marches: Violence and Narrative in an Arab Society* (Berkeley and Los Angeles: University of California Press, 1996).

84   Gellner's classical formulation of this argument was provided in: Ernest Gellner, *Nations and Nationalism*, Cornell Paperbacks (Ithaca, New York: Cornell University Press, 1983). This went to a second edition. Gellner's posthumous work on nationalism takes a more nuanced approach that recognizes the importance of culture in its own right, including cultural encounters and cultural transmission: *Nationalism*, Master Minds Series (London: Phoenix, 1998).

D. Smith and Daniele Conversi have proposed what are sometimes seen as alternative theories of nationalism compared to Gellner's. Smith suggested that nationalism has roots in the pre-industrial cultures of ethnic groups whose cultures are used as the socio-cultural bases of national cultures.[85] Conversi has proposed that there are socio-military bases of nationalism. It is not economic mobility that requires a national culture, but military mobilization, which brings together and into close contact and interaction large numbers of individuals from different regions of a country, who are mobilized for service in the country's army. Conversi's theory of nationalism is close to Tilly's bellicist theory of the state.[86] These three contributions to our understanding of nationalism are often seen as opposed because of the following false dichotomies: nationalism is a modern phenomenon, as suggested by Gellner, or has ancient roots, as suggested by Smith; the social bases of nationalism are in the economy, as suggested by Gellner, or in the military, as suggested by Conversi. Far from being opposed, these theories are complementary. For example, a modern industrial economy can leverage pre-existing ethnic cultures in order to build more speedily a national culture.[87] Mobilization in a national army can serve to spread the national language and national culture, which then

---

85   Smith's earlier formulation regarding the ethnic origins of nations can be found in: Anthony D. Smith, *The Ethnic Origins of Nations* (Oxford and Malden, Massachusetts: Blackwell, 1991). A recent reformulation that takes into account criticisms can be found in: *Ethno-Symbolism and Nationalism: A Cultural Approach* (New York and London: Routledge, 2009).

86   Conversi's argument was couched as a critique of Gellner's argument: Daniele Conversi, "Homogenisation, Nationalism and War: Should We Still Read Ernest Gellner?," *Nations and Nationalism* 13, no. 3 (2007); "'We Are All Equals!' Militarism, Homogenization and 'Egalitarianism'in Nationalist State-Building (1789–1945)," *Ethnic and Racial Studies* 31, no. 7 (2008). Conversi has also worked on what could be called, paraphrasing Mann, the dark side of nationalism: "Genocide, Ethnic Cleansing and Nationalism," *Handbook of Nations and Nationalism. London: Sage Publications* (2006). I think this is a more accurate characterization than Mann's suggestion that democracy has a dark side: Michael Mann, *The Dark Side of Democracy: Explaining Ethnic Cleansing* (Cambridge and New York: Cambridge University Press, 2005). Everything can be portrayed as having a dark side. I believe that ethnic cleansing arises from the manipulation of national culture, and it is done against democracy, not because of democracy. I had an interesting conversation with a political scientist who had studied at Padua University and who expressed a similar view to Mann's. The political scientist argued that too many discordant views are bad for a state and thus that there can be 'too much democracy.' This is an argument that is being made in Italy by those who want to rehabilitate fascism, claiming that it fought divisive tendencies in Italian culture. I believe this conflation of diversity with division is both misleading and problematic.

87   Haim Gerber, "The Limits of Constructedness: Memory and Nationalism in the Arab Middle East," *Nations and Nationalism* 10, no. 3 (2004).

helps the emerging industrial economy. Both of these causal chains can be expanded upon and can be incorporated in a theory regarding the impact of cultural development upon other forms of development.

Because these contributions are complementary, I refer to them, for conciseness, as the *Gellner-Smith-Conversi theory of nationalism*. This theory is especially useful to understand the effects of cultural development on other types of development, and why nation-states are successful at promoting development. This is because they are successful at promoting cultural development. *The concept of cultural development* formalizes ideas implicit in Gellner's notion of a universal high culture. Cultural development includes the following three important components: first, the spread of a single language over a territory; second, the spread of literacy and numeracy amongst a population; and third, the spread of a sense of identity amongst the majority of the population over a territory, which gives cohesion to a country. *Political-military development can contribute to cultural development.* Conversi's argument can in fact be reformulated as an argument regarding the impact of political-military development upon cultural development, because states that mobilize citizen armies contribute to spreading a single language and identity amongst the citizenry mobilized for service in armies, and in some cases also literacy and numeracy. In modern times states contribute also to higher education via military academies, at least amongst officer. Literacy and numeracy and higher education amongst soldiers and officers then contributes to the spread of the single identity and language amongst the citizenry. The introduction of mass conscription during the Napoleonic Wars and the vast numbers of citizens mobilized thereafter gave a major contribution to the spread a common language and of a sense of identity, which then led to nationalism in various European countries.[88] There can thus be a mutual influence between cultural development and political-military development, and a feedback mechanism whereby cultural development then contributes to political-military development. Figure 3 represents all these contributions, including the contributions that both cultural development and political-military development give to economic development.

One instance of the feedback mechanism is that *cultural development can contribute to political-military development* because a common language, literacy, and a common identity all give cohesion to society and give the state that knows how to leverage these factors greater military capabilities. Because of

---

88   Eugen Weber, *Peasants into Frenchmen: The Modernization of Rural France, 1870–1914* (Stanford, California: Stanford University Press, 1976).

cultural development

Public goods associated with nationalism:
literacy and numeracy
national language used throughout a territory
Other public goods:
education in economics
education in engineering and technical subjects
research and technology

a

b

Public goods associated with nationalism
Other public goods

political-military development

Political-military aspects of markets creation:
internal peace and stability
Geopolitical aspects of markets creation:
size of territory over which the market exists
transportation
Legal aspects of markets creation:
standard laws enforced throughout a territory

c

economic development

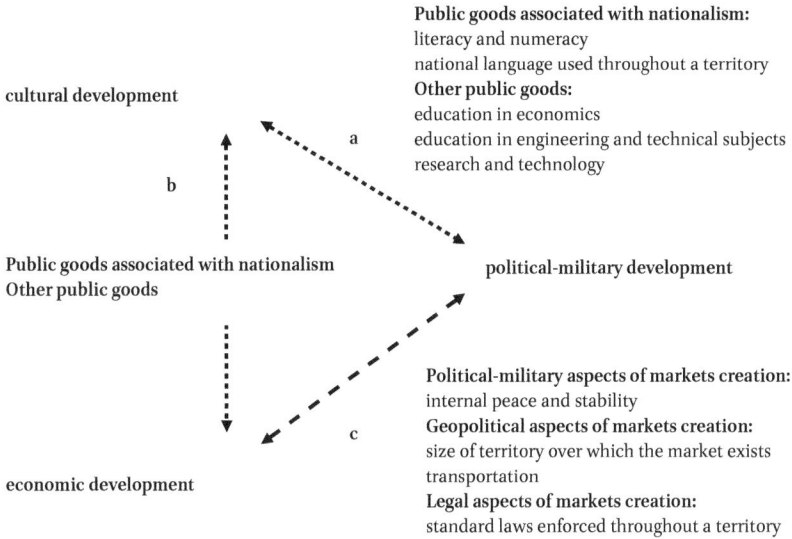

FIGURE 3   Non-economic contributions to economic development by nation-states

the feedback mechanism, cultural development and political-military development can reinforce each other. This feedback mechanism is represented in Figure 3 by the double arrow in segment a. There are feedback mechanisms between all three types of development. *The contribution that nation-states give to economic development* can usefully be divided into two parts, represented in Figure 3 by segments a and b, both of which concern the same public goods, and by segment c, which concerns the creation of markets. The part represented by segment c concerns *the constituent contribution given to economic development by nation-states, through the creation of large internal markets* that enable industrial capitalism, and through it economic development, as introduced above for the cases of Italy and Germany. In modern times the European Union and trading blocs like ASEAN have been similarly set up in order to create large and stable markets, and in order to compensate for the limitations of small nation-states.[89] Segment c is marked by a different arrow

---

89   On trading blocs, see: May T. Yeung, Nicholas Perdikis, and William A. Kerr, *Regional Trading Blocs in the Global Economy: The EU and ASEAN* (Cheltenham, UK and Northampton, Massachusetts: Edward Elgar, 1999). One focus of the debates on trading blocs is whether the global economy is being broken up into discreet regional economies. Here I am drawing attention to another phenomenon, associated with Arrighi's view that the hegemons grew in size, stressing that internal markets in a world system

than segments a and b in order to emphasize that its contribution is altogether different than the contribution of segments a and b. I refer to segment c as a *constituent* contribution because internal peace and stability, and standard laws enforced throughout a territory, are arguably more than a public good, they are constitutive of markets, and furthermore, they are part of the way in which a country works, not just markets within it.[90] Segment c thus represents the contribution from political-military development *directly* to economic development by creating markets, in particular large and stable markets associated with internal peace and stability, so that the markets are not subject to fluctuations or to market failures.

Segments a and b represent *the contribution from political-military development and from cultural development to economic development through public goods*. Technically, education is not a public good, but perhaps it is more accurate to say that it has a public good component to the extent that, for example, a certain level of education in most countries is available to everyone, and any company that hires workers in a given country can make use of the education that those workers have. Similarly, higher education is not a public good, but some research produced by universities, especially fundamental research that is accessible to anyone with the required knowledge, is arguably a public good.[91] Segments a and b effectively reformulate Gellner's argument by suggesting that *cultural development can contribute to economic development through public goods like* a shared language, literacy and numeracy that are necessary to industrial capitalism. Recently, Hall and his collaborators have shown, although not in these words, that cultural development contributes to both political-military development and economic development.[92] This can

---

riven with conflict are indispensable to provide protection against market fluctuations due to interstate conflict. Arguably the hegemons grew in size also because their internal markets provided the stability needed for economies of scale. Some of these questions are touched upon in: Josep Maria Colomer, "The Building of the American and European Empires," *Journal of Political Power* 4, no. 3 (2011).

90   I delve into the argument that laws and internal peace and stability are constitutive of markets in sections 3.3 and 3.4 below.

91   A good review of the arguments as to whether higher education is a public or a private good is provided by: Gareth Williams, "Higher Education: Public Good or Private Commodity?," *London Review of Education* 14, no. 1 (2016). Williams suggests that the best approach to higher education is neither a state monopoly nor an unrestricted market. For the different but related argument that higher education should work for the good of the public, see: Gert Biesta, "Philosophy of Education for the Public Good: Five Challenges and an Agenda," *Educational Philosophy and Theory* 44, no. 6 (2012).

92   Hall and his collaborators Patsiurko and Campbell have carried out empirical studies suggesting that a single national culture is associated with greater economic performance: Natalka Patsiurko, John L. Campbell, and John Anthony Hall, "Measuring Cultural

involve several causal chains, some of which have to do with the functioning of markets. Cultural development *enables occupational mobility*, as suggested by Gellner, and this mobility is especially important to capitalism, a society of perpetual growth within which competition leads to what economist Joseph Schumpeter called 'creative destruction,' the destruction of companies that are not economically viable and the creation of new ones that are more competitive.[93] The importance of cultural development to occupational mobility can also be due to the fact that in industrial capitalism there is mobility of workers from one company to another simply as part of career development. Lastly, cultural development also *facilitates the interaction of large numbers of individuals in large markets*, both labour markets and markets for goods, that is distinctive of industrial capitalism. The converse is also true. Interaction in markets has the effect of encouraging cultural development, by encouraging the spread of a single language, for example.

All of this suggests reasons why nation-states were successful, but it does not explain why they were more successful than empires. To explain this difference, we need to introduce *theories of empires, and the concept of internal dynamics, or dynamics that are internal to a state.* This argument is complementary to the argument that the state is not monolithic and constitutes a system, a point that is especially true in the case of large empires with very different cultures and administrations throughout their territories, part of their distinctive institutions and institutional histories, that sometime constitute

---

Diversity: Ethnic, Linguistic and Religious Fractionalization in the OECD," 35, no. 2 (2012); "Nation-State Size, Ethnic Diversity and Economic Performance in the Advanced Capitalist Countries," *New Political Economy* 18, no. 6 (2013). These studies also introduce additional concepts to measure cultural diversity, like fractionalization. I think instead it is important to encourage diversity and minimize divisions. The two, diversity and division, should not be conflated, and one does not necessarily lead to the other. I address this point in the book on the humanist theory of society. The problem of fragmentation that communitarian philosophies like Charles Taylor's can present for countries was addressed by: Mark Redhead, "Charles Taylor's Deeply Diverse Response to Canadian Fragmentation: A Project Often Commented on but Seldom Explored," *Canadian Journal of Political Science / Revue canadienne de science politique* 36, no. 1 (2003).

93 Hugo Reinert has suggested that the expression 'creative destruction' was introduced by sociologist Werner Sombart and was popularized by Nietzsche: Hugo Reinert and Erik S. Reinert, "Creative Destruction in Economics: Nietzsche, Sombart, Schumpeter," in *Friedrich Nietzsche (1844–1900)* (Berlin and Heidelberg: Springer, 2006). Arguably the most famous use of the expression however was by economist Joseph Schumpeter, as set out in: J. A. Schumpeter, *Capitalism, Socialism and Democracy* (New York and London: Routledge, 2013).

altogether different segmental states.[94] One such theory draws attention to a very important dynamic internal to territorial empires, whereby there was a long contention over the distribution of power between the central authority and peripheral administrations. It also draws attention to the political culture of empires. This theory has been put forward by Karen Barkey, a sociologist who has led the emergence of the contemporary sociological study of empires. Barkey's pioneering work has drawn attention to the accommodating culture of multiethnic empires like the Ottoman empire. She has introduced such key concepts as the 'bargaining' between center and periphery that characterized the Ottoman empire during much of its long history, and the change over time between the power of the central authority and peripheral administrations.[95] However, Barkey has oddly glossed over such appalling crimes as the Smyrna massacre of Greeks under Ottoman rule, implicitly attributing such crimes not to empires but to rising ethnic conflict stoked up by Turkish and Greek nationalisms. There is almost a longing in Barkey's work for a return to the age of empires, idealized and seen as tolerant of cultural differences, in contrast to nation-states that imposed cultural homogeneity in many parts of the world more or less violently.[96]

---

94   Roeder argues that these segmental states where the sites in which nationalism emerged in the Soviet Union, and suggests this argument can be generalized to other empires: Philip G. Roeder, *Where Nation-States Come From: Institutional Change in the Age of Nationalism* (Princeton and Oxford: Princeton University Press, 2007). Spruyt has focused on institutions in the core of European colonial empires, and suggested that in cases in which there was fragmentation of institutions in the core, which enabled some elites to hold vetoes, this led to stubborn resistance to decolonization: Hendrik Spruyt, *Ending Empire: Contested Sovereignty and Territorial Partition* (Ithaca and London: Cornell University Press, 2018).

95   Karen Barkey, *Bandits and Bureaucrats: The Ottoman Route to State Centralization* (Ithaca, New York: Cornell University Press, 1994).

96   Barkey's history of the Ottoman empire emphasizes its tolerance of differences, and focuses on state-society networks: *Empire of Difference: The Ottomans in Comparative Perspective* (Cambridge and New York: Cambridge University Press, 2008). Studies of the local press in Smyrna/Izmir suggest that it did not participate in tensions between the central authority and the local administration, which was closer to local communities, including Greek communities: Feryal Tansug, "The Greek Community of Izmir/Smyrna in an Age of Transition: The Relationship between Ottoman Centre-Local Governance and the Izmir/Smyrna Greeks, 1840–1866," *British Journal of Middle Eastern Studies* 38, no. 1 (2011). However, through committees and other venues, there was rising tension between the central authority and the local Greek community: Vangelis Kechriotis, "Civilization and Order: Middle-Class Morality among the Greek-Orthodox in Smyrna/Izmir at the End of the Ottoman Empire," in *Social Transformation and Mass Mobilization in the Balkan and Eastern Mediterranean Cities (1900–1923)*, ed. Andreas Lyberatos (Irakleio: Crete University Press, 2013). The Ottoman administration employed a variety

I do not share this view of empires as inherently more tolerant than nation-states, and in this project I emphasize that some empires, in particular European colonial empires, were responsible for as much violence as nation-states, and I especially emphasize that *there can be modern multiethnic polities that are not empires*. Barkey's theory, however, has the undoubted merit of drawing attention to specific features of the culture of territorial empires. She *characterizes territorial empires as multiethnic polities and implicitly contrasts them with nation-states* understood, as per Smith's theory, as being built around one ethnicity. Smith's argument can be reformulated as stating that cultural development will advance more quickly when there are pre-existing common cultural bases, for example linguistic bases whereby all the languages or dialects spoken in an area belong to a single language family. Smith's argument is more tenable if we focus on language, rather than ethnicity. Italy was arguably constituted of many different ethnicities that had begun speaking variants of Vulgar Latin following conquest by Rome. Other ethnicities settled in Italy following the barbarian invasions but they too began speaking variants of Vulgar Latin.[97] These and other similar cases suggest that, for a variety of reasons, *nation-states start from a more unified cultural base than empires and can better succeed in promoting cultural development*, that is, a single language, and a shared identity, within a given territory, compared to empires. This begins to suggest a reason as to why European territorial empires were less successful than nation-states and all broke up in the process of introducing industrial capitalism. Since empires are multiethnic, and industrial capitalism requires a certain level of cultural unification, empires fail to promote both capitalism and nationalism, and tend to break-up more easily than nation-states.

Another theory of empires that can help explain why they were less successful than nation-states focuses on the relationship between empires and democracy. Recently, the *argument has been made that there can be 'democratic*

---

of strategies to elicit allegiance, some of which stoked up conflict: Kamal Soleimani, *Islam and Competing Nationalisms in the Middle East, 1876–1926*, The Modern Muslim World (Cham, Switzerland: Springer, 2016).

97   On the history of the modern Italian language as a defining aspect of national culture, see: Tullio De Mauro, *Storia Linguistica dell'Italia Unita—Storia Linguistica dell'Italia Repubblicana*, Biblioteca Storica Laterza (Bari: Editori Laterza, 2017). Gramsci, like many Italian intellectuals, emphasized that modern Italian played a key role in defining a national culture, since around the time of unification in 1861 only a small percentage of Italians spoke the national language, and Italian was codified and spread only after unification, contributing to national identity. On Gramsci and language, see: Alessandro Carlucci, *Gramsci and Languages: Unification, Diversity, Hegemony* (Chicago: Haymarket Books, 2014).

empires' that could be successful at providing large internal markets, and also be viable multiethnic states, if only these empires gave autonomy to regional governments that are closer to the ethnically-defined peoples that they administer. This suggestion was made by Catalan political theorist Josep Colomer, who has described the United States and the European Union as 'democratic empires'.[98] I do not share this view of empires either, and below I argue that there is only one way in which empires have been democratic, and it was by accepting democracy at home but imposing empire abroad. I argue below that this eventually leads to undermining democracy at home too. This is because external dynamics that are part of interstate conflict can interact in very destructive ways with internal dynamics that are part of social conflict. This is part of the transition problems that accompany the introduction of capitalism. *The most important question to answer is not why empires are not democratic, but why empires cannot become democratic*, and it entails that we have to take into account political processes and the transition from one social organization to another, and from one political form to another. This is the question that we need to answer if we want to explain the breakup of the Habsburg, Ottoman and Romanov empires. This question is complementary to the question as to why empires failed to introduce and to advance capitalism, and the related question raised by Cipolla, amongst others, regarding the economic decline of empires, which facilitated their defeat and eventual breakup by capitalist states.[99] The answer to these two questions is that dynamics in the interstate system interacted in a destructive way with dynamics internal to territorial empires, in which there was a long-standing contention in the division of power between the central authority and peripheral administrations. The interaction between the external and internal dynamics was such that there was eventually a decisive shift in favor of power being concentrated

---

98   Josep Maria Colomer, *Great Empires, Small Nations: The Uncertain Future of the Sovereign State* (New York and London: Routledge, 2007). Colomer also looks at the history of these 'empires' in: "The Building of the American and European Empires." Alesina argued that both benefits and costs determine the size of an empire, and lists amongst the benefits economies of scale, internalization of externalities, and military strength, counterbalancing the costs that arise from heterogeneity of population: Alesina, "The Size of Countries: Does It Matter?." To these costs we should add the costs of war, which rise with the size of the empire, and greater borders, or greater geographic dispersal in the case of colonial empires. A discussion of these arguments for countries of all sizes is presented in: Alesina and Spolaore, *The Size of Nations*.

99   The question of the economic decline of empires was introduced by: Cipolla, *The Economic Decline of Empires*. This book was first published in 1970. In this book Cipolla also addresses the economic decline of Italy, which is central also to Toniolo's work: Toniolo, "An Overview of Italy's Economic Growth."

in the hands of peripheral administrations, and in the presence of interstate conflict this destroyed territorial empires.

This answer builds upon Gellner's theory of nationalism and it focuses upon the following mechanism. This is a mechanism that emphasizes the importance of culture and of social structures to collective action, and the need to model individual behavior by taking into account the cultural and structural foundations of social interaction, both of which are part of the structural-foundational view of social interaction that I sketch in greater detail in the book on the humanist theory of society. It can be integrated within a theory of the options that populations have when faced with the centralization of power within a state and growing demands by the state from society. Economist Albert O. Hirschman proposed that we should conceptualize the options the masses have in dealing with states as being exit, voice, and loyalty, in what can be referred to as an EVL *model of the interaction between the state and the masses within a country* that is especially useful to understand empires and nation-states, and more in general conflict in locations outside the core.[100] If we apply this model to empires negotiating the transition from a pre-capitalist economy to industrial capitalism, and the associated bargaining between the state and masses, then the following changes alter the options that the masses have in practice. In traditional societies loyalty tends to prevail because the masses do not have the means to challenge elite rule and the other options are effectively precluded. In modern societies the other two options become available, and cultural development heavily influences which one is chosen. In modern societies military mobilization and industrialization contribute to the emergence of nationalism and to greater or lesser cultural development. A possible explanation of the failure of empires to advance industrial capitalism is that they tend to be too big and stratified to develop embedded autonomy in state-society relations. Here I just want to emphasize that different state types have different effects upon cultural development, and in particular that empires are less successful at promoting cultural development.

In nation-states nationalism tends to lead to seeking voice and democracy. Nationalism helps to give rise to democracy because a common language and a shared sense of identity over a territory help the masses engage in collective action and demand a voice in the running of the state. This is preferred

---

100 Albert O. Hirschman, *Exit, Voice, and Loyalty: Responses to Decline in Firms, Organizations, and States*, American Council of Learned Societies, Humanities (Cambridge, Massachusetts and London: Harvard University Press, 1970). I reformulate the argument in terms of interactions between elites and masses because of the focus of this book. I revise and expand upon the EVL model in Section 7.4 below.

to seeking exit, because language and a shared identify make the masses also committed to the nation-state, and thus ultimately leads to democracy. *In European territorial empires,* all of which were multiethnic polities, the masses tended to choose exit and the breakup of the empire rather voice. Multiethnic polities are made up of vast areas with many cultural differences, and the latter tend to lead to many nationalisms, which lead to seeking exit rather than voice, because common collective action is made harder by the lack of a common culture, and a commitment to the multiethnic polity is undermined. This argument can help us *reformulate Skocpol's theory of social revolutions to include a theory of nationalist revolutions* in the following manner. In multiethnic polities, military mobilization and industrialization lead to the weakening of the central authority, and this leads to the breakup of the empire if any war further undermines the empire. *Breakup occurs because of a combination of the effects of war and transition organizational problems that affect the central authority.* The weakening of the central authority does not cause the breakup in and of itself. The Habsburg and the Ottoman empires broke up only after defeat in the First World War, whereas the Romanov empire, which had reinvented itself as the Soviet Union, broke up after defeat in the Cold War.[101] This theory can be further refined within a broader theory of development and democracy that takes into account hegemony, since the latter has a cultural component, and also relies upon social structures, all of which are important for collective action. This theory would have to take into account also the political dynamics of interstate conflict in the state system, because these empires all broke up after conflicts that occurred on a global scale.

5   The Interaction between External and Internal Dynamics

In order to understand the interaction between external and internal dynamics, a part of the interaction between interstate and social conflict, it is necessary to use the concept of *incorporation in the world economy and a number of related concepts, including incorporation in the state core.* These concepts help

---

101   This argument is analogous to the argument put forward by Skocpol for social revolutions: Skocpol, *States and Social Revolutions.* However, it emphasizes exit instead of voice. I explain revolutions as an instance of voice in Section 7.4 below. Some authors have pointed to an effort under the Soviet Union to accommodate minorities, which prevented an earlier breakup: Terry Dean Martin, *The Affirmative Action Empire: Nations and Nationalism in the Soviet Union, 1923–1939* (Ithaca, New York: Cornell University Press, 2001).

explain a number of cultural phenomena that arise in this process such as sectarianism and shifting employment and the associated culture. The concept of *incorporation in the state core* generalizes an important concept from World Systems Theory, namely, the concept of incorporation in the world economy. It is useful to expand this concept by suggesting that there is *a more general incorporation in the world system that has economic, cultural and political-military aspects*. The concept of *incorporation in the world economy,* first proposed by Wallerstein, was researched in detail for a specific geographical area by sociologist Resat Kasaba in his study of the Ottoman empire.[102] Countries that are incorporated in the world economy could be introducing capitalism of their own accord, typically for local markets, or could be based on non-capitalist economies, for example economies with limited or no private property. The expansion of long-distance trade relations and export-oriented capitalism, leading to incorporation in the world economy of areas in the semi-periphery and periphery, often brings about marked and very fast social changes that weaken civil society, for example because traditional agriculture and village communities, or traditional trade practices and trade guilds, are destroyed by the rapid expansion of production for international markets.[103] This can have long-lasting consequences that accentuate social conflict and negatively affect both development and democracy.

Incorporation in the world economy is accompanied by incorporation in world culture and incorporation in the state system, although these two processes both tend to be prominent at different times and to proceed more slowly. Incorporation in the state system tends to be the last phase, at least in some cases. Cultural contact and *incorporation in world culture* deeply affect civil society outside the core. This is because incorporation in world culture might undermine the authority of traditional intellectuals, and in particular of religious and other cultural elites, leading to a reaction that can be especially marked on the other side of the frontier, thus making these elites, and the local social groups they have ties to, more or less friendly towards states in the core, depending on whether they benefit or lose from the deep social changes introduced by increasing trade and cultural contact with states in

102   Resat Kasaba, *The Ottoman Empire and the World Economy: The Nineteenth Century,* SUNY Series in Middle Eastern Studies (State University of New York Press, 1988).

103   James A. Reilly, "Status Groups and Propertyholding in the Damascus Hinterland, 1828–1880," *International Journal of Middle East Studies* 21, no. 4 (1989); "From Workshops to Sweatshops: Damascus Textiles and the World-Economy in the Last Ottoman Century," *Review (Fernand Braudel Center)* 16, no. 2 (1993).

the core.[104] Incorporation in world culture heightens social conflict between the social groups negatively affected by social change and other social groups, and between some of these social groups and agents from the state core such as merchants and imperialists, also by acting on perceptions of threats. *Incorporation in the state system* occurs when states in other parts of the world are conquered or become allies of states in the state core, however distant they are from this core. Within Western Europe, which was involved all along in the state system, and where countries bordered with states in the state core, there was also, sooner or later, incorporation in the state core, as the state core expanded.

Incorporation into the state system can be especially harmful *in conjunction with divide-and-conquer and divide-and-rule tactics by imperialists*, which accentuate social conflict within the country that is subjected to these tactics. A more complete theory of the effects of states on development than Lange's would have to address these effects, because private companies and unscrupulous individuals with vast amounts of power had a huge impact on the territories they conquered and controlled. For example, private companies under especially unscrupulous individuals could take over entire countries and run them in a manner similar to indirect rule, through personal rule that introduced *especially harmful divide-and-conquer tactics*. Such was the case with the British South Africa Company ran by Rhodes.[105] Rhodes and his company conquered vast areas corresponding to modern-day Zambia and Zimbabwe, in southern Africa, and made them part of Rhodesia, a state that was Rhodes' private property and thus was not subject to true legal restraints. This lack of legal restraint might have enabled the massacres that took place during some of the wars that Rhodes undertook, for example in the First and Second Matabele

---

104   Part of the explanation of the rise of sectarianism in the Middle East during the nineteenth century is that the expansion of trade with the West made use, and in some cases enriched, an emergent Christian bourgeoisie. This sectarian conflict was arguably class conflict, or had a large class conflict component, but the ethno-religious aspect predominated because of the visibility of this new Christian bourgeoisie and its association with British and French merchants, and also because of Ottoman laws regarding Christian communities and Western interference. This conflict eventually contributed to the demise of the Ottoman empire: Fatma Muge Gocek, *Rise of the Bourgeoisie, Demise of Empire: Ottoman Westernization and Social Change* (Oxford and New York: Oxford University Press, 1996).

105   On sir Cecil Rhodes see: John Flint, *Cecil Rhodes* (New York: Warner Books, Hachette Book Group, 2009); R. I. Rotberg, *The Founder: Cecil Rhodes and the Pursuit of Power* (Oxford and New York: Oxford University Press, USA, 1988).

Wars.[106] The private companies had Royal Charters that gave them the right in British law to act in a given territory. It seems possible that Gordon's and Rhodes' activities, some of which defied the British government, had backing from other authorities, possibly Queen Victoria, and effectively bypassed the British government and also the parliament, showing they had little concern for British law, and no legal restraint in the colonies they conquered.[107] I argue below that these imperialists in the long run might have had, and might still have, negative impacts also upon development and democracy in Great Britain and the West more in general.

Trade with the West, whether part of conquest by European colonial empires or not, is also associated with the *rise of sectarianism throughout the nineteenth century*. Lebanon and Syria, Saudi Arabia and Egypt, as well as northern India, were all affected by the emergence of sectarian identities and by a wave of sectarian riots after the arrival of Western merchants and Western missionaries, a cultural phenomenon that was associated with European colonial ventures.[108] Sectarianism might be thought of as an ancient phenomenon, but it was

---

106   There are only popular accounts of the Matabele wars in English: Chris Ash, *Matabele: The War of 1893 and the 1896 Rebellions* (Pinetown, South Africa: 30° South Publishers, 2016). C. Peers, *The African Wars: Warriors and Soldiers of the Colonial Campaigns* (Barnsley, South Yorkshire, and Haverton, Pennsylvania: Pen & Sword Books, 2011). These wars resulted in large massacres despite the fact that the Matabele had British Army rifles, and the massacres resulted from the fact that forces of the British South Africa Company had Maxim machine guns with huge firepower for the time. The attacks against the Matabele might have been unprovoked and illegal.

107   On controversial imperial wars during Queen Victoria's reign, see: Stephen M. Miller, *Queen Victoria's Wars: British Military Campaigns, 1857–1902* (Cambridge and New York: Cambridge University Press, 2021). On Queen Victoria's private persona and its influence on her policies, see: Adrienne Munich, *Queen Victoria's Secrets* (New York: Columbia University Press, 1996); Paula Bartley, *Queen Victoria* (London and New York: Routledge, 2016).

108   There are many studies of the rise of sectarianism in Lebanon, for example: Leila Tarazi Fawaz, *An Occasion for War: Civil Conflict in Lebanon and Damascus in 1860* (Berkeley and Los Angeles: University of California Press, 1994). Ussama Makdisi, *The Culture of Sectarianism: Community, History, and Violence in Nineteenth-Century Ottoman Lebanon* (Berkeley and Los Angeles: University of California Press, 2000). Both Juan Cole and Christopher Bayly approached this subject from a comparative perspective that is complementary to World Systems Theory: Juan Ricardo Cole, "Of Crowds and Empires: Afro-Asian Riots and European Expansion, 1857–1882," *Comparative Studies in Society and History* 31, no. 1 (1989); Christopher Alan Bayly, *Imperial Meridian: The British Empire and the World, 1780–1830*, Studies in Modern History (London: Longman, 1989). This comparative approach was later embraced by many scholars, for example the contributors to: Leila Tarazi Fawaz, Christopher Alan Bayly, and Robert Ilbert, eds., *Modernity and Culture: From the Mediterranean to the Indian Ocean* (New York: Columbia University Press, 2002).

instead a modern phenomenon that built upon older ethno-religious divisions. *Deliberate divide-and-conquer tactics worsened the effects of trade and sectarianism,* all of which contributed to creating poverty and violence traps.[109] They were often used by imperialists from Europe, including in India before the establishment of the Raj in 1858, when colonies in India were placed directly under the British Crown. Imperial rule in India relied to a greater or lesser extent upon local administrators and native informants. Historian Christopher Bayly has pointed to the importance of intelligence and communications for British rule in India, and to the recruitment of runners to convey information, and of native informants to provide local knowledge. These individuals, runners and informants, came respectively from the Dalit, the untouchables outside castes, and from the Muslim minority.[110] Imperialists from Great Britain would have naturally selected intelligence agents from these groups, because, being outside castes or from religious minorities, they could not mobilize most of Indian society against the rule of the Raj if they decided to rebel. Members of the Sikh community might have been used in a similar manner, contributing in the past to stereotyping the Sikh as violent, thus further isolating them.[111]

---

109   Makdisi, *The Culture of Sectarianism.* There was also competition for influence between Russian, French, and English interests, all infiltrating the Ottoman empire, and all constituting differences sources of patronage and protection for local agents. Arguably, violence facilitated Western infiltration of these areas and the competition for influence in the region between different European powers (Great Britain, France, Russia) had the same effect as divide-and-conquer tactics. The Levantine trade with Europe had been mostly peaceful from the early seventeenth to the early nineteenth century.

110   See especially Chapter 2 in: Christopher Alan Bayly, *Empire and Information: Intelligence Gathering and Social Communication in India, 1780–1870,* Cambridge Studies in Indian History and Society (Cambridge and New York: Cambridge University Press, 1999). Benedict Anderson has suggested that some of these administrators constituted the elite that drove later nationalist projects: Benedict Anderson, *Imagined Communities: Reflections on the Origin and Spread of Nationalism* (London and New York: Verso, 1991). Some authors have suggested that British authorities in India feared too much violence: D. Omissi, *The Sepoy and the Raj: The Indian Army, 1860–1940,* Studies in Military and Strategic History (London and New York: Palgrave Macmillan, 2016). This does not rule out the idea that they also employed divide-and-rule tactics, however. They would have simply used these tactics only up to a point on most occasions, in such a way that it did not undermine their economic and political interests. But if this rule was challenged, European imperialist elites, including British imperialist elites, could resort to brutal methods, also setting one community against the other.

111   The religious boundaries between the Sikh and other ethnic groups were shaped by interaction with the British: Harjot Oberoi, *The Construction of Religious Boundaries: Culture, Identity, and Diversity in the Sikh Tradition* (Chicago: University of Chicago Press, 1994).

The concept of *shifting employment together with the associated culture* points to other important cultural phenomena, in particular cultural phenomena that are necessary to understand the emergence of a social war of maneuver, because they contribute to the rise of violent social movements. *Some cultural phenomena interact with the dynamics of the world system and reinforce them.* I clarify these arguments using two *phenomena from contemporary Italian culture* that are especially important to understand the rise of fascism. The first phenomenon is *an aesthetics of military feats that justifies violence.* It is often associated with a fascination with heroic gestures justified aesthetically as *beau geste*, or a beautiful heroic gesture, which can become associated with an eagerness to look for swift and drastic solutions to advance the cause that one fervently supports at one time. Fascists built an entire aesthetics upon this attitude, which they mis-used as an alternative to ethics, and even to justify ethically dubious and also unethical acts.[112] Remarkably, this aesthetics claimed to complement an ethics that addressed questions of modernity and that presented itself as a third way between Marxism and democracy and their unqualified advocacy of modernity, as part of an approach to democracy that recalls traditionalist critics of modernity and the rejection of modernity introduced in the Volume 1 of this book.[113] The aesthetics that fascism built upon is epitomized by the Italian Futurist art movement to which Umberto Boccioni belonged, and in particular by the Futurist Manifesto, the manifesto of this art movement. Similarly to Gabriele D'Annunzio's movement, Italian Futurism preceded fascism, and arguably laid the cultural foundations for it.[114]

---

112   This fascist aesthetic built upon the idealist philosophy, including the aesthetics, proposed by philosophers Croce and Gentile. On fascist aesthetics, see: Walter L. Adamson, "Fascism and Culture: Avant-Gardes and Secular Religion in the Italian Case," *Journal of Contemporary History* 24, no. 3 (1989); Ruth Ben-Ghiat, "Fascism, Writing, and Memory: The Realist Aesthetic in Italy, 1930–1950," *The Journal of Modern History* 67, no. 3 (1995); "Italian Fascism and the Aesthetics of the 'Third Way'," *Journal of Contemporary History* 31, no. 2 (1996). Unlike Ben-Ghiat, I think we should not take seriously the fascist claim that the theory of the ethical state proposed by fascists was an ethics. It was only a manipulation and trivialization of ethics.

113   In addition to the articles on fascist aesthetics, these questions are addressed in: Walter L. Adamson, "The Culture of Italian Fascism and the Fascist Crisis of Modernity: The Case of II Selvaggio," ibid. 30, no. 4 (1995); "Modernism and Fascism: The Politics of Culture in Italy, 1903–1922," in *Fascism*, ed. Jeremy Black and Michael S. Neiberg (London and New York: Routledge, 2006). Ben-Ghiat addressed the relationship between fascism and modernity in: Ruth Ben-Ghiat, *Fascist Modernities: Italy, 1922–1945*, Studies on the History of Society and Culture (Berkeley and Los Angeles: University of California Press, 2001). This book was re-printed in 2004.

114   This manifesto was published in 1909 on the French newspaper *Le Figaro* and it was penned by Filippo Tommaso Marinetti. It contains 11 statements, or theses, to use the

The second phenomenon is *an attitude that in Italian culture is known as qualunquismo*, a concept that is difficult to translate and that might be literally translated as anything-goes-ism. Qualunquismo might be accompanied and supported by different philosophies, but is invariably *associated with patronage networks and the need to shift patron*. It can become violent when patronage dries up, or when patronage itself turns violent in the search for spoils of politics, or what in the United States is called pork barrel politics. Both *the aesthetics of military feats* and *qualunquismo* are cultural traits associated with elite manipulation of popular culture and with the use of volunteers. Both of these cultural phenomena are part of the culture of individuals in shifting employment, whether déclassé aristocrats and downwardly mobile elites more in general, or individuals drawn from the masses who depend upon déclassé aristocrats.[115] Sometimes these individuals are military specialists in shifting military employment, the modern political-military equivalent of hired lances in medieval Europe, or of *ronin* in early modern Japan. The fascination with beautiful heroic gestures, especially when coupled with *qualunquismo*, can lead some individuals to accept the use of drastic means to achieve one's cause, and it can lead some individuals to change their allegiance from the extreme left to the extreme right. This is an elite attitude, associated with Gentile's actualist idealism and philosophy of the act, which gave ideological legitimacy to fascism, thus contributing to it.[116] This ideology, distant though it seems from today, arguably has had a lasting influence upon popular culture until our own time. It included a focus on machines, especially airplanes, as a symbol of modernity and daring, which arguably survives in much of contemporary film. Many contemporary films are pure action, and emphasize the excitement of action without considering the ethical and political implications of action.[117]

---

same language as Marx's *Theses on Feuerbach*. An English translation of the Futurist Manifesto can be found in: Umbro Apollonio, ed. *Futurist Manifestos* (London: Thames and Hudson, 1973). The first statement in the Futurist Manifesto reads 'We want to sing the love of danger, the way of energy and boldness,' the ninth reads 'We want to glorify war—the sole hygiene of the world—militarism, patriotism, the destructive gesture of libertarians, the beautiful ideas for which one dies, and contempt for woman.'

115   An example of déclassé aristocrat in shifting military employment is Carlo Pisacane, who in the mid-1800s served in the Neapolitan Army, and then ended up leading the first and ill-fated expedition by volunteers to seize the Kingdom of Naples, before Giuseppe Garibaldi's successful expedition. On Pisacane as anarchist: Manlio Cancogni, *Gli Angeli Neri. Storia Degli Anarchici Italiani da Pisacane Ai Circoli di Carrara* (Milan: Mursia, 2011).

116   Giovanni Gentile and Anthony James Gregor, *Origins and Doctrine of Fascism: With Selections from Other Works* (London and New York: Routledge, 2011).

117   On the use of imagery relating to airplanes that was made by fascism and nazism, see: Fernando Esposito, *Fascism, Aviation and Mythical Modernity*, trans. Patrick Camiller

The aesthetics of military feats and *qualunquismo*, far from being limited to Italy, are *a recurrent feature in the world system* related to social organization problems and transition problems. The general mechanism affecting any country that goes through these problems as it is incorporated in the world system can be summarized as stating that *heightened social conflict outside the core can create a poverty and violence trap*, often associated with social disaggregation, which includes loss of community and social ties. This heightened social conflict, and the associated poverty and violence trap, lead to conditions in which social movements are easily manipulated and easily degenerate into violence. This is because in the transition from a non-capitalist to a capitalist economy, social conditions initially deteriorate, and the poorer parts of the population are reduced to abject poverty, creating a reservoir of discontent and poverty that makes it possible to recruit large numbers of volunteers, who can be used to sustain violent social movements that harm both development and democracy. In addition, civil society and culture also suffer initially, so that there are no safety nets and no other outlets for the discontent than violence, and no alternatives to shifting military employment or criminality. The problems of development and democracy that affect southern Italy are arguably part of this violence and poverty trap. This trap can lead to prolonged violence and problems of development and democracy from which certain parts of the population, and sometimes entire communities, and even whole areas of a country, can find it very hard to lift themselves out of. This is also because the mix of poverty and violence can be such that there is little or no investment in an area, or the investment is intercepted by patronage networks that make use of volunteers. These are also the conditions that lead to the rise of violent social movements like fascism and nazism, and more recently populism and islamofascism. Equipped with these concepts, we can return to the question of the predominance of a social war of maneuver at the frontier, which includes the emergence of these violent social movements.

6 The Social War of Maneuver and Violent Social Movements

The concepts just sketched out are all useful to understand violent social movements that undermine democracy, starting with the argument that *fascism, nazism and populism might all be caused by a combination of social*

(London and New York: Palgrave Macmillan, 2015). First World War Aces like Boelcke in Germany and Francesco Baracca in Italy were used for nazi and fascist imagery, and are still important today.

conflict and interstate conflict in the world system, and the associated dynamics. World Systems Theory is again especially useful in this context. I refer to these violent social movements as *systemic movements*, however, in order to emphasize their difference from antisystemic movements, which is due to the fact that fascism, nazism and populism arguably contribute to the way in which power works within the state system and to its injustices, making them worse in fact.[118] They might be especially associated with attempts by imperialist elites to consolidate their power. There are *features of fascism and nazism, and today of populism*, that call for a geographic reference frame that transcends individual states and societies, and focuses on a larger scale of social processes affecting many state. This is because all three movements are clear instances of recurrent and widespread social phenomena.[119] All three movements are part of *recurrent phenomena* that share the same basic features. These features are: they claim to address similar social problems, namely, competition from other social groups or from other states; they similarly focus on scapegoats for social problems, as part of their bad rhetoric; they similarly use inflammatory language, with divisive effects; and they similarly use violence and undermine democracy. For example, populist politicians in Western democracies all blame migrants from the developing world or foreign workers and elites, from India or China, for the problems of development that beset most Western democracies. Fascism similarly blamed migrants, although from internal peripheries rather than different countries, or from internal minorities like Jewish minorities, and foreign elites, chiefly from Russia, for problems of development that beset Western countries experimenting with democracy like Italy and Germany, and for economic problems caused by the Great Depression.[120]

---

118 This argument regarding systemic movements builds upon the view that there are movements that participate in counter-revolutions: Brendan McQuade, "(Anti) Systemic Movements: Hegemony, the Passive Revolution, and (Counter) Revolutions," in *The World-System as Unit of Analysis*, ed. Immanuel M. Wallerstein and Roberto Patricio Korzeniewicz (London and New York: Routledge, 2017). I elaborate upon this argument in Section 7.4. Here I focus on the idea that fascism was part of successive waves of expansion of the world system. On this point, see: Kristin Plys, "Theories of Antifascism in the Interwar Mediterranean Part I: Fascism in the Longue Durée," *Journal of World-Systems Research* 28, no. 2 (2022). There were not just different waves of fascism, but different waves of violent social movements, that interacted in various ways with fascism.

119 On fascism and populism as global phenomena, see: Tim Jacoby, "Global Fascism: Geography, Timing, Support, and Strategy," *Journal of Global History* 11, no. 3 (2016). Marzia Maccaferri and Andrea Mammone, "Global Populism and Italy. An Interview with Federico Finchelstein," *Modern Italy* 27, no. 1 (2022).

120 Some of these points are addressed in: Jason Stanley, *How Fascism Works: The Politics of Us and Them* (New York: Random House, 2018). Federico Finchelstein, *A Brief History of Fascist Lies* (Berkeley and Los Angeles: University of California Press, 2020). On the

Fascism, nazism and populism were or are *widespread phenomena*. Fascism and nazism affected within the short time-span of two decades a number of different countries. Fascism started in Italy but it rapidly spread to Austria and Germany, where nazism explicitly modelled itself on precedents set in Italy. Great Britain, Hungary, Romania, Spain, all had their fascist parties and leaders.[121] Japan too had a fascist dictatorship, because the type of authoritarian rule, and the revolution that it implemented over society, can be compared to the fascist dictatorship in Italy and the nazi dictatorship in Germany.[122] We are witnessing today a similarly widespread phenomenon with populism. Populism has affected within the short time-span of two to three decades many different Western countries. It arguably started in Italy with the Northern League, a regionally based party calling for the independence of regions in northern Italy, that at first often used racist arguments against Italians from central Italy and southern Italy, who became scapegoats for problems affecting the Italian state, a tactics that foreshadowed the use of foreign migrants as scapegoats by populist parties, and the bad rhetoric of the populist Five Star Movement in Italy, which was also started in the north of the country.[123] Great Britain followed suit with the UK Independence Party, which was arguably a populist party. They were then followed by the emergence of populist parties in France,

---

ideological continuities and similarities between fascism and populism, see: *From Fascism to Populism in History* (Berkeley and Los Angeles: University of California Press, 2019).

121 Walter Laqueur's classic, first published in 1976 and then in 1978, addressed the international dimension of fascism and the many countries it affected: Walter Laqueur, *Fascism: A Reader's Guide: Analyses, Interpretations, Bibliography* (Wildwood House, 1976). Laqueur has recently published a new study that looks also at neofascism and postfascism: *Fascism: Past, Present, Future* (Oxford and New York: Oxford University Press, 1997). More recently, this international dimension has been emphasized in: Michael Mann, *Fascists* (Cambridge and New York: Cambridge University Press, 2004).

122 Barrington Moore Jr studied fascism in Japan as a revolution from above, and thus as comparable to fascism in Italy and nazism in Germany: Moore, *Social Origins of Dictatorship and Democracy*. On the difficulties in defining fascism, see: Robert O Paxton, "The Five Stages of Fascism," *The Journal of Modern History* 70, no. 1 (1998).

123 On Populism in Italy, see: Giuliano Bobba and Duncan McDonnell, "Italy: a Strong and Enduring Market for Populism," in *European Populism in the Shadow of the Great Recession*, ed. Hanspeter Kriesi and Takis Spyros Pappas (London and New York: ECPR Press with Palgrave Macmillan, 2015). On the role of the Northern League and Five Star Movement, see: Dwayne Woods, "The Crisis of Center-Periphery Integration in Italy and the Rise of Regional Populism: The Lombard League," *Comparative politics* (1995); "The Many Faces of Populism in Italy: The Northern League and Berlusconism," in *The Many Faces of Populism: Current Perspectives*, ed. Dwayne Woods and Barbara Wejnert, Research in Political Sociology (Bingley: Emerald, 2014). Maria Elisabetta Lanzone, "The 'Post-Modern' Populism in Italy: The Case of the Five Star Movement," ibid.

Germany, Hungary, Poland, Spain, and by the election of a populist President in the United States, Donald Trump.[124]

Historical phenomena that are recurrent and widespread must be the result of *causes that transcend the history of each state* and that affect many states at the same time. The most likely candidate for explaining such widespread and recurrent historical phenomena like fascism, nazism and populism is *the modern state system and the combination of social conflict and interstate conflict within it.* But what exactly in this state system, which features of social and interstate conflict, could have caused fascism, nazism and populism? Providing an answer to this question will take the rest of this book and a number of other books. Part of the answer is that all three movements were caused by *a combination of common conditions plus common causes. Common conditions* could be due to economic factors, or political factors, or a combination of both. *Cultural factors* like liberalism and neoliberalism play a role in creating economic problems, whether from internal crises like the 1929 and 2008 economic crises, or from the relocation of industry that occurred from the 1990s onwards.[125] Economic crises and the relocation of industry lead to hardship, which encourages extremist political positions amongst those parts of the masses that are most directly affected. *Political factors* that affect many countries, such as the balance of power within the state system, especially when this balance changes, encourage interstate conflict to replace the state that is the hegemon, by a state that has grown in power. The First and Second World War were arguably waged by states that sought to replace Great Britain as the hegemon.[126]

---

124   Luke March, "Left and Right Populism Compared: The British Case," *The British Journal of Politics and International Relations* 19, no. 2 (2017). For a study of the UK Independence Party that addresses its ties to populism, see: Robert Ford and Matthew J. Goodwin, *Revolt on the Right: Explaining Support for the Radical Right in Britain* (London and New York: Routledge, 2014). On populist parties in Europe, see: Stijn van Kessel, *Populist Parties in Europe: Agents of Discontent?* (London and New York: Palgrave Macmillan, 2015). Populism had an impact upon non-populist parties, some of which adopted its tactics: Daniele Albertazzi, Donatella Bonansinga, and Davide Vampa, "Introduction," in *Populism and New Patterns of Political Competition in Western Europe*, ed. Daniele Albertazzi and Davide Vampa (London and New York: Routledge, 2021).

125   Sara Hsu, *Financial Crises, 1929 to the Present* (Cheltenham, UK and Northampton, Massachusetts: Edward Elgar, 2013). On the history of economic theories dealing with crises, see the many contributions in: Annalisa Rosselli, Nerio Naldi, and Eleonora Sanfilippo, eds., *Money, Finance and Crises in Economic History: The Long-Term Impact of Economic Ideas* (London and New York: Routledge, 2018).

126   On the relation between economic cycles and crises and political hegemonies, see: Barry K. Gills, "Hegemonic Transitions in the World System," in *The World System: Five Hundred Years or Five Thousand?*, ed. Andre Gunder Frank and Barry K. Gills (London and

World Systems Theory, together with considerations from geopolitics, also *clarify the two comparisons between different types of violent social movements,* the first being a comparison between fascism and nazism and populism, and the second being a comparison between fascism and nazism and Muslim fundamentalism or islamofascism. I argue that all these violent social movements are caused by a combination of social conflict and interstate conflict at the frontier of the core of the state system, and more specifically by heightened conflict related to incorporation in the state core. This heightened conflict leads to an even more unequal distribution of power and thus undermines democracy, and sometimes enables violent social movements to seize power through a coup d'etat and put an end to democratic institutions, with a speedy seizure of power, thus enabling an even greater shift in the distribution of power, greatly favoring the elites compared to the masses. This explanation of violent social movements emphasizes their impact on democracy understood as distribution of power, an explanation that is closely associated with social conflict and the poverty and violence trap. This explanation does not rule out that populism might arise from other causes too, depending upon the geographical location. These causes might be additional to those proposed here.

Common causes can be causes that are part of a sequence of events, or they can be a shared cause, that is, the same cause that applies to multiple states, like heightened social conflict. *Fascism in Italy was the first cause in a sequence of events,* because it initiated a sequence of events that led to the emergence of other fascist movements. The spread of fascism was certainly aided by Mussolini's active policy to encourage fascism in other countries, which involved starting a fascist international committed to promoting, in other countries than Italy, what was variously called Universal Fascism or the Universality of Rome. Historian Michael Ledeen, a controversial figure for many years at the American Enterprise Institute for Public Policy Research, a think tank, wrote about this aspect of fascism.[127] Mussolini and Hitler especially played a

---

New York: Routledge, 1996). Barry K. Gills and Andre Gunder Frank, "World System Cycles, Crises, and Hegemonic Shifts, 1700 BC to 1700 AD," ibid. On Gramsci's and Gramscian approaches to these questions, see: Lorenzo Fusaro, *Crises and Hegemonic Transitions: From Gramsci's Quaderni to the Contemporary World Economy* (Leiden and Boston: Brill, 2018).

127   The alliance between Mussolini and Hitler sought to export the fascist and nazi vision for a new world order to other countries, notably to Spain: Matteo Albanese and Pablo del Hierro, *Transnational Fascism in the Twentieth Century: Spain, Italy and the Global Neo-Fascist Network*, A Modern History of Politics and Violence (London, Berlin, New York: Bloomsbury, 2016). J. F. Coverdale, *Italian Intervention in the Spanish Civil War*, Princeton Legacy Library (Princeton and Oxford: Princeton University Press, 2015). Coverdale has argued that fascist intervention in Spain was essential to Francisco Franco's

key role in Francisco Franco's rise to power in Spain, because without their military intervention Franco might not have won, or might not have won quickly and decisively enough to offset the international reaction against Franco.[128] These *common causes are important, but only in conjunction with the common conditions*, such as changes in social organization in the transition from traditional to capitalist society, and social disaggregation, both of which explain why the common causes could have the disastrous effects that they did, and were so hard to contain. The combination of common causes and conditions applies fairly well to fascism and nazism. In order to understand populism and islamofascism, and their relation to fascism and nazism, it is necessary to introduce additional concepts, and address heightened social conflict, an especially important common cause that applies to multiple states. These additional concepts that nuance and expand upon the geographic reference frame are especially important for this purpose.

Table 1 suggests how common causes and conditions apply in the broadest terms to the cases of Italy, Germany, and countries in the Middle East. It also explains the two comparisons mentioned above, between on the one hand, fascism and nazism, and on the other hand, populism, as in the first comparison, or islamofascism, as in the second comparison.

Fascism and nazism are compared to populism because there is likely some historical continuity as part of a sequence of events. In this case the social movement is at the actual same location as the previous social movement, and it uses *some* of the same symbolism, rhetoric, and possibly some of the same personnel, drawn from the same social groups. Conditions have changed, however, and whereas fascism and nazism were a social war of maneuver, populism is a social war of position. *Fascism and nazism are compared to islamofascism because they stem from a shared cause*: heightened conflict at the frontier at the time of incorporation in the state core. Both are instances of social

---

success but did not influence Franco, whereas Albanese and Hierro have suggested that networks were built at that time that lasted until the time of the Golpe Borghese in the 1970s and even until more recent times. For Mussolini and Hitler's cultural policies towards parts of occupied Europe, see: B. G. Martin, *The Nazi-Fascist New Order for European Culture* (Cambridge, Massachusetts and London: Harvard University Press, 2016).

128   There is also a growing body of scholarly work on the relationship between Mussolini's fascist movement and similar movements in other countries, for example Portugal: Annarita Gori and Rita Almeida de Carvalho, "Italian Fascism and the Portuguese Estado Novo: International Claims and National Resistance," *Intellectual History Review* 30, no. 2 (2020). The intervention of Mussolini and Hitler in the Spanish Civil War proved decisive: Albanese and del Hierro, *Transnational Fascism in the Twentieth Century*. Coverdale, *Italian Intervention in the Spanish Civil War*.

TABLE 1   Geographical location and violent social movements

		Time period	
Social movements compared		**1920s–1940s**	**1980s–2000s**
Actual location	Italy and Germany	Fascism and Nazism	Populism
Relative location	Frontier of the core	Fascism and Nazism	Islamofascism
Type of relationship		**1920s–1940s**	**1980s–2000s**
Actual location	Italy and Germany	*Historical continuity*	
Relative location	Frontier of the core	*Common cause: heightened conflict at the frontier* (possibly some historical continuity)	

war of maneuver, albeit with some important *differences due to the later historical period when incorporation in the state core was occurring.* In the first half of the twentieth century it was Italy and Germany that were being incorporated into the state core, and this led to violent social movements that seized power and ruled in the 1920s-1940s period. In the second half of the century it was countries in the Middle East that were being incorporated, and this led to similar violent social movements, from the PLO to Hezbollah, and more recently to the revival of power of the Muslim Brotherhood.

I want to add some hypotheses about historical continuity that help explain the *conditions for different social war types,* emphasizing both the different development of civil society, as pointed out at the end of Chapter 2, and also *heightened conflict due to a combination of social conflict and interstate conflict.* The historical continuity from fascism and nazism to islamofascism could have taken two forms. One form is continuity via Middle Eastern sympathizers of fascism who were recruited and active in the Middle East in the 1920s-1940s, and whose activities eventually might have contributed to the rise of Muslim fundamentalism up to and including the 1980s-2000s.[129] Another form is that of Italian sympathizers of fascism who contributed to the

---

129   On fascist interference and presence in the Middle East in the 1920s-40s, see: Nir Arielli, *Fascist Italy and the Middle East, 1933–40* (London and New York: Palgrave Macmillan,

terrorism that rocked Italy during the Years of Lead, over the 1960s-1980s, some of whom might however have established ties to groups in the Middle East and have continued their activities, just from different bases. Some of these terrorists, like the Nuclei Armati Rivouzionari, or NAR, had fascist sympathies. The attempted 1970 coup by Junio Valerio Borghese aimed to put in power a neo-fascist government in Italy.[130] These violent social movements failed at that time in Italy because they could never achieve a mass following, since Italy was going through a period of prosperity, it had built up civil society, and effective policing eventually put an end to terrorism. This proved that the conditions for a social war of maneuver in Italy no longer existed. The conditions had changed to favoring a social war of position. Populism has achieved more political success only thanks to the fact that economic growth has slowed, and most of the politicians involved have avoided openly advocating violence and thus have not been subjected to police repression of violent social movements. They instead made use for political purposes of the occasional violence from terrorists, or from petty criminals amongst migrants, who are outsiders that the populists can easily construe as a threat that they claim to be defending Italians from. The conditions are more fluid in the Middle East and North Africa, where there has been both the rise of violent social movements and the collapse of some states, paving the way for attempted coups and more conflict that can be classified as a social war of maneuver.

2010). I want to emphasize here that the concept of volunteers might be relevant to understand both fascism and islamofascism.

130   On violence during that period, see: Della Porta, *Social Movements, Political Violence, and the State*. Some associate the Years of Lead mostly with left-leaning extremists who created terrorist cells: Richard Drake, *Apostles and Agitators: Italy's Marxist Revolutionary Tradition* (Boston: Harvard University Press, 2009); *The Revolutionary Mystique and Terrorism in Contemporary Italy* (Bloomington: Indiana University Press, 2021). This last book was first published in 1989. However, there was a significant contribution to violence also from right-wing terrorist cells: Franco Ferraresi, "The Radical Right in Postwar Italy," *Politics & Society* 16, no. 1 (1988). *Threats to Democracy: The Radical Right in Italy after the War* (Princeton and Oxford: Princeton University Press, 2012). Most importantly, the terrorists on the left were part of a conspiratorial strain in Italian Marxist politics that was marginal, very small, and only gained visibility through their violence.

PART 3

*Development and Democracy and
the Division of Labour in Society*

∵

Quantity and Quality

In [Bukharin's] Popular Handbook of Sociology it is said [...] that every society is something more than the sum of the individuals composing [the society]. This is true in abstract terms, but what does it mean practically? [...] The most concrete theoretical-practical explanation [of this statement] is given in [Marx's] Critique of Political Economy, where it is demonstrated that in a factory's production system there is a production quota that is not attributable to any single worker, but to the ensemble of skilled workers [maestranze], to the collective man. Something similar happens for the whole of society, which is based on a division of labour and of [social] functions, and is therefore more than the sum of its component [parts].

ANTONIO GRAMSCI, *Prison Notebooks*, Notebook 11, Note 32, p.1446. My emphasis.[1]

• •
•

---

1   Gramsci, *Quaderni del Carcere*, 1446.

Theoretical Groundwork on Power and the Division of Labour in Society

In this chapter I introduce the theoretical groundwork that contributes to those *parts of the general theory of development and democracy that concern the sources of development* that I outline in the next chapter. These parts of the general theory are a further elaboration of Gramsci's theory of hegemony, and theory of power more in general, emphasizing that, in addition to the economic power that is central to Cohen's theory, there are also cultural power, and political-military power, both of which, sometimes together, play an important role in history. This chapter thus also extends *Weber's sociology, and the sociology multidisciplinary approach more in general*, since the specific multidisciplinary approach that I use is derived from a combination of Weber's work with Gramsci's work.[1] The sociology multidisciplinary approach, as practiced by Weber, and more recently by Mann, suggests that we should conceive of the different domains of human activity, namely, the economy, culture, politics, and the military, as equally important in history, because no domain is completely determined by the other domains, and all influence the way in which a country works. Mann explicitly formulated this argument in terms of power, suggesting that the different domains are each associated with a different source of power, namely, economic, cultural, political, and military power.[2] I expand upon Mann's theory suggesting that there are different arenas each specialized in one of the different sources of power. Since all domains and arenas are important to the way in which a country works, a multidisciplinary approach is necessary in order to provide a *comprehensive theory* to inform

---

1   The importance of some of Max Weber's ideas for Gramsci was highlighted by Frosini in: Fabio Frosini, *Gramsci e la Filosofia: Saggio sui Quaderni del Carcere* (Roma: Carocci, 2003). A comparison between Gramsci and Weber, both seen as theorists of modernity, and of 'mass society' in particular, is presented in: Michele Filippini, *Una Politica di Massa: Antonio Gramsci e la Rivoluzione della Società* (Roma: Carocci, 2015).

2   On Max Weber's theory as a theory of modernity, see: Ralph Schroeder, *Max Weber, Democracy and Modernization* (Basingstoke: Macmillan, 1998). Mann presents his theory of power as an IEMP model suggesting that there are ideological (cultural), economic, military, and political sources of power: "Introduction: The IEMP Model and Its Critics," in *An Anatomy of Power: The Social Theory of Michael Mann*, ed. John Anthony Hall and Ralph Schroeder (Cambridge and New York: Cambridge University Press, 2006).

policy and ensure that efficient policies are formulated in different domains that reinforce, rather than undermine, each other. A comprehensive theory is especially needed in order to avoid one-sidedness, that is, overemphasizing just one domain, a disastrous error that affected Western philosophy and social science during the past 150 years.[3] The increasingly specialized social science produced over this period is deeply flawed and could not contribute to policy.

The first section below suggests that the different arenas emerge as part of the Durkheimian division of labour in society, and that each arena produces capabilities that are distinctive to it. There are economic capabilities that include knowledge and skills that raise productivity, cultural capabilities that include the ability to formulate views and articulate grievances, and in the case of intellectuals to formulate and empirically test entire theories, political capabilities that include the ability to govern a country, and military capabilities that include the ability to dissuade an enemy and win a war. The second section places the concept of capability within the theory of power, which emphasizes conflict. Capabilities are relative to the capabilities of others, or to the needs associated with a harsh environment. They are used in conflict with others as well as in efforts to tame nature. This chapter emphasizes the conflict that capabilities participate in, arguing that there is productive as well as destructive conflict, the first being conflict that has become routinized, and from which all violence has been removed. The third section emphasizes that each arena provides to other arenas also capital. Capital includes social capital, that is, the networks that an individual participates in, an important factor in democracy, in conjunction with the number of NPOs and NGOs in civil society and the state. Cultural capital includes qualifications, and arguably also a shared language. Both social and cultural capital contribute to the emergence of embedded autonomy, which requires networks between institutions and organizations, and also a shared language that is spoken and written throughout a country, enabling communications. The fourth section focuses on the manner in which social and cultural capital, and also political-military and cultural capabilities, contribute to regulation needed by markets. Regulation includes both the planned provision of capabilities and capital needed by markets, and also the regulation of behavior, including the removal of all violence and thieving, from activities internal to a country. The fifth section redefines democracy in terms of power, emphasizing that democracy entails a distribution of power within a country that is favourable to the masses, and

---

3   I address the concepts of one-sidedness and reductiveness in Section 5.1 of: Olsaretti, *The Struggle for Development and Democracy, Vol. 1.* I delve into the errors of one-sidedness during the past 150 years in: *Towards a Humanist Social Science.*

also a separation of powers between arenas, whereby economic, cultural, and political-military power remain independent of each other. The sixth section places this definition of democracy in relation to the overall argument regarding development, embedded autonomy, and democracy, namely, that all three are necessary, as they reinforce each other.

1   The Division of Labour in Society and Capabilities

Gramsci's theory of hegemony emphasized that *there are different arenas in society, namely, the economic, cultural, and political-military arenas*, and that cultural power and political-military power are produced in different arenas. It is useful to conceptualize the division of society in different arenas as *an aspect of Emile Durkheim's concept of the division of labour in society*.[4] This is because in each arena a different type of activity is carried out, with its own principles of behavior, and with its own distinctive goals, that include: increasing wealth in the economic arena; increasing education and knowledge, including achieving truth, in the cultural arena; enabling collective action and defense in the political-military arena. In modern *capitalist* societies, the three arenas become distinctive arenas, with even more specific behaviors and goals than those just described. As emphasized by John Urry, *capitalist societies are distinguished by the coexistence of markets, civil society, and the state*.[5] These correspond respectively to the economic, cultural, and political-military arenas. This insight is present already in Gramsci's work, which addressed markets, civil society and the state, and also emphasized that all three are important, and that they have distinctive types of behavior.[6] *The growth of the division of labour is associated with uneven development.* With the increase in the division of labour in society, there comes also a differential access to the growing

4   Emile Durkheim and Lewis A. Coser, *The Division of Labor in Society*, trans. W. D. Halls, Free
    Press Paperback (New York: Free Press, 1997).
5   John Urry, *The Anatomy of Capitalist Societies: The Economy, Civil Society, and the State*
    (London and Basingstoke: Macmillan, 1981). Urry effectively extends to the whole of capitalist society the main argument of: Trigilia, *Economic Sociology*.
6   Gramsci's notes on each of these arenas are widely studied. For Gramsci's work on the state,
    see: Benedetto Fontana, "Gramsci on Politics and State," *Journal of Classical Sociology* 2, no. 2
    (2002). Gramsci's work on civil society has been the subject of many contributions: Walter
    L. Adamson, "Gramsci and the Politics of Civil Society," *Praxis International* 7, no. 3–4
    (1987–88); Joseph A. Buttigieg, "Gramsci on Civil Society," *boundary 2* 22, no. 3 (1995); "The
    Contemporary Discourse on Civil Society: A Gramscian Critique," *boundary 2* 32, no. 1 (2005);
    Benedetto Fontana, "Liberty and Domination: Civil Society in Gramsci," ibid. 33, no. 2 (2006).

power, due to the different position and function that individuals have in society as a consequence of the division of labour. Some of these positions and functions give more direct access to power than other positions and functions, and some positions and functions are more rewarded than other ones. Thus, the division of labour leads also to an unequal distribution of power in society and to a tendency to undermine democracy and lead to uneven development.

Durkheim was one of the founders of sociology, and his book *The Division of Labour in Society* first drew attention to the *division of labour in society as a crucially important aspect of modern societies*, as well as an important component of development. Durkheim made two interrelated points. The first point is that the division of labour in society leads to growth, the second is that, in a society in which there is an advanced division of labour, which is therefore divided into many different organizations, each with somewhat different values, new forms of social solidarity arise to give cohesion to society, constituting a distinctive type of social solidarity that provides cohesion in societies with an advanced division of labour.[7] Nationalism is arguably part of this distinctive type of social solidarity, and it is associated with the education provided in the cultural arena, whereby a single language comes to prevail throughout society. As argued by Gellner, nationalism becomes predominant with the introduction of industrial capitalism, which requires mobility in a society that is in perpetual growth and thus in constant flux.[8] Here I want to emphasize that, with the shared language and national culture associated with nationalism, there emerges also a shared sense of national identity, which provides the crucially important social solidarity in modern societies, in which social conflict would otherwise lead to the breakup of a state. Gramsci's theory of hegemony explains an important mechanism involved in creating this type of social solidarity in a country, namely, that the elites which guide a country also develop a philosophy or worldview to justify their rule and their vision for the country, a worldview that in modern times often takes the form of nationalism.[9]

---

7   Social solidarity is a key concept in: Durkheim and Coser, *The Division of Labor in Society*. Durkheim distinguishes between the mechanical solidarity that he attributes to traditional societies, and the type of social solidarity in societies with an advanced division of labour.

8   I am referring to Gellner's theory of nationalism as set out in: Gellner, *Nations and Nationalism*, and the revision to it is presented in: *Nationalism*. This theory was the subject of an edited volume with many important contributions: John Anthony Hall, ed. *The State of the Nation: Ernest Gellner and the Theory of Nationalism* (Cambridge and New York: Cambridge University Press, 1998).

9   This view of nationalism is set out in: Michelle Hartman and Alessandro Olsaretti, "'The First Boat and the First Oar': Inventions of Lebanon in the Writings of Michel Chiha.," *Radical History Review*, no. 86 (2003). I believe this is a better explanation than Gellner's functional explanation. Changes in social boundaries explain why nationalist visions

This is important because a national culture that the masses of a population identify with encourages them to pursue loyalty or voice, rather than exit, as social conflict flares up. It is all the more important because with the advancement of the division of labour in society there is lack of traditional social solidarity, as suggested by Durkheim, and also greater social conflict. Sociologist Dietrich Rueschemeyer has argued that *the divisions of labour in society also leads to greater conflict.*[10] This is because, with the advancement of both the division of labour in society and of development, there is growth in collective power, and an increase in social conflict, specifically conflict over the distribution of the fruits of development. I emphasize in this project that this conflict can be especially destructive in modern societies, in which mass mobilization and diffuse and random violence become possible, and I begin to explore the negative effects of destructive conflict on both development and democracy, emphasizing that it is very important for destructive conflict to be minimized and to be replaced by productive conflict.

These arguments involve *revisiting three important concepts for development* that together contribute to a significantly new approach to development and democracy. This significantly new approach can best be described with reference to Sen's seminal book *Development as Freedom*.[11] I build upon several of his key concepts, but in significantly new directions. I want to emphasize here three concepts that are central to Sen's work and that I build upon in new directions: the concept of division of labour, the concept of capabilities, and the concept of competition. Sen has renewed interest in *the concept of division of labour* that is central to Adam Smith's work, including Smith's view of the division of labour in a factory as a major contributor to productivity. This adds to the view of markets associated with mainstream economics and with neoliberalism, because it draws attention to other factors than just competition as the source of productivity.[12] In this book I begin to extend the Smithian concept

---

come to prevail. There can be more than one nationalist vision for a country, each emphasizing somewhat different values and different goals.

10   Dietrich Rueschemeyer, *Power and the Division of Labour*, Social and Political Theory from Polity Press (Cambridge, UK and Malden, Massachusetts: Polity, 1986). A detailed study of questions of fairness that emerge from the division of labour in the automotive industry is provided by: Hyeeong-Ki Kwon, *Fairness and Division of Labor in Market Societies: Comparison of the U.S. And German Automotive Industries* (New York and Oxford: Berghahn Books, 2004).

11   Sen, *Development as Freedom*. This book was first published in 1999.

12   Sen discusses Smith in Chapter 2 of: ibid. Sen has also specifically addressed Smith's work and emphasized Smith's continued relevance in: Amartya Sen, "Adam Smith's Prudence," in *Theory and Reality in Development: Essays in Honour of Paul Streeten*, ed. Sanjaya Lall and Frances Stewart (London and New York: Palgrave Macmillan, 1986); "Adam Smith and the

of the division of labour in a factory to the division of labour in society, seen as a source of productivity, as well as a source of conflict that can undermine social solidarity. The importance of this extension can be intuitively understood. Today, large manufacturers like car manufacturers do not produce all components in-house, but make use of more or less long supply chains. These range from providers of steel for the chassis to providers of components. They also use designers and research produced in universities to design a certain car model.[13] Clearly, there is a division of labour amongst companies that are part of supply chains, and sometimes also between designers and manufacturers, or between universities that produce scientific research and manufacturers who turn this research into technology, and ultimately into specific products. This chapter generalizes the concept of division of labour and focuses upon the division of labour in society, which involves groups of organizations specialized in producing altogether different products, for example, scientific research by universities in the cultural arena, and economic products such as cars in the economic arena.

The concept of capability introduced by Nussbaum and Sen as part of the capability approach to development conveys an important insight that development is related to what an individual can actually do, and is thus related to that individual's freedom.[14] I place the concept of capability within a more general theory of power that emphasizes the participation of capabilities in social conflict and interstate conflict. It is useful to begin by describing *the capability approach* proposed by Nussbaum and Sen. A defining feature of this approach is to introduce the concept of capability, in contrast to income, as a measure of development. Therefore, *development is defined as the growth in capabilities,*

Contemporary World," *Erasmus Journal for Philosophy and Economics* 3, no. 1 (2010); "The Contemporary Relevance of Adam Smith," in *The Oxford Handbook of Adam Smith,* ed. Christopher J. Berry, Maria Pia Paganelli, and Craig Smith (Oxford and New York: Oxford University Press, 2013).

13   Several authors approach the automotive industry as participating in the division of labour: Egon Endres and Theo Wehner, "Frictions in the New Division of Labour: Cooperation between Producers and Suppliers in the German Automobile Industry," in *The New Division of Labour: Emerging Forms of Work Organisation in International Perspective,* ed. Wolfgang Littek and Tony Charles (Berlin and New York: Walter de Gruyter, 1995); Kwon, *Fairness and Division of Labor in Market Societies.*

14   Sen, *Development as Freedom*; Martha C. Nussbaum, *Creating Capabilities: The Human Development Approach* (Cambridge, Massachusetts and London: Harvard University Press, 2011). For an overview of the approach, see: Ingrid Robeyns, "The Capability Approach: a Theoretical Survey," *Journal of Human Development* 6, no. 1 (2005). For a critical appraisal, see: John M. Alexander, *Capabilities and Social Justice: The Political Philosophy of Amartya Sen and Martha Nussbaum* (London and New York: Routledge, 2016).

rather than the growth in income. Capabilities describe what an individual can actually do, and arguably depend also upon knowledge and skills. Below I also emphasize capital, including social capital, as a source of capabilities.[15] For example, capabilities include literacy, and thus knowing a language and having the skills to read and write. They also include numeracy, and knowledge of mathematics and the skills to carry out calculations. Both literacy and numeracy are necessary to function in modern job markets and also to function as a citizen in modern democracies, since participation in democratic processes involves, amongst other things, reading the news and making informed decisions about them. This entails reassessing the achievements of certain policies, like the policies implemented by the Indian state Kerala, which does not have high income, but has high literacy and numeracy, and high life expectancy.[16]

A serious *criticism of the capability approach* is that, unlike income, capabilities are not easily quantified. One answer to this criticism is that indexes can provide a way to quantify at least certain capabilities, increasing the usefulness of capabilities as a measure of development, and also that composite indexes can be created, giving different weights to different components of the index.[17] For example, the overall development of a country can be measured by such indexes as a human development index taking many types of development

---

15 Sen discusses the capability approach in: Sen, *Development as Freedom*. Nussbaum applies the capability approach in: Martha C. Nussbaum, *Women and Human Development: The Capabilities Approach*, The Seeley Lectures (Cambridge and New York: Cambridge University Press, 2000). Useful surveys of the capability approach are provided in: Robeyns, "The Capability Approach: a Theoretical Survey."; "The Capability Approach in Practice," *Journal of Political Philosophy* 14, no. 3 (2006). For a discussion of Sen's capability approach, see: W. Kuklys, *Amartya Sen's Capability Approach: Theoretical Insights and Empirical Applications*, Studies in Choice and Welfare (Springer Berlin Heidelberg, 2006).

16 Sen makes this point in: Sen, *Development as Freedom*. Sen emphasizes that Kerala's achievement was not just good welfare, but also good public education. Why Kerala did not develop a strong presence in ICT compared to other parts of India is an interesting question for development.

17 For an overview of the issues that arise in applying the capability approach, see: Robeyns, "The Capability Approach in Practice." For a discussion of indexes used to measure capabilities, see: Sabina Alkire, "Dimensions of Human Development," *World Development* 30, no. 2 (2002). Nicolás Brando and Katarina Pitasse Fragoso, "Capability Deprivation and the Relational Dimension of Poverty: Testing Universal Multidimensional Indexes," in *Dimensions of Poverty: Measurement, Epistemic Injustices, Activism*, ed. Valentin Beck, Henning Hahn, and Robert Lepenies (Cham, Switzerland: Springer, 2020). On measurement of the related concept of functionings, that is, what capabilities achieve, see: Enrica Chiappero Martinetti, "A Multidimensional Assessment of Well-Being Based on Sen's Functioning Approach," *Rivista Internazionale di Scienze Sociali* 108, no. 2 (2000).

into account, while democracy in a country can be measured by a democracy index taking into account, for example, free and fair elections, and freedom of the press, that are respectively measures of political democracy and cultural democracy.[18] Another answer is that, although the capability approach cannot be used in alternative to income, it might be very useful in conjunction with income to define development. The capability approach thus introduces an important way to *conceptualize* development in addition to definitions of development based upon income alone, thus complementing measures of development based upon income.[19] This is important because a given investment can yield very different capabilities, and it is useful to compare, for given capabilities that one seeks, what is the level of investment that is required.

For example, capabilities in conjunction with investment can be used to compare economic capabilities by different organizations, whereby there are collective economic capabilities associated with a factory, like the output of a certain good or type of good, which can be compared to the output by another factory that uses the same machinery and the same labour, which cost the same investment.[20] Similarly, spending in the military is an important, but only rough measure, of the achievement of capabilities. China spends less, but also has lower costs, and can thus achieve some of the same capabilities with less spending. This might be corrected by measures of spending adjusted for the lower costs in China. However, capabilities are still very important as a baseline to be used in addition to measures of spending adjusted for costs in comparisons between countries. It is useful to compare, between the similar capabilities achieved by two different countries, the spending adjusted for costs that was necessary to achieve the similar capabilities. This would be a measure of the efficiency of industry and of the efficiency of research institutions. Lastly, there are capabilities that are not easily measured by spending, including quality of training, which can significantly increase capabilities given a certain level of spending, and including also innovation in basic scientific research, which gives the ability to develop altogether new capabilities that others do not have.[21]

---

18 Ambuj D. Sagar and Adil Najam, "The Human Development Index: a Critical Review," *Ecological Economics* 25, no. 3 (1998).

19 Robeyns, "The Capability Approach in Practice," 372.

20 The expression 'manufacturing production capacity' is used to refer to what is, for all intents and purposes, a collective capability of the workers and engineers in a factory. I address collective capabilities below.

21 One way to address such comparisons is to use Purchasing Power Parity (PPP). Some authors have suggested Relative Military Cost as a better measure of Chinese military spending than either market prices or PPP: Peter E. Robertson and Adrian Sin,

The arguments in this book also revise *the concept of competition itself and the concept of regulation*, including the Smithian concept of market self-regulation, by suggesting that competition is a type of conflict, and that the competition that leads to development is in particular one or more types of productive conflict. This book begins to elaborate upon the insight that social conflict can be either productive or destructive, focusing on a related question, namely, *how to avoid social conflict that is destructive* and bad for development and democracy alike. I define productive conflict by generalizing insights introduced by Tilly regarding the role of social movements in the democratization process, which led to the emergence of democracy in Western countries in modern times. Tilly's argument can be summarized as suggesting that conflict became routinized, and had violence removed from it, and that this type of conflict contributed to the democratization process.[22] Below I generalize this argument and suggest that productive conflict is conflict that has become routinized and has had all violence removed from it, and that this productive conflict led in the economic arena to market competition, in the cultural arena to productive cultural conflict that includes civil debates, as opposed to adversarial debates, and in the political arena to productive political conflict that includes competition for votes amongst political parties without partisanship. All these types of productive conflict became especially important with development. This book begins to elaborate upon this insight by focusing on a related question, namely, *how to avoid social conflict that is destructive* and bad for development and democracy alike. Violence is part of this destructive social conflict, and so is partisanship. The latter is associated with culture wars and adversarial debates, both of which are forms of narrow-minded partisanship in the cultural arena. They are also associated with political conflict that puts one's organization and partisan interests above principles and the common good.[23]

"Measuring Hard Power: China's Economic Growth and Military Capacity," *Defence and Peace Economics* 28, no. 1 (2017). On issues in using PPP in military spending, see: Michael Ward, "Appendix 8e. International Comparisons of Military Expenditures: Issues and Challenges of Using Purchasing Power Parities," *SIPRI Yearbook*.

22   Tilly, *Social Movements*. Tilly introduced also additional considerations than routinization and the removal of violence. For example, Tilly suggested that the series of criteria worthiness, unity, numbers and commitment, that he summarized with the unfortunate-sounding acronym WUNC, became accepted as measures of a movement whose grievances deserved to be redressed.

23   This is a central question to debates over partisanship that is touched upon also by: Jonathan White and Lea Ypi, *The Meaning of Partisanship* (Oxford and New York: Oxford University Press, 2016).

2   Capabilities within a Theory of Power and Conflict

The theory of development and democracy that I propose builds upon the capability approach first proposed by Nussbaum and Sen, that I refer to below simply as the capability approach, although I differ in significant ways from this approach because *I integrate capabilities within a theory of power*. By contrast with Nussbaum's and Sen's concept of capabilities, the concept of power emphasizes that what matters the most are not just capabilities in absolute terms, but capabilities relative to other groups, or states, or capabilities relative to a harsh environment.[24] This approach does not entail rejecting the concept of capability, but subsuming it under a more general theory of power that includes both capabilities and power, and entails expanding the concept of capability. I begin to expand upon the concept of capability in two new directions. The first involves combining the concept of capabilities with the concept of power. Similarly to the capability approach, I use the word capability to refer to the capability to carry out given tasks. However, I emphasize that what matters the most is power, which is based upon capabilities, but it also takes into consideration the capabilities of others.

The second direction involves integrating capabilities and power within a *conflict view of society* emphasizing that society is rife with conflict. Conceptualizing and introducing into theories of development *collective capabilities*, a concept that I derive from my reading of Gramsci's work and from Evans' work, is especially important in conjunction with this conflict view of society.[25] In particular, collective capabilities are especially important in order to integrate the military within the theory of development and democracy, since the military is based upon collective capabilities, and the military capabilities of armed forces are collective capabilities. Collective capabilities are important also in politics and in particular in social movements. The ability to engage in collective action, and in particular in deliberate and sustained collective action in the pursuit of shared goals, is essentially a collective capability that belongs to a social group or a social movement as a whole, and that

---

24   I sketched the importance of individualism and human nature for Gramsci's philosophy of science in the article: Alessandro Olsaretti, "From the Return to Labriola to the Anti-Croce: Philosophy, Praxis and Human Nature in Gramsci's *Prison Notebooks*," *Historical Materialism* 24, no. 4 (2016).

25   Peter B. Evans, "Collective Capabilities, Culture, and Amartya Sen's Development as Freedom," *Studies in Comparative International Development* 37, no. 2 (2002). The state capabilities that Migdal refers to are an instance of collective capabilities: Migdal, *Strong Societies and Weak States*.

I argue has to be measured relative to the ability of other social groups. This is the approach that is implicit in the concept of collective action advantage of the elites compared to the masses introduced in Volume 1. Lastly, this approach also has applications to the economy, for individuals competing on a labour market, because one's endowment in capabilities is measured compared to others' endowments, and for companies creating collective capabilities out of the many individuals and technologies that they employ, capabilities that are important compared to the collective capabilities of other companies.

I take a *sociological approach to the study of power*. Because of the crucial role of power in this approach, it is important to provide *a definition of power*. The concept of power that I use in this book builds upon work by Weber, but is limited to the concept of *herrschaft or authority, not macht,* which is associated with power over others.[26] I also take a considerably broader view of power, that includes *power compared to others*. As Gramsci pointed out, power includes also power over nature, and power over events, which includes the ability to make one's history rather than being at the mercy of it. This more general view of power is compatible with the concept of capabilities, which refers to what individuals, social groups, countries, and of course states, are capable of doing, in transforming nature for example. Furthermore, in the sociological approach that I take to the study of power, power includes both historical and geographical dimensions, as I study power within the world system and by taking a World Systems Theory approach. Lastly, the sociological approach emphasizes that there are different sources of power associated with each of the domains of human behavior, so that power can be said to have economic, cultural, political, and military sources.

The importance of differentiating between the power produced in each arena derives from the fact that, as Mann proposed, formalizing an insight that

---

26   This is the definition that Weber gave of power, for example in: Max Weber, Guenther Roth, and Claus Wittich, eds., *Economy and Society: An Outline of Interpretive Sociology* (Berkeley and Los Angeles: University of California Press, 1978). This interpretation of Weber's definition of power as *Macht* is subjected to a revisionist critique in: Lloyd I. Rudolph and Susanne Hoeber Rudolph, "Authority and Power in Bureaucratic and Patrimonial Administration: A Revisionist Interpretation of Weber on Bureaucracy," *World Politics* (1979). Interestingly, in Italian there are two words for power that correspond to the distinction made by Weber between different forms of power. The German word 'herrschaft' corresponds to the Italian 'potere,' which is a generic type of power that includes domination and also authority, whereas the German word 'macht' corresponds to the Italian 'potenza,' which is power over others. For a discussion of these differences see: B. Di Mauro, "Note sulla Legittimità in Max Weber," *Il Pensiero Politico* 24, no. 3 (1991). These differences are important.

was already present in Weber and Gramsci, *power has different sources*. These sources are of different types, and it is useful therefore to distinguish between economic, cultural, political and military sources of power.[27] These different sources of power are associated with distinctive ways to build power in the different domains: in the economy, it is productivity; in culture, the ability to formulate and spread ideas; in science, that I consider to be part of culture, the ability to achieve truth; in politics and the military, the ability to concentrate and direct collective action in the form of large cohesive forces. I differ from Mann in significant ways, however, because of the relationship between capabilities and power introduced above, which entails that what each arena produces are capabilities, both individual and collective, that then lead to power of one type or another, when these capabilities are measured in comparison to the capabilities of others, or to the capabilities required in a harsh environment, or to the capabilities required at a difficult historical conjuncture. We should distinguish, therefore, between economic, cultural, political, and military capabilities, each of which can be both individual and collective, and each of which is produced within an arena. The sociological approach to power is informed also by *a specific view of society as involving conflict* that is different than the economists' view.[28] It is very important to reconceptualize conflict away from reductive economic views of conflict, that see all conflict as economic conflict, and reduce economic conflict to market conflict, whether between individuals or organizations, that is, to conflict driven purely by self-interest.

Two aspects of the sociological approach to conflict are especially important to this book: the types of conflict, and the relationship between productive and destructive conflict. The first aspect emphasizes that there are *altogether different types of conflict,* because conflict in different arenas involves different types of human behavior, and also altogether different ends and means. One of the contributions of the general theory that I propose is to begin to conceptualize conflict within culture and politics as different than economic conflict. This is clear in terms of the *different ends* in these domains, so that we should not reduce conflict within culture to an economic calculus of profits or utilities, but recognize that different ends are at stake, achieving truth within culture, and ensuring the security of one's country and its allies within politics

---

27   See: Schroeder, "Introduction: The IEMP Model and Its Critics."
28   This conflict view of society, which was central to Marx's approach and later also to sociology, is set out in: Anthhony Giddens, *Capitalism and Modern Social Theory: An Analysis of the Writings of Marx, Durkheim and Max Weber* (Cambridge and NewYork: Cambridge University Press, 1973).

and the military. There are also *different means* to pursue ends in these different domains. Whereas within the economy individualistic behavior prevails, and the means are mostly private means, that is, means that are private to the individual or organization, within culture, and within politics and the military, collective action is more important, and the means are mostly public means, whereby for example in culture one uses the knowledge that is available, and also contributes to the common stock of knowledge that is available.

The second aspect of the sociological approach to power that informs this book concerns *the relationship between productive and destructive conflict.* In order to illustrate this difference, I focus here exclusively upon political-military conflict, also because this type of conflict greatly affects the economy. It is useful to begin by *defining both political-military conflict and collective action.* Political-military conflict is conflict in which at least one of the agents is a collective agent, for example a state, or a large organization more in general, that engages in collective action. Collective action then involves a large number of individuals who act in concert, as if they were a single collective agent. In some cases, we can still talk of collective action in this sense when a number of loosely coordinated SMOS act in concert, as if the social movement was the product of a single collective agent. A closely related *definition of conflict and collective action is based upon the scale* at which they occur, and it suggests that different agents are involved in collective action at different scales of conflict. At a local level, *micro conflict* occurs in which all agents are individuals or very small groups without a formal organization. Most studies of collective action claim that all collective action can be studied as arising from the interactions amongst individuals and the incentives and disincentives faced by individuals.[29] I focus in this book instead upon meso and macro conflict, which is conflict that involves different agents than individuals engaging in collective action. *Meso conflict* involves a scale greater than the local scale and at least one of the agents is an entire social group coordinated by one or more SMOS.[30] Social conflict tends to be meso conflict as per this definition, in which moreover several social groups are involved. *Macro conflict* is conflict that occurs at the largest scale, which can span large regions, continents, and increasingly with globalization, the entire world. Conflict at this scale involves

---

29   This approach was initiated by Mancur Olson, and was set out in: Mancur Olson, *The Logic of Collective Action*, Harvard Economic Studies (Cambridge, Massachusetts and London: Harvard University Press, 2009).

30   I define and discuss meso conflict and meso collective action problems in Chapter 6 of: Olsaretti, *The Struggle for Development and Democracy, Vol. 1*. I address social disaggregation, which affects meso collective action, in Section 5.4 below.

mostly states, since states are the only agents that have the organization and capabilities to engage in conflict on this scale. These states might engage in a series of local or regional conflicts in which large numbers of individuals and one or more social groups fight the state or states, typically in the form of irregular forces. Interstate conflict tends to be macro conflict as per this definition.

Whether conflict is productive or destructive depends in part upon whether the conflict includes violence and whether the conflict is regulated, as well as upon the scale of the conflict. Conflict can exclude or include violence, and it can be more or less well regulated. The two cases that are most important to the discussion in this book are non-violent conflict that is regulated, and violent conflict that is unregulated. Consider first the case of productive conflict. *Productive conflict arises from non-violent conflict that is regulated.* Tilly, in his studies of social movements in Europe, argued that democracy arose from a long process of democratization between each state and social movements, in which conflict had violence removed from it, at the same time as it became routinized and regulated.[31] There were numerous episodes of violence in this long process of democratization and several very violent revolutions. But most of the parties involved in this process sought in the long run to avoid the destruction associated with violence, and cooperated in providing regulation of conflict, including rules of civility, that are very important to avoid violence, and also more in general to limit all negative effects of conflict, as part of what sociologist Norbert Elias called the civilizing process.[32] Moreover, this conflict became productive as it led to a way to advance democracy and ensure that the grievances of social groups were taken into consideration.

This book adds to Tilly's theory of democratization the consideration that *productive conflict in European history includes mostly meso conflict*, and in particular meso conflict in countries in the core of the modern world system. Politics and the military are related in subtle yet important ways, because both are forms of collective action, and both were initially violent to a large extent. But within countries in the core, all violence was removed from internal collective action, over a long period of time, as an integral part of the civilizing

31   Tilly, Tarrow, and McAdam, *Contention and Democracy in Europe.*

32   Norbert Elias, *The Civilizing Process: Sociogenetic and Psychogenetic Investigations* (Oxford: Blackwell, 2000). This book was first translated into English as a two-volume book: *The Civilizing Process, Volume I: The History of Manners* (Oxford: Blackwell, 1969); *The Civilizing Process, Volume II: State Formation and Civilization* (Oxford: Blackwell, 1982). Some of these themes are touched upon also in: John Anthony Hall, *The Importance of Being Civil: The Struggle for Political Decency* (Princeton and Oxford: Princeton University Press, 2013).

process and the democratization process. The mechanism behind the civilizing process involves interstate conflict alongside social conflict. Arguably, the scale of police *repression* within a country is inversely related to the military strength of the country.[33] This can be for several reasons. One reason is that there is a trade-off between the two, whereby the resources that are absorbed for police repression of internal social conflict could be allocated instead to the military for defense against external threats. Another reason is that hegemony, which includes the spontaneous adhesion to a political project, for example a national project, limits social conflict and thus the need for police repression, and also creates a stronger military, not just by resources, but by greater commitment of the masses of the population.

Let us consider now the case of destructive conflict. *Destructive conflict arises from violent conflict*, and especially from unregulated violent conflict. Violent conflict that is unregulated is the most destructive, even when it is only micro conflict like diffuse criminality and terrorism, because the unpredictability of the conflict, and the appalling nature of the crimes, often deliberately targeting civilians, leaves a deep mark on a country and prevents social interaction in all arenas. There is destruction not just of life and property, which is the worst and most visible effect of violent conflict that is unregulated, but also of the most basic components of social life, like social capital, the importance of which I address below. This creates poverty and violence traps, because markets in the areas affected by this type of conflict do not work, or because there is little or no investment, and it is extremely difficult for an area affected by this type of conflict to lift itself out of poverty.

This book also expands upon Tilly's theory of democratization by emphasizing that *the most destructive conflict in European history was macro conflict.* There were two especially destructive forms of macro conflict, in the core or in the periphery of the world system. *In the core* there were massively destructive wars. This is because, as Tilly pointed out, states have become larger and larger in modern times, and they have also built considerably greater military capabilities than states in the past. This means that, while wars in European history have become rare, they have also become more destructive, culminating in the two massively destructive world wars, the First World War, and the Second World War.[34] *In the semi-periphery and periphery* there was massively destructive diffuse conflict involving macro conflict between one state and numerous individuals and social groups with their organizations, all associated with

---

33   I derive this argument from my reading of Gramsci's work.

34   Tilly, *Coercion, Capital and European States.*

institutional changes, leading first to the creation of empires, and then to their replacement by nation-states.[35] Arguably, the recent multiple wars fought by the United States, and recent conflicts that degenerated into civil wars, namely, the Libyan civil war, the South Sudan civil war, the Syrian civil war, and the Yemeni civil war,, and also the Eastern Ukraine civil war,, which recently escalated into a full-blown war, were all part of a new phase of expansion of the world system that brought further destruction, as these wars escalated and some agents behaved outside all rules of conflict.

3   The Provision of Capital and the Importance of Regulation

The negative effects of violence include both such obvious and visible effects as the destruction of life and capital, and also a more subtle and insidious problem. Violent conflict that is unregulated *undermines the smooth functioning of the division of labour in society*, and even the very foundations of social interaction. The contribution that the division of labour in society can give to development depends upon the interaction between arenas, and in particular upon what each arena contributes to the other arenas and how. I want to focus in this section upon what each arena contributes to other arenas, and in the next section upon the manner in which the different arenas contribute to development. Each arena contributes to other arenas its distinctive capabilities. It is useful, however, to differentiate between factors that contribute to these capabilities. Capabilities produced in one arena can be used in other arenas, for example cultural capabilities are used in the economic arenas to lead to economic capabilities. In addition to capabilities, each arena provides to other arenas both its own type of capital, and also regulation. Capital, whether private or public capital, by which we typically mean economic capital, enters in production processes as one of the factors of these processes.[36] Capabilities,

---

35   Wimmer and Min argue that the rise of empires, and the later emergence of nation-states, as part of decolonization, were important institutional transformations that lead however to great increase in war: Andreas Wimmer and Brian Min, "From Empire to Nation-State: Explaining Wars in the Modern World, 1816–2001," *American Sociological Review* 71, no. 6 (2006). Spruyt addresses the huge financial and human costs of colonial wars in: Spruyt, *Ending Empire*.

36   Neoclassical economics regards capital as a factor of production, together with land and labour, but there are disagreements about the details and especially about the importance of capital over and above the other factors: Klaus H. Hennings, "Capital as a Factor of Production," in *Capital Theory*, ed. John Eatwell, Murray Milgate, and Peter Newman (London and New York: Palgrave Macmillan, 1990). On capital in Marxian economics, see: Jayati Ghosh, "Capital," in *The Elgar Companion to Marxist Economics*, ed.

capital, and other factors such as values, are used for regulation, and are thus very important for productive conflict. In the case of values, they do not participate in production as a component of the process of production, but affect the behavior of individuals and organizations. In this section I begin to expand upon the concept of regulation by focusing on the regulation that politics and culture provide to markets. The overall argument is that each arena contributes to the capital of one form or another used by other arenas, and that both culture and politics contribute all-important regulation to the economy.

I use in this book an *extended and sociological concept of capital that includes social capital, and cultural capital,* in addition to the economic capital that we normally associate with the concept of capital. This concept of capital enables us better to understand how capital works, and how it favors or hinders development and democracy. It is useful first to delve into *the definition of social capital* that I use. There are numerous competing definitions of social capital, each of which emphasizes different aspects of this concept.[37] I use the expression social capital to refer to the number of social ties that an individual participates in. The qualities of these ties are also important. An important quality is whether they are strong or weak ties. Granovetter, for example, has argued that social capital in the form of weak ties is especially important in job markets, for the sharing of information that individuals need to find jobs.[38]

Ben Fine, Alfredo Saad-Filho, and Marco Boffo (Cheltenham, UK and Northampton, Massachusetts: Edward Elgar Publishing, 2012).

37   Overviews of the concept of social capital and associated debates are provided by: Alejandro Portes, "Social Capital: Its Origins and Applications in Modern Sociology," *Annual Review of Sociology* 24, no. 1 (1998). Michael Woolcock, "Social Capital: The State of the Notion," in *Social Capital. Global and Local Perspectives,* ed. Jouko Kajanoja and Jussi Simpura (Helsinki: Government Institute for Economic Research, 2000). Frane Adam and Borut Rončević, "Social Capital: Recent Debates and Research Trends," *Social Science Information* 42, no. 2 (2003); Humnath Bhandari and Kumi Yasunobu, "What Is Social Capital? A Comprehensive Review of the Concept," *Asian Journal of Social Science* 37, no. 3 (2009).

38   Rebecca L. Sandefur and Edward O. Laumann, "A Paradigm for Social Capital," in *Knowledge and Social Capital: Foundations and Applications* (London and New York: Routledge, 2009). Granovetter's argument extended the importance of weak ties also to political organization and social cohesion: Mark Granovetter, "The Strength of Weak Ties," *American Journal of Sociology* 78, no. 6 (1973); "The Strength of Weak Ties: A Network Theory Revisited," *Sociological Theory* 1 (1983). Empirical tests have confirmed Granovetter's theory: Deborah Wright Brown and Alison M. Konrad, "Granovetter Was Right: The Importance of Weak Ties to a Contemporary Job Search," *Group & Organization Management* 26, no. 4 (2001). Other empirical tests have confirmed it and modified it at the same time, showing the importance in some cases of strong ties as well as weak ties: Laura K. Gee et al., "The Paradox of Weak Ties in 55 Countries," *Journal of Economic Behavior & Organization* 133 (2017).

Another important quality is whether the ties are associated with trust. Trust is a quality of the social ties that constitute social capital, rather than being social capital itself. Typically, strong ties are associated with a high level of trust, but this is not necessarily the case. A despot or monarch might have strong ties to some of his or her subjects, but be a completely arbitrary and unreliable ruler, whose behavior is not and cannot be trusted by the subjects.[39] Trust instead can best be conceptualized as cultural capital, as part of a Weberian concept of cultural capital.

An important question concerns *the relationship between social capital and other types of capital,* including cultural capital. In keeping with the main argument of this book, namely that the economy, culture, politics, and the military are distinct yet complementary domains of human activity, I want to suggest that *there is economic, cultural, and political capital,* and that social capital complements each of these types of capital. Sociologists, including in particular Pierre Bourdieu, have emphasized that, in addition to economic capital, there is also social capital and cultural capital. Bourdieu defined cultural capital as qualifications, and by extension prestige.[40] Political capital can be taken to refer to the specific experience and qualifications that are derived from political activities, including endorsements. It uses other forms of capital but it is distinct from them. These include social capital in the form of specific networks that individuals engaged in politics participate in. These networks can be patronage networks, in which there are specific relations of power involved.[41]

---

39   On the relationship between trust and social capital, see: Arnaldo Bagnasco, "Trust and Social Capital," in *The Blackwell Companion to Political Sociology,* ed. Kate Nash and Alan Scott (2004). There are very different approaches in the literature. Some see social capital as consisting of trust relationships, thus trust is a component of social capital: Derrick Purdue, "Neighbourhood Governance: Leadership, Trust and Social Capital," *Urban Studies* 38, no. 12 (2001). Others consider trust to be a source of social capital: Florencia Torche and Eduardo Valenzuela, "Trust and Reciprocity: A Theoretical Distinction of the Sources of Social Capital," *European Journal of Social Theory* 14, no. 2 (2011).

40   Pierre Bourdieu, *Forms of Capital,* trans. Peter Collier, General Sociology, Volume 3: Lectures at the Collège de France 1983–84 (Cambridge, UK and Malden, Massachusetts: Polity, 2021). This approach differs from Putnam's: Martti Siisiainen, "Two Concepts of Social Capital: Bourdieu Vs. Putnam," *International Journal of Contemporary Sociology* 40, no. 2 (2003).

41   For a discussion of political capital and its definition, see: Kimberly L. Casey, "Defining Political Capital: A Reconsideration of Bourdieu's Interconvertibility Theory," (2008). Casey defines it as an amalgam of other types of capital that is applied to politics. As I use the expression, it includes both cultural and symbolic capital such as name recognition in politics, and qualifications relevant to politics, and it uses social capital such as political connections, but is not the same as social capital. This is because social capital is relevant to all other forms of capita. For example, investors benefit from social

Social capital is crucially important to the successful use of all other forms of capital, because social capital is very important to the sharing of information and coordination of activities amongst different agents. Let us consider the relation of social capital to cultural capital, and of both to economic capital. It is useful to extend the concept of cultural capital beyond qualifications, to include a Weberian cultural capital that consists in being known to be skilled, and being known to be reliable, a capital that Weber argued was essential to the accumulation of economic capital and to the emergence of capitalism.[42] Social capital complements this type of cultural capital, because the exchange of information that is enabled by social capital increases or diminishes knowledge of the reliability of a person, and thus their cultural capital. Together, both social capital and cultural capital strengthen economic capital. They make it possible to accumulate economic capital, as pointed out by Weber, and also to invest it thanks to reliable information, the lack of which is a major problem for entrepreneurs and investors alike.

In keeping with another important argument of this book, namely that the interactions amongst different agents in society occur at micro, meso, and macro scales of social interaction, there are different types of social capital depending on the agent and the scale at which we calculate the counts of social capital. As Alejandro Portes suggested, it is necessary to distinguish between social capital at the level of individuals and at the level of communities.[43] Social capital at the level of communities is very important because it *complements such measures of the extent of civil society* as the number of associations for a given population density, used by Putnam and Molotch amongst others. Social capital can include measures of the average number of

---

capital in investing economic capital, and researchers benefit from social capital in order to grow their cultural capital through funding for research. For a discussion of political capital and its applications in China, see: Victor Nee and Sonja Opper, "Political Capital in a Market Economy," *Social Forces* 88, no. 5 (2010). Social capital involved in patronage networks has negative effects. For a review of patronage in societies in which it is deeply rooted, see: Henk D. Flap, "Patronage: an Institution in Its Own Right," in *Social Institutions*, ed. Michael Hechter, Karl-Dieter Opp, and Reinhard Wippler (Londonand New York: Routledge, 2018). However, some researchers have found that access to patronage, alongside other types of resources, benefits individuals in communities: Bob Edwards and John D. McCarthy, "Strategy Matters: The Contingent Value of Social Capital in the Survival of Local Social Movement Organizations," *Social Forces* 83, no. 2 (2004).

42   This is one of the main arguments in: Max Weber, P. R. Baehr, and G. C. Wells, *The Protestant Ethic and the Spirit of Capitalism and Other Writings*, Penguin Classics (London: Penguin, 2002).

43   Alejandro Portes, "The Two Meanings of Social Capital," *Sociological Forum* 15, no. 1 (2000).

ties that individuals have to these associations, and as such is very important for democracy.[44] It is thus important to refine and extend Portes' approach. At the level of communities, one can arguably speak of the total social capital of communities. Part of this social capital can be characterized as public social capital, accessible to all. This contrasts with patronage networks, because the latter are exclusionary, and provide to clients of the patron preferential access to public goods, or even exclusive access. If the patron is a politician, this also runs counter to the bureaucratic requirement of impartiality, thus undermining trust in the state.[45] The rest of the total social capital of communities is an aggregate of the private social capital of members of the community. Arguably, in calculating the total social capital of a community, we should measure both the aggregate for individuals and for organizations. We can calculate counts of social capital available to at least three different types of agents: individuals, organizations, and the state. The count of social ties at the level of individuals is what is often meant by social capital. The count of social ties at the level of an organization is also important, at least for communities. It is the count of social ties between a given organization and other organizations, as well as to individuals and the state.[46] The count of social capital can also be at the level of the state, not just the level of the entire state, which is not so useful, but

---

44   Bob Edwards, Michael W. Foley, and Mario Diani, eds., *Beyond Tocqueville: Civil Society and the Social Capital Debate in Comparative Perspective* (Hanover and London: University Press of New England, 2001). Edwards and Foley have criticized Putnam for associating social capital with civil society, claiming that the boundaries between markets, civil society, and the state are not easy to demarcate: Bob Edwards and Michael W. Foley, "Civil Society and Social Capital Beyond Putnam," *American Behavioral Scientist* 42, no. 1 (1998). This is not a reason to renounce using the concept of civil society.

45   The importance of public social capital emerges in: Dietlind Stolle and Thomas R. Rochon, "Are All Associations Alike? Member Diversity, Associational Type, and the Creation of Social Capital," ibid. Membership in associations in France is *not* correlated with higher levels of civic behavior and trust: Nonna Mayer, "Democracy in France: Do Associations Matter?," in *Generating Social Capital: Civil Society and Insitutions in Comparative Perspective*, ed. Marc Hooghe and Dietlind Stolle (London and New York: Palgrave Macmillan, 2003). One possible explanation of this finding is the survival of patronage networks within and between associations. On the importance of impartiality to generalized trust and the use of social capital, see: Bo Rothstein and Dietlind Stolle, "Social Capital, Impartiality, and the Welfare State: an Institutional Approach," ibid. I discuss below public social capital.

46   For an overview of social capital within and across organizations, see: Olav Sorenson and Michelle Rogan, "(When) Do Organizations Have Social Capital?," *Annual Review of Sociology* 40 (2014). On the importance of this type social capital, see: Eric Lesser, "Leveraging Social Capital in Organizations," in *Knowledge and Social Capital: Foundations and Applications*, ed. Eric Lesser (London and New York: Routledge, 2009).

at the level of individual ministries or regional state institutions such as the administration in a region. At the level of ministries, there are ties between the ministry and NGOs within the political arena itself, and between ministries in the political arena and corporations in the economic arena, as part of a state-markets system. At the level of regional administrations, there are similar ties between the administration and local NGOs and local companies.[47]

In studying the effects of social capital on communities one can distinguish between negative and positive social capital, or as I suggest here, between different uses that are made of social capital. In order to contribute to development and democracy, *social capital has to be used as part of productive social conflict*, that is, as part of conflict that is subjected to laws and values, has become routinized, and from which all violence has been removed. This is part of *an alternative definition to the concept of negative social capital*. Political scientist Sheri Berman has argued that civil society can be associated with nazism, and other scholars have confirmed her argument by finding empirical evidence that social capital led to the rise of nazism.[48] Moreover, it has been suggested that, in communities in southern Italy affected by the mafia, and in the southern United States affected by the Ku Klux Klan, or KKK, mafia syndicates and their members, and KKK chapters and their members, use social capital in their activities, and therefore social capital can contribute to economic crime and racially and politically motivated crime.[49] Some authors

47   Robert D. Putnam, *Bowling Alone: The Collapse and Revival of American Community*, A Touchstone Book (New York: Simon & Schuster, 2000). A more recent index of state social capital was proposed by: Jennifer M. Mellor and Jeffrey Milyo, "State Social Capital and Individual Health Status," *Journal of Health Politics, Policy and Law* 30, no. 6 (2005). On the importance of social capital, including networks, for local government and local development, see: Carlo Trigilia, "Social Capital and Local Development," *European Journal of Social Theory* 4, no. 4 (2001). Joe Wallis and Brian Dollery, "Social Capital and Local Government Capacity," *Australian Journal of Public Administration* 61, no. 3 (2002).

48   Sheri Berman, "Civil Society and the Collapse of the Weimar Republic," *World Politics* 49, no. 3 (1997). "Civil Society and Political Insitutionalization," in *Beyond Tocqueville: Civil Society and the Social Capital Debate in Comparative Perspective*, ed. Bob Edwards, Michael W. Foley, and Mario Diani (Hanover and London: University Press of New England, 2001). A similar argument has been made for the use of social capital by nazis, whereby the denser the social networks, the faster the recruitment in the Nazi party, social capital thus contributing to the rise to power of the Nazi party: Shanker Satyanath, Nico Voigtländer, and Hans-Joachim Voth, "Bowling for Fascism: Social Capital and the Rise of the Nazi Party," *Journal of Political Economy* 125, no. 2 (2017).

49   Both Fukuyama and Putnam draw attention to the negative use of social capital by the mafia and the KKK, which grow their social capital at the expense of other groups: Francis Fukuyama, *The Great Disruption: Human Nature and the Reconstitution of Social Order* (New York, London, Toronto, Sydney, and Singapore: Simon & Schuster, 1999); "Social Capital, Civil Society and Development," *Third World Quarterly* 22, no. 1 (2001). Putnam,

have described the social capital used by criminal organizations as a type of negative social capital, in order to contrast it with the positive social capital, or civic capital, that benefits communities, and through them development and democracy.[50] The approach that I propose emphasizes instead that the same means, social capital, can be used for altogether different goals, and in altogether different manners.

The different goals entail growing only the social capital of the mafia syndicate and its members, or of the KKK chapter and its members, as opposed to the social capital of all members throughout the community, and the public social capital in the community. The different manners of using social capital also entail using social capital as part of destructive, as opposed to productive conflict. The uses of social capital made by the mafia and the KKK are part of destructive social conflict, as both organizations operate outside norms and values accepted by the majority, and also use violence, even random violence. *Diffuse violence, and especially random violence, has many negative effects* that affect both markets and civil society, both private companies and communities. Diffuse violence, or even the fear of violence, can affect the patterns of social interaction, leading to the *parcellization of a territory, and the markets within this territory.* Faced with violence, buyers and sellers stay in their communities, or in just one neighborhood that they know well, so that they know where not to go and whom to avoid. The same parcellization of activity can affect an entire territory, with disastrous effects for development. Diffuse violence can harm specific areas, or even entire regions in a country, and ultimately split a country into islands of legality and productive activity. This affects the entire country, and not just some areas. This is because, for the division of labour in society to function smoothly, and for different arenas to contribute to each other, it is necessary that most of a society be free from diffuse violence. The

---

Leonardi, and Nanetti, *Making Democracy Work*; Putnam, *Bowling Alone*. Acts of violence by the mafia, such as arson that destroys shops or factories, also create a climate of fear that destroys the total social capital of communities, and resemble terrorism in this respect.

50   An instance of a study that employs the concept of negative social capital is: Loïc Wacquant, "Negative Social Capital: State Breakdown and Social Destitution in America's Urban Core," *Netherlands Journal of Housing and the Built Environment* 13, no. 1 (1998). I find the approach proposed by Guiso and Pinotti more useful, as it emphasizes that political capital, in the form of voting rights and representation in parliament, only comes to fruition when it is accompanied by suitable cultural capital that they refer to as 'civic capital,' that is, capital that works for the entire community and not just for small groups within it: Luigi Guiso and Paolo Pinotti, "Democratization and Civic Capital," in *The Economic Development of Europe's Regions: A Quantitative History since 1900*, ed. Joan Ramon Rosés and Nolf Wolf (London and New York: Routledge, 2018).

structures linking institutions to organizations and citizens can similarly be broken up into separate, discrete structures, which are smaller, and link fewer institutions and fewer organizations, reducing their overall contribution to development.

By contrast, social capital that is used as part of productive social conflict can give many important contributions to development. Here I want to focus upon the contributions to embedded autonomy between arenas, and to regulation. The two are closely related. Social capital is very important to *understand embedded autonomy across arenas*. Embedded autonomy requires social capital, in particular networks amongst institutions and other organizations, and between institutions and individuals. As argued by Evans, the networks between institutions and organizations emerge where there are, to begin with, networks amongst individuals, who come to fill specific roles in institutions and organizations.[51] Later, the institutions might find these networks useful and might create permanent roles and official networks. These networks are important to start enterprises and make them competitive on the international stage. They are also important to promote development on the long run, amongst other reasons, because these networks are important to regulation, including regulation of the interaction between arenas. A very important use of social capital is for regulation. Regulation includes the provision of capital in the right quantities required by the economy. Regulation also includes constraints on behavior, including constraints in the manner in which one uses capital. In this last case, social capital and regulation contribute to each other, because social capital contributes to regulation, and regulation contributes to the growth of total social capital in a community, and ultimately to greater social capital, compared to communities thorn by the mafia or the KKK, for example. The two types of regulation are related. Without regulation of behavior, there cannot be adequate provision of economic capital, for example, since one party to a transaction might not provide the economic capital that they should provide and thus greatly harms productive activities.

Let us consider first *regulation that involves the provision of capital to the economy*. Social capital is an integral part of embedded autonomy between arenas, and through information sharing, it regulates the provision to markets of cultural capital, typically from civil society, and also of political capital, typically from the state. *Civil society contributes cultural capital* to markets in the

---

51   Evans, for example, studied a group of Brazilian computer scientists trained in the United
      States and known as the 'barbudos,' and their ties to the Brazilian state and corporations,
      as they tried to start a local computer industry after returning to Brazil: Evans, *Dependent
      Development*.

form of individuals with the qualifications, knowledge, and skills required by markets. It also makes other important contributions. The use of a standard language throughout a country that is measured by literacy levels, and that increases both individual and collective capabilities, is part of cultural development and the associated capabilities. Arguably, a standard language can be classified as a public good, and perhaps more specifically as collective cultural capital that is accessible to all.[52] This type of cultural capital is *closely related to, yet distinct from, regulation*. For example, teaching a language, which contributes to literacy in a country and to its cultural development, is distinct from codifying and standardizing the teaching of a language, which includes providing a standard grammar and vocabulary, and is a type of cultural regulation. They are also often implemented by different institutions. A ministry of education, or civil society institutions like Catholic schools, provide teaching in the standard language, whereas in at least some countries there are separate academies within civil society that are devoted to codifying the national language.[53] In practice, a ministry of education is partly involved in defining and standardizing the national language, but defining a standard language and teaching it are still two distinct functions, and different departments within a ministry would be involved in these different functions.

Similar considerations apply to political capital. The *state contributes political capital* to markets in the form of law and order. The police, which provides collective capabilities that are similar to the military, but for duties internal to a state, is an organization that provides political-military development

---

52   On language as a public good, see: Chris Chhim and Éric Bélanger, "Language as a Public Good and National Identity: Scotland's Competing Heritage Languages," *Nations and Nationalism* 23, no. 4 (2017). For instances of social capital seen as a public good, see: Ichiro Kawachi and Lisa Berkman, "Social Cohesion, Social Capital, and Health," *Social Epidemiology* 174, no. 7 (2000); Nan Lin, "Building a Network Theory of Social Capital," *Social capital* (2017). Fukuyama disagrees with this approach and suggests social capital is a private good with large positive and negative externalities: Francis Fukuyama, "Social Capital and Development," *SAIS Review (1989–2003)* 22, no. 1 (2002): 29–30. I suggest reasons to consider some public venues as providers of public social capital below, in the discussion of Aviram's work.

53   In Italy the Accademia della Crusca codified language: Giovanni Nencioni, "L'Accademia della Crusca e la Lingua Italiana," in *The History of Linguistics in Italy*, ed. Paolo Ramat, Hans-Josef Niederehe, and E. F. K. Koerner (Amsterdam: John Benjamins Publishing Company, 1986). In France the Académie Française codified language and produced the standard dictionary of French: Michael P. Fitzsimmons, *The Place of Words: The Académie Française and Its Dictionary During an Age of Revolution* (Oxford and New York: Oxford University Press, 2017). For an overview of the role of dictionaries in language policies, see: Dion Nkomo, "Dictionaries and Language Policy," in *The Routledge Handbook of Lexicography*, ed. Pedro A. Fuertes-Olivera (London and New York: Routledge, 2017).

and the associated capabilities, by providing law and order, something that includes maintaining the peace and preventing diffuse violence. Arguably, law and order can be classified as a public good, and perhaps more specifically as collective political capital that is accessible to all.[54] This type of political capital, similarly to cultural capital, is *also closely related to, yet distinct from, regulation*. For example, police work involves applying specific laws regarding violence and other aspects of human activity, such as preventing noise at night, or enforcing safety measures in factories and construction sites. It can be described as enforcing laws, and it is different than issuing laws and standardizing legal codes. These are the preserve of altogether different institutions within the state, being part respectively of the judiciary, and of the legislature.

Let us consider now *regulation that concerns behavior in social interactions*, including market interactions, for example avoiding opportunistic behavior, and avoiding violence. Social capital contributes to regulation through information sharing, and also through values. *Information sharing is crucial to regulation.* In particular, the availability of information is crucial to be able to identify infractions and bring forward the evidence that is necessary to apply sanctions against those who break contracts or show opportunistic behavior. Legal theorist Avitai Aviram suggests that this is an advantage that non-state agents have compared to the state, and that a crucial contribution to the availability of information comes from networks that benefit from network effects. These effects are related to the number of individuals who participate in the network, whereby a greater number of individuals tend to lead to greater information available within the network.[55] However, Aviram also includes amongst networks that benefit from network effects such venues as trade associations, commodity exchanges, and internet auction sites like eBay. In this book, I consider these instead as venues that are effectively public areas more or less open to anyone who works in a field, and in which transient networks thrive, providing public social capital.[56] I also differ from Aviram and

---

54   On law and order, including policing, as a public good, see: Tyler Cowen, "Law as a Public Good: The Economics of Anarchy," *Economics & Philosophy* 8, no. 2 (1992); Ian Loader and Neil Walker, "Policing as a Public Good: Reconstituting the Connections between Policing and the State," *Theoretical Criminology* 5, no. 1 (2001).

55   Amitai Aviram, "Regulation by Networks," *Brigham Young University Law Review* 29, no. 4 (2003).

56   Ibid., 1190, 1194. Transient networks can be a major contribution to public social capital, together with public areas. On transient networks in urban settings, see: Nigel Thrift, "An Urban Impasse?," *Theory, Culture & Society* 10, no. 2 (1993). On the concept of transient social capital and transient communities, see: Sibren Fetter, A. J. Berlanga, and Peter B. Sloep, "Using ad Hoc Transient Communities to Strengthen Social Capital: Design Considerations" (paper presented at the Proceedings of the 7th International Conference

sociologist Bruno Latour, the founder of a theoretical paradigm in sociology known as Actor-Network-Theory, or ANT, in that I see networks merely as a means, or tool, not as agents in their own right. It is not networks that regulate, but the individual agents or organizations who participate in the networks. The networks are an important means available to the agents to regulate, and in rare cases most agents in the network regulate, whether they are individuals or organizations.[57] Perhaps in these cases in which most agents in a network regulate, it might be appropriate to speak of regulation by networks. *Values are also crucial to regulation.* I use the word values to include norms. Values are not just involved in self-regulation, as suggested by Aviram, but also in community regulation, whereby if an individual in a community blatantly violates norms, other individuals in the same community intervene.

A growing literature addresses the importance of the interaction between values and laws in regulating behavior.[58] Sociologist James Coleman contributed to this literature and expressed concern at the decline of communities in which values are taught and implemented, and ultimately of values themselves, pointing to the serious consequences this decline would have for civil society.[59]

---

on Networked Learning, Lancaster, 2010); Louise Ryan et al., "Social Networks, Social Support and Social Capital: The Experiences of Recent Polish Migrants in London," *Sociology* 42, no. 4 (2008); Jonathan Ilan, "Street Social Capital in the Liquid City," *Ethnography* 14, no. 1 (2013).

57   Latour set out his theory in: Bruno Latour, *Reassembling the Social: An Introduction to Actor-Network-Theory* (Oxford and New York: Oxford University Press, 2005). He promoted it in: "On Actor-Network Theory: A Few Clarifications," *Soziale welt* (1996). "Network Theory| Networks, Societies, Spheres: Reflections of an Actor-Network Theorist," *International journal of communication* 5 (2011). Sociologist Loes Knaapen, who works on the sociology of medicine, has applied ANT to this field. For examples of Knaapen's work, see: Loes Knaapen, "Being 'Evidence-Based' in the Absence of Evidence: The Management of Non-Evidence in Guideline Development," *Social Studies of Science* 43, no. 5 (2013). "Science Needs More External Evaluation, Not Less," *Social Science Information* 60, no. 3 (2021). Latour also worked on studies of science and technology. He set out his arguments in this field in: Bruno Latour, *Pandora's Hope: Essays on the Reality of Science Studies* (Cambridge, Massachusetts and London: Harvard University Press, 1999).

58   A review of this literature is provided in: Richard H. McAdams, "The Origin, Development, and Regulation of Norms," *Michigan Law Review*, no. 96 (1997).

59   Portes points out that Coleman was concerned with the disappearance of social capital and the effects it had on norms and crime: Portes, "The Two Meanings of Social Capital," 2–3. Coleman's position on these questions is expressed in: James S. Coleman, "Social Capital in the Creation of Human Capital," *American Journal of Sociology* 94 (1988). Bagnasco reformulates Jane Jacob's argument on society's loss of self-organizational abilities in terms of loss of social capital: Bagnasco, "Trust and Social Capital."

4   Regulation and System States and System Change

In order to conceptualize how regulation works and what are its effects, it is
best to reformulate regulation as participating in systems, and particularly in
ensuring certain system states. This is also useful to conceptualize the fact that
regulation also contributes to the smooth functioning of the division of labour
by contributing to the sharing of information and coordination of activities
that are indispensable to the provision of capabilities, and capital, the latter
being widely recognized within economics. *It is useful to introduce the concepts
of system and system state in development,* in order better to conceptualize these
positive effects of regulation, and of sharing of information and coordination
of activities more in general. The concept of system is useful to development
because a system consists of separate institutions and organizations, without
a formal hierarchy between them, all of which are more or less autonomous to
pursue their growth plans. Each arena can be conceptualized as consisting of
a system or a number of related systems. For example, a market in which there
are many organizations and some economic institutions such as associations
of producers can be conceptualized as an economic system.

Most importantly, *systems can involve groups of institutions and organizations from different arenas.* As pointed out above, the cases of industrial development described by Evans can aptly be described as *state-markets systems.*
These systems range from one institution, a single government ministry, with
ties to one or a few corporations, to more complex cases that are aptly describable as state-market systems, because one or more state ministries interact
with many corporations. This concept of system, involving a mix of institutions and organizations, from two different arenas, can be usefully generalized,
and applied to a number of different cases. The concept of *innovation system* is
used to describe a combination of institutions and other organizations drawn
from the state, civil society, and markets, all of which interact in such a manner
as to produce scientific and technological innovations.[60] The concept of *welfare system* is used to describe a combination of state institutions and NGOS

---

60   On national innovation systems, see: Chris Freeman, "The 'National System of Innovation'
      in Historical Perspective," *Cambridge Journal of Economics* 19, no. 1 (1995). See also the
      many contributions in: R. R. Nelson, ed. *National Innovation Systems: A Comparative
      Analysis* (Oxford and New York: Oxford University Press, 1993). Eduardo Albuquerque
      et al., eds., *Developing National Systems of Innovation: University-Industry Interactions
      in the Global South* (Cheltenham, UK and Northampton, Massachusetts: Edward Elgar
      Publishing, 2015). On the spatial aspect of technology, see Thrift's work, including: Nigel
      Thrift, "From Born to Made: Technology, Biology and Space," *Transactions of the Institute
      of British Geographers* 30, no. 4 (2005).

that together offer different welfare mixes, which can address the diverse needs of welfare recipients, and also vary geographically. The concept of welfare system can arguably be extended to include donors, who act in between markets and civil society. Welfare systems participate in the state-society system, as approached by sociologist Emily Barman in her study of donors and private companies involved in donations.[61]

The usefulness of the concept of system to development is due to the fact that it allows us to conceptualize a situation in which different institutions and organizations are free to pursue their growth plans, but *through regulation, and through sharing of information and coordination of activities, they can achieve important common goals.* Regulation therefore is an important concept, and I generalize here the concept of regulation used by the regulation school in economics.[62] Sharing information and coordinating activities across arenas are distinct from regulation, although they can contribute to it, for example in order to formulate laws or policies that are especially useful, something that requires detailed and reliable information. *This concept of regulation involves an element of planning. However, this need not be rigid central planning* Soviet-style, which is the epitome of rigid planning that gets in the way of economic growth, rather than helping it. *There is some planning in all corporations*, and it is indispensable. For example, if a corporation intends to expand into a market, this entails that it has to plan ahead and be ready to increase its productive capacity, and its distribution capacity, which includes increasing its equipment, workforce, and IT department, from providing no goods in that market, to providing a certain number of goods.[63] Similarly, *there is some planning*

---

61   On Welfare systems, see: Adalbert Evers, "Mixed Welfare Systems and Hybrid Organizations: Changes in the Governance and Provision of Social Services," *International Journal of Public Administration* 28, no. 9–10 (2005). Alberta Andreotti and Enzo Mingione, "Local Welfare Systems in Europe and the Economic Crisis," *European Urban and Regional Studies* 23, no. 3 (2016). Barman approached donors and NGOs as part of a Bourdieaun field: Emily Barman, "An Institutional Approach to Donor Control: From Dyadic Ties to a Field-Level Analysis," *American Journal of Sociology* 112, no. 5 (2007). On the importance of social capital to the Swedish welfare state, see: Bo Rothstein, "Social Capital in the Social Democratic Welfare State," *Politics & Society* 29, no. 2 (2001).

62   On the regulation school, see: Alfredo C. Jr Robles, *French Theories of Regulation and Conceptions of the International Division of Labour*, International Political Economy Series (New York: St Martin's, 1994). A seminal work of this school is: Michel Aglietta, *A Theory of Capitalist Regulation: The US Experience* (London and New York: Verso Books, 2016).

63   The concept of steady state for the example of one corporation is associated with industrial engineering and economies of scale. In order to produce a good, a corporation has to buy one or more pieces of industrial machinery, and to hire a certain number of workers, in order to produce a certain amount of that good at a steady state. All industrial projects involve an element of planning, and this has generated specific processes: Stefano

in a system in which many different organizations interact, with coordination provided by institutions, but in a system this can bring government closer to the people, and make it flexible and better able to address diverse needs. This can best be conceptualized as a state-society system that can be applied also to regional planning.[64] As pointed out above, the concept of state-society system, in the case in which a state is divided into several different regional administrations, is useful to conceptualize *multi-level governance,* where there are different levels at which the state operates. This can be applied to explain the functioning of a state that is not one single rigidly-centralized state, but is divided into a number of different institutions, with a more or less formal hierarchical organization, and with different ties to civil society organizations and companies in their respective regions. State institutions thus can vary somewhat from one region to another, and they can be part of different innovation systems needed by different economic realities, and different welfare systems needed by the different citizenry, all of which makes the state less rigid and brings government closer to the people.[65]

The usefulness of the concept of system to development is also that systems have states, that can be steady or unsteady, and the concept of system state can help us conceptualize specific regulation challenges. In general, *regulation, and sharing of information and coordination of activities, are necessary to maintain a steady system state,* for example steady growth. Regulation can be of two kinds: self-regulation provided within an arena, and external regulation provided to an arena by other arenas. As far as regulation in the economic arena is concerned, including market regulation, there is self-regulation, and there are also external regulation provided by the political arena, and by the cultural arena.[66] This is because regulation includes both law and order,

---

Tonchia and F. Cozzi, *Industrial Project Management: Planning, Design, and Construction* (Cham, Switzerland: Springer, 2010). The concept of steady state for a system is different than the example for a corporation, as it involves several such companies. However, planning is involved in both, and the planning by a company includes also such things as forecasts of the total market size, and how this market grows, both of which are relevant to considerations of ensuring a steady state for a system.

64 The entire literature on regional planning involves planning in this sense, of coordinating amongst organizations, without imposing a rigid central plan. A classic in this type of planning is: Peter Hall, *Urban and Regional Planning* (London and New York: Routledge, 2002).

65 Colomer argues that greater autonomy to regions in Europe would serve the purpose of bringing the government closer to local realities: Colomer, *Great Empires, Small Nations.*

66 Adam Smith's theory, and liberal, and neoliberal theories, all emphasized self-regulation. However, Smith's theory also emphasized an element of cultural regulation, if only implicitly, by emphasizing that greed should not be part of markets: Heinz D Kurz, "Adam Smith on Markets, Competition and Violations of Natural Liberty," *Cambridge Journal of*

provided by the political arena, and values, provided by the cultural arena. I want to introduce *qualifications to what self-regulation of markets can achieve*. These qualifications are especially clear if we focus on the importance of both laws and values to regulate activities, reinforcing another point, namely, that *self-regulation and external regulation complement each other*, and the opposition between them is a false dichotomy. It is useful to distinguish between two cases. There are cases in which an appropriate combination of external regulation and self-regulation makes regulation more effective. In many cases it is necessary at least for political and cultural institutions to facilitate self-regulation of markets, for example by circulating information that is necessary for self-regulation, or facilitating such factors as social capital, which facilitate the circulation of information. There are also cases in which self-regulation is not sufficient and external regulation ought to be used to guarantee smooth system growth, for example when a change in the system (a system change) is necessary, or when the system expands, especially if it expands rapidly.

Let us consider the case in which *a combination of self-regulation and external regulation is most efficient, as it best contributes to a steady state*. Here I focus upon the importance of external regulation from both culture and politics to markets. Both ethical values and states that uniformly and efficiently apply laws are necessary to regulate social interaction. Since values are neglected in mainstream economic theory, I want to begin by emphasizing *the importance of values, as part of external regulation from both culture and politics, to markets*. Market self-regulation needs values, in addition to self-interested behavior. By contrast with Smith, Weber emphasized the importance of values for market behavior to work, especially on a large geographical scale, and also for capitalism to emerge.[67] Here I want to emphasize that behavior throughout a country, in markets, society, and the state, ought to conform to values, and in practice it often does in most countries in the West today, as there are values that prescribe amongst other things the means that can be used, and the manner in which to use them, as well as the ends that can be pursued. Where diffuse violence, and criminality more in general prevail, there is little or no development, and the costs of policing a city, a region, or a country riven with

---

    Economics 40, no. 2 (2016). Smith was also concerned to guarantee individual liberties. The latter have a political as much as an economic aspect. An overview of theories of regulation and criticism of Marxian regulation theory is provided by: Andrei Shleifer, "Understanding Regulation," *European Financial Management* 11, no. 4 (2005). Shleifer suggests that regulation has to find a middle way between dictatorship and disorder, an argument that is relevant to the extension of the EVL model in Section 7.4 below.

67 Weber, Baehr, and Wells, *The Protestant Ethic*.

conflict can become prohibitively high, creating poverty and violence traps. Tilly has studied how these traps affect entire social groups.[68] Values provided by culture are necessary, in addition to the negative incentives provided by policing through fear of arrest, because they lower the costs of policing. If there was no spontaneous adhesion to laws and individuals were always trying to cut corners, to break the law, and to make gains for themselves that are outside of the law, the costs of policing would be staggering.[69] Values are also necessary to undermine the sub-cultures that reinforce criminal behaviors. A range of very diverse criminal organizations and the behaviors associated with them, from the mafia, to the KKK, to terrorist organizations, whether by Muslim fundamentalists or by extremists in the West on both the left and right of the political spectrum, are reinforced by their own sub-cultures.[70] This

---

68   Violence often reinforces poverty traps by preventing the buildup of physical and human capital. Economic capital includes physical capital, and cultural capital includes human capital. On poverty traps, see: Costas Azariadis and John Stachurski, "Poverty Traps," in *Handbook of Economic Growth*, ed. Philippe Aghion and Steven Durlauf (Amsterdam, San Diego, Kidlington, Oxford, and London: Elsevier, 2005). See also the numerous contributions in: Samuel Bowles, Steven N. Durlauf, and Karla Hoff, eds., *Poverty Traps* (Princeton and New York: Princeton University Press, 2006). Tilly's argument is set out in: Charles Tilly, *Durable Inequality* (Berkeley and Los Angeles: University of California Press, 1998).

69   Policing is arguably part of a spectrum of regulation: Peter Gill, "Policing and Regulation: What Is the Difference?," *Social & Legal Studies* 11, no. 4 (2002). The spectrum of regulation includes policing, which can make use of coercion, and also soft regulation through values. As argued above, regulation includes values, or norms. The rising costs of policing in Great Britain are addressed by: Helen Mills, Arianna Silvestri, and Roger Grimshaw, Police Expenditure, (Centre for Crime and Justice Studies, 2010). Van Reenen touches upon police costs within the context of the effectiveness of cost reductions: Peter van Reenen, "The 'Unpayable' Police," *Policing* 22, no. 2 (1999). Policing also has non-monetary costs: Rachel A. Harmon, "Federal Programs and the Real Costs of Policing," *New York University Law Review* 90 (2015).

70   Nicaso has studied mafia culture in: Antonio Nicaso and Marcel Danesi, *Made Men: Mafia Culture and the Power of Symbols, Rituals, and Myth* (Lanham, Boulder, New York, and Oxford: Rowman & Littlefield Publishers, 2013). Nicaso takes mafia culture into consideration in his other books: Peter Edwards and Antonio Nicaso, *Business or Blood: Mafia Boss Vito Rizzuto's Last War* (Toronto: Vintage Canada, 2016); Lee Lamothe and Antonio Nicaso, *Bloodlines: The Rise and Fall of the Mafia's Royal Family* (New York: HarperCollins, 2001); Antonio Nicaso and Lee Lamothe, *Angels, Mobsters and Narco-Terrorists: The Rising Menace of Global Criminal Empires* (Mississagua, Ontario: John Wiley & Sons Canada, 2009). The culture of the KKK has been studied by: Felix Harcourt, *Ku Klux Kulture: America and the Klan in the 1920s* (Chicago and London: University of Chicago Press, 2019); James Ridgeway, *Blood in the Face: The Ku Klux Klan, Aryan Nations, Nazi Skinheads, and the Rise of a New White Culture* (New York: Basic Books, 1996). The culture of terrorism has been studied by: Michael Burleigh, *Blood and Rage: A Cultural History of Terrorism* (New York: Harper Press, 2008). On this and related topics see also

means that they have developed their own distinctive sub-cultures that can reinforce their specific criminal behaviors, both by encouraging individuals to indulge in these criminal behaviors, and by strengthening the commitment of members of the criminal organization that is based on these behaviors. This is one of the reasons why it is so hard to uproot such criminal organizations.

An important reason why a combination of self-regulation and external regulation is most efficient, is that in many markets there is little or no resilience to deviations from the norm. *Even a very small number of individuals who break or bend rules can ruin existing markets*. This can be very important. For example, if more than a small percent, say 1% or 5%, of sellers in a market sell defective goods, this can affect the steady system state of the entire market, by leading a large number of buyers to resorting to other markets, or to using only some sellers, who are not the most efficient, but are the most trusted, or to buying only some products.[71] The effects of the mafia and the KKK, for example, both of which operate outside the law, show that neither markets, nor civil society, really work even where a minority resorts to violence and other criminal behaviors like intimidation. This is *especially true in modern societies, including modern markets,* in which a large number of interactions are anonymous, and it is therefore necessary to use laws, as well as values, to regulate economic activity. Values ensure that most individuals in a society conform to discipline and honesty in the pursuit of profits. They especially ensure that the vast majority complies with rules spontaneously, and not just because of the threat of sanctions. States that uniformly enforce laws deal with the few individuals who break rules, and make sure than rule-bending or rule-breaking behavior does not spread beyond a certain point.[72] *Steady market growth requires trusting anonymous interaction*, as it often involves extending markets to new areas or taking in more agents. These additional anonymous interactions, if they

---

the many contributions in: Daniel J. Sherman and Terry Nardin, eds., *Terror, Culture, Politics: Rethinking 9/11* (Bloomington: Indiana University Press, 2006).

71   Yeniyurt and Townsend have argued that distance and uncertainty avoidance prevent the acceptance of new products: Sengun Yeniyurt and Janell D. Townsend, "Does Culture Explain Acceptance of New Products in a Country? An Empirical Investigation," *International Marketing Review* 20, no. 4 (2003). On the effects of organized crime, and its relation to states, see the many contributions in: Gianluca Fiorentini and Sam Peltzman, eds., *The Economics of Organised Crime* (Cambridge and New York: Cambridge University Press, 1997). On the effects of crime on the entire economy, see: Claudio Detotto and Edoardo Otranto, "Does Crime Affect Economic Growth?," *Kyklos* 63, no. 3 (2010).

72   States themselves are challenged by crime and rule-breaking more in general: David Garland, "The Limits of the Sovereign State Strategies of Crime Control in Contemporary Society," *The British Journal of Criminology* 36, no. 4 (1996).

are numerous, can make it harder for markets to participate in steady growth through self-regulation alone. The emergence of large markets can entail that buyers can go further afield to search for cheaper or better products, or that sellers reach more buyers. This requires trusting the law to regulate anonymous interaction, before this activity becomes routinized and buyers and sellers get to know each other, and self-regulation is sufficient.[73] Hence states that enforce honesty in the pursuit of profits are necessary in addition to values, which might not spread throughout a market, nor enable the market to expand, without a state.

Let us consider now the case in which *a combination of self-regulation and external regulation is indispensable, as it is necessary in changes of system states.* Here too I focus upon the importance of external regulation from both culture and politics to markets. The significant changes in system states that require external regulation can range from *significantly* expanding the scale at which a system works, for example a sudden expansion, to changing the manner in which a system works, for example introducing capitalism. In these cases regulation is important, because self-regulation would emerge too slowly or not emerge at all, especially if conflict increases dramatically and spirals out of control. For this purpose, the intervention of local government and police forces is important, not just to provide restraint and prevent violence, but also to grow communities and enable them to expand their social capital, which contributes to markets and welfare.[74] Regulation by the state is indispensable in *the case of significantly expanding the scale at which a system works*, and more specifically expanding markets. In this particular case laws are necessary because, when a market expands to new areas, and numerous new agents, or buyers and sellers, are brought into the market, market self-regulating mechanisms, and even cultural institutions, might not be sufficient at all to guarantee the smooth functioning of the market right after the change. Even with

---

73   One of the ways in which crime affects the economy is by eroding trust in institutions. On the erosion of trust in institutions, see: Luisa Blanco and Isabel Ruiz, "The Impact of Crime and Insecurity on Trust in Democracy and Institutions," *American Economic Review* 103, no. 3 (2013); Alexa J. Singer et al., "Victimization, Fear of Crime, and Trust in Criminal Justice Institutions: A Cross-National Analysis," *Crime & Delinquency* 65, no. 6 (2019).

74   Policing participates in the positive role of local government in growing social capital: Mildred Warner, "Building Social Capital: The Role of Local Government," *The Journal of Socio-Economics* 30, no. 2 (2001). Social capital in its turn can be useful for community policing: Nathan W. Pino, "Community Policing and Social Capital," *Policing: An International Journal of Police Strategies & Management* 24, no. 2 (2001). For a general overview of these questions, see: James Hawdon, "Legitimacy, Trust, Social Capital, and Policing Styles: A Theoretical Statement," *Police Quarterly* 11, no. 2 (2008).

cultural institutions, values do not spread fast enough, and therefore laws are necessary.[75] In addition, there are some things that only a state can provide. Removing barriers, like political barriers, or barriers of currency, requires the intervention of the state.

External regulation is necessary also for changing the manner in which a system works. This is a particular case of system change. Regulation by culture is arguably indispensable in such cases. The main point made by Weber was that, for capitalism to emerge and spread, certain ethical values had to spread first, and this required the previous intervention of cultural institutions, specifically, Protestant religious institutions, which for religious reasons spread widely some values, that then ended up contributing to the economy.[76] Weber's main point is that, before a certain type of economic activity can take place, a *whole* culture has to be in place. This is not a piecemeal change whereby some economic activity produces some culture, that in its turn encourages some more economic activity. In the case of markets, this is because *most* buyers and sellers in a market must share a number of important values for that market to work, and cultural institutions have to intervene to spread those values, or the market emerges much more slowly, or does not emerge at all.[77] In addition to a given culture, a whole set of laws needs to be devised and implemented in order for markets to arise and function. Economist Karl Polanyi argued that the English state played a crucial role in the emergence of modern markets in rural England and then in the rest of the country. This was at the cost of injustices associated with the enclosures movement, whereby village economies based on common lands, arguably dating back to feudalism, where privatized and sold to wealthy landowners, resulting in the destruction of communities.[78]

---

75   On the importance of the law to markets, see: Robin Paul Malloy, *Law and Market Economy: Reinterpreting the Values of Law and Economics* (Cambridge and New York: Cambridge University Press, 2000). On the importance of the law to development as part of a New Institutional Economics approach to development, see: Frank H. Stephen, *Law and Development: An Institutional Critique* (Cheltenham, UK and Northampton, Massachusetts: Edward Elga, 2018).

76   Weber, Baehr, and Wells, *The Protestant Ethic*. On the importance of culture to markets, see: Virgil Henry Storr, *Understanding the Culture of Markets* (London and New York: Routledge, 2013).

77   On the importance of culture to regulate interactions amongst buyers and sellers in a market, see: Mitchel Y. Abolafia, "Markets as Cultures: an Ethnographic Approach," *The Sociological Review* 46, no. 1 (1998). Culture is arguably important also to shape markets themselves, for example through expectations, and through customers' interest in lifestyle brands and their products.

78   Karl Polanyi, Joseph E. Stiglitz, and Fred Block, *The Great Transformation: The Political and Economic Origins of Our Time* (Boston: Beacon Press, 2001). On enclosures and the destruction of rural communities, see: Gordon E. Mingay, *Parliamentary Enclosure*

This paved the way for the introduction of capitalism in rural England, which contributed to the later emergence of industrial capitalism. The main point made by both Polanyi and Gramsci regarding the emergence of modern markets is that the state had to intervene, because there are things such as laws that only a state can provide, and furthermore, that a whole set of laws had to be put in place and enforced.[79] The intervention of the state, I want to add, need not be necessarily in favor of landowners and at the expense of communities. There are better ways to introduce markets that are also compatible with social justice, especially in modern times, in which there is a greater understanding of how markets work, and of the problems of transition from non-market to market economies. With this project, I seek to contribute to an understanding of these problems of transition.

5   The Balance of Power and Separation of Powers between Arenas

The sociology multidisciplinary approach, and the approach to development in terms of capabilities and a theory of power, have profound consequences for the definition of democracy, as well as for the definition of development. By development we usually refer to economic development only, which includes growth in income. By democracy we usually refer to political democracy only, which includes freedom of participation in political parties and regular and free elections of political leaders. Even in these restricted definitions of development and democracy, many would agree that greater development and democracy have been the two defining achievements of the last two hundred years in many Western countries. I argue that development and democracy are even more important and that this is because they affect even more domains of social life. Culture provides an especially clear example. In addition to economic development, there is cultural development, and in addition to political democracy, there is cultural democracy, which includes the freedom to express and practice one's culture and language, a freedom that is central to many ethnic communities and to all struggles for national independence or autonomy,

---

in England: An Introduction to Its Causes, Incidence and Impact, 1750–1850 (London and New York: Routledge, 2014).

79   For an overview of Gramsci's views on economics, including markets, see: Michael R. Kratke, "Antonio Gramsci's Contribution to a Critical Economics," *Historical Materialism* 19, no. 3 (2011). Burawoy argued that Gramsci's and Polanyi's work complemented each other: Michael Burawoy, "For a Sociological Marxism: The Complementary Convergence of Antonio Gramsci and Karl Polanyi," *Politics & Society* 31, no. 2 (2003).

including Quebec's.[80] Below I generalize these points and propose that, as far as development is concerned, there are economic development, cultural development, and political-military development, and as far as democracy is concerned, there are economic democracy, cultural democracy and political-military democracy. Furthermore, these types of development and democracy are each associated with a distinctive arena and power within that arena, and this means that democracy is dependent upon both a division of powers (or types of power) in a country, and also upon a balance of power in a country.

This definition of development and democracy is based upon the sociology multidisciplinary approach. In particular, two aspects of the sociology multidisciplinary approach affect the concepts of development and democracy. The first aspect involves laying *emphasis on how the whole of a country works, and thus taking into consideration culture and politics, as well as the economy, while studying development*, and taking a similar approach to democracy. This is important for policy, because such an approach to development enables the formulation of successful and efficient policies that are coherent across domains, such that an economic policy and a cultural policy reinforce each other, for example.[81] The second aspect of the sociology multidisciplinary approach that affects the concepts of development and democracy involves *social engineering and a specific approach to social structures*. Social engineering builds upon the emphasis of the sociology multidisciplinary approach on how the whole of a country works, and thus prescribes to study culture together with organization and social structures.[82] Social structures are seen

---

80   This book and the book on humanist political philosophy contain a significantly differ-ent approach than John Anthony Hall's approach to nationalism and Charles Taylor's approach to communitarianism. Nationalism and communitarianism sometimes overlap in the case of authors who see the national community as the most important commu-nity. Communitarianism is often seen as opposed to liberalism, for example as argued in: Charles Taylor, *The Malaise of Modernity*, The Massey Lectures Series (Toronto: House of Anansi Press, 2003). I argue instead that the search for cultural democracy that is at the base of communitarianism is complementary, not alternative, to political democracy and the political freedoms emphasized by classical liberal theorists like John Stuart Mill, as set out in: John Stuart Mill and John Gray, *On Liberty and Other Essays*, Oxford World's Classics (Oxford and New York: Oxford University Press, 2008).

81   The concept of cultural development is studied mostly in relation to communities and urban planning: Don Adams and Arlene Goldbard, *Creative Community: The Art of Cultural Development* (New York: Rockefeller Foundation, 2001); Carl Grodach and Anastasia Loukaitou-Sideris, "Cultural Development Strategies and Urban Revitalization: A Survey of US Cities," *International Journal of Cultural Policy* 13, no. 4 (2007). In this book I extend the concept of cultural development to entire countries.

82   I address these questions in the book on the humanist theory of society.

in a humanist social science as human constructs that are liable to be studied, understood, and improved. In some cases, social structures can be built as part of the social engineering for democracy introduced in Volume 1 of this book as an expansion of Putnam's and Molotch's approaches to civil society. Both of these approaches are based chiefly on counts of civil society organizations, neglecting the many features of social structures that exist amongst these organizations, and between these organizations and state institutions.[83] The approach that I advocate is aptly described as social engineering, rather than just economic incentives, because in addition to encouraging the creation of citizen associations and NGOs, I propose that we ought to build up ties amongst them and between them and institutions. This is what makes this approach to democracy an approach that promotes a structural-foundational view of democracy. This view entails that we approach relations in a manner analogous to structural design in buildings, and introduce the concepts of strength and resilience in social structures.

I want to emphasize and clarify the important point that this is a social engineering *for democracy, because the expression social engineering might be associated with the manipulation of society* imposed by totalitarian states following the ideologies of socialism-Marxism, fascism and nazism. Marx's theory of society, which contributed to totalitarianism in Russia, divided society into a base and superstructure, and has been described as an architectural view of society, which might be seen as an instance of social engineering that discredits this concept. I argue instead that social engineering, while not without its problems, is not inherently bad or dangerous. It all depends upon the uses that one makes of social engineering. I discuss elsewhere in this project the architectural-engineering analogy of society and show how it can be applied to advance democracy.[84] Here I want to emphasize that the social engineering that I propose is diametrically opposed to totalitarianism, and introduce reasons why we need to use social engineering to strengthen democracy. Democracy needs social engineering for both necessary and contingent reasons. The necessary reasons are perhaps most obvious. They all relate to the two complementary concepts of *separation of powers, and balance of power, as applied to a country*, both of which I use to reconceptualize development and democracy.

Let us consider the *separation of powers as applied to a country* and its implications for democracy. In the case of institutions, it is widely recognized that

---

83   See Section 1.5 in: Olsaretti, *The Struggle for Development and Democracy, Vol. 1.*

84   I address all these questions in the book on the humanist theory of society.

institutional design, which can aptly be described as institutional engineering, or more accurately as an engineering design of institutions, is indispensable to democracy.[85] For example, the institutions of all modern parliamentary democracies in the West have been designed and constructed in such a way as to embody the separation between executive, legislative, and judicial powers. I argue that this is necessary also in the case of society and that this is a defining feature of the social engineering for democracy that I propose. I argue in this project that there ought to be some kind of design that guarantees an analogous *division between state, society, and markets,* whereby each is built according to its own principles, and each is pre-eminent within its own arena, overlapping with and cooperating with the other arenas, but without taking over the other arenas, nor being taken over by them. By contrast, socialism-Marxism, fascism and nazism, all built totalitarian states that took over society and markets. Neoliberalism can be said to have contributed to totalitarian markets that are taking over society and to some extent also the state.[86]

There should also be an analogous *separation of powers in a country, or social division of powers between the different sources of power,* namely, economic power, cultural power, and political-military power. This is effectively a more basic way to reformulate the division between state, society, and markets, because markets are a source of economic power, society is a source of cultural power, as well as fulfilling other important functions, and the state is a source of political-military power. These sources of power, like the institutions and organizations that produce them, ought to be divided in order to ensure democracy.[87] This separation of powers in a country is related to development, besides democracy. The arguments introduced in Chapter 4 regarding embedded autonomy between the state and markets, and between the state and society, are effectively arguments regarding the way in which different sources of power can contribute to development, by interacting in certain ways, while remaining separate. The concept of *linguistic requirements of democracy,* associated with the concept of dialogue, can similarly be extended

---

85   Institutional design is touched upon in: B. Guy Peters, *Institutional Theory in Political Science,* 2nd ed. (London and New York: Continuum, 2005). On institutional design, see the many contributions in: Robert E. Goodin, ed. *The Theory of Institutional Design* (Cambridge and New York: Cambridge University Press, 1998).

86   By totalitarian markets I mean the view that seeks to rebuild the whole of society, or the totality of society, based upon market principles.

87   This is an extension to democracy, and to institutions in their interaction with society, of Mann's theory of power and his IEMP model, as set out in: Mann, *The Sources of Social Power, Vol. 1.*

to development.[88] Both development and democracy require that there should be a constant dialogue between institutions and other organizations, whether in markets or society, and between institutions and the masses in a country, in order to share information and coordinate activities, as explained in Chapter 4. The linguistic requirements of democracy, which include a shared language between intellectuals and the public, and thus less reliance by intellectuals upon specialist languages, contribute to development, because they ensure sharing of information and coordination of activities, as well as contributing to democracy, because in a democracy the policies and the theories that policies are based upon should be accessible to all.

Let us now consider the *balance of power as it applies to democracy.* The social engineering for democracy that I propose can be applied to ensure that there is a balance of power in society between elites and masses, in addition to the separation of powers. In each of the three cases, first the economy, second culture, third politics and the military, there ought to be an even distribution of power, that requires a balance of power and balance of forces.[89] The main reason for this is that, if power is all on the side of the elites, no separation of powers within the state, and no separation of powers within a country, will suffice to guarantee democracy. The concept of balance of power in society is also useful to reconceptualize democracy in ways that strengthen democracy. In this project I approach the balance of power in society by redefining in social engineering terms an important way to conceptualize democracy emphasized by political scientist Robert Dahl, namely, the concept of polyarchy, or plurality of centers of power.[90] Here I want to emphasize the significance of social engineering for both democratic and republican views of democracy, and why polyarchy has to be combined with social engineering. The social engineering for democracy that I propose emphasizes that we need to pursue, to some extent at least, both democratic and republican ideals. There ought to be a separation of powers and a balance of power in society, as per the democratic

---

88   There is a theory of dialogue that affects the way in which we conceive of language and also of democracy. Mikhail Bakhtin is the proponent of this theory, as emphasized by: Michael Holquist, *Dialogism: Bakhtin and His World* (London and New York: Routledge, 2003).

89   I address the relation between the balance of forces and balance of power in other parts of this project. As a preliminary definition, power arises from the ability to apply a given force repeatedly.

90   Robert Dahl first proposed the concept of polyarchy: Robert A. Dahl, *Polyarchy: Participation and Opposition* (New Haven and London: Yale University Press, 1973). I argue in the book on the humanist theory of society that the form of polyarchy proposed by Dahl can be dangerous for democracy, because it does not sufficiently address the problems that arise from the fact that there can be a very skewed distribution of power in favour of elites.

view of democracy, which reinforces, and is in its turn reinforced by, the separations of powers within institutions, as per the republican view of democracy. This requires that we should combine social engineering with institutional engineering.

There are also contingent reasons, in addition to the above necessary reasons, why we need a social engineering for democracy. The contingent reasons are that, for good or for worse, *social engineering is already happening*. This means that we have to respond to it by emphasizing a social engineering for democracy, rather than rejecting the idea altogether, because there is a real danger that someone will continue using social engineering, but in manners that work against democracy. There are already *good initiatives* that amount to a social engineering for democracy. In many states, there are initiatives that encourage building up civil society, an important part of society, by all sorts of incentives to the construction of citizen associations and NGOs for example, that are meant to ensure there is a vibrant life of civil society.[91] There are however also *negative initiatives* that amount to a social engineering that works against democracy, which ought to be opposed and replaced by good initiatives. Large real estate projects are effectively an instance of social engineering of communities. As highlighted by Putnam, some of their features, whether the community is gated or not, the provision of common recreation and sports facilities, clearly affect social life within these communities and their ties to other communities.[92] Some spatial aspects of communities are linked to long commuting times that deprive residents of free time, and thus contribute to destroying communal life. By contrast, Molotch argues that wealthy

---

91   Sabine Lang, *NGOs, Civil Society, and the Public Sphere* (Cambridge and New York: Cambridge University Press, 2012). On the mutual interaction between civil society and policy, see: Helmut K. Anheier, *Civil Society: Measurement, Evaluation, Policy*, Civicus, World Alliance for Citizen Participation (London and Sterling, Virginia: Earthscan, 2013).

92   This argument has been made by Putnam, who pointed out that gated communities, often wealthy communities, lack social capital internally and also links to other communities, a type pf social capital called by Putnam 'bridging capital,' which is close to the concept of structures that I propose: Putnam, *Bowling Alone*. Neighborhoods remain an important source of social capital and social cohesion: Ray Forrest and Ade Kearns, "Social Cohesion, Social Capital and the Neighbourhood," *Urban Studies* 38, no. 12 (2001). Ultimately, neighborhoods support social solidarity. Some have rightly argued that social capital is not enough for community building, and emphasized that questions of power and economic capital are important: James DeFilippis, "The Myth of Social Capital in Community Development," *Housing Policy Debate* 12, no. 4 (2001). However, this does not mean that we should ignore social capital, we should instead complement it with an approach that takes into consideration economic, cultural, and social capital, as well as power, as I do in this book.

communities have greater social capital, leading to more effective growth machines, or local elite coalitions that promote development.[93]

In the United States and many other countries, the move of the middle class to the suburbs has led in many cases to de facto segregated cities, with the working class in the city center that often suffered decay, and the middle class in sprawling suburbs that are often beautified. These two urban areas are de facto segregated by distance, which is an instance of a negative initiative that amounts to a social engineering that works against democracy, by undermining communities and also ties between communities that Putnam described as bridging social capital. The move of the middle class to the suburbs started with the work of city planner Robert Moses, whose practices in the wake of the Great Depression greatly affected New York City, can arguably be described as a social engineering that works against democracy, and have been harshly criticized.[94] The processes initiated by Moses can be taken very far and can ultimately undermine the cohesiveness of a society and encourage the rise of extremisms of various kinds, especially if culture wars are stoked up by pundits. Rudolph Giuliani's policies in New York City can similarly be described as a social engineering that works against democracy.[95] By contrast, a social engineering that works for democracy would emphasize providing more spaces and more time for social life, and avoiding segregated communities altogether or ensuring strong ties between communities, whether the de facto segregation is

93 Harvey Molotch, "The Political Economy of Growth Machines," *Journal of Urban Affairs* 15, no. 1 (1993). Logan and Molotch, *Urban Fortunes*. This is complemented by Flora's approach, which includes considerations of embeddedness alongside social conflict: Jan L. Flora, "Social Capital and Communities of Place," *Rural Sociology* 63, no. 4 (1998).

94 On Robert Moses' impact on New York City, seen as controversial today: H. Ballon, *Robert Moses and the Modern City: The Transformation of New York* (New York: W. W. Norton, 2007); Robert A. Caro, *The Power Broker: Robert Moses and the Fall of New York*, A Borzoi Book (New York: Alfred A. Knopf, 1974). For a popular culture depiction of Moses' work: Pierre Christin and Olivier Balez, *Robert Moses: The Master Builder of New York City* (Nobrow Limited, 2018).

95 Giuliani initiated urban policies that blamed the urban poor for urban decay: Neil Smith, "Giuliani Time: The Revanchist 1990s," *Social Text*, no. 57 (1998). These had influence as far as Turkey: Zeynep Gönen, "Giuliani in Izmir: Restructuring of the Izmir Public Order Police and Criminalization of the Urban Poor," *Critical Criminology* 21, no. 1 (2013). Giuliani's policies and urban segregation are placed in a broader historical context by: Susan S. Fainstein, "Assimilation and Exclusion in US Cities: The Treatment of African-Americans and Immigrants," in *Urban Segregation and the Welfare State: Inequality and Exclusion in Western Cities*, ed. Sako Musterd and Wim Ostendorf (London and New York: Routledge, 2013). On the expansion of penitentiaries and the incarceration of the urban poor, see: Loïc Wacquant, *Prisons of Poverty*, Expanded ed., Contradictions (Minneapolis and London: University of Minnesota Press, 2009).

by race, ethnicity, or class, thus discouraging processes that divide the masses
and make them easily dominated by elites that use divide-and-rule tactics.

6   The Argument Regarding Uneven Development within a Country

In addition to being associated with social engineering, development and
democracy are associated also with the four phenomena that are the explanans
of this volume: uneven development, neoliberalism, populism, and imperialism. The rest of this volume sets out the factors that give rise to development
and democracy in a country, and the ways in which these four phenomena
affect development and democracy. The overall argument is that the division
of labour in society gives a major contribution to development, but only where
there is productive social conflict, and only where a country is able to develop
without outside interference. Neoliberalism, populism, imperialism, and uneven development, all undermine development and democracy in one way or
another, ultimately because they alter the division of labour in society, or alter
the outcomes of conflict and the balance of power in society. This has various
negative effects that I discuss in greater detail below. Uneven development is
a pivotal concept in this volume because the main argument is that *imperialism leads to uneven development both across countries and within countries,
which undermines development and democracy in the long run.* Neoliberalism
and populism amplify this process. There are several different types of uneven development that this volume touches upon, including in particular the
uneven development across regions of a country that was central to Gramsci's
Southern Question. Here I want to begin by drawing attention to two types that
are understudied in the literature on development. Figure 4 is an extension of
Figure 3. It emphasizes the different types of development that there can be in
a country, and in addition associates each type of development with a specific
system.

Figure 4 is useful to summarize the different types of uneven development
and the system failures they might be associated with. As argued in Chapter 4,
in addition to economic development, there are also cultural development
and political-military development. The first type of uneven development
that this volume focuses upon is *uneven development in each arena,* the economic, cultural, and political-military arenas, that in modern capitalist societies roughly correspond to markets, civil society, and the state. In addition
to uneven economic development within a country, there can be also uneven
cultural development, and uneven political development. Uneven cultural
development occurs in cases in which a part of the masses, or an entire social

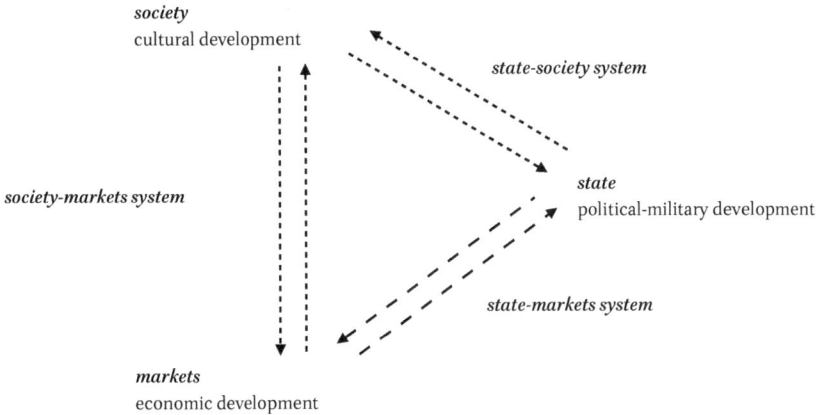

society
cultural development

state-society system

society-markets system

state
political-military development

state-markets system

markets
economic development

FIGURE 4   Overall development as development of a system of systems

group, has significantly lower levels of literacy and numeracy or of educational attainment than other parts of the masses. This can be across social classes, for example whereby the middle class and the working class have widely different educational attainments, or across different regions.[96] It also occurs in cases in which cultural life as measured by such proxies as number of cultural associations, such as arts and crafts NGOs, or theaters, whether popular theater or high-brow theater, varies widely in different social groups or geographical areas associated with different social groups. Uneven political development similarly occurs when the number of political associations, including interest groups, lobbies, SMOs and political parties, varies widely.

The second type of uneven development that this volume focuses upon and that is understudied in the literature on development is *uneven development*

---

96   Sullivan has argued that cultural capital does provide advantage to middle class students, but this is in addition to social class and the advantages that it confers: Alice Sullivan, "Cultural Capital and Educational Attainment," *Sociology* 35, no. 4 (2001). These questions are reviewed in: Michael Tzanakis, "Bourdieu's Social Reproduction Thesis and the Role of Cultural Capital in Educational Attainment: A Critical Review of Key Empirical Studies," *Educate* 11, no. 1 (2011). The cultural aspect of class divisions whereby working class boys are led by schooling to get working class jobs, was studied by: Paul Willis, *Learning to Labour: How Working Class Kids Get Working Class Jobs* (London and New York: Routledge, 2000). This book was first published in 1977. There are strong regional inequalities in educational attainment in Italy that are part of the Southern Question: Gabriele Ballarino, Nazareno Panichella, and Moris Triventi, "School Expansion and Uneven Modernization. Comparing Educational Inequality in Northern and Southern Italy," *Research in Social Stratification and Mobility* 36 (2014).

across arenas. Because of the synergies that there can be in development, it is important to develop, not just one arena to the maximum extent, but to have a balance whereby each arena develops considerably, and contributes to the development of the other arenas by providing to them the capabilities, capital, and regulation that they need to develop the most. States are best at producing defense, and they can also contribute to development through synergies. Different countries might place emphasis upon different types of development and might prioritize the development of one arena compared to the other ones. For example, some countries might give greater emphasis to cultural development. Let us consider as an example the cultural arena, and universities within it, which is where much or even most scientific research is produced, before being disseminated to other arenas.[97] It is clearly important for the cultural arena to develop and produce true scientific theories, which contribute to development in the economic arena. In economic history, it has been convincingly argued that the industrial revolution was preceded and made possible by a scientific revolution.[98]

Both of these types of development are relevant to understand *uneven development across regions of a country,* whereby some regions of a country are underdeveloped and become providers of cheap labour, and also *uneven development across social groups.* These two types of uneven development are usually associated with uneven economic, cultural, and political development, whereby the underdeveloped region has low measures of all three, and low economic development entails that there are few funds available for

---

97   This is different than G. A. Cohen's theory, which saw science as part of the econ-
       omy: Cohen, *Karl Marx's Theory of History*. There are many good reasons for classifying
       science as part of the cultural arena. One reason is that universities are part of the cul-
       tural arena, and universities advance both education and science. Another reason is that
       science includes both natural science and social science. Even as far as natural science
       alone is concerned, it is useful to classify it as part of the cultural arena, since most natural
       science is produced in universities, and is thus produced in the cultural arena and then
       disseminated to the economic arena. Some social science produced in universities is sim-
       ilarly disseminated to the economic arena. Most social science is disseminated first to the
       political arena, where it contributes to policy, and through it contributes to the economy.
       This social science is not strictly speaking part of the economic arena.
98   The effects of the scientific revolution were accentuated by high wages and the low cost
       of energy, which together encouraged the use of technology: Robert C. Allen, "Why the
       Industrial Revolution Was British: Commerce, Induced Invention, and the Scientific
       Revolution 1," *The Economic History Review* 64, no. 2 (2011). However, without a previous
       industrial revolution, the cost of scientific and technological innovation would have
       been prohibitively high. On the scientific revolution, see: Steven Shapin, *The Scientific
       Revolution* (Chicago and London: University of Chicago Press, 2018).

Basic factors:
division of labour
hegemony
social structures
shared language   segment 1:
                         · · · · · · · · · · ·▸   *National factors:*
                         social conflict   development
                         micro or meso   emb. autonomy
                         conflict   democracy   segment 2:
                                                               · · · · · · · · · · ·▸   *International factors:*
                                                               interstate   imperialism
                                                               conflict   uneven development
                                                               macro conflict   neoliberalism
                                                                                populism

                                                               social conflict
                                                               meso conflict

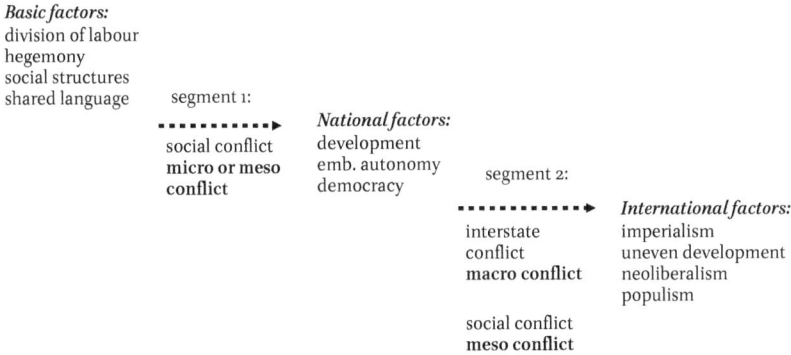

FIGURE 5   High-level summary of the entire argument of the general theory

cultural development and political development. But this is only an approximation and there are important exceptions. Similarly, a social group that is
lagging behind in economic development usually has few funds for cultural
and political development, which in many countries justifies providing free
education and subventions to politics, in order to enable the social groups
that lag behind in economic development to reach the cultural and political
development that is necessary to raise themselves to the same level as other
social groups.[99] *Uneven development across regions is produced by lack of productive conflict, or even destructive conflict,* which interferes with the basic processes that lead to development, and undermines the conditions that favor
democracy. The arguments in this part of the volume, and in particular in the
next chapter, focus on the effects of productive conflict on development and
democracy. These arguments are summarized by Figure 5, which provides a
refined high-level summary of the arguments of this book that were introduced in Section 3.3 of Chapter 3 and Figure 2. In these arguments I use the
word *country* to refer to the combination of a state, society, and markets, that
is, all of the main domains of human activity, within a given territory in modern times. The expression national factors refers to country factors in modern
times, since countries in the West have uniformly adopted nationalism of one
type or another. Development, embedded autonomy, and democracy, are all
national factors, that is, factors that describe important features of a country
in the age of capitalism and nationalism.

---

99   For example, studies of financial aid to students in the United States showed financial aid
      increased educational attainment: Susan M. Dynarski, "Does Aid Matter? Measuring the
      Effect of Student Aid on College Attendance and Completion," *American Economic Review*
      93, no. 1 (2003).

Figure 5 is an expanded version of Figure 2, with a number of additional concepts that were introduced in the theoretical groundwork above. It summarizes the arguments of this part of the volume, drawing attention to two very important additional factors compared to Figure 2, namely, the division of labour in society, and embedded autonomy. It also specifies the different types of conflict that are important to understand the sources of development, whether micro, meso, or macro conflict. The left part of this diagram, comprising segment 1, describes the manner in which basic factors, namely, the division of labour in society, hegemony, social structures, and a shared language, can lead to the national factors, namely, development, embedded autonomy, and democracy, through productive social conflict. It also suggests that the productive conflict that leads to development and democracy within a country is either micro or meso conflict. This part of the argument describes development and democracy in *a country that can develop free from major outside interference*, in which macro conflict, or interstate conflict, does not alter the outcomes of micro and meso conflict. This is not a purely hypothetical case. Great Britain, France, Spain, to some extent belong to this case, because they were the first proto nation-states with capacity to project power over long distances.

The right part of the diagram, comprising segment 2, summarizes the arguments of the last two chapters of this volume. The national factors, together with other factors such as the number and relative power of states in the world system, lead through macro conflict to a number of international factors, such as imperialism and uneven development across countries. These concepts are all necessary to understand the relations amongst neoliberalism, populism, imperialism, and uneven development, and suggest specific mechanisms whereby they undermine development and democracy within countries, that is, by interfering with the smooth functioning of the division of labour in society, and in some cases even by preventing the change from one system state to another, for example the introduction of capitalism, or the steady state functioning of the systems that are in existence. This is a fairly frequent case in history, as the expansion of north-western European states created a modern world system that sooner or later incorporated, often through conquest, much of the rest of the world.[100] In the countries thus incorporated in the modern world system, the outcomes of micro and meso conflict were fundamentally altered

---

100   This is a frequent argument in the literature on development. It also frequently appears in Wold Systems Theory. For a discussion of arguments regarding incorporation, see: Thomas D. Hall, "Incorporation into and Merger of World-Systems," in *Routledge Handbook of World-Systems Analysis* (Routledge, 2012).

by the more powerful European states, which often created, or exploited and amplified, social rents in other parts of the world, thus fundamentally affecting development there. Neocolonial companies similarly created social rents, or inherited and continued exploiting the social rents created by colonialists. The last part of this volume suggests that these rents, through neoliberalism and populism, might undermine development also in core, even in such countries as Great Britain, France, and the United States, that are widely thought to have strong democracies.

I argue in this part of the book that the division of labour in society contributes to development, but only where there are also embedded autonomy and democracy. This argument can be divided into different parts. The first part is that *the division of labour in society contributes to development.* This is because each arena is best at producing its type of capabilities, and thus at maximizing its own type of power, and all different capabilities are needed to advance development. The second part of the argument is that, in addition to the division of labour, *embedded autonomy is necessary to development.* Where there is embedded autonomy, each arena can develop its own type of capabilities thanks to autonomy, and yet while remaining autonomous contribute to the other arenas through embeddedness. For example, in order to produce true scientific theories, the cultural arena has to remain autonomous from the political arena, and scientists should be able to pursue truth first and foremost. At the same time, there should be embeddedness between the cultural arena and other arenas, so that the natural science produced in universities can be disseminated to the economic arena and contribute to productive activities within it, and the social science produced in universities can be disseminated to the political arena and contribute to the formulation of policies, which then contribute to the creation of wealth in the economic arena. Lastly, *democracy is also necessary to development.* This is because democracy guarantees embedded autonomy, and through it development. In particular, I propose a full definition of democracy that includes economic democracy, and cultural democracy, in addition to political democracy. This full definition of democracy includes also the balance of power and separation of powers, which guarantees embedded autonomy through various mechanisms that I describe below, and through embedded autonomy ultimately guarantees development.

Social conflict is involved in all of the above processes, whereby the division of labour in society, embedded autonomy, and democracy, together contribute to development within a country. In the discussion below I emphasize that *these contributions to development can only occur where productive social conflict predominates*, as opposed to destructive social conflict. The place of different types of conflict, whether micro or meso conflict, in the arguments of

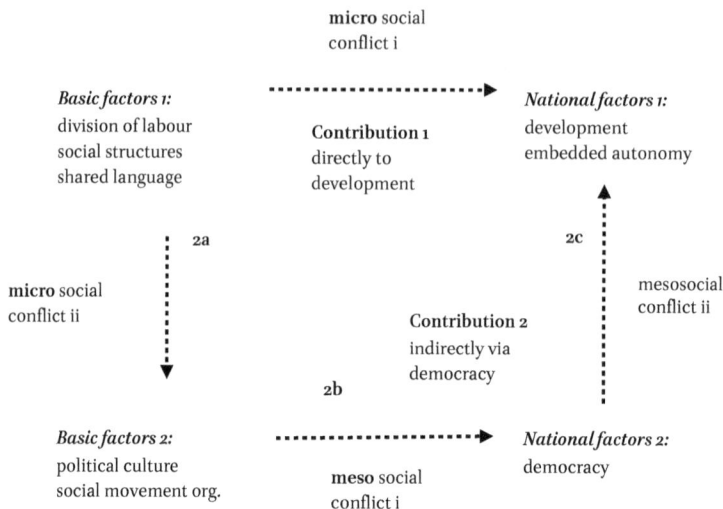

FIGURE 6   The effects of productive conflict on development, embedded
            autonomy, and democracy

this part of the book is clarified in the next diagram, which specifies details of
the left part, or segment 1, of Figure 5. The diagram in Figure 6 divides the basic
factors that cause national factors, and the national factors themselves, into
two groups of factors. I decided to represent development as closely related to
embedded autonomy, and both as part of the same group, National factors 1,
because both are arguably closely related to the division of labour in society.
Democracy is not, since it emerges also where there is little or no division of
labour. In fact, democracy in a country with an advanced division of labour in
society presents additional challenges, so that it is necessary to give what I call
below a full definition of democracy, therefore it is represented on its own, as
part of National factors 2.

Democracy is also involved in a different type of conflict than development and embedded autonomy. In suggesting this distinction, I build upon
Gramsci's work, which pointed out to two fundamentally different types of
social interaction, the micro conflict consisting mostly of individual interactions that predominates in the economic arena and in particular in markets,
and the meso conflict consisting mostly of collective action with participation by large numbers of individuals coordinated by SMOs and parties that

predominates in the political arena.[101] Figure 6 highlights the argument that different types of conflict are involved in processes that contribute to development, described in the diagram as Contribution 1 and Contribution 2. In Contribution 1, the first group of basic factors, Basic factors 1, are the division of labour, and the main components of embedded autonomy, namely, social structures and a shared language. They lead to development and embedded autonomy through productive *micro* social conflict, which is an important part of economic processes, and it includes the social interaction that predominates in markets. In Contribution 2, the same basic factors contribute to development and embedded autonomy through a more complex mechanism that involves mostly *meso* social conflict. First, through productive micro social conflict, they lead to Basic factors 2, that is, to the emergence of a political culture of protest that is routinized and avoids violent conflict, and to SMOs that take part in peaceful protests for redressing grievances. These basic factors in their turn, through collective action, including meso social conflict, contribute to democracy, which in its turn contributes to development by guaranteeing embedded autonomy, again through meso social conflict. Therefore, Contribution 2 occurs mostly through meso conflict, and it is an important part of political processes that include phenomena described in Volume 1 of this book as constituting meso collective action and meso collective action problems.[102] Meso collective action problems that prevent the emergence of productive meso social conflict, and ultimately of democracy, entail a fragile development, in which democracy does not guarantee embedded autonomy and development, so that development might be undermined in the long run.

---

101   I made these arguments in my dissertation: Alessandro Olsaretti, "Philosophy and Science in Gramsci's Reconstruction of Marxism" (McGill University, 2013). I argued there that Gramsci was attempting to formulate an economics that would focus on micro interactions, and a political science that would focus on interactions between organizations and social groups. I refer to the latter as meso interactions and meso collective action.

102   Meso collective action is affected both by social processes on a micro scale, like cooptation and defection, and by social processes on a meso scale, like the balance of power between social groups. Once organizations are created and micro collective action problems are solved, they make possible meso collective action.

Theses on the Sources of Development and Democracy

This chapter outlines the part of the general theory that concerns the sources of development and democracy, focusing upon development and democracy within countries. *The main argument is that development, embedded autonomy, and democracy, are all inter-related*, and all participate in a smoothly functioning division of labour in society. I expand upon the Durkheimian division of labour in society to include the Smithian division of labour in an organization, in order to explain the sources of the increases in capabilities that development is based upon.[1] The division of labour in society is a major contributor to development, because it enables efficiencies and synergies in producing capabilities. Embedded autonomy also contributes to development, because it ensures the smoothly functioning of division of labour in society. Democracy, in the full definition that includes a distribution of power and also a separation of powers in a country, maintains embedded autonomy, including the division into autonomous arenas, and thus ultimately contributes to development. This smoothly functioning division of labour in society is made possible by conflict that is regulated and turned into productive conflict. By contrast, destructive conflict undermines a smoothly functioning division of labour in society and can lead to uneven development, and ultimately to loss of development, embedded autonomy, and democracy. The theory in this chapter contributes to understand these social processes, and also *begins to suggest alternatives to neoliberal theories*. The theory proposes models of human behavior, and ultimately of society, that are not reductive and emphasize principles of human behavior that can be used to build models for the whole of society, including culture and politics, rather than those associated with *Homo Oeconomicus* that prevail in mainstream economic theory, including neoliberalism.

The theses in this chapter all propose *mechanisms that explain the processes introduced in the last section* (Section 5.6). The first section below introduces the first two theses, which define the most basic concepts that underpin the entire theory. Thesis 1 defines power and explains its relation to capabilities. It also introduces different types, measures, and forms of power, emphasizing

---

1 Durkheim and Coser, *The Division of Labor in Society*.

that the three basic types of power, namely, economic, cultural, and political-military power, correspond to the growth of *per-capita* capabilities, respectively economic, cultural, and political-military capabilities. Thesis II defines development and democracy with respect to power, suggesting that development is the growth in capabilities, and ultimately power, and democracy is an equitable distribution of power, a distribution of power that is favourable to the masses. The remaining sections each specify a part of the process outlined in Figure 6. The second section and third section concern Contribution 1 to development. The second section introduces Thesis III, which defines the division of labour in society as including the division of labour in an organization, and also the division of labour in a district, chiefly between organizations engaged in production and institutions engaged in education and research within industrial districts. The third section introduces arguments regarding the different arenas within a country. Sub-thesis III.c continues the arguments of Thesis III, suggesting that the division of labour in society includes a division of labour within a country into economic, cultural, and political-military arenas, which can be conceptualized as an extension of the division of labour in a district. Thesis IV defines embedded autonomy as a division of labour within a country whereby each arena remains autonomous from the other arenas, while through networks across arenas that provide embeddedness, they share information and coordinate activities, an essential part of regulation. Together, Theses III and IV define the social processes that lead to development through the division of labour in society. The remaining sections concern Contribution 2 to development, from democracy. The fourth section introduces Thesis V, which explains process 2b (1 skip 2a since it is widely addressed in the literature on democracy), provides a full definition of democracy as entailing a distribution of power and also a division of powers across the different arenas in a country, and emphasizing that some democracy in all three arenas, namely, economic and cultural, as well as political democracy, is necessary to avoid loss of democracy. The fifth section introduces Thesis VI, which explains process 2c, and argues that there is an interaction between development, embedded autonomy, and democracy, whereby these three factors can reinforce each other in a virtuous circle, or undermine each other in a vicious circle. The sixth section introduces Thesis VII, which argues that uneven development and imperfect embedded autonomy can set off a vicious circle, leading to loss of development and democracy even in countries in the core. Neoliberalism contributes to uneven development and imperfect embedded autonomy and can contribute to loss of both development and democracy in the long term.

1   Theses I and II and the Definitions of Basic Concepts

Theses I and II provide definitions of the basic concepts of the theory, namely, power, capabilities, development, and democracy. I propose in this project *definitions of development and democracy that build upon the definitions of capabilities and power* introduced in the previous chapter and emphasize that there are different sources of capabilities and thus different sources and forms of power. Thesis I defines the most basic concepts of power and capabilities, both of which are used in Thesis II to define development and democracy. Thesis I is divided into three parts, focusing respectively upon different types, measures, and forms of power. The types of power, namely, economic, cultural, and political-military power, were introduced above. The measures and forms of power, introduced in Thesis I below, require some explanation. It is necessary to *distinguish between different measures of power* because it is important to distinguish between development and other social phenomena that similarly lead to the growth in power of a country but are significantly different than development. A country that increases its power by conquering new territories is engaged in expansion, not development. A country that forces individuals to work longer hours to produce more is engaged in exploitation, not development. In addition, as emphasized by Harvey, in some cases there is also dispossession, as well as exploitation, as lands or natural resources were taken over by colonial companies, and today by neocolonial companies.[2] Accumulation by dispossession in foreign countries is arguably a type of conquest whereby, not an entire other country, but its resources, and sometimes parts of its territory, are effectively conquered. Many European companies engaged in colonialism were essentially engaged in conquest and exploitation, and today many neocolonial companies still engage in a mix of dispossession (just one component of conquest) and exploitation, not development. The main source of their wealth is not an increase in per-capita capabilities, for example by raising productivity, but simply undertaking the same economic processes where they can pay workers less. This is a very different type of development and perhaps not even really development.

---

2   Harvey, *The New Imperialism*. Harvey's concept of dispossession is more general than the
    concept of dispossession that I use here. Harvey extends dispossession to financial opera-
    tions and privatization, which lead to reducing wages or access to public goods. I find it more
    intuitive, and more useful from a theoretical point of view, to refer to these as exploitation,
    and to refer to dispossession only as the appropriation of assets such as land, or capital that
    is taken over.

It is similarly necessary to *distinguish between different forms of power* because the state type associated with different forms of power is very different, and it has altogether different effects upon development. The importance of this point will become clear in the next part of this volume, but it is useful to point here to the direction in which the argument is going. Emphasizing that development is the growth of per-capita capabilities is a relatively simple point, but it highlights *an important dynamic in the modern history of the West* that I address in the next chapter. Economist Thomas Piketty has pointed out that there is a physiological growth associated with demographic growth, and an additional growth associated with increases in productivity.[3] The above definition includes this difference and also an important point made by Mann regarding the forms of power in the modern history of the West, namely, that there are extensive and intensive forms of power.[4] In European history, these were respectively the forms of power associated with territorial empires, and with city-states and later with nation-states. For much of the history of the West, aristocratic-military elites tended to expand the total power available to them by adding territories. The sources of power that they specialized in, military power, lent themselves to this expansion in power. The physiocrats, a group of French economists who wrote during the eighteenth century that Gramsci was especially interested in, emphasized territory, in the form of land for agriculture, as the source of economic growth, although some began emphasizing also demographic growth within a given territory, that was successfully pursued by France around that time.[5] Both were ways of increasing the extensive form of power.

Other countries found ways of increasing the intensive form of power. A break occurred in the history of the West when cities, and then some entire countries, notably the Netherlands and England, began increasing their power chiefly by increasing per-capita capabilities, not by expanding territories, nor by expanding population. This required involvement by economic elites, who specialized in this type of power, and various alliances between the aristocratic-military elites and the emerging bourgeoisie, as part of hegemonic blocs. These were arguably the beginnings of development in the modern history of the West. It is therefore very important to introduce the following definitions regarding the types, measures, and forms of power.

---

3   Thomas Piketty, *Capital in the Twenty-First Century*, trans. Arthur Goldhammer (Cambridge, Massachusetts and London: Harvard University Press, 2017).
4   Mann, *The Sources of Social Power, Vol. 1*.
5   See entry for 'fisiocratici' in: Liguori and Voza, *Dizionario Gramsciano*.

I.   *There are different types, measures, and forms of power that are especially important to countries and populations within them.* They are all based upon capabilities, which constitute the bases of power when they are compared to the capabilities of others, or to the capabilities required in a harsh environment, or to the capabilities required at a certain historical conjuncture.

    a.   There are *three main types of power,* each based on specific capabilities produced in a different arena, with each arena being specialized in producing a different type of capabilities and ultimately of power:

        i.   The economic arena, specialized in economic capabilities.

        ii.   The cultural arena, specialized in cultural capabilities.

        iii.   The political-military arena, specialized in political and military capabilities.

    b.   It is useful to distinguish between *two measures of capabilities, namely, total and per-capita capabilities.* These are two ways of measuring the capabilities available to a country that can lead to very different types of growth:

        i.   *Total capabilities* are the sum of all capabilities available to a country, regardless of their source. In practice, because of the specificity of capabilities, it makes sense to measure separately the total economic, cultural, and political-military capabilities.

        ii.   *Per-capita capabilities are the capabilities per individual* in a country, which can vary more or less greatly around a country average. For the same reason as with total capabilities, it makes sense to measure separately the per-capita economic, cultural, and politica-military capabilities.

    c.   There are *two forms of power that define a country,* depending upon the distribution of capabilities within the country across individuals or social groups, and thus depending upon the distribution of power within the country, since the capabilities are compared across individuals or social groups. There are two forms of power.

        i.   There is an *extensive form of power,* with power concentrated in the hands of the elites, which derive their power from large numbers of individuals with low per-capita capabilities, for example low per-capita income. These elites can still raise total capabilities by expanding territory or population.

        ii.   There is an *intensive form of power,* with less concentration of power in the hands of elite, which derive their power from

a small number of individuals with high per-capita capabilities, for example high per-capita income. It tends to be associated with elites that could not greatly expand territory or
population.

The definitions in Thesis I are useful to Thesis II, and it is appropriate to show
the importance of these definitions by placing them within the context of the
argument of Thesis II, which they contribute to. Thesis II uses the above definitions and differentiations between measures and forms of power to *define
development and democracy*. There is a rough correspondence between sub-
theses, whereby II.a is based upon I.a, II.b is based upon I.b, and II.c is based
upon I.c. The main claim of Thesis II is that development is the growth of per-
capita capabilities and democracy is an even distribution of these capabilities.
However, this immediately raises the question of the differences between *even*
development, democracy, and *intensive* power.

These are three different concepts that closely interact with each other, and
yet which cannot be reduced one to the other. Let us consider the differences
between, on the one hand, even development, and on the other hand, democracy and forms of power. It is important to clarify these differences from the
beginning. As far as the *difference between even development and democracy* is
concerned, development is growth, and even development is an attribute of a
growth process, whereby the growth is evenly distributed. By contrast, democracy is based upon the distribution of capabilities, for example economic
democracy is based upon the distribution of income, which is a good proxy for
economic capabilities in many circumstances, and it refers to a static picture
at any one point in time. The Gini coefficient describes this distribution., but
it is effectively a snapshot, and it is important to remind ourselves that this
distribution changes.[6]

As far as the *difference between even development and forms of power* is concerned, development is a growth in capabilities, whereas forms of power are
similar to democracy, and they concern a distribution of power at any one point
in time. In addition, forms of power are based upon social interaction, and
they most clearly depend upon geographical and historical factors. Let us consider geographical factors first. In addition to an uneven distribution of capabilities, in the extensive form of power the population tends to be scattered
across vast territories and rarely interacts over long distances compared to the
elites. In the intensive form of power, the population tends to be concentrated

---

6   Graham Pyatt, "On the Interpretation and Disaggregation of Gini Coefficients," *The Economic
    Journal* 86, no. 342 (1976).

in one or more cities, and it more frequently interacts thanks to proximity and becomes capable of collective action. Marx first highlighted this relationship between collective action and geography, that was later studied by demographers.[7] Let us consider historical factors. They affect extensive and intensive power, because the outcomes of previous interactions lead to a distribution of power at any one point in time, which is more or less close to intensive power, or to extensive power. For example, intensive and extensive forms of power can be associated with cumulative loss or growth in social capital, because they are based upon social interaction and in particular upon the outcomes of previous social interactions. A sequence of historical events that leads to loss of social capital can have enduring consequences for a community by reducing basic capabilities within it and the basic ability of a community to participate in development.

The importance of the cumulative loss or growth of social capital, the loss of which leads to loss of other types of capital, was emphasized by Putnam and Molotch. Putnam expressed a major concern about contemporary American history, documenting the loss of social capital, and arguing that since the post-Second World War era there has been significant loss of social capital in American society.[8] This loss is not uniform throughout society. An important point highlighted by Molotch with his title *History repeats itself* is that under certain conditions some outcomes tend to occur and reoccur, and that typically the social capital of elite communities increases, whereas the social capital of working class and peasant communities is often destroyed, through cumulative processes whereby an earlier loss of social capital makes it more likely that there will be subsequent losses.[9] This also occurs with changes that affect small towns, often predominantly lower middle-class and working-class, and with a number of historical phenomena related to migration, whereby the move from villages and small towns to big cities, and from one region to another, or from one country to another, destroys communities, in which social capital thrives, and replaces them with anonymous interaction in big cities. This is only partly compensated for by the tendency for migrants in foreign countries to gather

---

7   Rodney Hilton, "Feudalism and the Origins of Capitalism," *History Workshop Journal* 1, no. 1 (1976). Richard Lachmann, "Origins of Capitalism in Western Europe: Economic and Political Aspects," *Annual Review of Sociology* (1989). On the importance of cities to wealth, see: E. A. Wrigley, *People, Cities, and Wealth: The Transformation of Traditional Society* (Oxford: Blackwell, 1987).

8   Putnam, *Bowling Alone*.

9   Logan and Molotch, *Urban Fortunes*; Harvey Molotch, William Freudenburg, and Krista E. Paulsen, "History Repeats Itself, but How? City Character, Urban Tradition, and the Accomplishment of Place," *American Sociological Review* (2000).

in Little Italies, Chinatowns, or other similar ethnic or cultural enclaves, since the culture of these enclaves is often different than the culture of the original community, and it participates in in national culture, not in community.[10] These points also highlight the importance of integrating in the definition of development the concept of social development, which is closely associated with social capital, and in studying the relationship between development and forms of power. Social capital includes the social networks that each individual participates in, their type, and their strength. Social capital is thus very useful to sharing of information and coordination of activities, and ultimately contributes to all other types of capital. In addition to social capital, there is also overall capital, or an aggregate measure of development that takes into consideration development in each of the arenas.

II.   *Development and democracy are both related to per-capita capabilities within a country*, and ultimately to power within that country.

    a.   There are *five main types of development,* each consisting in the growth of per-capita capabilities in one of the three arenas specialized in a specific type of capabilities, plus a fourth one consisting in the growth of per-capita basic capabilities that are based on social capital, and lastly an aggregate measure of the overall development of a country:

        i.   *Economic development* is the growth of economic per-capita capabilities

        ii.   *Cultural development* is the growth of cultural per-capita capabilities;

        iii.   *Political-military development* is the growth of political and military per-capita capabilities.

        iv.   *Social development* is the growth in basic per-capita capabilities that are needed by individual to function in society and engage in social interaction, and it includes social capital.

        v.   *Overall development* is the growth in all of the above per-capita capabilities that a country can achieve given its population and resources, whereby there is not just great economic development and little or no cultural development or political-military development, but considerable

10   On these enclaves, and how they change, see: Mohammad Qadeer, Sandeep K. Agrawal, and Alexander Lovell, "Evolution of Ethnic Enclaves in the Toronto Metropolitan Area, 2001–2006," *Journal of International Migration and Integration/Revue de l'integration et de la migration internationale* 11, no. 3 (2010).

or even maximum development in each and every type of development.

b. *It is useful to distinguish between different distributions of per-capita capabilities* according to the set of individuals across whom we measure the distribution. There are the following useful distributions:

    i. *A distribution of capabilities across individuals within the whole country,* whereby the distribution is measured across all individuals in a country. In practice, it makes sense to measure this distribution across all individuals in each of the different arenas in the whole country.

    ii. *Distributions of capabilities across individuals within a region, or social group,* whereby the distribution is measured across all individuals in a region, or across all individuals in a social group, that are part of a country.

    iii. *A distribution of capabilities across regions or social groups, not individuals,* within the whole country, whereby for example the average capabilities in one region are compared to the average capabilities in other regions, and whereby one measures the distributions of all the averages across regions.

c. *Democracy consists in a distribution of per-capita capabilities favorable to the masses.* Depending on how we measure the distribution, it is useful to distinguish between the following different types of democracy.

    i. There are *different types of democracy associated with each arena,* each of which is based upon the distribution of per-capita capabilities measured for one arena within the whole country:

        1. *Economic democracy* is based upon the distribution of economic capabilities.

        2. *Cultural democracy* is based upon the distribution of cultural capabilities.

        3. *Political and military democracy* is based upon the distribution of political and military capabilities.

    ii. *The intensive form of power is most often associated with democracy,* although there can be some democracy also in countries characterized by the extensive form of power. However, the likelihood of an intensive form of power and ultimately of democracy varies with the arena. Even in the case of a country in which intensive power predominates:

1. *The economic arena tends to be based upon inten-*
    sive power.

2. *The cultural arena tends to be based upon a mix* of
    intensive power and extensive power, varying greatly
    with the geography and history of the country.

3. *The political-military arena tends to be based upon*
    extensive power, since the military, and all legitimate
    violence more in general, is a natural monopoly, and
    those who ran this monopoly can most readily con-
    centrate power in their own hands, even where the
    intensive form of power predominates in the rest of
    society.

Many of the definitions in Thesis 11 follow from the previous discussions of
key concepts. Because of its important role, I want to dwell on *social develop-*
ment and its role in overall development. Social development is important for
several different reasons. *Social development is important because it is associ-*
ated with basic capabilities. As emphasized by Sen, who drew attention to the
importance of literacy and good health, there are very important capabilities
such as these that are not taken into consideration by standard measures of
development. Good health and literacy arguably constitute in themselves valuable types of development, as emphasized above with the concept of cultural development, for example. In addition, they contribute to other types
of development, such as economic development and military development,
because literate and skilled manpower increases both economic and military
capabilities.[11] The concept of social development includes both good health
and arguably also social capital. As such, social development contributes to
development in all other fields. The same capital in other fields, whether economic, cultural, or political capital, will yield very different results whether it
is accompanied by social capital or not. An entrepreneur with the right social
capital, or connections, will go much further than one without it, but with the
same amount of economic capital and cultural capital in the form of qualifications. The same consideration applies to a politician with the right social capital compared to one without it. This is because social capital is very important
to access information and also to access other types of capital, and to convert
one type into another.

Social development is also very important to productive social conflict. This is
because social development consists in the advancement of basic capabilities

---

11   Sen, *Development as Freedom.*

needed to function in society that I describe below, including social capital, and good health. Poverty and destructive social conflict, especially when interacting in poverty and violence traps, undermine basic capabilities and ultimately the very constituents of social interaction, and thus undermine all other forms of development. This is clear when we consider that social development includes support networks, and individuals who lack both economic capital and support networks can be reduced to a poverty and violence trap from which they never re-integrate in the workforce, because they are unable to change occupation, or retrain, or move to new locations and job markets. Under certain social conditions, this leads to a large part of the population who are unable to re-integrate in the workforce and grow their own capabilities, and ultimately the total capabilities of their country. The destruction of communities and social capital within them undermines the economic, cultural, and political capital of the social groups affected by it.

This destruction has taken place in many countries in the West, and it has taken many forms, with variations from one country to another, stretching far beyond the phenomenon highlighted by Putnam for loss of social capital in the United States. This had historical precedents. Some lower middle class communities, as well as working class communities that achieved gains in income and some personal property, buying up semi-detached houses in sprawling areas with little or no communal amenities, were affected by a similar loss of social capital, and ultimately of community, which was described by the phrase 'an Englishman's home is his castle,' whereby some social groups in parts of England withdrew into a private life with little or no social and communal dimensions.[12] Rural communities were also affected by this loss. This is clear in rural communities affected by what can be called the *pulverization of property*, resulting in very small farms, often weighed down by sharecropping, which distinguishes rural economies in the semi-periphery and to some extent in the periphery of the world system.[13] Marx's metaphor that the peasantry in France in the second half of the nineteenth century were like potatoes in a sack, a large number of individuals only loosely held together by common interests, and unable to engage in collective action, arguably pointed to the combination of reduced social capital, reduced economic capital, and inability to participate in politics and democracy, of many small farmers.[14] Gramsci's description

---

12   Amanda Vickery, "An Englishman's Home Is His Castle? Thresholds, Boundaries and Privacies in the Eighteenth-Century London House," *Past & Present* 199, no. 1 (2008).
13   Wallerstein, *The Modern World-System, Vol. 1.*
14   Claudio J Katz, "Marx on the Peasantry: Class in Itself or Class in Struggle?," *The Review of Politics* 54, no. 1 (1992).

of southern Italy as a vast social disaggregation pointed to this state of affairs taken to extremes, whereby many individuals in small towns and villages lost their farms or small workshops thus becoming laborers, and furthermore lost also all community, and all ability to pull themselves out of this trap, because of lack of all types of capital, including social capital and support networks. In this way, many descended into a spiral of brigandage or other forms of criminality, including the mafias, whereby they operated outside society or at its margins, forming criminal organizations permanently outside society.

2   Thesis III on the Division of Labour as a Source of Development

Not all micro conflict is destructive. Where productive micro conflict prevails, *the interactions of individuals lead to development thanks to the emergence of a suitable division of labour* that increases capabilities. This is the process described in Figure 6 as Contribution 1. Thesis III describes an important source of development, namely, the processes whereby, in Contribution 1, Basic factors 1 and in particular the division of labour, lead to National factors such as development. Before delving into this thesis, it is important to clarify in some detail *the type of division of labour that is involved in development*. For this purpose, we ought to begin by differentiating between aggregate and collective capabilities. *Aggregate capabilities* are obtained through adding by juxtaposition more individuals or more small organizations. Using Marx's metaphor, aggregate capabilities arise simply by adding more potatoes to the sack, for example more small farms, or more skilled artisans who work alone or in small workshops, or more skilled computer programmers who work alone or in small teams. For much of the middle ages economic growth occurred as part of demographic growth, followed by clearings of more land as more small farms were added, and sometimes more villages with artisans were added catering to these communities. By contrast, *collective capabilities* are different and can arise from the same number of individuals, and even from a smaller number of individuals, but with a different organization, technology, and capital. For the purposes of this book, *I focus chiefly upon organization*, without which investments and technology do not come to fruition. It is intuitive that the sum of many small farms has very different capabilities and potential for growth than a large centrally managed agro-business with a workforce specialized in different tasks, greater use of machinery, and a specialized management and marketing department.

Collective capabilities thus arise to a significant extent from changes in organization that are part of a well-functioning division of labour. There are *three different divisions of labour that contribute to development*, each involving a somewhat different way of organizing production: first, a division of labour within a single organization, amongst the individuals and departments within the organization; second, a division of labour in a district, amongst different organizations within the district, effectively a micro system; and third, a Durkheimian division of labour in society that I refer to below as a division of labour in a country, amongst the different types of organizations active in each arena, effectively a meso system with additional differentiation between arenas. Let us consider first *the division of labour within an organization.* This was first studied by Smith, who exemplified the manner in which it leads to development using as a case study the division of labour in a factory producing pins. As emphasized by Smith, *specialization in tasks leads to significant gains in productivity*, and thus to much greater collective economic capabilities. This is because gathering several workers under one roof, breaking up the process of producing pins into separate tasks such as creating the pin, creating the head of the pin, etc. etc., with each worker engaged in just one task, resulted in more pins being produced than the sum of pins that would have been produced simply by aggregating the output of the same number of workers each working on his own. In Smith's example, there is not much greater economic capital, and even less skills in each worker. It is the organization that leads to greater output. Later, this form of organization lent itself to further growth, by capital investment in machinery, and by further differentiation of tasks. Gramsci pointed out that with the division of labour within an organization, *better leveraging of greater skills also leads to significant gains in productivity*, whereby the maestranze, that is, senior and skilled shop floor workers, can significantly increase productivity, for example because the organization of shop floor work enables them to intervene and fix problems or errors in the production chain as soon as they arise.

These points can be generalized to all different types of organizations, involved in developing different types of capabilities, since some of the same considerations regarding internal organization apply also to organizations involved in different domains. Thus there are also cultural and military collective capabilities, that similarly arise from organization with specialization and better leveraging of skills. *Collective cultural capabilities* arise from the internal organization of universities, and especially of research teams. They can make a great difference to research, just like the internal organization of companies can make a great difference to their ability to innovate, besides their output.[15]

---

15   On the importance of organization to innovation, including universities, see the many contributions in: Alfonso Gambardella and Franco Malerba, eds., *The Organization of*

The internal organization of universities and research institutions is becoming ever more important because of the sheer number of scientists involved. There is at least since the Second World War, most markedly in the United States and other NATO countries, a big science approach to producing technological innovation, whereby the state grants large contracts to universities and other institutions, using ever larger groups of scientists, and leveraging the research capabilities of these institutions. Project Manhattan, which produced the first atom bomb, was an early instance of big science of this type.[16] Some sub-fields of physics, notably nuclear research, including research into sub-atomic particles, occurs on a very large scale, in part because of the very large machinery that is needed, and organization becomes very important. The research teams at CERN, a particle physics laboratory in Switzerland, are conducted by large research groups that consist of 1000s of scientists.[17]

Collective military capabilities arise from the internal organization of military units, and are measured as a whole, for an army, or an army unit. They can also vary greatly with the organization of the army or army unit. For example, the capability of individual soldiers to carry our specific operations can be measured and aggregated, simply as a sum across the individuals. But the most important military capabilities are derived from organization. To place suitably trained individuals with specific capabilities, in the positions in which these capabilities are best leveraged, is part of this organization. The very same number of soldiers, including individuals with the same capabilities, could contribute little or nothing to the collective capabilities, if the army or army unit organization did not leverage their individual capabilities. A simple example can clarify this concept. Medieval heavy cavalry was greatly limited in effectiveness when early modern infantry developed the capability to act in concert as a phalanx, that is, as a compact mass of soldiers, locking shields and using long spears to keep the cavalry at bay. Individual skilled infantry placed at key points, like the sides and especially the corners, of units within this

---

Economic Innovation in Europe (Cambridge and New York: Cambridge University Press, 1999). I address the negative effects of academic specialization in: Olsaretti, *Towards a Humanist Social Science.*

16   Jeff A. Hughes, *The Manhattan Project: Big Science and the Atom Bomb* (New York: Columbia University Press, 2003); Michael Hiltzik, *Big Science: Ernest Lawrence and the Invention that Launched the Military-Industrial Complex* (New York, London, Toronto, Sydney, New Delhi: Simon & Schuster, 2015).

17   The current General Director of CERN, Fabiola Gianotti, was previously the head of the ATLAS experiment at CERN, an experiment that employed 3000 scientists, researchers and IT experts, the size of an army light brigade: Wikipedia, "Fabiola Gianotti."

phalanx, greatly contributed to making the phalanx work.[18] As with the example of workers in a pin factory, this was first and foremost an organizational innovation, supported by some technological innovation like the introduction of longer and more effective spears.

Let us consider now *the division of labour within a district*. A district is a geographical area in which there are several companies all specialized in producing the same product, or similar products. Economist Alfred Weber, one of the founders of modern economic geography, initiated the academic study of industrial districts, emphasizing the importance of the availability in an area of key goods like technology and a skilled workforce.[19] Instances of industrial districts can be found amongst car manufacturers that specialize in sports cars, for example the districts near Bologna and Modena, or near Oxford, England. Companies in industrial districts, as well as companies participating in complex supply chains, have given rise to new forms of organization capable of both flexibility and innovation, both of which contribute to the competitive advantage of these companies, especially in high-tech sectors, and in sectors in which product innovation is important. As first emphasized by Vasta, these new forms of organization partly replaced mass production. Both Andrea Prencipe and Manuel Castells, from different perspectives, have studied these new forms of organization. Prencipe and his collaborators, including Stefano Brusconi, have focused especially upon systems integration and its contribution to companies in high-tech industries like the aeronautical industry.[20]

---

18   On new types of warfare in early modern Europe, see: Frank Tallett, *War and Society in Early Modern Europe: 1495–1715* (London and New York: Routledge, 2016).

19   Alfred Weber, "On the Location of Industries," *Progress in Human Geography* 6, no. 1 (2006). The study of industrial districts has drawn the attention of many Italian researchers: Fiorenza Belussi, Giorgio Gottardi, and Enzo Rullani, eds., *The Technological Evolution of Industrial Districts* (New York: Springer Science + Business Media, 2003). The literature on industrial clusters has continued the study of districts under a new name: Charlie Karlsson, Borje Johansson, and Roger Stough, *Industrial Clusters and Inter-Firm Networks* (Cheltenham, UK and Northampton, Massachusetts: Edward Elgar, 2005). A theory of districts is proposed by: David A. Lane, "Complexity and Local Interactions: Towards a Theory of Industrial Districts," in *Complexity and Industrial Clusters*, ed. Alberto Quadrio Curzio and Marco Fortis (Cham, Switzerland: Springer, 2002).

20   Andrea Prencipe, Andrew Davies, and Michael Hobday, eds., *The Business of Systems Integration* (Oxford And New York: Oxford University Press, 2003). Michael Hobday, Andrew Davies, and Andrea Prencipe, "Systems Integration: a Core Capability of the Modern Corporation," *Industrial and corporate change* 14, no. 6 (2005). Prencipe's work on the aero industry includes: Andrea Prencipe, "Technological Competencies and Product's Evolutionary Dynamics a Case Study from the Aero-Engine Industry," *Research policy* 25, no. 8 (1997); Massimo Paoli and Andrea Prencipe, "The Role of Knowledge Bases in Complex Product Systems: Some Empirical Evidence from the Aero Engine Industry,"

Castells, from an urban sociology and urban and regional planning perspective, has emphasized the network aspect of a new form of organization that is enabled in complex cases by systems integration.[21] These new forms of organization are made possible by the development of ICT and by systems integration that brings together in one production system disparate ICT systems.[22]

The concept of district can be extended to geographic areas in which other companies than factories predominate, for example Silicon Valley, which started off producing semiconductors but eventually became a major hub for software development and internet services.[23] Far from disappearing, districts like Silicon Valley have become an important paradigm for development, and have spawned numerous attempts at imitation, with varying degrees of success, from the ill-fated Silicon Alley in New York City, and the Multimedia City in Montreal, to the more successful Silicon Glen near Edinburgh, Glasgow, and Stirling, in Scotland, and Silicon Fen near Cambridge, in England.[24] Knowledge and technology are very important to the functioning of industrial districts. In big science the capabilities to carry out extensive research does not lie just in the organization of a single university and institution, but in in the more complex organizational arrangement associated with a given society-markets

Journal of Management and Governance 3, no. 2 (1999). Andrea Prencipe, "Breadth and Depth of Technological Capabilities in CoPS: The Case of the Aircraft Engine Control System," *Research policy* 29, no. 7–8 (2000). Brusconi and Prencipe have emphasized modularity as a key concept to describe the new forms of organization: Stefano Brusoni and Andrea Prencipe, "Unpacking the Black Box of Modularity: Technologies, Products and Organizations," *Industrial and corporate Change* 10, no. 1 (2001); "Patterns of Modularization: The Dynamics of Product Architecture in Complex Systems," *European Management Review* 8, no. 2 (2011). See also the many contributions in: Andrea Prencipe, *Strategy, Systems and Scope* (Thousand Oaks, London, and New Delhi: SAGE, 2020).

21 Castells set out his studies and vision for the network society in: Manuel Castells, *The Information Age, Volume 1. The Rise of the Network Society*, The Information Age: Economy, Society and Culture (Chichester, West Sussex: Wiley-Blackwell, 2000); *The Information Age, Volume 2. The Power of Indentity*; *The Information Age, Volume 3. End of Millennium*. This trilogy was re-published in 2009–2010. Castells provided an overview in: "Toward a Sociology of the Network Society," *Contemporary sociology* 29, no. 5 (2000).

22 On the systems integration aspect, see: Andrea Prencipe, "Corporate Strategy and Systems Inttegration Capabilities: Managing Networks in Complex Systems Industries," in *The Business of Systems Integration*, ed. Andrea Prencipe, Andrew Davies, and Michael Hobday (Oxford And New York: Oxfiord University Press, 2003).

23 On Silicon Valley as an industrial district, see: Bennett Harrison, "Concentrated Economic Power and Silicon Valley," *Environment and Planning A* 26, no. 2 (1994); Sean Digiovanna, "Industrial Districts and Regional Economic Development: a Regulation Approach," *Regional Studies* 30, no. 4 (1996).

24 Annika Steiber and Sverker Alänge, *The Silicon Valley Model*, Cham, Switzerland (Springer, 2016).

system, in which many universities and other research institutions interact, by a mix of cooperation and competition.[25] Sometimes this interaction is at a local level, and it involves both cultural institutions like universities and technical schools, and also many different companies, giving rise to industrial districts. As pointed out by Prencipe and his collaborators, different regions of Italy had a major impact upon the performance of companies within them[26] There is always some specialization and division of labour in districts, for example between cultural institutions like universities or technical schools, and economic organizations like factories and offices. Especially where the factories are Small or Medium Sized Enterprises, or SMEs, that do not have enough funds to run training programs internally, nor research budgets that enable them to fund research internally, separate universities or technical schools that are specialized in providing the specific training and technical knowledge required for a certain production process can give a major contribution to the competitiveness of the SMEs and ultimately of the entire industrial district.[27]

Districts also tend to be especially good at the economic capabilities needed for driving change, weathering crises, and resiliently bouncing back from failures. Culture and cultural institutions play an important role in the ability of districts to drive change, in the economy as much as in politics. AnnaLee Saxenian, in her comparative study of the two districts that drove the revolution in consumer electronics and in particular in computers, Silicon Valley, near San Francisco, and Route 128, near Boston, contrasted the ability to innovate of Silicon Valley, and introduce several new products, first semiconductors, then personal computers, then internet technologies, with the lack of this ability in Route 128, which pioneered microcomputers, but once this product went out of favor, it was displaced from markets, and went into a long economic decline.

---

25 A similar point is made by: Olof Hallonsten, *Big Science Transformed* (Cham, Switzerland: Springer, 2016).

26 An important argument in the literature is that there are knowledge spillovers, and that the whole region and its institutions participate in these knowledge spillovers: Keld Laursen, Francesca Masciarelli, and Andrea Prencipe, "Regions Matter: How Localized Social Capital Affects Innovation and External Knowledge Acquisition," *Organization science* 23, no. 1 (2012). See also: Alfonso Gambardella, Myriam Mariani, and Salvatore Torrisi, "How 'Provincial' is Your Region? Openness and Regional Performance in Europe," *Regional Studies* 43, no. 7 (2009). Alfonso Gambardella and Marco S. Giarratana, "Organizational Attributes and the Distribution of Rewards in a Region: Managerial Firms Vs. Knowledge Clusters," *Organization Science* 21, no. 2 (2010).

27 Gary Herrigel, *Industrial Constructions: The Sources of German Industrial Power* (Cambridge and New York: Cambridge University Press, 2000). On the importance of local schools to industrial districts in Italy, see: Claudio Gentili, *Scuola e Impresa. Teorie e Casi di Partnership Pedagogica* (Milan: Franco Angeli, 2013).

Saxenian emphasized the very different entrepreneurial culture in these two districts and the closely related way of financing new enterprises. In Silicon Valley there was more cultural tolerance for failures in investment, and also more informal investment, whether by angel investors or venture capitalists, both of which led to greater willingness to take risks, and ultimately to greater enterprise and innovation.[28] Other studies have emphasized the importance of universities to the success of districts, especially to Silicon Valley, whose Stanford University and University of California in Berkeley have contributed to the concept of the entrepreneurial university, which refers to universities that are successful both at carrying out research and at turning the research into business applications.[29]

Cities can often be conceptualized as consisting of one or more industrial districts, and some of the same considerations apply to the economy of cities that apply to industrial districts. Cities have continued attracting companies and remained important engines of growth, despite their high costs, at least in part because of the more or less elaborate division of labor within them, and the presence of numerous and diverse cultural institutions.[30] Development agencies that seek to attract new investments often emphasize the diverse industrial base of a city, as well as the presence of diverse cultural institutions that carry out research and training in disparate fields, both of which can lead to synergies in the creation of new products. The presence of universities and schools that train diverse professional profiles, from managers, to engineers, to IT experts, to scientists, is a major attraction for companies, and so is the presence of a diverse workforce.[31] A diversity of specialist skills, whether acquired

---

28   Saxenian, *Regional Advantage*.
29   On the role of universities in Silicon Valley, see: Josep M. Pique, Jasmina Berbegal-Mirabent, and Henry Etzkowitz, "Triple Helix and the Evolution of Ecosystems of Innovation: The Case of Silicon Valley," *Triple Helix* 5, no. 1 (2018). On Stanford University and UC Berkeley as a paradigm, see: Henry Etzkowitz, "Entrepreneurial University Icon: Stanford and Silicon Valley as Innovation and Natural Ecosystem," *Industry and Higher Education* 36, no. 4 (2022); Stephen B. Adams, "Follow the Money: Engineering at Stanford and UC Berkeley During the Rise of Silicon Valley," *Minerva* 47, no. 4 (2009).
30   Peter Hall, "Creativity, Culture, Knowledge and the City," *Built Environment* 30, no. 3 (2004). Hall places this argument in the framework of the emergence of civilizations: *Cities in Civilization* (New York: Pantheon, 1998).
31   Montreal International, the public-private partnership that has re-launched the Montreal economy over the past 25 years, highlights the importance of international workers and students as one of its pillars: Montreal International, 2020 Activity Report, (2021). Politicians as diverse as Denis Coderre, Valérie Plante, and François Legault, have all backed an approach to development that builds upon internationally-mobile workers and students as a pillar of growth. This is part of the creative cities development paradigm. On this paradigm, see the many contributions in: Philip Cooke and Luciana Lazzeretti, eds.,

locally or imported, also contributes to the division of labor within cities. Cities are attractive, not just for investors, but also for the increasingly mobile and increasingly transnational upper middle class, that is, those professionals who are very skilled and have skills that are high in demand. This is for some of the same reasons that attract investors, since professionals with great skills can progress the furthest in their career in cities that attract investors in new technologies. Cities are attractive also because of the presence of amenities, and because of good standards of living.[32]

Let us consider now *the division of labour within a country.* The interaction between cultural institutions and economic organizations can occur at the national level. Universities, for example, interact and sometimes compete with each other at the national level, not just at the level of a district or city, where there is just one or two universities or similar cultural institutions. They interact also with other organizations, as part of a division of labour within a country that is very important for development. States found out long ago that they could increase political-military development the most, their distinctive type of development, if they left some activities to other organizations. This is because universities are better at providing scientific innovations, and private companies are better at turning scientific innovations into technological innovations, including weapons needed by states.[33] It is important to remind ourselves that this is true also of other arenas. It is true for example of economic development. Private companies can increase their wealth the most if some activities are left to other arenas, for example an educated workforce is best provided by civil society institutions, and defense is best provided by nation-states. Basic research is clearly best provided by universities, because of the long-term investment necessary in basic research, which can be very important in the long run, although it does not immediately yield profits.[34]

Thesis 111 explains the mechanisms whereby the division of labour in society contributes to development. It argues that *the division of labour in society contributes to development* because it leads to specialization in skills and

Creative Cities, Cultural Clusters and Local Economic Development (Cheltenham, UK and Northampton, Massachusetts: Edward Elgar, 2008).

32   This argument has been reviewed by: Edward L. Glaeser, "Cities, Information, and Economic Growth," *Cityscape* 1, no. 1 (1994); John M. Quigley, "Urban Diversity and Economic Growth," *Journal of Economic Perspectives* 12, no. 2 (1998).

33   This is part of Saxenian's argument on differences between the Boston area and San Francisco area. The first was tied to big science and was closer to state investment as a model of development: Saxenian, *Regional Advantage.*

34   See the arguments in: Ammon J. Salter and Ben R. Martin, "The Economic Benefits of Publicly Funded Basic Research: a Critical Review," *Research Policy* 30, no. 3 (2001).

greater collective capabilities in all three different instances of the division of labor, namely, within an organization, within a district, and within a country. Collective capabilities in organizations are frequently studied as organizational capabilities, from Smith's days to our own.[35] In countries there emerges a very important division of labour amongst different arenas that is foreshadowed in the division of labour within districts. The creation of different arenas, each best at producing the type of development and the associated capabilities that are distinctive to it, is crucial to development, alongside the creation of large markets within nation-states. This insight can be articulated and formalized into the following thesis and sub-theses, which describe the mechanisms whereby the division of labour in society contributes to development.

III.   *The division of labour in society leads to a growth in capabilities through differentiation and specialization.* We can distinguish between three different types of division of labour, which co-exist and complement each other in the division of labour in society, as they lead to growth in capabilities through different mechanisms.

   a.   *There is a division of labour in an organization.* This type of division of labor leads to growth in capabilities through differentiation or specialization. It is necessary to distinguish between differentiation within a production process, and human specialization, since in some cases differentiation and specific equipment require less skills and thus less human specialization.

      i.   *At the level of the production process and equipment,* differentiation in processes enables the maximum development of capabilities for that activity, by minimizing waste of time in switching between different activities and by using very specific machinery.

      ii.   *At the level of the workforce, and its knowledge, know-how, and skills,* specialized workers and often entire specialized departments maximize capabilities through the specific knowledge, know-how, and skills they have that are needed for greater output in certain production processes.

---

35   On organizational capabilities, see the many contributions in: Giovanni Dosi, Richard R. Nelson, and Sydney G. Winter, eds., *The Nature and Dynamics of Organizational Capabilities* (Oxford and New York: Oxford University Press, 2000). An application of the concept of organizational capabilities is: Frederik Tell, "Integrating Electrical Power Systems: From Individual to Organizational Capabilities," in *The Business of Systems Integration,* ed. Andrea Prencipe, Andrew Davies, and Michael Hobday (Oxford And New York: Oxford University Press, 2003).

b. *There is a division of labour in a district.* In a district there are several, and sometimes numerous, organizations that compete and cooperate with each other at the same time, with differentiation combined with specialization leading to growth in capabilities in the following manners, each corresponding to a somewhat different mechanism.

    i.   *Differentiation and specialization in economic and cultural capabilities*, between on the one hand factories and offices, and on the other hand universities and schools associated with training.

    ii.   *Differentiation and specialization affecting the demand-side*, associated with product innovation, carving out market niches, or supplying variable demand, for a variety of different products, associated with economies of scope.

    iii.   *Differentiation and specialization affecting the supply side*, as part of more or less long supply chains that provide different inputs needed for a given product, which contributes to economies of scale.

There is also a division of labour in a country, item III.c, that I address in the next section, as it involves a somewhat different type of division of labour. The above thesis, and sub-theses III.a and III.b within it, suggest the *mechanisms* whereby the division of labour in society leads to development. The thesis suggests that the division of labour in society involves differentiation and specialization, often both differentiation and specialization, and that this specialization includes specialization in activities, and specialization in principles of behavior and the associated organizational forms. Let us consider first the mechanisms that lead to development in the *division of labour within one organization*. The division of labour in a factory described by Smith involves a differentiation in the production process whereby the production of a pin is divided into different parts, avoiding loss of time in switching from one part to another of the process. It is important to distinguish between differentiation and specialization, since the latter refers to the human knowledge and skills that are sometimes, but not always, associated with differentiation. Differentiation can require less skills, as in Smith's example, and in some cases this is amplified by the introduction of machinery, to the point of leading to brutal and de-humanizing production processes involving repetitive movements, as described in Marx's early work on alienation, and in Gramsci's notes on Taylorism and Fordism.[36] However, in some cases the introduction of modern machinery has required more skills and specialization, and assigned the repetitive tasks to machines. For example, with the introduction of modern automation and robots on car production lines, the de-humanizing aspects of production chains have been removed, and the level of technical knowledge required has increased, to the point that many workers on the shop floor of car manufacturers are required to have an engineering degree.[37]

In some cases differentiation within an organization is associated with altogether different knowledge and skills, leading to differentiation into different departments involved in different parts of a process. In many organizations, including many factories, there is today a separate department that handles Information Technology, or IT, more recently generalized to Information and Communications Technology, or ICT.[38] At CERN there is an internal department that writes and maintains the computer code that is needed to process the large amounts of data produced by the machinery. In large organizations that have been long at the cutting edge of data processing, these departments emerged through a piecemeal process of differentiation and specialization, whereby specific data and information requirements emerge that need either specific software or handling of data in a specific manner. In large organizations that undergo rapid growth, many different pieces of codes are written in a piecemeal fashion by different scientists, which soon become impossible to maintain, as the number of the pieces of code increases, and as the employees who wrote them leave as part of turnover. It is therefore necessary to create a specialized internal department to handle the code and impose uniform standards.[39] In these departments there is training both in the specific computer language or software used by the department, and also in even more specific software requirements faced by the department. This is part of processes of differentiation and specialization that affect training, even more than the actual production process. With the greater amount of knowledge and skills required in modern production processes, there emerge also greater requirements for training. In addition to saving time in switching between one

---

36   See entry for 'fordismo' in: Liguori and Voza, *Dizionario Gramsciano*.

37   On the importance of skilled work in modern societies, and on the need for further research on this topic, see: Francis Green, *Skills and Skilled Work: An Economic and Social Analysis* (Oxford and New York: Oxford University Press, 2013).

38   There is a correlation between high skills and ICT technologies used in industry: Martin Falk and Federico Biagi, "Relative Demand for Highly Skilled Workers and Use of Different ICT Technologies," *Applied Economics* 49, no. 9 (2017).

39   CERN, "Welcome to CERN IT Department."; "Browse Services by Department. Services for IT."

production process and another, some differentiation emerges that involves saving time switching between training and work, providing intensive training or training on the job.

Let us consider the mechanisms that lead to development in the *division of labour within a district*. Some of these mechanisms are essentially the same as those that give rise to training departments or groups devoted to training within an organization. In many organizations some training is carried out internally for specific tasks. But training in some other tasks that are less specific to the organization is best carried out externally to the organization. In order to understand differentiation and specialization in districts we have to focus upon two important concepts. One is the *size of the organization*, both in absolute terms, and relative to the markets that it operates in. Organization size is very important to understand the functioning of districts and also mechanisms of differentiation and specialization within districts. Arrighi, building upon arguments by Smith, suggested that SMEs are very important to the proper functioning of markets, including to increase productivity.[40] This is because SMEs truly participate in markets, whereas large corporations tend to form oligopolies and even cartels, which stifle market forces. Arrighi added that paradoxically SMEs have driven Chinese growth and are the key to the continued success of the Chinese economy, whereas large corporations have come to predominate in many sectors of the United States economy. Another important concept is *the concept of economies of scale and the related concept of economies of scope*. Large corporations tend to emerge that dominate large markets, because they can benefit from *economies of scale*, which entail that after an initial investment, a large company can produce a very large number of standardized goods or commodities, thanks to modern industrial production, that is, production differentiated as explained by Smith, that furthermore uses specialized machinery. This leads to such an expansion in economic capabilities, that there are massive economies of scale to be realized. The resulting goods are much cheaper than the goods produced by SMEs, especially if transportation costs are also lowered. Large corporations sometimes are also able to benefit from *economies of scope*, which entail that a manufacturer of a certain product can easily introduce one or more similar products, and with relatively low additional costs, compared to a manufacturer who wants to introduce a new product from scratch.

---

40   Giovanni Arrighi, *Adam Smith in Beijing: Lineages of the 21st Century* (London and New York: Verso, 2009).

The size of the organizations active in a district, their distribution, and the differentiation and specialization amongst them, all affect the division of labor within districts, and its ability to contribute to capabilities, in the following manner. *Both competitiveness and the long-term viability of a district* require a more or less advanced division of labour and a mix of large and small companies. In particular, the growth in capabilities within a district often includes *diverse economic capabilities* that are appropriate for a more diverse economic base, and include capabilities related to economies of scale and of scope, as well as the ability to change and innovate. Sub-thesis iii.b.i emphasizes that within a district, the differentiation and specialization between economic and cultural capabilities is very important to development, because it optimizes training requirements. This in its turn is both because smes do not have the budgets for internal training and research departments, and because training and research greatly benefit from being concentrated, even when large companies are active in districts.[41] There are gains in capabilities from having training and research concentrated in one cultural institution, so long as the professors or researchers have autonomy in their research and are not stifled by a centrally-managed bureaucratic organization. The dissemination of knowledge also benefits from some centralization and coordination. This is because training and research are not private goods, but largely club goods available only in the district, or public goods available to all. They benefit from sharing across companies, which greatly contributes to the growth of the club or public good.[42]

The next two sub-theses emphasize supply-side and demand-side gains to be had from differentiation and specialization amongst the organizations that are active in a district. The division of labour in a district directly contributes to these capabilities. This is because the division of labor in a district contributes to the *diverse economic capabilities needed to succeed in the long ran*, including driving change, weathering crises, and resiliently bouncing back from failures.[43] These are very important economic capabilities that are decisive to the

---

41   On the difficulties faced by smes in implementing training, see: Urban Pauli, "Training Professionalisation and sme Performance," *Human Resource Development International* 23, no. 2 (2020).

42   On education and research knowledge as club goods and public goods, see: Rita Locatelli, *Reframing Education as a Public and Common Good: Enhancing Democratic Governance* (London and New York: Palgrave Macmillan, 2019); Allen Batteau, *Technology and the Common Good: The Unity and Division of a Democratic Society* (New York and Oxford: Berghahn Books, 2022).

43   On innovation and resilience, see: Jennifer Clark, Hsin-I Huang, and John P. Walsh, "A Typology of 'Innovation Districts': What It Means for Regional Resilience," *Cambridge Journal of Regions, Economy and Society* 3, no. 1 (2010).

long-term success of a district, and are in addition to economies of scale and of scope, and overlap to some extent with these economies. Sub-thesis III.b. ii suggests that companies in industrial districts can increase economic capabilities related to economies of scope. The mechanism whereby the division of labor in a district leads to these capabilities is related to the fact that a distribution of companies of various sizes, all interacting with cultural institutions, are better able to introduce product innovations, carve out market niches, and supply variable demand. SMEs in districts tend to be better at all of these economic capabilities, which in their turn tend to contribute to more diversified and stable markets than markets defined by a few large commodities and a few large corporations focused exclusively on economies of scale.[44] These more diversified markets in some cases are capable of stable and sustained growth that in the long term amounts to greater growth than markets subject to periodic fluctuations that lead to crises and massive disruptions in the economy that it takes a long time to recover from. These more diversified markets have capabilities and features that contribute to self-regulation. There are market niches in specialty products, catering to different social groups and different communities, which tend to be more stable and less subject to fluctuation than large markets for commodities.

Sub-thesis III.b.iii suggests that the division of labor in a district contributes some of the *same diverse economic capabilities* also to the supply-side. The division of labour in districts includes differentiation and specialization within supply chains, and it is related to supply-side considerations that contribute both to economies of scale and to the capabilities necessary for driving change, weathering crises, and resiliently bouncing back from failures. For example, car manufacturers are greatly affected by economies of scale, and many have turned into corporations that benefited from the demand-side capabilities introduced above, by specializing in the design and marketing of these products, and also in the final assembly of their products, leveraging

---

44   On SMEs and innovation, see the many contributions to: Bjørn T. Asheim et al., eds., *SMEs and the Regional Dimension of Innovation*, Regional Innovation Policy for Small-Medium Enterprises (Cheltenham, UK and Northampton, Massachusetts: Edward Elgard, 2003). On product innovation by SMEs, see: Piore and Sabel, *The Second Industrial Divide*. The expression innovation district has been coined to describe the ability of districts with numerous companies of all sizes to produce innovation. On the role of universities in innovation districts, see: Costas Spirou, *Anchoring Innovation Districts: The Entrepreneurial University and Urban Change* (Baltimore: Johns Hopkins University Press, 2021).

systems integration.[45] However, this has gone hand-in-hand with heavy reliance on suppliers, and leaving many or even most components to be produced by suppliers. In this case, differentiation and specialization by the suppliers in a certain product leads to greater economic capabilities, including capabilities related to economies of scale and also to innovation, because suppliers produce a given component for different companies, and they have greater knowledge of that component than inhouse departments. This is at least in part because there is competition amongst SMEs in the supply chain, whereas there is no competition amongst internal departments of a corporation.[46] In addition, a supplier who produces the same or very similar products for several different corporations benefits from both economies of scale and of scope. There are also greater capabilities to innovate and to resiliently bounce back from failures in districts. Failure in one part of a supply chain, and even failure in the main corporation, can be more easily remedied by simply switching to different suppliers, or in more complex cases by reconfiguring the supply chain, while avoiding the loss incurred, and energy required, in re-building a company. Some of these very same mechanisms are at work also in the division of labour in a country, which involves arenas, and in the case of arenas additional requirements involving embedded autonomy become especially important.

3   Thesis IV on Embedded Autonomy as a Source of Development

Thesis IV describes the manner in which the two national factors, namely the division of labour in a country, and embedded autonomy, interact with each other to produce development. These are part of processes depicted in Figure 6 as National factors 1. There are two distinct mechanisms whereby the division of labour in a country leads to growth in capabilities. The first involves a geographical extension of the division of labour in a district, whereby the scale of a districts grows, and different districts co-exist in a country, sometimes

---

45   On the growing importance of lifestyle considerations, including design, see: Markus Seidel, Christoph H. Loch, and Satjiv Chahil, "Quo Vadis, Automotive Industry? A Vision of Possible Industry Transformations," *European Management Journal* 23, no. 4 (2005).

46   On the importance of suppliers, see: Thomas Klier and James Rubenstein, *Who Really Made Your Car?: Restructuring and Geographic Change in the Auto Industry* (Kalamazoo, Michigan: W.E. Upjohn Institute for Employment Research, 2008). On the greater power of some suppliers, see: Wilson Kia Onn Wong, *Automotive Global Value Chain: The Rise of Mega Suppliers* (London and New York: Routledge, 2017).

producing the same product, and thus in competition with one another, other times producing altogether different products. In this case the same mechanisms that lead to growth in the division of labour in a district, are at work also in a country, simply on a greater scale. There is also a second mechanism and an altogether different type of division of labour that is at work in a country. It is the division of labour between arenas, whereby each arena comes to specialize in a *type of development and the associated capabilities.* This division of labour emerges clearly only where a relatively large state is in existence that encompasses several districts, or when a smaller state, for example a city-state, participates in activities and cultural exchange with similar organizations in other countries. For example, the university or main cultural institution in a district begins to interact with other similar cultural institutions in other districts, whether in the same country or in other countries, sharing knowledge, sometimes hiring from the other institutions. The political institutions in a district or city similarly start interacting with other institutions in other districts and sharing political goals and tactics.

These two mechanisms are associated with different types of division of labour. It is important to emphasize that *the different arenas in a country are specialized in different types of activities,* instead of products. It is useful to dwell on this point at some length in order to differentiate between the division of labor in a district and the division of labor in a country. Within a country there is still differentiation, as in Smith's example. This is clear if we compare the military with the economy. Although there are exceptions, especially in modern armies, a soldier typically has skills that are different than those of a worker, and switching back and forth between one type of activity and the other can be costly in terms of time. Moreover, service in an army for long periods of time disrupts economic activities. Therefore, professional armies have become widely adopted, except in times of large-scale wars. This is also clear if we compare culture with the economy. Although there is overlap, especially in modern knowledge economies, a researcher typically has skills that are different than those of a white collar worker, and switching back and forth between one type of activity and the other would be costly. The important point that I am emphasizing here is that some of the same mechanisms at work in the division of labour in a factory that increase productivity are at work also in the division of labour in a country, and increase the capabilities produced in each arena, and thus contribute to development. Moreover, the most important contribution to development in the division of labour in a country comes from specialization, which involves activities as opposed to products. A university or institute might teach courses in design that are used to train designers of cars as much as designers of home appliances or household objects. It might teach mechanical engineering courses that serve to design cars or hospital equipment. A university, like much of culture, is specialized in research, and in education, not in specific products. In addition, cultural capital enters the economy as a factor of production, but culture is more than just providing this factor. Sub-thesis III.c emphasizes the two different mechanisms involved in producing growth in capabilities as part of the division of labour in a country. The following is *a continuation of Thesis III that shows only sub-thesis III.c.*

III. *The division of labour in society leads to a growth in capabilities through differentiation and specialization.* These affect also the third type of division of labour, namely, the division of labour in a country.

    c. *There is a division of labour in a country.* Within a country with a large territory and population, there are two divisions of labour that lead to growth in capabilities through different mechanisms.

        iii. *There is a division of labour associated with products* that is an extension to the entire country of the division of labour in a district, in which there emerges a single nation-wide market for a certain product, or group of similar products, that is produced in one or more districts.

        ii. *There is a division of labour in arenas* that involves different activities, in which the three different arenas, namely, the economic, the cultural, and the political-military arenas, each become heavily specialized in a different domain of human activity. The growth in arena-specific capabilities emerges from a combination of principles of behavior and organizational forms.

            1. *Arena-specific principles of behavior emerge that guide individual and organizational behavior in each arena,* and become widespread within that arena, as the type of behavior that is most successful within that arena comes to predominate, and is sanctioned by law.

            2. *Arena-specific organizational types emerge and become predominant in each arena,* as each type is best at developing the capabilities distinctive to that arena, sanctioned by law. In the West the organizational types that prevailed are:

                a. Private companies in the economic arena.

                b. Non-governmental organizations, or NGOs, and non-profit organizations, or NPOs, in the cultural arena, which overlaps with civil society.

     c.   Nation-states, political parties, and social move-
          ment organizations, or SMOs, in the political-
          military arena.

Since the mechanism involved in the division of labour in products is the same
as the mechanism involved in the division of labour in a district, I focus here
upon the second type of specialization that is part of the division of labour in
a country, *specialization amongst arenas in principles of behavior,* and *organizational forms,* both of which contribute to the growth in per-capita capabilities. The behaviors distinctive to each of the three arenas, namely, the
economic, cultural, and political-military arenas, arguably constitute altogether
different types of behavior that can be summarized as *Homo Oeconomicus,
Homo Culturalis, and Homo Politicus. Homo Oeconomicus* is a concept widely
used in early economic theory to describe a category of behavior that distinguishes individuals in markets, while *Homo Culturalis,* and *Homo Politicus*
are approaches that define the different behaviors in other arenas. They too
are based on widely used concepts. A central point emphasized by Gramsci
is that different behaviors come to prevail in markets, civil society, and the
state. Gramsci argued that *in markets* the type of behavior described by the
concept of *Homo Oeconomicus* prevails. This is acquisitive individualism, or
individualistic behavior in the search for profit, a behavior that under some
circumstances can create great wealth.[47] By contrast, in both civil society and
the state, solidarity is especially important. *In the state,* the type of behavior
described by the Aristotelian concept of *Zoon Politikon* (political animal) or
Homo Politicus prevail, a concept that emphasizes the ability to cooperate with
others in collective action, rather than acting individually. This is an important behavior outside markets. Recent social experiments by anthropologists
have confirmed that in most small scale societies outside the West this type of
behavior does prevail over *Homo Oeconomicus.*[48] In addition, studies of collective action in countries in the West, in which markets are the predominant way
to organize the economic arena, show that even in the West behaviors exist
in the political arena that are very different than the individualistic behavior
associated with *Homo Oeconomicu.* These studies have also emphasized the
importance of culture, and in particular of symbols and shared ideals, to collective action.[49]

---

47   Kratke, "Antonio Gramsci's Contribution to a Critical Economics."
48   Samuel Bowles and Herbert Gintis, "Social Preferences, Homo Oeconomicus and *Zoon
      Politikon,*" in *The Oxford Handbook of Contextual Political Analysis,* ed. Robert E. Goodin
      and Charles Tilly (Oxford and New York: Oxford University Press, 2006).
49   Ann Swidler, "Cultural Power and Social Movements," in *Culture and Politics*
      (Springer, 2000).

There is also a type of behavior that is distinctive to the cultural arena. Gramsci contributed to the emergence of modern cultural studies by drawing attention to the importance of culture in its own right as a factor in many social processes. Recent studies have suggested that many human behaviors can be described by the concept of *cultural animal*, a concept that emphasizes human behaviors are steeped in culture.[50] This affects behavior in all different arenas in one way or another, and it becomes a distinctive principle of behavior in the cultural arena. Here I want to contrast *Homo Culturalis* with the behavior of *Homo Oeconomicus* that prevails in markets. Behavior in civil society, as well as the state, is more cooperative compared to behavior in markets, as appropriate for behaviors that involve mostly club goods and collective goods.[51] Arguably in the cultural arena a number of different behaviors prevail, due to the size and internal differentiation of this arena in advanced capitalist societies. In the book on the humanist theory of society I suggest that we should conceive of civil society as part of a more general domain, society, that in advanced capitalist societies includes economic, cultural, and political society, as well as civil society.[52] There are types of behavior that are distinctive to each of these parts of society, is largely but not exclusively based on civil society and the cultural arena. For example, behaviors in society use means and pursue ends that are different than those that prevail in markets and also than in different parts of society other. The concept of *Homo Academicus* proposed by Bourdieu emphasizes that university professors are motivated by the search, not for profit, but for prestige.[53] This is a very different end, as evident also in the long hours they devote to their research would yield far greater profits in markets, compared to universities. The Enlightenment ideal of the scientist committed to truth is yet another type of behavior that prevails, at some times and places, within

---

50   Roy F. Baumeister, *The Cultural Animal: Human Nature, Meaning, and Social Life* (Oxford and New York: Oxford University Press, 2005). This concept is implicit in work by Stuart Hall, who emphasized that we are completely immersed in culture and that we function through culture. On Stuart Hall, see: James Procter and Robert Eaglstone, *Stuart Hall* (London and New York: Routledge, 2004).

51   Civil society is both a place where trust is produced, and in which cooperative behavior predominates. On this subject, see the many contributions in: Frank Tonkiss et al., eds., *Trust and Civil Society* (London and New York: Palgrave Macmillan, 2000).

52   On political society in Gramsci, see the entry for 'società politica' in: Liguori and Voza, *Dizionario Gramsciano*. The concept of economic society is proposed by: Juan J. Linz and Alfred Stepan, *Problems of Democratic Transition and Consolidation: Southern Europe, South America, and Post-Communist Europe* (Baltimore and London: Johns Hopkins University Press, 1996).

53   Pierre Bourdieu, *Homo Academicus*, trans. Peter Collier (Stanford, California: Stanford University Press, 1988).

society, and in particular within the cultural arena.[54] It involves pursuing ideals, rather than personal gains including prestige, and it complements collective action in the political arena.

These different principles of behavior are all very important to the different capabilities of the cultural and political-military arenas. In the cultural arena it is necessary to be motivated first and foremost by commitment to truth. Similarly, in the political-military arena, it is necessary to be motivated first and foremost by service to the nation and the state, and to the ideals they represent, and only in the second instance by a search for profits, which should be just rewards, rather than getting rich. This is clear when we consider what can go wrong when these priority rankings are reversed. *Putting profit first in the cultural arena can lower the cultural value of products.* Recent mass produced cultural products are a good example of this. Private companies seeking profits first and foremost can lower the cultural value of a product, or simply fail to increase the cultural value, and produce for example reality shows or other similar cultural products that sell fast and maximize profits by providing entertainment, but add little or nothing to knowledge and understanding.[55] *Similarly, putting profit first in the military arena can lower the level of security provided.* Private military contractors seeking profits first and foremost have to be subjected to strict rules. For example, such contractors can be allowed to search for profit in the service of one's country, but not in the service of other countries. This was a serious problem with mercenary companies in early modern Italy, compared with the armies of north-western European national states.[56] Moreover, even with strict rules, the search for profit still does not make the best soldiers, because the possibility of death threatens to put an end to all profits, and profit-maximizing individuals are more likely to cave in when faced with a tough battle. This criticism is important at the level of mercenary commanders, because if one seeks personal profits, one is more likely to switch to service of other countries that offer greater profits, which might be easy if

---

54   Thomas L. Hankins, *Science and the Enlightenment* (Cambridge and New York: Cambridge University Press, 1985). Roy Porter, *The Enlightenment,* 2nd ed. (London and New York: Palgrave Macmillan, 2001).

55   On the economic considerations affecting Reality TV shows, see: Chad Raphael, "The Political-Economic Origins of Reali-TV," in *Reality TV: Remaking Television Culture,* ed. Susan Murray and Laurie Ouellette (New York and London: New York University Press, 2009).

56   Michael Mallett and William Caferro, *Mercenaries and Their Masters: Warfare in Renaissance Italy* (Barnsley, South Yorkshire: Pen & Sword Military, 2009).

there are grey areas in laws, or one might be tempted to serve two masters, if these two masters are both NATO employers.[57]

In addition to different types of behavior, *different organizational forms emerge* in each arena. The organizational forms that prevail in society and the state are different than those that prevail in markets, and are related to the types of behavior that prevail in these other arenas. It is this *combination of organizational form with principles of behavior* that maximizes the capabilities produced in each arena. *In the economic arena*, in which markets prevail, various arena-specific organizational forms became predominant, most being types of for-profit private enterprises, best suited to the main principle of behavior in markets, namely, the search for profit through acquisitive individualism. They ensured the greatest creation of wealth.[58] Because of neoliberalism's emphasis upon markets alone, I want to emphasize that the organizational forms and principles of behavior in other arenas are very different than the organizational forms specific to markets and market principles of behavior that emphasize acquisitive individualism. *In the political-military arena*, there emerged nation-states, parties committed to voice or loyalty, and national armies, as the organizational forms that maximize military capabilities and ensure the best defense. Nation-states emerged and became the predominant *state* organizational form. The guiding principle in this case, a formalization of loyalty to one's country, is attachment to the nation, and service to the state that represents and protects the nation. Other organizational forms emerged rewarding those who pursue voice or loyalty first and foremost. In close interaction with nation-states, political parties emerged as an important organizational form in the political-military arena, mostly linked in various ways to the nation-state and pursuing voice or loyalty within it.[59] These organizational forms are associated with specific behaviors. In all these organizations rewards

---

57   On the problems that arise with the extensive use of military contractors, see the Symposium on Private Military Contractors and International Law introduced by: Francesco Francioni, "Private Military Contractors and International Law: An Introduction," *European Journal of International Law* 19, no. 5 (2008). On the problems in privatizing lethal force, see: Antenor Hallo de Wolf, "Modern Condottieri in Iraq: Privatizing War from the Perspective of International and Human Rights Law," *Indiana Journal of Global Legal Studies* 13, no. 2 (2006).

58   David J. Teece, "Management and Governance of the Business Enterprise: Agency, Contracting, and Capabilities Perspectives," in *The Oxford Handbook of Capitalism*, ed. Dennis C. Mueller (Oxford and New York: Oxford University Press, 2012).

59   Some authors have argued that there is a decline in the nation-state, but they only refer to ideological attachment, not organizational form: Karl-Dieter Opp, "Decline of the Nation State? How the European Union Creates National and Sub-National Identifications," *Social Forces* 84, no. 2 (2005). If a European state should ever emerge, it would still make

consist first and foremost in career advancement, rather than personal profit. Career advancement thus complements voice or loyalty. A worker in the job market is supposed to look for the best-paid employment for his skills, and switch employers accordingly, whereas loyalty to one's nation and state is expected of politicians and soldiers. Politicians who are in the service of foreign countries instead of their country, and captains of mercenary companies who switch employment for higher pay, are universally reviled, and this type of behavior is often prohibited by law. Mercenaries who steal other soldier's pay or who pillage lands they should protect, are against both sets of principles, market principles, and political principles prescribing loyalty.[60]

In the cultural arena, various organizational forms came to prevail, all complementing principles of behavior other than acquisitive individualism. *These organizational forms all tended to be non-profit organizations* that are best suited for maximizing capabilities in public goods.[61] In civil society, NPOs and those who work for them are driven first and foremost by service to the community and those in need, sometimes extended far beyond the community by some missionaries. The same can be said for most cultural institutions, from cultural foundations, to museums, to colleges, most of which are non-profits, and are thus part of civil society. These are principles that are very different than acquisitive individualism and the search for profit[62] The same can be said of scientists, including social scientists, who are supposed to be committed to the search for truth, or service to the scientific community and the public first and foremost, and those scientists who change theory only or mostly because of higher pay or greater prestige are universally reviled. The greatest rewards for scientists are the truths they discovered, or the theories useful to society that they put forward, with profits from research being largely re-invested in

---

use of culture like nation-states did, or like Great Britain did, which emerged from the union of England with Northern Ireland and Scotland, and earlier with Wales.

60   On these questions, see: Zoe Salzman, "Private Military Contractors and the Taint of a Mercenary Reputation," NYU *Journal of International Law & Politics* 40 (2007).

61   Solomon and Anheier define the civil society sector (here I use the word arena, I define sector in the book on the humanist theory of society) to consist of private non-profit organizations: Lester M. Salamon and Helmut K. Anheier, "The Civil Society Sector," *Society* 34, no. 2 (1997).

62   The importance of individual motivation, both to volunteering, and giving, is addressed by several contributors in: Michael Edwards, ed. *The Oxford Handbook of Civil Society* (Oxford and New York: Oxford University Press, 2011). Some have argued that cultural organizations driven by distinctive principles of behavior are emerging even in world culture. On this point, see also the many contributions in: John Boli and George M. Thomas, eds., *Constructing World Culture: International Nongovernmental Organizations since 1875* (Stanford, California: Stanford University Press, 1999).

research, and organizational form and organizational rewards have emerged that provide these rewards. In the above examples I have specified *first and foremost* because economic considerations affect us all, simply because we all have to live. One way of formulating this point is that individuals active in different arenas have different priority rankings by category of ends. In the economic arena, profit typically ranks first, and considerations relating to truth rank second or third, amongst the ends that we have to pursue. In the cultural arena, truth comes first, and profit second.[63] The increasing move towards market mechanisms in the cultural arena, and in some countries subordination to political and military pressures, means that the pursuit of truth suffers.

The advancement of the division of labour in a country requires the adoption of distinct principles of behavior and organizational forms by each arena, and it is ensured by embedded autonomy. Embedded autonomy between arenas describes an important type of interaction between the different arenas that contributes to development by enabling the *advancement* as well as smooth functioning of the division of labour between arenas. In particular, *it enables the efficient use of resources associated with the division of labour between arenas* and also other efficiencies, including the greatest contribution from each arena to the other arenas in its own type of development. *It also enables synergies in development between arenas,* whereby development occurs in all the different arenas, which can contribute to common pools of resources and knowledge, greatly advancing development in all the arenas that draw from these common pools. Embedded autonomy across arenas functions through the sharing of information and coordination of activities that is necessary for capitalizing on efficiencies and synergies between arenas, and also for the regulation in the production of capabilities by each of the different arenas. In addition to embedded autonomy, there must be comprehensive development across arenas, that is, considerable development across all arenas.

IV.   *Embedded autonomy between arenas in a country contributes to development.* Embedded autonomy consists of a type of interaction between arenas whereby there is smooth functioning of the division of labour between arenas, and also the greatest possible contribution to development from each arena.

  a.   *The definition of embedded autonomy* is that it is a type of interaction that involves both autonomy and embeddedness between

---

63   Philosophers refer to these features as epistemic virtues: Jason Kawall, "Other–Regarding Epistemic Virtues," *Ratio* 15, no. 3 (2002).

arenas and contributes to the smooth functioning of the division of labour between arenas.

    i.   *Through autonomy* each arena can adopt the principles of behavior and organizational forms that maximize the growth in capabilities that are distinctive to that arena.

    ii.   *Through embeddedness* there can be sharing of information and coordination of activities with the other arenas that maximize the contributions needed by other arenas from that arena.

b. *Embedded autonomy leads to the greatest growth in per-capita capabilities*, through the following mechanisms involving the division of labour.

    i.   *There is the most efficient use of resources by arenas,* since each arena is capable of optimizing the production of its distinctive type of capabilities through autonomy, and to receive the most capabilities that it needs from the other arenas through embeddedness.

    ii.   *There are synergies in development if comprehensive development is pursued,* because different arenas can share common pools of resources that these arenas contribute to and draw from, ensuring the greatest advances in such shared resources as human resources and technological base.

c. *Embeddedness ensures the sharing of information and coordination of activities that is necessary to capitalize on efficiencies and synergies, and also to ensure regulation.* Within the mechanisms involved, it is useful to differentiate between the structures and the processes that these structures enable.

    i.   *The structures that enable embeddedness facilitate interaction amongst institutions and organizations* like NGOs, NPOs, and SMOs, and also private companies and corporations, which exchange information and coordinate activities through all of the following structures and means.

        1.   *Networks amongst institutions and organizations,* which can be permanent or transient, and strong or weak, with degrees in between these parameters, for example from most permanent to most transient.

        2.   *Shared social areas and forums,* in which institutions and organizations more freely interact, typically through public goods and transient networks, and in

which there is transparency and accountability of all the networks, whether permanent or transient.

3. *A shared language and mutually intelligible professional dialects or jargons* are an integral means of interactions used in the networks and in the shared areas and forums, without which the networks and shared areas and forums cannot properly function.

ii. *Embeddedness enables important processes*, which include the following processes involving the contributions needed by other arenas.

1. *The formulation of new policies or adjustments to policies,* which guarantee that new capabilities are produced, and that the right type of capabilities needed by the other arenas are produced, in the right amount, and when and where they are needed.

2. *The formulation of new laws and values or adjustments to laws and values* that punish criminal behaviors, or put pressure on behaviors deemed unacceptable, and ensure productive social conflict free of violence, as well as rules of civility in debates and ultimately all interactions.

3. *The implementation of existing procedures within a given policy and legal framework* for addressing problems or needs that arise in the ordinary provision of capabilities from one arena to another, like the routine assignment of more policemen to an area, or of more funds to some NGOs, if the need arises.

Sub-thesis IV.a provides the very definition of embedded autonomy and how it contributes to development, emphasizing its contribution to the division of labour between arenas. It follows from the above discussion of the divisions of labour. The other two sub-theses, IV.b and IV.c, introduce new concepts and require some explanation to clarify their significance. Sub-thesis IV.b goes into detail explaining how embedded autonomy contributes to development, by enabling efficiencies and synergies. Sub-thesis IV.b.i focuses upon *efficiencies in the use of resources.* The mechanism whereby embedded autonomy leads to greater development is by promoting the division of labour across arenas, a division that entails two efficiencies. The first efficiency consists in *the most efficient production of capabilities within an arena.* This is because *through autonomy each arena* is able to adopt the principles of behavior and organizational forms that maximize the production of capabilities that are distinctive to it, and lead to the most efficient use of available resources and the greatest development of that arena. The second efficiency consists in *the greatest contribution to the capabilities needed by the other arenas.* This is because *through embeddedness each arena gives the greatest contribution to the development* of other arenas, by contributing to them the capabilities that they need, and that it is most efficient at producing, because through embeddedness there is the sharing of information and coordination of activities across arenas that is necessary to ensure that each arena produces the capabilities needed by the other arenas.

Sub-thesis IV.b.ii emphasizes that in addition to efficiencies, embedded autonomy enables *synergies in the development of each arena* that are associated with comprehensive development. *Comprehensive development* is development across the board, in all arenas. When comprehensive development is part of an interaction between arenas accompanied by embedded autonomy, embeddedness ensures that political-military development, not only provides the best and most efficient defense, but also contributes to economic development, especially in conjunction with cultural development. For example, if the political-military and economic arenas develop side-by-side, as part of comprehensive development, they can participate in a common pool of skilled manpower that both arenas contribute to and draw from, for example a pool of personnel for private security forces and today for cyber companies that infantry training and training for military cyber units contributes to.[64] Even more important, both the political-military and the economic arenas can participate in a shared technological base that they both contribute to and draw from. Silicon Valley and Route 128 emerged when market applications were found for defense technologies. The whole semiconductors industry, and ultimately much of the consumer electronics and the modern computers industry, arose from an initial state investment in machines that could compute trajectories of bombs.[65]

---

64   Pooling and sharing are becoming important to the militaries of different countries in Europe: Thomas Overhage, "Pool It, Share It, or Lose It: an Economical View on Pooling and Sharing of European Military Capabilities," *Defense & Security Analysis* 29, no. 4 (2013). An analogous concept applies to the political-military and economic arenas within one country, and it could provide a useful way of leveraging contractors' work without altering the state monopoly of legitimate violence, and without creating private military forces. In some countries it is the economic arena that has benefited from skills acquired in the military.

65   Saxenian, *Regional Advantage.* On the role played by Fairchild and its military contracts in the emergence of the microchip and ultimately of the modern computer industry, see: Christophe Lecuyer, David C. Brock, and Jay Last, *Makers of the Microchip: A Documentary History of Fairchild Semiconductor* (Cambridge, Massachusetts: MIT Press, 2010).

4   Thesis V and the Full Definition of Democracy

The theory suggests that a main challenge for development has to do with the need to maintain the different arenas separate, in a manner analogous to the separation of powers within a state, while each arena still contributes to all the other arenas. Thesis V proposes a full definition of democracy that explains the manner in which *democracy contributes to autonomy between arenas*. The key point is that the full definition of democracy ensures autonomy, and thus ensures at one and the same time a strong democracy and the embedded autonomy that is necessary for development. These are part of the processes depicted in Figure 6 as Contribution 2 to development, whereby Basic factors 2, namely political culture and SMOs, lead to National factors 2, namely democracy, which contributes to National factors 1, in particular embedded autonomy. The full definition of democracy combines two views, the democratic and republican views of democracy. As per the democratic view, it emphasizes an even distribution of power as an important component of democracy. As per the republican view, it adds institutions as a crucially important guarantee of an even distribution of power, and of the balance of power and separation of powers as applied to a country, namely the arenas producing economic, cultural, and political-military power. In addition, institutions have to be conceived of in relation to society, a view of institutions that is implicit in sub-thesis IV.c above, and a view of institutions as involved in social conflict, and participating in the crucially important social conflict equivalent of checks and balances, which ensure the balance of power and separation of powers.

Contribution 2 in Figure 6 is divided into three processes, numbered 2a, 2b, and 2c. I do not focus upon 2a and the role of micro social conflict in democracy, since it is widely addressed in the literature on democracy. I focus instead upon 2b and 2c, and thus upon *the role of meso social conflict in democracy*, a much under-theorized type of social conflict, and the related collective action problems.[66] Process 2b leads from political culture and SMOs, through meso social conflict, to democracy. Meso conflict, as discussed above, is largely social conflict that involves entire social groups as the largest and most important agents, which became involved in the democratization process described by Tarrow and Tilly with the emergence of a specific political culture that includes seeking to redress grievances as part of a voice strategy, a culture that drove an expanding sector of SMOs. For a long period in European history, following the expansion of capitalism, there were frequent riots that flared up into violent

---

66   I address contribution 2a in: Olsaretti, *The Struggle for Development and Democracy, Vol. 1.*

attempts at revolutions and seizures of power, all of which were part of crowd behavior, and all of which were very destructive, taking a toll on property, life, and also on social capital and smooth interactions amongst individuals.[67] Collective violence within a country can be extremely destructive of all activities, and can negatively affect both development and democracy. One reason is that steady system states spin out of control, or are completely destroyed, in a rapid and very destructive outburst of collective violence, or in a series of outbursts. Two important improvements in collective action were made in the long process of democratization that minimized collective violence within countries. One was the emergence, and eventual wide acceptance, of a political culture committed to redressing grievances. The other was a growth in the number of SMOs as part of an expanding civil society, that participated in the social conflict equivalent of checks and balances, whereby loss of democracy, if initiated, was nevertheless contained.

The process of democratization was made possible by the first improvement in collective action, consisting in the emergence of *a political culture committed to seeking the redress of grievances without violence*, which guided meso conflict and turned it into productive social conflict. This political culture included repertoires of contention that took a standard form, as performances repeated over time, in what was effectively mock conflict.[68] These forms of conflict remained within the bounds of laws and values, had violence removed from them, and became routinized. E. P. Thompson argued that the working class in England moved from such forms of protest as destruction of machinery, to more routinized and less harmful forms of protest such as loud music, initially an intimidation, to ordered and peaceful protests seeking the redress of grievances.[69] Tilly showed that a similar process was at work in France, and elsewhere in Europe, albeit at different times and with different speeds, which included *charivari*, a form of mock parade that was extended to social protests, from which all violence was eventually removed.[70] The emergence

---

67   Tilly, Tarrow, and McAdam, *Contention and Democracy in Europe*. On revolutions and riots as part of contention, see: Tilly, *Social Movements*; Charles Tilly, Louise Tilly, and Richard H. Tilly, *The Rebellious Century, 1830–1930* (Cambridge, Massachusetts and London: Harvard University Press, 1975).

68   Tilly was amongst the first to introduce the concept of repertoire in collective action, and to highlight the important of repertoires in the democratization process: Charles Tilly, *Regimes and Repertoires* (Chicago: University of Chicago Press, 2010).

69   E. P. Thompson, *The Making of the English Working Class*, Penguin Modern Classics (London: Penguin, 2002).

70   Charles Tilly, *The Contentious French* (Cambridge, Massachusetts: Belknap Press, 1986). Tilly generalized his points in: *Contentious Performances*, Cambridge Studies in Contentious Politics (Cambridge and New York: Cambridge University Press, 2008).

of a social group identity amongst the working classes, alongside the emergence of these repertoires and acceptable ways to seek redress of grievances, and with the establishment of ties to other social groups and the state, where an important part of the transition from collective action that was based on destructive and short-sighted crowd behavior, to orderly demonstrations to seek redress of grievances.[71] Tilly argued that eventually the whole of contention between social movements and states became routinized, and that the repertoires of contention developed by social movements were accepted by states, whereby displays of worthiness, unity, numbers, and commitment, or WUNC, meant that grievances were taken seriously and addressed, crucially dissuading agents within the state from using violence in order to deny the redress of grievances.[72]

The other important improvement in collective action was the growth in the number of SMOs, as part of a *social conflict equivalent of checks and balances,* whereby loss of democracy, if initiated, was contained. This improvement was important in both processes 2b and 2c. In process 2b, it contributed to keeping conflict within bounds and preventing conflict from escalating out of control and turning again into violent and destructive conflict. By keeping conflict within bounds, these checks and balances ensured instead that conflict continued contributing to democracy. In process 2c, the social conflict equivalent of checks and balances that became part of democracy contributes to embedded autonomy, and through it to development, because it ensures the autonomy of arenas, which contributes at one and the same time to both development and democracy. Gramsci's *analogy comparing civil society to the layered fortifications and deep defenses characteristic of a war of position* is especially useful to understand how the social checks and balances contribute to democracy in countries with a large and autonomous civil society. In a war of position, if one side in a battle achieves a victory against a first line of defense of the other side, they are faced with further defenses. In the case of democracy, if loss of democracy is initiated in the political-military arena, it cannot proceed. If there is also democracy, that is, an even distribution of power, within the cultural and economic arenas, and between these arenas and the political-military arena, this provides an especially important additional check against loss of political-military democracy. It is like a second line of defense that prevents further loss of democracy in the political-military arena, as well as preventing losses being initiated also in the other arenas.

---

71 *Social Movements.*

72 *Regimes and Repertoires*; "Charivaris, Repertoires and Urban Politics," in *French Cities in the Nineteenth Century* (Routledge, 2018).

The Gramscian concept of social war of position also begins to suggest *ways in which the social conflict equivalent of checks and balances work.* The concept of social war of position was associated both with the growth in the number of SMOs, part of a large and expansive civil society that is typical of certain geographical locations coinciding with the core of the world system, and also with the expansion of structures within civil society. *The growth in the number of SMOs as part of a large civil society is important to guarantee democracy itself,* as well as to criticize and improve upon policies. This can be measured, as proposed by Putnam and Molotch, by such aggregate measures as the number of NGOs and other organizations like SMOs in a given territory, or for a given population, as well as by additional measures such as the average wealth, and the average number of members, of these organizations.[73] Such a large civil society contributes to the smooth functioning of democracy through criticism and public debate. In addition, it can provide the above checks and balances that prevent loss of democracy, if there is also *reliable and speedy communication and coordination of activities across arenas* through embedded autonomy. This is facilitated by some of the same structures that enable embedded autonomy to foster development, and by specific structures that enable embedded autonomy to guarantee democracy. These specific structures are social structures between institutions and NGOs involved in democracy, such as NGOs that protect citizen rights, and between institutions and SMOs involved in democracy, such as SMOs campaigning for democracy in a specific geographic area, or against specific of government policies within a country.[74]

The above concepts all inform Thesis V, which puts forward a full definition of democracy and explains its interaction with autonomy between arenas. Democracy is very important both on its own, and also because it contributes to development. On its own, it guarantees basic human rights, and the conscious participation of citizens in political, cultural, and economic processes, which is arguably a very valuable end in itself. In order to understand how democracy contributes to development, we first have to *define democracy in*

---

73   Putnam, Leonardi, and Nanetti, *Making Democracy Work.* Logan and Molotch, *Urban Fortunes.* Resource Mobilization Theory on social movements adds the consideration that a movement divided into too many SMOs can disperse resources and raise costs: John D. McCarthy and Mayer N. Zald, "Resource Mobilization Theory: Vigorous or Outmoded?," in *Handbook of Sociological Theory,* ed. Jonathan H. Turner (Cham, Switzerland: Springer, 2006).

74   On the importance of SMOs, see: "Resource Mobilization Theory: Vigorous or Outmoded?." On the importance to social movements of networks, see the many contributions in: Mario Diani and Doug McAdam, eds., *Social Movements and Networks: Relational Approaches to Collective Action* (Oxford and New York: Oxford University Press, 2003).

greater detail, and introduce the full definition of democracy. In addition to the separation of powers within a state, there is a separation of powers in a country that is related to the division of labour in society, and functions best where there is a certain distribution of power. The division of society into different arenas is the social equivalent of the separation of powers in a state, and to understand how this separation of powers works to guarantee democracy, it is useful to begin by providing *a full definition of democracy that improves upon the definition of democracy as power of the people,* or *demos,* and includes considerations related to the division of society into different arenas. Such a definition emphasizes that there has to be at least some democracy in each of the arenas, and also across arenas.

v. *The full definition of democracy includes structures amongst institutions and organizations, as well as a certain distribution of power both within each arena and across arenas,* all of which act as the social conflict equivalent of checks and balances, ensuring advances in democracy and preventing losses in democracy.

 a. *Democracy emerges in the course of a long democratization process involving both cultural and organizational components,* chiefly a political culture and a large civil society with many SMOs, all of which interact to advance democracy, and help maintain democracy.

 i. *A political culture emerges that regulates interactions between protesters and the state,* and ensures that protesters seek voice, and also that they seek voice through productive social conflict, from which all violence was removed, and that the state too avoids resorting to violence.

 ii. *A large civil society emerges in which many SMOs participate in democratization,* and in which there are specific structures amongst NGOs, SMOs, and the state that ensure communication and coordination across all these organizations and the state in order to prevent the escalation of conflict into violence.

 b. *Democracy includes a distribution of power within each and every arena that is favorable to the masses,* a distribution of the power that is specific to that arena. This distribution of power ensures that democracy within each arena does not come to an end for reasons *internal* to that arena. This distribution depends upon specific capabilities.

 i. *Political-military democracy* is a distribution of power in the political-military arena that is favorable to the masses, and it depends upon the capability to engage in collective action.

ii.   *Cultural democracy* is a distribution of power in the cultural
      arena that is favorable to the masses, and it depends upon the
      capability to engage in collective action within the cultural
      arena, for example by student groups within colleges, or by
      associations of colleges, and upon the capability to formulate
      and spread philosophies and scientific theories.

iii. *Economic democracy* is a distribution of power in the eco-
      nomic arena that is favorable to the masses, and it depends
      upon the capability to engage in collective action in the econ-
      omy arena, for example by cooperatives, unions, or industri-
      alists' associations, and upon the distribution of wealth and
      the capability to engage in entrepreneurship, which requires
      access to economic capital.

c.   *Democracy includes an even distribution of power across arenas
     that ensures the autonomy of arenas*, since an even distribution of
     power guarantees both the autonomy of each arena, and democ-
     racy within each arena, in order to make sure that autonomy and
     democracy do not come to an end for reasons *external* to that arena.
     The distribution of power across arenas has the following features.

i.   *Each arena is able to resist takeover by other arenas*, for exam-
      ple by agents in other arenas.

ii.   *Each arena is able to exercise some influence over the other are-
      nas*, and thus to contribute to restoring democracy if democ-
      racy is lost in another arena.

The importance of a political culture and SMOs to advance democracy, as
stated in sub-thesis V.a, should be clear from the discussion that preceded
Thesis V. Here I want to clarify first the importance of sub-theses V.b and V.c to
maintain democracy, and then highlight the importance of a political culture
and SMOs highlighted in sub-thesis V.a, not only to advance democracy, but
also to maintain it. The two sub-theses V.b and V.c emphasize two features of
the distribution of power, respectively an even distribution of power within
each of the arenas, and also across the arenas, both of which are necessary to
ensure democracy. Sub-thesis V.b suggests that *a measure of democracy within
each and every arena contributes to democracy*. This argument is especially
clear if we consider economic democracy, which includes a distribution of
wealth that is in favor of the masses, or is at least not too skewed against the
masses. Some measure of economic democracy greatly contributes to political democracy, because it guarantees funding for NGOs and SMOs, without
which democracy is stunted. Most functioning democracies provide substantial economic funding, albeit in different ways, for political activities of one

form or another.[75] In the United States political parties are largely self-funded, through donations, whereas in Italy there is public funding of political parties and newspapers in order to ensure that social groups without much wealth can participate in politics. Some measure of economic democracy is also necessary to enable direct participation in politics, for example to allow small business owners and workers to take time off from work, in order to attend important political events such as major demonstrations. Sub-thesis v.c complements thesis v.b and suggests that *a measure of democracy across arenas contributes to democracy.* Democracy across arenas entails an even distribution of power across arenas, and thus a certain level of development in all arenas, that is, comprehensive development. If the other arenas, for example the economic arena, are sufficiently developed, they can bring more pressure upon the state.

The importance of these points, and of sub-thesis v.a to maintain democracy, and prevent a catastrophic loss of democracy, become clear also if we consider the *two main mechanisms whereby democracy can be lost.* One mechanism starts with *loss of political democracy first,* that is, democracy in the political-military arena. It is intuitive that if democracy is lost in the political-military arena, this will lead to a loss of democracy also in the cultural arena and in the economic arena, because the power of security forces, the police and the military, can easily be turned against intellectuals and the middle class and working class. This is what happened in Russia under Soviet communism, in Italy under fascism, and in Germany under nazism.[76] Although the process is obvious, I want to emphasize key aspects of the distribution of power across arenas that are involved in this mechanism. Sub-thesis v.b.i emphasizes that the distribution of political-military power should not be too skewed, because elites who have all power in their hands could put an end to democracy. This process typically starts in the political-military arena and can quickly spread to other arenas unless there is distribution of power across arenas, as emphasized by sub-thesis v.c. If there is distribution of power across arenas, other arenas can put pressure on the political-military arena. For example, in a country in which there is cultural democracy, including a vibrant civil society, if the

---

75   Koss Michael, *The Politics of Party Funding: State Funding to Political Parties and Party Competition in Western Europe* (Oxford and New York: Oxford University Press, 2010). For a comparative approach to party finance, see: Robert G. Boatright, *The Deregulatory Moment?: A Comparative Perspective on Changing Campaign Finance Laws* (Ann Arbor: University of Michigan Press, 2015).

76   On these seizures of power, see: Henry Ashby Turner, *Hitler's Thirty Days to Power: January 1933* (New York: Basic Books, 1997); Adrian Lyttelton, *The Seizure of Power: Fascism in Italy, 1919–1929* (London and New York: Routledge, 2004); Alexander Rabinowitch, *The Bolsheviks Come to Power: The Revolution of 1917 in Petrograd* (Chicago: Haymarket Books, 2004). The concept of seizure of power is important to the arguments of this book.

aristocratic-military elite starts gaining too much power over the masses and tries to put an end to political democracy, this triggers mass demonstrations supported by civil society, as well as other established means to bring pressure on the state, such as public debates, or electoral campaigns, because there is also cultural democracy.[77] A measure of economic democracy enables these mass demonstrations to take place repeatedly, through donations from supporters to SMOs fighting for democracy or to opposition political parties, and through the ability of participants to take part in repeated demonstrations, if necessary taking time off from work.

What is perhaps less obvious is that loss of democracy can be initiated by a second mechanism, that starts with *loss of democracy in other arenas than the political-military arena*, or is compounded by loss of democracy in other arenas, as happened in Italy. An important mechanism involves *loss of cultural democracy first*. This mechanism includes lack of networks and lack of a shared language and mutually intelligible professional dialects, between academics and the rest of the cultural arena, and also amongst organizations in the cultural and the political arenas. Lack of these factors deprives the political arena both of useful theories and of a moderating voice of reason that the cultural can exert on the political arena. This in its turn can lead to lack of communication and inability to coordinate activities between the cultural and the political-military arena, and ultimately to loss of autonomy of the cultural from the political-military arena. This seems to have been the mechanism exploited by Mussolini before and in the early stages of the fascist seizure of power in Italy, with the unwitting cooperation of liberal philosopher Croce. An important insight regarding this mechanism can be found in Gramsci's notes on fascism and on Croce. These notes can be interpreted to suggest that the lack of a truly autonomous civil society in Italy at the time, coupled with the inability to communicate and coordinate activities across the cultural and political arenas, meant that the struggle for cultural democracy was separated from the struggle for political democracy. Croce ostensibly defended academia from the restrictions imposed by fascism, but neglected to link cultural democracy to political democracy, and thus failed truly to defend democracy. The masses in Italy, deprived of the contribution that intellectuals, including academics, could give to political life, where more easily controlled by fascism, which rapidly destroyed political democracy after it forcibly seized political

---

77   Sen highlights the importance of public debate to development in: Sen, *Development as Freedom*. Tilly highlights the importance of demonstrations and public debates to contention and ultimately to democracy in: Charles Tilly, *Social Movements, 1768–2004* (New York and London: Routledge, 2019).

power. Shortly after, Mussolini completed the destruction of cultural democracy in Italy, also by demanding the allegiance of all academics to the fascist state that he had set up, and by setting up youth movements controlled by the fascist state that indoctrinated children from a young age, in an attempt to remove all dissent from Italian culture and enforce a stifling cultural as well as political conformism.[78]

The above discussion helps to understand the importance of a suitable political culture and large number of SMOs highlighted in sub-thesis v.a, not only to advance democracy, but also to maintain it. A political culture proscribing violence, and a large number of SMOs that participate in this political culture, are part of the social conflict equivalent of checks and balances that can avoid or delay a great loss of democracy in the political-military arena. These checks and balances are crucially important to avoid that this loss increases very quickly and becomes too great, in which case those responsible for this loss of democracy can turn a police force or an army that they came to control against demonstrators, and in some cases impose such casualties that mass demonstrations end. If they have sophisticated intelligence and communications networks, they can identify and arrest or kill all leaders of the opposition and of SMOs. In Italy under Mussolini the fascist blackshirts, and later the OVRA secret police, took on the task of killing opposition leaders in parliament and in social movements.[79] In addition to the political culture proscribing violence and large number of SMOs, structures amongst SMOs and institutions are also important to mobilize opposition and enable the intervention of the additional guarantee of political-military democracy provided by the other arenas. A free news media that brings attention accurately and speedily to abuses of power in the political-military arena is equally important. This is one reason why culture wars are harmful to democracy, namely, that they harm public debate and can prevent the accurate and speedy identification of threats to democracy by raising emotions and muddling issues.[80]

It is useful to place the above discussion within a broader historical and geographical framework. The two mechanisms whereby democracy can be lost are each associated with *countries with different extents of civil society, in which different types of social conflict prevail.* Meso social conflict can reach dimensions at which it is aptly called a war, because of the scale of the conflict, and

---

78   I propose all these arguments in: Olsaretti, *Towards a Humanist Social Science.*

79   On fascist political violence, see: Giovanna Tosatti, "Pericolosi per la Sicurezza dello Stato: Le Schedature della Polizia tra Periferia e Centro," in *1914–1945: L'Italia nella Guerra Europea dei Trent'anni,* ed. Simone Neri Serneri (Rome: Viella, 2011).

80   I make this argument in: Olsaretti, *Towards a Humanist Social Science.*

because such conflict tends often to be heightened, and spills into what can be called a social war. The type of social war is affected both by the size of civil society, and by the presence of suitable structures within it. As far as the size of civil society is concerned, the first mechanism, whereby loss of democracy starts in the political arena first, is associated with *countries with a small civil society, in which a social war of maneuver prevails*. In these countries, a political party can seize power through a military coup and lead to a complete loss of democracy in the political-military arena, after which it relatively quickly puts an end to democracy in the cultural and economic arenas too. This is what happened in Soviet Russia, where the end of political democracy was swiftly followed by the suppression of civil society, including freedom of the press, and suppression of economic democracy through forced collectivization.[81] The second mechanism, whereby loss of democracy is initiated in the cultural arena first, is associated with *countries with a large civil society, in which a social war of position prevails*, although there are intermediate cases like Italy. In these countries a coup d'etat to seize the state is difficult or impossible, but there can still be *some* loss of democracy in the cultural arena, and below I suggest in the economic arena, which in its turn leads to some loss of democracy in the political-military arena. Then a vicious circle can be set off that over a long period of time leads to loss of democracy in the country. This slower loss of democracy is analogous to the slow inroads made in a war of position. It entails a more complex mechanism than in the case of a social war of maneuver, a mechanism that requires considering development. Before focusing on the details of this mechanism, it is useful to focus in greater detail upon the inter-relations between development and democracy.

5   Thesis VI on Interactions between Development and Democracy

This section focuses upon a detailed description of the interaction between National factors 1, namely development and embedded autonomy, and National factors 2, namely democracy. Development and democracy are closely inter-related, as one influences the other, with embedded autonomy as an intermediate factor that ensures a positive interaction between development and

---

81   Since Stalin's time in power, arguably building upon earlier developments under Lenin, the Soviet Union established a stifling control over the press and over all aspects of culture, including arts and literature: Jeffrey Brooks, *Thank You, Comrade Stalin!: Soviet Public Culture from Revolution to Cold War* (Princeton and Oxford: Princeton University Press, 2000). On literature, see: Valeria D. Stelmakh, "Reading in the Context of Censorship in the Soviet Union," *Libraries & Culture* 36, no. 1 (2001).

democracy, whereby greater development leads to greater embedded autonomy, which leads to greater democracy. This in its turn leads to greater embedded autonomy, which leads to greater development. Clarifying the inter-relationship between development, embedded autonomy, and democracy begins to explain the negative effects of uneven development within a country, the focus of the next section. This is because in the interactions between development, embedded autonomy, and democracy, there can be either virtuous or vicious circles. In a virtuous circle, greater development leads to greater democracy, which in its turn leads to greater development, in a growth process that reinforces itself. In a vicious circle, loss in development leads to loss in democracy, which leads to further loss in development, in a downward spiral that reinforces itself and accelerates the loss in development and democracy, to the point that it might endanger even countries with a large civil society and a strong democracy.

Let us consider each of these processes in turn, namely, the interaction between development and democracy, the role of embedded autonomy as an intermediate factor in this interaction, and vicious and virtuous circles. The *interaction between development and democracy* includes the following key considerations. On the one hand, *development contributes to democracy*. For example, cultural development contributes to creating some of the conditions for democracy, because to be able to choose political leaders it is indispensable to read and to adopt informed and measured opinions, which requires literacy and a certain level of education, as well as a certain type of public debate. Here I add also the organizational aspect of cultural development, that is, the great expansion in civil society and the number of organizations within it. On the other hand, *democracy contributes to development*. For example, the fight for cultural democracy that is central to struggles for national independence can increase cultural development and contribute to economic development by providing a certain level of education, a common language that is indispensable for working with many others in large factories and offices, and also some of the conditions for the creation of a more skilled workforce. Thus, it contributes to economic development. The importance of *embedded autonomy as an intermediate factor* between development and democracy is due to the fact that it participates in both development and democracy. Embedded autonomy, which includes institutions and their ties to other institutions and to organizations, contributes at one and the same time to both development and democracy. It contributes to development by providing efficiencies and synergies to development, and also by ensuring the smooth functioning of the division of labour in society. It contributes to democracy by providing the social conflict equivalent of checks and balances, which contribute to the separation of powers in society.

Vicious and virtuous circles are important to understand a number of *processes of divergence or distancing in development*. Weber characterized the first emergence of capitalism, facilitated by values associated with Protestantism, as analogous to a switch in train tracks, after which subsequent processes were set on paths that lead in altogether different directions, growth or stagnation, development or underdevelopment.[82] The concept of industrial divide proposed by Piore and Sabel conveys a similar idea, in describing the later emergence of industrial capitalism in the first industrial revolution, and subsequent phenomena comparable to it, as leading to an industrial divide, or separation in development processes.[83] In order to understand the emergence of virtuous or vicious circles in development and democracy, it is useful to *conceptualize a country as a system of systems*. The institutions and organizations active in each arena can be conceived of as a system, and so can combinations of institutions and organizations that cross arenas, including the state-society, society-markets, and state-markets systems. In a country, there can be one or more of each of these last three types of systems, each developed to a greater or lesser extent. A country can be conceived of as the sum total of interactions within certain boundaries, in all of these systems, and thus as a system of systems, with the central institutions of the state providing the most general regulation that applies to all systems in a country. The *concepts of feed and feedback mechanisms* from systems theory can be useful to conceptualize virtuous and vicious circles in causal chains. Feed and feedback mechanisms apply to what can be called causal circles, as opposed to causal chains. In a causal circle, the last factor in the causal chains feeds back into earlier factors, that thus constitute a circle.[84] This is obviously important to understand virtuous and vicious circles, in which the feed and feedback mechanism reinforce or undermine each other. Thesis VI proposes a high-level summary of *the interactions between development and democracy, suggesting that embedded autonomy acts as an intermediate factor* in these interactions, such that it is possible to talk

---

82   Weber, Baehr, and Wells, *The Protestant Ethic*. Recently a similar argument has been
      proposed by Pomeranz. Paraphrasing Polanyi, Pomeranz has described the emergence
      of industrial capitalism in Europe as leading to a great divergence between Europe, or
      more accurately north-western Europe, and other Eurasian civilizations like China and
      Japan: Kenneth Pomeranz, *The Great Divergence: China, Europe, and the Making of the
      Modern World Economy* (Princeton and Oxford: Princeton University Press, 2000).
83   Piore and Sabel, *The Second Industrial Divide*.
84   I use the words feed and feedback in a general manner that conforms to systems theory.
      However, feed and feedback mechanisms usually refer to processes that involve flows of
      the same substance, for example capital. Below I use the words feed and feedback to refer
      to processes that contribute to capabilities, even though the flows might be different.

about the interaction between development and embedded autonomy, and between democracy and embedded autonomy.

VI.   *There is an interaction between development and democracy, with embedded autonomy as an intermediate factor,* which includes several processes that belong to each arena conceived of as a system, or to systems that cross arenas, like society-markets and state-society systems.

    a.   *The interaction between development and embedded autonomy occurs in each arena and also in a society-markets system,* a system in which civil society organizations interact with private companies and other economic organizations; this interaction can be conceptualized as consisting of two processes.

        i.   *Development contributes to embedded autonomy,* by creating the wealth that enables financing a large and thriving civil society, including the organizational means that contribute to democracy, namely, NPOs, NGOs, and SMOs, all of which benefit either from donations, or from volunteering, by individuals who have disposable wealth or time.

        ii.   *Embedded autonomy contributes to development,* as institutions emerge, and develop ties to each other and to civil society organizations that enable them to share information and coordinate activities, and thus to provide the club goods and public goods that are needed, and also the regulation that is needed, to ensure development.

    b.   *The interaction between democracy and embedded autonomy occurs in each arena and also as part of a state-society system,* a system in which state institutions interact with civil society organizations; this interaction can be conceptualized as consisting of two processes.

        i.   *Democracy contributes to embedded autonomy,* because a certain distribution of power helps maintain the autonomy of arenas that is part of embedded autonomy, and also guarantees such important rights as the right to free speech, and to freedom of enterprise, both of which contribute to a thriving civil society.

        ii.   *Embedded autonomy contributes to democracy,* because it ensures that each arena retains its independence but still contributes to preventing loss of democracy within that arena, or in other arenas.

    c.   *Several systems come to interact within a country, including state-society and society-markets systems, giving rise to more complex*

interactions, that can be part either of virtuous or vicious circles
between different systems, that is, interactions that mutually reinforce or undermine each other. The virtuous or vicious circles can
be conceptualized as involving feed and feedback mechanisms
that participate in, or undermine, comprehensive development.

iii. *There can be a virtuous circle between democracy and devel-*
      opment, whereby democracy guarantees embedded auton-
      omy and contributes to development, which in its turn
      contributes to embedded autonomy and democracy. Two
      mechanisms are involved in this virtuous circle between
      development and democracy, a feed mechanism and a
      feedback mechanism, that mutually reinforce each other.

iv.   *There can be a vicious circle between democracy and develop-*
      ment, whereby loss of democracy leads to loss of embedded
      autonomy, which leads to loss of development, and a fur-
      ther loss of embedded autonomy and democracy. The two
      mechanisms mutually reinforce each other, but with signs
      reversed, as the feed and feedback mechanisms mutually
      undermine each other, and loss in one increases loss in
      the other.

Conceptualizing a country as a system of systems is especially useful to understand Thesis VI. The main systems in a country in which there is an advanced
division of labour, and separate and autonomous arenas, are summarized in
Table 2 below. This table also shows the different systems in which the interaction between development and democracy via embedded autonomy takes
place. These include each arena conceived of as a system. They also include,
as the two most important systems within which this interaction plays out,
the society-markets system, and the state-society system. Let us take as an
example the first system listed in Table 2, namely, the political-military arena,
which can be conceived of as a system in which several political organizations, from SMOs to political parties, interact with each other and with the
state. Political-military development includes the number of these organizations, their degree of internal organization and cohesion, and their capability
to engage in collective action. Political democracy depends upon the distribution of political-military power, and thus on the distribution of the capability to engage in collective action across these different organizations, and
their social groups.[85] Embedded autonomy within the political arena refers to

---

85   I make this point in Chapter 6 of: Olsaretti, *The Struggle for Development and Democracy,*
     Vol. 1.

TABLE 2   Main systems involved in the interactions between development and democracy

Arenas	Development	Embedded autonomy	Democracy
Political-military arena	Political-military development	Political institutions	Political democracy
Cultural arena	Cultural development	Cultural institutions	Cultural democracy
Economic arena	Economic development	Economic institutions	Economic democracy
Political-military, cultural, and economic arenas	Economic development	Society-markets system and state-society system	Political democracy

the networks across these political organizations and the state, which provide embeddedness, while democracy helps maintain autonomy between the state and these organizations. The interaction between development and democracy within the cultural arena, and the economic arena, is subject to similar considerations as the interaction within the political arena just described.

Most importantly, similar considerations apply also to the interaction between development and democracy in the case of *the main cross-arena systems involved in democratization*. In this case, economic development, whereby the laboring classes had some disposable income, led to an expansion in the society-markets system, for example through the growth of trade unions, which contributed to the state-society system, through the foundation and support of working class political parties, which then contributed to political democracy.[86]

The *manner in which multiple systems within a country interact as part of virtuous or vicious circles* is best clarified by taking as an example only two such systems, the state-society system, and the state-markets system. As a general definition, in virtuous circles a given process is reinforced, whereas in vicious circles the process is undermined. The given process is reinforced or undermined either by two parts of this process, or by an external process associated

---

86   On the participation of trade unions in politics, see: Wolfgang Streeck and Anke Hassel, "Trade Unions as Political Actors," *International handbook of trade unions* 335 (2003).

with a different system. Let us consider first the case in which *a given process is reinforced or undermined by two parts of this process*. This case is represented in Figure 7, which shows a high-level summary of the relationship between democracy and development through embedded autonomy involving the society-markets system and the state-society system. Diagram A in Figure 7 shows two different processes, a and b, that are part of two different systems, respectively the society-markets system and the state-society system. Each process is divided into two parts. The first part shows the interaction between development and embedded autonomy, with part a1 representing the contribution from development to embedded autonomy, and part a2 representing the contribution from embedded autonomy to development. Similarly, in the process that is part of the interaction between democracy and embedded autonomy, part b1 represents the contribution from embedded autonomy to development, whereas part b2 represents the contribution from democracy to embedded autonomy.

Figure 7 thus represents two systems that coexist in the same country without interacting much, as they still work as two separate systems. One reason for this could be that there is not enough democracy, and the interaction between

DIAGRAM A - General relationship involving two systems and two virtuous or vicious circles, processes a1 and a2 within the society-markets system, and processes b1 and b2 within the state-society system.

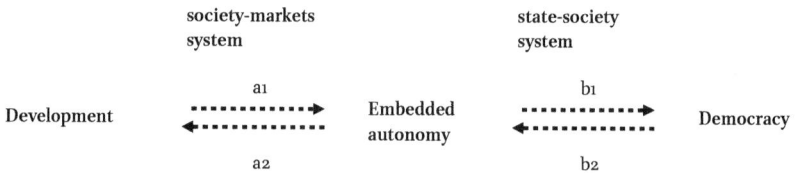

DIAGRAM B - Example in which one process is a virtuous circle in which the two parts a1 and a2 reinforce each other, while the other process is a vicious circle in which the two parts b1 and b2 undermine each other.

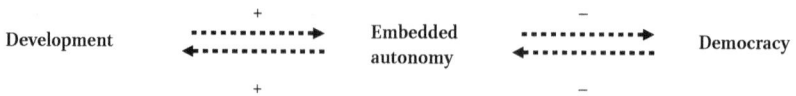

FIGURE 7   The relationship between development and democracy through embedded autonomy

embedded autonomy and democracy has little or no influence on the interaction between development and embedded autonomy, which is the only or
main driver of development. This situation could be encountered in a country
at the early stages of democratization. Another reason could be that embedded
autonomy is imperfect, or there is not much embedded autonomy. The country could have achieved some measure of democracy, but not have achieved
the smooth functioning of institutions described by embedded autonomy, and
the state only slowly interacts with society and markets outside of elections.

In such a system there can still be virtuous and vicious circles. Diagram B
shows process a as a virtuous circle, in which the two parts a_1 and a_2, a feed
and feedback, are both positive (+) and thus reinforce each other, and process
b as a vicious circle, in which the two parts b_1 and b_2 are both negative (-) and
thus undermine each other. Let us consider now the case in which a process
is reinforced or undermined by an external process associated with a different
system. In Diagram B of Figure 7, the vicious circle in the state-society system (two - signs), through the intermediate factor embedded autonomy, can
undermine development, which participates in the virtuous circle in society-
markets system (two + signs). In such a case, loss of democracy could undermine autonomy between arenas, and thus could undermine development. In
addition, if there are institutions that participate in both the society-markets
system and the state-society system, processes that negatively affect these
institutions and the way they function end up affecting both development and
democracy. This last mechanism also affects the case in which two systems are
closely coupled, to the extent that a single overarching system has emerged,
for example a markets-society-state system. For some interactions, it might
be appropriate to talk about a single system in which markets, society, and
the state, all seamlessly interact. Figure 8 illustrates the components of such
a single overarching markets-society-state system, and also the usefulness of
the concepts of feed and feedback mechanisms (these apply also to Figure 7,
but they are most useful to describe the interactions represented in Figure 8).

This system would be different than the two component systems, the
society-markets and state-society systems, in two important ways. In one way,
more organizations take part in this system, and thus more organizations
would be affected by failure of the system. In another way, this system would
be different because it would have longer cycles, or series of processes whereby
the circle is complete. In this system the parts of the process have been re-
labeled as c in order to emphasize that they are part of a single larger process
with four parts, c_1, c_2, c_3, and c_4, as opposed to the two processes a_1 and a_2,
and b_1 and b_2. In the larger process, c_1 and c_2 are part of a feed mechanism
that leads from development to democracy, whereas c_3 and c_4 are part of a

Diagram A: feed mechanism, from development to embedded autonomy to democracy

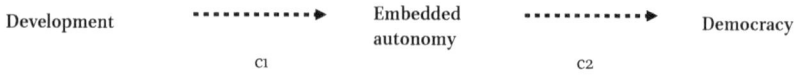

Development   ·············▶   Embedded   ············▶   Democracy
                            autonomy

                       c_1 c_2

Diagram B: feedback mechanism, from democracy to embedded autonomy to development

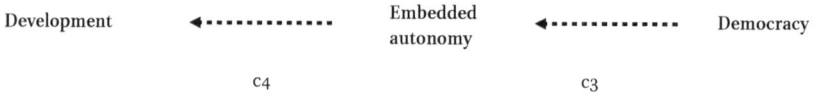

Development   ◀·············   Embedded   ◀·············   Democracy
                            autonomy

                       c_4 c_3

FIGURE 8   Feed and feedback mechanisms in the relationship between development and democracy

feedback mechanism that leads from democracy to development. The longer cycle could occur because changes in economic development affect first such organizations as unions, and only later and through them they affect political parties and the state, and thus democracy. In a shorter cycle, economic development leads directly to donations to political parties involved political elections to state offices, and thus directly affect democracy.

Figure 9 represents a combination of virtuous and vicious cycles for a case in which the two systems, the society-markets and state-society systems, closely interact as part of a broader state-society-markets system. Diagram A shows a virtuous circle, in which the feed mechanism from development to democracy positively contributes to embedded autonomy, as represented by the + sign. This is reinforced by the feedback mechanism from democracy to development, which further strengthens development, if embedded autonomy continues guaranteeing smooth growth. The vicious circle is simply the same process, but in a downward spiral in which loss in democracy is reinforced by loss in development, as shown in Diagram B, where the loss is represented by a negative sign.

Diagram C shows a combination of a positive feed mechanism with a negative feedback mechanism. In the case of a single overarching process, there are virtuous (Diagram A) and vicious (Diagram B) circles, and the intermediate case in Diagram C. The distinctive feature of Figure 9 is that it pertains to a longer process, and illustrates *virtuous and vicious circles that contribute to long-term development or the reversal of long-term development*. These circles are useful to explain processes of divergence like the rise of north-western

Diagram A: virtuous circle, both the feed and the feedback mechanism are positive

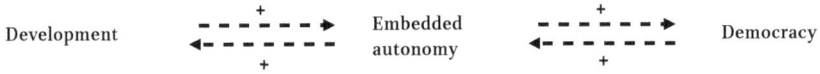

Development   + - - - ➤   Embedded   + - - - ➤   Democracy
               ◄ - - - -   autonomy   ◄ - - - -
                   +   +

Diagram B: vicious circle, both the feed and the feedback mechanism are negative

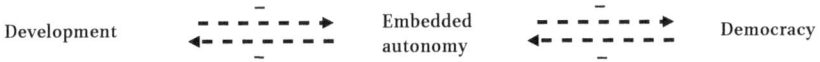

Development   ‾ - - - ➤   Embedded   ‾ - - - ➤   Democracy
               ◄ - - - -   autonomy   ◄ - - - -
                   ‾   ‾

Diagram C: Combination of a positive feed mechanism with a negative feedback mechanism

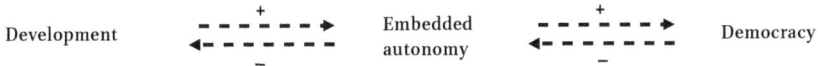

Development   + - - - ➤   Embedded   + - - - ➤   Democracy
               ◄ - - - -   autonomy   ◄ - - - -
                   ‾   ‾

FIGURE 9   Virtuous and vicious circles between development and democracy in a single
            markets-society-state system

Europe, which might be undermined if an external process started undermining democracy as part of a vicious circle that reinforces itself and is repeated
many times over.

6   Thesis VII and the Loss of Development and Democracy

Uneven development within countries can lead to the reversal of virtuous circles,
and even set off a vicious circle, in development and democracy, especially if it
is reinforced by imperfect embedded autonomy. This is because uneven development can undermine embedded autonomy, and through it democracy, in a
process that can be amplified by imperfect embedded autonomy, leading to a
vicious circle that can reverse a virtuous circle in the long term. This argument
involves *thinking about both development and democracy as long-term processes*
that are in their turn part of larger processes that take longer to complete,
all of which are internal to a country as a system of systems, and are further
reinforced by processes external to a country. In making this point, I expand
upon Tarrow and Tilly's concept of democratization process, which suggests
that we should think about democracy as part of a *long* process of contention

between states and social movements.[87] I argue in this project that, in addition to the democratization process, there are processes of development, and also institutional processes involving embedded autonomy, and that all are part of the advancement of the division of labour in society and of comprehensive development. In some cases, development might be undermined only in the long term, not in the short term. As a consequence, this can lead to the acceptance of policies that produce immediate gains but that undermine long-term processes involving the interaction between democracy, embedded autonomy, and development. Arguably, uneven development within a country leads to economic gains for the elite, and might lead initially to some economic gains for the middle class, but in the long term it undermines both development and democracy for the majority of the population in a country.

In order to understand these processes it is necessary to clarify the meaning of uneven development and imperfect embedded autonomy. One important clarification is that *uneven development is not the same as lack of democracy*, although there is a close relationship between the two. This can be clarified using as examples uneven economic development and economic democracy. Economic democracy is a political process in the economic arena, involving collective action between unions and large employers, for example. Uneven economic development is an economic process in the economic arena, involving individual interactions in markets, whereby some companies get richer than others, or some employers get rich at the expense of their employees. This reduces funds to unions and the ability of workers to engage in collective action, and thus undermines economic democracy, but it is not the same. Another important clarification is that *loss of democracy is not the same as imperfect embedded autonomy*. Democracy is a distribution of power that is favorable to the masses, and in the full definition it includes the distribution of power across arenas. It depends upon embedded autonomy, that is, a process whereby institutions intervene to guarantee a certain distribution of power that is not too skewed, but it is not the same thing as embedded autonomy. With specific reference to the above point, loss of democracy is a change in the distribution of power that makes it more skewed against the masses, something that might occur because of imperfect embedded autonomy, whereby imperfect interactions amongst institutions and organizations allows this loss to take place, but it is not the same thing as the loss.

Two especially important processes are processes that involve the cultural arena. These can be divided into processes that lead to loss of cultural

---

87   Tilly, Tarrow, and McAdam, *Contention and Democracy in Europe*.

democracy, and processes that lead to loss of embedded autonomy between the cultural arena and other arenas. Processes that lead to *loss of cultural democracy* can negatively affect development and democracy. Some measure of cultural democracy is indispensable to political democracy. This is because it provides the factors that Gramsci, and Tilly more recently, highlighted are important to successful collective action repertoires such as social group identity, support of a program, and ties to other social groups, who are made aware of the plight of a given social group.[88] They are also indispensable to deliberate and sustained collective action, which is central to the success of a movement, as Gramsci highlighted. Lastly, cultural democracy is also indispensable to provide the criticism and the theories that are necessary to guide the formulation and implementation of policies, and to prevent loss of political democracy, if loss of political democracy is initiated in the political arena. Yet in many countries in the West there has been a slow erosion of cultural democracy, and also of economic democracy. This is partly because the cultural and economic arenas have traditionally been neglected in theories of democracy, and partly because there are fewer institutional guarantees of democracy within these arenas.[89] These other types of democracy have been defended less, especially in the wake of neoliberalism, which essentially argued that we should forsake some or even all economic democracy, and some or even all cultural democracy, in exchange for greater development. It seems clear that this is leading to loss of democracy in other arenas, which will sooner or later lead to loss of development as a whole, in the long term.

Processes that lead to *loss of embedded autonomy between the cultural arena and other arenas* can also negatively affect development and democracy. *There is loss of autonomy that affects the cultural arena*. This too is increasing in many countries in the West. In Soviet Russia the state took over the political arena, ended democracy within it, then took over other arenas. In the West today, with the aftermath of neoliberalism, large economic corporations, instead of the state, are taking over other arenas, as market principles are being imposed on the cultural arena, with the re-organization of universities and publishers alongside market lines, as entrepreneurial universities and corporate publishers respectively, and upon the state, with the re-organization of the military and especially intelligence units alongside market lines as contractors, whose

---

88   Charles Tilly, *Stories, Identities, and Political Change* (Lanham, Boulder, New York, and Oxford: Rowman & Littlefield, 2002).

89   David Trend, *Cultural Democracy: Politics, Media, New Technology* (Albany: State University of New York Press).

use has grown significantly.[90] In the past, much emphasis has been placed upon the need to ensure an autonomous press from politics, but the equally important need to ensure an autonomous press from economic considerations has been largely overlooked. For example, books that are very important for culture can be rejected because they do not sell right away. In addition, there are institutional processes that can lead to loss of embeddedness of the cultural arena from other arenas. *There is also loss of embeddedness within the cultural arena itself.* Specialist languages in the West undermine both the linguistic requirements of democracy and embeddedness. The division of universities into specialized departments that do not talk to each other, and the distancing of higher education institutions from the rest of culture, as well as from society, can undermine embeddedness between the cultural arena and the political arena. If an arena becomes so remote from the other arenas that it largely loses embeddedness, for example because it develops its own specialist language, this too can diminish its contribution to development.[91]

Thesis VII and its sub-theses below all detail the conditions that can lead to loss of development and democracy. The sub-theses are intelligible in the light of previous theoretical groundwork. Here I just want to add a few clarifications. *Caporalato refers to the use of coercion in the economy.* It is a word that is commonly used in Italian political discourses to refer to specific market conditions and the social conditions that accompany them, and in particular to a mix of market mechanisms and coercion. The coercion is by *caporali,* or strongmen referred to as *caporali,* or 'corporals,' who effectively act as gang masters, to intimidate and sometimes coerce workers through beatings or even assassinations.[92] It is used in social conditions in which a social group is dominated by another, and workers are forced to work for very low wages by

---

90   On the entrepreneurial university, see: Holden Thorp and Buck Goldstein, *Engines of Innovation: The Entrepreneurial University in the Twenty-First Century* (Chapel Hill: University of North Carolina Press, 2013). See also the many contributions in: Alain Fayolle and Dana T. Redford, eds., *Handbook on the Entrepreneurial University* (Cheltenham, UK and Northampton, Massachusetts: Edward Elgar, 2014). On corporate publishing in the United States, see: Kim Becnel, *The Rise of Corporate Publishing and Its Effects on Authorship in Early Twentieth Century America* (London and New York: Routledge, 2012). On corporate universities and campus politics, see: AbdulHadi and Shehadeh, "Resisting the US Corporate University."

91   I address this argument in: Olsaretti, *Towards a Humanist Social Science.*

92   Ruth-Ben-Ghiat uses the word strongmen to refer to the leadership and their attitudes: Ruth Ben-Ghiat, *Strongmen: Mussolini to the Present* (New York and London: W. W. Norton, 2020). I make a different use of the word strongman, to refer to the rank and file, including early fascists who were involved in caporalato. I address this point below in Section 7.4.

unfavorable market conditions, and there is a reservoir of discontent amongst the workers that could lead to strikes, or to reporting illegal working conditions and other abuses of economic power by employers. The latter thus resort to labour gangs in order to ensure a smooth work process and to meet delivery schedules. Social conditions marked by great exploitation give rise to an economic need for coercion by labour gangs, for example in cases in which there are tight deadlines, as in agriculture at the time of harvests, or in construction when there are important deadlines for handing to a client a finished building, since strikes or reviews of working conditions can impose delays to tight delivery schedules.[93]

Thesis VII emphasizes that there are conditions in which there is no productive conflict, and conflict degenerates into violence and destructive conflict, undermining development, democracy, and embedded autonomy alike. *Caporalato is associated with the degeneration of development into social rents.* The social rents arise from market conditions in which there are only a few employers and a large workforce that is forced to work for very low wages by the sheer lack of employment in the economy, and in addition social conditions prevent these market conditions from changing in favor of the workforce. In theory, a large workforce and cheap labour costs should attract investment by employers, but this can be a very slow process. Moreover, it can be prevented altogether if there arise poverty and violence traps, in which case parts of the working class, in desperate economic conditions, lose all community, and all safety nets, and descend into a life of crime that prevents investment in an area by anyone other than the existing employers who have a large *caporalato* system, or by mafias whose work practices include *caporalato*.[94] In addition, attracting investment can be a temporary solution only, as some types of investment move on once employment and wages rise. Many employers in

---

93   Domenico Perrotta, "Vecchi e Nuovi Mediatori: Storia, Geografia ed Etnografia del Caporalato in Agricoltura," *Meridiana* 79, no. 1 (2014). Caporalato greatly affects migrants: Domenico Perrotta and Devi Sacchetto, "Migrant Farmworkers in Southern Italy: Ghettoes, Caporalato and Collective Action," *Workers of the World* 1, no. 5 (2014). In the case of construction, there can be very tight deadlines for handing over a factory that is meant to start producing at a certain time, for example because shop floor equipment has been bought and will be delivered at a certain time, by which time the factory must be ready to house the equipment. There are often also production schedules for the factory that must be adhered to. On caporalato as a mafia active in agriculture, see: Fiammetta Fanizza and Marco Omizzolo, *Caporalato. An Authentic Agromafia* (MIlan: Mimesis International, 2019).

94   Political violence like terrorism and revolutions reduces international investment, and arguably also internal investment. The same is true of crime in urban neighborhoods, especially neighborhoods affected by rising crime: Johanna Lacoe, Raphael W. Bostic, and

central and southern Italy who were active in textile and shoes manufacturing started buying raw materials from North Africa, and relocated to Eastern Europe in the search for a cheaper workforce. Some of these were employers who lacked the entrepreneurial culture and cultural institutions to drive development through organizational and technological innovation that introduces efficiencies or synergies, and instead just sought conditions in which they could create easy profits for themselves by cutting on inputs or wages.[95] Some cultural institutions capable of driving innovations have emerged in Italy, chiefly private universities like Bocconi University in Milan and LUISS University in Rome, and state universities like Milan Bicocca, all being amongst the top universities in Italy for social science, and rising in international ranks. However, Italian universities are still far from the achievements of equivalent universities in Great Britain, for example.

Thesis VII suggests the numerous ways in which a reversal of a virtuous circle that undermines both development and democracy can occur. The vicious circle represents a worst-case scenario, but *even a relatively long virtuous circle can be reversed by acting at various points in the causal circle*, and setting off a vicious circle. The reversal of a virtuous circle is important to understand the manner in which both democracy and development can be lost even in a country with a developed civil society in which a social war of position predominates, by undermining at least partially the second line of defense. The following thesis formalizes this insight, proposing a number of mechanisms that can be involved in undermining development and democracy, and embedded autonomy.

VII.   *There can be reversals of the democratization process whereby loss of democracy, or loss of embedded autonomy, or loss of development, lead to further losses in the other factors*, undermining both development and democracy in the long run. There are numerous combinations of these

---

Arthur Acolin, "Crime and Private Investment in Urban Neighborhoods," *Journal of Urban Economics* 108 (2018).

95   The root cause of this economic strategy is the lack of institutions free of red tape, capable of promoting different development strategies, including a suitable education and innovation sector: Emanuele Felice, Alessandro Nuvolari, and Michelangelo Vasta, "Alla Ricerca delle Origini del Declino Economico Italiano," *L'Industria* 40, no. 2 (2019). Rephrased in the arguments of this book, the root cause is the lack of suitable state-markets and society-markets systems, and embedded autonomy, including the lack of entrepreneurial universities. Italian companies also faced difficulties in access to international markets: Michelangelo Vasta, "Italian Export Capacity in the Long-Term Perspective (1861–2009): a Tortuous Path to Stay in Place," *Journal of Modern Italian Studies* 15, no. 1 (2010).

three factors that can lead to loss of development democracy under-stood as per the full definition of democracy. Reversal of a virtuous cir-cle can occur at one or more of the following points.

a. *Reversal can occur at development,* with changes in the feedback mechanism, so that loss of development leads to loss of embed-ded autonomy, and ultimately of democracy. This can be initiated by the following different types of uneven development within a country.

    i. *Uneven development across arenas,* which can lead to loss of comprehensive development, which in its turn can lead to loss of embedded autonomy, because an arena can be more easily taken over by the other arenas.

    ii. *Uneven development across social groups,* which creates social rents that enable companies that are not compet-itive to survive by leveraging a large reservoir of cheap labour, and thus leads to less economic development, and also to heavy reliance upon labour, which subtracts labour resources from other arenas, and thus leads to less com-prehensive development.

    iii. *Uneven development across regions,* which creates social rents similar to uneven development across social groups, and also specific social rents that use other large reservoirs of cheap factors such as cheap land and cheap existing real estate, that are widely available in the underdeveloped regions.

b. *Reversal can occur at embedded autonomy,* which stops reinforc-ing democracy. This is loss of embedded autonomy that is caused by other factors than uneven development, like purely institu-tional considerations, or considerations regarding the manner in which institutions interact with organizations. This can be ini-tiated by the following failures in institutions and their interac-tions with society.

    i. *Lack of networks amongst institutions and organizations,* which can be due to purely institutional factors such as specialization, whereby for example cultural institutions become very remote from the rest of culture and from other arenas.

    ii. *Lack of shared social areas and forums,* in which institu-tions and organizations can freely interact, which can be due to the same factors that lead to lack of networks amongst institutions and organizations, and also to more specific factors affecting the provision of public spaces, like the emergence of suburban sprawl that comes to dominate real estate, in which there are only private spaces linked to economic activities, and no truly public spaces in which economic, cultural, and political activities interact.

iii. *Lack of a shared language and mutually intelligible professional dialects or jargons*, which can be due to specialization within institutions, and also to turf wars, which compound the lack of networks, and of shared areas and forums, between institutions and organizations.

c. *Reversal can occur at democracy*, that is at the distribution of political-military power, and it can affect the types of conflict, including how widespread is violence, which affects all other processes. This can be initiated by the following failures in the regulation of conflict, all of which undermine productive conflict, or can lead to conflict spiraling out of control, to the point that one social group or one organization can impose semi-permanent social rents.

i. *Wars amongst social groups,* whereby there is sustained large scale conflict, with or without violence, and with or without direct participation of the state, which can take sides, or attempt to moderate or even solve the conflict. There can be different types of war amongst social groups, all of which undermine democracy. *Social wars*, or wars amongst *entire* social groups, which can include class conflict, or inter-ethnic conflict.

1. *Economic wars*, in which one side deliberately tries to prevent gains by the other side, for example by employers using *caporalato*, fascists, or mafias, in order to break strikes and intimidate workers, or by workers creating groups to break machinery and intimidate employers.

2. *Culture wars*, in which different groups of intellectuals take extreme positions, and forsake the goal of contributing to public goods like a shared stock of knowledge, and also forsake rules of civility, aiming first and foremost at putting down adversaries.

3. *Political wars,* or partisan wars, in which different groups of activists or politicians behave like

intellectuals in culture wars, and sometimes cooperate with these intellectuals.

ii.   *Diffuse violence, or diffuse thieving, associated with social disaggregation*, which lead to particular types of wars amongst social groups, in which there is no regulation and complete failure to play by acceptable rules of the game that are necessary for conflict to be productive.

1.   *Social banditry*, or social wars in which both sides involved in the conflict act outside the law, and small organized groups resort to banditry at the borderline between social conflict and thieving.

2.   *Illegal employment*, or economic wars in which employers completely dominate the other side, who have no contracts, and no resort to the law in case of grievances, and are completely subjected to *caporalato*, fascists, or mafias.

The next chapters go into greater detail in explaining the mechanisms that lead to wars amongst social groups, and to diffuse violence associated with social disaggregation, suggesting that these have an international dimension, and that neoliberalism and populism contribute to them. Here I want to provide a *summary of the argument regarding the loss of development and democracy*, and how this loss relates to neoliberalism and populism. Violence can lead to multiple losses that set off a vicious circle, whereby loss of development, loss of embedded autonomy, and loss of democracy, reinforce themselves. In addition, I want to highlight here the *importance of uneven development and imperfect embedded autonomy to initiate a vicious circle* that involves loss of development and loss of embedded autonomy. Figure 10 serves to clarify the mechanism whereby uneven development within a country might affect a virtuous circle. It illustrates the insight that uneven development and imperfect embedded autonomy have cumulative effects. The uneven development within countries (shown on the right-hand side of the diagram) could be initiated by causes that are external to the three processes represented in the picture and the causal circle they form in interacting with each other. These include external political and economic processes addressed in the next part of this volume. The next chapter suggests that a combination of political processes and economic processes in the world system can change development into uneven development within a country. This can undermine or even reverse the virtuous circle if other processes provide an additional negative contribution. The diagram shows a positive feed mechanism from democracy, to embedded autonomy, and on to development, that is undermined and possibly reversed by a combination of uneven development within a country and imperfect embedded autonomy, whose cumulative effect is represented by the two negative signs in segment 2d.

It is useful to add a few clarifications to the mechanisms shown in Figure 10. This diagram represents *processes that are internal to a country*, which can be at work in the entire country, or only in some regions. Segment 2a represents *a positive contribution from democracy to embedded autonomy*. This can include more than a guarantee of embedded autonomy, for example, additional institutions or additional networks between institutions and organizations that originate from productive meso conflict, which contributes to democracy, which then contributes to embedded autonomy by making the institutions available to processes involving embedded autonomy. Segment 2b represents *a positive contribution from embedded autonomy to development*, whereby these same institutions or ties guarantee the smooth functioning of the division of labour in society and thus guarantee to development. Segment 2c represents the *negative contribution from uneven development to embedded autonomy*, whereby some loss of development in an arena leads some organizations and also some institutions to shut down. Crime can also lead some organizations and institutions to shut down. Segment 2d represents *an additional negative contribution from embedded autonomy processes themselves*. This could be the distancing of higher education institutions from the rest of culture and from society that originates with specialization and exclusive reliance upon specialist languages, which is accentuated by culture wars and the withdrawal of some university professors into a detached behavior like a Crocean *Homo Academicus*. This adds another negative contribution, leading to a cumulative effect that can undermine democracy and reverse the virtuous circle, a cumulative effect that is represented in segment 2d by the two negative signs, where one sign represents the negative contribution from uneven development, while the other sign represents the negative contribution from imperfect embedded autonomy.

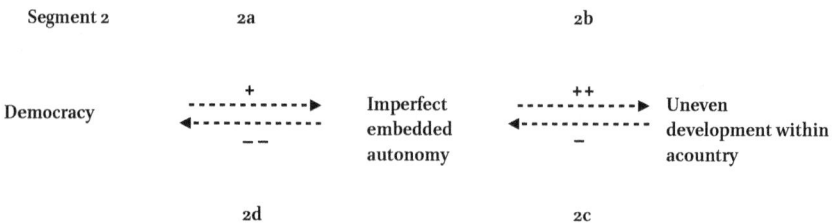

Segment 2   2a   2b

Democracy   ⊶ - - - - - - - - - - ▶ Imperfect   ⊶ - - - - - - - - - - ▶ Uneven
            ◀ - - - - - - - - - - ⊶ embedded   ◀ - - - - - - - - - - ⊶ development within
                    − −   autonomy   −   a country

                2d   2c

FIGURE 10   Reversal of the virtuous circle between development and democracy – the order
             of the factors in this diagram refers to Segment 2 in Figure 2

A number of *factors that are external to a country can contribute to setting off a vicious circle* between development, embedded autonomy, and democracy. These factors can intervene at various points in the above feed and feedback mechanisms, further reinforcing the vicious circle set off by uneven development within a country and by imperfect embedded autonomy. With the expansion of the modern world system to encompass most of the world, which is driven at least in part by the expansion of the modern state system, a combination of internal and external factors can cause uneven development and set off the negative feedback mechanism even in countries with advanced development and democracy, countries in the core. To understand the mechanisms involved, we have to address the emergence of the modern state system and of imperialism within it, since the two are related. The main argument of the next part of the book is that imperialism, which is a process that affects interactions amongst states whereby some states engage in imperialism and under-develop some countries, ultimately undermines also development in countries with a developed civil society. The outline of this process and the manner in which it reinforces vicious circles is represented in Figure 11. In this figure there are three processes that are external to the system whereby development and democracy interact within a country. These three processes are labeled e1, e2, and e3.

This diagram also begins to clarify the effects of neoliberalism and populism in undermining development and democracy in the long run, through uneven development. It is useful to distinguish between the effects of neoliberalism that are internal to a country and those that are external to it, although neoliberalism is arguably an international phenomenon associated with the world-elite. The effects e1, e2, e3 are all external to a country, or reinforced by processes

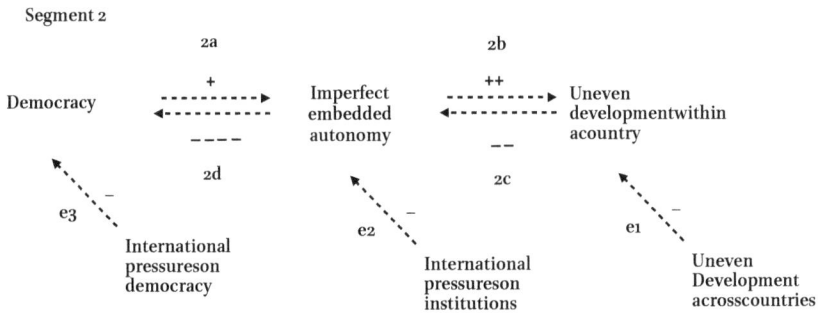

FIGURE 11   Reversal of the virtuous circle between development and democracy –
additional negative effects from processes external to a country up to the
maximum negative effect

external to a country. Effect e1 suggests that *uneven development across countries contributes to uneven development within countries*. This is the focus of the next part of the book. Here I just want to state the general argument. The availability of countries with low development and vast labour forces, in which entrepreneurs can realize high profits simply by living off social rents, or which can easily be controlled by neocolonial corporations, can lead to a large uneven development across social groups in countries in the west, as the economic elite who relocated factories to developing countries had major windfalls, while the masses had fewer gains or even lost out. Amongst the masses, the working class lost out, while the middle class benefited, at least temporarily, from cheaper imported goods.[96] Effect e2 represents *negative effects on embedded autonomy*. These include austerity measures associated with neoliberalism, which can be started internally, or imposed externally by the IMF as a condition for loans. The European Union similarly imposed austerity measures upon Greece as a condition for its loans. The problem with these austerity measures is that, while reducing unnecessary expenditures, they often indiscriminately affect institutions, and contribute to imperfect embedded autonomy, rather than fixing it.[97] Thus neoliberalism and debt crises created by large patronage networks also create the conditions for an intervention on institutions, which is typically a short-lived intervention that can undermine civil society and aggravate the imperfect embedded autonomy that led to the debt crises in the first place. Building a functioning embedded autonomy is instead a slow and progressive process like democratization. Some of the same institutions are involved that are involved in democratization, and they include cultural institutions and civil society.[98] Effect e3 represents *negative effects on democracy*. Both neoliberalism and the populist backlash that followed it are associated with underdevelopment and migration, which lead to populism, which then undermines democracy.

---

96   Some of these points are addressed in: Bagnasco and Thompson, "The Question of the Middle Class."; Andres Solimano, *Economic Elites, Crises, and Democracy: Alternatives Beyond Neoliberal Capitalism* (Oxford and New York: Oxford University Press, 2014).

97   Stiglitz, *Globalization and Its Discontents. The Stiglitz Report: Reforming the International Monetary and Financial Systems in the Wake of the Global Crisis* (New York and London: New Press, 2010).

98   *The Stiglitz Report*, 118, 136.

PART 4

Development and Democracy and the Division of Labour in the World System

∵

The problem of political leadership in the creation and development of the nation and of the modern state in Italy.

Crispi's imperialism [...] lacked any economic-financial basis. [...] This basis was replaced by the populist [popolare] passions of rural [intellectuals and politicians] blindly committed to the ownership of land: [Crispi's imperialism] was born of an internal political necessity [the excess rural population compared to the land available in Italy], delaying its solution to infinity. Therefore Crispi's [imperialist] policy was opposed by (northern) capitalists who would have much rather liked to see the substantial sums of money spent [on imperialist conquests] in Africa spent in Italy instead; but in southern Italy Crispi was popular [as a politician], for having crated the 'myth' of easy land.

ANTONIO GRAMSCI, *Prison Notebooks,* Notebook 19, Note 24, pp.2018–2019. My emphasis.[1]

∴

---

1 Gramsci, *Quaderni del Carcere,* 1446.

Theoretical Groundwork on Power and the Division of Labour in the World System

In this chapter I introduce the theoretical groundwork that contributes to those *parts of the general theory that concern international relations and questions of international development*, focusing upon processes external to countries that affect development and democracy. These parts too are a further elaboration of Gramsci's theory of hegemony, and theory of power more in general. The theory suggests that countries participate in a more or less marked form of uneven development analogous to the one highlighted by Gramsci for the Southern Question in Italy. In particular, this chapter and the next argue that uneven development within countries, which can set off a vicious circle undermining development and democracy even in countries in the core, can be caused by processes external to a country, including in particular imperialism and uneven development across countries. I focus in this part of the volume upon uneven *political-military* development across countries, which leads to uneven *economic* development across countries. In such cases interstate conflict leads, not to the best states for development and democracy to be selected, but to more or less marked deviations from the paradigm of the developmental state, including predatorial states. These deviations are due largely to two mechanisms, both of which involve social rents. One mechanism involves the projection of power by conquering states, or by powerful neighboring states, which skews the distribution of power in society and imposes underdevelopment, or severely limits development. The other mechanism involves social disaggregation, poverty and violence traps, and violent social movements. Both of these mechanisms create or accentuate social rents, because the conquering elite is much more powerful than the masses, or because national elites dominate the masses due to the social disaggregation of one or more social groups amongst the masses.

The first section below reviews the concept of division of labour in the world system. This is a concept derived from the concept of division of labour in the world economy that is central to World Systems Theory and contributes to explaining how power in the world system leads to deviations from the ideal Smithian division of labour across countries. The division of labour in the world system is a more general concept that draws attention to the importance also of politics and culture, and in particular of geopolitics and geoculture, in the world system. The second section revises the division into core, semi-periphery, and periphery of the world system, drawing attention to the importance that geopolitical and geocultural considerations have on the projection of power, predicting whether states engage in colonial expansion and whether they succeed. The first two sections entail a thorough revision of the Diamond-Wallerstein theory, as I add considerations from geopolitics and geoculture, including logistics, to understand the emergence of the state core. The third section delves into the first mechanism whereby conquest, and the projection of power more in general, leads to the underdevelopment or limited development of countries outside the core. It suggests that the division of labour in the world system is the product of uneven political-military development which, together with geopolitical and geocultural features of the state system, leads to imperialism and uneven development. The fourth section delves into the second mechanism whereby social disaggregation, together with violence, leads to violent social movements. It discusses the types of conflict and hegemony that prevail outside the core, extending the EVL model and highlighting the protracted and destructive nature of conflict outside the core, a conflict that is associated with social disaggregation, poverty and violence traps, and violent social movements. The third and fourth sections entail a thorough revision of the Cohen-Tilly theory, because interstate and social conflict outside the core lead to deeply flawed states, rather than developmental states, by various forms of domination, and by preventing alternative hegemonies, and even all redressing of grievances. The fifth section expands upon this point, by suggesting that we should not conceptualize the effects of the world system upon states as if they led to state selection, or selection of a particular state type, because they lead instead to interference with ongoing processes of state formation, that is, ongoing creation of states. In particular, violence distorts or even prevents the positive contributions that states can give to development.

1   The Division of Labour in the World System and Geopolitical Areas

In this chapter I propose an *extension of Gramsci's theory of hegemony to World Systems Theory* that builds upon the theses on power and its sources proposed in the previous chapter. I also take Arrighi's remarks on hegemony in the world system much further and I expand upon in new directions, all influenced by Gramsci's theory of hegemony, four concepts that are central to World Systems

Theory.[1] The four concepts are: the world system; the division of labour in the world economy; hegemony in the state system; interstate conflict in the state system. Let us focus upon the first two concepts, delving into detail in explaining how I expand upon these two concepts. This is sufficient to understand the entire argument, before focusing on the last two concepts. *The concept of world system* includes the view that there is a world system that transcends countries, which were conceptualized above as a system of systems. Any country is increasingly affected by interactions and system states that are external to itself, and that belong to the world system. The latter has become increasingly important with the passage of time, since with increasing globalization interactions in the world system increasingly affect interactions within each country, whether through the expansion of trade flows in the world economy, or through increased interstate conflict in the state system, and increased cultural exchange within world culture, which is often caught up in interstate conflict. There are even debates as to whether these flows are now more sizeable and more powerful that any flows and interactions that occur within a country, and whether they are beyond the control of individual states.[2] The expansion of state regional alliances, and a regional approach to trade, pioneered by the European Union, later followed by NAFTA, Merco Sur, and ASEAN, are at least in part a response by states to two needs that emerge within a world economy, namely, the need to open up entire regions to trade, and at the same time the need for states in those regions to maintain some kind of bargaining power

---

1   Giovanni Arrighi, "The Three Hegemonies of Historical Capitalism," in *Gramsci, Historical Materialism and International Relations*, ed. Stephen Gill (Cambridge and New York: Cambridge University Press, 1993). The approach set out in this article by Arrighi was continued in his book: *The Long Twentieth Century*.
2   The arguments on the effects of globalization on states are reviewed in: Suzanne Berger, "Globalization and Politics," *Annual Review of Political Science* 3 (2000). Tilly argued that the time of strong states is over, and that this is due in part to globalization: Charles Tilly, "The Time of States," *Social Research* (1994). Some authors have argued that not all states are challenged by the global economy, and that some states shaped the institutions of global capitalism. On this topic, see the many contributions in: David A. Smith, Dorothy J. Solinger, and Steven C. Topik, eds., *States and Sovereignty in the Global Economy* (London and New York: Routledge, 1999). Others have argued that states are coping both with globalization and with institutions associated with neoliberalism that guide globalization: Sean Ó Riain, "States and Markets in an Era of Globalization," *Annual Review of Sociology* 26 (2000). Others yet have argued that, alongside the challenges of globalization, there are also opportunities for developmental states in the global economy: Linda Weiss, "Guiding Globalization in East Asia: New Roles for Old Developmental States," in *States in the Global Economy: Bringing Domestic Institutions Back In*, ed. Linda Weiss (Cambridge and New York: Cambridge University Press, 2003); "Is the State Being 'Transformed' by Globalization?."

inside the modern state system, in negotiating and managing trade agreements, and in deciding which trade flows to encourage.[3]

The concept of division of labour in the world economy is an important concept in World Systems Theory. The latter emphasized from the beginning the division of the world economy into three parts, namely, a core, semi-periphery, and periphery, which participated in the division of labour in the world economy. This was associated with *a division of labour in the world economy between industrial capitalism in the core and agrarian capitalism and extraction of raw materials in the periphery.* Wallerstein argued that in the core industrial capitalism prevailed, based on large industrial corporations as the main organizational form, whereas in the periphery agricultural production and extraction of raw materials prevailed, based on large farms and large companies that extract raw materials, providing basic goods such as sugar for markets in the core, and raw materials for industries in the core.[4] *The methods of capital accumulation were also different.* Wallerstein argued that in the core market mechanisms for extracting profits and accumulating capital prevailed, whereas in the periphery coercion prevailed, including violence, to which we should add mechanisms like those described by Harvey as accumulation by dispossession. For example, Wallerstein likened American plantations to open-air factories in which extraction of profits occurred through coercion, including brutal violence, in what was an especially harsh form of exploitation that used racial differences to isolate and dominate those who worked in the fields.[5]

There were geographical exceptions, and there were also changes, in the division of labour between core and periphery just highlighted. *The semi-periphery was an exception because intermediate types of economic organizations*

---

3   On regionalism and trading blocs as a response to pressures from globalization, see: Theodore Pelagidis and Harry Papasotiriou, "Globalisation or Regionalism? States, Markets and the Structure of International Trade," *Review of International Studies* 28, no. 3 (2002). On the importance of links between trading blocs as another way to cope with globalization, see: Yeung, Perdikis, and Kerr, *Regional Trading Blocs in the Global Economy.* Kerry has approached the state as caught between internal pressures from agents seeking economies of scale and external pressures due to globalization: Kerry A. Chase, *Trading Blocs: States, Firms, and Regions in the World Economy* (Ann Arbor: University of Michigan Press, 2009).

4   Wallerstein, *The Modern World-System, Vol. I.*

5   On the place of plantations in the world economy, see: Terence K. Hopkins and Immanuel Wallerstein, "Commodity Chains in the World-Economy Prior to 1800," *Review (Fernand Braudel Center)* 10, no. 1 (1986). Wallerstein's argument has been criticized, and these critiques were reviewed in: Albert Bergesen, "The Critique of World-System Theory: Class Relations or Division of Labor?," *Sociological Theory* 2 (1984). Bergesen also compared Wallerstein's theory to Smith's theory, as far as the international division of labour is concerned, and criticized it: "Turning World-System Theory on Its Head," *Theory, Culture & Society* 7, no. 2–3 (1990).

prevailed, for example small companies, and small farms involved in share-cropping, as opposed to large-scale capitalist concerns, whether large industrial corporations or large farms, which prevailed in the core and periphery respectively. Wallerstein saw this as a limitation of economic organizations in the semi-periphery that condemned the countries that relied upon these economic organizations to lower productivity and a lower rank in the hierarchy of power in the world economy. *In more recent times, the division of labour in the world economy changed.* Several authors have argued that a New International Division of Labour emerged as industry relocated from the core to the periphery in search for a cheap workforce.[6] Arrighi suggested that in countries in the core there has been a shift from mercantile, to industrial, and later to financial capitalism, affecting also the division of labour between the core, semi-periphery, and periphery. *Mercantile capitalism* relies on profits from trade, especially price differences of some goods across different geographical areas. In early modern times, spices could be bought cheaply in markets in Asia and sold dearly in European markets. *Industrial capitalism* relies upon profits from economies of scale, which raise productivity, at least in some circumstances. *Financial capitalism* relies upon profits from lending capital to other users. Arrighi also suggested, in an argument that parallels Piore and Sabel's, that SME-based economies, which include China according to Arrighi, could gain an advantage upon economies based upon large corporations, which include the United States.[7] Arrighi further suggested that market gains like those advocated by Smith could only be achieved in countries where SMEs predominate, and true market mechanisms were at work, as opposed to countries where large corporations predominate. This is because large corporations often operate as oligopolies or monopolies, in imperfect markets in which there are few or no competitors. A suitable use of SMEs would lead to a more equal division of labour in the world economy that approximates Smith's ideal of a more equal distribution of wealth amongst nations.[8]

---

6 Folker Fröbel, Jurgen Heinrichs, and Otto Kreye, *The New International Division of Labour: Structural Unemployment in Industrialised Countries and Industrialisation in Developing Countries* (Cambridge and New York: Cambridge University Press, 1981). This argument has been confirmed by subsequent developments affecting Western economies. It is criticized and also nuanced and built upon in: Nicolas Grinberg, "Global Commodity Chains and the Production of Surplus-Value on a Global Scale: Bringing Back the New International Division of Labour Theory," *Journal of World-Systems Research* 22, no. 1 (2016). See also: Guido Charnock and Greig Charnock Starosta, eds., *The New International Division of Labour: Global Transformation and Uneven Development* (London and New York: Palgrave Macmillan, 2016).
7 Arrighi, *The Long Twentieth Century*.
8 *Adam Smith in Beijing.* On Smith's views on the division of labour, see: Lisa Hill, "Adam Smith, Adam Ferguson and Karl Marx on the Division of Labour," *Journal of Classical Sociology* 7,

In this project I emphasize a more general concept than the concept of division of labour in the world economy, namely, *the division of labour in the world system*. This concept is in addition, not in alternative, to the concept of division of labour in the world economy. The concept of division of labour in the world system is meant to highlight that there is *a rough division of labour within the world system that is comparable to the division of labour in society between arenas* highlighted above, namely, a division into political-military, cultural, and economic organizations that are active in the world system. These are active respectively in the state system, world culture, and the world economy. This specialization is important for two sets of reasons. One is that *the division of labour in the world system is imperfect, or even deeply flawed*, and there is little or nothing equivalent to embedded autonomy, and to regulate conflict and put pressure on those who use violence, compared to the division of labour in a country. Therefore, violence greatly affects the division of labour in the world system. This is changing, but only slowly, with the emergence of an international civil society, including SMOs active on a world stage, and of such forums as the World Social Forum, which brings together these SMOs.[9] State regional alliances sometimes also have a role in regulating conflict, and minimizing violence and exploitation, but this is even harder to achieve than regulating an individual state.

The concept of division of labour in the world system is important also for a second set of reasons, namely, that *there are numerous aspects of the division of labour in the world system that interact with both politics and the military*. In some cases at least, political-military development and interstate closely interact with and mutually shape the division of labour in the world system. Therefore, it is important to approach them as an important part of the division of labour in the world system, and not to consider them exclusively as phenomena that arise just from the division of labour in the world economy.

---

no. 3 (2007). Fleischacker argues that these views were part of Smith's philosophy: Samuel Fleischacker, *On Adam Smith's "Wealth of Nations": A Philosophical Companion* (Princeton and Oxford: Princeton University Press, 2005). Sun places Smith's views within the history of theorizing about the division of labour: Guang-Zhen Sun, *The Division of Labour in Economics: A History* (London and New York: Routledge, 2013).

9   Tarrow is critical of international civil society and transnational activist networks, and argues they are far from capable of governing globalization and even bringing pressure on transnational institutions: Sidney Tarrow, "Transnational Politics: Contention and Institutions in International Politics," *Annual Review of Political Science* 4 (2001). For a review of arguments regarding the impact of globalization on civil society, see: David Brady, Jason Beckfield, and Wei Zhao, "The Consequences of Economic Globalization for Affluent Democracies," *Annual Review of Sociology* 33 (2007).

These aspects include social processes that cannot be adequately described as being due just to economic factors, but always involve the interaction of politics and the military with culture and the economy. One of these aspects was introduced in Chapter 1, and it is that development, even within countries in the core, is not uniform, and there are *internal peripheries* that are part of uneven development within countries. They share important similarities with peripheries in the world system that are part of uneven development across countries. Both internal peripheries and peripheries of the world system tend to be less democratic, and to have a less developed civil society. Another aspect concerns migration flows, since both internal peripheries and the periphery of the world system became *providers of labour*. With the expansion of the division of labour, inequalities arose whereby some regions within a country, the internal peripheries, and entire countries within the world system, the peripheries, became providers of labour, often cheap labour that can be exploited in one way or another. Yet another aspect is that there arose *asymmetric threats*, from irregular forces composed of volunteers, or from organized crime, all typically based in, or reliant upon, the internal peripheries or the peripheries of the world system. The 9/11 attacks are an instance of asymmetric threats that became so powerful as to be able to strike *command centers of American financial power*.[10]

A very important question concerning the division of labour in the world system is how it arose and *what was the role of political-military power in this process*. In order better to understand the role of conflict in the division of labour in the world system, it is necessary to *use additional concepts to the concepts of state core and frontier of the state core*, in particular geopolitical concepts that pertain to the balance of power between states. For reasons of space, I focus only upon Europe. The European state system that became the basis for the modern state system had some peculiarities that are best understood using the concept of *geopolitical area* to complement the concept of frontier introduced above. Gellner has suggested that, in the spread of nationalism from north-western Europe, it is useful to distinguish between two areas, both in

---

10   For a definition of asymmetric threats, see: Kenneth F. Jr McKenzie, *The Revenge of the Melians: Asymmetric Threats and the Next QDR*, Mcnair Paper (Washington, D.C.: Instute for National Strategic Studies, 2001). Thornton provides a very insightful view on the 9/11 attacks as an asymmetric threat: Rod Thornton, *Asymmetric Warfare: Threat and Response in the 21st Century* (Cambridge, UK and Malden, Massachusetts: Polity, 2007). However, his claim that the terrorists relied exclusively upon training and box cutters is hard to believe, and is not consistent with his view that that the terrorists struck 'the nerve center of American military might:' ibid., 1.

Europe, but outside the core. I adapt Gellner's argument here to *three geopolitical areas, one of which became part of the state core, and two of which became geopolitical bands beyond this core.* I describe their location using a geographic reference frame centered in north-western Europe, in Paris, and sometimes oscillating between London and Paris. Similarly to the frame of reference of the Habsburg empire, centered in Vienna and Budapest, and sometimes oscillating between these cities and Lisbon and Madrid. *The first geopolitical area* was north-western Europe, and initially all of western Europe, including Portugal and Spain. The combination of capitalism and nationalism first emerged in countries in north-western Europe, especially England and France, which is also where capitalism and nationalism initially expanded the most. These countries and their states would form the state core, and ultimately the core of the modern world system, including the world economy and world culture, as their economies and cultural institutions greatly expanded. The next two geopolitical areas contained other states, which would form two geopolitical bands that can be measured from the center of the geographic reference frame, moving south and east from this center. Immediately on the other side of the frontier, there was a first geopolitical band, including states in the Italian peninsula and the central European states corresponding to modern-day Germany. Further south and east there was also a second geopolitical band, including the Habsburg, Ottoman, and Romanov empires.[11]

These three geopolitical areas were affected by the following *considerations that concern state type and that are very important to understand macro conflict in Europe.* In the modern state system *each area was clearly distinguished by a different state type. States in the core* were all proto nation-states. They included England, later to become part of Great Britain, France, the Netherlands, and also initially Portugal and Spain. The two geopolitical areas outside the state core of the emerging modern world system were also distinguished by the predominance of one state type, a peculiarity highlighted by both Gellner and Tilly that I am reformulating here in terms of geopolitical bands.[12] The *first geopolitical band*, which included areas corresponding to modern-day Italy and Germany, contained mostly city-states and derived state types, like regional

---

11   This argument is set out in Gellner's second book on nationalism, posthumously published: Gellner, *Nationalism*. There are some similarities between Gellner's argument in this book and arguments about cultural influence made by Bernard Lewis in: Bernard Lewis, *Cultures in Conflict: Christians, Muslims, and Jews in the Age of Discovery* (Oxford and New York: Oxford University Press, 1996). However, Gellner does not share the same view as Lewis of Islam as inherently engaged in conflict with Christianity.

12   Tilly, *Coercion, Capital and European States*. Gellner, *Nationalism*.

states that developed around a city-state, or leagues of city-states and other small states, like the Hanseatic League and the Swiss Confederation.[13] *The second geopolitical band* contained mostly territorial empires, the Habsburg, Ottoman, and Romanov empires. These geopolitical considerations contribute to World Systems Theory by *adding state type and logistics as important considerations to understand macro conflict,* including capitalism and nationalism as geoeconomic and geocultural features associated with state type. World Systems Theory describes the distribution of states in terms of economic power and the type of capitalism, attributing the following types of capitalism to different geographical areas: capitalism to states in the core, which in World Systems Theory does not include Spain and Portugal; agrarian capitalism, or forms of extraction of tribute by violence, to states in the periphery, which included the second geopolitical band; and different forms of economic organization such as SMEs than industrial and agrarian capitalism in countries in the semi-periphery, which included the first geopolitical band.

There are arguably important reasons for this correlation between, on the one hand geopolitical areas, and on the other hand state type and type of capitalism and extent of economic development. The latter arise from the different ability to produce and project political-military power, which is associated both with state type and with features of the state system. In order to understand the dynamics of conflict and how conflict played out, we have to understand *the interaction of state type with geographical features of the state system.* As suggested above, different state types had different abilities in producing political-military development, with proto nation-states producing the greatest, and also being able to sustain military forces for a considerable period of time. Spruyt pointed out that city-states were often capable of fielding large armies for their size, and hold their ground against larger states.[14] But their divisions meant that they could not sustain in the field military forces sufficient

---

13   Hendrik Spruyt, *The Sovereign State and Its Competitors: An Analysis of Systems Change,* Princeton Studies in International History and Politics (Princeton and Oxford: Princeton University Press, 1994). On the origins of the state in Italy, as part of the movement to 'bring the state back in' to social science studies, see the many contributions in: Julius Kirshner, ed. *The Origins of the State in Italy, 1300–1600* (Chicago and London: University of Chicago Press, 2009). This book was based on a 1993 conference.

14   Spruyt compares the size of armies fielded by different state types in: Spruyt, *The Sovereign State and Its Competitors.* However, this was relative to state size. In addition, although several different Italian states made alliances and joined forces, thus fielding large armies, these alliances were not long-lasting, and as pointed out above, they were subject to macro collective action problems relating to difficulties in coordinating collective action involving states of different types.

to oppose those fielded by proto nation-states, for example the forces fielded by France and Spain during the Italian Wars. These divisions, in addition to reliance upon mercenary captains and their companies, rather than citizen armies motivated by nationalism, proved disastrous, and explains why parts of northern Italy and the whole of southern Italy were contested between France and Spain and eventually conquered by Spain.[15] The long-term perspective is especially important in conjunction with logistics, and the ability to project power, which depends in part upon logistics and the transportation technology and infrastructure available at any one time, and in part upon geographical features of a system that I address below. What sealed the fate of the small Italian states was that the Italian peninsula was within relatively easy reach of both France and Spain, which could project and sustain relatively large armies in the Italian peninsula.

Before proceeding with a discussion of the manner in which state type and geographical features of the state system affect the projection of power, it is necessary to clarify the importance of logistics in the definition of geopolitical bands, and differentiate the concept of geopolitical band from the concept of sphere of influence. *Geopolitical band is not the same as a sphere of influence*, although it can overlap with a sphere of influence. The concept of geopolitical band is a geographical concept related to logistics and the limits it sets upon the ability to move armies and to project military power over land. There is in civilian logistics an economic equivalent to military logistics that is related to the ability to move goods. Sphere of influence involves being under hegemony, and it thus includes also geoculture, in various combinations with geopolitics and geoeconomics. It can predate conquest, and this is what happened to the Ottoman empire. This broad outline of a general theory clearly applies to two cases of states within Europe but outside the core, both of which are addressed below. One case is Italy, which was in the first geopolitical band. The other case is the Ottoman empire, and some of its successor states, Greece, Lebanon, and Syria, all of which were in the second geopolitical band.[16] The eastern Mediterranean has long been drawn into conflict at the near frontier, with enduring negative consequences for development, all arguably related to

---

15   Guido Ruggiero, *The Renaissance in Italy: A Social and Cultural History of the Rinascimento* (Cambridge and New York: Cambridge University Press, 2015), 154–204. The classic treatment of mercenary captains is provided by: Mallett and Caferro, *Mercenaries and Their Masters*. This book was first published in 1974. Mallett argues that the captains' companies were efficiently organized, like other European armies at the time. However, their interests and incentives were different.

16   See Sections 7.3 and 7.4 below.

the difficulty in introducing capitalism and nationalism, after they had been greatly developed by north-western European states.

It is equally important to differentiate the concept of geopolitical band from the concept of buffer zone. *The first geopolitical band in Europe is not the same as a buffer zone.* This is for several reasons, two of which stand out as especially important. One reason is that *participation in a geopolitical band is relatively stable, whereas participation in conflict as a buffer zone can change.* The concept of geopolitical band emphasizes that the main participants in the conflict are part of a state system that is relatively stable. A buffer zone emphasizes that the two states or groups of states on either side of the buffer zone are the main agents involved in conflict, and the areas in between are merely a buffer, but this can change as conflict in the state system changes. For example, the first geopolitical band might have acted as a buffer zone at certain times, after north-western European states emerged and consolidated and were in competition with the Habsburg empire. But at other times, for example after a unified Germany emerged and industrialized rapidly, thus becoming very powerful, Germany was no longer a buffer state, but a contender for power over continental Europe against France, and a threat to England. Thus the main conflict or threat of conflict was at the near frontier, and states at the far frontier, notably the Romanov empire, were drawn into this conflict and participated in the First World War on the side of France and England.[17] The Romanov empire, from contender for power over continental Europe against France, became an ally in what was a strategic outflanking maneuver. In this maneuver England and France, concerned about the rise in power of Germany and its alliance with the Ottoman empire, and with the Habsburg empire, which was centered on Austria by this time, sought allies further away, amongst their former contenders, and against a former buffer state, which was outflanked and forced to fight on two fronts in major conflicts.[18]

---

17   On the First World War as a war involving chiefly empires, and the participation of the Romanov and Ottoman empires, see the many contributions in: Robert Gerwarth and Erez Manela, eds., *Empires at War: 1911–1923* (Oxford and New York: Oxford University Press, 2014).

18   Anglo-Russian relations were affected by England's desire for an ally on the eastern front: Keith Neilson, *Strategy and Supply: The Anglo-Russian Alliance 1914–1917* (London and New York: Routledge, 2014). Despite rivalries, there were efforts to develop Anglo-Russian relations also in Asia: Ian Nish, "Politics, Trade and Communications in East Asia: Thoughts on Anglo-Russian Relations, 1861–1907," *Modern Asian Studies* 21, no. 4 (1987). For an overview of Anglo-Russian relations, see: Elmo E. Roach, "Anglo-Russian Relations from Austerlitz to Tilsit," *The International History Review* 5, no. 2 (1983). On Franco-Russian relations and the need to contain Bismarck's Germany, see: George Frost

Another reason is that *buffer zone is based upon status in conflict, whereas geopolitical band is based upon geographical distance and other features* that affect logistics, such as the presence of mountain ranges and access to sea lanes. Location in a geopolitical band is based upon geographical distance with respect to the state core, which provides the center of the geographic reference frame. This is a more important parameter than buffer zone because the geographic reference frame and the location of the geopolitical band with respect to it have been relatively stable since the beginning of the modern era in the 1500s, affecting conflict whether a state acted as a buffer or in another role. Although the state core has expanded, the geographic reference frame has not changed, and neither has the type of conflict described by geopolitical band. The goal of the hegemon and other states in the core has always been to prevent powerful contenders from arising and replacing them as hegemon. Whether these contenders were in the first or second geopolitical band varied with time. In early modern Europe, during the 1500s and 1600s, the main contenders for power over continental Europe that north-western European states faced where the Habsburg and Ottoman empires, whereas since the late 1800s and most strikingly after the early 1900s, they were Germany and to some extent Italy, after Germany and Italy expanded in power and fell under the rule of dictators.[19] Whether a buffer zone or a strategic outflanking maneuver were the main strategies pursued to contain the emerging contender depended upon all of these considerations, and upon the mutable changes in political alliances and relative power in the world system. It is an empirical question whether using buffer zones or a strategic outflanking maneuver prevailed. Probably both strategies co-existed, and one prevailed as the main strategy at one time or another.

Kennan, *The Decline of Bismarck's European Order: Franco-Russian Relations 1875–1890* (Princeton and Oxford: Princeton University Press, 1979).

19   The rise of new contenders or challengers for the status of hegemon in the world system, including Germany and Italy, and the decline of previous hegemons, is addressed in different ways in: Wallerstein, *The Modern World-System, Vol. IV*; Arrighi, *The Long Twentieth Century*. Arguably, the First and Second World Wars were wars fought against Germany over hegemony in Europe, and led to the decline of British hegemony, alongside the cultural convergence between Great Britain and the United States: Kori Schake, *Safe Passage: The Transition from British to American Hegemony* (Cambridge, Massachusetts and London: Harvard University Press, 2017). The cultural convergence, if there was one, was arguably due to the hegemony of the British aristocratic-military elite over the United States, and it minimized the effects of the transition, as the differences in international policies were not as marked as they could have been.

2   Geopolitical Areas and the Rules of Projection of Power

In the modern state system, *the interaction of state type with geographical features of the state system greatly influenced which states were taken over or brought under a sphere of influence*, and whether they were subjected to one form of exploitation and underdevelopment or another. *Conquest was affected to some extent by uneven political-military development and geographical distance between states.* Uneven political-military development is the difference between a state engaged in imperial expansion and another state, and it predicts that the larger this difference in power, the more likely the expanding state is to take over the other state. Geographical distance similarly predicts that the closer the other state is, the easier it is to take it over, because the costs of logistics involved in moving armies to a territory, and keeping them in the field, are lower. In addition, in some cases at least conquering a nearby state contributes to strengthening the natural boundaries of the expanding state, or provides a route for further conquests, whether a land route, or access to the sea.[20] This is not what happened in Europe, and the main reasons are that a state system had emerged, in which several states were all trying to expand, and the balance of power within the system, and the peculiarities of the system, affected the dynamics within the system. It is not that uneven political-military development or logistics had no effect, but that the emergence of new state types interacted with geographical features of the state system to impose *deviations from predictions based only upon uneven political-military development and logistics.* It is necessary to add other factors in order to predict expansion and conquest, and these factors include geopolitics and its interactions with geoculture. Later I will add the interaction between geopolitics and geoeconomics. Geoculture here refers to the fact that there are cultural influences in the system, whereby countries in spheres of influence are influenced at least in part through hegemony. There is also learning in the system.

Let us consider in greater detail the two points above, regarding the limitations of uneven political-military development and logistics to predict conquest, and their relation to geopolitics. In order to predict conquest, *the effects*

---

20   On the importance of proximity and sheer power in war between two states, see: Stuart A Bremer, "Dangerous Dyads: Conditions Affecting the Likelihood of Interstate War, 1816–1965," *Journal of Conflict Resolution* 36, no. 2 (1992). Bremer argues that other factors like lack of democracy were also important. Most world systems analysis focuses on the economic origins of wars. On this topic, see the many contributions in: Robert K. Schaeffer, ed. *War in the World-System* (New York, Westport Connecticut, and London: Greenwood Press, 1989).

of uneven political-military development have to be complemented by geopolitics and geoculture, and in particular the combination of state type and geopolitical area. These effects can be aptly summarized as involving a combination of geopolitics with geoculture that influenced system dynamics. This was in part because there emerged over a period of protracted conflict in the core a relatively stable balance of power that led to a *tendency to maintain the status quo within Europe,* both within the core and on the other side of the frontier. This is because the balance of power was such that no single state in the core could conquer other states in the core. It was also in part because within the core of north-western European states, and to some extent also across the frontier, there was cultural exchange, or greater cultural exchange than with countries outside Europe. For example, military innovations quickly spread from one state to another. So did cultural influence, and north-western European states became hegemonic within the emerging state system. Since states in the core were all considerably powerful, they could not conquer each other, nor their weak nearest neighbors. Some Italian states, notably the Kingdom of Naples and the Duchy of Milan, were conquered by Spain, one of the states in the first geopolitical area. However, other Italian states were not conquered, despite the marked power gap between, for example, France and Piedmont, or the Habsburg empire and Venice, two dyads each of which shared borders or where within short geographical distance of each other.[21] This was because of the tendency of the state system to maintain the status quo, whereby if a state in the core tried to conquer small nearby states and increase its power, other powerful states in the core or in the two other two geopolitical areas, the geopolitical bands, would intervene to prevent it.

The tendency to maintain the status quo within Europe clearly emerged in the course of the first two centuries of modern European history, by 1648 or 1714 at the latest, after which these states concentrated on expansion further away, outside Europe, and ended up building large colonial empires. The Italian Wars, which were fought on an off over the period 1494–1559, clearly showed this tendency to maintain the status quo. The king of France, Charles

---

21   The Republic of Venice and the Republic of Genoa remained independent until the Napoleonic Wars. The Duchy of Savoy, including Piedmont, and the Grand Duchy of Tuscany, remained independent, but were under the hegemony and political influence of France. On the different diplomatic practices and politics of Italian states, see the many contributions to: Daniela Frigo, ed. *Politics and Diplomacy in Early Modern Italy: The Structure of Diplomatic Practice, 1450–1800* (Cambridge and New York: Cambridge University Press, 2000). See also: John A. Marino, *Early Modern Italy: 1550–1796*, Short Oxford History of Italy (Oxford a nd New York: Oxford University Press, 2002).

VIII, initiated these wars by invading Italy in order to seize the Kingdom of Naples, to which he had a claim, but this led Spain to intervene for fear that France would become too powerful. Eventually Spain emerged victorious, but at a huge cost.[22] Later, the French Wars of Religion and the Thirty Years War of 1618–48, in which geoculture in the form of religious influence over political alliances emerged, showed a similar dynamic as the Italian Wars. The Habsburg empire that emerged from the marriage alliance of Austria and Spain was huge, and it sought to conquer the rest of Europe, starting with the Netherlands, leading to alliances to contain Habsburg expansionism. In the Thirty Years' War, other Protestant countries than the Netherlands, notably England, and at times Sweden, entered these wars against the Habsburg empire for fear that this empire would become too powerful.[23] France, a Catholic power, was at times allied with one side, at other times with the other. The Ottoman empire, long at war with the Habsburg empire, was also drawn into this conflict over control of Europe, notably by granting trading agreements to England and the Netherlands in order to contain Habsburg power.[24] This escalation in conflict, compounded by the cost of the wars that the Habsburg empire engaged in, led it to bankruptcy, stalemate in the Thirty Years War, and the end of Habsburg expansionism within Europe.[25]

There were large wars in Europe after 1648 that were started and doggedly pursued by Luis XIV, as part of his efforts to build a larger French state and rise to power over continental Europe. They similarly led to alliances to contain

---

22   On the Italian Wars, see: Mallett and Shaw, *The Italian War*. As pointed out above, both Mallet and Sella address the question as to whether there was a new system of states in Italy. Sella set out his argument in: Sella, *Italy in the Seventeenth Century*.

23   For the effects of religion on warfare in Europe, see: Norman Housley, *Religious Warfare in Europe, 1400–1536* (Oxford and New York: Oxford University Press, 2008). Various authors have emphasized that the wars of religion were due to a complex mix of factors that included as causes religion itself, and also emerging states. A similar picture emerges from: R. J. Knecht, *The French Wars of Religion 1559–1598*, 3rd ed. (London and New York: Routledge, 2014). On the complexity and destructiveness of the Thirty Years War, see: Peter H. Wilson, *The Thirty Years War: Europe's Tragedy* (Cambridge, Massachusetts: Belknap Press, 2011).

24   On the participation of the Ottoman empire in religious warfare in Europe, see: Housley, *Religious Warfare in Europe*. However, the effort to contain the Habsburg empire also led to a Franco-Ottoman alliance: Christin Isom-Verhaaren, *Allies with the Infidel: The Ottoman and French Alliance in the Sixteenth Century* (London and New York: I. B. Tauris, 2011). This alliance confirms that the wars were not exclusively over religion, but were driven to a significant extent by geopolitics and the tendency to maintain the status quo.

25   On the expansion of the Spanish Habsburgs, and Habsburg decline following the increased scale of war and bankruptcy, see: William S. Maltby, *The Rise and Fall of the Spanish Empire* (London and New York: Palgrave Macmillan, 2008).

Bourbon expansionism (Luis XIV was a member of the Bourbon ruling house), again with huge costs for the state that sought expansion, leading to the end of Bourbon expansionism within Europe by 1714 and the close of the War of the Spanish Succession.[26] Maintaining the status quo in Europe prevailed for two centuries after the end of Luis XIV reign. The only exceptions were wars initiated by drastic social change, namely, the French Revolutionary Wars and the Napoleonic Wars of 1792–1815, both of which were triggered by the French Revolution, during which drastic social change was introduced in France, and by the execution of the French king Luis XVI, which led to a reaction by other European countries committed to maintaining the status quo, including the rights of kings, and large-scale war broke out and spiraled out of control after Napoleon's seizure of power in France.[27] These were followed by the long peace of the Concert of Europe, after which there were only internal revolutions, and the wars over Italian and German unification, which were relatively small or short, while European powers concentrated upon colonial expansion.[28] Major wars in Europe returned with the First World War of 1914–18 and the Second World War of 1939–45, in which the ruling houses of Italy and Germany, and later totalitarian dictators who had seized power in these countries, sought to challenge England, by then part of Great Britain, and its ally France, in two massively destructive wars over control of Europe.[29]

The usefulness of logistics to predict conquest, similarly to uneven political-military development, is limited. In order to predict conquest, *logistics has to be complemented by geopolitics and geoculture,* and in particular by the

---

26   On the continuous warfare, large armies, and consequent escalating costs of Luis XIV's wars that ultimately undermined the French state, see: John A. Lynn, *The Wars of Louis XIV, 1667–1714* (London and New York: Routledge, 2013).

27   On the Napoleonic Wars, see: Alexander Mikaberidze, *The Napoleonic Wars: A Global History* (Oxford and New York: Oxford University Press, 2020). Mikaberitze emphasizes the international dimension of these wars, and their ties to the dynastic wars of the eighteenth century. Both were arguably part of efforts to raise France or the Habsburg empire to power over Europe.

28   The Concert of Europe was part of defensive realism, whereby states that were of comparable power restrained themselves from attempting to impose their power over Europe, in order to avoid major wars amongst these states: Matthew Rendall, "Defensive Realism and the Concert of Europe," *Review of International Studies* 32, no. 3 (2006). This was arguably influenced by the previous centuries of costly and fruitless wars for control over Europe.

29   Both the First and Second World War were affected by the rise of Germany to Great Power status, since this altered the balance of power in Europe: Andreas Hillgruber, *Germany and the Two World Wars*, trans. William C. Kirby (Cambridge, Massachusetts and London: Harvard University Press, 1981).

combination of state type and geopolitical area. All of the north-western European states, namely, Spain and then the Habsburg empire, France, England and then Great Britain, Portugal and the Netherlands, built large colonial empires.[30] This was in part because there emerged over the same period of protracted conflict in the core a *tendency towards expansion through colonial ventures*, as the north-western European states began expanding further away, over sea lanes, and creating trading colonies or settler colonies. This expansion, whether by design, or by a trial-and-error learning process, became a more important route to expansion than conquest in Europe. Conquering nearby states proved impossible, and this led north-western European states to focus mostly on conquests further away. Logistics still played a part, in the form of seafaring technology for ocean-going vessels that enabled expansion and trade further away. Portugal, soon followed by the Netherlands, first expanded into the silk and spice trade in Asia by circumnavigating Africa, displacing from this trade Italian states, notably Venice and Genoa, which bought these luxury goods on Levantine markets, as part of the last leg in the overland trade through Central Asia. Both Venice and Genoa went into a long period of economic and political decline. Spain started expanding into the Americas and creating a large colonial empire by conquest and settler colonies soon after Christopher Columbus' voyages and initial conquests.[31] As these colonies expanded, so did

---

30 On Anglo-Dutch relations since the Napoleonic Wars, see the many contributions in: Nigel J. Ashton and Duco Hellema, eds., *Unspoken Allies: Anglo-Dutch Relations since 1780* (Amsterdam: Amsterdam University Press, 2001). The ties between Great Britain and Portugal dated back to the middle ages and developed into a semi-colonial tutelage: Sandro Sideri, *Trade and Power: Informal Colonialism in Anglo-Portuguese Relations* (Rotterdam: Rotterdam University Press, 1970). These lasted into the time of the Salazar regime and the Spanish Civil War: Glyn Stone, *The Oldest Ally: Britain and the Portuguese Connection, 1936–1941*, Royal Historical Society Studies in History (Woodbridge, Suffolk: Boydell, 1994). See also: Bruno Cardoso Reis, "Myths of Decolonization: Britain, France, and Portugal Compared," in *The Ends of European Colonial Empires: Cases and Comparisons*, ed. Miguel Bandeira Jeronimo and Antonio Costa Pinto (London and New York: Palgrave Macmillan, 2016).

31 Wallerstein thought Portugal had started the modern world economy: Wallerstein, *The Modern World-System, Vol. 1*, 38–39, 49. Whereas Portugal built, at least initially, a trading empire, Spain built a territorial and tributary empire that was unsustainable: ibid., 165–195. Eventually this paved the way for the rise of the Netherlands and Great Britain. For the role of trade in these early empires, see the many contributions in: James D. Tracy, ed. *The Rise of Merchant Empires: Long Distance Trade in the Early Modern World 1350–1750* (Cambridge and New York: Cambridge University Press, 1990). For a comparison between British and Spanish expansion in the Americas, see: John H. Elliott, *Empires of the Atlantic World: Britain and Spain in America, 1492–1830* (New Haven and London: Yale University Press, 2006).

wars over these colonies, which became the first global wars in history, like the Seven Years War, and later the wars of independence that saw the involvement of one north-Western European state against another.[32] France and Spain lost many of their colonies, but still retained colonial empires. Portugal and the Netherlands retained their colonial empires, and England and then Great Britain kept expanding its colonial empire until it became the largest empire in European history.[33]

The importance of geopolitical and geocultural considerations relating to state type and geopolitical area all suggest *a revision of the concepts of core, semi-periphery, and periphery that emphasizes uneven political-military development, logistics, and also geopolitical and geocultural considerations* that affect the projection of power. Arrighi made an important point when he criticized the tendency in much of World Systems Theory to explain many phenomena simply by classifying a state as being in the core, semi-periphery, or periphery.[34] The important point that follows from Arrighi's criticisms is that it is necessary to provide an explanation as to why some states constitute the core, semi-periphery, or periphery, rather than invoke this classification as if it were an explanation in itself. Another difficulty with World Systems Theory is that definitions of the core tend to be made by identifying first a hegemonic state as the center of the core, and then defining the core with reference to the hegemonic state. Wallerstein and Arrighi disagreed over the question as to which was the first hegemonic state, Wallerstein suggesting it was Portugal, and Arrighi suggesting it was the Netherlands. However, both shared the assumption that the state dominating the trade between Europe and Asia had

---

32 The Seven Years War has been described as the first global war, as it was waged at the same time in Europe and North America, with major engagements in both theaters: Daniel A. Baugh, *The Global Seven Years War 1754–1763: Britain and France in a Great Power Contest* (London and New York: Routledge, 2011). The Seven Years War changed the balance of power in North America, and included the British conquest of French colonies in Canada. It also set off forces that would eventually undermine the British empire in North America: Fred Anderson, *Crucible of War: The Seven Years' War and the Fate of Empire in British North America, 1754–1766* (New York: Vintage Books, 2000).

33 The size and dispersal of colonial empires, which become unsustainable, is a central theme in: David B. Abernethy, *The Dynamics of Global Dominance: European Overseas Empires, 1415–1980* (New Haven and London: Yale University Press, 2000). Taagepera suggests that a communications revolution around 1600 made possible larger empires: Rein Taagepera, "Size and Duration of Empires: Systematics of Size," *Social Science Research 7*, no. 2 (1978).

34 Arrighi, "Capitalism and the Modern World-System." On the Netherlands as a state that played an important role in the modern world economy, greater than Portugal's role, see: *The Long Twentieth Century*.

the greatest wealth and the greatest power at its disposal, an assumption that is only partially true, since political-military power, and the projection of this power, was central both to define the core, and to decide which state became hegemonic within this core, but trade with Asia was an important, but by no means the only, defining feature of the core. The mechanism behind the emergence of the core, semi-periphery, and periphery divisions within the modern world system has to include all of the above considerations, namely, power gap, logistics, and also geopolitical and geocultural considerations that affected the projection of power. These different factors could be the bases for a *rules of projection of power*, which could be a contemporary reformulation of Mahan's rules of sea power, or general conditions affecting sea power, that were set out by naval commander and historian Alfred Thayer Mahan.[35] These rules would be rules of thumb, suggesting the likely occurrence of the projection of power, and whether it results in conquest, given some existing conditions.

Mahan's theory is especially interesting as it anticipated the modern concept of projection of power, emphasizing especially sea power, and it thus complements Wallerstein's theory, which did include interstate conflict in the study of European colonial expansion and an historical study of the wars that European colonial powers engaged in, but arguably failed to appreciate the importance of the projection of power.[36] This modern version of Mahan's rules of sea power would be concerned with the projection of power more in general, rather than just with sea power. It would combine land power with sea power, and logistics over land with logistics over sea lanes. In particular, I want to further expand upon Mahan's theory than George Modelski and William Thompson did. The latter wrote a seminal work on sea power from a World Systems Theory perspective that emphasizes sea power as a crucial military capability in the world economy and for all hegemons.[37] Most importantly, it

---

35   Alfred Thayer Mahan, *The Influence of Sea Power Upon History, 1660–1783*, Dover Military History, Weapons, Armor (Dover Publications, 2012). The six general conditions affecting sea power are laid out in Chapter II of Mahan's book. Mahan contributed to the build-up of the United States Navy and had an enduring influence also through his teachings. This influence is commemorated today by Mahan Hall at the United States Naval Academy at Annapolis.

36   There are interesting similarities between Mahan's theory and Wallerstein's theory. Both gave war an important dimension. Both tried to relate military power to other forms of power, especially economic power. However, Wallerstein neglected to theorize sea power, a point made and obviated by: Jan Glete, *Warfare at Sea, 1500–1650: Maritime Conflicts and the Transformation of Europe* (London and New York: Routledge, 2000), 13.

37   George Modelski and William R. Thompson, *Seapower in Global Politics, 1494–1993* (Houndmills, Basingstoke, Hampshire and London: Macmillan, 1988). In this book Modelski and Thompson presented first and foremost empirical data that correlates the

would reformulate some old concepts using the latest concepts from historical geography and sociology, in the manner suggested in Tables 3 and 4 below. Here I begin by describing the concepts in these tables, before showing how they explain the emergence of the core. The C in front of the Roman numeral serves to distinguish Mahan's conditions and corresponding contemporary concepts from the theses in this part of the book. C1 refers to concepts from contemporary geography and sociology, and C2 refers to concepts from World Systems Theory, all of which are useful to formulate rules of projection of power. These rules are useful to understand the emergence of the core and of the first geopolitical band, which was part of the semi-periphery, out of inter-state competition that resulted in specific dynamics, like the two tendencies highlighted above, to maintain the status quo in Europe, and to seek expansion mostly further away over sea lanes, resulting in the construction of colonial empires. Here I begin by sketching the rules of projection of power, before applying them to define the core of the modern state system. Table 3 refers to conditions of projection of power related to *actual geographical position* in a continent, and ultimately in the globe.

Conditions C1.I and C1.II both refer to actual geography and are self-explanatory. Conditions C1.III and C1.IV are components of extensive or intensive power. Territory is an important component of extensive power, because territory can be used for agriculture, which was especially important in the past, and because territory can contain natural resources that can be mined or extracted. Population relative to territory and development is a measure of intensive power. Mahan's condition C1.V, character of the people, is close to the concept of psychology of people, a concept that has been discredited by its association with *völkerpsychologie* and its racial overtones. It is best reformulated as the culture of a country, that in modern times includes national identity and the national language, both of which are part of geoculture. Mahan's condition C1.VI, character of government, is best reformulated as the extent of democracy, as measured by democracy indexes and by measures of the extent of civil society and of the separation of powers. Arguably, there is also a political culture that is important for the smooth functioning of government, and that includes principles of behavior that are specific to politics. This is not a complete list. The same conditions proposed by Mahan can be reformulated also using additional concepts from World Systems Theory. Table 4 refers to conditions relating to *relative geographical position*, derived from contemporary

---

rise and fall of hegemons with long cycles in the expansion of the world economy, and with growing military capabilities, in particular sea power. They also discuss whether Portugal or the Netherlands was the first hegemon.

TABLE 3   Mahan's conditions of sea power and corresponding contemporary geographical and sociological concepts I. Actual geographical location

No.	Mahan's condition	Contemporary geographical or sociological equivalent
C1.I	Geographical position	Geographical location: location alongside mountains, rivers, coastlines
C1.II	Physical conformation	Physical geography: terrain, whether plains or mountainous
C1.III	Extent of territory	Extensive power: territorial contribution to power
C1.IV	Number of population	Intensive power: population relative to territory and development
C1.V	Character of the people	Culture: shared culture, national identity, national language
C1.VI	Character of the government	Politics: extent of civil society, separation of powers

historical sociology and World Systems Theory, that are useful to understand the projection of power.

The above two tables and all the conditions, whether concerning actual or relative geographical location, together with the concept of projection of power, can serve to *reformulate the concept of core,* and ultimately also of semi-periphery and periphery. The latter were both areas that became semi-peripheral and peripheral areas with respect to the core because of political and military events. By the late 1400s there had emerged in Europe a new type of state, fairly large territorial states that were proto nation-state, namely, England, France, and Spain, with Portugal and the Netherlands as limiting cases. Let us consider again Table 3, which summarizes the *features of these states that made them into proto nation-states and thus into relatively powerful states* for their times. These states were all located alongside coastlines and all had access to sea lanes (C1.I). They all contained fairly large agricultural areas capable of sustaining large populations at a time in which most persons lived in the countryside, yet they also contained fairly large towns and the beginnings of capitalism, combining both extensive and intensive power (C1.II, III, and IV). All had the beginnings of national identity (C1.V), an identity initially built largely around the monarchy and religion. England and the Netherlands built the beginnings of a national identity around their Protestantism and

TABLE 4   Mahan's conditions of sea power and corresponding contemporary geographical
            and sociological concepts II. Relative geographical location

No.	Mahan's condition	Contemporary world system equivalent
C2.I	Geographical position	Relative geographical location in the state system: whether in the core, or the frontier, or other locations
C2.II	Physical conformation	Relative physical geography with respect to the system: state surface area as percentage of the area of the state core, number and rank of states in the core
C2.III	Extent of territory	Power gap: contribution from extensive power
C2.IV	Number of population	Power gap: contribution from intensive power
C2.V	Character of the people	Rank in world culture: hegemonic, subaltern, subject
C2.VI	Character of the government	Rank in the state system: core, semi-periphery, periphery

opposition to Catholic powers, while Spain built it around its Catholicism
and opposition to the Muslim states that remained as of the late 1400s in the
Iberian peninsula and were conquered by the close of the century as part of
the Reconquista.[38] The important point is that these proto nation-states had
started using culture, and in particular religion, in order to buttress their power,
whereas during the Middle Ages culture and religion had been monopolized

---

38   Religion was the basis of national identity in the proto nation-states of early modern
      Europe. This is strikingly visible in England, as discussed by the many contributions
      in: Tony Claydon and Ian McBride, eds., *Protestantism and National Identity: Britain
      and Ireland, C.1650–C.1850* (Cambridge and New York: Cambridge University Press,
      1998). Religion was arguably the basis of national identity also in Spain: Jose Álvarez
      Junco, *Spanish Identity in the Age of Nations* (Manchester and New York: Manchester
      University Press, 2016). Kumar has argued that there was an imperial dimension to
      English identity: Krishan Kumar, *The Making of English National Identity* (Cambridge
      and New York: Cambridge University Press, 2003). I believe this argument *might* apply
      to British identity, which was built around the union of kingdoms and was *initially* influ-
      enced by imperialist adventures, but not to English identity, which placed greater empha-
      sis upon Protestantism and freedom. On Catholicism and French identity, see: Joseph

by the Catholic Church. Their type of government was also distinctive, as these states had parliaments and had started developing representative democracy, giving voice to the most powerful aristocrats and other political entities (C1.VI). Some of these countries had parliaments originally made up mostly of powerful aristocrats, but in some cases there was representation also for wealthy cities with their own charters.[39]

As pointed out above, it was not just the state type that predicted expansion and conquest, but the combination of state type with geopolitical area, and in particular with features of the state system relating to geopolitics and geoculture. These features explain both the tendency to maintain the status quo and the tendency towards colonial expansion, both of which entailed that *the north-western European states constituted a system with its own dynamics that continued expanding and evolving, until it became the core of the modern state system* and ultimately of the world system, including the world economy and world culture. It is necessary to contrast this system, which emerged in the course of the early modern period, by 1648 or 1714 at the latest, with the earlier state system. Up to the late 1400s, the north-western European states were arguably part of the core of a European state system that included also the states in the Italian peninsula and in central Europe corresponding to modern-day Germany, in the first geopolitical band, all of which participated in the trade with North Africa described by Braudel, and in the trade with Asia that went through the Levant.[40] Venice and other Italian states played a central role in this trade, getting rich by buying luxury goods in Levantine ports from the overland trade through Asia, and selling them on European markets. At least part of this trade went north through the Rhine river to reach central and northern European markets including the Netherlands. Barcelona and Genoa participated in this trade by selling luxury goods on western European markets.[41]

F. Byrnes, *Catholic and French Forever: Religious and National Identity in Modern France* (University Park, Pennsylvania: Pennsylvania State University Press, 2005).

39 Ertman addresses early parliaments within a discussion of patrimonial and bureaucratic state infrastructures: Ertman, *Birth of the Leviathan*. On the political thought that supported medieval governments, see: Arthur P. Monahan, *Consent, Coercion, and Limit: The Medieval Origins of Parliamentary Democracy* (Leiden and Boston: Brill, 1987).

40 Braudel, *The Mediterranean, Vol. 1*; *The Mediterranean, Vol. 2*; *Civilization and Capitalism, Vol. 2*.

41 The Hanseatic League, a league of trading cities alongside the Baltic and North Sea coasts, benefited from inland trade coming from the Rhine River: Philippe Dollinger, *The German Hansa* (London and Basingstoke: Macmillan, 1970). On the role of German merchants in Venice as brokers, and the Fondaco dei Tedeschi, see: Uwe Israel, "Brokers as

The north-western European states, as they grew in size and power by the late 1400s, began constituting a significantly new state system. Let us consider again Table 4, which summarizes *the geopolitical and geocultural features of the first geopolitical area, in which European proto nation-states were located, that eventually made it into the core of the modern state system*, including its tendency to maintain the status quo, and its tendency towards expansion in colonial ventures over sea lanes. The north-western European states were all part of the core of the previous state system (C2.I), and in addition they shared a number of important features relating to physical geography, as they all constituted a solid block of territory including all of north-western Europe, within which three large and fairly evenly matched states had emerged by the late 1400s, namely, England and then Great Britain, France, and Spain (C2.II), none of which could prevail over the other states in the wars that followed, between 1494 and 1714. Nor could they conquer the smaller states in the core, the Netherlands and Portugal, both of which eventually became allies of Great Britain, although they embraced their innovations, which spread through the system, as first Portugal, then the Netherlands, began introducing important organizational and economic innovations that England was to take up and develop even more in expanding extensive power and sea trade. In this, the north-western European states were aided by their geographic position in Europe as described in Figure 3, all on the Atlantic coast (C1.I), a position that was far from Asian markets, but ideally suited to project power over sea lanes, into the Americas, and later into Asia, especially once ocean-going vessels were introduced and perfected, and all to a greater or lesser extent built and also maintained for a long time colonial empires. It was the balance of power in the core, together with the ability to project power over sea lanes, that led to the tendency towards expansion into colonial empires highlighted above. This balance of power, in conjunction with the presence of intensive as well as extensive power, and the fact that uneven political-military development between these states in both intensive and extensive power was not decisive, as described in Figure 4 (C2.III and IV), entailed that they all continued expanding over sea lanes, and expanding capitalism to some extent, and thus intensive power, with the exception of Spain and Portugal, both of which were eventually marginalized as powers within Europe.

German-Italian Cultural Mediators in Renaissance Venice," in *Migrating Words, Migrating Merchants, Migrating Law: Trading Routes and the Development of Commercial Law*, ed. Stefania Gialdroni, et al. (Leiden and Boston: Brill, 2020).

3   The Effects of the Projection of Power outside the Core

The semi-periphery and periphery of the world system come into existence because of the projection of power by states in the core, and were deeply influenced by it. This revision of the Diamond-Wallerstein theory suggests that political-military development and state type explain conquest and underdevelopment in the semi-periphery and periphery. In considering the effects of uneven political-military development, and more in general of the projection of power including geopolitical and geocultural considerations, it is useful to distinguish between areas reachable by sea lanes that were to become the periphery of the world system, and areas in Europe, but outside the core, in the first and second geopolitical bands, that were to become the semi-periphery. The areas reachable by sea lanes included countries in the Americas, Asia, and Africa, all of which were to become part of the periphery of the modern world system and its artificial division of labour. Domination and harsh exploitation prevailed, accompanied by limited hegemony in the form of conversion to Catholicism. The areas in Europe but outside the new core included countries in the first and second geopolitical bands, in what was to become the semi-periphery of the world system. In this case, the projection of power was to affect revolution from above and the ability to introduce capitalism and nationalism. In these areas hegemony between states prevailed, and some kind of imitation occurred that led some states to introduce capitalism and nationalism as part of revolutions from above, but geopolitical influences always accompanied geocultural ones, and limited the autonomy of the states in the semi-periphery in evolving as they could have otherwise, leading to other forms of underdevelopment.

Below I provide an account of the manner in which *the projection of power affected both the likelihood of conquest and the harshness of exploitation.* This was affected by geopolitical considerations, which determined that areas most easily reachable through sea lanes were conquered first. When we consider expansion in colonial ventures, over sea lanes, the two factors, extent of uneven political-military development, and logistics, are fairly good predictors of expansion and conquest, and also of the extent of exploitation and underdevelopment that ensued. In colonialism the greater uneven political-military development lead to a skewed distribution of power in favor of political-military elites that profoundly affected the behavior of these elites.[42] However,

---

42   Higley suggests that elites that were less securely in power tended to resort to intrigue and violence more easily: John Higley, "Patterns of Political Elites," in *The Palgrave Handbook of Political Elites*, ed. Heinrich Best and John Higley (London and New York: Palgrave

these factors have to be complemented by geopolitical factors. This suggests a modification of Lange's argument, beginning to explain why some colonies of the British empire were subjected to direct rule, while other ones were subjected to the more damaging indirect rule.[43] As a first approximation, the greatest the uneven political-military development, the earliest the conquest, and the greatest the exploitation and underdevelopment, but amongst conquered countries that were of comparable political-military development, logistics predicted conquest and the extent of exploitation, in particular, India was conquered first, then China. The two factors above also have to be complemented by a third one, namely, cost-benefit tradeoffs, which explain why China was conquered last, because the cost of gaining access to its markets was fairly large, and why Africa was conquered last, because the opportunities for imperialists from Europe to get rich were least compared to the costs. One factor influencing costs were the costs of holding on to conquered countries, and of preventing revolts within them that demanded exit or voice.

Let us consider first the expansion of European proto nation-states in the Americas, Asia, and Africa, and the effects it had on underdevelopment. Initially, *European proto nation-states states concentrated upon conquest of territory mainly in the Americas, which led to very large settler colonies* or colonies dominated by settlers from Europe, with Africa initially exploited and underdeveloped through the slave trade. These countries were easier to conquer for a number of reasons, several of which have been highlighted by Diamond: the lower population densities, or the later time when high population densities were achieved, meant that these countries did not have enough means or time to develop advanced technologies before early modern European conquests. *Conquest of countries in the Americas presented a low cost-benefit tradeoff* as they could be conquered relatively easily and rapidly (low costs) and vast amounts of wealth could be extracted, in the form of gold and silver, tribute, or extraction of profits from local populations by European colonialists who built plantations or other large farms (high benefits).[44] Imperialist elites from

Macmillan, 2018). However, more factors have to be taken into consideration, including the culture of these elites, and their relation to other elites, and consideration involving the projection of power.

43   This distinction is discussed in Section 4.1 above. Lange does not explain why there were these two different types of rule in the British empire, focusing instead on their effects: Lange, *Lineages of Despotism and Development*.

44   See Chapter 4 in: Elliott, *Empires of the Atlantic World*. The broader aspects of this exploitation are addressed in: Eduardo Galeano and Isabelle Allende, *Open Veins of Latin America: Five Centuries of the Pillage of a Continent*, trans. Cedric Belfrage (New York: Monthly Review Press, 1997). The broader monetary and financial context, including the rise in

Europe could conquer vast tracts of land that could quickly be settled by colonists and brought under cultivation, both because there was great uneven political-military development across countries, and also because logistics meant that ports in the Americas all alongside the Atlantic coast, with access to these vast tracts of land, could easily ship the agricultural goods produced to Europe.[45] In this case, *uneven political-military development across countries rapidly lead to uneven economic development within the countries* that were conquered, because the conquering elites were aristocratic-military elites who came from abroad with more advanced military technologies, and more advanced techniques of power, including divide-and-conquer and divide-and-rule tactics. These aristocratic-military elites could dictate their terms without any restraints.[46]

The general mechanism that led to underdevelopment in the Americas, and the settler colonies that imperialists from Europe built there, was that *a skewed balance of power across countries directly led to a very skewed balance of power in society and to social rents,* whereby the elite could easily extract profits, and engage in exploitation rather than development. The only (initially partial) exception were the United States, in which there was a south whose economy was based upon plantations, and a north in which there was a large number of settlers who built local economies that were not so reliant upon export of

---

prices caused by bullion exported to Europe, is addressed in: Pierre Vilar, *A History of Gold and Money, 1450 to 1920,* trans. Judith White (London and New York: Verso, 1991). Imperialists from Spain, France and Great Britain also built large plantations throughout the Caribbean: Frank Moya Pons, *History of the Caribbean: Plantations, Trade, and War in the Atlantic World* (Princeton: Markus Wiener Publishers, 2007). Both in Central America and North America there was progressive build-up of settler colonies that created large farms and other economic enterprises: Edward Cavanagh and Lorenzo Veracini, eds., *The Routledge Handbook of the History of Settler Colonialism* (London and New York: Routledge, 2016).

45   There were still important differences due to the state that the colonists came from, and the trade policies that were implemented: John DeWitt, *Early Globalization and the Economic Development of the United States and Brazil* (Westport, Connecticut, and London: Praeger, 2002).

46   Elites in Latin America tended also to be involved in an economy based on the export of natural resources, and this led also to internal struggles amongst the elites: Cristóbal Rovira Kaltwasser, "Political Elites in Latin America," in *The Palgrave Handbook of Political Elites,* ed. Heinrich Best and John Higley (London and New York: Palgrave Macmillan, 2018). This left a legacy of powerful elites and weak states that has affected many countries in Latin America: Barry Cannon, *The Right in Latin America: Elite Power, Hegemony and the Struggle for the State* (London and New York: Routledge, 2016). See also: Stanley J. Stein, "Bureaucracy and Business in the Spanish Empire, 1759–1804: Failure of a Bourbon Reform in Mexico and Peru," *Hispanic American Historical Review* 61, no. 1 (1981).

goods to Europe, resulting in high development in the north.[47] Except for the United States, the balance of power in society within the American colonies created by aristocratic-military elites from Europe tended to be heavily skewed towards the elites, who enjoyed a huge collective action advantage, and this led to great uneven development within these countries. In Latin America there was polarization between very wealthy elites and the colonized masses, with intermediate groups of settlers that were under the leadership of the elites and constituted subaltern social groups that contributed to elite power.[48] There also tended to be no embedded autonomy between different arenas in these colonies. There was therefore uneven development and lack of democracy within these colonies in all arenas: economic and cultural, as well as political-military. In Latin America, the elites controlled completely politics and the military, and also had great influence over culture, which was dominated by the Catholic Church, controlling through domination, or at most limited hegemony, the large plantations or mines and large mercantile concerns that sold agricultural products and raw materials or ores, especially gold and silver, to Europe.[49]

European proto nation-states focused also upon conquest in Asia. However, *conquest in Asia followed a different route due to the lesser extent of uneven development across countries.* There was still uneven political-military development across European proto nation-states and these countries, but it was not as marked as the uneven development between European proto nation-states and countries in the Americas. As a result, *in Asia uneven development across countries lead to uneven development within the countries much more slowly.* Conquest was slower and took place over a long period of time. It also involved a somewhat different mechanism. Countries in Asia had high population densities, more advanced technologies, and possibly more advanced techniques of power, than countries in the Americas and Africa. The most powerful amongst these countries were territorial empires: India, still nominally under the

---

47   This point was made by Barrington Moore Jr in explaining the origins of the American Civil War, as the economic interests, as well as political allegiances, of north and south, ended up diverging: Moore, *Social Origins of Dictatorship and Democracy.*

48   On the long-lasting effects of conquest, see: Regina Grafe and Maria Alejandra Irigoin, "The Spanish Empire and Its Legacy: Fiscal Redistribution and Political Conflict in Colonial and Post-Colonial Spanish America," *Journal of Global History* 1, no. 2 (2006). This was also true of some colonies in North Africa such as Tunisia and Libya, in which the colonists built especially powerful states, and the process of state formation proceeded much more rapidly and drastically, from above, than if it had been driven by local forces: Anderson, *The State and Social Transformation in Tunisia and Libya.*

49   The ties of the Catholic Church in Latin America to elites are addressed in: Schwaller, *The History of the Catholic Church in Latin America,* 83, 114–15.

Mughal empire; and China, still an empire under the Qing dynasty. Conquest was not as easy, and where there was conquest it was initially limited to port cities that were important for trade, leading in India to the creation of important Portuguese commercial enclaves like Bombay and Goa, and the French enclave of Pondicherry.[50] Imperialists from Europe concentrated upon trade first, and progressively penetrated these countries through trade, which made them and their trading companies like the East India Company richer, until they could field sizeable armies and conquer these countries. In this case there was some uneven political-military development across countries, which was compounded by uneven economic development, whereby European imperialist elites knew how to exploit markets, and dominated the trade flows between Asian markets and European markets, driving this early form of globalization to their advantage. This eventually led to growing uneven political-military development and the later conquest of India, a conquest that occurred over a one-hundred year period.

By contrast with countries in the Americas, *conquests of countries in Asia presented a medium-high cost-benefit tradeoff*, as conquest was hard (high costs), although the returns were high too (high or very high benefits), and these countries could not be conquered rapidly, because they were both large and fairly advanced in political-military development. In this case, conquest was preceded by penetration through trade, which was spearheaded by the mercantile bourgeoisie in alliance with aristocratic-military elites, and trade prevailed over conquest for a long time. *Within Asia too the extent of uneven political-military development across countries influenced the timing and effects of conquest.* Arguably, South Asia, and in particular India, were conquered before East Asia, and in particular China, because of their lower political-military development, combined with shorter geographical distance from Europe. In India the Mughal empire had entered decline, and the whole Indian subcontinent was divided into a number of states, a division that made India less powerful politically and militarily than it could have been, if it had been unified, and made it easier for imperialists from Europe to apply divide-and-conquer tactics in order to conquer one or a few Indian states at a time.[51] These tactics might have continued later in the form of divide-and-rule tactics.

---

50   Thompson describes these enterprises as initially based upon a Venetian model of trade expansion, making use of networks of bases/entrepots and sea power: Thompson, "The Military Superiority Thesis," 153–55, 169.

51   Thompson highlights the importance of local allies in: ibid. This entails that imperialists from Europe used divide-and-conquer and divide-and-rule tactics, allying with one social group in a country against other social groups, in order to take over that country.

By contrast, imperial China under the Qing dynasty was more unified, and was also further away, therefore it was only subjected to some form of colonial tutelage later, when imperialists from Europe had become wealthier and more powerful from their trade and conquests in South Asia and South East Asia, that also served as bases from which to project power, or staging posts for European conquests in China, since China was further from Europe than India.[52] In the absence of reliable statistics presenting the extent of development before European conquest and before independence, we should consider the explanation that the length of European colonialism might have influenced the current difference in development between India and China, not the alleged negative effects upon development of democracy in India.[53]

In the case of Africa uneven political-military development did not lead to conquest initially because of the high cost-benefit tradeoff. In this case, conquest might have been relatively easy (low costs), but the returns were low too (low or very low benefits). Africa was conquered last by European colonialists, in what became known as the Scramble for Africa, whereby numerous European powers, including France, Great Britain, and Portugal, and also the newly formed states Germany and Italy, conquered most of Africa in the late 1800s to early 1900s, in a series of belated colonial ventures, all associated with indirect rule.[54] In this case there was great uneven development between European states and the countries in Africa that they conquered, but also fewer opportunities for enrichment, leading to smaller numbers of colonists (except in South Africa) than in the Americas and possibly Asia. One of the reasons for the late conquest of Africa is that the climate in most of Africa was considerably different than Europe's and it would not attract European settlers, whose farming animals and knowledge were specific to a different climate. Perhaps this is the reason why South Africa attracted larger numbers of European settlers compared to other parts of Africa from an early time, because its climate is quite similar to Europe's, and this, in addition to its strategic location along sea lanes

---

52   On European trade and imperialism in China, see: John E. Wills et al., *China and Maritime Europe, 1500–1800: Trade, Settlement, Diplomacy, and Missions* (Cambridge and New York: Cambridge University Press, 2010); Anne Reinhardt, *Navigating Semi-Colonialism: Shipping, Sovereignty, and Nation Building in China, 1860–1937*, Harvard East Asian Monographs (Leiden and Boston: Brill, 2020).

53   Sen oddly supports what is effectively a Stalinist argument that democracy in India slowed down development compared to China, since India made compromises demanded by democratic forces, whereas China did not: Sen, *Development as Freedom*. There are likely many other factors than democracy that explain the post-independence differences in development between China and India.

54   M.E. Chamberlain, *The Scramble for Africa*, 3rd ed. (London and New York: Routledge, 2014).

and importance for IC lines, attracted settlers from Europe.[55] Another reason, compared to parts of Latin America, might have been the limited transportation infrastructure such as trade routes, especially lack of trade routes that reached deep into the interior, and the consequent difficulty in penetrating many parts of Africa, whether by conquest and settlers, or by trade. Where these trade routes existed, in North Africa and parts of West Africa, both of which had participated in trade with Europe since early modern times, conquest proceeded more quickly.[56]

The general mechanism that led to underdevelopment in Asia and Africa, and the trading colonies that imperialists from Europe built there, was that *a skewed balance of power was also affected by different demographic ratios*, or ratios between colonists and local population. These ratios were initially, or remained, less than those in the Americas, and imperialists from Europe resorted far more to indirect rule, including extensive use of divide-and-conquer and divide-and-rule tactics, to maintain themselves in power in areas in which there were only small numbers of colonists compared to the local population. In India this was because the entire Indian subcontinent had high population densities, and even the wealthy East India Company did not maintain large numbers of colonists relative to the local population, and relied upon indirect rule. British colonies in India, initially trading concerns that made alliances with local rulers, and thus participated in indirect rule, moved to direct rule only as the number of British colonists increased over a long period of time and built their own local armies that they controlled. The First War of Indian Independence, in 1857, originally referred to by imperialists from Great Britain

---

55 On the attractiveness of South Africa to early settlers from Europe because of its climate, see: John Hunt and Heather-Ann Campbell, *Dutch South Africa: Early Settlers at the Cape, 1652–1708* (Leicester: Matador, 2005). On colonialism in South Africa, see: Leonard Monteath Thompson, *A History of South Africa*, 3rd ed. (New Haven and London: Yale University Press, 2001). On the importance of guns and European military superiority in South Africa, see: William Kelleher Storey, *Guns, Race, and Power in Colonial South Africa* (Cambridge and New York: Cambridge University Press, 2012). On the process of peripheralization of the whole of southern Africa, see: Arrighi, "Peripheralization of Southern Africa, I."; Immanuel Maurice Wallerstein and William G. Martin, "Peripheralization of Southern Africa, II: Changes in Household Structure and Labor-Force Formation," *Review (Fernand Braudel Center)*. 3, no. 2 (1979).

56 Modelski and Thompson address the importance of geographical barriers to expansion in the interior or hinterland of countries that imperialists from Europe reached by sea: Geroge Modelski and William R. Thompson, "The Evolutionary Pulse of the Wolrd System: Hinterland Incursions and Migrations, 4000 BC to AD 1500," in *World-Systems Theory in Practice: Leadership, Production, and Exchange*, ed. Nick P. Kardulias (Lanham, Boulder, New York, and Oxford: Rowman & Littlefield Publishers, 1999).

as the Sepoy Revolt, was both a sign of difficulty in controlling these local armies, and a tightening of the screw in direct control of India.[57]

In many parts of Africa population densities were lower than in Asia, as pointed out by Diamond, but since the *cost-benefit tradeoff* of conquest for imperialists from Europe were high, so was the density of European colonists, which reflected the gains that imperialists could have. This meant that imperialists from Europe resorted extensively to divide-and-conquer and divide-and-rule tactics, even more than elsewhere. The effects on Africa were disastrous, and endured to this day in the lower development of most countries in Africa.[58] This also led to great uneven development and shortcomings in democracy of most countries in Africa, between the very few wealthy rulers and European colonists, and the vast majority of the population. They might also have led to geographical uneven development within some countries. As Lange argued, India represents an intermediate case between direct and indirect rule. Imperialists from Europe might have conquered first areas in India that were least developed and were going to become internal peripheries to India, and thus providers of cheap labour, including cheap military labour, as well as staging posts from which to proceed to conquer the rest of India. This is another mechanism whereby uneven political-military development across countries, namely Great Britain and India, might have led to accentuating uneven economic development within a country, India.[59]

Let us consider now *the expansion of power of European proto nation-states in Europe,* and their eventual hegemony over Europe. European proto nation-states had become nation-states that constituted the core of north-western European states and exercised hegemony over the state system. This hegemony, buttressed by political-military power, still had profound effects on the underdevelopment of areas in Europe that were outside the core, in the first and second geopolitical bands, most of which were to become the semi-periphery of the modern world system, with its own distinctive variety of capitalism.[60] The expansion of the hegemony of north-western European

---

57   On the increased British power after the establishment of the Raj, see: Lawrence James, *Raj: The Making and Unmaking of British India* (New York: St. Martin's Griffin, 1997).

58   Lange discusses the development statistics that show the lower development of most countries in Africa compared to other countries in the world: Lange, *Lineages of Despotism and Development.*

59   Lange argues that India was an intermediate case between indirect rule and direct rule: ibid.

60   See the contributions in: Giovanni Arrighi, *Semiperipheral Development: The Politics of Southern Europe in the Twentieth Century* (Thousand Oaks, London, and New Delhi: SAGE, 1985). These long-standing processes of peripheralization were accentuated by the

states was accompanied by the creation of new states in Europe by two routes. In the first geopolitical band two new states, Italy and Germany, were created in 1861 and 1871 respectively by bringing together many smaller states within a larger proto nation-state or nation-state.[61] In the second geopolitical band, states were created by the breakup of territorial empires, as the Ottoman empire was broken up into numerous states. In the Balkans, these were Serbia and Greece, then Bulgaria and Rumania, in the course of the nineteenth century. In the Middle East, these were Lebanon, Syria, Iraq, Israel, and Jordan in the early to mid-twentieth century. The Habsburg empire, which no longer included Spain, was broken up following defeat in the First World War into Austria, Hungary, Czechoslovakia.[62] All these states were created because by the mid eighteenth century to early nineteenth century the balance of power in Europe had changed significantly. Colonial expansion, accompanied by industrialization, had made states in the core very powerful, and Great Britain and France had become allies, from the Entente Cordiale, down to the current Entente Frugale.[63] This changed the balance of power in Europe significantly, to the point that north-western European states could challenge the large territorial empires, notably the Habsburg and Ottoman empires, for supremacy in Europe. In addition, Great Britain and France had started penetrating the

---

European Monetary Union, and its effects on institutions and development policies in southern Europe: Francesca Gambarotto and Stefano Solari, "The Peripheralization of Southern European Capitalism within the EMU," *Review of International Political Economy* 22, no. 4 (2015). Some authors have highlighted the low development of many successor states of empires in what I refer to as the second geopolitical band, including Baltic countries and Balkan countries: Derek H. Aldcroft, *Europe's Third World: The European Periphery in the Interwar Years* (London and New York: Routledge, 2016).

61   In some ways Italy around the time of unification was still a proto nation-state because of the lack of industrial capitalism and the lack of a single language and culture.

62   On the breakup of these empires, see the contributions in Part One of: Barkey and von Hagen, *After Empire*. Roeder shows that most modern states originated from the breakup of empires, whether territorial or colonial empires: Roeder, *Where Nation-States Come From*.

63   The Entente Cordiale was the alliance between France and Great Britain, buttressed by a number of agreements, that took shape in the early 1900s. The Entente Cordiale has been strained many times, but amidst growing similarities and ties. See the introduction and many contributions in: Richard Mayne, Douglas Johnson, and Robert Tombs, eds., *Cross Channel Currents: 100 Years of the Entente Cordiale* (London and New York: Routledge, 2004). The Entente Frugale is a formal military alliance aimed, amongst other things, at containing the costs of the projection of military power. On the Entente Frugale in the context of Anglo-French relations, see: Alice Pannier, *Rivals in Arms: The Rise of UK-France Defence Relations in the Twenty-First Century* (Montreal, Kingston, London, Ithaca: McGill-Queen's University Press, 2020).

Ottoman empire through trade, in a manner that presaged later conquest, like the penetration through trade and then conquest that imperialists had implemented in India and South East Asia.

All the new states created were small compared to the empires and were easily brought under the hegemony of states in the core. *In the case of Italy and Germany the new states altered the status quo within Europe the least.* From the point of view of the balance of power between states in Europe, Italian and German unification took place in the form that altered the status quo the least, because of the size of the resulting state. It was not another large and powerful state that conquered the Italian peninsula or that conquered central European states that correspond to modern-day Germany. This is clear in the case of Italy. It was not France or Spain, nor the Habsburg empire, that conquered all the small states in the Italian peninsula, which would have altered the status quo in Europe, but a unified state was created by one of the many small states, in such a way that this unified state was not by itself a threat to France or Great Britain, and it could offset Habsburg power. Similar considerations apply to Germany. Had the Habsburg empire conquered states that are today part of Germany, and unified all speakers of German (and dialects of German), this would have created a very large and powerful state that would have radically altered the balance of power in central Europe and in Europe as a whole. Instead, a new state was created out of many small states, by one of these small states, that was not significantly bigger and more powerful than France or Great Britain, and could offset Habsburg power. When a unified Germany allied itself with the Austrian Habsburgs, this triggered the First World War, together with other factors.[64] *The breakup of the Habsburg and Ottoman empires created many small states*, all of which were easily brought and maintained under the hegemony of states in the core, an hegemony that at times became colonial tutelage. Greece was from the start under the semi-colonial tutelage of France and Great Britain. Lebanon and Mandate Palestine, later to become Israel, were similarly under the tutelage of these powers, and Syria

---

64   Joll's classic on the origins of the First World War takes into account Germany's rise in power, and it has recently been re-published: James Joll and Gordon Martel, *The Origins of the First World War* (London and New York: Routledge, 2013). The argument regarding the importance of Germany's rise in power in triggering the First World War was put forward by: Fritz Fischer, *Germany's Aims in the First World War* (New York: w.w. Norton, 1967). This argument has been criticized in: David E. Kaiser, "Germany and the Origins of the First World War," *The Journal of Modern History* 55, no. 3 (1983). For an overview of these debates, see: Annika Mombauer, *The Origins of the First World War: Controversies and Consensus* (London and New York: Routledge, 2013).

and Iraq were briefly French and British colonies.[65] Egypt, a country that had always occupied a very important strategic position in sea lanes from Europe to Asia, and in IC lines more in general, was brought briefly under French and then under British rule, since its rulers could pose a threat to the trade with India, increasingly important after the creation of the Suez Canal. French and British hegemony over Egypt arguably continues to this day.[66]

Let us consider first the *effects upon states in the first geopolitical band of uneven political-military development across countries*. These were similar to the effects that uneven development had upon states in Asia. Similarly to India and China, there was less uneven development between European proto nation-states and other states in Europe, compared to the uneven development between European proto nation-states and states or stateless countries in the Americas and Africa. For example, the greater political-military development of European proto nation-states enabled them to conquer some states in the Italian peninsula, notably the Kingdom of Naples and the Duchy of Milan. The conquest of these states might have led to *some* uneven development within countries through the same mechanism whereby conquest led to uneven development in countries in the Americas, but it was nowhere near as marked as in these countries. The same can be said for the conquest of the Kingdom of Naples at the time of the unification of Italy.[67] This was because the conquering

---

65 For an overview of the British and French mandates in the Middle East, including the mandates in Lebanon, Syria, Israel/Palestine, Transjordan, and Iraq, and the effects of the mandates on these countries, see the many contributions in: Nadine Méouchy and Peter Sluglett, *The British and French Mandates in Comparative Perspectives/Les Mandats Français et Anglais dans une Perspective Comparative* (Leiden and Boston: Brill, 2004). On the failure of the mandates in establishing stable and democratic countries in the Middle East, see: D.K. Fieldhouse, *Western Imperialism in the Middle East, 1914–1958* (Oxford and New York: Oxford University Press, 2006).

66 On Napoleon's invasion, see: Juan Ricardo Cole, *Napoleon's Egypt: Invading the Middle East* (London and New York: Palgrave, 2007). On the importance of strategic considerations affecting the British empire and its trade routes to individual countries including Egypt, see the many contributions in: Andrew N. Porter, ed. *The Oxford History of the British Empire: The Nineteenth Century* (Oxford and New York: Oxford University Press, 1999).

67 For an overview of the history of southern Italy, see: Tommaso Astarita, *Between Salt Water and Holy Water: A History of Southern Italy* (New York: W. W. Norton, 2006). For Napoleon's invasion of Italy and its effect on southern Italy, within the context of the European revolutions of the time, see: John A. Davis, *Naples and Napoleon: Southern Italy and the European Revolutions, 1780–1860* (Oxford and New York: Oxford University Press, 2006). Some authors have argued that the Kingdom of Naples was on its way to becoming its own nation-state: Girolamo Imbruglia, ed. *Naples in the Eighteenth Century: The Birth and Death of a Nation State*, Cambridge Studies in Italian History and Culture (Cambridge and New York: Cambridge University Press, 2000). On economic policies after unification,

elites who came from abroad did not have much more advanced technologies and techniques of power and could not completely dictate their terms, therefore the balance of power in society between the conquering elites and the rest of society was not so skewed towards the conquering elites. *Uneven political-military development affected economic development through the tendency of the modern world system to maintain the status quo within Europe.* For example, the greater political-military development of European proto nation-states, and later of north-western European states, undermined the economy of much of Italy, including states that were not conquered, by preventing the positive interaction between political-military, cultural, and economic development.[68] This was because Italian states could not develop the economy by expanding internal markets and advancing industrial capitalism, since they were all small and could not expand because of the tendency to maintain the status quo. The positive mechanisms whereby nation-states could develop culture and the economy were also not at work in the Italian peninsula, which remained divided until 1861 into many small states with different languages, different currencies, sometimes still suspicious of each other from previous wars.

What is worse, the new states that were created and brought under the hegemony of north-western European states all tended to be led by a strong aristocratic-military elite, in a manner similar to conquered states in the Americas, although the mechanism involved hegemony and a semi-colonial tutelage, rather than conquest. All thus suffered from lack of democracy, and heightened social conflict. Eventually, *a unified Italian state emerged, but it suffered for a long time from uneven development within a country, as well as lack of democracy.* The mechanism that led to continued uneven development across countries involves revising Moore's theory of revolution from above in the light of Gramsci's theory of hegemony and the concept of geopolitical band. Moore pointed out that interstate conflict leads some states to introduce capitalism from above, in order to become more powerful, but that capitalism introduced from above, instead of leading to democracy, leads to dictatorship. This is an important insight, but the mechanism was more complex than suggested by Moore, and it involved uneven development.[69] The effect of the state system and its tendency to maintain the status quo in Europe is that *Italian and German unification took place in the manner that altered the status quo in*

---

see the last chapter in: Derek Beales and Eugenio F. Biagini, *The Risorgimento and the Unification of Italy* (London and New York: Routledge, 2014).

68   I address this positive interaction in Sections 2.3 and 2.4. I further expand upon it in Section 7.5 below.

69   Moore, *Social Origins of Dictatorship and Democracy.*

Europe the least, because of the limits to both democracy and development that it imposed, hampering these states, and especially Italy, from the time they were created. I want to emphasize that pointing to this mechanism does not diminish in any way the responsibilities of ruling houses like the House of Savoy that ruled over Piedmont, and later of fascists, just to mention two collective agents that had *enduring* negative effects upon Italy as well as other countries. It only explains why they won and were able to influence Italy for such a long time.

Both Italy and Germany were unified by states, Piedmont and Prussia respectively, that were less economically advanced than some of the other states they unified, but that had strong martial traditions and had advanced political-military development the most.[70] In these states the social conditions for democracy were less advanced than in other Italian and German states respectively. In particular, there was little democracy understood as a distribution of power across arenas. Aristocratic-military elites in the core might have backed the aristocratic-military elites in these less economically advanced states in order to avoid the emergence of a more powerful state that could become a competitor. Aristocratic-military elites in the core would also have been less alarmed by a unified state built around similar elites as themselves than by one built around a completely different social group, especially if this group was the bourgeoisie that was challenging them in their own countries, and forcing compromises upon aristocratic-military elites.[71] The latter accepted to share power with the emerging bourgeoisie partly because of fear of another revolution like the French Revolution, and partly because it produced wealth and ultimately greater power for themselves too. Thus, the balance of power between states in the modern state system favored a balance of power in society within Italy and Germany that was skewed towards elites, and particularly towards aristocratic-military elites. This is an additional factor contributing to dictatorship that predisposed Italy to uneven development, and also to especially negative effects for democracy of introducing capitalism from above.

The uneven development across arenas characterized by an overly powerful political-military arena led to uneven development within the political-military arena, and also within the economic arena, for the following reasons. In the case

---

70   I draw this point from Philip Gorski, who has emphasized that Prussia was poorer and less powerful than other German states. Prussia's economy was largely agrarian: Gorski, *The Disciplinary Revolution.* Gorski describes in his book what is arguably a cultural revolution from above, or a cultural revolution accentuated and exploited from above.

71   On class alliances, see: Nicos Poulantzas, *Classes in Contemporary Capitalism,* trans. David Fernbach, reprint ed. (Verso, 2018). Arrighi addresses how class alliances change with changing opportunities for investment: Arrighi, *The Long Twentieth Century.*

of the Piedmontese aristocratic-military elite, it enjoyed a marked collective action advantage compared to the masses from the very beginning, and this entailed that there was little political-military democracy. It could therefore introduce capitalism from above in such a manner as to maintain this advantage. The aristocratic-military elite could dictate its own terms to the masses, as well as the bourgeoisie, when it introduced capitalism. Uneven economic development in the south of the country had already created a situation in which some social groups lost cohesiveness and underwent disaggregation, producing an underclass of individuals in shifting employment, including shifting military employment. In the south disaggregation led to many thousands of volunteers who joined Garibaldi and contributed to the conquest of the Kingdom of Naples by the Piedmontese elite. Most of them were disbanded after this conquest, receiving little or nothing in return for their efforts, not even better social conditions in the south, which became part of a Kingdom of Italy dominated heavily by the Piedmontese elite, not an Italian Republic. The political-military power of the Piedmontese elite enabled them to impose their own agenda, including economic policies that favored them the most at the expense of other parts of the country. This had lasting negative effects upon Italy, especially upon southern Italy, and to some extend upon central Italy too.

Let us consider now the *effects upon states in the second geopolitical band of uneven political-military development across countries*. These were different than the effects upon states in the first geopolitical band. Further away, in the second geopolitical band and at the far frontier, there were territorial empires, the Habsburg, Ottoman, and Romanov empires. In this case, revolution from above, specifically the introduction of capitalism from above, did not produce dictatorship, but breakup at first, and later dictatorship. In addition to encouraging aristocratic-military elites in these areas, the splinter states were arguably treated in a manner similar to indirect rule.[72] For reasons of space,

---

72 The Mandates in Lebanon, Israel/Palestine, Syria, Transjordan, and Iraq were effectively colonial tutelage over the successor states created in the Middle East from the breakup of the Ottoman empire. On the Mandate period in these countries, see: Roza El-Eini, *Mandated Landscape: British Imperial Rule in Palestine, 1929–1948* (London and New York: Routledge, 2004); Peter Sluglett, *Britain in Iraq: Contriving King and Country, 1914–1932* (New York: Columbia University Press, 2007); Idir Ouahes, *Syria and Lebanon under the French Mandate: Cultural Imperialism and the Workings of Empire* (London and New York: I. B. Tauris, 2018). Harrison B. Guthorn, *Capital Development: Mandate Era Amman and the Construction of the Hashemite State (1921–1946)* (London: Gingko Library, 2021). On the role of violence in crushing dissent in the mandate states, see: Daniel Neep, *Occupying Syria under the French Mandate: Insurgency, Space and State Formation* (Cambridge and New York: Cambridge University Press, 2012). Local elites, often in continuity with Ottoman times, still played an important role: Philip Shukry Khoury, *Syria*

I focus only upon the Ottoman empire, and below I draw attention to the similarities with southern Italy, which in many ways belonged, and in some ways still belongs, to the periphery of the world system, and after Italian unification constituted an internal periphery.

In the Ottoman empire, similarly to Italy, there were clear efforts to carry out a revolution from above and introduce both an advanced military and capitalism. In the course of the nineteenth century, with the Tanzimat reforms, the Ottoman empire sought to further advance and to take charge of this process, by introducing laws that created a modern army and laws that advanced markets.[73] It hoped to set up a virtuous circle whereby economic development created also the wealth that would finance political-military development and enable it not to be conquered by north-western European states. Showing a remarkable understanding for its times of the importance of nationalism, it also sought to introduce Ottomanism, an Ottoman nationalism that would have increased both political-military development, through attachment to the Ottoman state, and also cultural development.[74] Yet within half a century of introducing these reforms the Ottoman empire broke up. The Habsburg empire similarly broke up as it was introducing reforms that included capitalism. The Romanov empire was seized by revolutionary forces from within, and narrowly avoided breakup, only to break up some 70 years later. Breakup was always due to a combination of interstate and social conflict. Interstate conflict, as pointed out by Skocpol for Russia, was very important. For example,

---

and the French Mandate: The Politics of Arab Nationalism, 1920–1945 (Princeton and Oxford: Princeton University Press, 2014). The mandate period had an important impact on the built environment, a point discussed by: El-Eini, Mandated Landscape; Guthorn, Capital Development.

73   For an overview of the reform period, known as Tanzimat, see: Donald Quataert, "The Age of Reforms, 1812–1914," in An Economic and Social History of the Ottoman Empire. Volume Two: 1600–1914, ed. Halil İnalcık and Donald Quataert (Cambridge and New York: Cambridge University Press, 1994). Davison's book on the Tanzimat reforms is a classic: Roderic H. Davison, Reform in the Ottoman Empire, 1856–1876 (Princeton and Oxford: Princeton University Press, 2015). It was first published in 1963. There are interesting studies of cities and local elites during the reform period: Yonca Köksal, The Ottoman Empire in the Tanzimat Era: Provincial Perspectives from Ankara to Edirne (London and New York: Routledge, 2019). John K. Bragg, Ottoman Notables and Participatory Politics: Tanzimat Reform in Tokat, 1839–1876 (London and New York: Routldge, 2014).

74   Ottomanism competed with Arabism, a pan-Arab nationalism, and with Islamism: Hasan Kayali, Arabs and Young Turks: Ottomanism, Arabism, and Islamism in the Ottoman Empire, 1908–1918 (Berkeley and Los Angeles: University of California Press, 1997). On Ottomanism in a comparative perspective, see the many contributions in: Johanna Chovanec and Olof Heilo, eds., Narrated Empires: Perceptions of Late Habsburg and Ottoman Multinationalism (Cham, Switzerland: Springer, 2021).

defeat in the First World War led to the breakup of the Ottoman empire, but this breakup was facilitated by heightened social conflict within it, which was exploited by imperialist elites.

However important, interstate conflict was not sufficient on its own, and breakup was due to its interaction with social conflict, heightened by the introduction and subsequent expansion of capitalism, in a process similar in some respects to the conquest of large and powerful states in Asia, notably India and China, whereby trade laid the ground for later conquest. The efforts to reform the Ottoman state and expand capitalism took place against the backdrop of an already advanced agrarian and mercantile capitalism in some areas, in particular the Balkan and Levantine provinces of the Ottoman empire. Much of the Mediterranean was being drawn into international markets dominated by the emerging industrial economies, France and Great Britain, and local notables turned into a mercantile bourgeoisie and agrarian capitalist class, cooperating with French and British merchants in exporting raw material to industrial economies.[75] It is debatable whether the external trade of the areas being drawn into international trade surpassed the internal trade, in addition to the fact that local merchants were involved in both of these trades. The important point is that the expanding external trade included mass produced goods, and this had a great impact on social change, at least in some parts of the Mediterranean, including Sicily and the Balkan and Levantine provinces of the Ottoman empire.[76] Sicily and other parts of southern Italy were also being drawn into the expanding international markets. There was a similar expansion of trade between *the Balkan provinces of the Ottoman empire* and Europe, particularly France and Great Britain, and also to some extent the Habsburg

---

75   There was expansion of trade with the West and the emergence of capitalist agriculture: Sevket Pamuk, *The Ottoman Empire and European Capitalism, 1820–1913: Trade, Investment and Production* (Cambridge and New York: Cambridge University Press, 1987). On the expansion of trade between the West and Istanbul, the center of power of the Ottoman empire, see: Edhem Eldem, *French Trade in Istanbul in the Eighteenth Century* (Leiden and Boston: Brill, 1999). Fariba Zarinebaf, *Mediterranean Encounters: Trade and Pluralism in Early Modern Galata* (Oakland, California: University of California Press, 2018).

76   This was part of an expansion of internal trade driven by local agents: Bruce McGowan, "The Age of the Ayans," in *An Economic and Social History of the Ottoman Empire. Volume Two:1600–1914*, ed. Halil İnalcık and Donald Quataert (Cambridge and New York: Cambridge University Press, 1994). The expansion of trade coincided with the introduction of capitalism, and the export of cheap European industrially-produced textiles altered local production and local trade: Huri Islamogu-Inan and Caglar Keyder, in *The Ottoman Empire and the World-Economy*, ed. Huri Islamogu-Inan (Cambridge and New York: Cambridge University Press, 2004). See also the other contributions in this edited volume.

empire. This trade used Greek Orthodox merchants who traded with the interior of the country and sold goods to European merchants in port cities.[77] There was also a similar expansion of trade between Europe and *the Levantine provinces* of the Ottoman empire during the eighteenth century and the first half of the nineteenth century. This trade similarly used Christian merchants, whether Maronite, Syrian Christian, or Greek Orthodox merchants, who similarly traded with the interior of the country and sold goods to European merchants in port cities.[78]

All these are cases of *incorporation in the world system*, whereby areas were being turned into the periphery of this system, through the creation of large farms that catered to international markets. The mechanism involved in incorporation was slightly different and more complex than envisaged by World Systems Theory.[79] Even when considering only incorporation in the world economy, it is necessary to emphasize broader changes than just changes in economic organizations. The latter were undoubtedly important. One aspect of these changes was *the emergence of large farms and heightened conflict in the countryside*. In Italy large farms known as *latifondi* emerged that made use of agricultural laborers. This led to the emergence of deep economic grievances that were to lead parts of the population to support Italian unification in the hope that the new state would redress their grievances.[80] In the Ottoman

---

77   There was one wave of trade globalization in 1820–70: Giovanni Federico and Antonio Tena-Junguito, "A Tale of Two Globalizations: Gains from Trade and Openness 1800–2010," *Review of World economics* 153, no. 3 (2017). On trade in the Balkans, see: Trajan Stoianovich, "The Conquering Balkan Orthodox Merchant," *The Journal of Economic History* 20, no. 2 (1960).

78   On trade alongside the Levantine coast and the role of international and local elites, see: Richard Van Leeuwen, *Notables and Clergy in Mount Lebanon: The Khāzin Sheikhs and the Maronite Church, 1736–1840* (Leiden and Boston: Brill, 1994). Beshara Doumani, *Rediscovering Palestine: Merchants and Peasants in Jabal Nablus, 1700–1900* (Berkeley, Los Angeles, and London: University of California Press, 1995). This trade reached into the interior, at least as far as Damascus: James A Reilly, "Damascus Merchants and Trade in the Transition to Capitalism," *Canadian Journal of history/Annales canadiennes d'histoire* 27, no. 1 (1992).

79   The World Systems Theory approach to the Ottoman empire was set out in: Immanuel Maurice Wallerstein, "The Ottoman Empire and the Capitalist World-Economy: Some Questions for Research," *Review (Fernand Braudel Center)* 2, no. 3 (1979). There is a literature on this topic: Kasaba, *The Ottoman Empire and the World Economy*; Huri Islamogu-Inan, ed. *The Ottoman Empire and the World-Economy* (Cambridge and New York: Cambridge University Press, 2004).

80   For a review of the importance of latifundia in Sicilian history and their ties to migration, see: John Paul Russo, "The Sicilian Latifundia," *Italian Americana* 17, no. 1 (1999). Riall has pointed to the importance of discontent to rural unrest in Sicily and to Garibaldi's expedition: Lucy Riall, *Sicily and the Unification of Italy: Liberal Policy and Local Power, 1859–1866*

empire the expansion of external trade was associated with the emergence of large farms known as *çiftliks* in the Anatolian provinces of the Ottoman empire, corresponding to modern day Turkey, and to some extent also in the Balkans and the Levant, accompanied by the impoverishment of peasants, who were turned into agricultural laborers.[81] Sharecropping, the arrangement whereby a peasant family lived in a small farm that it cultivated in exchange for paying a share of its crop to the landowner, tended to disappear, although not as fast and uniformly as World Systems Theory assumed, since sharecropping was adaptable enough to survive, although it is typically associated with small farms and less capital investment and technological innovation.[82]

As part of incorporation in the world economy, there were also *the emergence of port cities and new urban neighborhoods, and heightened urban conflict*, all part of an expansion in physical and social infrastructure. Small Levantine towns alongside the coast were turned into thriving port cities engaged in trade with the interior, importing European industrial goods, and exporting agricultural raw materials.[83] This expansion in infrastructure led also to the creation of new neighborhoods in old cities, with local merchants in this trade, and sometimes to Ottoman outposts built for defense that were engaged in

---

(Oxford: Clarendon Press, 1998). Latifundia were associated with a skewed distribution of power in markets: Pablo Martinelli, "Latifundia Revisited: Market Power, Land Inequality and Agricultural Efficiency. Evidence from Interwar Italian Agriculture," *Explorations in Economic History* 54 (2014).

81   The edited volume by Keyder and Tabak was a landmark book for the study of large farms in the Ottoman empire: Caglar Keyder and Faruk Tabak, eds., *Landholding and Commercial Agriculture in the Middle East: Globalization, Revolution, and Popular Culture* (Albany: State University of New York Press, 1991).

82   For an overview of sharecropping in France and Italy, with the addition of the interesting case of California, see: Ulf Jonsson, "The Paradox of Share Tenancy under Capitalism: A Comparative Perspective on Late Nineteenth-and Twentieth-Century French and Italian Sharecropping," *Rural History* 3, no. 2 (1992). Some Italian towns like Casalecchio, just outside Bologna, saw the decline of sharecropping and the emergence of rural capitalism, together with migration to the city during the nineteenth century: David I. Kertzer and Dennis P. Hogan, *Family, Political Economy, and Demographic Change: The Transformation of Life in Casalecchio, Italy, 1861–1921* (Madison, Wisconsin: University of Wisconsin Press, 1989). There might have been even earlier roots of this phenomenon: Domenico Sella, "Household, Land Tenure, and Occupation in North Italy in the Late XVIth Century," *Journal of European Economic History* 16, no. 3 (1987).

83   For an overview of the expansion of port cities, see: Çaglar Keyder, Y. Eyüp Ozveren, and Donald Quataert, "Port-Cities in the Ottoman Empire: Some Theoretical and Historical Perspectives," *Review (Fernand Braudel Center)* 16, no. 4 (1993); Caglar Keyder, "Peripheral Port-Cities and Politics on the Eve of the Great War," *New Perspectives on Turkey* 20 (1999). On the expansion of Beirut, see: Leila Tarazi Fawaz, *Merchants and Migrants in Nineteenth-Century Beirut* (Harvard University Press: Cambridge, Massachusetts and London, 1983).

the caravan trade with the interior.[84] This expansion was associated with the impoverishment of artisans and entire craft guilds, and massive migration, as happened both in the Ottoman empire and Italy. This is because the export to the Levant of textiles produced in north-western Europe with modern industrial machinery impoverished local craftsmen producing textiles, at the same time as the Tanzimat reforms were removing their privileges.[85]

Together with the heightened social conflict, whether in rural or urban areas, there was also the emergence of new forms of conflict, associated with anonymous interactions and crowd behavior. Crowd behavior, in social conflict, led to rioting in areas affected by accelerated urbanization, including expanding port cities, and new neighborhoods in Damascus, all affected by anonymous interaction and the volatile conditions associated with crowd behavior. This is what lead to the wave of riots in the Middle East and northern India in the 1850s, stretching till the 1880s.[86] They were all part of social disaggregation lower down social hierarchies of power, whereby some social groups, mostly peasants who were sharecroppers, and artisans in traditional craft guilds, were impoverished, losing both what little economic capital they had, and all social capital and community. As a result, entire social groups lost cohesion and were caught in poverty and violence traps. The overall picture is that, with the introduction of capitalism, there was initially much hardship, together with social disaggregation and also diffuse violence, whether in the form of banditry or crime. *Southern Italy, the Balkans, and the Levant are clear cases* in which social disaggregation led to conditions that undermined development, because of the violence that became endemic at some times and places in these regions. This violence undermined development both directly

---

84   Linda Schatkowski Schilcher, *Families in Politics: Damascene Factions and Estates of the 18th and 19th Centuries* (Stuttgart: Franz Steiner Verlag, 1985). On the expansion of physical infrastructure, see the many contributions in: Thomas Philipp and Birgit Schäbler, eds., *The Syrian Land: Processes of Integration and Fragmentation: Bilād Al-Shām from the 18th to the 20th Century* (Stuttgart: Franz Steiner Verlag, 1998).

85   Reilly has focused on the impoverishment of artisans or craft workers in Lebanese and Syrian cities, and also of small farmers in the hinterlands of these cities, as well as on social and military conflict: Reilly, "From Workshops to Sweatshops: Damascus Textiles and the World-Economy in the Last Ottoman Century." Reilly placed these trends within the history of the Middle East, and in particular of the Levant: *The Ottoman Cities of Lebanon: Historical Legacy and Identity in the Modern Middle East* (London and New York: I. B. Tauris, 2016). *Fragile Nation, Shattered Land: The Modern History of Syria* (London and New York: I.B.Tauris, 2019).

86   Schilcher, *Families in Politics*. The historical study of crowd behavior was pioneered by: George F. E. Rudé, *The Crowd in History: A Study of Popular Disturbances in France and England, 1730–1848* (London: Serif, 1995). This book was first published in 1964.

and through social conditions favoring dictatorship and undermining democracy, which further undermined development. The mechanism involved social disaggregation, which gave rise to large numbers of bandits, sometimes in the shifting military employment of local rulers in the Ottoman empire. It also led to the emergence of the conditions for nationalism that included the beginnings of national identity that led to the independence of Serbia and Greece, and in Italy to the formation of large forces of volunteers, Garibaldi's redshirts and later Mussolini's blackshirts.

4   The Effects of Conflict on Hegemony outside the Core

The projection of power altered the outcomes of conflict outside the core and in order to be able to conceptualize this effect we have to formulate a better classification of the outcomes of conflict than the EVL model, since the latter is too limited. The following refined categories compared to exit, voice, and loyalty, serve to conceptualize the manner in which the balance of power in the state system due to uneven political-military development, sometimes compounded by uneven economic development across countries, alters the balance of power in society. In combination with social disaggregation, this can strengthen aristocratic-military elites in various ways, and lead to many problems of development and democracy. Here I begin by revising the EVL model by focusing on the outcomes of conflict. The EVL model lends itself to describe the outcomes of combinations of social and interstate conflict, specifically conflict between on the one hand states, and on the other hand social movements and political parties seeking exit, voice, or loyalty. The EVL model is however incomplete, and it is useful to extend the EVL model by taking into consideration a number of more specific outcomes of social and interstate conflict.[87] Table 5 presents a generalized form of the EVL model with more outcomes of conflict.

The columns in this table represent *more specific outcomes than exit, voice, and loyalty,* for conflict involving contention between states and social movements and political parties within them, focusing on the success of the

---

87   Hirschman, *Exit, Voice, and Loyalty.* Hirschman's EVL model has generated several interesting applications that also nuanced this model: Steven Pfaff and Hyojoung Kim, "Exit-Voice Dynamics in Collective Action: An Analysis of Emigration and Protest in the East German Revolution," *American Journal of Sociology* 109, no. 2 (2003); Sarah Gammage, "Exercising Exit, Voice and Loyalty: A Gender Perspective on Transnationalism in Haiti," *Development and Change* 35, no. 4 (2004).

TABLE 5   Outcomes of social and interstate conflict

		Outcome of conflict		
		Exit	Voice	Loyalty
Decisiveness	*Clear-cut*	Independence	Democracy	Social status quo
of outcome	*Protracted*	Irredentism	Revolution	Domination
	Undecided	Ethnic strife	Social banditry	Wretched conditions

movements and parties seeking the outcomes exit, voice, and loyalty.[88] This table classifies conflict, and at the same time begins to provide *a possible explanation for the different outcomes of conflict.* The columns in Table 5 represent an increasingly skewed balance of power in society, which can be affected by the state system. This balance of power depends upon internal conditions that influence whether social movements are sufficiently strong to achieve exit or voice, so that the balance of power might influence whether these social movements seek exit, voice, or loyalty. Factors external to a state might also influence whether exit, voice, or loyalty are pursued. Culture, especially national culture, influences whether movements seek exit or voice, because it influences how committed social movements are to a state. Interstate conflict might stoke up differences and lead some movements to seek independence, with the help of other states. Other states might also intervene and decide the outcomes of social conflict. As a result of these factors, and also as a result of sequences of events in which other states might intervene, there can be different outcomes, which can be more or less clear-cut.

---

88   Hirschman's EVL model also generated a literature dealing with this model: Albert O. Hirschman, "'Exit, Voice, and Loyalty': Further Reflections and a Survey of Recent Contributions," *Social Science Information* 13, no. 1 (1974). In subsequent years, this literature was summarized by: David M. Saunders, "Introduction to Research on Hirschman's Exit, Voice, and Loyalty Model," *Employee Responsibilities and Rights Journal* 5, no. 3 (1992); Keith Dowding et al., "Exit, Voice and Loyalty: Analytic and Empirical Developments," *European Journal of Political Research* 37, no. 4 (2000). There have been calls for revising and applying Hirschman's models to international migration: Bert Hoffmann, "Bringing Hirschman Back in: 'Exit,' 'Voice,' and 'Loyalty' in the Politics of Transnational Migration," *The Latin Americanist* 54, no. 2 (2010).

The rows in Table 5 represent outcomes that are clear-cut, other outcomes that are less clear-cut and associated with more protracted conflict, all the way to undecided conflict with no end in sight. More than one such conflict might affect a country at any one time. Moving down the rows represents conflict of increasing duration, just like moving down the columns represents a balance of power that is more skewed in favor of one side. *The first row shows clear-cut outcomes*, in which conflict results in the outcomes independence, democracy, or social status quo within a country, corresponding respectively to exit, voice, and loyalty. These are the most obvious outcomes for contention between states and social movements. Here I just want to add that there might be cycles of conflict, in which social movements continue demanding democracy, after the movements achieve some democracy, while remaining committed to the state and without engaging in violence. The other two rows represent outcomes that are not so clear-cut, in which there is a long period of conflict, involving violence to a greater or lesser extent, that can leave a deep mark on a country.

The second row shows outcomes associated with protracted conflict and much violence. In this case, exit, voice, and loyalty take the form respectively of irredentism, revolution, and domination. *Irredentism* is a name derived from the Risorgimento, Italy's protracted struggle for national unification, that is applicable also to other cases in which a new state is formed, but neighboring states contain large numbers of co-nationals, and the state and movements and parties aligned with it, all engage with neighboring states in a protracted conflict that includes ethnic conflict, in order to annex areas with many co-nationals that the state deems *irredente*, or unredeemed, because still subject to foreign rule.[89] *Revolution* is another outcome associated with protracted conflict that is not clear-cut. In this outcome, social forces seeking to achieve voice engage in a long and violent conflict in which voice is not granted, and some social movements therefore resort to violence in order to gain control of the state. Revolution is a long-drawn out process, typically without a clear outcome

---

89   An early instance of interest in the concept of irredentism in English-language scholarship was the edited volume: Naomi Chazan, ed. *Irredentism and International Politics* (Boulder: Lynne Rienner, 1991). An application of the concept of irredentism to the post-Cold War world, including Yugoslavia, is provided by: Thomas Ambrosio, *Irredentism: Ethnic Conflict and International Politics* (Westport, Connecticut, and London: Praeger, 2001). Kornprobst provides an overview of irredentism in European history with a focus on the two very interesting cases of German and Irish irredentism: Markus Kornprobst, *Irredentism in European Politics: Argumentation, Compromise and Norms* (Cambridge and London: Cambridge University Press, 2008).

for a long time, as there are cycles of revolution and reaction.[90] For example, between the French Revolution of 1789 and the formation of the modern French Republic in 1870, there were Napoleon's dictatorship and the very bloody Napoleonic Wars, with the restoration of the monarchy in their wake, followed by a Second Republic and a second dictatorship under Napoleon III.[91] *Domination* is an outcome in which some social groups are largely or completely dominated by the state, because they are incapable of deliberate and sustained collective action. This results in neither exit nor voice, not even loyalty. These social groups do not accept the domination they are subjected to, and are thus not loyal, and could rebel if international conditions change.

Since irredentism is little studied compared to revolutions, yet very important, I want to describe it in greater detail. *Irredentism is associated with especially harmful mixes of interstate and social conflict*, in which protracted interstate conflict stokes up social conflict, which takes the form of ethnic conflict that leads to ethnic cleansing. The Risorgimento began in the 1820s, with the Carbonari and the first insurrectionary movements, leading to the creation of a unified Italian state by 1861.[92] However, important parts in the north-east of Italy remained unredeemed and were the object of a protracted conflict lasting nearly 85 years. In particular, Trieste remained under the Habsburg empire until 1918, when it joined Italy as a result of Italy's participation in the First World War on the side of Great Britain and France.[93] So did Istria, a small peninsula just south-east of Trieste, were large numbers of the population, although not a majority, considered themselves Italian. Some Italian nationalists, led by

90   I derive this view from my reading of Gramsci's work, and I will address this topic in the book on the theory of history that is part of this project.

91   For a review of these developments, see: Pamela Pilbeam, *Republicanism in Nineteenth-Century France, 1814–1871* (Houndmills, Basingstoke, Hampshire, and London: Macmillan, 1995). An overview of French history during the nineteenth century is provided by: Robert Tombs, *France, 1814–1914* (London and New York: Routledge, 1996). The social changes behind these developments are detailed in: Roger Price, *A Social History of Nineteenth-Century France* (London and New York: Routledge, 2021).

92   On the Risorgimento, see: Lucy Riall, *The Italian Risorgimento: State, Society and National Unification*, Historical Connections (New York and London: Routledge, 2002); Beales and Biagini, *The Risorgimento and the Unification of Italy*.

93   Trieste changed from being a cosmopolitan city in the Habsburg empire to being part of Italy, a change detailed in: Maura Hametz, *Making Trieste Italian, 1918–1954*, Royal Historical Society (Woodbridge, Suffolk, and Rochester, New York: Boydell Press, 2005). Irredentism at some point intertwined with fascism, which left a mark on both the culture and the landscape of Triste: Fabio Capano, "From a Cosmopolitan to a Fascist Land: Adriatic Irredentism in Motion," *Nationalities Papers* 46, no. 6 (2018); Borut Klabjan, "Erecting Fascism: Nation, Identity, and Space in Trieste in the First Half of the Twentieth Century," ibid. By contrast, Hametz emphasizes civic nationalism in Trieste.

D'Annunzio, tried to annex also Fiume, today called Rijeka, in 1919. Zara, the Italian name of Zadar, the city that is today part of Croatia, was also temporarily annexed.[94] These areas and cities remained contested between Italy and Yugoslavia, the successor state of the Habsburg and Ottoman empires in these areas. In the wake of violence and massacres by fascists and Yugoslav nationalists, an early form of ethnic cleansing that resulted in the *foibe* massacres of Italians, Istria and Zara were permanently given to Yugoslavia.[95] Greece lived through an even longer and more violent irredentism. Greece was first formed as an independent state by secession from the Ottoman empire during a protracted war that lasted from 1821 to 1832, which was won with the intervention of Great Britain and France on the side of Greek nationalists, so that Greece had to accept as ruler a king from an aristocratic house close to the royal house of Great Britain.[96] The modern Greek state, initially only including southern Greece, emerged over the next decades from a protracted struggle that lasted for nearly 100 years, during which there was much violence between Greek and Turkish populations and armed forces, including massacres like the Smyrna massacre, arguably part of ethnic cleansing, which led to the formation of ethnically homogeneous Greek and Turkish states.[97] During those 100 years

---

94   D'Annunzio stoked up irredentism: Milou van Hout, "In Search of the Nation in Fiume: Irredentism, Cultural Nationalism, Borderlands," *Nations and Nationalism* 26, no. 3 (2020). Interestingly, tourism seems to have played a similar role: Maura Hametz, "Replacing Venice in the Adriatic: Tourism and Italian Irredentism, 1880–1936," *Journal of Tourism History* 6, no. 2–3 (2014).

95   Gaia Baracetti, "Foibe: Nationalism, Revenge and Ideology in Venezia Giulia and Istria, 1943—5," *Journal of Contemporary History* 44, no. 4 (2009). Large numbers of Italians fled these areas: Gustavo Corni, "The Exodus of Italians from Istria and Dalmatia, 1945–56," in *The Disentanglement of Populations*, ed. Jessica Reinisch and Elizabeth White (London and New York: Palgrave Macmillan, 2011).

96   Douglas Dakin, *The Greek Struggle for Independence, 1821–1833* (Berkeley and Los Angeles: University of California Press, 1973); Mark Mazower, *The Greek Revolution: 1821 and the Making of Modern Europe* (New York: Penguin, 2021). On Prince Philip, part pf the Greek Monarchy, see: Constantinos Lagos and John Carr, *Philip, Prince of Greece: The Duke of Edinburgh's Early Life and the Greek Succession* (Barnsley, South Yorkshire, and Haverton, Pennsylvania: Pen & Sword History, 2021).

97   John S. Koliopoulos and Thanos M. Veremis, *Modern Greece: A History since 1821* (Chichester, West Sussex: Wiley-Blackwell, 2009). On the wars fought by Greece during this period, see: Richard C. Hall, *The Balkan Wars, 1912–1913: Prelude to the First World War* (London and New York: Routledge, 2002); Konstantinos Travlos, ed. *Salvation and Catastrophe: The Greek-Turkish War, 1919–1922* (Lanham, Maryland: Lexington Books, 2020). There were also important revolts: Pinar Senisik, *The Transformation of Ottoman Crete: Revolts, Politics and Identity in the Late Nineteenth Century* (London: I. B. Tauris, 2011). Greek irredentism also aimed at incorporating parts of the Middle East: Paschalis M. Kitromilides, "Greek Irredentism in Asia Minor and Cyprus," *Middle Eastern Studies* 26, no. 1 (1990).

the Greek state expanded by successive conquests during a series of wars that stoked up ethnic conflict, until the collapse of the Ottoman empire in 1918.

The third row shows outcomes associated with undecided conflict, or conflict without an outcome, that is, conflict so protracted that it remains for all intents and purposes undecided. Diffuse *ethnic strife* is a type of undecided conflict that is associated with separatism and results in many and frequent acts of violence across divisions between ethnic groups. In the long struggle for a modern Greek state there was both irredentism with the direct participation of the Greek state, and also diffuse ethnic strife involving irregular forces, the *klephts*, who participated in irredentism, hence the official status that they achieved, and other times acted exclusively through their own raids, which stoked up ethnic conflict, and bordered on criminality.[98] *Social banditry* was banditry by similar groups to the *klephts*, that were active however in social conflict without an ethnic dimension, participating mostly in conflict between social classes. The expression social bandits was promoted in modern social science by historian Eric Hobsbawm, who focused on class conflict that did not take the dimensions of an outright class war.[99] The ties between bandits and states could be variable. In Greece the klephts had ties to the emerging Greek state, whereas in Italy they were part of a reaction against the Italian state.[100] In the long struggle for a modern Italian state, Garibaldi achieved a swift and successful outcome in the south of the country with the conquest of the whole Kingdom of Naples in southern Italy, during a short military campaign in 1860–61.[101] But the social grievances of large numbers of the population

---

98   Koliopoulos describes a distinctive military class that lived between brigandage and pastoralism: John S. Koliopoulos, "Brigandage and Irredentism in Nineteenth-Century Greece," *European History Quarterly* 19, no. 2 (1989). Their image has changed over time: Gerassimos Karabelias, "From National Heroes to National Villains: Bandits, Pirates and the Formation of Modern Greece," in *Subalterns and Social Protest*, ed. Stephanie Cronin (London and New York: Routledge, 2012).

99   Eric J. Hobsbawm, *Bandits* (London: Abacus, 2001). This book was first published in 1969. It complements Hobsbawm's research on understudied types of revolt: *Primitive Rebels* (London: Abacus, 2017). This book was first published in 1971. For a review of debates on this topic, see: Slatta Richard, "Eric J. Hobsbawm's Social Bandit: A Critique and Revision," *A Contracorriente* 1, no. 2 (2004).

100   Victor Roudometof, *Nationalism, Globalization, and Orthodoxy: The Social Origins of Ethnic Conflict in the Balkans* (Westport, Connecticut: Greenwood Press, 2001). The state also used different mechanisms of repression: Baris Cayli, "Peasants, Bandits, and State Intervention: The Consolidation of Authority in the Ottoman Balkans and Southern Italy," *Journal of Agrarian Change* 18, no. 2 (2018).

101   Garibaldi's biographies describe the swiftness of his campaigns. The Kingdom of Naples, after the restoration in the wake of the Napoleonic Wars, had been re-united with Sicily and renamed the Kingdom of the Two Sicilies.

went unaddressed, as one king replaced another. In the decades 1870–90 there were large groups of social bandits, some fairly well organized and constituting large permanent bands, who scoured the countryside through much of southern Italy, engaging in a protracted low-level war against the newly formed Italian Army.[102] *Wretched conditions* are social conditions in which there is a large reservoir of discontent, but not even the organization present in groups of bandits, just large numbers of individuals subject to complete domination by other social groups. Sometimes these large numbers of individuals live in ghettoes or enclaves with diffuse criminality, and without any community or opportunities for a stable income, all of which destroys their ability to participate in politics.[103] Wretched conditions is a better word than subaltern status to refer to this outcome, and I reserve the word subaltern to refer instead to the social equivalent of subaltern officers in armies, namely, individuals who take part in social movements, but have no initiative in driving social change, and no say in making plans, as they implement plans made by higher-ranking officers or high-ranking politicians. Individuals in wretched conditions do not take part in any social movements, but exclusively in crime, and in occasional outbursts of violence such as riots.[104]

There are important similarities between protracted and undecided conflict. In particular, there are similarities between on the one hand irredentism and revolutions, and on the other hand diffuse ethnic strife and social banditry. Some of these similarities arise from *both conceptual and political-military ties.* Conceptually, the point at which to consider a conflict undecided, as opposed to protracted, that is, the number of years or decades at which one draws the line, is somewhat arbitrary. It is better to conceptualize conflict as moving progressively from clear-cut, to protracted, and on to undecided. Politically

---

102   This point is emphasized in: Andrea Carteny, "Il Brigantaggio in Italia tra Risorgimento e Questione Meridionale: Un'introduzione al Tema," *Chronica Mundi* 11, no. 1 (2016).

103   I borrow the word 'wretched' from Fanon: Frantz Fanon, Homi K. Bhabha, and Jean-Paul Sartre, *The Wretched of the Earth*, trans. Richard Philcox (New York: Grove Atlantic, 2007). Unlike Fanon and Marx, I prefer to speak of wretched conditions, rather than a wretched *lumpenproletariat*. These conditions lead, not to productive social conflict, but to terrorist movements like Boko Haram: William W. Hansen and Umma Aliyu Musa, "Fanon, the Wretched and Boko Haram," *Journal of Asian and African studies* 48, no. 3 (2013).

104   I make this argument in Chapter 6 of: Olsaretti, *The Struggle for Development and Democracy, Vol. 1.* Marx called this group the *lumpenproletariat*. For a critique of this concept, see: Mark Cowling, "Marx's Lumpenproletariat and Murray's Underclass: Concepts Best Abandoned," in *Marx's Eighteenth Brumaire:(Post) Modern Interpretations*, ed. Mark Cowling and James Martin (London: Pluto, 2002). Fanon derived several concepts from his reading of Marx: Nigel C. Gibson, "Fanon and Marx Revisited," *Journal of the British Society for Phenomenology* 51, no. 4 (2020).

and militarily, protracted conflict leads to undecided conflict. The protracted conflict in southern Italy after unification led to greater poverty, contributing to uneven development and to poverty and violence traps, and even greater social disaggregation, as large numbers of individuals lower down social hierarchies were pushed to the margins of society, and ended up participating in activities at the border between what is legal and what is not, some permanently pushed into the criminal underworld, outside of all legality and social life.[105] As the struggle dragged on, the conflict moved from a failed revolution to social banditry, and as the conditions of the masses in southern Italy worsened and the balance of power became even more skewed against them, they moved from social banditry to wretched conditions with much crime, whether petty crime or organized crime. Organized crime, likely in the service of landlords, thrived where there was domination, whereas social banditry and crime, sometimes involving kidnappings, prevailed in the most desperate economic conditions.[106]

There are also important differences between protracted and undecided conflict, although these outcomes share the same social origins. The shared social origins are in social conflict, or conflict between social groups, whether ethnically defined social groups, or economically defined social groups like classes. However, there are very important differences related to values, and ultimately to hegemony. Hobsbawm defined social banditry as different than crime because it has a clear social dimension. Social banditry overlaps with criminality, but is justified in the eyes of part of the population by a social cause.[107] This can be either an ethnic cause, whereby bandits and the social groups they are drawn from have grievances that are fairly widely recognized against a different ethnic group, or a class cause, whereby the grievances are economic and against a different social class. The klephts were irregular forces that shaded

105   Reviews of the literature on brigandage in southern Italy emphasize various factors, including state repression, alongside economic conditions: Alessandro Capone, "Il Brigantaggio Meridionale: una Rassegna Storiografica," *Le Carte e la Storia* 21, no. 2 (2015); Carteny, "Il Brigantaggio in Italia." The protracted violence led to greater poverty, and thus to poverty and violence traps: Pierluigi Ciocca, "Brigantaggio ed Economia nel Mezzogiorno d'Italia, 1860–1870," *Rivista di Storia Economica* 29, no. 1 (2013).

106   Alfredo Del Monte and Luca Pennacchio, "Agricultural Productivity, Banditry and Criminal Organisations in Post-Unification Italy," *Rivista Italiana degli Economisti* 17, no. 3 (2012). Brigandage was also greater where large farms prevailed, and less where small farms prevailed: "Struttura Fondiaria, Brigantaggio e Associazioni Criminali nel Mezzogiorno nei Decenni Post-Unitari," (working paper, Università Parthenope, 2011).

107   Hobsbawm, *Bandits*.

into social bandits with an ethnic-national cause.[108] The difference between protracted and undecided conflict is that in ethnic strife and social banditry, one side is even more militarily powerful than the other, whether because of its sheer size and cohesion, or because of a favorable international conjuncture. This means that both irredentism and revolution are precluded. In addition, the balance of cultural power is also more skewed, and there is no capability to formulate an alternative hegemony, and sometimes not even the ability to articulate grievances. Whereas in social banditry the rebellion might be backed by values, in wretched conditions this inability is even more marked.

Hegemony plays an important part in conflict, both at the level of social groups, and at the level of the state. Gramsci's theory of hegemony suggests that *hegemony is related both to social groups and to the state*, and is thus involved in both social and interstate conflict. It suggests that a hegemonic social group exercises hegemony over allied social groups, and domination over other social groups within the same country, and also that hegemony shapes the state, and is in its turn shaped by it.[109] I add to these insights that there is a dominant hegemony and at times also an alternative hegemony. The *dominant hegemony* is associated with a hegemonic social group that holds most political-military power and cultural power, and is usually at the head of a hegemonic bloc, or bloc of social groups, that includes other social groups allied with it, and that controls the state. The *alternative hegemony* is associated with other social groups yet. Amongst the social groups that are not part of the hegemonic bloc, there are either groups that lack a worldview of their own and do not participate in any hegemonic bloc in any position, or groups that have begun formulating their own worldview, by themselves or through class alliances, and thus participate in an alternative hegemony. This alternative hegemony is sometimes described as a counter-hegemony, a term associated chiefly with work by sociologist William Carroll, but I prefer to use the expression counter-hegemony for different social phenomena.[110] *Hegemony*

---

108   Anscombe describes the common social origins of Albanian bandits and Ottoman irregular forces active in the Balkans: Frederick Anscombe, "Albanians and 'Mountain Bandits'," in *The Ottoman Balkans, 1750–1830, Pp 87–114*, ed. Frederick Anscombe (Princeton, New Jersey: Markus Wiener Publishers, 2006). Greek bandits still retained some social ties, as entire kinship groups or parts of kinship groups were part of bands of bandits: Thomas W Gallant, "Greek Bandits: Lone Wolves or a Family Affair?," *Journal of Modern Greek Studies* 6, no. 2 (1988).

109   I make this argument in Chapter 6 of: Olsaretti, *The Struggle for Development and Democracy, Vol. 1.*

110   William K. Carroll, "Hegemony, Counter-Hegemony, Anti-Hegemony," *Socialist Studies/ Études Socialistes* 1, no. 3 (2006). The concept has been applied to the study of social movements: William K. Carroll and Robert S. Ratner, "Between Leninism and Radical

relates to productive social conflict that contributes to both development and democracy. There is productive social conflict only in cases in which an alternative *hegemony* engages in conflict with a dominant hegemony. This applies also to the orderly process of democratization studied by Tilly, a process that involves social groups in showing their worthiness, unity, numbers, and commitment, and thus in convincing other social groups and the state to redress their grievances.[111] Participating in an alternative hegemony, and having one's own philosophy or worldview, enables social groups to articulate their grievances and to pursue them in an orderly manner, through deliberate and sustained collective action, and also through dialogue with other social groups. It is thus a prerequisite for productive social conflict, including democratization, whereas dominated social groups and social groups that have undergone disaggregation engage only in random acts of violence and occasional rioting, and are incapable of pursuing any political goals, on their own, or in dialogue with other social groups.

The role of hegemony in the outcomes of social and interstate conflict introduced above is illustrated by Table 6 below, which summarizes how each of the outcomes of conflict is related to hegemony. I focus upon the dominant hegemony and its relation to the country and the state that rules over it. Here I begin by considering the cases that are not highlighted in grey, all of which are cases in which there is no hegemony, only domination and similar outcomes in which one side is incapable of articulating grievances and pursuing them through deliberate and sustained collective action. The following are all *outcomes that do not involve hegemony* in Table 6, and thus cannot lead to productive social conflict. In the case of domination, one group is dominated by another through sheer political-military power, and does not share

Pluralism: Gramscian Reflections on Counter-Hegemony and the New Social Movements," *Critical Sociology* 20, no. 2 (1994); "Social Movements and Counter-Hegemony: Lessons from the Field," *New Proposals* 4, no. 1 (2010). I followed Carroll's use of the expression counter-hegemony in: Alessandro Olsaretti, "Croce, Philosophy and Intellectuals: Three Aspects of Gramsci's Theory of Hegemony," *Critical Sociology* 42, no. 3 (2016). I explain my use of the expression counter-hegemony below. I use the expression counter-hegemony in order to distinguish this concept from Carroll's, who writes 'counter hegemony' as two separate words, since they refer to two altogether different phenomena.

111   Tilly put forward this argument in: Tilly, *Social Movements, 1768–2004*. It has been shown that all four features of protest in wunc affect the manner in which politicians respond to protest: Ruud Wouters and Stefaan Walgrave, "Demonstrating Power: How Protest Persuades Political Representatives," *American Sociological Review* 82, no. 2 (2017). The four features also affect donations: Erica Bailey et al., "What the wunc? Perceptions of wunc and Social Movement Mobilization" (paper presented at the Academy of Management Proceedings, 2020).

the dominant group's worldview and philosophy, and is unable to produce its own, because it lacks the ability and its own organic intellectuals. In the case of social banditry, there is rebellion against a hegemonic social group and its worldview, which is justified in the eyes of part of the population by values that support the grievances of the social bandits, but there is no ability to produce its own worldview or philosophy, and even little or no ability to articulate these grievances, as the social bandits lack this ability, and typically they also lack ties to intellectuals who could articulate their grievances. In the case of wretched conditions, there is a similar rebellion, but at the level of individuals or very small groups who also lack any justification by values.

By contrast, the cases highlighted in grey in Table 6 are *the cases that involve hegemony.* It is useful to distinguish between cases in which the dominant hegemony is contested or uncontested. *Uncontested hegemony* applies to the case in which the social status quo is maintained. In this case, the groups involved in the conflict all subscribe to the same worldview and philosophy, and all participate in the same hegemony, thus there is no alternative hegemony. The loyalty associated with this case refers to social groups that are part of a hegemonic bloc, and have at most minor grievances that they seek to redress within the bounds of this hegemonic bloc and its worldview and philosophy. The other cases are cases of *contested hegemony*, and they all involve a dominant hegemony and an alternative hegemony. It is important to differentiate in these cases how much of the dominant hegemony is contested, and in particular whether the alternative hegemony contests both the country and the state, or only the state. There are important differences that call for classifying these alternative hegemonies in different categories. Gramsci made a *distinction between cultural and political hegemony.* This is an important distinction that it is useful to spell out in greater detail.[112] The following reformulation builds upon the theory that I propose in this book. Nationalism challenges the project for the country, and then often extends this challenge to the state, and arguably corresponds to a cultural hegemony, that is, an alternative hegemony that arises first in the cultural arena, or that is promoted chiefly by intellectuals, at least initially. Revolutionary ideologies like communism seek instead to change the state, and arguably correspond to a political hegemony only, that is, an alternative hegemony that arises first in the political arena, or is promoted chiefly by politicians and political activists.

---

112   On this distinction, see the entries 'cultura,' and 'egemonia' in: Liguori and Voza, *Dizionario Gramsciano*, 191, 267. The concept of cultural hegemony has been adopted by some historians: T. J. Jackson Lears, "The Concept of Cultural Hegemony: Problems and Possibilities," *The American Historical Review* 90, no. 3 (1985).

TABLE 6   Status of dominant hegemony in the outcomes of social and interstate conflict. The status of hegemony acts as an overlay compared to Table 5, but only in the cases shaded in grey. No hegemony is involved in cases of domination, social banditry, and wretched conditions

		Status of dominant hegemony		
		Contested-country + state	Contested-state	Uncontested
Decisiveness of outcome	Clear-cut	Independence	Democracy	Social status quo
	Protracted	Irredentism	Revolution	Domination
	Undecided	Ethnic strife	Social banditry	Wretched conditions

Cases in the first column are cases in which *the alternative hegemony contests both the country and the state*. These are cases of cultural hegemony, or that start as a project for cultural hegemony, which then takes a political dimension. Typically, the alternative hegemony involves outright rejection of the national project for the country that is pursued by the hegemonic social group, a group that also controls the state, and represents its political project through the language and imagery of nationalism.[113] In the case of *independence*, there is contested hegemony that rejects both the country and the state, and achieves a decisive outcome, thanks also to its ability to articulate grievances, and formulate an alternative hegemony, with a distinctive vision for both the country and the state that attracts wide support. The American War of Independence is arguably an instance of alternative hegemony that included an important component of cultural hegemony from the beginning and that achieved an initial decisive outcome.[114] In the case of *irredentism*, there is less ability to articulate grievances and formulate a successful alternative hegemony, sometimes

---

113   This is the approach to nationalism as hegemony proposed in: Hartman and Olsaretti, "'The First Boat and the First Oar'." In this case, Lebanese nationalists challenged Ottomanism, proposing an alternative local nationalism with the backing of France that was sometimes referred to as Phoenicianism.

114   On cultural hegemony in American history, see: George Lipsitz, "The Struggle for Hegemony," *The Journal of American History* 75, no. 1 (1988); Lee Artz and Bren Ortega

accompanied by difficulties such as a geographically mixed population. The Greek War of Independence is arguably an instance of alternative hegemony that achieved a partial and much protracted outcome.[115]

Cases in the second column are cases in which *the alternative hegemony contests only the state*. These are cases of political hegemony that contests only the state, whereas there is at least partial adherence to the cultural hegemony associated with nationalism, which ensures that the aggrieved social groups remain committed to the country and do not seek to break it up, only to change the state. In the case of *democracy*, there is contested hegemony, and thus both a dominant hegemony and an alternative hegemony, but these two are not so far apart and irreconcilable. Since the social movements or political parties are committed to the country, they seek a voice in running the state, typically to redress economic grievances.[116] In some cases different ethnic groups participate in conflict that leads to democracy, not in order drastically to change the national project, but simply to bring the national project more in line with their interests. In the case of *revolution* there is an alternative political hegemony that contests the dominant hegemony, and is committed to the country but not to the state, and thus seeks to seize the state in order to implement

---

Murphy, *Cultural Hegemony in the United States* (Thousand Oaks, California: Sage Publications, 2000). This cultural hegemony was internal as much as external, and contrasts with Arrighi's use of the word hegemony to refer to external hegemony only: Arrighi, "Hegemony Unravelling."; "Hegemony Unravelling–II."

115   The Phanariot Greeks, elite Greek families in Istanbul with ties to the Ottoman state, remained in some cases committed to the Ottoman state: Christine Philliou, "Communities on the Verge: Unraveling the Phanariot Ascendancy in Ottoman Governance," *Comparative Studies in Society and History* 51, no. 1 (2009). The mutually exclusive Greek and Turkish nationalisms emerged during the course of the nineteenth and early twentieth centuries: Resat Kasaba, "Greek and Turkish Nationalism in Formation: Western Anatolia 1919–1922," *European University Institute Working Papers*, no. 17 (2002); Dimitris Kamouzis, *Greeks in Turkey: Elite Nationalism and Minority Politics in Late Ottoman and Early Republican Istanbul* (London and New York: Routledge, 2020). Before the nineteenth century there had been centuries of coexistence: Nicholas Doumanis, *Before the Nation: Muslim-Christian Coexistence and Its Destruction in Late-Ottoman Anatolia* (Oxford and New York: Oxford University Press, 2012). Some authors have suggested this should be part of an approach to nationalism that studies how nationalism changes over the course of history: John Breuilly, ed. *Bringing History Back into Nationalism?*, New Perspectives on South-East Europe (London and New York: Palgrave Macmillan, 2010). See also the other contributions in this edited volume.

116   This argument is strengthened by the view that there is enduring national diversity within a globalizing economy: John Anthony Hall, "Globalization and Nationalism," *Thesis Eleven* 63, no. 1 (2000). In some cases, a political party like Mexico's PRI ensures commitment to the state: Joy Langston, "Breaking out Is Hard to Do: Exit, Voice, and

change. In this case, there is ability to formulate grievances and pursue them through deliberate and sustained collective action, but the balance of power in society is such that there is great opposition to redressing the grievances at the level of the state, and the groups seeking redressal decide to seize the state in order to obtain redressal. The orderly process of democratization studied by Tilly is impossible.[117] The conflict degenerates into much violence that can last for considerable lengths of time. In these cases, interstate conflict can significantly alter outcomes and make them protracted. Skocpol pointed out that the French and Russian revolutions were both precipitated by interstate conflict that increased grievances and at the same time weakened the state.[118]

The social movements that participate in undecided outcomes, and also the ones that participate in protracted outcomes in which there is much violence, are arguably *systemic movements*. The reason why they are systemic, rather than antisystemic movements, is that they contribute to the dominant hegemony. *The general mechanism involved in these systemic movements is based on disaggregation and diffuse violence.* In the transition to capitalism, a transition that in the periphery was often initiated by trade with north-western European countries, there is often social disaggregation, as a large part of the population, belonging to one of more social groups, is impoverished, is unable to organize, has deep grievances, and constitutes a large reservoir of discontent for protracted and undecided conflict, which continues in numerous and diffuse acts of violence.[119] This has two disastrous effects, both of which prevent the emergence of any antisystemic social movements, and encourage instead systemic movements. Both effects were at work in the *wave of riots that followed the expansion of European trade*, and swept through the Ottoman provinces corresponding to modern-day Lebanon and Syria in the mid-1800s, part of an even

---

Loyalty in Mexico's One-Party Hegemonic Regime," *Latin American Politics & Society* 44, no. 3 (2002). Economic considerations, for example in the form of economic performance that affects elite defection at the time of elections, are still important to hegemony: Ora John Reuter and Jennifer Gandhi, "Economic Performance and Elite Defection from Hegemonic Parties," *British Journal of Political Science* 41, no. 1 (2011).

117   Tilly, *Social Movements.*

118   Skocpol, *States and Social Revolutions.* This book was first published in 1979. Skocpol has collected her later work on the subject and her responses to critics in: *Social Revolutions in the Modern World* (Cambridge and New York: Cambridge University Press, 1994).

119   In Fawaz' reconstruction of the massacres in Mount Lebanon around 1859 there was a considerable role of individuals without strong communal ties in initiating unrest and stoking up conflict, including muleteers, and other individuals who moved from one village to another: Fawaz, *An Occasion for War.* A similar role was played by individuals in the new neighborhood in Damascus tied to internal trade: Schilcher, *Families in Politics.*

larger wave of riots in the Middle East and also northern India that followed
the expansion of trade with Europe, and included also the riots associated with
the First War of Indian Independence.[120]

The first effect is that *disaggregation creates volatile conditions associated
with crowd behavior that can lead to rioting, and can be manipulated by elites.*
Rioting can be manipulated to target other elites, and specific social groups, in a
variety of different ways. For example, the riots against Christians in Damascus
in 1861 were partly aimed against the rising Christian mercantile bourgeoisie.
They were preceded by diffuse violence against Christians in nearby Mount
Lebanon, they were triggered by rumors, and were part of a conflict between
old and new elites that made no difference to the economic grievances of the
population.[121] Rioting can also be manipulated by elites to encourage and justify elite repression of social movements, or foreign intervention, whether the
rioting is initiated by *agents provocateurs* or not. After the riots in the Levant,
France created what was effectively a protectorate in Mount Lebanon, initiating a form of semi-colonial tutelage over the area, that was to last until the
creation of modern Lebanon, whereas Ottoman authorities proceeded with
a stern repression in Damascus, and continued advancing Ottomanism by
emphasizing the threat of violence.[122] The violence against British residents
in India during the First War of Indian Independence similarly lead to very
harsh repression and crimes against Indian troops that surrendered, arguably
a type of racially and politically motivated crime, and eventually led to the
annexation of India to the British Crown.[123] Garibaldi's expedition to conquer

---

120   Cole, "Of Crowds and Empires."

121   Schilcher, *Families in Politics.*

122   The effects of international rivalries on local culture are detailed in: Makdisi, *The
      Culture of Sectarianism.* Institutions were set up to deal with religious and ethnic rival-
      ries that for a time prevented conflict, but unfortunately reinforced sectarianism: Engin
      Deniz Akarli, *The Long Peace: Ottoman Lebanon, 1861–1920* (Berkeley, Los Angeles, and
      London: University of California Press, 1993); Makdisi, *The Culture of Sectarianism.* The
      Ottoman reaction to the riots, and Ottomanism as an ideology of order, both sought to
      deal sternly with the rioters and to set up a more stable modern society: Philip Shukry
      Khoury, *Urban Notables and Arab Nationalism: The Politics of Damascus 1860–1920*
      (Cambridge and New York: Cambridge University Press, 2003).

123   Juan Cole has emphasized that the riots were part of profound social changes initiated
      by trade and conquest, which stoked up religious violence, rather than the effect of reli-
      gion alone: Juan Ricardo Cole, *Roots of North Indian Shiism in Iran and Iraq: Religion
      and State in Awadh, 1722–1859* (Berkeley and Los Angeles: University of California Press,
      1988); *Sacred Space and Holy War: The Politics, Culture and History of Shi'ite Islam* (London
      and New York: I. B. Tauris, 2002). The British reaction against the First War of Indian

southern Italy similarly lead to riots against landlords by aggrieved populations that were harshly repressed. In the case of Italy, the threat of a possible French intervention, had Garibaldi marched on Rome after conquering Naples, led to the intervention of Piedmont ostensibly to prevent further conquests, but effectively resulting in handing over of the Kingdom of Naples to form another kingdom, rather than an Italian Republic.[124]

The second effect is that *disaggregation aggravated by undecided conflict leads to the conditions for violent social movements that often become stable systemic movements manipulated by elites.* In a case in which several elites are in conflict with each other, and there are social disaggregation and diffuse violence associated with banditry and criminality, there are often also large numbers of volunteers, who can be mobilized around an ideology and organization provided by the elites to form violent social movements, and sometimes fairly large and permanent irregular forces, both of which can be said to participate in a *counter-hegemony*, that is, a bogus alternative hegemony that is set up or manipulated by elites in order to buttress their own power, and is used in a manner analogous to counter-insurgency, but specifically in order to counter alternative hegemonies.[125] Counter-hegemony is arguably the continuation or extension, in a society that is undergoing transition to capitalism, of loyalist movements that were used as counter-insurgency forces. Loyalist movements built around an ideology of loyalty to kings that was provided by the Catholic Church were a powerful force in European history. For example, loyalist movements in the Vendee region of France, and in the Calabria region of southern Italy, played a major role in elites' reaction against revolutions. The Vendee provided forces against the French Revolution. In the case of Calabria,

---

Independence / 1857 uprising shaped British rule in India and throughout the British empire: Jill C. Bender, *The 1857 Indian Uprising and the British Empire* (Cambridge and New York: Cambridge University Press, 2016). For European perceptions of this uprising, see: Shaswati Mazumdar, ed. *Insurgent Sepoys: Europe Views the Revolt of 1857* (London and New York: Routledge, 2012). In the period leading up to the revolt and its aftermath, there were institutional changes: Thomas R. Metcalf, *Aftermath of Revolt: India 1857–1970* (Princeton and Oxford: Princeton University Press, 2015). These changes were similar to the institutional changes in Mount Lebanon.

124   Garibaldi's repression of a revolt in Sicily is analyzed by: Lucy Riall, *Under the Volcano: Revolution in a Sicilian Town* (Oxford and New York: Oxford University Press, 2013).

125   I exclusively use 'counter-hegemony' in this sense. This is similar to the expression counter-insurgency, and refers to the manipulation of culture in order to put down social movements. By contrast, Carroll uses the expression counter hegemony to refer to any alternative hegemony, and anti-hegemony to refer to the rejection of all cultural work and organization that are necessary to buttress hegemony: Carroll, "Hegemony, Counter-Hegemony, Anti-Hegemony."

a loyalist movement known as *sanfedisti* played a major role in the suppression of the Neapolitan Republic set up in the wake of the Neapolitan Revolution of 1799.[126]

In at least some cases, *systemic movements are used by the elites as loyalist counter-insurgency forces, in order to repress antisystemic movements*. Later reactionary movements like the francoist forces that started the Spanish Civil War and quashed the First Spanish Republic arguably shared some features with earlier loyalist movements like the *sanfedisti*, including the ideology provided by the Catholic Church.[127] This point is sometimes used as an argument to classify francoism as a loyalist movement that led to a traditional authoritarian regime, and thus different than fascism and nazism, two violent social movements that are seen more as a new type of movement that led to totalitarian regimes.[128] However, the social origins of the irregular forces that sustained

---

126   On the Vendee in the context of the counter-revolution against the French Revolution, see: James Roberts, *The Counter-Revolution in France, 1787–1830* (London, New Delhi, New York, Sydney: Bloomsbury Publishing, 1990). For a popular account of the Vendee Revolt against the French Revolution, see: Robert Harper, *Fighting the French Revolution: The Great Vendée Rising of 1793* (Barnsley, South Yorkshire, and Haverton, Pennsylvania: Pen & Sword Books, 2019). The Neapolitan Revolution of 1799 and its reception in historiography is detailed in: John A. Davis, "The Neapolitan Revolution, 1799–1999: Between History and Myth," *Journal of Modern Italian Studies* 4, no. 3 (1999). John Robertson, "Enlightenment and Revolution: Naples 1799," *Transactions of the Royal Historical Society* 10 (2000). On the *sanfedisti* as part of counter-revolution, see: Antonino De Francesco, "Dal Sanfedismo al Brigantaggio: la Controrivoluzione nel Mezzogiorno d'Italia (1799–1863)," in *Blancs et Contre-Révolutionnaires en Europe. Espaces, Réseaux, Cultures et Mémoires, Fin xviiie-Début xxe Siècles: France, Italie, Espagne, Portugal*, ed. Bruno Dumons and Marco Folin (Rome: Collection de l'École française de Rome, 2011).

127   The Spanish monarchy, despite initial (mild) opposition, came to terms with Francoism: Joseph Dunthorn, "The Spanish Monarchy and Early Francoism: Alternative or Complement?," *Totalitarian Movements and Political Religions* 1, no. 2 (2000). Francoism also relied upon the Catholic Church: Julián Casanova, "Franco, the Catholic Church and the Martyrs," in *The Spanish Civil War: Exhuming a Buried Past*, ed. Anindya Raychaudhuri (Cardiff: University of Wales Press, 2013).

128   Linz argues that Francoism was an authoritarian rather than a totalitarian movement like fascism and nazism: Juan J. Linz, *Totalitarian and Authoritarian Regimes* (Boulder, Colorado, and London: Lynne Rienner Publishers, 2000). This has raised objections: Thomas Jeffrey Miley, "Franquism as Authoritarianism: Juan Linz and His Critics," *Politics, Religion & Ideology* 12, no. 1 (2011). Francoism's reliance upon traditional sources of power have also been emphasized by others. Francoism lacked the reliance on one party and on a totalitarian ideology of fascism and nazism, relying instead upon traditional sources of elite power, the army and the church: Robert Paxton, "Franco's Spain in Comparative Perspective," in *Falange. Las Culturas Políticas del Fascismo en la España de Franco (1939–1975)*, ed. Miguel Ángel Ruiz Carnicer (Zaragoza: Institución Fernando el Católico, 2013).

fascism were in old phenomena associated with social disaggregation that led to banditry, the mafia, and also fascism. Some bandits had no social dimension, and even worked for landlords, or found makeshift employment in the service of landlords.[129] Sicilian bandit Salvatore Giuliano, who became famous for his exploit, which included infamous assassinations of policemen and a massacre of workers, served landlords, rather than the aggrieved masses in Sicily.[130] The Sicilian mafia, and also other mafias in southern Italy, might have started as, or been reinforced by, armed guards on landlords' estates, and early *caporalato*, labour gangs used to coerce agricultural laborers, a task that in the Apulia region, where there were numerous large farms, was taken up by fascist gangs. There was a similar use of fascist gangs on rural estates in northern Italy, where fascists were also used to threaten workers.[131] Thus fascism in Italy at first lived in a close relationship with organized crime, and built its irregular forces out of the same pool of cheap labour, and was reactionary in many of the same ways as loyalist movements. However, fascism built an entire pseudo-revolutionary ideology, showing a level of sophistication in cultural power not found in loyalist movements, suggesting that in many ways fascism was a counter-hegemony aimed at breaking up and derailing attempts to build alternative hegemonies.[132]

---

129 For a review of debates on this subject, see: Carlo Verri, "Un Dibattito Marxista: Mafia e Latifondo," *Meridiana*, no. 63 (2008). This is a reformulation of the argument that the mafia are stationary bandits, proposed by: Filippo Sabetti, "Stationary Bandits. Lessons from the Practice of Research from Sicily," *Sociologica*, no. 2 (2011). This argument does not rule out the possibility that the mafia, from its origins, changed over time into a different social phenomenon. On the history of the mafia, see: Salvatore Lupo, *History of the Mafia*, trans. Antony Shugaar (New York: Columbia University Press, 2009). At certain times and places the mafia was rooted in village communities: Anton Blok, *The Mafia of a Sicilian Village, 1860–1960: A Study of Violent Peasant Entrepreneurs* (Oxford: Basil Blackwell, 1974).

130 Hobsbawm presents a flattering image of Giuliano as a social bandit: Hobsbawm, *Bandits*. This is part of mythologizing about bandits: Graham Seal, "The Robin Hood Principle: Folklore, History, and the Social Bandit," *Journal of folklore research* (2009). Reporting on Giuliano was especially sensationalist: Jonathan Dunnage, "Sicilian Bandits and the Italian State: Narratives About Crime and (in) Security in the Post-War Italian Press, 1948–1950," *Cultural and Social History* 19, no. 2 (2022).

131 Fascism in Apulia and Tuscany recruited from the same social groups, and filled the same role, as mafia gangs did in several parts of southern Italy: Frank M. Snowden, *Violence and the Great Estates in the South of Italy: Apulia, 1900–1922* (Cambridge and New York: Cambridge University Press, 2004); *The Fascist Revolution in Tuscany, 1919–22* (Cambridge and New York: Cambridge University Press, 2004).

132 This makes my argument different than: Mancur Olson, "Dictatorship, Democracy, and Development," *American Political Science Review* 87, no. 3 (1993).

5   Political-Military Development and State and Market Formation

Protracted and undecided conflict, including diffuse violence, has major negative effects upon development. Some of these effects are direct, as violence
takes a toll upon daily interactions, for example market interactions that are
distorted or even made impossible by the presence of diffuse violence. Violence
also affects development indirectly, because it has major negative effects upon
state formation, and it prevents or limits political-military development, thus
introducing major deviations from the Cohen-Tilly theory. The effects of the
projection of power on the semi-periphery and periphery are more widespread than the legacy of failed states, the worst case scenario highlighted
by Lange, in which violence is rife and there is much destructive conflict.[133]
They include many intermediate cases, like India in Lange's study, to which
we should add cases such as Greece and Italy in Europe, and arguably most
of the semi-periphery, in which the projection of power by states in the core
fundamentally altered the balance of power in society, including the balance
of political-military and also cultural power, and thus the hegemony that could
be formed in a state.[134] In all these cases the projection of power on the semi-
periphery and periphery negatively affected state formation, and through it
the emergence of markets that I describe below as market formation. State
formation refers both to the creation of new states, like Italy, Germany, Greece,
and Lebanon, and later of new states in postcolonial locations that emerged
from anticolonial struggles.[135] State formation also refers to processes within
a state such as the emergence of a bureaucracy based on rules, instead of a
patrimonial administration based on patronage networks. State formation is
thus very important, and it affects all states, including states in the core, like
England and France, and states in the semi-periphery and periphery, in which
case state formation was distorted from what it could have been by the projection of power from states in core.

    I focus here upon *political-military development*, because this is an underthe-
orized concept within development studies. Yet it is a very important concept.
Political-military development offers us a better way to conceptualize the manner in which states work and affect development, than the economics-based

---

133   Lange, *Lineages of Despotism and Development*.
134   Distortions to development introduced by imperialism are central to World Systems
      Theory's argument: Wallerstein, *The Modern World-System, Vol. 1*. One of the effects of the
      projection of power is dispossession: Harvey, *The New Imperialism*.
135   Most states were created by the breakup of empires: Roeder, *Where Nation-States
      Come From*.

view of the state as provider of public goods like defense. This is a reductive, economics-based conception of the state. By contrast, *the concept of political-military development emphasizes a different way to conceive of the state itself* than as an institution devoted to defense alone. Moreover, defense itself is a more complex social affair than one might initially assume. Political-military development is a way to conceptualize a development of collective capabilities distinctive to the political-military arena that includes the production of political-military power though a number of factors. Some are political-military factors that include the creation of political and military institutions and other organizations, ranging from the state and armies to political parties, and their subjection to more or less clearly codified rules, a combination of factors that ideally also removes all violence from within a state, and limits the use of the military to defense, rather than imperial expansion, and rather than seizing power internally through the military, or *manu militari*. This is a complex process best described as *state formation*, whereby from the private armies and tax-levying organizations of medieval kings, there progressively emerged modern states as public organizations subject to rules of behavior, and to the sovereignty of the people, not of kings.[136] In state formation institutions were designed and perfected, and entire arenas were created, with the state dominating the political-military arena, and with structures spanning from the political-military into other arenas and enabling coordination of activities and interaction across arenas.

The concept of political-military development also emphasizes a different way to conceive of the interactions between the state and markets and society, that is interactions between, on the one hand the political-military arena, and on the other hand the economic and cultural arenas. The state is closely involved in markets and gives crucially important contributions to them, to the point that it is appropriate to argue that *the state is constitutive of modern markets and plays a key role in the process of market formation*.[137] This is an extension of the argument introduced above that external regulation is necessary for changing

---

136 State formation is the process whereby states are created. For a comparison of state formation in Europe and China, see: V. T. Hui, *War and State Formation in Ancient China and Early Modern Europe* (Cambridge and New York: Cambridge University Press, 2005). There were analogous process of state formation in the Ottoman empire. I address one of them in: Olsaretti, "Political Dynamics in the Rise of Fakhr al-Din."

137 Market formation refers to the creation of new markets, and it is closely related to collective action: Brandon H. Lee, Jeroen Struben, and Christopher B Bingham, "Collective Action and Market Formation: An Integrative Framework," *Strategic Management Journal* 39, no. 1 (2018). Here I emphasize that the state plays an important role in market formation, also through its intervention in collective action.

the manner in which a system works. Gramsci argued that states are constitutive of modern markets because without states no modern markets would
have come into existence, and no modern markets could function.[138] His argument has been compared to the argument put forward by Polanyi, since both
emphasized that the emergence of markets occurred alongside the emergence
of modern states, and that modern states sanctioned market competition
and enlarged the areas and number of behaviors subject to this competition.
Polanyi especially argued that modern states enlarged the scope of markets,
creating markets for land and also labour markets, whereas previously land
and labour had been closely regulated, and markets had included mostly or
only consumer products.[139] Business historian Alfred Chandler has made a
similar argument, and formulated it explicitly as an alternative against Smith's
argument regarding the self-regulation of markets, arguing that top managers
and state officials were actively involved in the regulation of markets, as a 'visible hand,' an argument similar to the argument more recently put forward by
those who studied South Korean conglomerates, including Evans.[140]

The state is constitutive of markets in two important ways highlighted by
Gramsci. The first is that the state contributes to codifying and enforcing market behavior, which does not necessarily emerge of its own accord, and the
second is that the state physically participates in market formation through
state formation. Both of these ways emphasize the modern state as the driving force in market formation, not just a provider of public goods, because
without state action no modern markets would exist. Let us consider the first
way. Gramsci emphasized in particular that competition in markets was not a

---

138   On Gramsci's views of markets as a historical rather than natural product, see: Kratke,
       "Antonio Gramsci's Contribution to a Critical Economics." Gramsci suggests that mod-
       ern markets came into existence in the eighteenth century. Historiography has confirmed
       that the behaviors associated with markets can be found around that time: Margaret
       C. Jacob and Matthew Kadane, "Missing, Now Found in the Eighteenth Century: Weber's
       Protestant Capitalist," *The American Historical Review* 108, no. 1 (2003).

139   On the similarities between Gramsci's and Polanyi's work, see: Burawoy, "For a Sociological
       Marxism." On their similar views regarding the emergence of markets, see: Terenzio
       Maccabelli, "La 'Grande Trasformazione:' I Rapporti tra Stato ed Economia nel *Quaderni
       del Carcere*," in *Gramsci nel Suo Tempo*, ed. Francesco Giasi (Roma: Carocci, 2008).

140   Alfred D. Jr Chandler, *The Visible Hand: The Managerial Revolution in American Business*
       (Cambridge, Massachusetts and London: Harvard University Press, 1993). A similar
       argument has been made for the interaction between nation and state in the industrial
       revolution, which was arguably aided by nationalism: Magnusson, *Nation, State and
       the Industrial Revolution*. Evans' argument regarding intervention by developmental
       states implicitly makes a similar argument regarding the visible hand: Evans, *Embedded
       Autonomy*.

naturally occurring phenomenon, based on interactions in a state of nature, but was based on interactions that are part of society and hence subject to regulation by laws and values.[141] This insight is complemented by the argument put forward by philosopher Thomas Hobbes, in what was an early argument for centralized states, that in the absence of laws restraining individuals, a conflict of all against all can occur, which makes a state of nature a brutish condition.[142] Recent sociological research on the negative effects of violence, for example research by Dawson and Lange, while emphasizing the modernity of ethnic violence and its relation to the state, has continued and expanded upon the very important insight of Hobbesian philosophy regarding the necessity of the state in order to avoid the brutality of a state of nature.[143] From these arguments it becomes clear that *creating markets did not involve simply removing laws and values*, and reverting to a state of nature, but changing laws and values from one set of laws and values to another. Market behavior is a very specific type of competition, prescribing that one cannot use violence against one's competitors, nor cunning and deception, which contribute instead to thieving of one form or another. Market competition prescribes that, not the militarily strongest or the most cunning and deceitful wins, but the one who applies their intelligence to manufacture more cheaply a given product, or to manufacture a better product. Thus it rules out selling defective products, for example.

Creating markets required changing behavior and completely removing violence from activities internal to a country. This was a long process that both the state and culture participated in, and that the state was indispensable to push through, as part of state formation. The removal of violence from all

---

141   Kratke, "Antonio Gramsci's Contribution to a Critical Economics." Gramsci referred to his view of markets as involving a specific culture and state intervention as 'mercato determinato.' See entry for 'mercato determinato' in: Liguori and Voza, *Dizionario Gramsciano*.

142   On Hobbes' theory, see: Norberto Bobbio, *Thomas Hobbes and the Natural Law Tradition*, trans. Daniela Gobetti (Chicago and London: University of Chicago Press, 1993). On Hobbes's justification of the state as an institutions indispensable to avoid a war of all against all, see: Gregory S. Kavka, "Hobbes's War of All against All," *Ethics* 93, no. 2 (1983). David Schmidtz, "Justifying the State," ibid. 101, no. 1 (1990).

143   The state contributed to violence through education emphasizing ethnic differences, and by institutionalizing violence: Andrew Dawson, "Political Violence in Consolidated Democracies: The Development and Institutionalization of Partisan Violence in Late Colonial Jamaica (1938–62)," *Social Science History* 40, no. 2 (2016); Lange, *Killing Others*. Regarding the positive effects of the state, police legitimacy is associated with a decrease in homicide rates: Andrew Dawson, "Police Legitimacy and Homicide: A Macro-Comparative Analysis," *Social Forces* 97, no. 2 (2018).

activities internal to a country was part of what Elias called *the civilizing process*.[144] This was a process that states were closely involved in and that affected the aristocratic-military elites as much as, or even more than, the masses. As emphasized by Weber, with the emergence of modern states, all *legitimate* violence was concentrated in the hands of the state, and violence was ruled out as an acceptable means for individuals to use in their daily interactions.[145] Individual behavior was deeply changed in the civilizing process. In early modern Europe it was very common for aristocrats and other wealthy individuals to carry swords, and make use of them to defend themselves, but also to defend what they perceived of as their honor, and to kill others when they felt challenged, or to challenge others to duels, a practice that reached epidemic proportions at some points in European history, as there was nothing to restrain these individuals.[146] This diffuse violence compounded a mechanism highlighted by Tilly, who pointed out that the size of European states also affected diffuse violence. When there were many small states, each with its own lord and small army, there were also more frequent wars between these small states.[147] The civilizing process led to the removal of violence from everyday interactions and went alongside with the diffusion of rules of civility that applied to the cultural arena and debate, as well as to the economic arena, arguably contributing to both scientific advances and advances in productivity.[148] The civilizing process was not uniform, and applied only or mostly to activities within European countries, while the activities outside of Europe were unaffected, and the aristocratic-military elites involved in imperialism continued using violence, sometimes brutal violence.

In addition to the removal of violence from everyday interactions, *creating markets required also the removal of all cunning and deception, and ultimately*

---

144   Elias, *The Civilizing Process*. Elias saw these changes as an integral part of state formation.
145   On Max Weber's view on the state, including parallels with Hobbes' view, see: Andreas Anter, *Max Weber's Theory of the Modern State: Origins, Structure and Significance*, trans. Keith Tribe (London and New York: Palgrave Macmillan, 2014).
146   Elias, *The Civilizing Process*. Recent historiography has confirmed the widespread nature of this violence, including in particular dueling: Julius R. Ruff, *Violence in Early Modern Europe, 1500–1800* (Cambridge and New York: Cambridge University Press, 2001).
147   Tilly, *Coercion, Capital and European States*.
148   Elias, *The Civilizing Process*. The epitome of the well-mannered courtesan was formulated in Italy by Castiglione, and had widespread circulation in Europe, becoming a model of standards of conduct: Peter Burke, *The Fortunes of the Courtier: The European Reception of Castiglione's Cortegiano* (University Park, Pennsylvania: Pennsylvania State University Press, 1996). On the effects of this civilizing process on language as well as manners in England, see: Andreas H. Jucker, *Politeness in the History of English: From the Middle Ages to the Present Day* (Cambridge and New York: Cambridge University Press, 2020).

of all thieving. The state contributed also to codifying and enforcing honest and transparent market behavior. Laws and values that removed all violence from activities internal to a country were very important for the emergence of markets in conjunction with complementary laws and values that enforced honesty and transparency. Weber highlighted a very important point regarding capitalism when he emphasized that capitalism involves making many small profits repeatedly, and that this involves routinization. With frequently repeated transactions, and even more with routinization, ethical values emerge and are strengthened that regulate interactions, for example values that prescribe discipline and honesty in the pursuit of profits.[149] In repeated routine interactions, buyers and sellers in a market get to know each other, and those who sell a product on that market can reliably make small profits repeated over many times, if they are trusted by buyers, who seek honest sellers. Hence discipline and honesty in the pursuit of profits spread and facilitate further market interactions. But routinization and ethical values do not always emerge of their own accord, for example because there might be diffuse violence that is difficult to regulate since it is widespread and affects many different social settings. Moreover, as emphasized above, routinization and ethical values do not always emerge of their own accord if markets are rapidly expanding, or at least do not emerge sufficiently quickly.

The latter is a case that often requires the intervention of the state, both to enlarge the market, and to guarantee that market behavior applies throughout the enlarged market. This discussion leads to the second way in which states contributed to market formation, whereby *the state physically participates in market formation through state formation.* State formation contributes to market formation by creating or by gaining access to markets, which requires political intervention in order both to provide the legal framework and the transportation infrastructure, without which markets cannot function, and which only be provided by states, at least in some circumstances. Colomer considers the two processes of state formation and market formation together, highlighting that both are central to the European Union, and that both are ultimately driven by economies of scale. Defense, an important part of state formation, is subject to economies of scale, and so are markets, whether for

---

149   Weber, Baehr, and Wells, *The Protestant Ethic.* The importance of repeated transactions
      to stable economic behavior and structures is emphasized by: Richard Swedberg, *Max
      Weber and the Idea of Economic Sociology* (Princeton and Oxford: Princeton University
      Press, 2018), 42, 66.

defense goods, or for other goods.[150] State formation is involved in market formation through the *legal framework* that creates new political boundaries delimiting internal markets, or through the negotiation of trade agreements with other states that give access to external markets.[151] There is arguably also a process of global markets formation, whereby international markets are created by joining several markets that are internal to different countries, for example as part of a trading block, which then expand to achieve a near-global or global scale. The European Union and NAFTA are the most notable such agreements, and at one point in time they were engaged in talks to form a single trading block, now superseded in part by the Canada-European Union agreement, and driven largely by states and defense considerations.[152]

States physically participate in market formation also through the construction of *transportation infrastructure*, without which markets could not function. This is another instance in which activities by the state cannot be described exclusively as providing public goods, in the form of defense and transportation infrastructure, because they are constitutive of markets, and also more in general because they affect all interactions within a country, and have important effects upon the political-military, cultural, and economic arenas, especially when they set off synergies between political-military, economic, and cultural development. Transportation infrastructure is perhaps most obviously constitutive of markets, since it is initiated by states and has huge impacts upon markets. *This infrastructure was greatly enlarged by state*

---

150 Colomer, *Great Empires, Small Nations*; "The Building of the American and European Empires." For Colomer regional states are more important to ethnic and national culture than nation-states like Spain.

151 On the importance of a legal framework to global markets, see: David Gerber, *Global Competition: Law, Markets, and Globalization* (Oxford and New York: Oxford University Press, 2010). The importance of the law to American corporate capitalism, not just as regulation from a minimal state, is brought out in: Martin J. Sklar, *The Corporate Reconstruction of American Capitalism, 1890–1916: The Market, the Law, and Politics* (Cambridge and New York: Cambridge University Press, 1988).

152 Duina argues that law and politics play a major role in the creation of large regional markets associated with trading blocs: Francesco Duina, *The Social Construction of Free Trade: The European Union, NAFTA, and Mercosur* (Princeton and Oxford: Princeton University Press, 2013). On the importance of initiatives and mergers between the European Union and NAFTA, see: Nicholas V. Gianaris, *The North American Free Trade Agreement and the European Union* (Westport, Connecticut, and London: Praeger, 1998). This process is advanced in financial markets. On the Transatlantic Trade and Investment Partnership supported by the Obama administration in order to create a very large trade block uniting the United States and the European Union, see: Ferdi De Ville and Gabriel Siles-Brügge, *TTIP: The Truth About the Transatlantic Trade and Investment Partnership* (Cambridge, UK and Malden, Massachusetts: Polity Press, 2015).

activities initiated for political-military reasons. This was clear in cases like Ottoman investment in railways, roads, and telegraph communications in the late 1800s, all part of efforts both to assert Ottoman authority in the Levantine provinces, and also to create large internal markets that would favor capitalism, which in the case of the Hijaz railway from Anatolia to Saudi Arabia served also to provide cultural capital to the Ottoman Sultan as a defender of Islam.[153] A similar investment was made decades later by the United States. Dwight D. Eisenhower is said to have ordered the construction of motorways in the United States because as a soldier it had taken him an inordinate amount of time to travel from coast to coast by road, and he thought it was important to be able to move military units rapidly across the country in order to ensure the country's defense.[154] Roads most obviously facilitated travel and interactions, and also IC and C2 capabilities. In Eisenhower's time, radio towers and telephone cables served for IC and C2, but deploying and maintaining these was facilitated by roads. This important role of the state has continued in our time. There is today both a transportation infrastructure and an electrical and electronic infrastructure. The latter has expanded greatly with the internet, which originated in the application of military technology to civilian uses.[155] Its effects on IC and C2 are obvious. However, more traditional transportation infrastructure also has very important effects upon social interaction, and ultimately upon IC and C2, especially in an age in which most mobile phones, and even cars, can connect to the internet, and can receive GPS coordinates, while moving.

---

153   These Ottoman investments are detailed in: Philipp and Schäbler, *The Syrian Land*. On Ottoman railways, see: Murat Özyüksel, *The Hejaz Railway and the Ottoman Empire: Modernity, Industrialisation and Ottoman Decline* (London and New York: I. B. Tauris, 2014). Peter H. Christensen, *Germany and the Ottoman Railways: Art, Empire, and Infrastructure* (New Haven and London: Yale University Press, 2017).

154   On the importance of Eisenhower's policies for the construction of transportation infrastructure in the United States, and its place in transportation planning, see: Mark H. Rose, *Interstate: Express Highway Politics, 1939–1989* (Univiversity of Tennessee Press, 1990). Mark H. Rose and Raymond A. Mohl, *Interstate: Highway Politics and Policy since 1939* (University of Tennessee Press, 2012); Tom Lewis, *Divided Highways: Building the Interstate Highways, Transforming American Life* (Ithaca, New York: Cornell University Press, 2013).

155   On the role of military projects and academic research in the invention of internet, see: Janet Abbate, *Inventing the Internet* (Cambridge, Massachusetts: MIT Press, 2000). Since its military beginnings, the internet was shaped also by academics (many still part of the state, or at least funded by the state), and by its many users: Tommaso Detti and Giuseppe Lauricella, *The Origins of the Internet* (Rome: Viella, 2017).

This infrastructure also participated in *synergies between political-military and cultural and economic development.* The synergies arise from the fact that the political-military, cultural, and economic arenas, all end up benefiting from, and contributing to, the same infrastructure, which is associated with an increase in the geographical scale of social interaction.[156] Activities by the state such as investment in transportation and electronic infrastructure increase political-military development, and also contribute to both culture and the economy. The growth of internal economic and cultural arenas, including markets for books, directly contributes to the spread of a common language and culture and also to the creation of larger markets, and thus contributes to both cultural and economic development at one and the same time. It is perhaps less obvious, but nevertheless important, that bridges and roads can also become cultural icons and even participate directly in certain cultural trends. Route 66, which crosses much of the United States and ends in California, is a good example of a road with iconic status. This and other roads in the United States are associated with the Beat Generation and such novels as Steinbeck's *Grapes of Wrath*, and *On the Road*, that preceded and arguably paved the way for the 'British Invasion' and the counterculture movement of the 1960s.[157] *These investments in infrastructure benefit the state and are thus part of political-military development,* as well as cultural and economic development. As argued above, the concept of political-military development suggests that the best defense is provided by nation-states, and that this includes a sense of national identity and consequent identification with the nation-state, and also powerful shared symbols that enable collective action. The national flag is one such symbol. I argue elsewhere that there are other similarly powerful symbols, including the names and imagery associated with navy vessels, or cultural symbols associated with cultural icons, for example the imagery of knights or cowboys, or stock-in trade characters from popular culture and folk tales. The samurai is arguably an instance of these powerful symbols outside the West.[158]

---

156   Infrastructure contributes to political-military development because it enables greater collective action. It is associated with a growth in both the scale and also the frequency of social interaction made possible also by transportation infrastructure. I address these arguments in the book on the humanist theory of society.

157   On Steinbeck as part of a narrative tradition, see: Ronald Primeau, *Romance of the Road: The Literature of the American Highway* (Bowling Green, Ohio: Bowling Green State University Popular Press, 1996).

158   Olsaretti, *Towards a Humanist Social Science.*

6   The Argument Regarding Uneven Development across Countries

Political-military development is arguably the single factor that has greatest influence upon the division of labour in the world system. This is through uneven political-military development. *Imperialism poses a major problem for development.* Outside interference imposes major deviations from social processes that advance development and democracy in a country, and the outside interference can impose an enduring underdevelopment associated with an artificial division of labour in the world system. Outside interference in the form of imperialism also suggests revisions of the Cohen-Tilly theory and its conception of interstate conflict. Social conflict is distorted by imperialism from what it would be according to the Cohen-Tilly theory, and it leads, not to developmental states or democratic states being adopted throughout the world, but to less powerful states being taken over and exploited, more or less severely, condemning these states to enduring underdevelopment and to dictatorship. Which countries are taken over, and which ones are exploited more severely, depends upon uneven political-military development across countries, and the rules of projection of power, including the geocultural and geopolitical features of the state system that are outlined above. *Uneven political-military development can lead to imperialism*, which leads to economic exploitation, creating or accentuating uneven development across countries, and a division of labour in the world system distorted by imperialism. Countries that are taken over and exploited end up being providers of raw materials or workforce. Their cultures are not represented on a world stage, as they either lack their intellectuals active in world culture, or these intellectuals are few and easily coopted. This means that these countries find it harder to formulate policies that would enable them to change their position in the division of labor in the world system, and to rally their citizens around their own developmental policies, instead of IMF ones.

This leads to two major revisions of the Cohen-Tilly model. The first is that any model of the impact of interstate conflict on the selection of a state type has to take into consideration *state formation, not just state selection*. Any state is involved in a long process of state formation that can be steered in one direction or another, whether towards a developmental and democratic state type, or a predatorial state type, or in other directions yet. The presence of other states that have pioneered a developmental state type and democracy poses as much of a problem as an aid to implementing such a state type. This is because one does not just implement from above this state type, as if one were working on a blank slate, but tries to intervene in ongoing processes of state formation. The difficulties that states found in implementing revolution from above are instructive. Many of the states that tried this route to state formation ended up with some capitalist development but dictatorship instead of democracy, as emphasized by Moore for Italy, Germany, Japan, to which we should add Russia and Spain.[159] Other states that tried ended up with some reforms encouraging ongoing capitalist development, but broke up, and also ended in many cases with dictatorship in the successor states. In all these cases there was a link between underdevelopment and dictatorship, analogous to poverty and violence traps, but active on the level of the entire country. This is because state formation was embroiled in social conflict, and social conflict and its outcomes were significantly altered by the presence of a state system. States were being formed in a long process of contention between the emerging state organization and social movements. However, in addition to states, the state system was also coming into being and expanding. Rather than leading to a selection process, this led either to conquest, in the case of countries in the periphery that became colonies, or to the balance of power in society being fundamentally altered, in the case of countries in the semi-periphery, ultimately always leading to underdevelopment and dictatorship.

The effects on countries that were conquered was stark. It is intuitive that weaker countries are exploited the most. What is perhaps less obvious is that there can be negative effects in the long term also on countries that participate in imperialism and take over other countries. David Abernethy, in *The Dynamics of Global Dominance*, has argued that European colonial empires, by their very success and expansion, were doomed to failure.[160] This was due both to the high costs of maintaining an empire, which increased as the empire grew in size, and also to the fact that the introduction of capitalism changed conditions in the colonies, and eventually led to the emergence of nationalist movements in the colonies that fought for and won independence.[161] This book emphasizes that *imperialism can lead to loss of development and democracy even in countries in the core of the modern world system*, because *imperialist elites* are strengthened by imperialism and sooner or later expand their power to such an extent that they can undermine development and democracy in the core too. The theoretical groundwork in this chapter serves to provide explanations of underdevelopment within parts of Europe like southern Italy, and the possible loss of democracy in the core of the state system, in countries like

---

159   Moore, *Social Origins of Dictatorship and Democracy.*
160   Abernethy, *The Dynamics of Global Dominance.* Spruyt has added to this argument that the international institutional environment also contributed to the costs of empire: Spruyt, *Ending Empire.*
161   Abernethy, *The Dynamics of Global Dominance.*

Great Britain and the United States, that are thought of as bastions of democracy and unlikely to undergo a loss of democracy.

The *overall argument* of this part of the volume uses the concepts of world system and of division of labour in the world system. A high-level summary of the entire argument is that the aristocratic-military elites of north-western European countries concentrated their efforts at expansion abroad, in the world system, building vast colonial empires, which enabled them to build their extensive power. Their activities led to a division of labour in the world system into core, semi-periphery, and periphery that was dictated at least in part by the projection of power, which made use of violence and also of very damaging divide-and-conquer and divide-and-rule tactics. This greatly increased uneven development across countries by underdeveloping the periphery and to some extent the semi-periphery too. While social conflict within countries in the core was subjected to effective regulation, and all violence was removed from it, turning it into productive social conflict, outside these countries there was little or no regulation of conflict, and no restraint to what aristocratic-military elites and their allies could do, therefore destructive conflict continued for a very long time. There was in particular destructive interstate conflict, which led to destructive social conflict within countries and much violence, leading to lasting forms of underdevelopment outside the core. This was also through social disaggregation and violent social movements, which led to the creation of poverty and violence traps, and underdevelopment and dictatorship. Neoliberalism, with its emphasis on unregulated markets, enabled the use of the large reservoirs of cheap labour thus created in countries outside the core, and living off social rents. This led to uneven development across social groups within countries in the core, as the working class was effectively excluded from development.

I argue in the next chapter that imperialism led to or amplified uneven development across countries, leading to uneven development within countries in the core, which in its turn could set off a vicious circle undermining development and democracy in the core. The different parts of this argument are illustrated by Figure 12, which shows the various mechanisms at work. Figure 12 is an extension of Figure 6 at the end of Chapter 5, which argued that National factors 1, namely development and embedded autonomy, and National factors 2, namely democracy, can positively interact with each other and reinforce each other, leading to lasting and perhaps also greater development and democracy in the long run. However, the argument illustrated by Figure 6 applies only to countries that were able to develop free of outside interference. With the expansion of the world system, and the emergence of the division of labour in the world system, most countries were either conquered or brought under the hegemony, and also the influence, of north-western European states in the core of the state system. Figure 12 includes National factors 1 and 2, and also a number of additional factors that belong to *a longer process affecting development and democracy that is external to countries* and involves imperialism and uneven development across countries, all part of the division of labour in the world system.

Figure 12 is divided into three parts, all of which are explain the longer processes. In the part on the left hand side there are factors concerning countries in the core, namely, National factors 1 and National factors 2. National factors 1 include uneven development within countries, and imperfect embedded autonomy, which together can set off a vicious circle in countries in the core. In the other two parts there are factors that concern countries in the semi-periphery and periphery. The part on the right hand side includes factors and conflict that lead to the division of labour in the world system, by affecting social conflict in countries in the semi-periphery and periphery. The part in the middle of the picture includes conflict that spills from the core to the semi-periphery and periphery, represented by segment a in the bottom of the picture, and conflict that spills from the semi-periphery and periphery to the core, represented by segments d and e.

Let us consider each of the segments a to e in turn. Segment a represents *conflict that spilled from the core*, leading north-western European countries to expand into colonial ventures and build vast colonial empires. The next chapter builds upon the discussion above of the origins of the state core in the projection of power, and proposes that a combination of social conflict in countries in the core that had begun the transition to capitalism, with inter-state conflict subject to the rules of projection of power outlined above, led to a spiral in interstate competition to build up political-military power, driven by aristocratic-military elites that were seeking to expand their extensive power. This led to International factors 1, namely uneven political-military development across countries and imperialism. The uneven political-military development was initially driven by north-western European proto nation-states, which were larger than other European states, and also pioneered the use of culture and eventually nationalism for building state power. They engaged in imperialism in colonial ventures as the only way to expand their power, a strategy that lead these states to become very powerful and continue building uneven political-military power across countries, whether other countries in Europe or in the world. Segments b to c represent the *effects of imperialism on countries in the semi-periphery and periphery*. Segment b represents conflict in the world system initiated or heightened by the mix of trade and conquest practiced by imperialist elites from the core. The introduction or expansion of

countries in the core   countries in the semi-periphery and periphery

conflict in the world system   division of labour in the world system

criminality
microconflict

social conflict   ***International factors 3:***
meso conflict   migration
                                             relocation of industry
◄ · · · · · · · · · · · · · ·   neoliberalism
                                             populism
        d

National factors 1:
uneven development
within a country,
imperfect embedded
autonomy,
loss of democracy.
                                             ▲
                                             ┊   c
        ◄ ·.
            ·.
              ·.
                ·.
        e   ·.   ***International factors 2:***
                  ·.   uneven social development
                    ·.   across countries,
interstate conflict   uneven economic
macro conflict   development across
                                             countries.

                                             ▲
                                             ┊   b
        a
· · · · · · · · · · · · ·►   ***International factors 1:***
National factors 2:   uneven political-military
democracy   development across
interstate conflict   countries,
macro conflict   imperialism.

social conflict
meso conflict

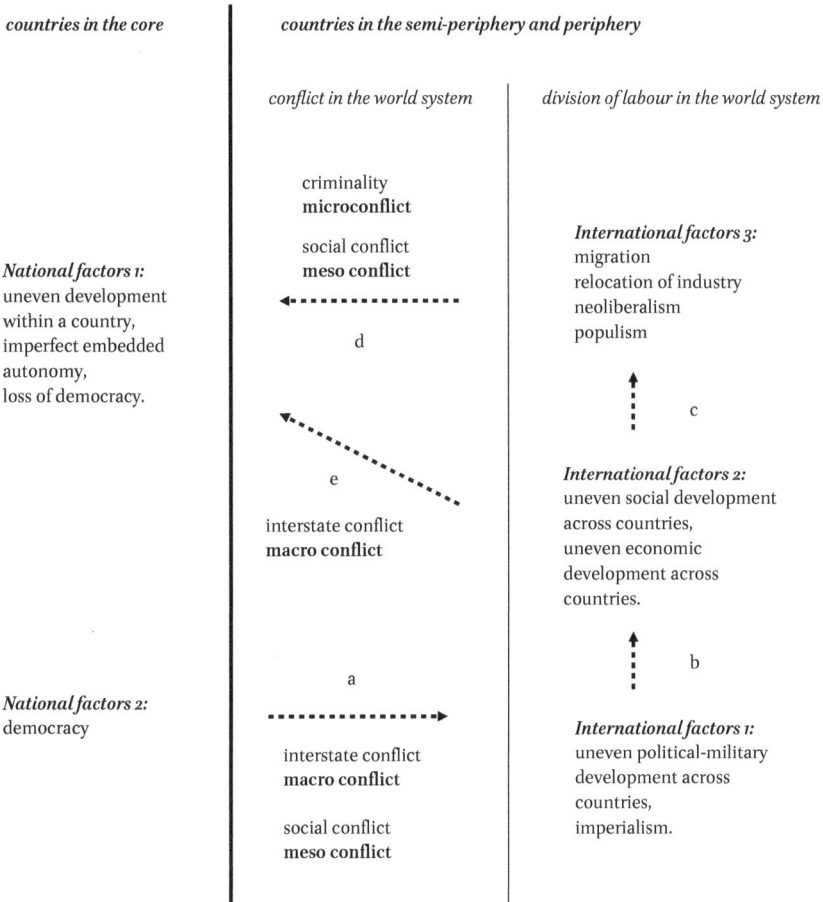

FIGURE 12   The effects on countries in the core, and on countries in the semi-periphery and
             periphery, of uneven development across countries

capitalism that they drove was accompanied by social disaggregation made
worse by divide-and-conquer and divide-and-rule tactics widely practiced by
imperialists from Europe. These led to social disaggregation, and the undermining of social development and economic development for the masses in
the semi-periphery and periphery, through the mechanisms introduced above
that included poverty and violence traps, violent social movements, and dictatorship for entire countries. Segment c represents the mechanism whereby
uneven social and economic development led to large underpaid labour forces
which, together with neoliberalism, led to migration or the relocation of
industry.

Segments d and e represent *conflict that spilled from the semi-periphery and periphery*, and had *effects on countries in the core*, leading to uneven development within countries, and also to imperfect embedded autonomy and loss of democracy. Segment d represents the effects on countries in the core of migration from the periphery to the core, which in many countries in the West has reached considerable proportions. In the past, migration has contributed to the development of countries in the core, at the cost of underdeveloping the semi-periphery and periphery, but the more recent widespread illegal migration has had negative effects throughout the world system, including the core, since it creates in the core the social conditions associated with social disaggregation, because many of the immigrants involved have no legal status, and instead of reaching the better life that they sought, fall into poverty and violence traps, providing workforce controlled by *caporalato* and other similar mixes of market mechanisms and coercion. The widespread relocation of industry has the negative effect of creating uneven development across countries, since it affects mostly the working class and lower middle class. It also compounds the social disaggregation associated with illegal migration. Neoliberalism and populism exacerbate these effects, as they encourage both migration and social conflict lower down social hierarchies of power. Segment e represents interstate conflict. The dictatorships that thrive at the frontier of the state core, because of the social disaggregation and violent social movements, lead to military and paramilitary threats, in the form of the interstate conflict started by fascism and nazism, and more recently the direct threat from violent social movements associated with islamofasism, all of which undermine democracy in the core.

CHAPTER 8

Theses on the Sources of Imperialism and Uneven Development

This chapter outlines the part of the general theory of development and democracy that concerns questions of international relations and international development, focusing upon uneven development across countries and dictatorship. *The main argument is that imperialism and uneven development* affect the division of labour in the world system, and in the long run could lead to loss of development and democracy even in countries in the core, as they lead to uneven development within these countries, and imperfect embedded autonomy. *The division of labour in the world system is due chiefly to interference from aristocratic-military elites in social processes* that would otherwise have greater chances of leading to development and democracy. It leads instead to some countries becoming providers of agricultural goods, raw materials, and more recently of cheap labour. However, unlike neoliberal theories, *this theory does not advocate the removal of all politics from development policies*. This is first and foremost because politics is indispensable to development, since it provides defense, which is indispensable in order to ensure that a country is not conquered or brought under the sphere of influence of another country, whose elite is then in a position to exploit the country in various ways and underdevelop the country. It is also because politics can give a positive contribution to development. As argued above, the state provides its own type of development, political-military development, which is valuable in its own right, and is also constitutive of markets, which would not exist, nor be able to expand at a steady state, without the intervention and regulation provided by the state, together with civil society. The theses in this chapter contribute instead to the argument that less uneven political-military development across countries is beneficial in the long run for development and democracy, because it is the best guarantee we have against imperialism.

The theses in this chapter all propose *mechanisms that explain the processes introduced in the last section* (Section 7.6). The first section below introduces Thesis VIII, which defines the social conditions for democracy. Thesis VIII complements Thesis V and the full definition of democracy, by proposing clear definitions of the balance of power in society, as a balance of power amongst social groups that depends to a large extent upon the ability to engage in collective action. Thesis VIII also serves to introduce social conflict in this part of the theory. The second section introduces Theses IX and X, both of which concern the manner in which the social conditions for democracy change as a society transitions from the organization and the balance of power typical of agrarian society, to those typical of capitalist society. In brief, the collective action advantage of the elites over the masses is reduced in this transition, but there is a more or less long transition period during which elites can strike back. Together, Theses VIII, IX, and X define the social processes that would have greater chances of leading to democracy if a country was mostly free of outside interference. These are the conditions that would encourage outcomes of social conflict in favor of the masses. The remaining sections each specify a part of the process outlined in Figure 12, whereby democracy in the core leads to uneven development within countries in the core and imperfect embedded autonomy through a number of processes that involve imperialism underdeveloping countries in the semi-periphery and periphery. The third section introduces Theses XI and XII, both of which explain process a, whereby democracy led to uneven political-military development and imperialism. These two theses respectively explain the social conflict and the interstate conflict that are involved in the emergence of imperialism. They also begin to explain the apparent paradox whereby Great Britain was the country in the West that advanced the most democracy internally, but also that built the largest colonial empire. This was because the British aristocratic-military elite, who saw their power reduced at home, focused their efforts upon expansion abroad. This elite, and other elites who became their allies, when deprived of social rents at home, moved further and further away in their search for social rents. The fourth section introduces Thesis XIII, which explains process b, whereby imperialism led to or exacerbated uneven development across countries, especially uneven social and economic development between the core on the one hand, and the semi-periphery and periphery on the other hand. The fifth section introduces Thesis XIV, which explains processes c and d, whereby migration and relocation of industry, exacerbated by neoliberalism and populism, lead to uneven development within countries in the core. Lastly, the sixth section introduces Thesis XV, which explains process e, whereby uneven development across countries lead to dictatorship in the semi-periphery and periphery, and also to the interstate conflict associated with fascism and nazism, and more recently islamofascism, all of which lead to loss of democracy in the semi-periphery and periphery, which threatens democracy in the core.

1   Thesis VIII on Democracy and the Balance of Power

The first three theses all concern the likely outcomes of social conflict. They provide the background for the theses that explain the processes in Figure 12. The first three theses all *focus upon the struggle for democracy in the political-military arena.* They are part of an argument regarding the social origins of dictatorship and democracy that builds upon Gramsci's and Moore's work. In particular, I build upon Gramsci's discussion of the social conditions that lead to a social war of maneuver in certain geographical locations, and to the likely emergence of dictatorship in these locations.[1] The argument sets the social origins of dictatorship and democracy within the unified theory of development and democracy, by focusing on the balance of power in society. The importance of the argument regarding the social origins of dictatorship and democracy follows from the discussion in Part 3 of this volume regarding ways in which democracy can be lost. The struggle for democracy in the political-military arena is especially important because this is where loss of democracy can be initiated by a military seizure of power, that uses military means outside of the law. This is also where loss of democracy as a whole can proceed very quickly and spread to other arenas, resulting in complete loss of democracy, since loss of democracy in the political-military arena can rapidly lead to loss of democracy in other arenas too. It is also important to address the evolution of the political-military arena because democracy arose in the West as part of a long process of democratization that often involved violence and more or less open military conflict. It is therefore important to understand how this process of democratization might go wrong and democracy could be lost in the West, where we have become used to take democracy for granted. As both Gramsci and Tilly emphasized, in different ways, the social conflict involved in the process of democratization centered around collective action, and the associated organizations.[2] The masses achieved gains by organizing

---

1   I discuss these points in Sections 1.6 and 2.3 above. See: Moore, *Social Origins of Dictatorship and Democracy.* See also entries for 'democrazia' and 'ditttatura' in: Liguori and Voza, *Dizionario Gramsciano.* Owen's work on states in the Middle East addresses the origins of dictatorships in the Middle East: Roger Owen, *State, Power and Politics in the Making of the Modern Middle East,* 3 ed. (London and New York: Routledge, 2013).

2   Charles Tilly, *Democracy* (Cambridge and New York: Cambridge University Press, 2007). There is a literature on Gramsci that rejects his emphasis on organization as indispensable to social movements. Some new social movements emphasize instead identity and spontaneity: Richard B. Day, *Gramsci Is Dead: Anarchist Currents in the Newest Social Movements* (London: Pluto, 2005). Organization and professionalization have their drawbacks, as argued by Choudry and Kapoor in the introduction to the volume: Choudry and Kapoor, *Ngoization.* However, organization is still indispensable and the answer to its drawbacks should not be

themselves to the point that they demanded and achieved redressal of grievances, and a voice in running their countries.

Thesis VIII details the changes in the balance of power in society involving
collective action that made it possible for the masses to organize themselves,
and to demand and achieve gains in the democratization process. This thesis formalizes and expresses in concise form arguments that I introduced in
Volume 1 and detail elsewhere.[3] The masses had not always been capable of
organizing themselves and achieving gains against the elite. However, with the
introduction of capitalism, social conditions changed, and there was a shift in
the balance of power in society that drastically reduced the elites' collective
action advantage.

VIII.   *The balance of power between social groups in society affects the likely
outcomes of social conflict.* In particular, the outcomes of social conflict depend upon the following factors influencing the balance of
power between social groups.

    a.   *The balance of power between social groups in society affects
democracy.* A group that is powerful, if it is faced by an even
more powerful group, will not achieve democracy.

        i.   *Political-military power is immediately decisive in social con-
flict,* since quickly raising this power can settle open social
conflict or routinized social conflict such as elections.

        ii.   *Political-military power still requires contributions from
other sources of power,* without which it cannot achieve
decisive victories in the long run.

            1.   *Cultural power provides the cultural means to engage
in collective action,* including the theories needed
to guide deliberate and sustained collective action,
and a sense of identity needed to sustain collective
action.

            2.   *Economic power provides the economic means to
engage in collective action,* such as the means needed
to take time off from work, the means to finance

---

anarchy. NGOs and professionalization can stifle social movements, but lack of organization
is equally, or even more, damaging for social movements.

3   Chapter 6 in Volume 1 defines and discusses the concept of collective action advantage, and
the factors that enable elites to enjoy such an advantage compared to the masses: Olsaretti,
The Struggle for Development and Democracy, Vol. 1. I make some of these arguments also in
the book on the humanist theory of society.

strikes, and the donations to pay for campaigns and organizations.

b. *The balance of power between social groups in society depends upon the ability to engage in collective action* of different social groups, and it is the difference in this ability from one social group to another, or collective action advantage, that affects democracy.

  i. *The ability to engage in collective action in large countries* in which many different social groups participate in political life depends upon the relative unity of different blocs of social groups. The following factors affect the ability of each social bloc to engage in collective action.

    1. The number, type, and relative position of social groups within the social bloc.

    2. The existence within the social bloc of organizations of one type or another enables coordination of the different social groups.

    3. Features of each social group within the social bloc such as the group's cohesiveness, which is related to the presence of community and of dense networks, and also to the presence of organizations such as NPOS, NGOS, and SMOS.

  ii. *The collective action advantage depends upon both of the following factors* regarding two blocs involved in social conflict.

    1. The comparison in the abilities to engage in collective action of the two different blocs.

    2. The ability of one bloc to compound the collective action problems of the other bloc, whether micro or meso collective action problems, also by cooptation and defection.

c. *The collective action advantage of the elites can be very different between one type of society and another,* in particular between agrarian-artisanal society and capitalist society.

  i. *In agrarian-artisanal society the elites enjoy a marked collective action advantage* over the masses that is very hard to undo, except in cities.

  ii. *In capitalist society the elites see their collective action advantage reduced* and a long period of social conflict starts in which there can be both victories and reversals for democracy.

Thesis VIII, by formulating the argument in terms of *social conditions*, rather than social origins, shifts the argument away from determinism and towards statistical thinking, as an argument regarding the likely outcome of conflict. It is intuitive that in a struggle between two opposing sides in which one side enjoys a marked collective action advantage, especially if this side is both larger and also better organized than the opposing side, this side will most likely win, but there is no guarantee of victory. In some cases, the balance of power between the two camps is so uneven that a victory of the larger and better organized side is almost guaranteed. But in many cases the outcome of conflict is by no means guaranteed, and errors or weaknesses of the larger and better organized side can still lead it to lose. Sub-thesis VIII.a clarifies both what Gramsci meant by his argument that political-military power is immediately decisive in social conflict, and also the relationship between political-military and other types of power. *Collective action is key to political-military power*. Gramsci's emphasis upon political-military power seen as deliberate and sustained collective action was not meant as a replacement for economic power, but emphasized different roles for different types of power.[4] The difference between political-military power and other types of power is one of time-horizon. Political-military power is based upon collective action, and it is immediately decisive in social conflict. It still requires a contribution from cultural power, in the form of adequate theories, and education, both of which are indispensable to deliberate and sustained collective action (statement VIII.a.ii.1). Similarly, political-military power still requires a contribution from economic power, which is necessary to sustain and grow the ability to engage in collective action (VIII.a.ii.2). This contribution, and also to some extent the contribution from cultural power, is decisive only in the long-run, and presupposes sufficient political-military power to protect the economic agents involved in developing economic power. Sub-theses VIII.b and VIII.c relate political-military power to collective action, and define the social conditions

---

4   Gramsci's work is different than the political Marxism of Ellen Meiksins Wood because of his emphasis upon a multidisciplinary approach to social science. Wood's views are set out in: Ellen Meiksins Wood, *Democracy against Capitalism: Renewing Historical Materialism* (London and New York: Verso, 2016). Gramsci's work is also different than the economic approach based exclusively upon micro conflict and utility proposed by Acemoglu: Daron Acemoglu and James A. Robinson, *Economic Origins of Dictatorship and Democracy* (Cambridge and New York: Cambridge University Press, 2005). Acemoglu's work is arguably an instance of the kind of work in political theory and in the theory of history that G. A. Cohen and the September Group practiced.

that affect meso collective action, including the conditions that lead to more or less pronounced collective action problems. These two sub-theses are a formalization of arguments in Volume 1 and of the hypotheses introduced above regarding the collective action advantage of elites.[5] They both describe the mechanisms whereby some social groups enjoy a collective action advantage.

2   Theses IX and X on Conflict and Transitions to Capitalism

The next two theses both concern the change in the social conditions for democracy between one type of society and another. The *two types of society* that I address are agrarian society and capitalist society. In making this distinction, I build upon Gellner's distinction between agrarian society and industrial society, and I further generalize it using points made by Wallerstein, who built upon historical research, and highlighted that there was an agrarian capitalism that was very important for development in the West, as well as industrial capitalism. I draw from this point and other points the insight that we should classify society as capitalist, rather than industrial, because capitalist agriculture paved the way for capitalist industry.[6] This classification is different than, and alternative to, the classification of European society as feudal or capitalist that is central to much of Marxist scholarship, including scholarship by Perry Anderson.[7] Feudal society was a very specific type of society that was found in some parts of Europe, such as parts of France and England, but by no means in all parts. It also underwent considerable transformations, and by the sixteenth century the military organization associated with feudal society and its

---

5 I make the arguments regarding meso collective action and meso collective action problems in Chapter 6 of: Olsaretti, *The Struggle for Development and Democracy, Vol. 1.* This formalized argument provides an axiomatic-deductive approach to hypotheses 1 and the refined hypotheses 1′, 1″, and 1‴ that I set out in Section 1.4 in this volume, and to the additional refined hypotheses 1g′, 1g″, and 1g‴ that I set out in Section 2.3 in this volume.

6 Ernest Gellner and John Breuilly, *Nations and Nationalism*, Cornell Paperbacks (Ithaca, New York: Cornell University Press, 2008). Gellner's distinction is addressed by several of the contributors in: Hall, *The State of the Nation.* I discuss in the book on the theory of history the importance for Gellner's theory of the concept of capitalist rather than industrial society. Wallerstein emphasized the importance of capitalist agriculture since his first book on the world system: Wallerstein, *The Modern World-System, Vol. 1.*

7 The concept of feudalism is central to: Anderson, *Lineages of the Absolutist State; Passages from Antiquity to Feudalism* (London and New York: Verso, 2013). Anderson's work on absolutist states is criticized in: Richard Lachmann, "Comparisons within a Single Social Formation: A Critical Appreciation of Perry Anderson's Lineages of the Absolutist State," *Qualitative sociology* 25, no. 1 (2002).

corresponding economic organization had disappeared.[8] This military organization had been replaced by increasingly centralized armies under absolutist rulers, which were more or less standing armies, rather than levies. The economic organization was replaced by small farms, engaged in sharecropping and also selling on markets for agricultural produce, and by an increasing number of large farms that became capitalist concerns with considerable capital investment, largely or completely producing for markets. Historical research has emphasized that large farms existed also in rapidly industrializing countries like England, and initially contributed to industrialization by sustaining the growing urban population. Small and medium-sized farms disappeared in the course of the seventeenth and eighteenth centuries, decisively going into decline with the repeal of the Corn Laws in 1832, after which the British market for agricultural products was flooded with very cheap grain from North America.[9]

The concept of *transition from one type of society to another* is important. Historians and historical sociologists have argued that in European history there were transitions from antiquity to feudalism, and from feudalism to capitalism. Each country went through a somewhat different transition, and at different times, an insight that is supported by the concept of social formation, whereby a country is not purely feudal or purely capitalist, but combines features of both types of society in different manners that depend upon the history and geography of the country, and also upon the history and geography of the systems that the country participated in.[10] In addition, World Systems Theory suggests that capitalism had from the very beginning, in the sixteenth century, an international dimension. This raises the very important question as to whether this international dimension interfered with the transition from

---

8   There was a debate on the transition from feudalism to capitalism: Paul Sweezy et al., *The Transition from Feudalism to Capitalism* (London: Verso, 1987). This debate is relevant to Moore's book: Moore, *Social Origins of Dictatorship and Democracy*.

9   On the place of the Corn Laws in free trade, see: Anthony Howe, *Free Trade and Liberal England, 1846–1946* (Oxford: Clarendon Press, 1997); Cheryl Schonhardt-Bailey, *From the Corn Laws to Free Trade: Interests, Ideas, and Institutions in Historical Perspective* (Cambridge, Massachusetts: MIT Press, 2006).

10   The concept of transition is central to the debate on feudalism and the rise of capitalism: Sweezy et al., *The Transition from Feudalism to Capitalism*. Wallerstein explored the concept in: Immanuel Maurice Wallerstein, "From Feudalism to Capitalism: Transition or Transitions?," *Social Forces* 55, no. 2 (1976). Anderson uses a similar concept to transition in: Anderson, *Passages from Antiquity to Feudalism*. Wood has recently argued that the transition to capitalism in the West was the product of fortuitous historical circumstances: Ellen Meiksins Wood, *The Origin of Capitalism: A Longer View* (London and New York: Verso, 2016).

one type of society to another, and whether this interference was negative or positive. In the case of the flooding of British markets with cheap corn produced abroad, and similar phenomena that affected many countries, it is also worth to raise a counterfactual question and ask whether the change was as beneficial as it could have been, and to whom.

As part of this counterfactual question, it is important to ask what does the change consist in, and who drives it. In this project I argue that *the most important change in European history was in the scale of production* and, closely coupled with this change, in the scale of social interaction. Hence the definition that it was a change from agrarian-artisanal society, based on small scale production of agricultural and manufactured goods, to capitalist society, in which there was large scale production through heavy investment in capital and technology, in both agriculture and industry. There was also at the same time *an increase in the scale of social interaction*, which depends upon the infrastructure and logistics, including means of transportation and communication. This made possible for the first time in European history mass political mobilization, undermining the collective action advantage of elites. Some of this change was important for productivity. There are some agricultural goods like grain that are subject to economies of scale and can be produced more cheaply in other countries that have a natural competitive advantage. But not all goods are subject to economies of scale, or equally subject to economies of scale.

Who drove the process is also very important. Arguably, *aristocratic-military elites drove change in many European countries*, as they remained at the head of their countries by leading hegemonic blocs that included other elites who cooperated with them, such as factions of the bourgeoisie. The composition and leadership of these hegemonic blocs affects change. For example, it decides what goods are subject to competition, and the speed and manner in which change takes place. These details greatly affect such outcomes as who pays transition costs, and whose communities are destroyed in the transition. Here I begin by describing *the manner in which elites as a whole retained their collective action advantage* compared to the masses during the transition from agrarian-artisanal society to capitalist society. *Thesis IX* describes the combination of social organization and political-military organization that give elites a marked collective action advantage in agrarian-artisanal society.

IX.   *The elites in agrarian-artisanal society enjoy a marked collective action advantage over the masses* because of the following organization and social structures that act on a meso scale.

    a.   *Social organization*, including social stratification considerations such as relative position in the hierarchy of power of social groups. This is affected by culture and social boundaries, both of which affect the number and relative position of different social groups in the hierarchy of power.

    i.   Social boundaries amongst the elites are fewer, are porous, and are less affected by geographical distance, enabling the elites to engage in collective action even across large distances.

    ii.   Social boundaries amongst the masses are more numerous, are stronger, and are more affected by geographical distance, making it harder for the masses to engage in collective action because they are divided into many communities.

b. *Political-military organization*, which includes networks of individuals and networks of organizations like SMOs and political parties, can reinforce the effects of social organization by providing, or failing to provide, IC and C2 capabilities.

    i.   Social networks across the elites can be of the same form as the above stratification, and are such as to endow them with C2 capabilities that enable them to coordinate their forces across large distances and also with IC capabilities that enable them to identify which community amongst the masses poses the greatest threat.

    ii.   Social networks across the masses, from one community to another, are non-existent or weak or do not stretch very far.

c. *International alliances*, which can range from alliances of equals, all the way to conquest, and provide support to one elite or another. All have the effect of altering the balance of power in society, through external support, and sometimes through the transfer of organizational innovations and technology.

    i.   *Alliances of equals*, in which different elites participate who help each other, sharing in benefits and costs of the alliance.

    ii.   *Hegemony*, in which one elite leads politically and culturally, and other elites follow the leadership and implement the policies of the leading elite without compulsion.

    iii. *Incorporation in a sphere of influence*, in which there is some compulsion, or the threat of compulsion, which can have negative effects compared to hegemony, depending upon the timing and the manner of incorporation.

iv.   *Conquest*, whereby the elite of the conquered country is left partially in command, but is under the compulsion to implement all the orders of the conquering elite.

The above thesis, Thesis IX, details the reasons why agrarian-artisanal society rarely achieves democracy, except in cities that are part of social formations that include agrarian-artisanal society and pockets of capitalism in the cities and their surrounding regions. This is because the elites enjoy a marked collective action advantage, thanks to both social organization and political-military organization. Sub-thesis IX.a details social organization in agrarian-artisanal society, including the division of the masses into a large number of discrete social groups, separated by both distance and culture, and engaged chiefly in small scale social interaction. This leads to meso collective action problems amongst the masses. Sub-thesis IX.b details political-military organization, focusing upon networks that constitute another contribution to the elites' collective action advantage. The argument is that political-military organization can reinforce social organization. The consequences for the elites' collective action advantage are clear. The main consequence is that social interaction amongst elites occurs on a larger scale than amongst the masses, and elites are capable of collective action across greater distances than the masses.

Sub-thesis IX.c introduces considerations from international political alliances, which can alter the balance of power in society, including the collective action advantage due to favorable social and political-military organization. These political alliances can become especially important in the transition from agrarian-artisanal to capitalist society. As the social organization of agrarian-artisanal society changes, the masses are able to mobilize larger forces, but initially not decisively, because of the lack of a favorable political-military organization, which prevents collective action over great distances. International alliances are necessary to understand one way in which imperialism alters processes that otherwise would have greater chances of leading to democracy, by bringing a country within the sphere of influence of countries in the core. In particular, international alliances can buttress elites, like the aristocratic-military elite, whose power would wane faster without support from international alliances. The next thesis, *Thesis x, introduces the mechanisms that enable elites to retain their collective action advantage in the transition to capitalist society.* This is because the masses lack the organization to secure stable gains for democracy, and a long drawn out process of contention starts, that under some circumstances contributes to the democratization process. In other circumstances it leads to dictatorship.

x.   *The elites in capitalist society see their collective action advantage reduced because of changes in social boundaries* that make mass political mobilization possible and favor collective action by the masses on a large scale.

a. There is however a *tradeoff between social organization and political-military organization*. A favorable social organization to the masses, a social organization with fewer boundaries, requires also greater political-military organization and the accompanying IC and C2 capabilities, which arise from networks that take time and resources to build.

    i. *A favorable social organization to the masses is especially undermined by social disaggregation*, which entails at the level of individuals lack of social capital, and at the level of social groups lack of community, both of which remove safety nets and also make collective action harder, through lack of knowledge and trust.

    ii. *Rapid urbanization initially destroys the favorable social conditions for collective action that existed in cities*, as it destroys neighborhoods with strong communities, and leads to anonymous interaction.

b. This tradeoff creates a *window of opportunity for the elites*. At least initially, the masses lack the required political-military organization to make use of the favorable changes in social boundaries, and this offsets their advantage in numbers. The elites can take advantage of this opportunity to expand their extensive power before the masses could build sufficient political-military organization and intensive power to challenge elite rule.

    i. During this window of opportunity the elites can especially implement the following *political-military tactics outside control of the state*, control of which is changing in favor of the masses:

        1. *Create irregular forces controlled by the elites* that can range from thugs and hit squads, to more or less large armed retinues, to private armies and private police forces, all using volunteers or cheap military labour more in general.

        2. *Divide-and-conquer and divide-and-rule tactics* that involve setting one social group against another, to prevent the emergence of social blocs amongst the masses that could challenge elite power.

ii.   Elites can also implement the following *criminal tactics that make use of criminals or encourage criminality*, all of which are also outside control of the state.

1.   *Banditry* that either undermines a region by preventing investment, or by directly targeting inhabitants of that region.

2.   *Pogroms and other riots* against specific individuals or specific social groups, as part of crowd behavior that is manipulated by elites.

This thesis explains why, *where capitalist social organization emerges, it is often associated with more social conflict*, at least initially. The elites, including the aristocratic-military elite, see their collective action advantage disappear in the transition from the social organization of agrarian-artisanal society to that of capitalist society. Rebellions and revolutions follow, accompanied by the expansion of state power as part of state formation. However, social conflict makes state formation especially difficult, and in addition elites can resort to irregular forces and criminal organizations that are altogether outside the state, and are thus not part of the democratization process. England, which was the first proto nation-state in Europe to undergo the transition to capitalism, and the first to undertake the long process of democratization, went through heightened conflict and the difficulties in state formation just outlined. There was widespread brigandage in parts of England up to the eighteenth century, there was crime in cities affected by rapid expansion, and migration from Ireland created tensions.[11] At the same time as internal peripheries like Ireland and Scotland were used as cheap reservoirs of labour for industry within Great Britain, they were used also to raise regiments for imperial expansion abroad. The latter became especially important. Another way in which elites continued building their power outside the state, and thus outside of democratization, was by seeking territorial expansion abroad.

Sub-thesis x.a suggests the mechanism whereby elites can maintain their collective action advantage. This is because of the tradeoff between social

---

11   There was a marked rise in criminality in England during the seventeenth and eighteenth centuries, and in the associated representation of crime in the press: Robert B. Shoemaker, "The Street Robber and the Gentleman Highwayman: Changing Representations and Perceptions of Robbery in London, 1690–1800," *Cultural and Social History* 3, no. 4 (2006). This rise in crime was arguably part of the agrarian revolution that predated the industrial revolution and included the introduction of capitalism in the countryside. The English agrarian or agricultural revolution is described in: Mark Overton, *Agricultural Revolution in England: The Transformation of the Agrarian Economy 1500–1850* (Cambridge and New York: Cambridge University Press, 1996).

organization and political-military organization. As social organization begins to change in favor of the masses, which begin to engage in social interaction on a larger scale, and are able to participate in mass mobilization, the required political-military organization for deliberate and sustained collective action by the masses on a large scale lags behind, as it takes time to build this political-military organization. As a consequence, crowd behavior and brief revolts initially predominate in collective action by the masses. Sub-thesis x.b suggests the mechanisms whereby elites can exploit crowd behavior and compound the meso collective action problems faced by the masses. These mechanisms include illegal or criminal means, which can be used in divide-and-conquer and divide-and-rule tactics that exploit the social disaggregation faced by some social groups, which is arguably the greatest meso collective action problem during the transition from agrarian-artisanal to capitalist society. When these mechanisms play out on a world stage, they can lead to the wave of riots and sectarian violence introduced above, and to poverty and violence traps associated with social disaggregation and the inability to build an alternative hegemony, as detailed above.[12]

3   Theses XI and XII on Transitions from Democracy to Imperialism

The concept of *transition* is very important to understand interstate conflict, and more in general macro conflict, as well as the question of the Rise of the West. Some authors maintained that countries in the West, or more specifically countries in north-western Europe, rose to power over other countries because they made the transition to capitalism earlier than these other countries, and capitalism gave countries in north-western Europe great economic power, and ultimately great military power, enabling them to conquer other parts of the world.[13] The reasons why some countries made the transition to capitalism earlier than other countries are complex. There was likely an important contribution from politics, since as Gramsci and Polanyi pointed out, the

---

12   These mechanisms explain the problems detailed in Section 4.5, as part of the expansion of the world system and the growing interaction between internal and external dynamics. They also explain the processes detailed in Section 7.4, whereby social disaggregation and heightened conflict, intensified by incorporation in the world system and the projection of power by states in the core, lead to especially prolonged and violent conflict.

13   This question was central to Hall's early work: Hall, *Powers and Liberties*. For a review of recent debates, see: Eric H. Mielants, *The Origins of Capitalism and the "Rise of the West"* (Philadelphia: Temple University Press, 2008).

state played an important part in creating markets. Most importantly, there was greater social conflict during the transition to capitalism, which interacted with the greater interstate conflict that was part of state formation and in particular of the wars amongst proto nation-states that led to the emergence of the state core.

The next two theses, Theses XI and XII, both of which were introduced in Volume 1, explain *why there emerged a tendency towards expansion that drove imperialism* in some European countries. They detail process a in Figure 12, which involves a combination of social and interstate conflict associated with democracy, leading to a tendency towards expansion and ultimately to states developing more power, and in particular political-military power, contributing to uneven political-military development across countries. There were actually *two tendencies towards expansion* at work, both of which led from democracy to imperialism, or more accurately from gains by the masses in the democratization process, to efforts by elites whose power had been challenged to seek imperial expansion abroad. *The first tendency involved social conflict,* and it was especially at work in England and then Great Britain, where the social conflict over democracy was greatest, and where the masses secured early some victories in their struggle for democracy, at least temporarily, so that the elites reacted by taking advantage of the window of opportunity they had and expanding their extensive power and seeking easier victories abroad. *The second tendency towards expansion involved interstate conflict,* and in particular it involved interstate conflict amongst proto nation-states in western Europe, namely, England and then Great Britain, France, Spain, as well the Netherlands and Portugal. *Thesis XI* outlines the social conflict that led to the first tendency towards expansion.

XI.   *In modern Europe there was competition between two forms of power, the intensive power distinctive of democracies and the extensive power distinctive of empires. There was no decisive victory between these forms of power, but a dynamic balance of power that kept changing.*

    a.   *This balance of power was internal to states* and consisted in a dynamic balance of power between social groups within the state, whereby if some groups increased their power, so did the other groups.

    b.   *The balance of power between social groups overlapped with the balance between intensive and extensive forms of power.* It was distinguished by the following features.

        i.   Democracies achieved a breakthrough in developing intensive power by advancing economic development in city-states, where population was concentrated, and proved a match for feudal lords.

ii.   Feudal lords, and later imperialist elites, reacted by further extending their power, typically in areas that were poorer and less densely populated and were thus easier to conquer, but they developed this extensive power to the point that they could fight back against democracies and conquer some of them.

iii. This social conflict led to a first tendency towards state expansion. This is because there was no fixed balance of power between the intensive and extensive forms of power, but a tendency whereby each form tried to outgrow the other, leading to both economic development and imperial expansion.

Sub-thesis x.a suggests that the mechanism driving imperial expansion was internal to states, and sub-thesis x.b argues that this mechanism involved a *dynamic* balance of power that kept changing, in which there were elites specialized in extensive power, notably aristocratic-military elites, that sought to increase their power by adding population and territories, and also elites, notably the bourgeoisie, that sought to increase intensive power. This social conflict led to the first tendency towards expansion, and ultimately to imperialism, because it led aristocratic-military elites that were specialized in extensive power to attempt to increase their own power by conquering new territories in order to maintain their power compared to the bourgeoisie. This tendency was greatest in England and then Great Britain, because of its distinctive social features, and because of its location in north-western Europe, where it competed with other states that had or were developing some of the same features. These states were all part of the emerging state core, which was shaped by war, until it found a balance of power that led to expansion outside Europe, on sea lanes. Much of western Europe was engulfed in conflict through most of the 1500s, and then during the Thirty Years War, between 1618 and 1648, after which a truce was agreed and there emerged a new state type in Europe that was partly fashioned by war, as suggested by Tilly. Unlike Tilly, I emphasize that these states were shaped both by social conflict and by interstate conflict that escalated into war. They also began developing culture and the economy in new directions compared to their medieval predecessors. *Thesis XII* outlines the interstate conflict that led to the second tendency towards expansion.

XII.   *In modern Europe there emerged a number of powerful states of a new kind for Europe, namely, proto nation-states.* These were *England, France, Spain, with the Netherlands and Portugal as intermediate cases* between city-states and proto nation-states. There was no decisive victory nor permanent peace amongst these states, or between these states and other states, but a dynamic balance of power that kept changing.

a. *This balance of power was external to states* and consisted in a dynamic balance of power between states, whereby if one state increased its power, so did the other states.

b. *The balance of power between these states kept changing slowly* through a mix of external and internal factors. It was distinguished by the following features.

    i. There was, post 1648, a relatively stable balance of power between states, whereby major wars within Europe were rare compared to the previous two centuries.

    ii. The proto nation-states concentrated in expanding outwards, in areas outside Europe, by a mix of trade and conquest, expanding extensive power.

    iii. The net effect was that European proto nation-states engaged in a sustained outward expansion, and then occasional very destructive wars in Europe when expansion altered the balance of power between states.

    iv. Some of these proto nation-states also developed the internal economy to a great extent, and this led to more of the competition highlighted in thesis IX and thus even more expansion, especially within one state, England, which went through a historically unprecedented expansion.

Sub-thesis XI.a suggests that the mechanism driving imperial expansion was external to states, and sub-thesis XI.b argues that this mechanism too, like the mechanism based on social conflict, involved a *dynamic* balance of power that kept changing, whereby if some states increased their power, this would prompt other states to attempt to increase their power too. This mechanism was at work in the state core of the modern world system, which gave rise to the Atlantic world system, as states in the core, that is, states in north-western Europe (England, France, and the Netherlands), and initially also states in western Europe (Spain and Portugal), sought expansion. Sub-thesis XI.b emphasizes in particular that conflict within the state core involved both extensive and intensive power.[14] This mechanism in particular is useful to explain the

---

14   The following argument is a modification of the argument put forward in: Thompson, "The Military Superiority Thesis." Compared to Thompson's argument in this article, I draw attention to the importance of interstate conflict in the core for the dynamic balance power. See also: *Power Concentration in World Politics: The Political Economy of*

emergence of capitalism in north-western Europe, which encouraged pursuing intensive power, leading to capitalism. Spain and Portugal initially drove
state expansion in the core, with Spain focusing first and foremost on extensive
power and adding population and territories, while Portugal sought a combination land-based extensive power, with its expansion in South America that
was to lead to the formation of Brazil, and trade-based extensive power with its
trade in Asia, and colonies alongside sea lanes that served to provide bases for
this trade. Arguably, both Spain and Portugal greatly favored extensive power,
and in their expansion soon ran into problems in maintaining vast empires
with diverse populations. Countries in north-western Europe, chiefly England
and the Netherlands, faced with the massive expansion by Spain, which they
could not initially outpace, started promoting intensive power even more. This
led to the emergence of the Netherlands, and then England, as capitalist countries at the center of the new capitalist world economy.

4   Thesis XIII on the Effects of Imperialism upon Development

The outward expansion that north-western European proto nation-states
engaged in became part of imperialism. Initially it led to heightened interstate
conflict in the core, as these states fought each other for supremacy in Europe,
which in its turn led these proto nation-states to build powerful military forces,
as predicted by Tilly and the bellicist school of the state. This contributed to
uneven political-military development across states between states in the core
and states outside it. The conquest and colonization that followed subjected
countries outside north-western Europe to exploitation and enduring forms
of underdevelopment or accentuated uneven development across countries,
by leading to uneven social development and uneven economic development
across countries. *Thesis XIII* details process b in Figure 12, whereby uneven
political-military development across countries leads to imperialism and
uneven development within countries. The most general considerations that
applied to these states, and to the core of the state system that they constituted, can be summarized as involving *macro collective action*, which refers to
collective action on a macro geographical scale, in which all sides mobilize
large numbers of individuals, in organizations that are more or less tightly
organized, whether they are states or private armies. Macro collective action

Systemic Leadership, Growth, and Conflict, World-Systems Evolution and Global Futures
(Berlin and Heidelberg: Springer, 2020).

includes many of the same considerations, but for states as opposed to social groups, as the meso collective action described above for conflict amongst social groups. These include considerations like the number, type and relative position of states in the state system, including both geographical position and position in the hierarchy of power. They all affected the ability of states to produce and project power.

Moreover, a particular tendency emerged in the core of the state system. *The balance of power in the entire system affects conquest,* and this balance was greatly affected by the distribution of power across states in the entire system, and in particular by the presence of two or more powerful states. This balance of power was such as to prevent further conquests, because if a powerful state with great political-military development tried to conquer a less powerful one, another powerful state would intervene for fear that the first state would enlarge itself and get very powerful and pose a threat. This meant that the modern state system tended to maintain the status quo after a certain number of powerful states emerged in the core, and a certain balance of power had been reached amongst these states, and between these states and other powerful states, the territorial empires. This balance of power changed, but slowly.

XIII.   *Uneven political-military development across states leads to imperialism,* because of the dynamic balance of power between states in northwestern Europe, initially throughout western Europe. Imperialism has the effect of producing or accentuating uneven social and economic development within countries that are conquered, thus strengthening uneven political-military development.

a.   *The balance of power that was distinctive to the core of the modern state system,* which had the following features that affected its dynamics.

i.   *State type,* which includes differences in size, and varies with both time and geographical distance. The following classification is important to understand states in early modern Europe.

1.   *North-western European proto nation-states,* which proved more successful than the other state types, and were initially all concentrated in western Europe.

2.   *City-states,* like the city-states in Italy, Germany, and Switzerland, which were concentrated in the first geopolitical band, and initially acted as buffer states.

3.   *Territorial empires,* like the Habsburg, Ottoman, and Romanov empires, which were concentrated in the

second geopolitical band, and initially threatened proto nation-states.

ii. *Geopolitics*, which includes more than just logistics, and in particular the following important factors.

1. Geographical position relative to each other as a bloc of territories that shared land borders or were within close proximity of each other by sea.

2. Physical conformation as a state system dominated by three large states of approximately equal size and power, namely England, France, and Spain, and two smaller states, namely, the Netherlands and Portugal.

3. A mix of extensive power with intensive power, whereby these states were fairly large territorially, and also included pockets of capitalism, which would continue expanding.

iii. *Geoculture*, which includes the uses of culture made by states, whatever the origins of the culture. In particular, proto nation-states had begun using culture to ensure loyalty, and at most also voice, but not exit.

1. The use of religion for political purposes to ensure loyalty to the ruling houses, whose rule was claimed to be sanctioned by God.

2. The beginnings of nationalism as a non-religious identity that ensured attachment to a specific state, initially overlapping with a specific religious identity, such as Anglicanism in England.

b. *The projection of power by north-western European states was subject to rules due to the balance of power, and also to the geography and history of individual states and of the state system* that they were part of, which led to expansion alongside sea lanes, first into the Americas, then into Asia, and lastly into Africa, because of the following factors.

i. Geographical position alongside the Atlantic coast of Europe, such that they could not easily tap into Levantine ports and the trade across Asia, in which there was much competition by more established players, including Genoa and Venice, but they could easily expand into the Atlantic.

    ii.   Cost-benefit tradeoffs associated with the fact that expansion across sea lanes, while increasingly possible, was still expensive, and the Americas offered the greatest opportunities to get rich from conquest, Asia the greatest opportunities but also the greatest costs, and Africa fewer opportunities as well as fewer costs.

  c. *The effects of the projection of power were disastrous upon the countries that were conquered or colonized,* because of the following factors, all of which contributed to either uneven social development, or uneven economic development across countries, or both these types of uneven development.

    i.   *Colonies,* which can be more or less extensive, whereby a number of colonists move permanently to the country that has been taken over, and form part of the elite and sometimes also of the subaltern social groups that are necessary for the exercise of power by the elite, who are much more militarily powerful, and live off of social rents rather than developing the countries they colonized.

    ii.   *A mix of trade and conquest,* whereby trade pays for and thus facilitates conquest and later pays for keeping the country under foreign control, and also facilitates domination and living off of social rents, because the introduction of capitalism creates social disaggregation.

    iii.   *Techniques of power,* including widespread use of divide-and-conquer and divide-and-rule tactics, which heightened conflict in already volatile situations associated with social disaggregation.

In order fully to understand the effects of state type and state system upon imperialism we have to delve into *geopolitical and historical features of the state system* that contribute to explain both the rise of north-western Europe and the emergence of the modern state system, in a process that started in the 1500s and accelerated after 1648.[15] An example as to why these features are important is that the combination of intensive and extensive power changed

---

15   The period from the 1500s to 1648 saw the emergence of the sovereign state. Spruyt refers to proto nation-states as sovereign states because of their legal features, as well as geopolitical features: Spruyt, *The Sovereign State and Its Competitors.* For the legal features of sovereign states, see: Michael Ross Fowler and Julie Marie Bunck, *Law, Power, and the Sovereign State: The Evolution and Application of the Concept of Sovereignty* (University Park, Pennsylvania: Pennsylvania State University Press, 2010).

over time and so did uneven development across countries, whether uneven political-military, or uneven cultural, or uneven economic development. This is because the proto nation-states also began developing in new directions compared to their neighbors in other parts of Europe and the world, fostering the military, but also culture and the economy. This was for two reasons. One was internal to these states, and it has to do with the amount of power that a state could produce, which was due to the state type, whereby proto nation-states, for a number of reasons introduced in Chapter 4, were better suited for developing capitalism and nationalism than other state types, and this made the proto nation-states more powerful by enabling them to expand intensive power. The other reason was external to the states and requires that we take into consideration *the balance of power between states, and also the course of imperial expansion*, in other words, how imperialism evolved and advanced. The balance of power between states is important in its own right. The point made above for the balance of power between social groups, in Thesis VIII.a, that what one can achieve depends both upon one's power and the power of other agents, also applies to states. In addition, the balance of power changes, depending upon the course of imperial expansion. Initial success in expansion can make a state even more powerful by expanding extensive power, to the point that it becomes capable of defeating other states yet, even states much larger than itself. The north-western European states pursued both avenues to expanding their power, intensive power and extensive power.

5   Thesis XIV on Economic Effects on the Core

Imperial expansion has long-term effects on the development and democracy of states in the core. It is useful to divide these effects into economic effects due to social rents, and political-military effects. I begin here by considering the economic effects. *Imperial expansion led to growth in the power of aristocratic-military elites*, and enabled these elites to favor the type of growth that benefited them the most, namely growth in extensive power that involved growth in territories, and sometimes in population, not in per-capita capabilities, and thus to concentrate on expansion rather than development. This included leading the transition to capitalism in such a manner that benefited them the most and enabled them to navigate through social change while maintaining their collective action advantage. *Thesis XIV* details processes c and d, whereby uneven social and economic development across countries, plus neoliberalism and populism, lead to uneven development within countries in the core. Aristocratic-military elites living off of social rents abroad had negative effects upon development throughout the world system, as they continued using a mix of violence and economic means that is far from optimal for development, because it rewards the strongest and the most cunning (for example in terms of divide-and conquer and divide-and-rule tactics), not the most efficient or innovative economic agents. Imperial expansion also highlights the continued importance of political-military power, over and above economic power and cultural power, in driving development, also by imposing compromises, whereby aristocratic-military elites let intensive power be advanced at home, while they sought extensive power abroad, and accepted civilization and democratization at home, while they continued to use violence and to rule with an iron fist abroad. This had consequences for development both in the core and also in the semi-periphery and periphery. Imperialism led to under-development and a division of labour in the world system dictated by a skewed distribution of political-military power, which created *two types of social rents, both of which were central to neoliberalism*. In the first type, some countries became providers of cheap land and agricultural goods. In the second type, some countries became providers of cheap labour.[16]

In the first type of social rent, *imperialism stunted demographic growth and through it development*, with effects on countries throughout the world system. This argument is an extension of Diamond's argument and it takes into consideration the effects of imperialism in accentuating and prolonging low demographic growth.[17] As a consequence of imperialism, some countries became providers of cheap land for agricultural goods sold on international markets, and the social rents were associated with depressing demographic growth, a social mechanism that kept the value of land permanently low. Imperialism acted through both political-military and cultural power. Let us consider first the *effects of political-military on economic power*. According to the free trade account of the division of labour in the world system, countries in North America had a competitive advantage in the production of some agricultural goods, and it was beneficial for the British economy to open up its markets to these agricultural goods, in exchange exporting to North America

---

16   There have been long-term studies of the labour share, or portion of national income allo-
      cated to labour, which suggest there is a mixed record for countries in the core: Giovanni
      Federico, Alessandro Nuvolari, and Michelangelo Vasta, "Inequality in Pre-Industrial
      Europe (1260–1850): New Evidence from the Labor Share," *Review of Income and Wealth*
      Online Version of Record (2021). This article takes a very long-term approach that is simi-
      lar to the macro historical sociology and geography that I advocate in this book. However,
      this article focuses only upon European countries.
17   Diamond, *Guns, Germs, and Steel*.

industrial goods produced in Great Britain.[18] This is the equivalent for international competition of the argument criticized above that markets entail a removal of restrictions and a return to a state of nature. It is appropriate to speak in some cases of a *natural competitive advantage* arising from physical geography. There is a natural competitive advantage for some goods like grains, which could be cheaply produced in vast North American plains with heavy investment of capital, and shipped to Europe through rivers and sea ports making for cheap bulk transportation. The Saint Lawrence river and Canadian grain are a clear instance of this natural competitive advantage.[19] However, if land was plentiful in North America partly for geographical reasons, there were also demographic reasons involved, whereby Native American populations were thinly distributed across vast territories, whereas there was high population density in Great Britain making for expensive land and giving industry an advantage. Both of these factors, low population density in North America, and high population density in Great Britain, relative to the agricultural and industrial base, were not the product of a state of nature, but at least partly the product of imperial expansion that depressed the demographic base in North America, making available vast amounts of land at very low prices in North America. Imperial expansion led both to large numbers of death, also due to diseases, and to uneven social and economic development that kept demographic growth low.

The export of grain is an especially clear case that illustrates *the effects of political-military power upon economic power, via imperialism and incorporation in state systems* creating an artificial division of labour in the world system. Diamond, building upon recent scholarship on the effects of the European conquest of the Americas, has pointed to the massive loss of population from diseases that were introduced by Europeans, and in at least some cases by exploitative practices that bordered on genocide.[20] North Africa and West Africa likely suffered from similar damage to demographic growth, condemning them to an enduring low demographic growth and underdevelopment. I have introduced above the point that West Africa likely had rice cultivation and could have sustained large populations, had it not been incorporated in

---

18   On competitive advantage, see: Michael E. Porter, *Competitive Advantage of Nations: Creating and Sustaining Superior Performance* (New York: Free Press, 2011).

19   On the natural advantage of North American plains and waterways, and its effect on Canadian economic history, see: William Thomas Easterbrook and Mel Watkins, *Approaches to Canadian Economic History: A Selection of Essays* (Montreal, Kingston, London, Ithaca: McGill-Queen's University Press, 1967).

20   Diamond, *Guns, Germs, and Steel.*

the world system at the time and in the manner in which it was incorporated, being exploited and underdeveloped through the slave trade. North Africa suffered a similar fate that similarly presents an exception to Diamond's argument requiring that we take into consideration the effects of imperialism. In the case of North Africa, incorporation in earlier systems, later reinforced by incorporation in the modern world system, was similarly responsible for a depressed demographic base and position as provider of grain. North Africa had plains that could produce grain. In ancient times it had cavalry, Numidian cavalry, yet with the exception of Egypt, North Africa did not develop large populations, and this had to do with political-military events. Already in ancient times the Italian peninsula grew demographically and conquered North Africa, which became a provider of grain at the time of the Roman empire. In the sixteenth century individual Italian cities, notably Venice, were importing North African grain. Incorporation in earlier state systems meant that the land was used to grow grain for export markets, rather than to support demographic growth and internal markets.[21]

Let us consider now *the effects of cultural power upon political-military power* in underdevelopment through stunted demographic growth. The decisions taken by elites were also justified and sustained over a long period of time through cultural power and the ability to formulate and disseminate entire theories, updating them over time in order to keep them relevant and address changes in circumstances. These decisions might have exploited differences that seem natural, but were in fact the product of previous political decisions. In addition, these decisions accentuated these seemingly natural differences, and harnessed them to specific ideological and political projects, that is, to different hegemonic projects. This is strikingly clear when we consider Canada in comparison to the United States. Both Canada and the United States have vast amounts of land in plains that can be used for agrarian capitalism. Both have access to sea that enables them to ship these agricultural goods. However, the Canadian and United States economies developed in altogether different ways, because of different political decisions, and different hegemonic projects.[22]

---

21   Diana K. Davis, *Resurrecting the Granary of Rome: Environmental History and French Colonial Expansion in North Africa* (Athens: Ohio University Press, 2007). Braudel mentions the grain trade in: Braudel, *The Mediterranean, Vol. 1*; *The Mediterranean, Vol. 2*. Issawi links the grain trade in early modern and modern times to the ancient Roman trade: Charles Issawi, *An Economic History of the Middle East and North Africa* (London and New York: Routledge, 2013). The destruction of Carthage might have set North Africa on a different path to development.

22   Lipset started the comparative sociology of Canada and the United States: Seymour Martin Lipset, *Continental Divide: The Values and Institutions of the United States and*

Canada has to this day low population density, and an economy that is heavily based upon agrarian capitalism and the extraction of raw materials. It has only in recent history began to industrialize and encourage immigration. This is the product of its historic ties to Great Britain and its enduring relationship as a provider of agricultural goods and raw materials for the British economy, which exported industrial gods to Canada.[23] By contrast, the United States has a far higher population density, and a far larger industrial base, as well as a large agricultural base. It encouraged industry and immigration, and more reliance on internal markets, rather than exporting goods to Great Britain, since very early in its history. This is the product of a different hegemonic project, which led to a different political history that began diverging with the American War of Independence, when Canada became a refuge for British loyalists, while the United States sought and won its independence. This different political history was later reinforced by the American Civil War and developments in its wake.[24]

In the second type of social rent, *imperialism stunted local economic growth and through it development*, with effects on countries throughout the world system. Some countries, as well as some internal peripheries like southern Italy, had demographic growth but no economic growth, including little or no industrialization. As a consequence, they became providers of cheap labour for the production of industrial goods sold on international markets, and the social rents were associated with depressed economic growth, through the mechanisms highlighted in Chapter 7, including social disaggregation and poverty and violence traps. Cheap labour was provided either through migration,

---

Canada (London and New York: Routledge, 2013). This book was first printed in 1990. Unlike Lipset, I emphasize that the differences between Canada and the United States are not due to a static culture and the institutions that buttress it, but to political decisions, and political economy decisions, along the lines that Lipset did acknowledge in: *The First New Nation: The United States in Historical and Comparative Perspective* (New Brunswick, New Jersey: Transaction Publishers, 2003).

23   Harold A. Innis, *Essays in Canadian Economic History*, ed. Mary Q. Innis (Toronto, Buffalo, London: University of Toronto Press, 2017). This is still a feature of the Canadian economy, now producing raw materials for world markets: Roger Hayter and Trevor J. Barnes, "Canada's Resource Economy," *Canadian Geographer/Le Géographe Canadien* 45, no. 1 (2001).

24   On the importance to the economic growth of the United States of political economy, including national politics and government policies, see: Ronald Seavoy, *An Economic History of the United States: From 1607 to the Present* (London and New York: Routledge, 2013); Frederick S. Weaver, *An Economic History of the United States: Conquest, Conflict, and Struggles for Equality* (Lanham, Boulder, New York, Toronto and Oxford: Rowman & Littlefield Publishers, 2015).

often with continued exploitation, or through industry relocation. *Migration* played an important part in the world system.[25] After slavery was banned in the British empire in 1833, some plantation owners, and also investors in industrial enterprises like railway construction, had recourse to indentured servitude. The latter involved using workers from South Asia, and sometimes East Asia, who signed up to work for a number of years outside their countries, after which they supposedly became free of contractual obligations and would have been able to earn a better living for themselves in their new countries.[26] Migrants from Italy, and especially southern Italy, participated in a wave of migration to the Americas in the late 1800s to early 1900s, in some cases lasting till the 1950s. Some of these migrants, who were too poor to buy themselves the ship fare to migrate and to support themselves until they found employment outside their countries, were similarly exploited through a system known as the *padrone system*.[27]

In more recent times, *industry relocation* tapped into reservoirs of cheap labour by recruiting workers and putting them to work in their country of origin, but still in conditions that were far from ideal. Moreover, these conditions still involved social rents that depressed economic growth. The latter were the product of previous imperialism, which left a large pool of cheap labour created by demographic growth without economic growth, because of the social disaggregation and poverty and violence traps initially created or accentuated by imperialism and the introduction of capitalism by imperialists. These conditions meant that for a long time there was little or no capital investment, and that what industry existed was not efficient, but simply relied upon cheap labour.[28] The countries that found themselves in this position could not easily

---

25   On these questions, see: Alejandro Portes and John Walton, *Labor, Class, and the International System* (New York, London, Toronto, Sydney, San Francisco: Academic Press, 1981); Denis O'Hearn and Paul S. Ciccantell, *Migration, Racism and Labor Exploitation in the World-System* (London and New York: Routledge, 2021).

26   Ashutosh Kumar, *Coolies of the Empire* (Cambridge and New York: Cambridge University Press, 2017). This phenomenon had older roots, as indentured servants from Great Britain and Ireland were used as labour in the earliest colonies: Anna Suranyi, *Indentured Servitude: Unfree Labour and Citizenship in the British Colonies* (Montreal, Kingston, London, Ithaca: McGill-Queen's University Press, 2021).

27   On the wave of Italian migration starting in the 1870s and 1880s, see the relevant book part in: William J. Connell and Stanislao G. Pugliese, eds., *The Routledge History of Italian Americans* (London and New York: Routledge, 2017). On the *padrone* system, see: Gunther Peck, *Reinventing Free Labor: Padrones and Immigrant Workers in the North American West, 1880–1930* (Cambridge and New York: Cambridge University Press, 2000).

28   This is the industrialization described by Evans for the 1970s in: Evans, *Dependent Development*. There was an earlier industrialization in parts of the British empire, but only as the Second World War started and changed policies: Lawrence J. Butler, *Industrialisation*

escape it, and participation in international markets only slowly improved these conditions. The countries with large reservoirs of cheap labour that sold industrial goods on international markets had no interest in improving working conditions and raising salaries for the workforce. In addition, since vast workforces were mobilized in numerous developing countries, from Mexico and Central America, to North Africa, the New Asian Tigers, and especially India and China with their very large populations, the industrialists who relocated could live off of social rents for a long time.[29]

This had a cultural dimension, as some large parts of the population in these internal peripheries, or in countries in the periphery, belonging to one or more social groups, were unable to develop their own alternative hegemonies, and even to articulate their grievances. Neoliberalism was and to a large extent still is the economic theory of the dominant hegemony associated with elites active on the international stage. *Thesis XIV* details processes c and d, whereby uneven social and economic development across countries, together with neoliberalism, lead to industry relocation, which negatively affected the working class and lower middle class in countries in the West, and thus lead to uneven development within countries, in particular uneven development across social groups.

XIV.   *The division of labour in the world system brings about uneven development in countries in the core through the following mechanisms,* all of which involve social rents.

    a.   *Elites can tap into, and compound through political means, two different types of social rents outside the core,* which enable elites to extract profits and even be competitive, not by introducing organizational and technological innovations, but by paying less for certain factors.

        i.   *Social rents associated with low population density and cheap land in the periphery,* which typically lead to export

---

and the British Colonial State: West Africa 1939–1951 (London and New York: Routledge, 1997). Arguably, the investment in developing countries promoted by neoliberalism sought a cheap labour force, and was forced to make some concessions to the countries where they invested. Labour-intensive firms tend to relocate more: Enrico Pennings and Leo Sleuwaegen, "International Relocation: Firm and Industry Determinants," *Economics Letters* 67, no. 2 (2000).

29   For example, some firms are re-locating from China to South-East Asia: Chun Yang, "Relocating Labour-Intensive Manufacturing Firms from China to Southeast Asia: a Preliminary Investigation," *Bandung* 3, no. 1 (2016). However, China, although with a huge labour market, was not the only developing country to attract investment, and this arguably contributed to keep labour costs low for a certain time.

       of agricultural goods from the periphery to the core that
       benefit from cheap land.

   ii.   *Social rents associated with high population density and
       cheap labour in the periphery,* which typically lead to export
       of industrial goods from the periphery to the core that ben-
       efit from cheap labour, such as goods in labor-intensive
       industries.

b.   *Social rents outside the core lead to uneven development* in the core
   through the following mechanisms:

   i.   *Migration,* which lowers the costs of labour in the core, and
       in the case of illegal immigration creates social disaggrega-
       tion lower down the hierarchy of power in society, an also
       a vast pool of cheap labour with no rights that is exploited
       through such practices as *caporalato.*

   ii.   *Relocation of industry* from countries in the core to coun-
       tries in the periphery, which affects especially the working
       class and the lower middle class of countries in the core.

c.   *Neoliberalism and populism compound these effects by providing
   ideological legitimation* to policies that enable these effects, or
   that make them worse.

   i.   *Neoliberalism* provides ideological legitimation to reliance
       upon international markets, and to cuts in state funding
       rather than making it efficient, thus enabling social rents
       and imperfect markets in which some social groups have no
       bargaining power.

   ii.   *Populism* enables social rents to continue by blaming scape-
       goats, and by encouraging divisions amongst social groups
       that belong to the masses, especially between the middle
       class and the working class, and the existing population and
       migrants.

Thesis xiv describes the economic effects of social rents on countries in the
core. It focuses in particular upon *uneven development in countries in the core.*
Sub-thesis xiv.a emphasizes the political origins of both types of social rents.
However, social rents leverage social conditions affecting the economy, like
demographic base in relation to available land, or demographic base in relation
to available capital for investment. To this we could add the effects of violence
on society, associated with disaggregation and heightened social conflict, that
are the focus of Thesis xiii. Sub-thesis xiv.a thus emphasizes the importance
of macro historical sociology and geography in setting what Braudel called

the limits of the possible, or what can be achieved, given certain social conditions.[30] These social conditions include the demographic base, which affects both the price of land and the price of labour. As emphasized by Diamond, the demographic base is the product of long-term trends that are difficult to change. This is at least in part because this base affects the balance of power in society. In the case of low population densities, these tend to consign the masses to a position in which they are dominated by the elites in their country, because of the lack of numbers and thin distribution over a territory. Canada is a partial exception to this argument, due to its strategic position as a gateway to access North American resources that the British aristocratic-military elite wanted to retain in the wake of the American War of Independence. In the case of high population densities, uneven social and economic development within these countries, whereby the elites enjoy greater social capital and economic capital, with the masses often lacking both, still consigns the latter to a position in which they are dominated by the elites in their country, because the masses lack the organizational means necessary to leverage their greater numbers and engage in deliberate and sustained collective action. Sub-thesis XIV.b suggests that these mechanisms affect countries in the core, accentuating uneven development in these countries, whether because of the relocation of industry to countries in the semi-periphery and periphery, which affects the working class hardest, or because of migration from these countries to the core, which accentuates poverty lower down the hierarchies of power, as migrants, especially illegal migrants, often lack rights and are unable to seek redressal of grievances. Sub-thesis XIV.c suggests that neoliberalism sanctions ideologically and in terms of policies this state of affairs, maintaining social conditions characterized by a very skewed distribution of power.

6   Thesis XV on Political-Military Effects on the Core

Uneven social and economic development across countries, and social disaggregation, also lead to violent social movements and to dictatorship in many countries in the semi-periphery and periphery. These processes were part of a social war of maneuver that had destabilizing effects in countries in the semi-periphery and periphery, and also in countries in the core. These effects worked mostly through interstate conflict between, on the one hand,

---

30   Fernand Braudel, *The Structures of Everyday Life: The Limits of the Possible*, Civilisation Matérielle, Économie et Capitalisme (Collins, 1981).

dictatorships and violent social movements that emerged in countries in the semi-periphery and periphery, and on the other hand countries in the core. *Thesis XV* details process e, a process that involves interstate conflict, and more in general macro conflict that includes asymmetric conflict between states and other agents such as violent social movements, leading to loss of democracy. It also details part of process d, which leads to imperfect embedded autonomy because neoliberalism applies international pressures on institutions, such as pressures to reduce debt, rather than increase efficiency, especially on countries in the semi-periphery and periphery. This part of process d interacts with process e, whose components e1 to e3 are represented in Figure 11, since social wars and culture wars are amplified by migration and populism, and imperfect embedded autonomy and lack of communication across different arenas further contribute to the negative effects of populism.

All the mechanisms proposed by the theses in this part of the volume seek to explain the longer process affecting development and democracy than the processes studied in the previous part. This longer process leads to the emergence of uneven development in countries in the core, as a consequence of a division of labour in the world system driven by political-military power and social rents. This longer process is rapidly bringing about a decline of United States hegemony, or what appeared to be United States hegemony. What is worse, this longer process is arguably beginning to undermine also democracy (e3) and embedded autonomy (e2) in the core. The mix of traditional military conflict, like in the early stages of the Iraq War and the Afghanistan War, followed by endless asymmetric conflict with massive costs, have placed a huge drain upon United States finances.[31] This has affected economic democracy (e3), since at the same time there are growing inequalities in all Western countries, including the United States, requiring investment to improve the conditions of the laboring classes, and of SMEs. The latter instead are largely and increasingly excluded from the model of development advanced by neoliberalism, and forced to compete with the working and middle classes of developing countries, and with migrants, by lowering labor costs, rather than by increasing skills, or by product innovation. In addition, there is a very real threat of war in Europe, with the rearmament pursued by the Russian Federation and the recent war in Ukraine. The longer process is affecting also embedded autonomy (e2), as international institutions like the United Nations and the European Union, both of which are very remote from realities on the ground, and thus are even more affected by imperfect embedded autonomy

---

31   Ref on financial effects of Afghanistan and Iraq wars.

than national institutions, are compounding, rather than solving, the imperfect embedded autonomy of national institutions. This became strikingly clear at the time of the Greece debt crisis, when the European Union adopted policies similar to the IMF, and sought to impose draconian austerity measures.[32] Thesis XV suggests the mechanisms involved in the process whereby uneven social and economic development in the world system is leading to *imperfect embedded autonomy and loss of democracy in countries in the core*, which could set off a vicious circle in development and democracy even in countries in the core like the United States.

XV. *The division of labour in the world system brings about imperfect embedded autonomy and loss of democracy in countries in the core through the following mechanisms,* all of which involve macro conflict.

    a. *There is a political side to uneven social development in the world system, which leads to a social war of maneuver* in semi-peripheral and peripheral locations of the world system. This social war of maneuver has different effects depending upon uneven economic development.

        i. *In the case of Italy and Germany in the 1920s-40s,* it gave rise to violent social movements, and when the violent social movements seized power, they could pose a symmetric threat to countries in the core because of fairly advanced economic development.

        ii. *In the case of countries in the Middle East and North Africa in the 1980s-2000s,* it gave rise to dictatorships and violent social movements that lead to asymmetric threats because of low economic development, and often inability to seize the state, so that the threat remained asymmetric.

    b. *Macro conflict leads to imperfect embedded autonomy* through international pressures on institutions, some of which are reinforced by neoliberalism and populism.

        i. *High military expenditures can lead to pressures to make savings on expenditures by institutions,* which can harm institutions and reduce their ability to interact with organizations.

        ii. *Security threats can reduce investment,* both because investors are directly concerned by security threats, and because

---

32 Silvia Ardagna and Francesco Caselli, "The Political Economy of the Greek Debt Crisis: A Tale of Two Bailouts," *American Economic Journal: Macroeconomics* 6, no. 4 (2014).

they are concerned by the effects of the security threats on markets, including international markets for strategic resources like oil, and markets that the investment would produce for.

c. *Macro conflict leads to loss of democracy* through pressure on social conflict within countries in the core, which can escalate into war, in conjunction with migration, neoliberalism, and populism, whereby violent social movements stoke up social conflict inside countries in the core, and turn it into war.

   i. *Economic wars* lower down hierarchies of power are stoked up by increasing numbers of immigrants.

   ii. *Culture wars* between different ideological camps, or between the state and churches, are stoked up by populism, aided indirectly by large numbers of immigrants, as well as by foreign dictatorships, and by violent social movements which contribute to creating a perception of imminent threats by immigrants, instead of by elites or by more complex problems.

   iii. *Political wars* between politicians, *some* of whom tap into culture wars, participate in populism, and cooperate with intellectuals engaged in culture wars, and are indirectly aided by dictatorships and violent social movements.

Thesis xv describes the political-military effects of interstate conflict on countries in the core. It focuses on imperfect embedded autonomy and on the loss of democracy in countries in the core, both of which follow from interstate conflict with countries in the semi-periphery and periphery that are mired in social conflict, and are taken over by dictators and rocked by violent social movements. This thesis makes use of the broad classification of violent social movements in the semi-periphery and periphery that include fascism, nazism, populism, and islamofascism. Sub-thesis xv.a emphasizes the political origins of these violent social movements, as well as their origins in the social conditions associated with the social war of maneuver in the semi-periphery and periphery, social conditions that can also lead to social rents. These conditions could lead either to dictatorships, or to simmering undecided conflict that strengthens violent social movements. After the Second World War, and the passing of the French and British mandates in the Middle East, a number of dictatorships arose, notably in Libya, Syria, and Iraq, because military officers and high-ranking party officials could easily effect seizures of power.[33] In the case of Libya, the dictatorship actively used terrorist groups, creating cadres trained in terrorist activities. The resulting macro conflict, including both interstate conflict with dictators and asymmetric threats posed by violent social movements that engage in terrorist activities, did and can further undermine both embedded autonomy and democracy in the core. Sub-thesis xv.b suggests a mechanism whereby these security threats, whether by dictators or violent social movements, lead to imperfect embedded autonomy in countries in the core. The high expenditures to face up to these threats can lead to cutting budgets and reforming institutions with the only or main goal to realize immediate savings in state budgets. They can also lower investments due to the climate created by the security threat, a climate that can deeply affect international markets.[34] Sub-thesis xv.c suggests a mechanism whereby the security threats can undermine democracy in countries in the core, by exacerbating or starting internal social conflict that can escalate into wars, including economic wars at the bottom of the hierarchy of power in society, and culture wars.

---

33   Owen, *State, Power and Politics in the Middle East.*
34   Internal instability is associated with flight of capital: Paul Collier, "On the Economic Consequences of Civil War," *Oxford Economic Papers* 51, no. 1 (1999).

Conclusions

This book, including this volume, seeks to provide theoretical alternatives to neoliberalism and in particular to encourage a reevaluation of the role of culture and politics in development, including the role of civil society and the state in development. The state is indispensable to development, and the most important task we face is not to fall back onto a minimal state, but how to build a better state that maximizes the returns on investment and avoids wasting public money. Civil society is similarly indispensable to development, also because cultural institutions are indispensable to produce the theories to improve the state and the criticism to hold it accountable. This book suggests the following two arguments that are alternative to neoliberal theories. The first argument is that *the division of labour in society is a major source of development*, and a very important part of the division of labour in society is the division of labour within a country between the economic, cultural, and political-military arenas. In countries in the West today, this division largely overlaps with the division between markets, civil society, and the state. All three are necessary to development, because the greatest development of each arena, and the maximum synergies between arenas, are realized only when each arena is free to pursue its own type of development, also by adopting specific organizational forms and principles of behavior that become distinctive to it. In order to achieve a smoothly functioning division of labour in society, the different arenas in a country should remain in constant dialogue with each other, and share information and coordinate activities, while remaining autonomous. This type of interaction is best described as embedded autonomy between arenas, whereby each arena remains autonomous from the other arenas, while through embeddedness it shares information and coordinates activities with the other arenas. Democracy is very important to development, because it contributes to embedded autonomy, ensuring that no arena is taken over by the other arenas, and thus that all arenas remain autonomous. Moreover, with democracy, the networks between arenas that ensure sharing of information and coordination of activities, are also useful to hold the political arena, including the state, accountable.

The second argument is that *the division of labour in the world system is the product of imperialism, which ultimately leads to loss of development, embedded autonomy, and democracy*, even in countries in the core. Social conflict and interstate conflict in the core lead to imperialism. Imperialism, through a mix of trade and conquest, creates or accentuates social rents, or conditions whereby elites are able to extract profits without development, taking advantage of a skewed distribution of power in society. This is because with trade and the introduction of capitalism there is social disaggregation and uneven social and economic development, to the point that some groups are reduced to abject poverty, and are caught in poverty and violence traps. Imperialism is thus associated with the survival of violence in the world system, and with organizational forms that use combinations of market mechanisms and violence, that are far from optimal for productivity. It is also associated with violent social movements that make use of volunteers to man large irregular forces, and sometimes seize power. Imperialism thus creates or accentuates uneven development across countries, and an artificial division of labour in the world system whereby some countries become providers of cheap land or cheap labour. This has profound effects on development and democracy in the core. The availability of cheap land and labour are due to social rents, which undermine development, since they are not based on organizational or technological innovations that increase productivity, but rely instead on paying less for land and labour. While some fast-developing countries, notably India and China, have made progresses in development, they have progressed at the expense of the laboring classes of Western countries, so that uneven development has decreased across countries, but it has increased within countries in the West. Other countries have been affected by migration, and violent social movements, both which are also undermining development and democracy in Western countries. There must be other ways, and better ways, to ensure development for all social groups that belong to the masses.

Like all theories, the general theory proposed in this book has to be subjected to empirical tests. Besides Hypotheses 5 and 6, both of which are derived from the theses of the general theory, the following would be especially promising locations to start testing the theory, starting with the hypothesis that an imperialist world elite existed in the past. Amsterdam and the Hague could yield valuable clues to the existence of such an imperialist world-elite in the past, since the Dutch imperialist elite built ties to the French and British imperialist elites. Very important locations whose contemporary history could yield valuable clues about the existence of an imperialist world-elite in the past include its centers of power in Paris and London, united by very old ties, from the Entente Cordiale to the more recent Entente Frugale. Other promising locations and important centers of power of imperialist world-elites of the past are in former colonies. The British imperialist world-elite became fabulously rich through its rule in India. It was able to exercise this rule through Scotland, which became an important power base and provider of labour for imperialism, and through the Royal Navy, which became the main instrument to project power over sea lanes. Other important power bases are port cities and entire countries alongside sea lanes used for trade with India and also with East Asia, which include in the Mediterranean Gibraltar, Sicily, Cyprus, and in Africa Egypt, and South Africa. Centers of power in Italy could yield important information about national elites that became clients of this world-elite, and have continued basing their power upon domination, rather than hegemony, leading to an especially virulent populism, bordering on militarism, that is increasingly similar to fascism. Surprisingly, perhaps, some of the most important locations for testing the theory are likely those associated with the other imperialist world-elite that emerged in the past, before the British imperialist world-elite. This other elite was the elite at the head of the Habsburg empire, and its two centers of power in Budapest and Vienna, such important centers as Salzburg, as well as major centers of power such as Madrid and Lisbon. The Habsburg elite included the Spanish imperialist world-elite, at the head of that part of the Habsburg empire that built a vast colonial empire, through its navy and port cities and entire countries along sea lanes, including Argentina, Mexico, Uruguay, and the colonies of the Portuguese imperialist elite, chiefly Brazil. The Habsburg elite also included the Austrian Habsburgs, one of whose members was the last emperor of Mexico. The Caribbean and most of Central America, including Mexico, suffered at the hands of all different imperialists from Europe, including the Habsburgs, and are to this day affected by enduring uneven development, and poverty and violence traps, and so is Brazil.

This book also proposes a *theory about the social origins of neoliberalism and the populist backlash*, and their participation in processes that undermine development and democracy. Neoliberalism is part of cycles of expansion of the world economy that are dominated by imperialist elites in search for social rents. It is an economic theory that destabilizes countries in the core by setting off a longer cycle that builds upon imperialism and the uneven development across countries that it produced or accentuated, by exploiting and amplifying social rents in the semi-periphery and periphery that were created by imperialism. It thus amplifies a distorted division of labour in the world system that enables the survival of non-optimal organizational forms that combine market mechanisms and violence. Moreover, neoliberalism, by relocating industry to countries that are imperfect democracies, and even dictatorships for all intents and purposes, enriches dictators and oligarchs, and by transferring organizational and technological innovations, it stunts cultural democracy in these countries, and ultimately democracy, since the innovations that are necessary to be competitive are imported from abroad, and placed in the hands of unaccountable rulers, who use them to increase their power compared to the masses in their countries, either strengthening the dictatorship, or delaying the advance of democracy. This leads to migration, and to security threats, whether from states, criminal organizations, or violent social movements, that destabilize countries in the core. Populism, together with fascism, nazism, and islamofascism, is part of the same cycles of expansion of the world economy, and it followed neoliberalism, further strengthening its negative effects by blaming scapegoats and encouraging knee-jerk reactions, rather than careful and well-thought out solutions to social problems. The recent development of BRICS countries represents a major problem for development and democracy in the core if only because these imperfect democracies could easily slip back into outright dictatorships, re-playing on a world scale the emergence of industrialized countries in the semi-periphery and periphery, Italy, Germany, and Japan, that were imperfect democracies, and quickly turned into dictatorships, leading to the Second World War.

The general theory in this volume has clear *applications also to international relations and international development.* Pointing to possible threats from BRICS countries that might turn into outright dictatorships does *not* amount to a call to engage in thoughtless wars outside our borders in the name of democracy. To the contrary, the theory also entails that the elites responsible for imperialism, and more recently for neoliberalism and populism, originated and still have their most important power bases in the West. The emergent imperialist world-elite and its most powerful allies, the establishments of major countries in the West, are the key elites that pose a threat to security. We should not allow them to have a free rein outside our borders, for ethical reasons, and also for political reasons, which can be readily summarized. There are no such things as democratic empires. In the history of Europe, elites who had to grant democracy at home, continued and even expanded exploitation and social rents abroad, building vast colonial empires that made them especially powerful, and then turned back on their home countries and undermined, and could still undermine, democracy at home. In other words, defeated at home, the empire further expanded, adapting to the times, and then struck back. This entails that democracies in the West should not tolerate the use of violence, nor exploitation, by Western elites acting outside their borders, since in the long run this presents a security threat, perhaps even an existential threat, to our democracies. The uneven development that imperialism creates or accentuates, and the dictatorships, organized crime, and violent social movements that it leads to, eventually undermine development and democracy in the West too. It follows that the most important fight for development and democracy is within the West, and in particular within NATO countries. Long term applications of the theory include constructing the theoretical and organizational means to build alternative hegemonies, from below, and in an inclusive manner, in order to provide valid alternatives to neoliberalism, and encourage a more even development throughout the world, within countries in the West, and across countries throughout the world. This book seeks to contribute to these alternatives, to a development that benefits the masses, and to a more peaceful world, removing the spectre of yet another world war once and for all from our foreseeable future.

Bibliography

A'Hearn, Brian, and Anthony J. Venables. "Regional Disparities: Internal Geographies and External Trade." In *The Oxford Handbook of the Italian Economy since Unification*, edited by Gianni Toniolo. Oxford and New York: Oxford University Press 2013.

Abbate, Janet. *Inventing the Internet*. Cambridge, Massachusetts: MIT Press, 2000.

Abdelal, Rawi. "Dignity, Inequality, and the Populist Backlash: Lessons from America and Europe for a Sustainable Globalization." *Global Policy*. 11, no. 4 (2020): 492–500.

Abdulhadi, Rabab. "The Palestinian Women's Autonomous Movement: Emergence, Dynamics, and Challenges." *Gender & Society*. 12, no. 6 (1998): 649–673.

Abdulhadi, Rabab. "Where Is Home? Fragmented Lives, Border Crossings, and the Politics of Exile." *Radical History Review*. 86, no. 1 (2003): 89–101.

Abdulhadi, Rabab Ibrahim. "Framing Resistance Call and Response: Reading Assata Shakur's Black Revolutionary Radicalism in Palestine." *Women's Studies Quarterly*. 46, no. 3 & 4 (2018): 226–231.

AbdulHadi, Rabab Ibrahim, and Saliem Shehadeh. "Resisting the US Corporate University: Palestine, Zionism, and Campus Politics." In *The University and Social Justice: Struggles across the Globe*, edited by Aziz Choudry and Salim Vally. Toronto: Between the Lines publisher, 2020.

Abernethy, David B. *The Dynamics of Global Dominance: European Overseas Empires, 1415–1980*. New Haven and London: Yale University Press, 2000.

Abernethy, David B. *Education and Politics in a Developing Society: The Southern Nigerian Experience*. Harvard University, 1965.

Abernethy, David B. *The Political Dilemma of Popular Education: An African Case*. Stanford Studies in Comparative Politics. Stanford, California: Stanford University Press, 1969.

Abolafia, Mitchel Y. "Markets as Cultures: an Ethnographic Approach." *The Sociological Review*. 46, no. 1 (1998): 69–85.

Abu-Lughod, Janet L. *Before European Hegemony: The World System A.D. 1250–1350*. Oxford, New York, Toronto: Oxford University Press, 1991.

Acemoglu, Daron, and James A. Robinson. *Economic Origins of Dictatorship and Democracy*. Cambridge and New York: Cambridge University Press, 2005.

Adam, Frane, and Borut Rončević. "Social Capital: Recent Debates and Research Trends." *Social Science Information*. 42, no. 2 (2003): 155–183.

Adams, Don, and Arlene Goldbard. *Creative Community: The Art of Cultural Development*. New York: Rockefeller Foundation, 2001.

Adams, Stephen B. "Follow the Money: Engineering at Stanford and UC Berkeley During the Rise of Silicon Valley." *Minerva*. 47, no. 4 (2009): 367–390.

Adamson, Walter L. "The Culture of Italian Fascism and the Fascist Crisis of Modernity: The Case of II Selvaggio." *Journal of Contemporary History*. 30, no. 4 (1995): 555–575.

Adamson, Walter L. "Fascism and Culture: Avant-Gardes and Secular Religion in the Italian Case." *Journal of Contemporary History*. 24, no. 3 (1989): 411–435.

Adamson, Walter L. "Gramsci and the Politics of Civil Society." *Praxis International*. 7, no. 3–4 (1987–88): 320–39.

Adamson, Walter L. "Modernism and Fascism: The Politics of Culture in Italy, 1903–1922." In *Fascism*, edited by Jeremy Black and Michael S. Neiberg. London and New York: Routledge, 2006.

Aglietta, Michel. *A Theory of Capitalist Regulation: The US Experience*. London and New York: Verso Books, 2016.

Agoston, Gabor. *The Last Muslim Conquest: The Ottoman Empire and Its Wars in Europe*. Princeton and Oxford: Princeton University Press, 2021.

Akarli, Engin Deniz. *The Long Peace: Ottoman Lebanon, 1861–1920*. Berkeley, Los Angeles, and London: University of California Press, 1993.

Albanese, Matteo, and Pablo del Hierro. *Transnational Fascism in the Twentieth Century: Spain, Italy and the Global Neo-Fascist Network*. A Modern History of Politics and Violence. London, Berlin, New York: Bloomsbury, 2016.

Albertazzi, Daniele, Donatella Bonansinga, and Davide Vampa. "Introduction." In *Populism and New Patterns of Political Competition in Western Europe*, edited by Daniele Albertazzi and Davide Vampa. London and New York: Routledge, 2021.

Albuquerque, Eduardo, Wilson Suzigan, Glenda Kruss, and Keun Lee, eds. *Developing National Systems of Innovation: University-Industry Interactions in the Global South*. Cheltenham, UK and Northampton, Massachusetts: Edward Elgar Publishing, 2015.

Aldcroft, Derek H. *Europe's Third World: The European Periphery in the Interwar Years*. London and New York: Routledge, 2016.

Alesina, Alberto. "The Size of Countries: Does It Matter?." *Journal of the European Economic Association*. 1, no. 2–3 (2003): 301–316.

Alesina, Alberto, and Enrico Spolaore. *The Size of Nations*. Cambridge, Massachusetts, and Lndon, England: MIT Press, 2005.

Alexander, John M. *Capabilities and Social Justice: The Political Philosophy of Amartya Sen and Martha Nussbaum*. London and New York: Routledge, 2016.

Alkire, Sabina. "Dimensions of Human Development." *World Development*. 30, no. 2 (2002): 181–205.

Allen, Robert C. "Why the Industrial Revolution Was British: Commerce, Induced Invention, and the Scientific Revolution 1." *The Economic History Review*. 64, no. 2 (2011): 357–384.

Amable, Bruno. *The Diversity of Modern Capitalism*. Oxford and New York: Oxford University Press, 2003.

Ambrosio, Thomas. *Irredentism: Ethnic Conflict and International Politics*. Westport, Connecticut, and London: Praeger, 2001.

Amsden, Alice H. *Asia's Next Giant: South Korea and Late Industrialization*. Oxford and New York: Oxford University Press, 1992.

Amsden, Alice H. *Escape from Empire: The Developing World's Journey through Heaven and Hell*. MIT Press, 2009.

Anderson, Benedict. *Imagined Communities: Reflections on the Origin and Spread of Nationalism*. London and New York: Verso, 1991.

Anderson, Fred. *Crucible of War: The Seven Years' War and the Fate of Empire in British North America, 1754–1766*. New York: Vintage Books, 2000.

Anderson, Lisa. *The State and Social Transformation in Tunisia and Libya, 1830–1980*. Princeton and Oxford: Princeton University Press, 1986.

Anderson, Perry. *Lineages of the Absolutist State*. London: Verso, 2013.

Anderson, Perry. *Passages from Antiquity to Feudalism*. London and New York: Verso, 2013.

Andreotti, Alberta, and Enzo Mingione. "Local Welfare Systems in Europe and the Economic Crisis." *European Urban and Regional Studies*. 23, no. 3 (2016): 252–266.

Anheier, Helmut K. *Civil Society: Measurement, Evaluation, Policy*. Civicus, World Alliance for Citizen Participation. London and Sterling, Virginia: Earthscan, 2013.

Anheier, Helmut K., and Lester M. Salamon. "Volunteering in Cross-National Perspective: Initial Comparisons." *Law and Contemporary Problems*. 62 (1999): 43.

Anscombe, Frederick. "Albanians and 'Mountain Bandits.'" In *The Ottoman Balkans, 1750–1830, Pp 87–114*, edited by Frederick Anscombe. Princeton, New Jersey: Markus Wiener Publishers, 2006.

Anter, Andreas. *Max Weber's Theory of the Modern State: Origins, Structure and Significance*. Translated by Keith Tribe. London and New York: Palgrave Macmillan, 2014.

Apollonio, Umbro, ed. *Futurist Manifestos*. London: Thames and Hudson, 1973.

Ardagna, Silvia, and Francesco Caselli. "The Political Economy of the Greek Debt Crisis: A Tale of Two Bailouts." *American Economic Journal: Macroeconomics*. 6, no. 4 (2014): 291–323.

Arielli, Nir. *Fascist Italy and the Middle East, 1933–40*. London and New York: Palgrave Macmillan, 2010.

Armitage, David. *The Ideological Origins of the British Empire*. Ideas in Context. Cambridge and New York: Cambridge University Press, 2000.

Armitage, David, and Michael J. Braddick, eds. *The British Atlantic World, 1500–1800*, Problems in Focus Series. London and New York: Palgrave Macmillan, 2002.

Arreguín-Toft, Ivan. *How the Weak Win Wars: A Theory of Asymmetric Conflict*. Cambridge and New York: Cambridge University Press, 2005.

Arrighi, Giovanni. *Adam Smith in Beijing: Lineages of the 21st Century*. London and New York: Verso, 2009.

Arrighi, Giovanni. "Capitalism and the Modern World-System: Rethinking the Nondebates of the 1970's." *Review (Fernand Braudel Center)*. 21, no. 1 (1998): 113–129.

Arrighi, Giovanni. "Hegemony and Antisystemic Movements." In *The Modern World-System in the Long Duree*, edited by Immanuel Maurice Wallerstein, 2004.

Arrighi, Giovanni. "Hegemony Unravelling." *New Left Review*. 32 (2005): 23.

Arrighi, Giovanni. "Hegemony Unravelling–II." *New Left Review*. 33, no. May–June (2005): 83–116.

Arrighi, Giovanni. *The Long Twentieth Century: Money, Power, and the Origins of Our Times*. London and New York: Verso, 1994.

Arrighi, Giovanni. "Peripheralization of Southern Africa, I: Changes in Production Processes." *Review (Fernand Braudel Center)*. 3, no. 2 (1979): 161.

Arrighi, Giovanni. *The Political Economy of Rhodesia*. Vol. 16: Mouton The Hague, 1967.

Arrighi, Giovanni. *Semiperipheral Development: The Politics of Southern Europe in the Twentieth Century*. Thousand Oaks, London, and New Delhi: SAGE, 1985.

Arrighi, Giovanni. "The Three Hegemonies of Historical Capitalism." In *Gramsci, Historical Materialism and International Relations*, edited by Stephen Gill. Cambridge and New York: Cambridge University Press, 1993.

Arrighi, Giovanni, Terence K. Hopkins, and Immanuel Maurice Wallerstein. *Antisystemic Movements*. London and New York: Verso, 2012.

Arrighi, Giovanni, Beverly J. Silver, and Benjamin D. Brewer. "Industrial Convergence, Globalization, and the Persistence of the North-South Divide." *Studies in Comparative International Development*. 38, no. 1 (2003): 3.

Artz, Lee, and Bren Ortega Murphy. *Cultural Hegemony in the United States*. Thousand Oaks, California: Sage Publications, 2000.

Ash, Chris. *Matabele: The War of 1893 and the 1896 Rebellions*. Pinetown, South Africa: 30° South Publishers, 2016.

Asheim, Bjørn T., Arne Isaksen, Claire Nauwelaers, and Franz Tödtling, eds. *SMEs and the Regional Dimension of Innovation*, Regional Innovation Policy for Small-Medium Enterprises. Cheltenham, UK and Northampton, Massachusetts: Edward Elgard, 2003.

Asher, Michael. *Khartoum: The Ultimate Imperial Adventure*. London: Penguin, 2005.

Ashton, Nigel J., and Duco Hellema, eds. *Unspoken Allies: Anglo-Dutch Relations since 1780*. Amsterdam: Amsterdam University Press, 2001.

Astarita, Tommaso. *Between Salt Water and Holy Water: A History of Southern Italy*. New York: W. W. Norton, 2006.

Aviram, Amitai. "Regulation by Networks." *Brigham Young University Law Review*. 29, no. 4 (2003): 1179–1235.

Azariadis, Costas, and John Stachurski. "Poverty Traps." In *Handbook of Economic Growth*, edited by Philippe Aghion and Steven Durlauf. Amsterdam, San Diego, Kidlington, Oxford, and London: Elsevier, 2005.

Bagnasco, Arnaldo. "Trust and Social Capital." In *The Blackwell Companion to Political Sociology*, edited by Kate Nash and Alan Scott, 230–239, 2004.

Bagnasco, Arnaldo, and Doug Thompson. "The Question of the Middle Class." *Italian Politics*. 20 (2004): 204–222.

Bailey, Erica, Dan Jun Wang, Hayagreeva Rao, and Sarah A Soule. "What the wunc? Perceptions of wunc and Social Movement Mobilization." Paper presented at the Academy of Management Proceedings, 2020.

Ballarino, Gabriele, Nazareno Panichella, and Moris Triventi. "School Expansion and Uneven Modernization. Comparing Educational Inequality in Northern and Southern Italy." *Research in Social Stratification and Mobility*. 36 (2014): 69–86.

Balleriaux, Catherine. *Missionary Strategies in the New World, 1610–1690: An Intellectual History*. London and New York: Routledge, 2016.

Ballon, H. *Robert Moses and the Modern City: The Transformation of New York*. New York: W. W. Norton, 2007.

Baracetti, Gaia. "Foibe: Nationalism, Revenge and Ideology in Venezia Giulia and Istria, 1943—5." *Journal of Contemporary History*. 44, no. 4 (2009): 657–674.

Baran, Paul A. *Monopoly Capital*. New York: Monthly Review Press, 1966.

Barkey, Karen. *Bandits and Bureaucrats: The Ottoman Route to State Centralization*. Ithaca, New York: Cornell University Press, 1994.

Barkey, Karen. *Empire of Difference: The Ottomans in Comparative Perspective*. Cambridge and New York: Cambridge University Press, 2008.

Barkey, Karen, and Mark von Hagen, eds. *After Empire: Multiethnic Societies and Nation-Building. The Soviet Union and the Russian, Ottoman, and Habsburg Empires*. London and New York: Routledge, 1997.

Barman, Emily. "An Institutional Approach to Donor Control: From Dyadic Ties to a Field-Level Analysis." *American Journal of Sociology*. 112, no. 5 (2007): 1416–1457.

Bartley, Paula. *Queen Victoria*. London and New York: Routledge, 2016.

Bates, Robert Hinrichs. *Markets and States in Tropical Africa: The Political Basis of Agricultural Policies*. California Series on Social Choice and Political Economy. Berkeley and Los Angeles: University of California Press, 1981.

Batteau, Allen. *Technology and the Common Good: The Unity and Division of a Democratic Society*. New York and Oxford: Berghahn Books, 2022.

Baugh, Daniel A. *The Global Seven Years War 1754–1763: Britain and France in a Great Power Contest*. London and New York: Routledge, 2011.

Baumeister, Roy F. *The Cultural Animal: Human Nature, Meaning, and Social Life*. Oxford and New York: Oxford University Press, 2005.

Bayly, Christopher Alan. *Empire and Information: Intelligence Gathering and Social Communication in India, 1780–1870*. Cambridge Studies in Indian History and Society. Cambridge and New York: Cambridge University Press, 1999.

Bayly, Christopher Alan. *Imperial Meridian: The British Empire and the World, 1780–1830.* Studies in Modern History. London: Longman, 1989.

Beales, Derek, and Eugenio F. Biagini. *The Risorgimento and the Unification of Italy.* London and New York: Routledge, 2014.

Beck, Thorsten, and Asli Demirguc-Kunt. "Small and Medium-Size Enterprises: Access to Finance as a Growth Constraint." *Journal of Banking & finance.* 30, no. 11 (2006): 2931–2943.

Becnel, Kim. *The Rise of Corporate Publishing and Its Effects on Authorship in Early Twentieth Century America.* London and New York: Routledge, 2012.

Behnke, Nathalie, Jörg Broschek, and Jared Sonnicksen. "Introduction: The Relevance of Studying Multilevel Governance." In *Configurations, Dynamics and Mechanisms of Multilevel Governance,* edited by Nathalie Behnke, Jörg Broschek and Jared Sonnicksen. London and New York: Palgrave Macmillan, 2019.

Belussi, Fiorenza, Giorgio Gottardi, and Enzo Rullani, eds. *The Technological Evolution of Industrial Districts.* New York: Springer Science + Business Media, 2003.

Ben-Ghiat, Ruth. "Fascism, Writing, and Memory: The Realist Aesthetic in Italy, 1930–1950." *The Journal of Modern History.* 67, no. 3 (1995): 627–665.

Ben-Ghiat, Ruth. *Fascist Modernities: Italy, 1922–1945.* Studies on the History of Society and Culture. Berkeley and Los Angeles: University of California Press, 2001.

Ben-Ghiat, Ruth. "Italian Fascism and the Aesthetics of the 'Third Way'." *Journal of Contemporary History.* 31, no. 2 (1996): 293–316.

Ben-Ghiat, Ruth. *Strongmen: Mussolini to the Present.* New York and London: W. W. Norton, 2020.

Bender, Jill C. *The 1857 Indian Uprising and the British Empire.* Cambridge and New York: Cambridge University Press, 2016.

Berger, Suzanne. "Globalization and Politics." *Annual Review of Political Science.* 3 (2000): 43–62.

Bergesen, Albert. "The Critique of World-System Theory: Class Relations or Division of Labor?." *Sociological Theory.* 2 (1984): 365–372.

Bergesen, Albert. "Turning World-System Theory on Its Head." *Theory, Culture & Society.* 7, no. 2–3 (1990): 67–81.

Bergesen, Albert James. "Pre Vs. Post 1500ers." *Comparative Civilizations Review.* 30, no. 30 (1994): 11.

Berman, Sheri. "Civil Society and Political Institutionalization." In *Beyond Tocqueville: Civil Society and the Social Capital Debate in Comparative Perspective,* edited by Bob Edwards, Michael W. Foley and Mario Diani. Hanover and London: University Press of New England, 2001.

Berman, Sheri. "Civil Society and the Collapse of the Weimar Republic." *World Politics.* 49, no. 3 (1997): 401–429.

Bhandari, Humnath, and Kumi Yasunobu. "What Is Social Capital? A Comprehensive Review of the Concept." *Asian Journal of Social Science.* 37, no. 3 (2009): 480–510.

Bhatt, Swati. *How Digital Communication Technology Shapes Markets: Redefining Competition, Building Cooperation.* London and New York: Palgrave Macmillan, 2016.

Bieler, Andreas, and Adam David Morton. "A Critical Theory Route to Hegemony, World Order and Historical Change: Neo-Gramscian Perspectives in International Relations." *Capital & Class.* 28, no. 1 (2004): 85–113.

Biesta, Gert. "Philosophy of Education for the Public Good: Five Challenges and an Agenda." *Educational Philosophy and Theory.* 44, no. 6 (2012): 581–593.

Blanco, Luisa, and Isabel Ruiz. "The Impact of Crime and Insecurity on Trust in Democracy and Institutions." *American Economic Review.* 103, no. 3 (2013): 284–88.

Block, Fred, and Peter Evans. "The State and the Economy." In *The Handbook of Economic Sociology,* edited by Neil J. Smelser and Richard Swedberg. Princeton and Oxford: Princeton University Press, 2010.

Blok, Anton. *The Mafia of a Sicilian Village, 1860–1960: A Study of Violent Peasant Entrepreneurs.* Oxford: Basil Blackwell, 1974.

Boatright, Robert G. *The Deregulatory Moment?: A Comparative Perspective on Changing Campaign Finance Laws.* Ann Arbor: University of Michigan Press, 2015.

Bobba, Giuliano, and Duncan McDonnell. "Italy: a Strong and Enduring Market for Populism." In *European Populism in the Shadow of the Great Recession,* edited by Hanspeter Kriesi and Takis Spyros Pappas, 163–179. London and New York: ECPR Press with Palgrave Macmillan, 2015.

Bobbio, Norberto. *Thomas Hobbes and the Natural Law Tradition.* Translated by Daniela Gobetti. Chicago and London: University of Chicago Press, 1993.

Boli, John, and George M. Thomas, eds. *Constructing World Culture: International Nongovernmental Organizations since 1875.* Stanford, California: Stanford University Press, 1999.

Boli, John, and George M. Thomas. "World Culture in the World Polity: A Century of International Non-Governmental Organization." *American Sociological Review.* 62, no. 2 (1997): 171–190.

Bond, Sheryl, and Jean-Pierre Lemasson, eds. *A New World of Knowledge: Canadian Universities and Globalization.* Ottawa, Cairo, Dakar, Johannesburg, Montevideo, Nairobi, New Delhi, Singapore: International Development Research Centre, 1999.

Borg, Carmel, Joseph A. Buttigieg, and Peter Mayo, eds. *Gramsci and Education,* Culture and Politics Series. Lanham, Boulder, New York, and Oxford: Rowman & Littlefield, 2002.

Bourdieu, Pierre. *Forms of Capital.* Translated by Peter Collier. General Sociology, Volume 3: Lectures at the Collège de France 1983–84. Cambridge, UK and Malden, Massachusetts: Polity, 2021.

Bourdieu, Pierre. *Homo Academicus*. Translated by Peter Collier. Stanford, California: Stanford University Press, 1988.

Bowles, Samuel, Steven N. Durlauf, and Karla Hoff, eds. *Poverty Traps*. Princeton and New York: Princeton University Press, 2006.

Bowles, Samuel, and Herbert Gintis. "Social Preferences, Homo Oeconomicus and *Zoon Politikon*." In *The Oxford Handbook of Contextual Political Analysis*, edited by Robert E. Goodin and Charles Tilly. Oxford and New York: Oxford University Press, 2006.

Bowring, Finn. "From the Mass Worker to the Multitude: A Theoretical Contextualization of Hardt and Negri's Empire." *Capital & Class*. 28, no. 2 (2004): 101–132.

Braddick, Michael J. *State Formation in Early Modern England, C.1550–1700*. Cambridge and New York: Cambridge University Press, 2000.

Brady, David, Jason Beckfield, and Wei Zhao. "The Consequences of Economic Globalization for Affluent Democracies." *Annual Review of Sociology*. 33 (2007): 313.

Bragg, John K. *Ottoman Notables and Participatory Politics: Tanzimat Reform in Tokat, 1839–1876*. London and New York: Routldge, 2014.

Brando, Nicolás, and Katarina Pitasse Fragoso. "Capability Deprivation and the Relational Dimension of Poverty: Testing Universal Multidimensional Indexes." In *Dimensions of Poverty: Measurement, Epistemic Injustices, Activism*, edited by Valentin Beck, Henning Hahn and Robert Lepenies. Cham, Switzerland: Springer, 2020.

Braudel, Fernand. *Civilization and Capitalism 15th-18th Century, Volume 2: The Wheels of Commerce*. Translated by Sian Reynolds. New York: Harper & Row, 1982.

Braudel, Fernand. *Civilization and Capitalism, 15th-18th Century Volume 3: The Perspective of the World*. Translated by Sian Reynolds. 1st ed. New York: Harper & Row, 1984.

Braudel, Fernand. *Civilization and Capitalism, 15th-18th Century, Volume 1: The Structure of Everyday Life*. Translated by Sian Reynolds. New York: Harper & Row, 1981.

Braudel, Fernand. *The Mediterranean and the Mediterranean World in the Age of Philip II, Vol. 1*. Translated by Sian Reynolds. New York: Harper & Row, 1972.

Braudel, Fernand. *The Mediterranean and the Mediterranean World in the Age of Philip II, Vol. 2*. Translated by Sian Reynolds. New York: Harper & Row, 1973.

Braudel, Fernand. *The Structures of Everyday Life: The Limits of the Possible*. Civilisation Matérielle, Économie et Capitalisme. Collins, 1981.

Braverman, Harry, and John Bellamy Foster. *Labor and Monopoly Capital: The Degradation of Work in the Twentieth Century. New Introduction by John Bellamy Foster*. New York: Monthly Review Press, 1998.

Bremer, Stuart A. "Dangerous Dyads: Conditions Affecting the Likelihood of Interstate War, 1816–1965." *Journal of Conflict Resolution*. 36, no. 2 (1992): 309–341.

Breuilly, John, ed. *Bringing History Back into Nationalism?*, New Perspectives on South-East Europe. London and New York: Palgrave Macmillan, 2010.

Brewer, Anthony. *Marxist Theories of Imperialism: A Critical Survey*. London and New York: Routledge, 1990.

Brewer, John, and Eckhart Hellmuth, eds. *Rethinking Leviathan: The Eighteenth-Century State in Britain and Germany,* German Historical Institute London. Oxford and New York: Oxford University Press, 1999.

Brooks, Jeffrey. *Thank You, Comrade Stalin!: Soviet Public Culture from Revolution to Cold War.* Princeton and Oxford: Princeton University Press, 2000.

Brown, Deborah Wright, and Alison M. Konrad. "Granovetter Was Right: The Importance of Weak Ties to a Contemporary Job Search." *Group & Organization Management.* 26, no. 4 (2001): 434–462.

Brown, Nicholas, and Imre Szeman. "What Is the Multitude? Questions for Michael Hardt and Antonio Negri." *Cultural Studies.* 19, no. 3 (2005): 372–387.

Brusoni, Stefano, and Andrea Prencipe. "Patterns of Modularization: The Dynamics of Product Architecture in Complex Systems." *European Management Review.* 8, no. 2 (2011): 67–80.

Brusoni, Stefano, and Andrea Prencipe. "Unpacking the Black Box of Modularity: Technologies, Products and Organizations." *Industrial and corporate Change.* 10, no. 1 (2001): 179–205.

Bryant, Joseph M. "A New Sociology for a New History? Further Critical Thoughts on the Eurasian Similarity and Great Divergence Theses." *Canadian Journal of Sociology/Cahiers canadiens de sociologie.* 33, no. 1 (2008).

Bryant, Joseph M. "The West and the Rest Revisited: Debating Capitalist Origins, European Colonialism, and the Advent of Modernity." *Canadian Journal of Sociology/Cahiers canadiens de sociologie.* (2006): 31, no. 4 403–444.

Bulmer, Simon, and William E. Paterson. *Germany and the European Union: Europe's Reluctant Hegemon?* London: Red Globe Prss, 2018.

Burawoy, Michael. "For a Sociological Marxism: The Complementary Convergence of Antonio Gramsci and Karl Polanyi." *Politics & Society.* 31, no. 2 (2003): 193–261.

Burke, Peter. *The Fortunes of the Courtier: The European Reception of Castiglione's Cortegiano.* University Park, Pennsylvania: Pennsylvania State University Press, 1996.

Burleigh, Michael. *Blood and Rage: A Cultural History of Terrorism.* New York: Harper Press, 2008.

Butler, Lawrence J. *Industrialisation and the British Colonial State: West Africa 1939–1951.* London and New York: Routledge, 1997.

Buttigieg, Joseph A. "The Contemporary Discourse on Civil Society: A Gramscian Critique." *boundary 2.* 32, no. 1 (2005): 33–52.

Buttigieg, Joseph A. "Gramsci on Civil Society." *boundary 2.* 22, no. 3 (1995): 1–32.

Byrnes, Joseph F. *Catholic and French Forever: Religious and National Identity in Modern France.* University Park, Pennsylvania: Pennsylvania State University Press, 2005.

Callinicos, Alex. "The Limits of "Political Marxism."" *New Left Review.* 184, no. 1 (1990): 110–15.

Cancogni, Manlio. *Gli Angeli Neri. Storia Degli Anarchici Italiani da Pisacane Ai Circoli di Carrara*. Milan: Mursia, 2011.

Cannon, Barry. *The Right in Latin America: Elite Power, Hegemony and the Struggle for the State*. London and New York: Routledge, 2016.

Capano, Fabio. "From a Cosmopolitan to a Fascist Land: Adriatic Irredentism in Motion." *Nationalities Papers*. 46, no. 6 (2018): 976–991.

Capone, Alessandro. "Il Brigantaggio Meridionale: una Rassegna Storiografica." *Le Carte e la Storia*. 21, no. 2 (2015): 32–40.

Cardoso Reis, Bruno. "Myths of Decolonization: Britain, France, and Portugal Compared." In *The Ends of European Colonial Empires: Cases and Comparisons*, edited by Miguel Bandeira Jeronimo and Antonio Costa Pinto. London and New York: Palgrave Macmillan, 2016.

Carlucci, Alessandro. *Gramsci and Languages: Unification, Diversity, Hegemony*. Chicago: Haymarket Books, 2014.

Carney, Judith Ann. *Black Rice: The African Origins of Rice Cultivation in the Americas*. Cambridge, Massachusetts and London: Harvard University Press, 2001.

Caro, Robert A. *The Power Broker: Robert Moses and the Fall of New York*. A Borzoi Book. New York: Alfred A. Knopf, 1974.

Carroll, William K. "Hegemony, Counter-Hegemony, Anti-Hegemony." *Socialist Studies/ Études Socialistes*. 1, no. 3 (2006): 9–43.

Carroll, William K., and Robert S. Ratner. "Between Leninism and Radical Pluralism: Gramscian Reflections on Counter-Hegemony and the New Social Movements." *Critical Sociology*. 20, no. 2 (1994): 3–26.

Carroll, William K., and Robert S. Ratner. "Social Movements and Counter-Hegemony: Lessons from the Field." *New Proposals*. 4, no. 1 (2010): 7–22.

Carteny, Andrea. "Il Brigantaggio in Italia tra Risorgimento e Questione Meridionale: Un'Introduzione al Tema." *Chronica Mundi*. 11, no. 1 (2016).

Casanova, Julián. "Franco, the Catholic Church and the Martyrs." In *The Spanish Civil War: Exhuming a Buried Past*, edited by Anindya Raychaudhuri. Cardiff: University of Wales Press, 2013.

Casanova, Pascale. *The World Republic of Letters*. Translated by M.B. DeBevoise. Cambridge, Massachusetts and London: Harvard University Press, 2004.

Casey, Kimberly L. "Defining Political Capital: A Reconsideration of Bourdieu's Interconvertibility Theory." (2008). https://cpb-us-w2.wpmucdn.com/about.illino isstate.edu/dist/e/34/files/2019/09/Casey.pdf.

Castells, Manuel. *The Information Age, Volume 1. The Rise of the Network Society*. The Information Age: Economy, Society and Culture. Chichester, West Sussex: Wiley-Blackwell, 2000.

Castells, Manuel. *The Information Age, Volume 2. The Power of Indentity*. The Information Age: Economy, Society and Culture. Chichester, West Sussex: Wiley-Blackwell, 2000.

Castells, Manuel. *The Information Age, Volume 3. End of Millennium.* The Information Age: Economy, Society and Culture. Chichester, West Sussex: Wiley-Blackwell, 2000.

Castells, Manuel. "Toward a Sociology of the Network Society." *Contemporary sociology.* 29, no. 5 (2000): 693–699.

Cavanagh, Edward, and Lorenzo Veracini, eds. *The Routledge Handbook of the History of Settler Colonialism.* London and New York: Routledge, 2016.

Cayli, Baris. "Peasants, Bandits, and State Intervention: The Consolidation of Authority in the Ottoman Balkans and Southern Italy." *Journal of Agrarian Change.* 18, no. 2 (2018): 425–443.

Cepiku, Denita. "A Network Approach to Asymmetric Federalism: The Italian Case Study." In *Making Multi-Level Public Management Work: Stories of Success and Failure from Europe and North America.*, edited by Denita Cepiku, Dabvid K. Jesuit and Ian Roberge. Boca Raton, Florida: CRC Press, 2013.

CERN. "Browse Services by Department. Services for IT." https://cern.service-now.com /service-portal?id=services_department&dep=IT, accessed October 16, 2022.

CERN. "Welcome to CERN IT Department." https://information-technology.web.cern .ch/services, accessed October 16, 2022.

Chamberlain, M.E. *The Scramble for Africa.* 3rd ed. London and New York: Routledge, 2014.

Chandler, Alfred D. Jr. *The Visible Hand: The Managerial Revolution in American Business.* Cambridge, Massachusetts and London: Harvard University Press, 1993.

Charnock, Guido, and Greig Charnock Starosta, eds. *The New International Division of Labour: Global Transformation and Uneven Development.* London and New York: Palgrave Macmillan, 2016.

Chase, Kerry A. *Trading Blocs: States, Firms, and Regions in the World Economy.* Ann Arbor: University of Michigan Press, 2009.

Chase-Dunn, Christopher. *Global Formation: Structures of the World-Economy.* Oxford: Basil Blackwell, 1991.

Chase-Dunn, Christopher. "Interstate System and Capitalist World-Economy: One Logic or Two?." *International Studies Quarterly.* 25, no. 1 (1981): 19–42.

Chazan, Naomi, ed. *Irredentism and International Politics.* Boulder: Lynne Rienner, 1991.

Chhim, Chris, and Éric Bélanger. "Language as a Public Good and National Identity: Scotland's Competing Heritage Languages." *Nations and Nationalism.* 23, no. 4 (2017): 929–951.

Chirot, Daniel. "The Rise of the West." *American Sociological Review.* 50, no. 2 (1985): 181–195.

Choudry, Aziz. *Learning Activism: The Intellectual Life of Contemporary Social Movements.* Toronto, Buffalo, London: University of Toronto Press, 2015.

Choudry, Aziz, and Dip Kapoor, eds. *Ngoization: Complicity, Contradictions and Prospects.* London and New York: Zed Books, 2013.

Chovanec, Johanna, and Olof Heilo, eds. *Narrated Empires: Perceptions of Late Habsburg and Ottoman Multinationalism*. Cham, Switzerland: Springer, 2021.

Christensen, Peter H. *Germany and the Ottoman Railways: Art, Empire, and Infrastructure*. New Haven and London: Yale University Press, 2017.

Christin, Pierre, and Olivier Balez. *Robert Moses: The Master Builder of New York City*. Nobrow Limited, 2018.

Chu, Yin-wah, ed. *The Asian Developmental State: Reexaminations and New Departures*. London and New York: Palgrave Macmillan, 2016.

Ciocca, Pierluigi. "Brigantaggio ed Economia nel Mezzogiorno d'Italia, 1860–1870." *Rivista di Storia Economica*. 29, no. 1 (2013): 3–30.

Cipolla, Carlo M., ed. *The Economic Decline of Empires*, Economic History. London and New York: Routledge, 2013.

Cipolla, Carlo M. *Guns, Sails and Empires: Technological Innovations and the Early Phases of European Expansion, 1400–1700*. New York: Pantheon Books, 1965.

Cipolla, Carlo M. *Miasmas and Disease: Public Health and the Environment in the Pre-Industrial Age*. Translated by Elizabeth Potter. New Haven and London: Yale University Press, 1992.

Citino, Robert Michael. *Blitzkrieg to Desert Storm: The Evolution of Operational Warfare*. Kansas: University Press of Kansas, 2004.

Citino, Robert Michael. *The Path to Blitzkrieg: Doctrine and Training in the German Army, 1920–39*. Mechanicsburg, Pennsylvania: Stackpole Books, 2007.

Clark, Jennifer, Hsin-I Huang, and John P. Walsh. "A Typology of 'Innovation Districts': What It Means for Regional Resilience." *Cambridge Journal of Regions, Economy and Society*. 3, no. 1 (2010): 121–137.

Claydon, Tony, and Ian McBride, eds. *Protestantism and National Identity: Britain and Ireland, C.1650–C.1850*. Cambridge and New York: Cambridge University Press, 1998.

Cochrane, Eric. *Italy 1530–1630*. Longman History of Italy. London and New York: Routledge, 2014.

Cohen, Gerald Allan. *History, Labour, and Freedom: Themes from Marx*. Oxford: Clarendon Press, 1988.

Cohen, Gerald Allan. *Karl Marx's Theory of History: A Defence*. Princeton Paperbacks. Princeton and Oxford: Princeton University Press, 2001.

Cole, Juan Ricardo. *Napoleon's Egypt: Invading the Middle East*. London and New York: Palgrave, 2007.

Cole, Juan Ricardo. "Of Crowds and Empires: Afro-Asian Riots and European Expansion, 1857–1882." *Comparative Studies in Society and History*. 31, no. 1 (1989): 106–133.

Cole, Juan Ricardo. *Roots of North Indian Shiism in Iran and Iraq: Religion and State in Awadh, 1722–1859*. Berkeley and Los Angeles: University of California Press, 1988.

Cole, Juan Ricardo. *Sacred Space and Holy War: The Politics, Culture and History of Shi'ite Islam*. London and New York: I. B. Tauris, 2002.

Coleman, James S. "Social Capital in the Creation of Human Capital." *American Journal of Sociology*. 94 (1988): S95–S120.

Colli, Andrea, and Michelangelo Vasta. *Forms of Enterprise in 20th Century Italy: Boundaries, Structures and Strategies*. Cheltenham, UK and Northampton, Massachusetts: Edward Elgar, 2010.

Collier, Paul. "On the Economic Consequences of Civil War." *Oxford Economic Papers*. 51, no. 1 (1999): 168–183.

Collins, John, Ned Hall, and L. A. Paul, eds. *Causation and Counterfactuals*. Cambridge, Massachusetts and London: MIT Press, 2004.

Colomer, Josep Maria. "The Building of the American and European Empires." *Journal of Political Power*. 4, no. 3 (2011).

Colomer, Josep Maria. *Great Empires, Small Nations: The Uncertain Future of the Sovereign State*. New York and London: Routledge, 2007.

Conklin, Alice L. *A Mission to Civilize: The Republican Idea of Empire in France and West Africa, 1895–1930*. Stanford, California: Stanford University Press, 1997.

Connell, William J., and Stanislao G. Pugliese, eds. *The Routledge History of Italian Americans*. London and New York: Routledge, 2017.

Conversi, Daniele. "Genocide, Ethnic Cleansing and Nationalism." *Handbook of Nations and Nationalism*. London: Sage Publications. (2006): 320–333.

Conversi, Daniele. "Homogenisation, Nationalism and War: Should We Still Read Ernest Gellner?." *Nations and Nationalism*. 13, no. 3 (2007): 371–394.

Conversi, Daniele. "'We Are All Equals!' Militarism, Homogenization and 'Egalitarianism' in Nationalist State-Building (1789–1945)." *Ethnic and Racial Studies*. 31, no. 7 (2008): 1286–1314.

Cooke, Philip, and Luciana Lazzeretti, eds. *Creative Cities, Cultural Clusters and Local Economic Development*. Cheltenham, UK and Northampton, Massachusetts: Edward Elgar, 2008.

Corni, Gustavo. "The Exodus of Italians from Istria and Dalmatia, 1945–56." In *The Disentanglement of Populations*, edited by Jessica Reinisch and Elizabeth White. London and New York: Palgrave Macmillan, 2011.

Coverdale, J. F. *Italian Intervention in the Spanish Civil War*. Princeton Legacy Library. Princeton and Oxford: Princeton University Press, 2015.

Cowen, Tyler. "Law as a Public Good: The Economics of Anarchy." *Economics & Philosophy*. 8, no. 2 (1992): 249–267.

Cowling, Mark. "Marx's Lumpenproletariat and Murray's Underclass: Concepts Best Abandoned." In *Marx's Eighteenth Brumaire:(Post) Modern Interpretations*, edited by Mark Cowling and James Martin. London: Pluto, 2002.

Crossick, Geoffrey, and Heinz-Gerhard Haupt. *The Petite Bourgeoisie in Europe 1780–1914: Enterprise, Family and Independence*. London and New York: Routledge, 2013.

Currie, Janice K., and Janice Newson, eds. *Universities and Globalization: Critical Perspectives.* Thousand Oaks, London, and New Delhi: SAGE, 1998.

D'Auria, Matthew. "The Ventotene Manifesto: The Crisis of the Nation State and the Political Identity of Europe." In *European Identity and the Second World War,* edited by Menno Spiering and Michael Wintle. London and New York: Palgrave Macmillan, 2011.

Dahl, Robert A. *Polyarchy: Participation and Opposition.* New Haven and London: Yale University Press, 1973.

Dakin, Douglas. *The Greek Struggle for Independence, 1821–1833.* Berkeley and Los Angeles: University of California Press, 1973.

Daly, Jonathan. *Historians Debate the Rise of the West.* London and New York: Routledge, 2014.

Damrosch, David. *What Is World Literature?* Princeton and Oxford: Princeton University Press, 2003.

Damrosch, David, ed. *World Literature in Theory.* Chichester, West Sussex and Malden, Massachusetts: Wiley-Blackwell, 2014.

Dant, Tim. "Material Civilization: Things and Society." *The British Journal of Sociology.* 57, no. 2 (2006): 289–308.

Davidson, Alastair. "Gramsci, the Peasantry and Popular Culture." *The Journal of Peasant Studies.* 11, no. 4 (1984): 139–154.

Davidson, Basil. *West Africa before the Colonial Era: A History to 1850.* London and New York: Routledge, 2014.

Davies, Tim, Setphen B. Walker, Mor Rubinstein, and Fernando Perini, eds. *The State of Open Data: Histories and Horizons.* Cape Town and Ottawa: African Minds and the International Development Research Center, 2019.

Davis, Diana K. *Resurrecting the Granary of Rome: Environmental History and French Colonial Expansion in North Africa.* Athens: Ohio University Press, 2007.

Davis, John A. *Naples and Napoleon: Southern Italy and the European Revolutions, 1780–1860.* Oxford and New York: Oxford University Press, 2006.

Davis, John A. "The Neapolitan Revolution, 1799–1999: Between History and Myth." *Journal of Modern Italian Studies.* 4, no. 3 (1999): 350–358.

Davison, Roderic H. *Reform in the Ottoman Empire, 1856–1876.* Princeton and Oxford: Princeton University Press, 2015.

Dawson, Andrew. "Police Legitimacy and Homicide: A Macro-Comparative Analysis." *Social Forces.* 97, no. 2 (2018): 841–866.

Dawson, Andrew. "Political Violence in Consolidated Democracies: The Development and Institutionalization of Partisan Violence in Late Colonial Jamaica (1938–62)." *Social Science History.* 40, no. 2 (2016): 185–218.

Day, Richard B. *Gramsci Is Dead: Anarchist Currents in the Newest Social Movements.* London: Pluto, 2005.

De Francesco, Antonino. "Dal Sanfedismo al Brigantaggio: la Controrivoluzione nel Mezzogiorno d'Italia (1799–1863)." In *Blancs et Contre-Révolutionnaires en Europe. Espaces, Réseaux, Cultures et Mémoires, Fin XVIIIe-Début XXe Siècles: France, Italie, Espagne, Portugal*, edited by Bruno Dumons and Marco Folin. Rome: Collection de l'École Françoise de Rome, 2011.

De Mauro, Tullio. *Storia Linguistica Dell'italia Unita – Storia Linguistica Dell'italia Repubblicana*. Biblioteca Storica Laterza. Bari: Editori Laterza, 2017.

De Ville, Ferdi, and Gabriel Siles-Brügge. *TTIP: The Truth About the Transatlantic Trade and Investment Partnership*. Cambridge, UK and Malden, Massachusetts: Polity Press, 2015.

Dedman, Martin. *The Origins and Development of the European Union 1945–1995: A History of European Integration*. London and New York: Routledge, 1996.

DeFilippis, James. "The Myth of Social Capital in Community Development." *Housing Policy Debate*. 12, no. 4 (2001): 781–806.

Del Monte, Alfredo, and Luca Pennacchio. "Agricultural Productivity, Banditry and Criminal Organizations in Post-Unification Italy." *Rivista Italiana degli Economisti*. 17, no. 3 (2012): 347–378.

Del Monte, Alfredo, and Luca Pennacchio. "Struttura Fondiaria, Brigantaggio e Associazioni Criminali nel Mezzogiorno nei Decenni Post-Unitari." working paper, Università Parthenope, 2011.

Delbourgo, James, and Nicholas Dew, eds. *Science and Empire in the Atlantic World*, New Directions in American History. New York and London: Routledge, 2008.

Della Porta, Donatella. *Social Movements, Political Violence, and the State: A Comparative Analysis of Italy and Germany*. Cambridge Studies in Comparative Politics. Cambridge and New York: Cambridge University Press, 1995.

Della Sala, Vincent. "A New 'Confindustria' for a New Model of Italian Capitalism?." *Italian Politics*. 16 (2000): 205–222.

Dennis, Michael. *Lessons in Progress: State Universities and Progressivism in the New South, 1880–1920*. Urbana and Chicago: University of Illinois Press, 2001.

Deriglazova, Larisa. *Great Powers, Small Wars: Asymmetric Conflict since 1945*. Woodrow Wilson Center Press, Washington D.C.: Johns Hopkins University Press, Baltimore, 2020.

Deschaux-Dutard, Delphine. "L'Europe et Sa Défense: La Coopération Structurée Permanent, Est-Elle une Panacée?." *Défense & Sécurité Internationale*. no. 149 (2020): 40–41.

Detotto, Claudio, and Edoardo Otranto. "Does Crime Affect Economic Growth?." *Kyklos*. 63, no. 3 (2010): 330–345.

Detti, Tommaso, and Giuseppe Lauricella. *The Origins of the Internet*. Rome: Viella, 2017.

DeWitt, John. *Early Globalization and the Economic Development of the United States and Brazil*. Westport, Connecticut, and London: Praeger, 2002.

Di Mauro, B. "Note sulla Legittimità in Max Weber." *Il Pensiero Politico*. 24, no. 3 (1991): 313.

Diamond, Jared. *Collapse: How Societies Choose to Fail or Succeed: Revised Edition.* London: Penguin, 2011.

Diamond, Jared. *Guns, Germs, and Steel: The Fates of Human Societies.* New York and London: W. W. Norton, 1999.

Diani, Mario, and Doug McAdam, eds. *Social Movements and Networks: Relational Approaches to Collective Action.* Oxford and New York: Oxford University Press, 2003.

Diez-Minguela, Alfonso, Julio Martinez-Galarraga, and Daniel A. Tirado-Fabregat. *Regional Inequality in Spain: 1860–2015.* Palgrave Studies in Economic History. London and New York: Palgrave MacMillan, 2018.

Digiovanna, Sean. "Industrial Districts and Regional Economic Development: a Regulation Approach." *Regional Studies*. 30, no. 4 (1996): 373–386.

Dollinger, Philippe. *The German Hansa.* London and Basingstoke: Macmillan, 1970.

Domhoff, G. William. *State Autonomy or Class Dominance?: Case Studies on Policy Making in America.* Social Institutions and Social Change. Hawthorne, New York: Aldine de Gruyter, 1996.

Dosi, Giovanni, Richard R. Nelson, and Sydney G. Winter, eds. *The Nature and Dynamics of Organizational Capabilities.* Oxford and New York: Oxford University Press, 2000.

Doumani, Beshara. *Rediscovering Palestine: Merchants and Peasants in Jabal Nablus, 1700–1900.* Berkeley, Los Angeles, and London: University of California Press, 1995.

Doumanis, Nicholas. *Before the Nation: Muslim-Christian Coexistence and Its Destruction in Late-Ottoman Anatolia.* Oxford and New York: Oxford University Press, 2012.

Dowding, Keith, Peter John, Thanos Mergoupis, and Mark Van Vugt. "Exit, Voice and Loyalty: Analytic and Empirical Developments." *European Journal of Political Research*. 37, no. 4 (2000): 469–495.

Doyle, Don Harrison. *Nations Divided: America, Italy, and the Southern Question.* Athens, Georgia, and London: University of Georgia Press, 2002.

Drake, Richard. *Apostles and Agitators: Italy's Marxist Revolutionary Tradition.* Boston: Harvard University Press, 2009.

Drake, Richard. *The Revolutionary Mystique and Terrorism in Contemporary Italy.* Bloomington: Indiana University Press, 2021.

Duina, Francesco. *The Social Construction of Free Trade: The European Union, NAFTA, and Mercosur.* Princeton and Oxford: Princeton University Press, 2013.

Dunnage, Jonathan. "Sicilian Bandits and the Italian State: Narratives About Crime and (in) Security in the Post-War Italian Press, 1948–1950." *Cultural and Social History*. 19, no. 2 (2022): 185–202.

Dunthorn, Joseph. "The Spanish Monarchy and Early Francoism: Alternative or Complement?." *Totalitarian Movements and Political Religions*. 1, no. 2 (2000): 47–76.

Durkheim, Emile, and Lewis A. Coser. *The Division of Labor in Society.* Translated by W. D. Halls. Free Press Paperback. New York: Free Press, 1997.

Dynarski, Susan M. "Does Aid Matter? Measuring the Effect of Student Aid on College Attendance and Completion." *American Economic Review.* 93, no. 1 (2003): 279–288.

Easterbrook, William Thomas, and Mel Watkins. *Approaches to Canadian Economic History: A Selection of Essays.* Montreal, Kingston, London, Ithaca: McGill-Queen's University Press, 1967.

Edwards, Bob, and Michael W. Foley. "Civil Society and Social Capital Beyond Putnam." *American Behavioral Scientist.* 42, no. 1 (1998): 124–139.

Edwards, Bob, Michael W. Foley, and Mario Diani, eds. *Beyond Tocqueville: Civil Society and the Social Capital Debate in Comparative Perspective.* Hanover and London: University Press of New England, 2001.

Edwards, Bob, and John D. McCarthy. "Strategy Matters: The Contingent Value of Social Capital in the Survival of Local Social Movement Organizations." *Social Forces.* 83, no. 2 (2004): 621–651.

Edwards, Michael, ed. *The Oxford Handbook of Civil Society.* Oxford and New York: Oxford University Press, 2011.

Edwards, Peter, and Antonio Nicaso. *Business or Blood: Mafia Boss Vito Rizzuto's Last War.* Toronto: Vintage Canada, 2016.

Egan, Daniel. *The Dialectic of Position and Maneuver: Understanding Gramsci's Military Metaphor.* Leiden and Boston: Brill, 2016.

El-Eini, Roza. *Mandated Landscape: British Imperial Rule in Palestine, 1929–1948.* London and New York: Routledge, 2004.

Eldem, Edhem. *French Trade in Istanbul in the Eighteenth Century.* Leiden and Boston: Brill, 1999.

Elias, Norbert. *The Civilizing Process, Volume I: The History of Manners.* Oxford: Blackwell, 1969.

Elias, Norbert. *The Civilizing Process, Volume II: State Formation and Civilization.* Oxford: Blackwell, 1982.

Elias, Norbert. *The Civilizing Process: Sociogenetic and Psychogenetic Investigations.* Oxford: Blackwell, 2000.

Elliott, John H. *Empires of the Atlantic World: Britain and Spain in America, 1492–1830.* New Haven and London: Yale University Press, 2006.

Endres, Egon, and Theo Wehner. "Frictions in the New Division of Labour: Cooperation between Producers and Suppliers in the German Automobile Industry." In *The New Division of Labour: Emerging Forms of Work Organization in International Perspective,* edited by Wolfgang Littek and Tony Charles. Berlin and New York: Walter de Gruyter, 1995.

Ertman, Thomas. *Birth of the Leviathan: Building States and Regimes in Medieval and Early Modern Europe.* Cambridge and New York: Cambridge University Press, 1997.

Esping-Andersen, Gosta. *The Three Worlds of Welfare Capitalism*. Princeton and Oxford: Princeton University Press, 1990.

Esposito, Fernando. *Fascism, Aviation and Mythical Modernity*. Translated by Patrick Camiller. London and New York: Palgrave Macmillan, 2015.

Etzkowitz, Henry. "Entrepreneurial University Icon: Stanford and Silicon Valley as Innovation and Natural Ecosystem." *Industry and Higher Education*. 36, no. 4 (2022): 361–380.

Evans, Peter B. "The Challenges of the Institutional Turn: New Interdisciplinary Opportunities in Development Theory." In *The Economic Sociology of Capitalism*, edited by Victor Nee and Richard Swedberg. Princeton and New Jersey: Princeton University Press, 2005.

Evans, Peter B. "Collective Capabilities, Culture, and Amartya Sen's Development as Freedom." *Studies in Comparative International Development*. 37, no. 2 (2002): 54–60.

Evans, Peter B. *Dependent Development: The Alliance of Multinational, State, and Local Capital in Brazil*. Princeton and Oxford: Princeton University Press, 1979.

Evans, Peter B. *Embedded Autonomy: States and Industrial Transformation*. Princeton and Oxford: Princeton University Press, 1995.

Evans, Peter B. "Predatory, Developmental, and Other Apparatuses: A Comparative Political Economy Perspective on the Third World State." *Sociological Forum*. 4, no. 4 (1989): 561–587.

Evans, Peter B., Dietrich Rueschemeyer, and Theda Skocpol. *Bringing the State Back In*. Papers from a Conference Held at Mount Kisco, New York, in February 1982. Cambridge and New York: Cambridge University Press, 1985.

Evers, Adalbert. "Mixed Welfare Systems and Hybrid Organizations: Changes in the Governance and Provision of Social Services." *International Journal of Public Administration*. 28, no. 9–10 (2005): 737–748.

Evrensel, Ayse Y., and Tiffany Minx. "An Institutional Approach to the Decline of the Ottoman Empire." *Cogent Economics & Finance*. 5, no. 1 (2017): 1380248.

Exenberger, Andreas, and Simon Hartmann. "Extractive Institutions in the Congo: Checks and Balances in the *Longue Durée*." In *Colonial Exploitation and Economic Development: The Belgian Congo and the Netherlands Indies Compared*, edited by Ewout Frankema and Frank Buelens. London and New York: Routledge, 2013.

Fainstein, Susan S. "Assimilation and Exclusion in US Cities: The Treatment of African-Americans and Immigrants." In *Urban Segregation and the Welfare State: Inequality and Exclusion in Western Cities*, edited by Sako Musterd and Wim Ostendorf. London and New York: Routledge, 2013.

Falk, Martin, and Federico Biagi. "Relative Demand for Highly Skilled Workers and Use of Different ICT Technologies." *Applied Economics*. 49, no. 9 (2017): 903–914.

Fanizza, Fiammetta, and Marco Omizzolo. *Caporalato. An Authentic Agromafia*. MIlan: Mimesis International, 2019.

Fanon, Frantz, Homi K. Bhabha, and Jean-Paul Sartre. *The Wretched of the Earth.* Translated by Richard Philcox. New York: Grove Atlantic, 2007.

Fawaz, Leila Tarazi. "The City and the Mountain: Beirut's Political Radius in the Nineteenth Century as Revealed in the Crisis of 1860." *International Journal of Middle East Studies.* 16, no. 4 (1984): 489–495.

Fawaz, Leila Tarazi. *Merchants and Migrants in Nineteenth-Century Beirut.* Harvard University Press: Cambridge, Massachusetts and London, 1983.

Fawaz, Leila Tarazi. *An Occasion for War: Civil Conflict in Lebanon and Damascus in 1860.* Berkeley and Los Angeles: University of California Press, 1994.

Fawaz, Leila Tarazi, Christopher Alan Bayly, and Robert Ilbert, eds. *Modernity and Culture: From the Mediterranean to the Indian Ocean.* New York: Columbia University Press, 2002.

Fayolle, Alain, and Dana T. Redford, eds. *Handbook on the Entrepreneurial University.* Cheltenham, UK and Northampton, Massachusetts: Edward Elgar, 2014.

Federico, Giovanni, Alessandro Nuvolari, and Michelangelo Vasta. "Inequality in Pre-Industrial Europe (1260–1850): New Evidence from the Labor Share." *Review of Income and Wealth.* Online Version of Record before inclusion in an issue (2021): 1–29.

Federico, Giovanni, Alessandro Nuvolari, and Michelangelo Vasta. "The Origins of the Italian Regional Divide: Evidence from Real Wages, 1861–1913." *The Journal of Economic History.* 79, no. 1 (2019): 63–98.

Federico, Giovanni, and Antonio Tena-Junguito. "A Tale of Two Globalizations: Gains from Trade and Openness 1800–2010." *Review of World economics.* 153, no. 3 (2017): 601–626.

Felice, Emanuele. "Regional Income Inequality in Italy in the Long Run (1871–2010): Patterns and Determininants." In *The Economic Development of Europe's Regions: A Quantitative History since 1900,* edited by Joan Ramon Rosés and Nolf Wolf. London and New York: Routledge, 2018.

Felice, Emanuele, Alessandro Nuvolari, and Michelangelo Vasta. "Alla Ricerca delle Origini del Declino Economico Italiano." *L'Industria.* 40, no. 2 (2019): 197–222.

Ferraresi, Franco. "The Radical Right in Postwar Italy." *Politics & Society.* 16, no. 1 (1988): 71–119.

Ferraresi, Franco. *Threats to Democracy: The Radical Right in Italy after the War.* Princeton and Oxford: Princeton University Press, 2012.

Fetter, Sibren, A. J. Berlanga, and Peter B. Sloep. "Using ad Hoc Transient Communities to Strengthen Social Capital: Design Considerations." Paper presented at the Proceedings of the 7th International Conference on Networked Learning, Lancaster, 2010.

Fieldhouse, D.K. *Western Imperialism in the Middle East, 1914–1958.* Oxford and New York: Oxford University Press, 2006.

Filippini, Michele. *Una Politica di Massa: Antonio Gramsci e la Rivoluzione della Società*. Roma: Carocci, 2015.

Finchelstein, Federico. *A Brief History of Fascist Lies*. Berkeley and Los Angeles: University of California Press, 2020.

Finchelstein, Federico. *From Fascism to Populism in History*. Berkeley and Los Angeles: University of California Press, 2019.

Fiorentini, Gianluca, and Sam Peltzman, eds. *The Economics of Organised Crime*. Cambridge and New York: Cambridge University Press, 1997.

Fischer, Fritz. *Germany's Aims in the First World War*. New York: W.W. Norton, 1967.

Fitzsimmons, Michael P. *The Place of Words: The Académie Française and Its Dictionary During an Age of Revolution*. Oxford and New York: Oxford University Press, 2017.

Flap, Henk D. "Patronage: an Institution in Its Own Right." In *Social Institutions*, edited by Michael Hechter, Karl-Dieter Opp and Reinhard Wippler. London and New York: Routledge, 2018.

Fleischacker, Samuel. On Adam Smith's "Wealth of Nations": *A Philosophical Companion*. Princeton and Oxford: Princeton University Press, 2005.

Flint, John. *Cecil Rhodes*. New York: Warner Books, Hachette Book Group, 2009.

Flora, Jan L. "Social Capital and Communities of Place." *Rural Sociology*. 63, no. 4 (1998): 481–506.

Fontana, Benedetto. "Gramsci on Politics and State." *Journal of Classical Sociology*. 2, no. 2 (2002): 157–178.

Fontana, Benedetto. "Liberty and Domination: Civil Society in Gramsci." *boundary 2*. 33, no. 2 (2006): 51–74.

Fontana, Benedetto. "Logos and Kratos: Gramsci and the Ancients on Hegemony." *Journal of the History of Ideas*. 61, no. 2 (2000): 305–326.

Ford, Robert, and Matthew J. Goodwin. Revolt on the Right: Explaining Support for the Radical Right in Britain. London and New York: Routledge, 2014.

Forrest, Ray, and Ade Kearns. "Social Cohesion, Social Capital and the Neighbourhood." *Urban Studies*. 38, no. 12 (2001): 2125–2143.

Foster, John Bellamy. *The Theory of Monopoly Capitalism: An Elaboration of Marxian Political Economy*. New York: Monthly Review Press, 2014.

Fowler, Michael Ross, and Julie Marie Bunck. *Law, Power, and the Sovereign State: The Evolution and Application of the Concept of Sovereignty*. University Park, Pennsylvania: Pennsylvania State University Press, 2010.

Francioni, Francesco. "Private Military Contractors and International Law: An Introduction." *European Journal of International Law*. 19, no. 5 (2008): 961–964.

Frank, Andre Gunder, and Barry K. Gills, eds. *The World System: Five Hundred Years or Five Thousand?* London and New York: Routledge, 1996.

Frank, Andre Gunter. *Reorient: Global Economy in the Asian Age*. Berkeley and Los Angeles: University of California Press, 1998.

Freeman, Chris. "The 'National System of Innovation' in Historical Perspective." *Cambridge Journal of Economics.* 19, no. 1 (1995): 5–24.

Friedman, Debra, and Michael Hechter. "The Contribution of Rational Choice Theory to Macrosociological Research." *Sociological Theory.* 6, no. 2 (1988): 201–218.

Frigo, Daniela, ed. *Politics and Diplomacy in Early Modern Italy: The Structure of Diplomatic Practice, 1450–1800.* Cambridge and New York: Cambridge University Press, 2000.

Fröbel, Folker, Jurgen Heinrichs, and Otto Kreye. *The New International Division of Labour: Structural Unemployment in Industrialised Countries and Industrialisation in Developing Countries.* Cambridge and New York: Cambridge University Press, 1981.

Frosini, Fabio. *Gramsci e la Filosofia: Saggio sui Quaderni del Carcere.* Roma: Carocci, 2003.

Frosini, Fabio. "Riforma e Rinascimento." In *Le Parole di Gramsci: Per un Lessico dei Quaderni del Carcere* edited by Fabio Frosini and Guido Liguori. Roma: Carocci, 2004.

Fukuyama, Francis. *The Great Disruption: Human Nature and the Reconstitution of Social Order.* New York, London, Toronto, Sydney, and Singapore: Simon & Schuster, 1999.

Fukuyama, Francis. "Social Capital and Development." *SAIS Review (1989–2003).* 22, no. 1 (2002): 23–37.

Fukuyama, Francis. "Social Capital, Civil Society and Development." *Third World Quarterly.* 22, no. 1 (2001): 7–20.

Fusaro, Lorenzo. *Crises and Hegemonic Transitions: From Gramsci's Quaderni to the Contemporary World Economy.* Leiden and Boston: Brill, 2018.

Galeano, Eduardo, and Isabelle Allende. *Open Veins of Latin America: Five Centuries of the Pillage of a Continent.* Translated by Cedric Belfrage. New York: Monthly Review Press, 1997.

Gallagher, Patrick L. "Andreu Nin on Fascism in Italy: Translator's Introduction." *Historical Materialism.* 30, no. 2 (2022): 185–195.

Gallant, Thomas W. "Greek Bandits: Lone Wolves or a Family Affair?." *Journal of Modern Greek Studies.* 6, no. 2 (1988): 269–290.

Gambardella, Alfonso, and Marco S. Giarratana. "Organizational Attributes and the Distribution of Rewards in a Region: Managerial Firms Vs. Knowledge Clusters." *Organization Science.* 21, no. 2 (2010): 573–586.

Gambardella, Alfonso, and Franco Malerba, eds. *The Organization of Economic Innovation in Europe.* Cambridge and New York: Cambridge University Press, 1999.

Gambardella, Alfonso, Myriam Mariani, and Salvatore Torrisi. "How 'Provincial' is Your Region? Openness and Regional Performance in Europe." *Regional Studies.* 43, no. 7 (2009): 935–947.

Gambarotto, Francesca, and Stefano Solari. "The Peripheralization of Southern European Capitalism within the EMU." *Review of International Political Economy.* 22, no. 4 (2015): 788–812.

Gammage, Sarah. "Exercising Exit, Voice and Loyalty: A Gender Perspective on Transnationalism in Haiti." *Development and Change.* 35, no. 4 (2004): 743–771.

Gardner, Leigh. "Fiscal Policy in the Belgian Congo in Comparative Perspecctive." In *Colonial Exploitation and Economic Development: The Belgian Congo and the Netherlands Indies Compared*, edited by Ewout Frankema and Frank Buelens. London and New York: Routledge, 2013.

Garland, David. "The Limits of the Sovereign State Strategies of Crime Control in Contemporary Society." *The British Journal of Criminology.* 36, no. 4 (1996): 445–471.

Gee, Laura K., Jason J. Jones, Christopher J. Fariss, Moira Burke, and James H. Fowler. "The Paradox of Weak Ties in 55 Countries." *Journal of Economic Behavior & Organization.* 133 (2017): 362–372.

Geertz, Clifford. *The Interpretation of Cultures.* New York: Basic Books, 1973.

Geertz, Clifford. *Local Knowledge: Further Essays in Interpretive Anthropology.* New York: Basic Books, 1983.

Gellner, Ernest. *Nationalism.* Master Minds Series. London: Phoenix, 1998.

Gellner, Ernest. *Nations and Nationalism.* Cornell Paperbacks. Ithaca, New York: Cornell University Press, 1983.

Gellner, Ernest, and John Breuilly. *Nations and Nationalism.* Cornell Paperbacks. Ithaca, New York: Cornell University Press, 2008.

Gentile, Giovanni, and Anthony James Gregor. *Origins and Doctrine of Fascism: With Selections from Other Works.* London and New York: Routledge, 2011.

Gentili, Claudio. *Scuola e Impresa. Teorie e Casi di Partnership Pedagogica.* Milan: Franco Angeli, 2013.

Gerber, David. *Global Competition: Law, Markets, and Globalization.* Oxford and New York: Oxford University Press, 2010.

Gerber, Haim. "The Limits of Constructedness: Memory and Nationalism in the Arab Middle East." *Nations and Nationalism.* 10, no. 3 (2004): 251–268.

Gerwarth, Robert, and Erez Manela, eds. *Empires at War: 1911–1923.* Oxford and New York: Oxford University Press, 2014.

Ghosh, Jayati. "Capital." In *The Elgar Companion to Marxist Economics*, edited by Ben Fine, Alfredo Saad-Filho and Marco Boffo. Cheltenham, UK and Northampton, Massachusetts: Edward Elgar Publishing, 2012.

Gianaris, Nicholas V. *The North American Free Trade Agreement and the European Union.* Westport, Connecticut, and London: Praeger, 1998.

Giannetti, Renato, and Michelangelo Vasta, eds. *Evolution of Italian Enterprises in the 20th Century*: Physica-Verlag, 2009.

Giannetti, Renato, ed. *Nel Mito di Prometeo. L'innovazione Tecnologica Dalla Rivoluzione Industriale ad Oggi. Temi, Inventori e Protagonisti dall'Ottocento al Duemila.* Firenze: Ponte alle Grazie, 1996.

Gibson, Nigel C. "Fanon and Marx Revisited." *Journal of the British Society for Phenomenology.* 51, no. 4 (2020): 320–336.

Giddens, Anthhony. *Capitalism and Modern Social Theory: An Analysis of the Writings of Marx, Durkheim and Max Weber.* Cambridge and NewYork: Cambridge University Press, 1973.

Gill, Peter. "Policing and Regulation: What Is the Difference?." *Social & Legal Studies.* 11, no. 4 (2002): 523–546.

Gill, Stephen. *American Hegemony and the Trilateral Commission.* Cambridge and New York: Cambridge University Press, 1991.

Gill, Stephen, ed. *Gramsci, Historical Materialism and International Relations,* Cambridge Studies in International Relations. Cambridge and New York: Cambridge University Press, 1993.

Gill, Stephen. *Power and Resistance in the New World Order.* 2nd ed.: Palgrave Macmillan, 2008.

Gills, Barry K. "Hegemonic Transitions in the World System." In *The World System: Five Hundred Years or Five Thousand?*, edited by Andre Gunder Frank and Barry K. Gills. London and New York: Routledge, 1996.

Gills, Barry K., and Andre Gunder Frank. "World System Cycles, Crises, and Hegemonic Shifts, 1700 BC to 1700 AD." In *The World System: Five Hundred Years or Five Thousand?*, edited by Andre Gunder Frank and Barry K. Gills. London and New York: Routledge, 1996.

Gilsenan, Michael. *Lords of the Lebanese Marches: Violence and Narrative in an Arab Society.* Berkeley and Los Angeles: University of California Press, 1996.

Glaeser, Edward L. "Cities, Information, and Economic Growth." *Cityscape.* 1, no. 1 (1994): 9–47.

Glete, Jan. *Warfare at Sea, 1500–1650: Maritime Conflicts and the Transformation of Europe.* London and New York: Routledge, 2000.

Go, Julian. *Postcolonial Thought and Social Theory.* Oxford and New York: Oxford University Press, 2016.

Gocek, Fatma Muge. *Rise of the Bourgeoisie, Demise of Empire: Ottoman Westernization and Social Change.* Oxford and New York: Oxford University Press, 1996.

Goldstone, Jack A. "Capitalist Origins, the Advent of Modernity, and Coherent Explanation: a Response to Joseph M. Bryant." *Canadian Journal of Sociology/ Cahiers canadiens de sociologie.* 33, no. 1 (2008).

Goldstone, Jack A. "Efflorescences and Economic Growth in World History: Rethinking the 'Rise of the West' and the Industrial Revolution." *Journal of world history.* (2002): 323–389.

Goldstone, Jack A. "The Rise of the West—or Not? A Revision to Socio-Economic History." *Sociological Theory.* 18, no. 2 (2000): 175–194.

Gomellini, Matteo, and Cormac Ó Gráda. "Migrations." In *The Oxford Handbook of the Italian Economy since Unification*, edited by Gianni Toniolo. Oxford and New York: Oxford University Press 2013.

Gönen, Zeynep. "Giuliani in Izmir: Restructuring of the Izmir Public Order Police and Criminalization of the Urban Poor." *Critical Criminology*. 21, no. 1 (2013): 87–101.

González, Sara. "The North/South Divide in Italy and England: Discursive Construction of Regional Inequality." *European Urban and Regional Studies*. 18, no. 1 (2011): 62–76.

Goodin, Robert E., ed. *The Theory of Institutional Design*. Cambridge and New York: Cambridge University Press, 1998.

Gori, Annarita, and Rita Almeida de Carvalho. "Italian Fascism and the Portuguese Estado Novo: International Claims and National Resistance." *Intellectual History Review*. 30, no. 2 (2020): 295–319.

Gorski, Philip S. *The Disciplinary Revolution: Calvinism and the Rise of the State in Early Modern Europe*. Chicago: University of Chicago Press, 2003.

Grafe, Regina, and Maria Alejandra Irigoin. "The Spanish Empire and Its Legacy: Fiscal Redistribution and Political Conflict in Colonial and Post-Colonial Spanish America." *Journal of Global History*. 1, no. 2 (2006): 241–267.

Gramsci, Antonio. *La Questione Meridionale*. Roma: Editori Riuniti, 1974.

Gramsci, Antonio. *Quaderni del Carcere*. Edited by Valentino Gerratana. 4 vols. Torino: Einaudi, 2007. 1975, 2001.

Gramsci, Antonio, and Pasquale Verdicchio. *The Southern Question*. Translated by Pasquale Verdicchio. Picas. Toronto, Buffalo, Chicago, Lacaster: Guernica Editions, 2005.

Gran, Peter. *Beyond Eurocentrism: A New View of Modern World History*. Syracuse: Syracuse University Press, 1996.

Granovetter, Mark. "Economic Action and Social Structure: The Problem of Embeddedness." *American Journal of Sociology*. 91, no. 3 (1985): 481–510.

Granovetter, Mark. "The Strength of Weak Ties." *American Journal of Sociology*. 78, no. 6 (1973): 1360–1380.

Granovetter, Mark. "The Strength of Weak Ties: A Network Theory Revisited." *Sociological Theory*. 1 (1983): 201–233.

Graziano, Manlio. *The Failure of Italian Nationhood: The Geopolitics of a Troubled Identity*. London and New York: Palgrave Macmillan, 2010.

Geary, Frank, and Tom Stark. "150 Years of Regional GDP: United Kingdom and Ireland." In *The Economic Development of Europe's Regions: A Quantitative History since 1900*, edited by Joan Ramon Rosés and Nolf Wolf. London and New York: Routledge, 2018.

Green, Francis. *Skills and Skilled Work: An Economic and Social Analysis*. Oxford and New York: Oxford University Press, 2013.

Green, Toby. *A Fistful of Shells: West Africa from the Rise of the Slave Trade to the Age of Revolution*. London: Penguin, 2019.

Grinberg, Nicolas. "Global Commodity Chains and the Production of Surplus-Value on a Global Scale: Bringing Back the New International Division of Labour Theory." *Journal of World-Systems Research.* 22, no. 1 (2016): 247–278.

Grodach, Carl, and Anastasia Loukaitou-Sideris. "Cultural Development Strategies and Urban Revitalization: A Survey of US Cities." *International Journal of Cultural Policy.* 13, no. 4 (2007): 349–370.

Guiso, Luigi. "Small Business Finance in Italy." *EIB papers.* 8, no. 2 (2003): 121–149.

Guiso, Luigi, and Paolo Pinotti. "Democratization and Civic Capital." In *The Economic Development of Europe's Regions: A Quantitative History since 1900*, edited by Joan Ramon Rosés and Nolf Wolf. London and New York: Routledge, 2018.

Guthorn, Harrison B. *Capital Development: Mandate Era Amman and the Construction of the Hashemite State (1921–1946).* London: Gingko Library, 2021.

Haggard, Stephan. *Developmental States.* Elements in the Politics of Development. Cambridge and New York: Cambridge University Press, 2018.

Hall, John Anthony. "Confessions of a Eurocentric." *International Sociology.* 16, no. 3 (2001): 488–497.

Hall, John Anthony. "Globalization and Nationalism." *Thesis Eleven.* 63, no. 1 (2000): 63–79.

Hall, John Anthony. *The Importance of Being Civil: The Struggle for Political Decency.* Princeton and Oxford: Princeton University Press, 2013.

Hall, John Anthony. "Nationalisms: Classified and Explained." *Daedalus.* 122, no. 3 (1993): 1–28.

Hall, John Anthony. *Powers and Liberties: The Causes and Consequences of the Rise of the West.* Berkeley and Los Angeles: University of California Press, 1986.

Hall, John Anthony, ed. *The State of the Nation: Ernest Gellner and the Theory of Nationalism.* Cambridge and New York: Cambridge University Press, 1998.

Hall, Peter. *Cities in Civilization.* New York: Pantheon, 1998.

Hall, Peter. "Creativity, Culture, Knowledge and the City." *Built Environment.* 30, no. 3 (2004): 256–258.

Hall, Peter. *Urban and Regional Planning.* London and New York: Routledge, 2002.

Hall, Peter A., and David W. Soskice, eds. *Varieties of Capitalism: The Institutional Foundations of Comparative Advantage.* Oxford and New York: Oxford University Press, 2001.

Hall, Richard C. *The Balkan Wars, 1912–1913: Prelude to the First World War.* London and New York: Routledge, 2002.

Hall, Thomas D. *Comparing Globalizations: Historical and World-Systems Approaches.* World-Systems Evolution and Global Futures. Cham, Switzerland: Springer, 2017.

Hall, Thomas D. "Incorporation into and Merger of World-Systems." In *Routledge Handbook of World-Systems Analysis*: Routledge, 2012.

Hallo de Wolf, Antenor. "Modern Condottieri in Iraq: Privatizing War from the Perspective of International and Human Rights Law." *Indiana Journal of Global Legal Studies*. 13, no. 2 (2006): 315–356.

Hallonsten, Olof. *Big Science Transformed*. Cham, Switzerland: Springer, 2016.

Hametz, Maura. *Making Trieste Italian, 1918–1954*. Royal Historical Society. Woodbridge, Suffolk, and Rochester, New York: Boydell Press, 2005.

Hametz, Maura. "Replacing Venice in the Adriatic: Tourism and Italian Irredentism, 1880–1936." *Journal of Tourism History*. 6, no. 2–3 (2014): 107–121.

Hampton, Rosalind. *Black Racialization and Resistance at an Elite University*. Toronto, Buffalo, London: University of Toronto Press, 2020.

Hampton, Rosalind. "Nous Who? Racialized Social Relations and Quebec Student Movement Politics." In *The University and Social Justice: Struggles across the Globe*, edited by Aziz Choudry and Salim Vally. Toronto: Between the Lines publisher, 2020.

Hampton, Rosalind, and Désirée Rochat. "To Commit and to Lead: Black Women Organizing across Communities in Montreal." In *African Canadian Leadership: Continuity, Transition, and Transformation*, edited by Tamari Kitossa, Erica S. Lawson and Phiilip S.S. Howard. Toronto, Buffalo, London: University of Toronto Press, 2019.

Hankins, Thomas L. *Science and the Enlightenment*. Cambridge and New York: Cambridge University Press, 1985.

Hansen, William W., and Umma Aliyu Musa. "Fanon, the Wretched and Boko Haram." *Journal of Asian and African studies*. 48, no. 3 (2013): 281–296.

Harcourt, Felix. *Ku Klux Kulture: America and the Klan in the 1920s*. Chicago and London: University of Chicago Press, 2019.

Hardt, Michael, and Antonio Negri. "Adventures of the Multitude: Response of the Authors." *Rethinking Marxism*. 13, no. 3–4 (2001): 236–243.

Hardt, Michael, and Antonio Negri. *Empire*. Cambridge, Massachusetts and London: Harvard University Press, 2000.

Hardt, Michael, and Antonio Negri. *Multitude: War and Democracy in the Age of Empire*. London: Penguin, 2005.

Harkavy, Robert E. *Bases Abroad: The Global Foreign Military Presence*. SIPRI: Stockholm International Peace Research Institute. Oxford and New York: Oxford University Press, 1989.

Harmon, Rachel A. "Federal Programs and the Real Costs of Policing." *New York University Law Review*. 90 (2015): 870–960.

Harper, Robert. *Fighting the French Revolution: The Great Vendée Rising of 1793*. Barnsley, South Yorkshire, and Haverton, Pennsylvania: Pen & Sword Books, 2019.

Harrison, Bennett. "Concentrated Economic Power and Silicon Valley." *Environment and Planning A*. 26, no. 2 (1994): 307–328.

Harrison, Nick. *Our Civilizing Mission: The Lessons of Colonial Education*. Contemporary French and Francophone Cultures Series. Liverpool: Liverpool University Press, 2019.

Hartman, Michelle, and Alessandro Olsaretti. "'The First Boat and the First Oar': Inventions of Lebanon in the Writings of Michel Chiha." *Radical History Review*. no. 86 (2003): 37–65.

Harvey, David. *A Brief History of Neoliberalism*. Oxford and New York: Oxford University Press, 2007.

Harvey, David. *The New Imperialism*. Oxford and New York: Oxford University Press, 2003.

Hawdon, James. "Legitimacy, Trust, Social Capital, and Policing Styles: A Theoretical Statement." *Police Quarterly*. 11, no. 2 (2008): 182–201.

Hayter, Roger, and Trevor J. Barnes. "Canada's Resource Economy." *Canadian Geographer/Le Géographe Canadien*. 45, no. 1 (2001): 36–41.

Hechter, Michael. *Internal Colonialism: The Celtic Fringe in British National Development*. Sociology, History, Political Science. New York: Columbia University, 1972.

Hennings, Klaus H. "Capital as a Factor of Production." In *Capital Theory*, edited by John Eatwell, Murray Milgate and Peter Newman. London and New York: Palgrave Macmillan, 1990.

Herrigel, Gary. *Industrial Constructions: The Sources of German Industrial Power*. Cambridge and New York: Cambridge University Press, 2000.

Hess, Martin. "'Spatial' Relationships? Towards a Reconceptualization of Embeddedness." *Progress in Human Geography*. 28, no. 2 (2004): 165–186.

Higley, John. "Patterns of Political Elites." In *The Palgrave Handbook of Political Elites*, edited by Heinrich Best and John Higley. London and New York: Palgrave Macmillan, 2018.

Hill, Lisa. "Adam Smith, Adam Ferguson and Karl Marx on the Division of Labour." *Journal of Classical Sociology*. 7, no. 3 (2007): 339–366.

Hill, Mike, and Warren Montag. *Masses, Classes and the Public Sphere*. London and New York: Verso, 2000.

Hillgruber, Andreas. *Germany and the Two World Wars*. Translated by William C. Kirby. Cambridge, Massachusetts and London: Harvard University Press, 1981.

Hilton, Rodney. "Feudalism and the Origins of Capitalism." *History Workshop Journal*. 1, no. 1 (1976): 9–25.

Hiltzik, Michael. *Big Science: Ernest Lawrence and the Invention that Launched the Military-Industrial Complex*. New York, London, Toronto, Sydney, New Delhi: Simon & Schuster, 2015.

Hintz, Arne. *Civil Society Media and Global Governance: Intervening into the World Summit on the Information Society*. Münster: Lit Verlag, 2009.

Hirschman, Albert O. *Exit, Voice, and Loyalty: Responses to Decline in Firms, Organizations, and States*. American Council of Learned Societies, Humanities. Cambridge, Massachusetts and London: Harvard University Press, 1970.

Hirschman, Albert O. "" Exit, Voice, and Loyalty": Further Reflections and a Survey of Recent Contributions." *Social Science Information.* 13, no. 1 (1974): 7–26.

Hitzler, Ronald, and Reiner Keller. "On Sociological and Common-Sense Verstehen." *Current Sociology.* 37, no. 1 (1989): 91–101.

Hobday, Michael, Andrew Davies, and Andrea Prencipe. "Systems Integration: a Core Capability of the Modern Corporation." *Industrial and corporate change.* 14, no. 6 (2005): 1109–1143.

Hobsbawm, Eric J. *Bandits.* London: Abacus, 2001.

Hobsbawm, Eric J. *Primitive Rebels.* London: Abacus, 2017.

Hobson, John M. *The Eastern Origins of Western Civilisation.* Cambridge and New York: Cambridge University Press, 2004.

Hoffmann, Bert. "Bringing Hirschman Back in: 'Exit,' 'Voice,' and 'Loyalty' in the Politics of Transnational Migration." *The Latin Americanist.* 54, no. 2 (2010): 57–73.

Holquist, Michael. *Dialogism: Bakhtin and His World.* London and New York: Routledge, 2003.

Hopkins, Terence K., and Immanuel Wallerstein. "Commodity Chains in the World-Economy Prior to 1800." *Review (Fernand Braudel Center).* 10, no. 1 (1986): 157–170.

Hornborg, Alf, J. R. McNeill, and Joan Martinez-Alier, eds. *Rethinking Environmental History: World-System History and Global Environmental Change.* Lanham, New York, Toronto, Plymouth: AltaMira Press, 2007.

Housley, Norman. *Religious Warfare in Europe, 1400–1536.* Oxford and New York: Oxford University Press, 2008.

Howe, Anthony. *Free Trade and Liberal England, 1846–1946.* Oxford: Clarendon Press, 1997.

Hsu, Sara. *Financial Crises, 1929 to the Present.* Cheltenham, UK and Northampton, Massachusetts: Edward Elgar, 2013.

Hughes, Jeff A. *The Manhattan Project: Big Science and the Atom Bomb.* New York: Columbia University Press, 2003.

Hui, V. T. *War and State Formation in Ancient China and Early Modern Europe.* Cambridge and New York: Cambridge University Press, 2005.

Hunt, John, and Heather-Ann Campbell. *Dutch South Africa: Early Settlers at the Cape, 1652–1708.* Leicester: Matador, 2005.

Ilan, Jonathan. "Street Social Capital in the Liquid City." *Ethnography.* 14, no. 1 (2013): 3–24.

Imbruglia, Girolamo, ed. *Naples in the Eighteenth Century: The Birth and Death of a Nation State,* Cambridge Studies in Italian History and Culture. Cambridge and New York: Cambridge University Press, 2000.

Inalcık, Halil, and Donald Quataert, eds. *An Economic and Social History of the Ottoman Empire. Volume Two: 1600–1914.* Cambridge and New York: Cambridge University Press, 1994.

Innis, Harold A. *Essays in Canadian Economic History*. Edited by Mary Q. Innis. Toronto, Buffalo, London: University of Toronto Press, 2017.

Isaacson, Walter. *Einstein: His Life and Universe*. New York, London, Toronto, Sydney, New Delhi: Simon & Schuster, 2017.

Islamogu-Inan, Huri, ed. *The Ottoman Empire and the World-Economy*. Cambridge and New York: Cambridge University Press, 2004.

Islamogu-Inan, Huri, and Caglar Keyder. In *The Ottoman Empire and the World-Economy*, edited by Huri Islamogu-Inan. Cambridge and New York: Cambridge University Press, 2004.

Isom-Verhaaren, Christin. *Allies with the Infidel: The Ottoman and French Alliance in the Sixteenth Century*. London and New York: I. B. Tauris, 2011.

Israel, Uwe. "Brokers as German-Italian Cultural Mediators in Renaissance Venice." In *Migrating Words, Migrating Merchants, Migrating Law: Trading Routes and the Development of Commercial Law*, edited by Stefania Gialdroni, Albrecht Cordes, Serge Dauchy and Heikki Pihlajamäki. Leiden and Boston: Brill, 2020.

Issawi, Charles. *An Economic History of the Middle East and North Africa*. London and New York: Routledge, 2013.

Iuzzolino, Giovanni, Guido Pellegrini, and Gianfranco Viesti. "Regional Convergence." In *The Oxford Handbook of the Italian Economy since Unification*, edited by Gianni Toniolo. Oxford and New York: Oxford University Press 2013.

Ives, Peter, and Nicola Short. "On Gramsci and the International: a Textual Analysis." *Review of International Studies*. 39, no. 3 (2013): 621–642.

Jacob, Margaret C., and Matthew Kadane. "Missing, Now Found in the Eighteenth Century: Weber's Protestant Capitalist." *The American Historical Review*. 108, no. 1 (2003): 20–49.

Jacoby, Tim. "Global Fascism: Geography, Timing, Support, and Strategy." *Journal of Global History*. 11, no. 3 (2016): 451–472.

James, Lawrence. *Raj: The Making and Unmaking of British India*. New York: St. Martin's Griffin, 1997.

Joll, James, and Gordon Martel. *The Origins of the First World War*. London and New York: Routledge, 2013.

Jones, Philip. *The Italian City-State: From Commune to Signoria*. Oxford: Clarendon Press, 1997.

Jonsson, Ulf. "The Paradox of Share Tenancy under Capitalism: A Comparative Perspective on Late Nineteenth-and Twentieth-Century French and Italian Sharecropping." *Rural History*. 3, no. 2 (1992): 191–217.

Jucker, Andreas H. *Politeness in the History of English: From the Middle Ages to the Present Day*. Cambridge and New York: Cambridge University Press, 2020.

Junco, Jose Álvarez. *Spanish Identity in the Age of Nations*. Manchester and New York: Manchester University Press, 2016.

Kaiser, David E. "Germany and the Origins of the First World War." *The Journal of Modern History*. 55, no. 3 (1983): 442–474.

Kamouzis, Dimitris. *Greeks in Turkey: Elite Nationalism and Minority Politics in Late Ottoman and Early Republican Istanbul*. London and New York: Routledge, 2020.

Kapoor, Dip, and Aziz Choudry, eds. *Learning from the Ground Up: Global Perspectives on Social Movements and Knowledge Production*. London and New York: Palgrave Macmillan, 2010.

Karabelias, Gerassimos. "From National Heroes to National Villains: Bandits, Pirates and the Formation of Modern Greece." In *Subalterns and Social Protest*, edited by Stephanie Cronin. London and New York: Routledge, 2012.

Karlsson, Charlie, Borje Johansson, and Roger Stough. *Industrial Clusters and Inter-Firm Networks*. Cheltenham, UK and Northampton, Massachusetts: Edward Elgar, 2005.

Kasaba, Resat. "Greek and Turkish Nationalism in Formation: Western Anatolia 1919–1922." *European University Institute Working Papers*. no. 17 (2002).

Kasaba, Resat. *The Ottoman Empire and the World Economy: The Nineteenth Century*. SUNY Series in Middle Eastern Studies. State University of New York Press, 1988.

Katz, Claudio J. "Marx on the Peasantry: Class in Itself or Class in Struggle?." *The Review of Politics*. 54, no. 1 (1992): 50–71.

Kavka, Gregory S. "Hobbes's War of All against All." *Ethics*. 93, no. 2 (1983): 291–310.

Kawachi, Ichiro, and Lisa Berkman. "Social Cohesion, Social Capital, and Health." *Social Epidemiology*. 174, no. 7 (2000): 290–319.

Kawall, Jason. "Other–Regarding Epistemic Virtues." *Ratio*. 15, no. 3 (2002): 257–275.

Kayali, Hasan. *Arabs and Young Turks: Ottomanism, Arabism, and Islamism in the Ottoman Empire, 1908–1918*. Berkeley and Los Angeles: University of California Press, 1997.

Kechriotis, Vangelis. "Civilization and Order: Middle-Class Morality among the Greek-Orthodox in Smyrna/Izmir at the End of the Ottoman Empire." In *Social Transformation and Mass Mobilization in the Balkan and Eastern Mediterranean Cities (1900–1923)*, edited by Andreas Lyberatos. Irakleio: Crete University Press, 2013.

Kennan, George Frost. *The Decline of Bismarck's European Order: Franco-Russian Relations 1875–1890*. Princeton and Oxford: Princeton University Press, 1979.

Kerstenetzky, Celia Lessa. "The Brazilian Social Developmental State: A Progressive Agenda in a (Still) Conservative Political Society." In *The End of the Developmental State?*, edited by Michelle Williams. London and New York: Routledge, 2014.

Kertzer, David I., and Dennis P. Hogan. *Family, Political Economy, and Demographic Change: The Transformation of Life in Casalecchio, Italy, 1861–1921*. Madison, Wisconsin: University of Wisconsin Press, 1989.

Keyder, Caglar. "Peripheral Port-Cities and Politics on the Eve of the Great War." *New Perspectives on Turkey*. 20 (1999): 27–45.

Keyder, Çaglar, Y. Eyüp Ozveren, and Donald Quataert. "Port-Cities in the Ottoman Empire: Some Theoretical and Historical Perspectives." *Review (Fernand Braudel Center)*. 16, no. 4 (1993): 519–558.

Keyder, Caglar, and Faruk Tabak, eds. *Landholding and Commercial Agriculture in the Middle East: Globalization, Revolution, and Popular Culture.* Albany: State University of New York Press, 1991.

Khoury, Philip Shukry. *Syria and the French Mandate: The Politics of Arab Nationalism, 1920–1945.* Princeton and Oxford: Princeton University Press, 2014.

Khoury, Philip Shukry. *Urban Notables and Arab Nationalism: The Politics of Damascus 1860–1920.* Cambridge and New York: Cambridge University Press, 2003.

Kidd, John B., and Frank-Jurgen Richter, eds. *Development Models, Globalization and Economies: A Search for the Holy Grail?* London and New York: Palgrave Macmillan, 2005.

Kirshner, Julius, ed. *The Origins of the State in Italy, 1300–1600.* Chicago and London: University of Chicago Press, 2009.

Kitromilides, Paschalis M. "Greek Irredentism in Asia Minor and Cyprus." *Middle Eastern Studies.* 26, no. 1 (1990): 3–17.

Klabjan, Borut. "Erecting Fascism: Nation, Identity, and Space in Trieste in the First Half of the Twentieth Century." *Nationalities Papers.* 46, no. 6 (2018): 958–975.

Klein, Alexander. "Regional Inequality in the United States: Long-Term Patterns, 1880–2010." In *The Economic Development of Europe's Regions: A Quantitative History since 1900,* edited by Joan Ramon Rosés and Nolf Wolf. London and New York: Routledge, 2018.

Klieger, P. Christiaan. *The Microstates of Europe: Designer Nations in a Post-Modern World.* Lanham, Boulder, New York, Toronto, and Plymouth UK: Lexington Books, 2012.

Klier, Thomas, and James Rubenstein. *Who Really Made Your Car?: Restructuring and Geographic Change in the Auto Industry.* Kalamazoo, Michigan: W.E. Upjohn Institute for Employment Research, 2008.

Knaapen, Loes. "Being 'Evidence-Based' in the Absence of Evidence: The Management of Non-Evidence in Guideline Development." *Social Studies of Science.* 43, no. 5 (2013): 681–706.

Knaapen, Loes. "Science Needs More External Evaluation, Not Less." *Social Science Information.* 60, no. 3 (2021): 338–344.

Knafo, Samuel, and Benno Teschke. "Political Marxism and the Rules of Reproduction of Capitalism: A Historicist Critique." *Historical Materialism.* 29, no. 3 (2020): 54–83.

Knecht, R. J. *The French Wars of Religion 1559–1598.* 3rd ed. London and New York: Routledge, 2014.

Köksal, Yonca. *The Ottoman Empire in the Tanzimat Era: Provincial Perspectives from Ankara to Edirne.* London and New York: Routledge, 2019.

Koliopoulos, John S. "Brigandage and Irredentism in Nineteenth-Century Greece." *European History Quarterly*. 19, no. 2 (1989): 193–228.

Koliopoulos, John S., and Thanos M. Veremis. *Modern Greece: A History since 1821*. Chichester, West Sussex: Wiley-Blackwell, 2009.

Kornprobst, Markus. *Irredentism in European Politics: Argumentation, Compromise and Norms*. Cambridge and London: Cambridge University Press, 2008.

Kratke, Michael R. "Antonio Gramsci's Contribution to a Critical Economics." *Historical Materialism*. 19, no. 3 (2011): 63–105.

Krippner, Greta, Mark Granovetter, Fred Block, Nicole Biggart, Tom Beamish, Youtien Hsing, Gillian Hart, Giovanni Arrighi, Margie Mendell, and John Hall. "Polanyi Symposium: a Conversation on Embeddedness." *Socio-economic Review*. 2, no. 1 (2004): 109–135.

Krippner, Greta R. "The Elusive Market: Embeddedness and the Paradigm of Economic Sociology." *Theory and Society*. 30, no. 6 (2001): 775–810.

Krippner, Greta R., and Anthony S. Alvarez. "Embeddedness and the Intellectual Projects of Economic Sociology." *Annual Review of Sociology*. 33 (2007): 219–240.

Kuklys, W. *Amartya Sen's Capability Approach: Theoretical Insights and Empirical Applications*. Studies in Choice and Welfare. Springer Berlin Heidelberg, 2006.

Kumar, Ashutosh. *Coolies of the Empire*. Cambridge and New York: Cambridge University Press, 2017.

Kumar, Krishan. *The Making of English National Identity*. Cambridge and New York: Cambridge University Press, 2003.

Kurz, Heinz D. "Adam Smith on Markets, Competition and Violations of Natural Liberty." *Cambridge Journal of Economics*. 40, no. 2 (2016): 615–638.

Kwon, Hyeeong-Ki. *Fairness and Division of Labor in Market Societies: Comparison of the U.S. And German Automotive Industries*. New York and Oxford: Berghahn Books, 2004.

Lachmann, Richard. *Capitalists in Spite of Themselves: Elite Conflict and Economic Transitions in Early Modern Europe*. Oxfiord and New York: Oxford University Press, 2000.

Lachmann, Richard. "Chinese Powers: A Critical Appreciation of Dingxin Zhao's *the Confucian-Legalist State*." *Chinese Sociological Review*. 51, no. 1 (2019): 57–64.

Lachmann, Richard. "Comparisons within a Single Social Formation: A Critical Appreciation of Perry Anderson's Lineages of the Absolutist State." *Qualitative sociology*. 25, no. 1 (2002): 83–92.

Lachmann, Richard. "Elite Self-Interest and Economic Decline in Early Modern Europe." *American Sociological Review*. (2003): 346–372.

Lachmann, Richard. "Hegemons, Empires, and Their Elites." *Sociologia, Problemas e Práticas*. no. 75 (2014): 9–38.

Lachmann, Richard. "Origins of Capitalism in Western Europe: Economic and Political Aspects." *Annual Review of Sociology*. (1989): 47–72.

Lacoe, Johanna, Raphael W. Bostic, and Arthur Acolin. "Crime and Private Investment in Urban Neighborhoods." *Journal of Urban Economics*. 108 (2018): 154–169.

Lagos, Constantinos, and John Carr. *Philip, Prince of Greece: The Duke of Edinburgh's Early Life and the Greek Succession*. Barnsley, South Yorkshire, and Haverton, Pennsylvania: Pen & Sword History, 2021.

Lamothe, Lee, and Antonio Nicaso. *Bloodlines: The Rise and Fall of the Mafia's Royal Family*. New York: HarperCollins, 2001.

Lane, David A. "Complexity and Local Interactions: Towards a Theory of Industrial Districts." In *Complexity and Industrial Clusters*, edited by Alberto Quadrio Curzio and Marco Fortis. Cham, Switzerland: Springer, 2002.

Lang, Sabine. *NGOs, Civil Society, and the Public Sphere*. Cambridge and New York: Cambridge University Press, 2012.

Lange, Matthew. *Educations in Ethnic Violence: Identity, Educational Bubbles, and Resource Mobilization*. Cambridge and New York: Cambridge University Press, 2011.

Lange, Matthew. *Killing Others: A Natural History of Ethnic Violence*. Ithaca, New York: Cornell University Press, 2017.

Lange, Matthew. *Lineages of Despotism and Development: British Colonialism and State Power*. Chicago: University of Chicago Press, 2009.

Lange, Matthew, and Andrew Dawson. "Dividing and Ruling the World? A Statistical Test of the Effects of Colonialism on Postcolonial Civil Violence." *Social Forces*. 88, no. 2 (2009): 785–817.

Lange, Matthew, and Andrew Dawson. "Education and Ethnic Violence: a Cross-National Time-Series Analysis." *Nationalism and Ethnic Politics*. 16, no. 2 (2010): 216–239.

Lange, Matthew, and Dietrich Rueschemeyer, eds. *States and Development: Historical Antecedents of Stagnation and Advance*, Political Evolution and Institutional Change. London and New York: Palgrave Macmillan, 2005.

Langston, Joy. "Breaking out Is Hard to Do: Exit, Voice, and Loyalty in Mexico's One-Party Hegemonic Regime." *Latin American Politics & Society*. 44, no. 3 (2002): 61–88.

Lanzone, Maria Elisabetta. "The 'Post-Modern' Populism in Italy: The Case of the Five Star Movement." In *The Many Faces of Populism: Current Perspectives*, edited by Dwayne Woods and Barbara Wejnert. Research in Political Sociology. Bingley: Emerald, 2014.

Laqueur, Walter. *Fascism: A Reader's Guide: Analyses, Interpretations, Bibliography*. Wildwood House, 1976.

Laqueur, Walter. *Fascism: Past, Present, Future*. Oxford and New York: Oxford University Press, 1997.

Latour, Bruno. "Network Theory| Networks, Societies, Spheres: Reflections of an Actor-Network Theorist." *International journal of communication*. 5 (2011): 15.

Latour, Bruno. "On Actor-Network Theory: A Few Clarifications." *Soziale welt.* (1996): 369–381.

Latour, Bruno. *Pandora's Hope: Essays on the Reality of Science Studies.* Cambridge, Massachusetts and London: Harvard University Press, 1999.

Latour, Bruno. *Reassembling the Social: An Introduction to Actor-Network-Theory.* Oxford and New York: Oxford University Press, 2005.

Laursen, Keld, Francesca Masciarelli, and Andrea Prencipe. "Regions Matter: How Localized Social Capital Affects Innovation and External Knowledge Acquisition." *Organization science.* 23, no. 1 (2012): 177–193.

Law, Robin, and Kristin Mann. "West Africa in the Atlantic Community: The Case of the Slave Coast." *The William and Mary Quarterly.* 56, no. 2 (1999): 307–334.

Lears, T. J. Jackson. "The Concept of Cultural Hegemony: Problems and Possibilities." *The American Historical Review.* 90, no. 3 (1985): 567–593.

Lechner, Frank J., and John Boli. *World Culture: Origins and Consequences.* Oxford: Blackwell, 2008.

Lecuyer, Christophe, David C. Brock, and Jay Last. *Makers of the Microchip: A Documentary History of Fairchild Semiconductor.* Cambridge, Massachusetts: MIT Press, 2010.

Lee, Brandon H., Jeroen Struben, and Christopher B Bingham. "Collective Action and Market Formation: An Integrative Framework." *Strategic Management Journal.* 39, no. 1 (2018): 242–266.

Lenin, Vladimir Ilych. *Imperialism, the Highest Stage of Capitalism: A Popular Outline.* Unabridged with Original Tables and Footnotes ed. Auckland, United Kingdom: Aziloth Books, 2018.

Lesser, Eric. "Leveraging Social Capital in Organizations." In *Knowledge and Social Capital: Foundations and Applications*, edited by Eric Lesser. London and New York: Routledge, 2009.

Lewis, Bernard. *Cultures in Conflict: Christians, Muslims, and Jews in the Age of Discovery.* Oxford and New York: Oxford University Press, 1996.

Lewis, Tom. *Divided Highways: Building the Interstate Highways, Transforming American Life.* Ithaca, New York: Cornell University Press, 2013.

Liguori, Guido, and Pasquale Voza, eds. *Dizionario Gramsciano: 1926–1937.* Roma: Carocci, 2009.

Lin, Nan. "Building a Network Theory of Social Capital." *Social capital.* (2017): 3–28.

Linz, Juan J. *Totalitarian and Authoritarian Regimes.* Boulder, Colorado, and London: Lynne Rienner Publishers, 2000.

Linz, Juan J., and Alfred Stepan. *Problems of Democratic Transition and Consolidation: Southern Europe, South America, and Post-Communist Europe.* Baltimore and London: Johns Hopkins University Press, 1996.

Lipset, Seymour Martin. *Continental Divide: The Values and Institutions of the United States and Canada.* London and New York: Routledge, 2013.

Lipset, Seymour Martin. *The First New Nation: The United States in Historical and Comparative Perspective.* New Brunswick, New Jersey: Transaction Publishers, 2003.

Lipsitz, George. "The Struggle for Hegemony." *The Journal of American History.* 75, no. 1 (1988): 146–150.

Little, Daniel. *Microfoundations, Method, and Causation: On the Philosophy of the Social Sciences.* Transaction Publishers, 1998.

Liu, William Guanglin. *The Chinese Market Economy, 1000–1500.* State University of New York Press, 2015.

Loader, Ian, and Neil Walker. "Policing as a Public Good: Reconstituting the Connections between Policing and the State." *Theoretical Criminology.* 5, no. 1 (2001): 9–35.

Locatelli, Rita. *Reframing Education as a Public and Common Good: Enhancing Democratic Governance.* London and New York: Palgrave Macmillan, 2019.

Logan, John R., and Harvey L. Molotch. *Urban Fortunes: The Political Economy of Place. With a New Preface.* 20th Anniversary ed. Berkeley, Los Angeles, and London: University of California Press, 2007.

Lopez-Basagueren, Alberto, and Leire Escajedo San Epifanio, eds. *The Ways of Federalism in Western Countries and the Horizons of Territorial Autonomy in Spain,* Cham, Switzerland. Springer, 2013.

Lovejoy, Paul E. "The Impact of the Atlantic Slave Trade on Africa: A Review of the Literature." *The Journal of African History.* 30, no. 3 (1989): 365–394.

Lowe, John. *The Concert of Europe: International Relations 1814–70.* London: Hodder & Stoughton, 2000.

Lucchese, Salvatore. *Federalismo, Socialismo e Questione Meridionale in Gaetano Salvemini.* Meridiana. Manduria, Taranto: Piero Lacaita, 2004.

Lupo, Salvatore. *History of the Mafia.* Translated by Antony Shugaar. New York: Columbia University Press, 2009.

Lynn, John A. *The Wars of Louis XIV, 1667–1714.* London and New York: Routledge, 2013.

Lyttelton, Adrian. *The Seizure of Power: Fascism in Italy, 1919–1929.* London and New York: Routledge, 2004.

Maccabelli, Terenzio. "La 'Grande Trasformazione:' I Rapporti tra Stato ed Economia nel *Quaderni del Carcere*." In *Gramsci nel Suo Tempo*, edited by Francesco Giasi. Roma: Carocci, 2008.

Maccaferri, Marzia, and Andrea Mammone. "Global Populism and Italy. An Interview with Federico Finchelstein." *Modern Italy.* 27, no. 1 (2022): 61–66.

Magnusson, Lars. *Nation, State and the Industrial Revolution: The Visible Hand.* Routledge Explorations in Economic History. London and New York: Routledge, 2009.

Mahan, Alfred Thayer. *The Influence of Sea Power Upon History, 1660–1783.* Dover Military History, Weapons, Armor. Dover Publications, 2012.

Makdisi, Ussama. *The Culture of Sectarianism: Community, History, and Violence in Nineteenth-Century Ottoman Lebanon.* Berkeley and Los Angeles: University of California Press, 2000.

Mallett, Michael, and William Caferro. *Mercenaries and Their Masters: Warfare in Renaissance Italy.* Barnsley, South Yorkshire: Pen & Sword Military, 2009.

Mallett, Michael Edward, and Christine Shaw. *The Italian Wars, 1494–1559: War, State and Society in Early Modern Europe.* London and New York: Routledge, 2012.

Malloy, Robin Paul. *Law and Market Economy: Reinterpreting the Values of Law and Economics.* Cambridge and New York: Cambridge University Press, 2000.

Maltby, William S. *The Rise and Fall of the Spanish Empire.* London and New York: Palgrave Macmillan, 2008.

Mangiameli, Stelio, ed. *Italian Regionalism: Between Unitary Traditions and Federal Processes: Investigating Italy's Form of State.* Cham, Swiztzerland: Springer, 2014.

Mann, Michael. *The Dark Side of Democracy: Explaining Ethnic Cleansing.* Cambridge and New York: Cambridge University Press, 2005.

Mann, Michael. *Fascists.* Cambridge and New York: Cambridge University Press, 2004.

Mann, Michael. *The Sources of Social Power, Vol. 1: A History of Power from the Beginning to AD 1760.* Cambridge and New York: Cambridge University Press, 2012.

Mann, Michael. *The Sources of Social Power, Vol. 2: The Rise of Classes and Nation-States, 1760–1914.* The Sources of Social Power. Cambridge and New York: Cambridge University Press, 2012.

Mann, Michael. *The Sources of Social Power, Vol. 3: Global Empires and Revolution, 1890–1945.* Cambridge and New York: Cambridge University Press, 2012.

Mann, Michael. *The Sources of Social Power, Vol. 4: Globalizations, 1945–2011.* Cambridge and New York: Cambridge University Press, 2012.

March, Luke. "Left and Right Populism Compared: The British Case." *The British Journal of Politics and International Relations.* 19, no. 2 (2017): 282–303.

Marino, John A. *Early Modern Italy: 1550–1796.* Short Oxford History of Italy. Oxford a nd New York: Oxford University Press, 2002.

Martin, B. G. *The Nazi-Fascist New Order for European Culture.* Cambridge, Massachusetts and London: Harvard University Press, 2016.

Martin, Terry Dean. *The Affirmative Action Empire: Nations and Nationalism in the Soviet Union, 1923–1939.* Ithaca, New York: Cornell University Press, 2001.

Martinelli, Pablo. "Latifundia Revisited: Market Power, Land Inequality and Agricultural Efficiency. Evidence from Interwar Italian Agriculture." *Explorations in Economic History.* 54 (2014): 79–106.

Martinetti, Enrica Chiappero. "A Multidimensional Assessment of Well-Being Based on Sen's Functioning Approach." *Rivista Internazionale di Scienze Sociali.* 108, no. 2 (2000): 207–239.

Marx, Karl, Friedrich Engels, and Yanis Varoufakis. *The Communist Manifesto. Introduction by Yanis Varoufakis.* Vintage Classics. New York: Vintage Books, 2019.

Mattingly, Garrett. *Renaissance Diplomacy.* New York: Dover Publications, 1988.

Mayer, Nonna. "Democracy in France: Do Associations Matter?." In *Generating Social Capital: Civil Society and Insitutions in Comparative Perspective*, edited by Marc Hooghe and Dietlind Stolle. London and New York: Palgrave Macmillan, 2003.

Mayne, Richard, Douglas Johnson, and Robert Tombs, eds. *Cross Channel Currents: 100 Years of the Entente Cordiale.* London and New York: Routledge, 2004.

Mayo, Peter. *Gramsci, Freire and Adult Education: Possibilities for Transformative Action.* London and New York: Zed Books, 1999.

Mayo, Peter. *Hegemony and Education under Neoliberalism: Insights from Gramsci.* London and New York: Routledge, 2015.

Mazower, Mark. *The Greek Revolution: 1821 and the Making of Modern Europe.* New York: Penguin, 2021.

Mazumdar, Shaswati, ed. *Insurgent Sepoys: Europe Views the Revolt of 1857.* London and New York: Routledge, 2012.

Mazzei, Julie M., ed. *Non-State Violent Actors and Social Movement Organizations: Influence, Adaptation, and Change*, Research in Social Movements, Conflicts, and Change. Bingley, United Kingdom: Emerald Publishing Limited, 2017.

McAdams, Richard H. "The Origin, Development, and Regulation of Norms." *Michigan Law Review.* no. 96 (1997): 338–433.

McCann, Philip. *The UK Regional-National Economic Problem: Geography, Globalisation and Governance.* Regions and Cities. London and New York: Routledge, 2016.

McCarthy, John D., and Mayer N. Zald. "Resource Mobilization Theory: Vigorous or Outmoded?." In *Handbook of Sociological Theory*, edited by Jonathan H. Turner. Cham, Switzerland: Springer, 2006.

McGinnis, Michael D., and Elinor Ostrom. "Social-Ecological System Framework: Initial Changes and Continuing Challenges." *Ecology and Society.* 19, no. 2 (2014).

McGowan, Bruce. "The Age of the Ayans." In *An Economic and Social History of the Ottoman Empire. Volume Two: 1600–1914*, edited by Halil İnalcık and Donald Quataert. Cambridge and New York: Cambridge University Press, 1994.

McGowan, Winston. "African Resistance to the Atlantic Slave Trade in West Africa." *Slavery and Abolition.* 11, no. 1 (1990): 5–29.

McKenzie, Kenneth F. Jr. *The Revenge of the Melians: Asymmetric Threats and the Next QDR.* Mcnair Paper. Washington, D.C.: Insitute for National Strategic Studies, 2001.

McNally, Mark. "The Neo-Gramscians in the Study of International Relations: an Appraisal." *Materialismo Storico.* 2, no. 1 (2017): 93–114.

McNeill, J. R. *Something New under the Sun: An Environmental History of the Twentieth-Century World.* New York and London: W. W. Norton, 2001.

McNeill, William H. *The Rise of the West: A History of the Human Community.* Chicago and London: University of Chicago Press, 2009.

McQuade, Brendan. "(Anti) Systemic Movements: Hegemony, the Passive Revolution, and (Counter) Revolutions." In *The World-System as Unit of Analysis*, edited by Immanuel M. Wallerstein and Roberto Patricio Korzeniewicz. London and New York: Routledge, 2017.

Mellor, Jennifer M., and Jeffrey Milyo. "State Social Capital and Individual Health Status." *Journal of Health Politics, Policy and Law.* 30, no. 6 (2005): 1101–1130.

Méouchy, Nadine, and Peter Sluglett. *The British and French Mandates in Comparative Perspectives/Les Mandats Français et Anglais dans une Perspective Comparative.* Leiden and Boston: Brill, 2004.

Messina, Patrizio. *Finance for SMEs: European Regulation and Capital Markets Union: Focus on Securitization and Alternative Finance Tools.* European Monographs. Alphen aan den Rijn, the Netherlands: Wolters Kluwer, 2019.

Metcalf, Thomas R. *Aftermath of Revolt: India 1857–1970.* Princeton and Oxford: Princeton University Press, 2015.

Meyer, Carrie A. "The Political Economy of NGOs and Information Sharing." *World Development.* 25, no. 7 (1997): 1127–1140.

Meyer-Fong, T. *What Remains: Coming to Terms with Civil War in 19th Century China.* Stanford, California: Stanford University Press, 2013.

Michael, Koss. *The Politics of Party Funding: State Funding to Political Parties and Party Competition in Western Europe.* Oxford and New York: Oxford University Press, 2010.

Mielants, Eric H. *The Origins of Capitalism and the "Rise of the West."* Philadelphia: Temple University Press, 2008.

Migdal, Joel S. *Strong Societies and Weak States: State-Society Relations and State Capabilities in the Third World.* Princeton and Oxford: Princeton University Press, 1988.

Mikaberidze, Alexander. *The Napoleonic Wars: A Global History.* Oxford and New York: Oxford University Press, 2020.

Miley, Thomas Jeffrey. "Franquism as Authoritarianism: Juan Linz and His Critics." *Politics, Religion & Ideology.* 12, no. 1 (2011): 27–50.

Mill, John Stuart, and John Gray. *On Liberty and Other Essays.* Oxford World's Classics. Oxford and New York: Oxford University Press, 2008.

Miller, Stephen M. *Queen Victoria's Wars: British Military Campaigns, 1857–1902.* Cambridge and New York: Cambridge University Press, 2021.

Mills, Helen, Arianna Silvestri, and Roger Grimshaw. *Police Expenditure.* Centre for Crime and Justice Studies, 2010. https://www.crimeandjustice.org.uk/sites/crimeandjustice.org.uk/files/Police%20expenditure%201999-2009.pdf.

Mingay, Gordon E. *Parliamentary Enclosure in England: An Introduction to Its Causes, Incidence and Impact, 1750–1850.* London and New York: Routledge, 2014.

Modelski, George, and William R. Thompson. *Seapower in Global Politics, 1494–1993.* Houndmills, Basingstoke, Hampshire and London: Macmillan, 1988.

Modelski, Geroge, and William R. Thompson. "The Evolutionary Pulse of the Wolrd System: Hinterland Incursions and Migrations, 4000 BC to AD 1500." In *World-Systems Theory in Practice: Leadership, Production, and Exchange*, edited by Nick P. Kardulias. Lanham, Boulder, New York, and Oxford: Rowman & Littlefield Publishers, 1999.

Molotch, Harvey. "The Political Economy of Growth Machines." *Journal of Urban Affairs.* 15, no. 1 (1993): 29–53.

Molotch, Harvey, William Freudenburg, and Krista E. Paulsen. "History Repeats Itself, but How? City Character, Urban Tradition, and the Accomplishment of Place." *American Sociological Review.* (2000): 791–823.

Mombauer, Annika. *The Origins of the First World War: Controversies and Consensus.* London and New York: Routledge, 2013.

Monahan, Arthur P. *Consent, Coercion, and Limit: The Medieval Origins of Parliamentary Democracy.* Leiden and Boston: Brill, 1987.

Montreal International. *2020 Activity Report.* 2021. https://www.montrealinternatio nal.com/en/publications/2020-activity-report/.

Moore, Barrington Jr. *Social Origins of Dictatorship and Democracy: Lord and Peasant in the Making of the Modern World.* Boston: Beacon Press, 2015.

Moore, Jason W. "Capitalism as World-Ecology: Braudel and Marx on Environmental History." *Organization & Environment.* 16, no. 4 (2003): 514–517.

Moreno, Luis. *The Federalization of Spain.* London and New York: Routledge, 2013.

Moretti, Franco. *Atlas of the European Novel: 1800–1900.* London and New York: Verso, 1999.

Moretti, Franco. *Distant Reading.* London and New York: Verso, 2013.

Muller, Jan-Werner. *What Is Populism?* Philadelphia: University of Pennsylvania Press, 2016.

Munich, Adrienne. *Queen Victoria's Secrets.* New York: Columbia University Press, 1996.

Nayyar, Deepak. "BRICS, Developing Countries and Global Governance." *Third World Quarterly.* 37, no. 4 (2016): 575–591.

Nee, Victor, and Sonja Opper. "Political Capital in a Market Economy." *Social Forces.* 88, no. 5 (2010): 2105–2132.

Neep, Daniel. *Occupying Syria under the French Mandate: Insurgency, Space and State Formation.* Cambridge and New York: Cambridge University Press, 2012.

Neilson, Keith. *Strategy and Supply: The Anglo-Russian Alliance 1914–1917.* London and New York: Routledge, 2014.

Nelson, R. R., ed. *National Innovation Systems: A Comparative Analysis.* Oxford and New York: Oxford University Press, 1993.

Nencioni, Giovanni. "L'Accademia della Crusca e la Lingua Italiana." In *The History of Linguistics in Italy*, edited by Paolo Ramat, Hans-Josef Niederehe and E. F. K. Koerner. Amsterdam: John Benjamins Publishing Company, 1986.

Nicaso, Antonio, and Marcel Danesi. *Made Men: Mafia Culture and the Power of Symbols, Rituals, and Myth*. Lanham, Boulder, New York, and Oxford: Rowman & Littlefield Publishers, 2013.

Nicaso, Antonio, and Lee Lamothe. *Angels, Mobsters and Narco-Terrorists: The Rising Menace of Global Criminal Empires*. Mississagua, Ontario: John Wiley & Sons Canada, 2009.

Nicoll, F. *Gladstone, Gordon and the Sudan Wars: The Battle over Imperial Invention in the Victorian Age*. Pen & Sword Books, 2013.

Nik-Khah, Edward. "Chicago Neoliberalism and the Genesis of the Milton Friedman Institute (2006–2009)." In *Building Chicago Economics: New Perspectives on the History of America's Most Powerful Economics Program*, edited by Robert Van Horn, Philip Mirowski and Thomas A. Stapleford. Cambridge and New York: Cambridge University Press New York, 2011.

Nik-Khah, Edward, and Robert Van Horn. "The Ascendancy of Chicago Neoliberalism." In *The Handbook of Neoliberalism*, edited by Simon Springer, Kean Birch and Julie MacLeavy. London and New York: Routledge, 2016.

Nish, Ian. "Politics, Trade and Communications in East Asia: Thoughts on Anglo-Russian Relations, 1861–1907." *Modern Asian Studies*. 21, no. 4 (1987): 667–678.

Nkomo, Dion. "Dictionaries and Language Policy." In *The Routledge Handbook of Lexicography*, edited by Pedro A. Fuertes-Olivera. London and New York: Routledge, 2017.

Nolte, Hans-Heinrich. "Internal Peripheries: From Andalucia to Tatarstan." *Review (Fernand Braudel Center)*. *18, No. 2* (1995): 261–280.

Nolte, Hans-Heinrich. "Why Is Europe's South Poor? A Chain of Internal Peripheries Along the Old Muslim-Christian Borders." *Review (Fernand Braudel Center)*. *26, No. 1* (2003): 49–66.

Nussbaum, Martha C. *Creating Capabilities: The Human Development Approach*. Cambridge, Massachusetts and London: Harvard University Press, 2011.

Nussbaum, Martha C. *Women and Human Development: The Capabilities Approach*. The Seeley Lectures. Cambridge and New York: Cambridge University Press, 2000.

Ó Riain, Sean. "States and Markets in an Era of Globalization." *Annual Review of Sociology*. 26 (2000): 187–213.

O'Hearn, Denis, and Paul S. Ciccantell. *Migration, Racism and Labor Exploitation in the World-System*. London and New York: Routledge, 2021.

O'Laughlin, Bridget. "Making People 'Surplus Population' in Southern Africa." In *Reclaiming Development Studies: Essays for Ashwani Saith*, edited by Murat Arsel, Anirban Dasgupta and Servaas Storm. London: Anthem Press, 2021.

Oberoi, Harjot. *The Construction of Religious Boundaries: Culture, Identity, and Diversity in the Sikh Tradition.* Chicago: University of Chicago Press, 1994.

Obikili, Nonso. "The Impact of the Slave Trade on Literacy in West Africa: Evidence from the Colonial Era." *Journal of African Economies.* 25, no. 1 (2016): 1–27.

OECD. *Education Policy Analysis.* Paris: OECD Publishing, 2003. https://www.oecd.org /education/skills-beyond-school/35747684.pdf.

Olsaretti, Alessandro. "Beyond Class: The Many Facets of Gramsci's Theory of Intellectuals." *Journal of Classical Sociology.* 14, no. 4 (2014): 363–81.

Olsaretti, Alessandro. "Croce, Philosophy and Intellectuals: Three Aspects of Gramsci's Theory of Hegemony." *Critical Sociology.* 42, no. 3 (2016): 337–355.

Olsaretti, Alessandro. "From the Return to Labriola to the Anti-Croce: Philosophy, Praxis and Human Nature in Gramsci's *Prison Notebooks*." *Historical Materialism.* 24, no. 4 (2016): 193–220.

Olsaretti, Alessandro. "Philosophy and Science in Gramsci's Reconstruction of Marxism." McGill University, 2013.

Olsaretti, Alessandro. "Political Dynamics in the Rise of Fakhr al-Din, 1590–1633: Crusade, Trade, and State Formation Along the Levantine Coast." *The International History Review.* 30, no. 4 (2008): 709–740.

Olsaretti, Alessandro. *The Struggle for Development and Democracy, Volume 1: New Approaches.* Leiden and Boston: Brill, 2022.

Olsaretti, Alessandro. *Towards a Humanist Social Science.* Essays in Philosophy, Sociology, and the History of Culture. forthcoming.

Olsaretti, Alessandro. "Urban Culture, Curiosity and the Aesthetics of Distance: The Representation of Picturesque Carnivals in Early Victorian Travelogues to the Levant." *Social History.* 32, no. 3 (2007): 247–270.

Olson, Mancur. "Dictatorship, Democracy, and Development." *American Political Science Review.* 87, no. 3 (1993): 567–576.

Olson, Mancur. *The Logic of Collective Action.* Harvard Economic Studies. Cambridge, Massachusetts and London: Harvard University Press, 2009.

Olutayo, Akinpelu Olanrewaju. "'Verstehen,' Everyday Sociology and Development: Incorporating African Indigenous Knowledge." *Critical Sociology.* 40, no. 2 (2014): 229–238.

Omissi, D. *The Sepoy and the Raj: The Indian Army, 1860–1940.* Studies in Military and Strategic History. London and New York: Palgrave Macmillan, 2016.

Opp, Karl-Dieter. "Decline of the Nation State? How the European Union Creates National and Sub-National Identifications." *Social Forces.* 84, no. 2 (2005): 653–680.

Ostrom, Elinor. "Beyond Markets and States: Polycentric Governance of Complex Economic Systems." *American Economic Review.* 100, no. 3 (2010): 641–72.

Ostrom, Elinor. "A General Framework for Analyzing Sustainability of Social-Ecological Systems." *Science.* 325 (2009): 419–422.

Ouahes, Idir. *Syria and Lebanon under the French Mandate: Cultural Imperialism and the Workings of Empire.* London and New York: I. B. Tauris, 2018.

Overhage, Thomas. "Pool It, Share It, or Lose It: an Economical View on Pooling and Sharing of European Military Capabilities." *Defense & Security Analysis.* 29, no. 4 (2013): 323–341.

Overton, Mark. *Agricultural Revolution in England: The Transformation of the Agrarian Economy 1500–1850.* Cambridge and New York: Cambridge University Press, 1996.

Owen, Roger. *State, Power and Politics in the Making of the Modern Middle East.* 3 ed. London and New York: Routledge, 2013.

Özyüksel, Murat. *The Hejaz Railway and the Ottoman Empire: Modernity, Industrialisation and Ottoman Decline.* London and New York: I. B. Tauris, 2014.

Pamuk, Sevket. *A Monetary History of the Ottoman Empire.* Cambridge Studies in Islamic Civilization. Cambridge and New York: Cambridge University Press, 2000.

Pamuk, Sevket. *The Ottoman Empire and European Capitalism, 1820–1913: Trade, Investment and Production.* Cambridge and New York: Cambridge University Press, 1987.

Pannier, Alice. *Rivals in Arms: The Rise of UK-France Defence Relations in the Twenty-First Century.* Montreal, Kingston, London, Ithaca: McGill-Queen's University Press, 2020.

Paoli, Massimo, and Andrea Prencipe. "The Role of Knowledge Bases in Complex Product Systems: Some Empirical Evidence from the Aero Engine Industry." *Journal of Management and Governance.* 3, no. 2 (1999): 137–160.

Parboteeah, K. Praveen, John B. Cullen, and Lrong Lim. "Formal Volunteering: A Cross-National Test." *Journal of World Business.* 39, no. 4 (2004): 431–441.

Pasquier, Michael. *Fathers on the Frontier: French Missionaries and the Roman Catholic Priesthood in the United States, 1789–1870.* Oxford and New York: Oxford University Press, 2010.

Patsiurko, Natalka, John L. Campbell, and John Anthony Hall. "Measuring Cultural Diversity: Ethnic, Linguistic and Religious Fractionalization in the OECD." 35, no. 2 (2012): 195–217.

Patsiurko, Natalka, John L. Campbell, and John Anthony Hall. "Nation-State Size, Ethnic Diversity and Economic Performance in the Advanced Capitalist Countries." *New Political Economy.* 18, no. 6 (2013): 827–844.

Pauli, Urban. "Training Professionalisation and SME Performance." *Human Resource Development International.* 23, no. 2 (2020): 168–187.

Pavone, Claudio, and Stanislao Pugliese. *A Civil War: A History of the Italian Resistance.* Translated by Peter Levy and David Broder. London and New York: Verso, 2013.

Paxton, Robert. "Franco's Spain in Comparative Perspective." In *Falange. Las Culturas Políticas del Fascismo en la España de Franco (1939–1975),* edited by Miguel Ángel Ruiz Carnicer. Zaragoza: Institución Fernando el Católico, 2013.

Paxton, Robert O. "The Five Stages of Fascism." *The Journal of Modern History*. 70, no. 1 (1998): 1–23.

Pazos-Vidal, Serafin. *Subsidiarity and EU Multilevel Governance: Actors, Networks and Agendas*. London and New York: Routledge, 2019.

Peck, Gunther. *Reinventing Free Labor: Padrones and Immigrant Workers in the North American West, 1880–1930*. Cambridge and New York: Cambridge University Press, 2000.

Peers, C. *The African Wars: Warriors and Soldiers of the Colonial Campaigns*. Barnsley, South Yorkshire, and Haverton, Pennsylvania: Pen & Sword Books, 2011.

Pelagidis, Theodore, and Harry Papasotiriou. "Globalisation or Regionalism? States, Markets and the Structure of International Trade." *Review of International Studies*. 28, no. 3 (2002): 519–535.

Pelfrey, Patricia A., and Margaret Cheney. *A Brief History of the University of California*. Berkeley: University of California Press, 2004.

Pennings, Enrico, and Leo Sleuwaegen. "International Relocation: Firm and Industry Determinants." *Economics Letters*. 67, no. 2 (2000): 179–186.

Perrotta, Domenico. "Vecchi e Nuovi Mediatori: Storia, Geografia ed Etnografia del Caporalato in Agricoltura." *Meridiana*. 79, no. 1 (2014): 193–220.

Perrotta, Domenico, and Devi Sacchetto. "Migrant Farmworkers in Southern Italy: Ghettoes, Caporalato and Collective Action." *Workers of the World*. 1, no. 5 (2014): 75–98.

Pescosolido, Guido. *La Questione Meridionale in Breve: Centocinquant'anni di Storia*. Rome: Donzelli Editore, 2017.

Peters, B. Guy. *Institutional Theory in Political Science*. 2nd ed. London and New York: Continuum, 2005.

Pfaff, Steven, and Hyojoung Kim. "Exit-Voice Dynamics in Collective Action: An Analysis of Emigration and Protest in the East German Revolution." *American Journal of Sociology*. 109, no. 2 (2003): 401–444.

Philipp, Thomas, and Birgit Schäbler, eds. *The Syrian Land: Processes of Integration and Fragmentation: Bilād Al-Shām from the 18th to the 20th Century*. Stuttgart: Franz Steiner Verlag, 1998.

Philliou, Christine. "Communities on the Verge: Unraveling the Phanariot Ascendancy in Ottoman Governance." *Comparative Studies in Society and History*. 51, no. 1 (2009): 151–181.

Piketty, Thomas. *Capital in the Twenty-First Century*. Translated by Arthur Goldhammer. Cambridge, Massachusetts and London: Harvard University Press, 2017.

Pilbeam, Pamela. *Republicanism in Nineteenth-Century France, 1814–1871*. Houndmills, Basingstoke, Hampshire, and London: Macmillan, 1995.

Pino, Nathan W. "Community Policing and Social Capital." *Policing: An International Journal of Police Strategies & Management*. 24, no. 2 (2001): 200–215.

Piore, Michael. *Birds of Passage: Migrant Labor and Industrial Societies.* Cambridge and New York: Cambridge University Press, 1979.

Piore, Michael, and Charles Sabel. *The Second Industrial Divide: Possibilities for Prosperity.* New York: Basic Books, 1986.

Pique, Josep M., Jasmina Berbegal-Mirabent, and Henry Etzkowitz. "Triple Helix and the Evolution of Ecosystems of Innovation: The Case of Silicon Valley." *Triple Helix.* 5, no. 1 (2018): 1–21.

Pizzolato, Nicola, and John D. Holst, eds. *Antonio Gramsci: A Pedagogy to Change the World*, Critical Studies of Education. Cham, Switzerland: Springer, 2017.

Plys, Kristin. "Theories of Antifascism in the Interwar Mediterranean Part 1: Fascism in the Longue Durée." *Journal of World-Systems Research.* 28, no. 2 (2022): 344–358.

Polanyi, Karl, Joseph E. Stiglitz, and Fred Block. *The Great Transformation: The Political and Economic Origins of Our Time.* Boston: Beacon Press, 2001.

Pomeranz, Kenneth. *The Great Divergence: China, Europe, and the Making of the Modern World Economy.* Princeton and Oxford: Princeton University Press, 2000.

Pons, Frank Moya. *History of the Caribbean: Plantations, Trade, and War in the Atlantic World.* Princeton: Markus Wiener Publishers, 2007.

Porter, Andrew N., ed. *The Oxford History of the British Empire: The Nineteenth Century.* Oxford and New York: Oxford University Press, 1999.

Porter, Michael E. *Competitive Advantage of Nations: Creating and Sustaining Superior Performance.* New York: Free Press, 2011.

Porter, Roy. *The Enlightenment.* 2 ed. London and New York: Palgrave Macmillan, 2001.

Portes, Alejandro. "Social Capital: Its Origins and Applications in Modern Sociology." *Annual Review of Sociology.* 24, no. 1 (1998): 1–24.

Portes, Alejandro. "The Two Meanings of Social Capital." *Sociological Forum.* 15, no. 1 (2000): 1–12.

Portes, Alejandro, and John Walton. *Labor, Class, and the International System.* New York, London, Toronto, Sydney, San Francisco: Academic Press, 1981.

Poulantzas, Nicos. *Classes in Contemporary Capitalism.* Translated by David Fernbach. reprint ed.: Verso, 2018.

Poulantzas, Nicos. *Fascism and Dictatorship: The Third International and the Problem of Fascism.* London and New York: Verso, 2019.

Prawer, S. S. *Karl Marx and World Literature.* London and New York: Verso, 2014.

Prencipe, Andrea. "Breadth and Depth of Technological Capabilities in CoPS: The Case of the Aircraft Engine Control System." *Research policy.* 29, no. 7–8 (2000): 895–911.

Prencipe, Andrea. "Corporate Strategy and Systems Inttegration Capabilities: Managing Networks in Complex Systems Industries." In *The Business of Systems Integration*, edited by Andrea Prencipe, Andrew Davies and Michael Hobday. Oxford And New York: Oxfiord University Press, 2003.

Prencipe, Andrea. *Strategy, Systems and Scope*. Thousand Oaks, London, and New Delhi: SAGE, 2020.

Prencipe, Andrea. "Technological Competencies and Product's Evolutionary Dynamics a Case Study from the Aero-Engine Industry." *Research policy*. 25, no. 8 (1997): 1261–1276.

Prencipe, Andrea, Andrew Davies, and Michael Hobday, eds. *The Business of Systems Integration*. Oxford And New York: Oxfiord University Press, 2003.

Price, Roger. *A Social History of Nineteenth-Century France*. London and New York: Routledge, 2021.

Primeau, Ronald. *Romance of the Road: The Literature of the American Highway*. Bowling Green, Ohio: Bowling Green State University Popular Press, 1996.

Procter, James, and Robert Eagleton. *Stuart Hall*. London and New York: Routledge, 2004.

Przeworski, Adam, Michael E. Alvarez, Jose Antonio Cheibub, and Fernando Limongi. *Democracy and Development: Political Institutions and Well-Being in the World, 1950–1990*. Cambridge Studies in the Theory of Democracy. Cambridge and New York: Cambridge University Press, 2000.

Purdue, Derrick. "Neighbourhood Governance: Leadership, Trust and Social Capital." *Urban Studies*. 38, no. 12 (2001): 2211–2224.

Putnam, Robert D. *Bowling Alone: The Collapse and Revival of American Community*. A Touchstone Book. New York: Simon & Schuster, 2000.

Putnam, Robert D., Robert Leonardi, and Raffaella Y. Nanetti. *Making Democracy Work: Civic Traditions in Modern Italy*. Princeton and Oxford: Princeton University Press, 1994.

Pyatt, Graham. "On the Interpretation and Disaggregation of Gini Coefficients." *The Economic Journal*. 86, no. 342 (1976): 243–255.

Qadeer, Mohammad, Sandeep K. Agrawal, and Alexander Lovell. "Evolution of Ethnic Enclaves in the Toronto Metropolitan Area, 2001–2006." *Journal of International Migration and Integration/Revue de l'integration et de la migration internationale*. 11, no. 3 (2010): 315–339.

Quataert, Donald. "The Age of Reforms, 1812–1914." In *An Economic and Social History of the Ottoman Empire. Volume Two: 1600–1914*, edited by Halil İnalcık and Donald Quataert. Cambridge and New York: Cambridge University Press, 1994.

Quigley, John M. "Urban Diversity and Economic Growth." *Journal of Economic Perspectives*. 12, no. 2 (1998): 127–138.

Rabinowitch, Alexander. *The Bolsheviks Come to Power: The Revolution of 1917 in Petrograd*. Chicago: Haymarket Books, 2004.

Raphael, Chad. "The Political-Economic Origins of Reali-TV." In *Reality TV: Remaking Television Culture*, edited by Susan Murray and Laurie Ouellette. New York and London: New York University Press, 2009.

Redhead, Mark. "Charles Taylor's Deeply Diverse Response to Canadian Fragmentation: A Project Often Commented on but Seldom Explored." *Canadian Journal of Political Science / Revue canadienne de science politique*. 36, no. 1 (2003): 61–83.

Reilly, James A. "Damascus Merchants and Trade in the Transition to Capitalism." *Canadian Journal of history/Annales canadiennes d'histoire*. 27, no. 1 (1992): 1–27.

Reilly, James A. *Fragile Nation, Shattered Land: The Modern History of Syria*. London and New York: I.B. Tauris, 2019.

Reilly, James A. "From Workshops to Sweatshops: Damascus Textiles and the World-Economy in the Last Ottoman Century." *Review (Fernand Braudel Center)*. 16, no. 2 (1993): 199–213.

Reilly, James A. *The Ottoman Cities of Lebanon: Historical Legacy and Identity in the Modern Middle East*. London and New York: I. B. Tauris, 2016.

Reilly, James A. "Status Groups and Propertyholding in the Damascus Hinterland, 1828–1880." *International Journal of Middle East Studies*. 21, no. 4 (1989): 517–539.

Reinert, Hugo, and Erik S. Reinert. "Creative Destruction in Economics: Nietzsche, Sombart, Schumpeter." In *Friedrich Nietzsche (1844–1900)*, 55–85. Berlin and Heidelberg: Springer, 2006.

Reinhardt, Anne. *Navigating Semi-Colonialism: Shipping, Sovereignty, and Nation Building in China, 1860–1937*. Harvard East Asian Monographs. Leiden and Boston: Brill, 2020.

Rendall, Matthew. "Defensive Realism and the Concert of Europe." *Review of International Studies*. 32, no. 3 (2006): 523–540.

Reuter, Ora John, and Jennifer Gandhi. "Economic Performance and Elite Defection from Hegemonic Parties." *British Journal of Political Science*. 41, no. 1 (2011): 83–110.

Riall, Lucy. *The Italian Risorgimento: State, Society and National Unification*. Historical Connections. New York and London: Routledge, 2002.

Riall, Lucy. *Sicily and the Unification of Italy: Liberal Policy and Local Power, 1859–1866*. Oxford: Clarendon Press, 1998.

Riall, Lucy. *Under the Volcano: Revolution in a Sicilian Town*. Oxford and New York: Oxford University Press, 2013.

Richard, Slatta. "Eric J. Hobsbawm's Social Bandit: A Critique and Revision." *A Contracorriente*. 1, no. 2 (2004): 22–30.

Ridgeway, James. *Blood in the Face: The Ku Klux Klan, Aryan Nations, Nazi Skinheads, and the Rise of a New White Culture*. New York: Basic Books, 1996.

Rinaldi, Alberto, and Michelangelo Vasta. "The Italian Corporate Network after the 'Golden Age' (1972–1983): From Centrality to Marginalization of State-Owned Enterprises." *Enterprise & Society*. 13, no. 2 (2012): 378–413.

Roach, Elmo E. "Anglo-Russian Relations from Austerlitz to Tilsit." *The International History Review*. 5, no. 2 (1983): 181–200.

Roberts, James. *The Counter-Revolution in France, 1787–1830.* London, New Delhi, New York, Sydney: Bloomsbury Publishing, 1990.

Robertson, John. "Enlightenment and Revolution: Naples 1799." *Transactions of the Royal Historical Society.* 10 (2000): 17–44.

Robertson, Peter E., and Adrian Sin. "Measuring Hard Power: China's Economic Growth and Military Capacity." *Defence and Peace Economics.* 28, no. 1 (2017): 91–111.

Robeyns, Ingrid. "The Capability Approach in Practice." *Journal of Political Philosophy.* 14, no. 3 (2006): 351–376.

Robeyns, Ingrid. "The Capability Approach: a Theoretical Survey." *Journal of Human Development.* 6, no. 1 (2005): 93–117.

Robinson, William I. "Globalization and the Sociology of Immanuel Wallerstein: A Critical Appraisal." *International Sociology.* 26, no. 6 (2011): 723–745.

Robinson, William I. "The Transnational State and the BRICS: a Global Capitalism Perspective." *Third World Quarterly.* 36, no. 1 (2015): 1–21.

Robles, Alfredo C. Jr. *French Theories of Regulation and Conceptions of the International Division of Labour.* International Political Economy Series. New York: St Martin's, 1994.

Roeder, Philip G. *Where Nation-States Come From: Institutional Change in the Age of Nationalism.* Princeton and Oxford: Princeton University Press, 2007.

Roemer, John E. *A General Theory of Exploitation and Class.* Cambridge, Massachusetts and London: Harvard University Press, 1982.

Roemer, John E. *Value, Exploitation, and Class.* Fundamentals of Pure and Applied Economics. Harwood Academic Publishers, 1986.

Rose, Mark H. *Interstate: Express Highway Politics, 1939–1989.* Univiversity of Tennessee Press, 1990.

Rose, Mark H., and Raymond A. Mohl. *Interstate: Highway Politics and Policy since 1939.* University of Tennessee Press, 2012.

Rosselli, Annalisa, Nerio Naldi, and Eleonora Sanfilippo, eds. *Money, Finance and Crises in Economic History: The Long-Term Impact of Economic Ideas.* London and New York: Routledge, 2018.

Rotberg, R. I. *The Founder: Cecil Rhodes and the Pursuit of Power.* Oxford and New York: Oxford University Press, USA, 1988.

Rothstein, Bo. "Social Capital in the Social Democratic Welfare State." *Politics & Society.* 29, no. 2 (2001): 207–241.

Rothstein, Bo, and Dietlind Stolle. "Social Capital, Impartiality, and the Welfare State: an Institutional Approach." In *Generating Social Capital: Civil Society and Insitutions in Comparative Perspective*, edited by Marc Hooghe and Dietlind Stolle. London and New York: Palgrave Macmillan, 2003.

Roudometof, Victor. *Glocalization: A Critical Introduction.* Routledge Studies in Global and Transnational Politics. London and New York: Routledge, 2016.

Roudometof, Victor. *Nationalism, Globalization, and Orthodoxy: The Social Origins of Ethnic Conflict in the Balkans*. Westport, Connecticut: Greenwood Press, 2001.

Rovira Kaltwasser, Cristóbal. "Political Elites in Latin America." In *The Palgrave Handbook of Political Elites*, edited by Heinrich Best and John Higley, 255–271. London and New York: Palgrave Macmillan, 2018.

Rudé, George F. E. *The Crowd in History: A Study of Popular Disturbances in France and England, 1730–1848*. London: Serif, 1995.

Rudolph, Lloyd I., and Susanne Hoeber Rudolph. "Authority and Power in Bureaucratic and Patrimonial Administration: A Revisionist Interpretation of Weber on Bureaucracy." *World Politics*. (1979): 195–227.

Rueschemeyer, Dietrich. *Power and the Division of Labour. Social and Political Theory from Polity Press*. Cambridge, UK and Malden, Massachusetts: Polity, 1986.

Ruff, Julius R. *Violence in Early Modern Europe, 1500–1800*. Cambridge and New York: Cambridge University Press, 2001.

Ruggiero, Guido. *The Renaissance in Italy: A Social and Cultural History of the Rinascimento*. Cambridge and New York: Cambridge University Press, 2015.

Russo, John Paul. "The Sicilian Latifundia." *Italian Americana*. 17, no. 1 (1999): 40–57.

Ryan, Louise, Rosemary Sales, Mary Tilki, and Bernadetta Siara. "Social Networks, Social Support and Social Capital: The Experiences of Recent Polish Migrants in London." *Sociology*. 42, no. 4 (2008): 672–690.

Sabetti, Filippo. *The Search for Good Government: Understanding the Paradox of Italian Democracy*. Montreal, Kingston, London, Ithaca: McGill-Queen's University Press, 2000.

Sabetti, Filippo. "Stationary Bandits. Lessons from the Practice of Research from Sicily." *Sociologica*. no. 2 (2011): 1–22.

Sagar, Ambuj D., and Adil Najam. "The Human Development Index: a Critical Review." *Ecological Economics*. 25, no. 3 (1998): 249–264.

Said, Edward W. *Orientalism*. Vintage Books, 1994.

Salamon, Lester M., and Helmut K. Anheier. "The Civil Society Sector." *Society*. 34, no. 2 (1997): 60–65.

Salter, Ammon J., and Ben R. Martin. "The Economic Benefits of Publicly Funded Basic Research: a Critical Review." *Research Policy*. 30, no. 3 (2001): 509–532.

Salzman, Zoe. "Private Military Contractors and the Taint of a Mercenary Reputation." *NYU Journal of International Law & Politics*. 40 (2007): 853–892.

Samford, Steven. "Networks, Brokerage, and State-Led Technology Diffusion in Small Industry." *American Journal of Sociology*. 122, no. 5 (2017): 1339–1370.

Sandefur, Rebecca L., and Edward O. Laumann. "A Paradigm for Social Capital." In *Knowledge and Social Capital: Foundations and Applications*. London and New York: Routledge, 2009.

Sassen, Saskia. *Deciphering the Global: Its Scales, Spaces and Subjects.* New York and London: Routledge, 2013.

Sassen, Saskia. *Sociology of Globalization.* Contemporary Societies. w.w. Norton, 2007.

Satyanath, Shanker, Nico Voigtländer, and Hans-Joachim Voth. "Bowling for Fascism: Social Capital and the Rise of the Nazi Party." *Journal of Political Economy.* 125, no. 2 (2017): 478–526.

Saunders, David M. "Introduction to Research on Hirschman's Exit, Voice, and Loyalty Model." *Employee Responsibilities and Rights Journal.* 5, no. 3 (1992): 187–190.

Saxenian, AnnaLee. *The New Argonauts: Regional Advantage in a Global Economy.* Cambridge, Massachusetts and London: Harvard University Press, 2007.

Saxenian, AnnaLee. *Regional Advantage: Culture and Competition in Silicon Valley and Route 128, with a New Preface by the Author.* Cambridge, Massachusetts and London: Harvard University Press, 1996.

Schaeffer, Robert K., ed. *War in the World-System.* New York, Westport Connecticut, and London: Greenwood Press, 1989.

Schake, Kori. *Safe Passage: The Transition from British to American Hegemony.* Cambridge, Massachusetts and London: Harvard University Press, 2017.

Schilcher, Linda Schatkowski. *Families in Politics: Damascene Factions and Estates of the 18th and 19th Centuries.* Stuttgart: Franz Steiner Verlag, 1985.

Schluchter, Wolfgang, and Guenther Roth. *The Rise of Western Rationalism: Max Weber's Developmental History.* Translated by Guenther Roth. Berkeley, Los Angeles, and London: University of California Press, 1985.

Schmidtz, David. "Justifying the State." *Ethics.* 101, no. 1 (1990): 89–102.

Schneider, Jane, ed. *Italy's 'Southern Question': Orientalism in One Country.* London and New York: Routledge, 2020.

Schonhardt-Bailey, Cheryl. *From the Corn Laws to Free Trade: Interests, Ideas, and Institutions in Historical Perspective.* Cambridge, Massachusetts: MIT Press, 2006.

Schroeder, Ralph. "Introduction: The IEMP Model and Its Critics." In *An Anatomy of Power: The Social Theory of Michael Mann,* edited by John Anthony Hall and Ralph Schroeder. Cambridge and New York: Cambridge University Press, 2006.

Schroeder, Ralph. *Max Weber, Democracy and Modernization.* Basingstoke: Macmillan, 1998.

Schumpeter, J. A. *Capitalism, Socialism and Democracy.* New York and London: Routledge, 2013.

Schwaller, John Frederick. *The History of the Catholic Church in Latin America: From Conquest to Revolution and Beyond.* New York and London: New York University Press, 2011.

Seal, Graham. "The Robin Hood Principle: Folklore, History, and the Social Bandit." *Journal of folklore research.* (2009): 67–89.

Seavoy, Ronald. *An Economic History of the United States: From 1607 to the Present.* London and New York: Routledge, 2013.

Seckelmann, Margrit, Lorenza Violini, Cristina Fraenkel-Haeberle, and Giada Ragone, eds. *Academic Freedom under Pressure?: A Comparative Perspective.* Cham, Switzerland: Springer, 2021.

Seferiades, Seraphim, and Hank Johnston, eds. *Violent Protest, Contentious Politics, and the Neoliberal State.* London and New York: Routledge, 2016.

Seidel, Markus, Christoph H. Loch, and Satjiv Chahil. "Quo Vadis, Automotive Industry? A Vision of Possible Industry Transformations." *European Management Journal.* 23, no. 4 (2005): 439–449.

Sella, Domenico. "Household, Land Tenure, and Occupation in North Italy in the Late XVIth Century." *Journal of European Economic History.* 16, no. 3 (1987): 487.

Sella, Domenico. *Italy in the Seventeenth Century.* Longman History of Italy. London and New York: Routledge, 2014.

Sen, Amartya. "Adam Smith and the Contemporary World." *Erasmus Journal for Philosophy and Economics.* 3, no. 1 (2010): 50–67.

Sen, Amartya. "Adam Smith's Prudence." In *Theory and Reality in Development: Essays in Honour of Paul Streeten*, edited by Sanjaya Lall and Frances Stewart. London and New York: Palgrave Macmillan, 1986.

Sen, Amartya. "The Contemporary Relevance of Adam Smith." In *The Oxford Handbook of Adam Smith*, edited by Christopher J. Berry, Maria Pia Paganelli and Craig Smith. Oxford and New York: Oxford University Press, 2013.

Sen, Amartya. *Development as Freedom.* Oxford and New York: Oxford University Press, 2001.

Senisik, Pinar. *The Transformation of Ottoman Crete: Revolts, Politics and Identity in the Late Nineteenth Century.* London: I. B. Tauris, 2011.

Seymour, Michael John. *The Transformation of the North Atlantic World, 1492–1763: An Introduction.* Studies in Military History and International Affairs. Wesport, Connecticut, and London: Praeger, 2004.

Shapin, Steven. *The Scientific Revolution.* Chicago and London: University of Chicago Press, 2018.

Sherman, Daniel J., and Terry Nardin, eds. *Terror, Culture, Politics: Rethinking 9/11.* Bloomington: Indiana University Press, 2006.

Shleifer, Andrei. "Understanding Regulation." *European Financial Management.* 11, no. 4 (2005): 439–451.

Shoemaker, Robert B. "The Street Robber and the Gentleman Highwayman: Changing Representations and Perceptions of Robbery in London, 1690–1800." *Cultural and Social History.* 3, no. 4 (2006): 381–405.

Sideri, Sandro. *Trade and Power: Informal Colonialism in Anglo-Portuguese Relations.* Rotterdam: Rotterdam University Press, 1970.

Siisiainen, Martti. "Two Concepts of Social Capital: Bourdieu Vs. Putnam." *International Journal of Contemporary Sociology*. 40, no. 2 (2003): 183–204.

Silver, Beverly J., and Giovanni Arrighi. "Workers North and South." *Socialist Register*. 37 (2001).

Singer, Alexa J., Cecilia Chouhy, Peter S. Lehmann, Jessica N. Walzak, Marc Gertz, and Sophia Biglin. "Victimization, Fear of Crime, and Trust in Criminal Justice Institutions: A Cross-National Analysis." *Crime & Delinquency*. 65, no. 6 (2019): 822–844.

Skinner, Quentin. *The Return of Grand Theory in the Human Sciences*. Canto. Cambridge and New York: Cambridge University Press, 1990.

Sklair, Leslie. *The Transnational Capitalist Class*. Oxford: Blackwell, 2000.

Sklar, Martin J. *The Corporate Reconstruction of American Capitalism, 1890–1916: The Market, the Law, and Politics*. Cambridge and New York: Cambridge University Press, 1988.

Skocpol, Theda. *Democracy, Revolution, and History*. The Wilder House Series in Politics, History and Culture. Ithaca, New York: Cornell University Press, 2018.

Skocpol, Theda. *The Missing Middle: Working Families and the Future of American Social Policy*. New York: W.W. Norton, 2000.

Skocpol, Theda. *Social Revolutions in the Modern World*. Cambridge and New York: Cambridge University Press, 1994.

Skocpol, Theda. *States and Social Revolutions: A Comparative Analysis of France, Russia, and China*. Canto Classics. Cambridge and New York: Cambridge University Press, 2015.

Sluglett, Peter. *Britain in Iraq: Contriving King and Country, 1914–1932*. New York: Columbia University Press, 2007.

Smith, Anthony D. *The Ethnic Origins of Nations*. Oxford and Malden, Massachusetts: Blackwell, 1991.

Smith, Anthony D. *Ethno-Symbolism and Nationalism: A Cultural Approach*. New York and London: Routledge, 2009.

Smith, David A., Dorothy J. Solinger, and Steven C. Topik, eds. *States and Sovereignty in the Global Economy*. London and New York: Routledge, 1999.

Smith, David Horton, Robert A. Stebbins, and Jurgen Grotz, eds. *The Palgrave Handbook of Volunteering, Civic Participation, and Nonprofit Associations*. London and New York: Palgrave Macmillan, 2017.

Smith, Michael E. "The Aztec Empire and the Mesoamerican World System." In *Empires: Perspectives from Archaeology and History*, edited by Susan E. Alcock, Terence N. D'Altroy, Kathleen D. MIorrison and Carla M. Sinopoli. Cambridge and New York: Cambridge University Press, 2001.

Smith, Neil. "Giuliani Time: The Revanchist 1990s." *Social Text*. no. 57 (1998): 1–20.

Smith, Neil. *Uneven Development: Nature, Capital, and the Production of Space.* Athens: University of Georgia Press, 2008.

Snowden, Frank M. *The Fascist Revolution in Tuscany, 1919–22.* Cambridge and New York: Cambridge University Press, 2004.

Snowden, Frank M. *Violence and the Great Estates in the South of Italy: Apulia, 1900–1922.* Cambridge and New York: Cambridge University Press, 2004.

Soleimani, Kamal. *Islam and Competing Nationalisms in the Middle East, 1876–1926.* The Modern Muslim World. Cham, Switzerland: Springer, 2016.

Solimano, Andres. *Economic Elites, Crises, and Democracy: Alternatives Beyond Neoliberal Capitalism.* Oxford and New York: Oxford University Press, 2014.

Sorenson, Olav, and Michelle Rogan. "(When) Do Organizations Have Social Capital?." *Annual Review of Sociology.* 40 (2014): 261–280.

Soss, Joe. *Unwanted Claims: The Politics of Participation in the U.S. Welfare System.* Ann Arbor: University of Michigan Press, 2002.

Spirou, Costas. *Anchoring Innovation Districts: The Entrepreneurial University and Urban Change.* Baltimore: Johns Hopkins University Press, 2021.

Spruyt, Hendrik. *Ending Empire: Contested Sovereignty and Territorial Partition.* Ithaca and London: Cornell University Press, 2018.

Spruyt, Hendrik. *The Sovereign State and Its Competitors: An Analysis of Systems Change.* Princeton Studies in International History and Politics. Princeton and Oxford: Princeton University Press, 1994.

Staggenborg, Suzanne. *Social Movements.* 2nd ed. Oxford and New York: Oxford University Press, 2016.

Stanley, Jason. *How Fascism Works: The Politics of Us and Them.* New York: Random House, 2018.

Stantchev, Stefan. "The Medieval Origins of Embargo as a Policy Tool." *History of Political Thought.* 33, no. 3 (2012): 373–399.

Steiber, Annika, and Sverker Alänge. *The Silicon Valley Model.* Cham, Switzerland. Springer, 2016.

Stein, Stanley J. "Bureaucracy and Business in the Spanish Empire, 1759–1804: Failure of a Bourbon Reform in Mexico and Peru." *Hispanic American Historical Review.* 61, no. 1 (1981): 2–28.

Steinmetz, George, ed. *Sociology and Empire: The Imperial Entanglements of a Discipline.* Durham and London: Duke University Press, 2013.

Stekelenburg, Jacquelien van, Conny Roggeband, and Bert Klandermans. *The Future of Social Movement Research: Dynamics, Mechanisms, and Processes.* Social Movements, Protest and Contention. Minneapolis: University of Minnesota Press, 2013.

Stelmakh, Valeria D. "Reading in the Context of Censorship in the Soviet Union." *Libraries & Culture.* 36, no. 1 (2001): 143–151.

Stepanova, Ekaterina. *Terrorism in Asymmetrical Conflict: Ideological and Structural Aspects.* Stockholm International Peace Research Institute. Oxford and New York: Oxford University Press, 2008.

Stephen, Frank H. *Law and Development: An Institutional Critique.* Cheltenham, UK and Northampton, Massachusetts: Edward Elga, 2018.

Stiglitz, Joseph E. *Globalization and Its Discontents.* New York: w.w. Norton, 2003.

Stiglitz, Joseph E. *The Stiglitz Report: Reforming the International Monetary and Financial Systems in the Wake of the Global Crisis.* New York and London: New Press, 2010.

Stoianovich, Trajan. "The Conquering Balkan Orthodox Merchant." *The Journal of Economic History.* 20, no. 2 (1960): 234–313.

Stolle, Dietlind, and Thomas R. Rochon. "Are All Associations Alike? Member Diversity, Associational Type, and the Creation of Social Capital." *American Behavioral Scientist.* 42, no. 1 (1998): 47–65.

Stone, Glyn. *The Oldest Ally: Britain and the Portuguese Connection, 1936–1941.* Royal Historical Society Studies in History. Woodbridge, Suffolk: Boydell, 1994.

Storey, William Kelleher. *Guns, Race, and Power in Colonial South Africa.* Cambridge and New York: Cambridge University Press, 2012.

Storr, Virgil Henry. *Understanding the Culture of Markets.* London and New York: Routledge, 2013.

Streeck, Wolfgang, and Anke Hassel. "Trade Unions as Political Actors." *International handbook of trade unions.* 335 (2003).

Sullivan, Alice. "Cultural Capital and Educational Attainment." *Sociology.* 35, no. 4 (2001): 893–912.

Sun, Guang-Zhen. *The Division of Labour in Economics: A History.* London and New York: Routledge, 2013.

Suranyi, Anna. *Indentured Servitude: Unfree Labour and Citizenship in the British Colonies.* Montreal, Kingston, London, Ithaca: McGill-Queen's University Press, 2021.

Swedberg, Richard. *Max Weber and the Idea of Economic Sociology.* Princeton and Oxford: Princeton University Press, 2018.

Sweezy, Paul, Maurice Dobb, Kohachiro Takahashi, Rodney Hilton, Christopher Hill, Geirges Lefebvre, Domenico Procacci, Eric Hobsbawm, and John Merrington. *The Transition from Feudalism to Capitalism.* London: Verso, 1987.

Swidler, Ann. "Cultural Power and Social Movements." In *Culture and Politics*, 269–283: Springer, 2000.

Taagepera, Rein. "Size and Duration of Empires: Systematics of Size." *Social Science Research.* 7, no. 2 (1978): 108–127.

Tallett, Frank. *War and Society in Early Modern Europe: 1495–1715.* London and New York: Routledge, 2016.

Tampio, Nicholas. "Assemblages and the Multitude: Deleuze, Hardt, Negri, and the Postmodern Left." *European Journal of Political Theory*. 8, no. 3 (2009): 383–400.

Tansug, Feryal. "The Greek Community of Izmir/Smyrna in an Age of Transition: The Relationship between Ottoman Centre-Local Governance and the Izmir/Smyrna Greeks, 1840–1866." *British Journal of Middle Eastern Studies*. 38, no. 1 (2011): 41–72.

Tarrow, Sidney. *Power in Movement: Social Movements and Contentious Politics*. Cambridge and New York: Cambridge University Press, 1998.

Tarrow, Sidney. "Transnational Politics: Contention and Institutions in International Politics." *Annual Review of Political Science*. 4 (2001): 1–20.

Taylor, Charles. *The Malaise of Modernity*. The Massey Lectures Series. Toronto: House of Anansi Press, 2003.

Teece, David J. "Management and Governance of the Business Enterprise: Agency, Contracting, and Capabilities Perspectives." In *The Oxford Handbook of Capitalism*, edited by Dennis C. Mueller. Oxford and New York: Oxford University Press, 2012.

Tell, Frederik. "Integrating Electrical Power Systems: From Individual to Organizational Capabilities." In *The Business of Systems Integration*, edited by Andrea Prencipe, Andrew Davies and Michael Hobday. Oxford And New York: Oxfiord University Press, 2003.

Terlouw, Kees. "Semi-Peripheral Developments: From World-Systems to Regions." *Capitalism Nature Socialism*. 14, no. 4 (2003): 71–90.

Thompson, E. P. *The Making of the English Working Class*. Penguin Modern Classics. London: Penguin, 2002.

Thompson, Elizabeth. *Colonial Citizens: Republican Rights, Paternal Privilege, and Gender in French Syria and Lebanon*. New York: Columbia University Press, 2000.

Thompson, Judy, Judy Hall, and Leslie Heyman Tepper, eds. *Fascinating Challenges: Studying Material Culture with Dorothy Burnham*. Ottawa: University of Ottawa Press, 2001.

Thompson, Leonard Monteath. *A History of South Africa*. 3rd ed. New Haven and London: Yale University Press, 2001.

Thompson, William R. "The Military Superiority Thesis and the Ascendancy of Western Eurasia in the World System." *Journal of World History*. (1999): 143–178.

Thompson, William R. *Power Concentration in World Politics: The Political Economy of Systemic Leadership, Growth, and Conflict*. World-Systems Evolution and Global Futures. Berlin and Heidelberg: Springer, 2020.

Thornton, John, ed. *Africa and Africans in the Making of the Atlantic World, 1400–1800*. Cambridge and New York: Cambridge University Press, 1998.

Thornton, Rod. *Asymmetric Warfare: Threat and Response in the 21st Century*. Cambridge, UK and Malden, Massachusetts: Polity, 2007.

Thorp, Holden, and Buck Goldstein. *Engines of Innovation: The Entrepreneurial University in the Twenty-First Century.* Chapel Hill: University of North Carolina Press, 2013.

Thrift, Nigel. "From Born to Made: Technology, Biology and Space." *Transactions of the Institute of British Geographers.* 30, no. 4 (2005): 463–476.

Thrift, Nigel. "An Urban Impasse?." *Theory, Culture & Society.* 10, no. 2 (1993): 229–238.

Tilly, Charles. *Big Structures, Large Processes, Huge Comparisons.* New York: Russell Sage Foundation, 1984.

Tilly, Charles. "Charivaris, Repertoires and Urban Politics." In *French Cities in the Nineteenth Century,* 73–91: Routledge, 2018.

Tilly, Charles. *Coercion, Capital and European States: AD 990–1992.* Studies in Social Discontinuity. Oxford: Blackwell, 1993.

Tilly, Charles. *The Contentious French.* Cambridge, Massachusetts: Belknap Press, 1986.

Tilly, Charles. *Contentious Performances.* Cambridge Studies in Contentious Politics. Cambridge and New York: Cambridge University Press, 2008.

Tilly, Charles. *Democracy.* Cambridge and New York: Cambridge University Press, 2007.

Tilly, Charles. *Durable Inequality.* Berkeley and Los Angeles: University of California Press, 1998.

Tilly, Charles. *Regimes and Repertoires.* Chicago: University of Chicago Press, 2010.

Tilly, Charles. *Social Movements, 1768–2004.* Boulder: Paradigm Publishers, 2004.

Tilly, Charles. *Social Movements, 1768–2004.* New York and London: Routledge, 2019.

Tilly, Charles. *Stories, Identities, and Political Change.* Lanham, Boulder, New York, and Oxford: Rowman & Littlefield, 2002.

Tilly, Charles. "The Time of States." *Social Research.* (1994): 269–295.

Tilly, Charles. "War Making and State Making as Organized Crime." In *Bringing the State Back In,* edited by Peter Evans, Dietrich Rueschemeyer and Theda Skocpol. New York: Cambridge University Press, 1985.

Tilly, Charles, and Willem Pieter Blockmans. *Cities and the Rise of States in Europe, AD 1000 to 1800.* [in English] Boulder, Colorado: Westview Press, 1994.

Tilly, Charles, and Sidney G. Tarrow. *Contentious Politics.* Oxford and New York: Oxford University Press, 2015.

Tilly, Charles, Sydney Tarrow, and Doug McAdam. *Contention and Democracy in Europe, 1650–2000.* Cambridge Studies in Contentious Politics. Cambridge and New York: Cambridge University Press, 2004.

Tilly, Charles, Louise Tilly, and Richard H. Tilly. *The Rebellious Century, 1830–1930.* Cambridge, Massachusetts and London: Harvard University Press, 1975.

Tilly, Richard H., and Michael Kopsidis. *From Old Regime to Industrial State: A History of German Industrialization from the Eighteenth Century to World War I.* Markets and Governments in Economic History. Chicago and London: University of Chicago Press, 2020.

Tombs, Robert. *France, 1814–1914*. London and New York: Routledge, 1996.

Tonchia, Stefano, and F. Cozzi. *Industrial Project Management: Planning, Design, and Construction*. Cham, Switzerland: Springer, 2010.

Toniolo, Gianni. *An Economic History of Liberal Italy: 1850–1918*. Routledge Revivals. London and New York: Routledge, 2014.

Toniolo, Gianni. "An Overview of Italy's Economic Growth." In *The Oxford Handbook of the Italian Economy since Unification*, edited by Gianni Toniolo. Oxford and New York: Oxford University Press 2013.

Tonkiss, Frank, Andrew Passey, Natalie Fenton, and Leslie C. Hems, eds. *Trust and Civil Society*. London and New York: Palgrave Macmillan, 2000.

Torche, Florencia, and Eduardo Valenzuela. "Trust and Reciprocity: A Theoretical Distinction of the Sources of Social Capital." *European Journal of Social Theory*. 14, no. 2 (2011): 181–198.

Tosatti, Giovanna. "Pericolosi per la Sicurezza dello Stato: Le Schedature della Polizia tra Periferia e Centro." In *1914–1945: L'italia nella Guerra Europea dei Trent'anni*, edited by Simone Neri Serneri. Rome: Viella, 2011.

Tracy, James D., ed. *The Rise of Merchant Empires: Long Distance Trade in the Early Modern World 1350–1750*. Cambridge and New York: Cambridge University Press, 1990.

Travlos, Konstantinos, ed. *Salvation and Catastrophe: The Greek-Turkish War, 1919–1922*. Lanham, Maryland: Lexington Books, 2020.

Trend, David. *Cultural Democracy: Politics, Media, New Technology*. Albany: State University of New York Press.

Trigilia, Carlo. *Economic Sociology: State, Market, and Society in Modern Capitalism*. Oxford: Blackwell, 2008.

Trigilia, Carlo. "Social Capital and Local Development." *European Journal of Social Theory*. 4, no. 4 (2001): 427–442.

Trigilia, Carlo. *Sviluppo Senza Autonomia. Effetti Perversi delle Politiche nel Mezzogiorno*. Bologna: Il Mulino, 1992.

Trigilia, Carlo, and Luigi Burroni. "Italy: Rise, Decline and Restructuring of a Regionalized Capitalism." *Economy and Society*. 38, no. 4 (2009): 630–653.

Tucker, William T. "Max Weber's Verstehen." *The Sociological Quarterly*. 6, no. 2 (1965): 157–165.

Turcan, Romeo V., John E. Reilly, and Larissa Bugaian. "The Challenge of University Autonomy." In *(Re)Discovering University Autonomy: The Global Market Paradox of Stakeholder and Educational Values in Higher Education*, edited by Romeo V. Turcan, John E. Reilly and Larissa Bugaian. London and New York: Palgrave Macmillan, 2016.

Turco, Catherine J., and Ezra W. Zuckerman. "Verstehen for Sociology: Comment on Watts." *American Journal of Sociology*. 122, no. 4 (2017): 1272–1291.

Turner, Henry Ashby. *Hitler's Thirty Days to Power: January 1933*. New York: Basic Books, 1997.

Tzanakis, Michael. "Bourdieu's Social Reproduction Thesis and the Role of Cultural Capital in Educational Attainment: A Critical Review of Key Empirical Studies." *Educate.* 11, no. 1 (2011): 76–90.

Urry, John. *The Anatomy of Capitalist Societies: The Economy, Civil Society, and the State.* London and Basingstoke: Macmillan, 1981.

Van den Berg, Axel. *The Immanent Utopia: From Marxism on the State to the State of Marxism.* Princeton and Oxford: Princeton University Press, 1988.

Van Horn, Robert, Philip Mirowski, and Thomas A. Stapleford. *Building Chicago Economics: New Perspectives on the History of America's Most Powerful Economics Program.* Historical Perspectives on Modern Economics. Cambridge and New York: Cambridge University Press, 2013.

van Hout, Milou. "In Search of the Nation in Fiume: Irredentism, Cultural Nationalism, Borderlands." *Nations and Nationalism.* 26, no. 3 (2020): 660–676.

van Kessel, Stijn. *Populist Parties in Europe: Agents of Discontent?* London and New York: Palgrave Macmillan, 2015.

Van Leeuwen, Richard. *Notables and Clergy in Mount Lebanon: The Khāzin Sheikhs and the Maronite Church, 1736–1840.* Leiden and Boston: Brill, 1994.

van Reenen, Peter. "The 'Unpayable' Police." *Policing.* 22, no. 2 (1999): 133–152.

Vasta, Michelangelo. "Italian Export Capacity in the Long-Term Perspective (1861–2009): a Tortuous Path to Stay in Place." *Journal of Modern Italian Studies.* 15, no. 1 (2010): 133–156.

Vasta, Michelangelo, and Alberto Baccini. "Banks and Industry in Italy, 1911–36: New Evidence Using the Interlocking Directorates Technique." *Financial History Review.* 4, no. 2 (1997): 139–159.

Vasta, Michelangelo, Carlo Drago, Roberto Ricciuti, and Alberto Rinaldi. "Reassessing the Bank–Industry Relationship in Italy, 1913–1936: a Counterfactual Analysis." *Cliometrica.* 11, no. 2 (2017): 183–216.

Vaubel, Roland. "Enforcing Competition among Governments: Theory and Application to the European Union." *Constitutional Political Economy.* 10, no. 4 (1999): 327–338.

Verri, Carlo. "Un Dibattito Marxista: Mafia e Latifondo." *Meridiana.* no. 63 (2008): 135–56.

Vickery, Amanda. "An Englishman's Home Is His Castle? Thresholds, Boundaries and Privacies in the Eighteenth-Century London House." *Past & Present.* 199, no. 1 (2008): 147–173.

Vilar, Pierre. *A History of Gold and Money, 1450 to 1920.* Translated by Judith White. London and New York: Verso, 1991.

Vogelsang, Ingo. *Public Enterprise in Monopolistic and Oligopolistic Industries.* Fundamentals of Pure and Applied Economics. Chur, London, Paris, New York, and Melbourne: Harwood academic publishers, 1990.

Wacquant, Loïc. "Negative Social Capital: State Breakdown and Social Destitution in America's Urban Core." *Netherlands Journal of Housing and the Built Environment.* 13, no. 1 (1998): 25–40.

Wacquant, Loïc. *Prisons of Poverty.* Contradictions. Expanded ed. Minneapolis and London: University of Minnesota Press, 2009.

Wallerstein, Immanuel Maurice. *Africa, the Politics of Independence.* NewYork: Vintage Books, 1961.

Wallerstein, Immanuel Maurice. *Africa: The Politics of Unity.* NewYork: Random House, 1967.

Wallerstein, Immanuel Maurice. *The Decline of American Power.* New York and London: New Press, 2012.

Wallerstein, Immanuel Maurice. "The Development of the Concept of Development." *Sociological Theory.* (1984): 102–116.

Wallerstein, Immanuel Maurice. "From Feudalism to Capitalism: Transition or Transitions?." *Social Forces.* 55, no. 2 (1976): 273–283.

Wallerstein, Immanuel Maurice. *Geopolitics and Geoculture: Essays on the Changing World-System.* Cambridge and New York: Cambridge University Press, 1991.

Wallerstein, Immanuel Maurice. "The Inter-State Structure of the Modern World-System." *International theory: positivism and beyond.* (1996): 87–107.

Wallerstein, Immanuel Maurice. "The Itinerary of World-Systems Analysis; or, How to Resist Becoming a Theory." In *Uncertain Worlds,* edited by Immanuel Maurice Wallerstein, Carlos Aguirre Rojas and Charles C. Lemert. London and New York: Routledge, 2015.

Wallerstein, Immanuel Maurice. *The Modern World-System, Vol. I: Capitalist Agriculture and the Origins of the European World-Economy in the Sixteenth Century.* Berkeley and Los Angeles: University of California Press, 2011.

Wallerstein, Immanuel Maurice. *The Modern World-System, Vol. II: Mercantilism and the Consolidation of the European World-Economy, 1600–1750.* Modern World-System. Berkeley and Los Angeles: University of California Press, 2011.

Wallerstein, Immanuel Maurice. *The Modern World-System, Vol. III: The Second Era of Great Expansion of the Capitalist World-Economy, 1730s–1840s, with a New Prologue.* Modern World-System. Berkeley and Los Angeles: University of California Press, 2011.

Wallerstein, Immanuel Maurice. *The Modern World-System, Vol. IV: Centrist Liberalism Triumphant, 1789–1914.* Berkeley and Los Angeles: University of California Press, 2011.

Wallerstein, Immanuel Maurice. *The Modern World-System: Capitalist Agriculture and the Origins of the European World-Economy in the Sixteeth Century.* Studies in Social Discontinuity. New York: Academic Press, 1976.

Wallerstein, Immanuel Maurice. "The Ottoman Empire and the Capitalist World-Economy: Some Questions for Research." *Review (Fernand Braudel Center)*. 2, no. 3 (1979): 389–398.

Wallerstein, Immanuel Maurice. *The Politics of the World-Economy: The States, the Movements and the Civilizations*. Cambridge and New York: Cambridge University Press, 1984.

Wallerstein, Immanuel Maurice. *The Road to Independence: Ghana and the Ivory Coast*. Paris and the Hague: Mouton, 1964.

Wallerstein, Immanuel Maurice. "What Are We Bounding, and Whom, When We Bound Social Research." *Social Research*. 62, no. 4 (1995): 839–856.

Wallerstein, Immanuel Maurice. *The World-System and Africa*. New York: Diasporic Africa Press, 2016.

Wallerstein, Immanuel Maurice. "A World-System Perspective on the Social Sciences." *The British Journal of Sociology*. 27, no. 3 (1976): 343–352.

Wallerstein, Immanuel Maurice. "World-Systems Analysis: The Second Phase." *Review (Fernand Braudel Center)*. 13, no. 2 (1990): 287–293.

Wallerstein, Immanuel Maurice, M. Aymard, and J. Revel. *The Capitalist World-Economy*. Studies in Modern Capitalism. Cambridge and New York: Cambridge University Press, 1979.

Wallerstein, Immanuel Maurice, and William G. Martin. "Peripheralization of Southern Africa, II: Changes in Household Structure and Labor-Force Formation." *Review (Fernand Braudel Center)*. 3, no. 2 (1979): 193–207.

Wallis, Joe, and Brian Dollery. "Social Capital and Local Government Capacity." *Australian Journal of Public Administration*. 61, no. 3 (2002): 76–85.

Ward, Michael. "Appendix 8e. International Comparisons of Military Expenditures: Issues and Challenges of Using Purchasing Power Parities." *SIPRI Yearbook*.

Warner, Mildred. "Building Social Capital: The Role of Local Government." *The Journal of Socio-Economics*. 30, no. 2 (2001): 187–192.

Waters, M. *Modern Sociological Theory*. London, Thousand Oaks, New Delhi: SAGE Publications, 1994.

Watts, Ronald L. "Federalism, Federal Political Systems, and Federations." *Annual Review of Political Science*. 1, no. 1 (1998): 117–137.

Weaver, Frederick S. *An Economic History of the United States: Conquest, Conflict, and Struggles for Equality*. Lanham, Boulder, New York, Toronto and Oxford: Rowman & Littlefield Publishers, 2015.

Weber, Alfred. "On the Location of Industries." *Progress in Human Geography*. 6, no. 1 (2006): 120–128.

Weber, Eugen. *Peasants into Frenchmen: The Modernization of Rural France, 1870–1914*. Stanford, California: Stanford University Press, 1976.

Weber, Max, P. R. Baehr, and G. C. Wells. *The Protestant Ethic and the Spirit of Capitalism and Other Writings*. Penguin Classics. London: Penguin, 2002.

Weber, Max, Guenther Roth, and Claus Wittich, eds. *Economy and Society: An Outline of Interpretive Sociology*. Berkeley and Los Angeles: University of California Press, 1978.

Weiss, Linda. "Demythologising the Petite Bourgeoisie: The Italian Case." *West European Politics*. 9, no. 3 (1986): 362–375.

Weiss, Linda. "Guiding Globalization in East Asia: New Roles for Old Developmental States." In *States in the Global Economy: Bringing Domestic Institutions Back In*, edited by Linda Weiss. Cambridge and New York: Cambridge University Press, 2003.

Weiss, Linda. "Is the State Being 'Transformed' by Globalization?." In *States in the Global Economy: Bringing Domestic Institutions Back In*, edited by Linda Weiss. Cambridge and New York: Cambridge University Press, 2003.

Whatley, Warren. "The Transatlantic Slave Trade and the Evolution of Political Authority in West Africa." *Africa's Development in Historical Perspective*. (2014): 460–88.

White, Jonathan, and Lea Ypi. *The Meaning of Partisanship*. Oxford and New York: Oxford University Press, 2016.

Wikipedia. "Fabiola Gianotti." https://it.wikipedia.org/wiki/Fabiola_Gianotti, accessed June 11, 2021.

Williams, Gareth. "Higher Education: Public Good or Private Commodity?." *London Review of Education*. 14, no. 1 (2016): 131–142.

Williams, Michelle, ed. *The End of the Developmental State?* London and New York: Routledge, 2014.

Willis, Paul. *Learning to Labour: How Working Class Kids Get Working Class Jobs*. London and New York: Routledge, 2000.

Wills, John E., John Cranmer-Byng, Willard J. Peterson, and John W. Witek. *China and Maritime Europe, 1500–1800: Trade, Settlement, Diplomacy, and Missions*. Cambridge and New York: Cambridge University Press, 2010.

Wilson, Peter H. *The Thirty Years War: Europe's Tragedy*. Cambridge, Massachusetts: Belknap Press, 2011.

Wimmer, Andreas, and Brian Min. "From Empire to Nation-State: Explaining Wars in the Modern World, 1816–2001." *American Sociological Review*. 71, no. 6 (2006): 867–897.

Wong, R. B. *China Transformed: Historical Change and the Limits of European Experience*. Cornell Paperbacks. Ithaca, New York: Cornell University Press, 1997.

Wong, Wilson Kia Onn. *Automotive Global Value Chain: The Rise of Mega Suppliers*. London and New York: Routledge, 2017.

Woo-Cumings, Meredih, ed. *The Developmental State*, Cornell Studies in Political Economy. Ithaca and New York: Cornell University Press, 2019.

Wood, Ellen Meiksins. *Democracy against Capitalism: Renewing Historical Materialism*. London and New York: Verso, 2016.

Wood, Ellen Meiksins. *The Origin of Capitalism: A Longer View.* London and New York: Verso, 2016.

Woods, Dwayne. "The Crisis of Center-Periphery Integration in Italy and the Rise of Regional Populism: The Lombard League." *Comparative politics.* (1995): 187–203.

Woods, Dwayne. "The Many Faces of Populism in Italy: The Northern League and Berlusconism." In *The Many Faces of Populism: Current Perspectives*, edited by Dwayne Woods and Barbara Wejnert. Research in Political Sociology. Bingley: Emerald, 2014.

Woolcock, Michael. "Social Capital: The State of the Notion." In *Social Capital. Global and Local Perspectives*, edited by Jouko Kajanoja and Jussi Simpura. Helsinki: Government Institute for Economic Research, 2000.

Worth, Owen, and Phoebe Moore, eds. *Globalization and the 'New' Semi-Peripheries*, International Political Economy Series. London and New York: Palgrave Macmillan, 2009.

Wouters, Ruud, and Stefan Walgrave. "Demonstrating Power: How Protest Persuades Political Representatives." *American Sociological Review.* 82, no. 2 (2017): 361–383.

Wright, Erik Olin. *Approaches to Class Analysis.* Cambridge and New York: Cambridge University Press, 2005.

Wright, Erik Olin. *Understanding Class.* London and New York: Verso, 2015.

Wrigley, E. A. *People, Cities, and Wealth: The Transformation of Traditional Society.* Oxford: Blackwell, 1987.

Yang, Chun. "Relocating Labour-Intensive Manufacturing Firms from China to Southeast Asia: a Preliminary Investigation." *Bandung.* 3, no. 1 (2016): 1–13.

Yeniyurt, Sengun, and Janell D. Townsend. "Does Culture Explain Acceptance of New Products in a Country? An Empirical Investigation." *International Marketing Review.* 20, no. 4 (2003): 377–396.

Yeung, May T., Nicholas Perdikis, and William A. Kerr. *Regional Trading Blocs in the Global Economy: The EU and ASEAN.* Cheltenham, UK and Northampton, Massachusetts: Edward Elgar, 1999.

Young, Robert J. C. *Postcolonialism: An Historical Introduction.* Chichester, West Sussex and Malden, Massachusetts: Wiley-Blackwell, 2016.

Zarinebaf, Fariba. *Mediterranean Encounters: Trade and Pluralism in Early Modern Galata.* Oakland, California: University of California Press, 2018.

Zellars, Rachel. "'Too Tedious to Mention:' Pondering the Border, Black Atlantic, and Public Schooling in Colonial Canada." *Left History: An Interdisciplinary Journal of Historical Inquiry and Debate.* 23, no. 1 (2019): 62–93.

Zellars, Rachel B. "'As If We Were All Struggling Together:' Black Intellectual Traditions and Legacies of Gendered Violence." *Women's Studies International Forum.* 77 (2019).

Zhao, Dingxin. *The Confucian-Legalist State: A New Theory of Chinese History.* Oxford Studies in Early Empires. Oxford and New York: Oxford University Press, 2015.

Zolberg, Aristide R. "Origins of the Modern World System: a Missing Link." *World Politics*. 33, no. 2 (1981): 253–281.

Zucman, Gabriel, and Thomas Piketty. *The Hidden Wealth of Nations: The Scourge of Tax Havens*. Translated by Teresa Lavender Fagan. Chicago and London: University of Chicago Press, 2016.

Index

www.ingramcontent.com/pod-product-compliance
Lightning Source LLC
Chambersburg PA
CBHW070048030426
42335CB00016B/1829